MH-CET

MBA/ MMS 7 PAST PAPERS + 6 Mock Tests

Fully Solved

- **Head Office :** B-32, Shivalik Main Road, Malviya Nagar, New Delhi-110017
- **Sales Office :** B-48, Shivalik Main Road, Malviya Nagar, New Delhi-110017

Tel. : 011-26691021 / 26691713

Price : ₹ 300

Typeset by Disha DTP Team

DISHA PUBLICATION

For further information about books from DISHA,

Log on to **www.dishapublication.com** or email to **info@dishapublication.com**

CONTENTS

SOLVED PAPERS

MOCK PAPERS

SOLUTIONS

MAHARASHTRA COMMON ENTRANCE TEST

PAST EIGHT QUESTION PAPERS : At a glance

Topics	2014	2012	2011	2010	2009	2008	2007	2006
English Language		**50**	**50**	**50**	**50**	**50**	**50**	**50**
• Passage	10	15	32	15	15	15	9	15
• Synonyms	4	5	*	*	5	15	9	15
• Cloze Test	10	10	10	10	10	10	10	10
• Analogies	*	*	*	*	5	*	6	10
• Spelling Correction	*	*	*	*	*	*	5	5
• Sentence Correction	10	5	5	5	*	10	15	5
• Fill in the Blanks	*	5	*	5	10	*	5	*
• Para Jumble	5	5	3	5	5	*	*	5
• Naration	10	*	*	*	*	*	*	10
• Grammatically correct phrase	5	5	*	5	*	15	*	*
• Connector based Sentence starters	5	*	*	*	*	*	*	*
Quant	**20**	**20**	**25**	**20**	**15**	**20**	**20**	**10**
• Advance Maths	4	2	3	1	2	6	3	5
• Binary Operation	*	*	*	5	1	2	*	*
• Number System	2	8	7	10	5	1	5	*
• Arithmetic	5	8	8	7	3	11	5	5
• Linear equation	*	1	2	1	*	1	2	*
• Mensuration	2	1	5	1	*	1	3	*
• Geometry	7	*	*	*	*	*	*	*

Topics	2014	2012	2011	2010	2009	2008	2007	2006
Reasoning		**90**	**100**	**100**	**105**	**105**	**100**	**105**
• Non-verbal/ visual	25	10	25	30	25	30	30	30
• Ordering	*	5	3	3	4	30	30	30
• Cause/effect	2	5	5	5	5	*	5	*
• Syllogism	7	5	6	5	5	5	5	5
• Analogy	*	*	*	*	3	*	*	*
• Coding/ Decoding	7	5	5	10	15	14	9	*
• Blood Relation	5	5	*		4	5	*	*
• Series (number/letter)	6	5	2	5	10	5	13	15
• English Alphabet	*	*	5	2	*	*	*	
• Data arrangment Input and Output	6	*	5	5	5	5	10	15
• Odd-one out	*	5	5	*	2	3	5	5
• Data analysis/ Puzzle Test	28	20	15	5	*	5	5	*
• Statement / Assumption / Conclusion / Assertion	4	5	5	10	15	25	*	
• Logical deduction/ Selection procedure / Course of Action/ Argument/ Inference	6	5	19	15	15	10	10	15
• Decision Making	*	5	10	*	30	30	30	30
• Others	6	10	9	7	7	9	*	*
Data Interpretation	**20**	**35**	**20**	**15**	**20**	**20**	**20**	**20**
(Based on pie chart, table, bar and line graph)								
Data Sufficiency	**10**	**5**	**5**	**5**	**10**	**5**	**10**	**15**

CET 2014 AS COMPARED TO CET 2012, 2011, 2010 and 2009

	2014	2012	2011	2010	2009
Total Duration of Exam	150 minutes	150 minutes	150 minutes	150 minutes	150 minutes
Total number of Questions	200	200	200	200	200
Total marks	200	200	200	200	200
Marks per Question	1 mark	1 mark	1 mark	1 mark	1 mark
Negative marking	No	No	No	No	No
Number of Sections	Not Applicable	Not Applicable	Not Applicable	Not Applicable	Not Applicable
Number of choices per question	5	5	5	5	5
Mode of marking the ovals	Online mode	Black Ball point pen	Black Ball point pen	Black Ball point pen	Black Ball point pen

	2014	2012	2011	2010	2009
Quantitative Aptitude	20	20	22	15	15
Data Interpretation	20	40	20	20	25
Data Sufficiency	10	10	5	5	10
Logical Reasoning	60	50	48	54	53
Visual Reasoning	25	15	25	30	30
Verbal Ability and Verbal Reasoning	55	50	48	61	52
Reading Comprehension	10	15	32	15	15
Total	200	200	200	200	200

SOLVED PAPER
(Based on Memory)
COMMON ENTRANCE TEST
MAHARASHTRA-CET MBA/MMS
15th MARCH 2014

1. In a certain language 'to be polite' is coded as 'fa so la', 'she is polite' is coded as 'so me pa' and 'to have manners' is coded as 'na la ma'. Which of the following is the code for 'be' in that language?
(a) so (b) fa
(c) la (d) me
(e) na

2. If in a certain code 'GRIM' is coded as 'RMOS' and 'DUSK' is coded as 'LQPI' how will 'STOP' be coded in the same code language?
(a) MJIS (b) PJGB
(c) JPJIS (d) MJGB
(e) PGJB

Directions (Qs. 3-7) : Study the following arrangement carefully and answer the questions that follow :

7 R E T 4 A 9 % D F 1 U # B @ 8 H I © W M ★ 3 2 V $ 5 N P 6 Q

3. How many such consonants are there in the above arrangement, each of which is immediately preceded by a consonant and immediately followed by a number ?
(a) None (b) One
(c) Two (d) Three
(e) More than three

4. How many such numbers are there in the above arrangement, each of which is immediately preceded by a letter but not immediately followed by a symbol?
(a) None (b) One
(c) Two (d) Three
(e) More than three

5. How many such vowels are there in the above arrangement, each of which is immediately followed by a symbol ?
(a) None (b) One
(c) Two (d) Three
(e) More than three

6. Four of the following five are alike in a certain way based on their position in the above arrangement and so form a group. Which is the one that does not belong to the group?
(a) RTA (b) 9DF
(c) #@H (d) 3V5
(e) IW ★

7. Which of the following is the fourth to the left of the twelfth from the left end ?
(a) % (b) 8
(c) 2 (d) H
(e) None of these

Directions (Qs. 8-10) : Study the following information carefully and answer the questions that follow :

A television channel has scheduled five half-hour shows between 9.30 pm and midnight. Out of the three family drama shows 'Main Sati Hoon' has social message for audience. The family dramas bring in maximum revenues for the channel and they are scheduled one after another. The show 'Detective Doom' is a suspense thriller, a family drama and also has social message. Two of the family dramas have social message and one not having social message has adult content. There are two shows which have adult content and they have been scheduled at 10.30 pm and 11.30 pm. The show 'HIV and India' is a news based program and also has social message. 'Midnight Murders' neither has social message nor is a family drama and is scheduled at 11.30 pm. The two news based programs but are not family dramas have been given two adjacent slots. The show 'Main Sati Hoon' has been scheduled for 10.00 to 10.30 pm slot and has a family drama preceding it. 'Laugh a While' is the fifth program.

8. When is 'Laugh a While' scheduled ?
(a) 9:00 pm to 9:30 pm
(b) 9:30 pm to 10:00 pm
(c) 10:00 pm to 10:30 pm
(d) 10:30 pm to 11:00 pm
(e) None of these

9. Based on the information above which of the following is not implied ?
(a) 'Midnight Murders' is a news based program
(b) 'Laugh a While' has adult content
(c) 'Detective Dooms' has adult content
(d) 'HIV and India' has social message
(e) None of these

10. When is 'HIV and India' scheduled ?
(a) 11:00 pm to 11:30 pm
(b) 9:30 pm to 10:00 pm
(c) 10:00 pm to 10:30 pm
(d) 10:30 pm to 11:00 pm
(e) None of these

Directions (Qs. 11-15) : In the following questions, two equations numbered I and II are given. You have to solve both the equations and give answers.

(a) if $x > y$
(b) if $x \geq y$
(c) if $x < y$
(d) if $x \leq y$
(e) if $x = y$ or the relationship cannot be established

11. I. $12x^2 + 11x + 12 = 10x^2 + 22x$
II. $13y^2 - 18y + 3 = 9y^2 - 10y$

12. I. $\frac{18}{x^2}+\frac{6}{x}-\frac{12}{x^2}=\frac{8}{x^2}$

II. $y^3+9.68+5.64=16.95$

13. I. $\sqrt{1225x}+\sqrt{4900}=0$

II. $(81)^{1/4}y+(343)^{1/3}=0$

14. I. $\frac{(2)^5+(11)^3}{6}=x^3$

II. $4y^3=-(589\div 4)+5y^3$

15. I. $(x^{7/5}\div 9)=169\div x^{3/5}$

II. $y^{1/4}\times y^{1/4}\times 7=273\div y^{1/2}$

Directions (Qs.16-20): Read the following passage carefully and answer the questions given below it.

The evolution of Bring Your Own Device (BYOD) trend has been as proxfound as it has been rapid. It represents the more visible sign that the boundaries between personal life and work life are blurring. The 9 am - 5 pm model of working solely from office has become archaic and increasingly people are working extended hours from a range of locations. At the vary heart of this evolution is the ability to access enterprise networks from anywhere and anytime. The concept of cloud computing serves effectively to extend the office out of office. The much heralded benefit of BYOD is greater productivity. However, recent research has suggested that this is the greatest myth of BYOD and the reality is that BYOD in practice poses new challenges that may outweigh the benefits. A worldwide survey commissioned by Fortinet chose to look at attitudes towards BYOD and security from the users's point of view instead of the IT managers. Specifically the survey was conducted in 15 territories on a group of graduate employees in their early twenties because they represent the first generation to enter the workplace with an expectation of own devide use. Moreover, they also represent tomorrow's influences and decision makers. The survey findings reveal that for financial organizations, the decision to embrace BYOD is extremely dangerous. Larger organizations will have mature IT strategies and policies in place. But what about smaller financial businesses? They might not have such well developed strategies to protect confidential data. Crucially, within younger employee group, 55% of the people share an expectation that they should be allowed to use their own devices in the workplace or for work purposes. With this expectation comes the very real risk that employees may consider contravening company policy banning the use of own devices. The threats posed by this level of subversion cannot be overstated. The survey casts doubt on the idea of BYOD leading to greater productivity by revealing the real reason people want to use their own devices. Only 26% of people in this age group cite efficiency as the reason they want to use their own devices, while 63% admit that the main reason is so they have access to their favourite applications. But with personal applications so close to hand, the risks to the business must surely include distraction and time wasting. To support this assumption 46% of people polled acknowledged time wasting as the greatest threat to the organization, while 42% citing greater exposure to theft or loss of confidential data. Clearly, from a user perspective there is great deal of contradiction surrounding BYOD and there exists an undercurrent of selfishness where users except to use their own devices, but mostly for personal interest. They recognize the risks to the organization but are adamant that those risks are worth taking.

16. According to the passage, for which of the following reasons did Fortinet conduct the survey on a group of graduate employees in their early twenties?
    (A) As this group represents the future decision makers
    (B) As this group represents the first generation who entered the workforce with a better understanding of sophisticated gadgets
    (C) As this group represents the first generation to enter the workplace expecting that they can use their own devices for work purpose
    (a) All (A), (B) and (C) (b) Only (C)
    (c) Both (A) and (C) (d) Only (A)
    (e) Only (B)

17. Which of the following is **not true** about BYOD?
    (a) BYOD enables employees to access enterprise network from anywhere and anytime
    (b) Due to evolution of BYOD trend the 9am - 5pm model of working solely from office has become outdated
    (c) Recent research has confirmed that BYOD boosts organisational productivity
    (d) The concept of cloud computing facilates the BYOD trend

18. According to the passage, why would the decision to embrace BYOD prove dangerous to smaller financial businesses?
    (a) Their employees have poor knowledge about their devices which in turn pose a threat to the confidential data of the organisation
    (b) Their employees are more vulnerable to misplacement of devices
    (c) They may lack mature IT strategies and policies required to protect confidential data
    (d) They cannot afford to deal with damage liability issues of employee-owned devices
    (e) Their employees have a tendency to change jobs frequently

19. According to the passage, the expectation of younger employees that they should be allowed to use their own devices in the workplace, entails which of the following risks?
    (A) Younger employees may deliberately transfer confidential data of their companies to rivals if they are not allowed to use their own devices for work purpose
    (B) Younger employees may strongly feel like leaving the company if it presents usage of own device and join some other company that does not have such stringent policies
    (C) Younger employees may consider flouting company policy prohibiting usage of their own devices in the workplace or for work purposes
    (a) Only (C) (b) Only (B)
    (c) Both (A) and (C) (d) Only (A)
    (e) All (A), (B) and (C)

20. According to the findings of the survey conducted by Fortinet, why do majority of employees prefer using their own devices for work purpose?

(a) As they often find that the devices provided by the company lack quality

(b) As they have access to their favourite applications while working

(c) As majority of them believe that output doubles when they use their own devices for work purpose

(d) As handling data from their own devices reinforces their sense of responsiblity

Directions (Qs. 21-25) : Read the following passage carefully and answer the questions given below it.

Delays of several months in National Rural Employment Guarantee Scheme (NREGS) wage payments and work sites where labourers have lost all hope of being paid at all have become the norm in many states. How are workers who exist on the margins of subsistence supposed to feed their families? Under the scheme, workers must be paid within 1 5 days, failing which they are entitled, to compensation under the Payment of Wages Act - upto 3000 per aggrieved worker. In reality, compensation is received in only a few isolated instances. It is often argued by officials that the main reason for the delay is the inability of banks and post offices to handle mass payments of NREGS wages. Though there is a grain of truth in this, as a diagnosis it is misleading. The 'jam' in the banking system has been the result of the hasty switch to bank payments imposed by the Central Government against the recommendation of the Central Employment Guarantee Council which advocated a gradual transition starting with villages relatively close to the nearest bank. However, delays are not confined solely to the banking system. Operational hurdles include implementing agencies taking more than fifteen days to issue payment orders, viewing of work measurement as a cumbersome process resulting in procrastination by the engineering staff and non maintenance of muster rolls and job card etc. But behind these delays lies a deeper and deliberate 'backlash' against the NREGS. With bank payments making it much harder to embezzle NREGS funds, the programme is seen as a headache by many government functionaries the workload has remained without the "inducements". Slowing down wage payments is a convenient way of sabotaging the scheme because workers will desert NREGS worksites.

The common sense solution advocated by the government is to adopt the business correspondent model. Where in bank agents will go to villages to make cash payments and duly record them on handheld, electronic devices. This solution is based on the wrong diagnosis that distance separating villages from banks is the main issue. In order to accelerate payments, clear timelines for every step of the payment process should be incorporated into the system as Programme Officers often have no data on delays and cannot exert due pressure to remedy the situation. Workers are both clueless and powerless with no provision for them to air their grievances and seek redress. In drought affected areas the system of piece rate work can be dispensed with where work measurement is not completed within a week and wages may be paid on the basis of attendance. Buffer funds can be provided to gram panchayats and post offices to avoid bottlenecks in the flow of funds. Partial advances could also be considered provided wage payments are meticulously tracked. But failure to recognise problems and unwillingness to remedy them will remain major threats to the NREGS.

21. What impact have late wage payments had on NREGS workers?

(a) They cannot obtain employment till their dues are cleared

(b) They have benefited from the compensation awarded to them

(c) They have been unable to provide for their families

(d) They have been ostracised by their families who depend on them for sustenance

(e) None of the above

22. Which of the following factors has not been responsible for untimely payment of NREGS wages?

(a) Communication delays between agencies implementing the scheme

(b) Improper record keeping

(c) Behind schedule release of payments by banks

(d) Drought conditions prevalent in the country

(e) Delays in work measurement

23. What has the outcome of disbursing NREGS wages through banks been?

(a) Theft of funds by administration officials responsible for the scheme has reduced

(b) Increased work load for local government officials

(c) Protests by workers who have to travel long distances to the nearest bank to claim their wages

(d) Time consuming formalities have to be completed by workers

(e) None of the above

24. According to the passage, which of the following has/have been the consequence (s) of delayed wage payments?

A. Compensation to victimised workers has amounted to crores.

B. Banks will no longer be entrusted with remitting wages.

C. Regulations to ensure punctual wage payments have come into force.

(a) None of these (b) Only (A)

(c) (A) and (C) (d) (A) and (B)

(e) (B) and (C)

25. To which of the following has the author attributed the delay in wage payments?

(a) Embezzlement of funds by corrupt bank staff

(b) Lack of monitoring by the Central Employment Guarantee Council

(c) An attempt to derail the NREGS by vested interests

(d) Overworked bank staff deliberately delay payments to protest against extra work

(e) Engineers efforts to wreck the NREGS because of low wages

Directions (Qs. 26-29) : Read the following information carefully and answer the questions that follow :

Six friends Abhishek, Deepak, Mridul, Pritam, Ranjan and Salil married within a year in the months of February, April, July, September, November and December and in the cities of Ahmedabad, Bengaluru, Chennai, Delhi, Mumbai and Kolkata, but not necessarily following the above order. The brides' names were Geetika, Jasmine, Hema, Brinda, Ipsita and Veena, once again not following any order. The following are some facts about their weddings.

(i) Mridul's wedding took place in Chennai, however he was not married to Geetika or Veena
(ii) Abhishek's wedding took place in Ahmedabad and Ranjan's in Delhi; however neither of them was married to Jasmine or Brinda
(iii) The wedding in Kolkata took place in February
(iv) Hema's wedding took place in April, but not in Ahmedabad
(v) Geetika and Ipsita got married in February and November and in Chennai and Kolkata but not following the above order
(vi) Pritam visited Bengaluru and Kolkata only after his marriage in December
(vi) Salil was married to Jasmine to September

26. Hema's husband is
(a) Abhishek (b) Deepak
(c) Ranjan (d) Pritam
(e) Mridul

27. Deepak's wedding took place in
(a) Bengaluru (b) Mumbai
(c) Kolkata (d) Delhi
(e) Chennai

28. In Mumbai, the wedding of one of the friends took place in the month of
(a) April (b) September
(c) November (d) December
(e) July

29. Salil's wedding was held in
(a) Bengaluru (b) Chennai
(c) Kolkata (d) Delhi
(e) Mumbai

30. In the arrangement P26 M9 K S 4 V 7, the positions of the 1st and the 6th elements are interchanged, those of the 2nd and the 7th are interchanged, and so on. Then, which of the following will be the 4th element from the left end in the fresh, arrangement?
(a) M (b) 7
(c) 4 (d) 9
(e) None of these

Directions (Qs. 31-35) : In each of the following questions, a related pair of figures is followed by five lettered pairs of figures. Select the pair that has relationship similar to that in the question figure.

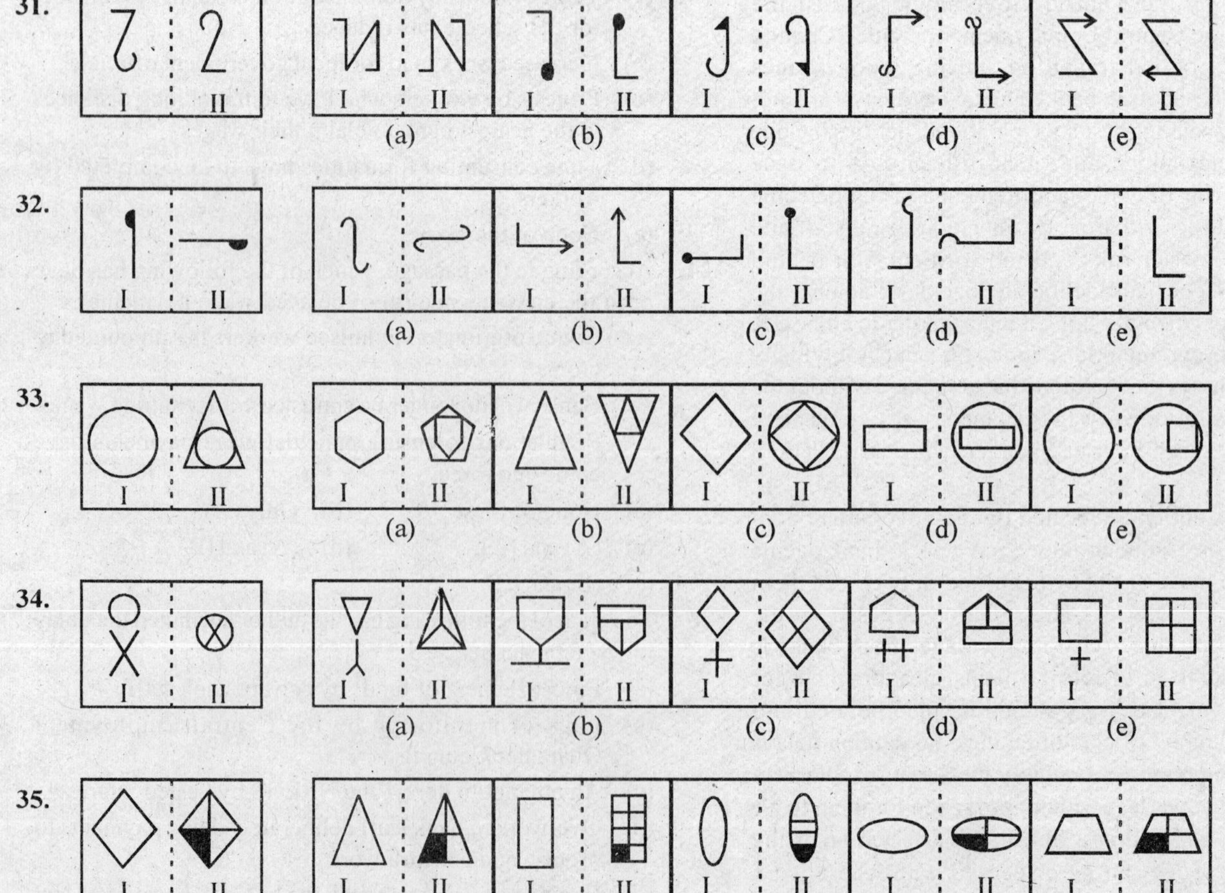

Directions (Qs. 36-37) : In the following number series, a wrong number is given. Find out the wrong number.

36. 29, 37, 21, 43, 13, 53, 5
(a) 37 (b) 53
(c) 13 (d) 21
(e) 43

37. 150, 290, 560, 1120, 2140, 4230, 8400
(a) 2140 (b) 560
(c) 1120 (d) 4230
(e) 290

38. The difference between the simple interest received from two different sources on ₹ 1500 for 3 years is ₹ 13.50. The difference between their rates of interest is:
(a) 0.1% (b) 0.2%
(c) 0.3% (d) 0.4%
(e) None of these

39. A man sells an article at 5% profit. If he had bought it at 5% less and sold it for ₹ 1 less, he would have gained 10%. The cost price of the article is :
(a) ₹200 (b) ₹150
(c) ₹240 (d) ₹280
(e) None of these

40. On a journey across Bombay, a tourist bus averages 10 km/h for 20% of the distance, 30 km/h for 60% of it and 20 km/h for the remainder. The average speed for the whole journey was
(a) 10 km/h (b) 30 km/h
(c) 5 km/h (d) 20 km/h
(e) None of these

Directions (Qs. 41-44) : In each of the following questions below, the figures follow a series/sequence. One and only one out of the five figures does not fit in the series/sequence. The number of that figure is your answer.

41.

(a)	(b)	(c)	(d)	(e)
D N A T S	N A D S T	A N S T D	S N A D T	S N D T A

42.

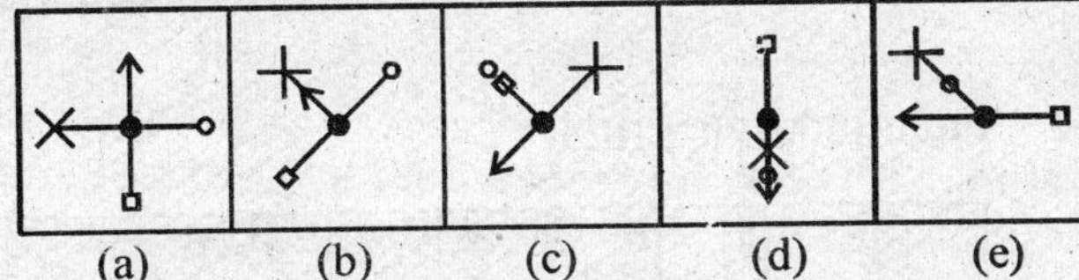

(a) (b) (c) (d) (e)

43.

(a) SSS □□ □□ OO △
(b) OOO S S S S △△ I
(c) △△△ O O O O II ★
(d) III △△ △△ ★★ O
(e) ★★ ★ I I I I LL C

44.

(a) (b) (c) (d) (e)

Directions (Qs. 45-49) : Which of the phrases (a), (b), (c) and (d) given below each sentence should replace the phrase printed in bold in the sentence to make it grammatically correct? If the sentence is correct as it is given and no correction is required, mark (e) as the answer.

45. Seeing that there was an ongoing sale in one of her favourite stores, Seeta **made a bee line for** it immediately after entering the mall.
(a) made a bee's line for
(b) make bees lined to
(c) made a bee line to
(d) make bee line to
(e) No correction required

46. Sharon made it to work in the **nicks of times**, or else she would have missed the meeting.
(a) nick of time (b) nicked time
(c) nick of timeliness (d) nick and time
(e) No correction required

47. Varun was **on cloud nine** after having stood first in his class.
(a) in ninth cloud (b) on nine clouds
(c) a cloudy nine (d) cloud on nine
(e) No correction required

48. Vithal had a habit of **pass the buck** when it came to important issues at work.
(a) pass to bucking (b) passing buck
(c) passing the buck (d) pass buck
(e) No correction required

49. Puneet **raked his brains** and tried to find an answer to a tricky question given in the paper but couldn't find one.
(a) rake his brain (b) racked his brains
(c) racked brains (d) raked brain
(e) No correction required

Directions (Qs. 50-54) : In each of the questions below are given four statements followed by three conclusions numbered I, II and III. You have to take the given statements to be true even if they seem to be at variance from commonly known facts. Read all the conclusions and then decide which of the given conclusions logically follows from the given statements disregarding commonly known facts.

50. Statements: All petals are flowers. Some flowers are buds. Some buds are leaves. All leaves are plants.
Conclusions: I. Some petals are not buds.
II. Some flowers are plants.
III. No flower is plant.
(a) Only I follows (b) Either II or III follows
(c) I and II follow (d) Only III follows
(e) None of the above

51. Statements: Some pens are keys. Some keys are locks. All locks are cards. No card is paper
Conclusions:
I. No lock is paper.
II. Some cards are keys.
III. Some keys are not paper.
(a) I and II follow (b) Only I follows
(c) Only II follows (d) All follow
(e) None follows

52. Statements: Some pearls are gems. All gems are diamonds. No diamond is stone. Some stones are corals.
Conclusions:
I. Some stones are pearls.
II. Some corals being diamond is a possibility.
III. No stone is pearl.
(a) Only I follows (b) Only II follows
(c) Either I or III follows (d) I and II follow
(e) None of these

53. Statements: Some apartments are flats. Some flats are buildings. All buildings are bungalows. All bungalows are gardens.
Conclusions:
I. All apartments being building is a possibility
II. All bungalows are not buildings.
III. No flat is garden.
(a) None follows (b) Only I follows
(c) Either I or III follows (d) II and III follow
(e) Only II follows

54. Statements: All chairs are tables. All tables are bottles. Some bottles are jars. No jar is bucket.
Conclusions:
I. Some tables being jar is a possibility.
II. Some bottles are chairs.
III. Some bottles are not bucket.
(a) Only I follows (b) I and II follow
(c) All follow (d) Only II follows
(e) None of these

55. A person starts from point P in East and moves 12 m to point Q. Then, he moves right 8 m to point R. Again he moves right for 6 m to point S. Then, he moves 6 m in the North to point T. Finally from there he goes to left for 6 m to point U. Which of three point he would form a triangle whose all the angles are less than 90°?
(a) PTQ (b) QTR
(c) UTS (d) TSR
(e) SQR

Directions (Qs. 56-60) : Study the following information carefully and answer the questions that follow :

If A + B means A is the father of B
If A × B means A is the sister of B
If A $ B means A is the wife of B
If A % B means A is the mother of B
If A ÷ B means A is the son of B

56. What should come in place of the question mark, to establish that J is the brother of T in the expression?
J ÷ P % H ? T % L
(a) × (b) ÷
(c) $ (d) Either ÷ or ×
(e) Either + or ÷

57. Which among the given expressions indicate that M is the daughter of D?
(a) L % R $ D + T × M (b) L + R $ D + M × T
(c) L % R % D + T ÷ M (d) D + L $ R + M × T
(e) L $ D ÷ R % M ÷ T

58. Which among the following options is true if the expresssion 'I + T % J × L ÷ K' is **definitely true**?
(a) L is the daughter of T (b) K is the son-in-law of I
(c) I is the grandmother of L (d) T is the father of L
(e) J is the brother of L

59. Which among the following expression is true if Y is the son of X is **definitely false**?
(a) W % L × T × Y ÷ X (b) W + L × T × Y ÷ X
(c) X + L × T × Y ÷ W (d) W $ X + L + Y + T
(e) W % X + T × Y ÷ L

60. What should come in place of the question mark, to establish that T is the sister-in-law of Q in the expression?
R % T × P ? Q + V
(a) ÷ (b) %
(c) × (d) $
(e) Either $ or ×

Directions (Qs. 61-65) : In each of the questions given below which one of the five answer figures should come after the problem figures, if the sequence were continued?

61. **PROBLEM FIGURES**

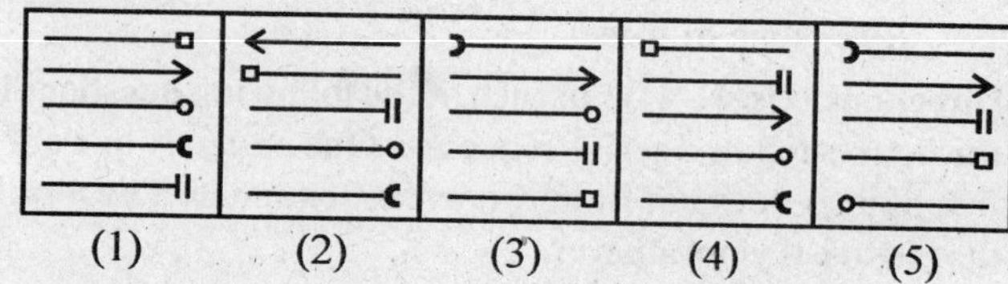
(1) (2) (3) (4) (5)

ANSWER FIGURES

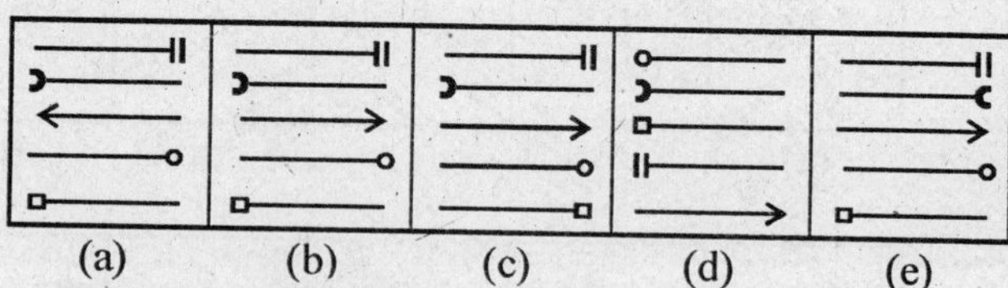
(a) (b) (c) (d) (e)

62. **PROBLEM FIGURES**

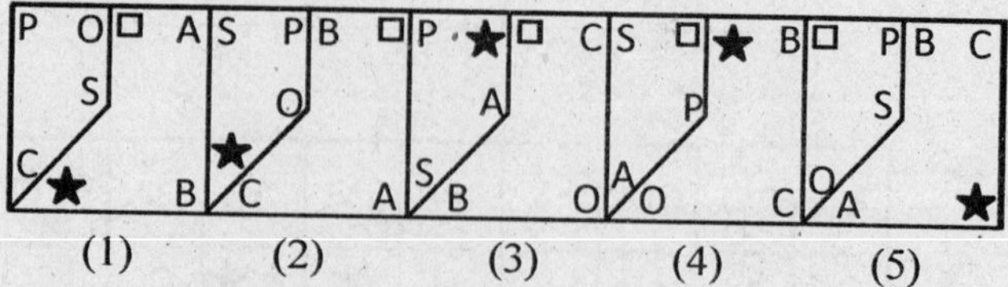
(1) (2) (3) (4) (5)

ANSWER FIGURES

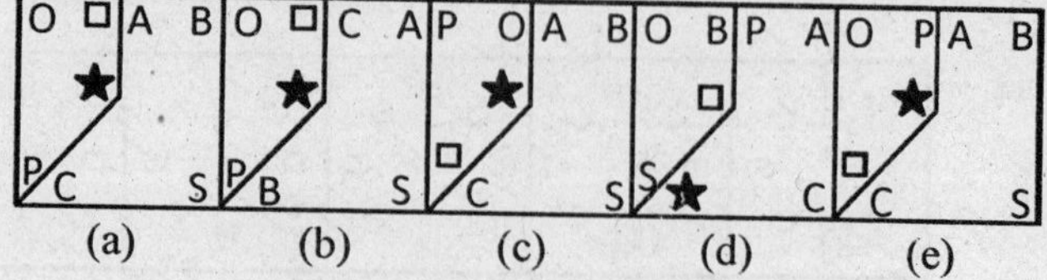
(a) (b) (c) (d) (e)

63. PROBLEM FIGURES

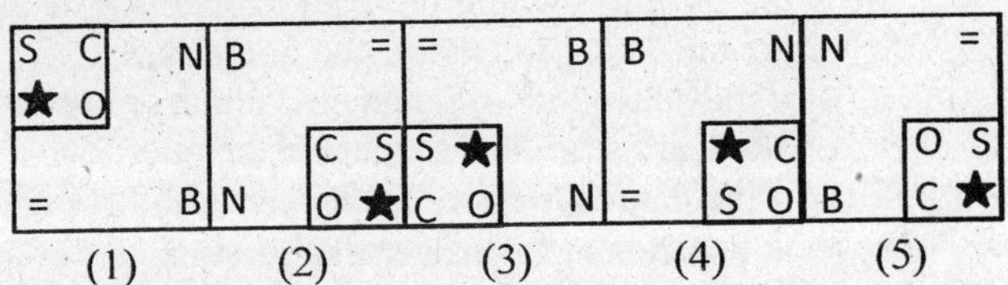

ANSWER FIGURES

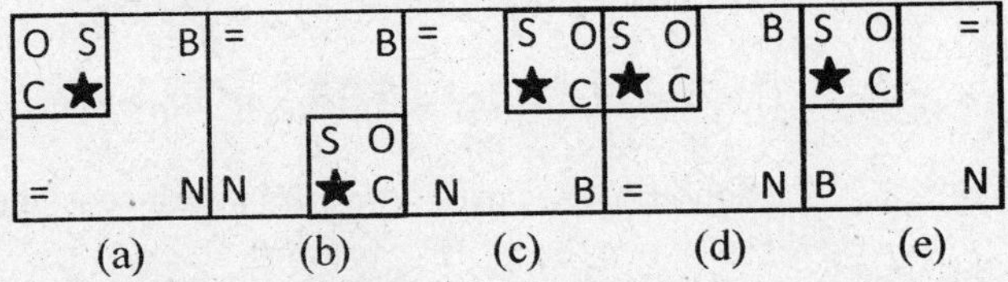

64. PROBLEM FIGURES

(1)	(2)	(3)	(4)	(5)
T □ O	A O △	3 A O	★ 3 B	3 □ K
A △	S □	K T	□ O	★ B
S L ★	K ★ T	△ □ ★	K △ T	△ T 6

ANSWER FIGURES

(a)	(b)	(c)	(d)	(e)
★ B □	★ K B	★ K B	★ B K	★ K B
△ K	△ □	△ □	△ □	3 □
P 6 3	T 6 3	C 6 3	C 6 3	Z 6 T

65. PROBLEM FIGURES

(1)	(2)	(3)	(4)	(5)
△ C T O □	△ □ O T C	C □ S T △	△C□ST	△ S B C T

ANSWER FIGURES

(a)	(b)	(c)	(d)	(e)
T △ S B C	S B C T △	S B C T △	T △ S B C	△ S ★ C T

Directions (Qs. 66-70) : Each of the following questions consists of six figures, the first of which is unnumbered and marks the beginning of the series continued in the sucessive figures numbered from (a) to (e). However, the series will be established only if the positions of two of the numbered figures are interchanged. The number of the first of the two figures is the answer. If no figure need to be interchanged then the answer is (e).

66.

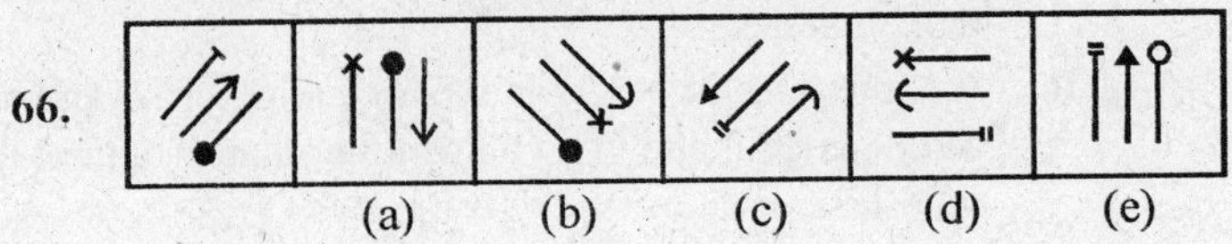

67.

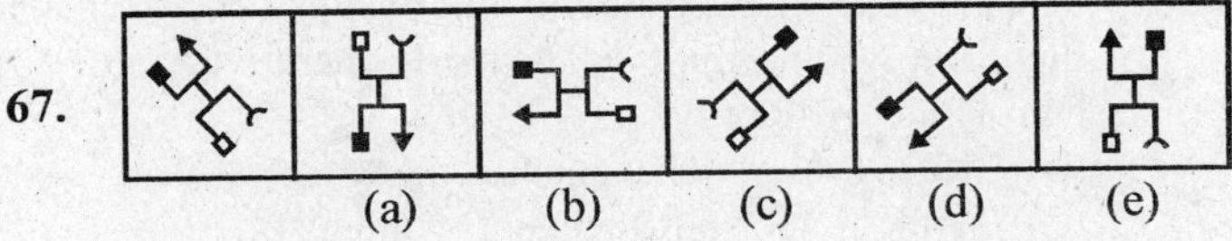

68.

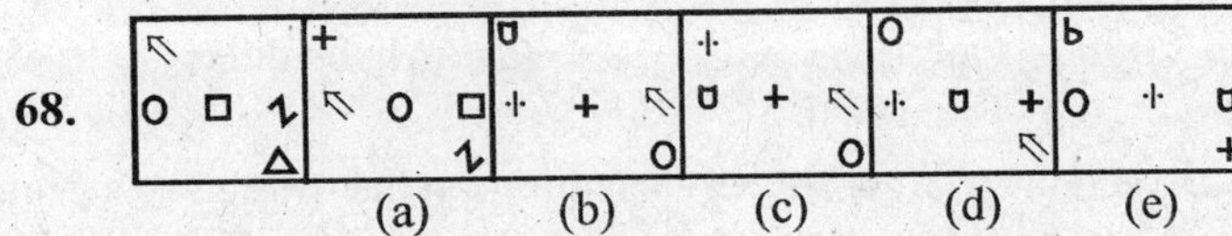

69.

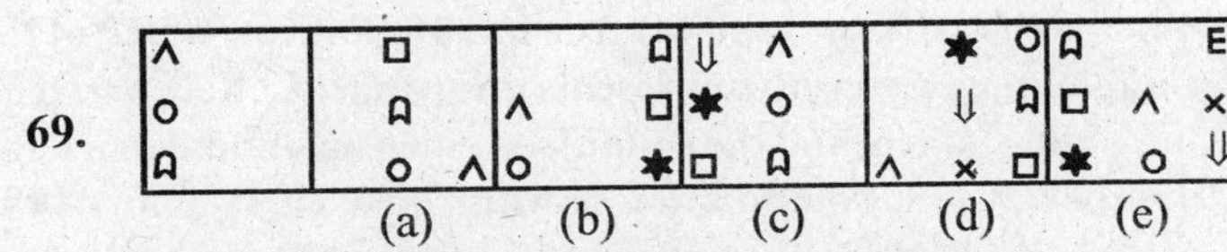

70.

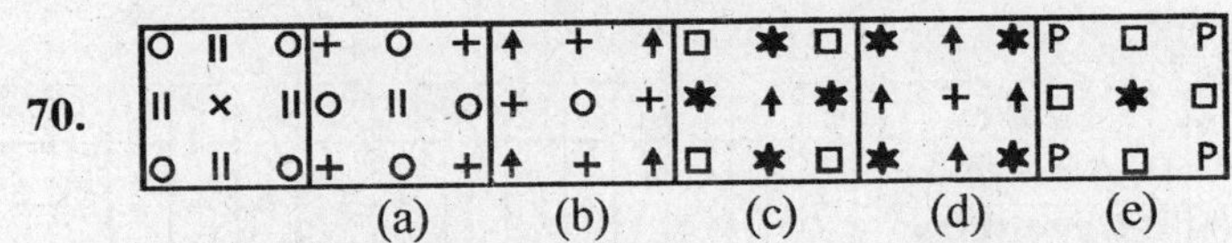

Directions (Qs. 71-75): In each question below, two sentences are given. These two sentences are to be combined into a single sentence without changing their meaning. Three probable starters of the so combined sentence are given which are denoted by (A), (B) and (C). Any one or more or none of them may be correct. Find out the correct starter(s), if any, and accordingly select your answer from among the given five answer choices.

71. He has lost his immunity. Therefore, he is vulnerable to any disease.
(A) His loss of immunity....
(B) Because of his vulnerability to his...
(C) His vulnerability to any disease...
(a) Only (A)
(b) Only (B)
(c) Only (C)
(d) Only (A) and (C)
(e) Only (A) and (B)

72. You must sign your railway ticket, write your name and age on it. It becomes valid only after that.
(A) To make your railway ticket valid, the railway authorities should sign...
(B) Without validating your railway ticket, you cannot...
(C) To validate your railway ticket, you must...
(a) Only (A)
(b) Only (B)
(c) Only (C)
(d) (A) and (B) only
(e) (B) and (C) only

73. Are you satisfied with this information? Please contact me for any further clarification.
(A) If you need...
(B) In case you need...
(C) Should you need...
(a) None
(b) All the three
(c) (A) and (C) only
(d) (A) and (B) only
(e) (B) and (C) only

74. How much you earn is less important. What is more important is how you earn, i.e., your methods of earning?
(A) How you earn is as important
(B) How much you earn is as important
(C) How you earn is not as important
(a) Only (A)
(b) Only (B)
(c) Only (C)
(d) All the three
(e) None of these

75. You must submit the proof of your being a US citizen. Only then your NRI account will be made operative.
   (A) Unless you prove...
   (B) Unless your NRI account is made operative...
   (C) Without your NRI account, you must...
   (a) Only (A) (b) Only (B)
   (c) Only (C) (d) All the three
   (e) None of these

Directions (Qs. 76-80): In each question below is given a group of letters followed by four combinations of digits/symbols numbered (a), (b), (c) and (d). You have to find out which of the combinations correctly represents the group of letters based on the coding system and the conditions given below and mark the number of that combination as your answer. If none of the combinations correctly represents the group of letters, mark (e) i.e. 'None of these' as your answer.

Letters	P	M	A	E	J	K	D	R	W	H	I	U	T	F
Digits/symbols Conditions	4	$	1	2	3	#	5	@	©	6	%	δ	7	9

(i) If the first letter is a consonant and the last letter is a vowel, the codes of both these are to be interchanged.
(ii) If both the first and the last letters are consonants both these are to be coded as per the code of the last letter.
(iii) If the first letter is vowel and the last letter is a consonant both these are to be coded as 'V'

Note: All the remaining letters are to be coded as per their original codes.

76. ERWHKA
   (a) 2@©6#1 (b) 1@©6#2
   (c) 1@©6#1 (d) 2@©6#2
   (e) None of these
77. MPEKDU
   (a) $42#5δ (b) $42#5$
   (c) δ42#5δ (d) δ425#$
   (e) None of these
78. TMEIUF
   (a) 7$2%δ9 (b) 7$2%δ7
   (c) 9$2%δ7 (d) 9$2%δ9
   (e) None of these
79. JTAERI
   (a) % 712@3 (b) 3712@3
   (c) V712@V (d) %712@%
   (e) None of these
80. UKTMIH
   (a) V#7$%6 (b) 6#7$%δ
   (c) V#7$%V (d) V7#$%6
   (e) None of these

Directions (Qs. 81-90) : Each of the questions below consists of a questions and two statements numbered I and II given below it. Use the data given to decide whether the data provided in the statements are sufficient to answer the question.

Read both the statements and Give answer
(a) if the data in statement I alone are sufficient to answer the question, while the data in statement II alone are not sufficient to answer the question.
(b) if the data in statement II alone are sufficient to answer the question, while the data in statement I alone are not sufficient to answer the question.
(c) if the data either in statement I alone or in statement II alone are sufficient to answer the question.
(d) if the data in both the statements I and II together are not sufficient to answer the question.
(e) if the data in both the statements I and II together are necessary to answer the question.

81. What will be the cost of the second necklace?
   I. The cost of the first necklace is more than $\frac{1}{5}$ of the second and the cost of the third necklace is more than $\frac{2}{5}$ of the second. The total cost of all the three necklaces is Rs. 120000.
   II. The cost of the first necklace is $\frac{2}{5}$ more than the second. The cost of the third necklace is the least and total cost of all the three necklaces is Rs. 1,20,000.
82. How many children are there in the class?
   I. Numbers of boys and girls are in the respective ratio of 3 : 4.
   II. Number of girls is more than the number of boys by 18.
83. What was the population of State 'A' in 1999?
   I. Population of the State increases every year by 20% and its population in 1997 was 1,20,000.
   II. Population of State A in 1997 was twice that of State B in the same year.
84. What is the cost of laying carpet in a rectangular hall?
   I. Cost of the carpet is ₹ 450 per square metre.
   II. Perimeter of the hall is 50 metres.
85. What is the rate of interest p.c.p.a.?
   I. Difference between compound interest and simple interest on an amount of ₹ 10,000 for two years is ₹225.
   II. The amount doubles itself on simple interest in $6\frac{2}{3}$ years.
86. Among M, K, B, D and W, who is the youngest?
   I. B is younger than D.
   II. W is younger than K but older than M.
87. What does 'Ne' stands for in the code language?
   I. 'Na Ni Nok Ne' means 'I will tell you' and 'Ni Nok Ne Nam' means 'he will tell you' in that code language.
   II. 'Ni Ne Mo Nam' means 'will he call you' and 'Ne Mok Sac Ni' means 'how will you go' in that code language.
88. Who amongst P, Q, R, S, T and U is the tallest?
   I. P is taller than R and T but not as tall as U, who is taller than Q and S.
   II. R is the third in height in the ascending order and not as tall as U, P and Q, Q being taller than P but not the tallest.

89. Who is paternal uncle of P?

I. P is brother of L, who is daughter of Q, who is sister of N, who is brother of S.

II. M is brother of K, who is husband of L, who is mother of G, who is sister of P.

90. What is Sudin's rank in the class of 44 students?

I. Ramesh, whose rank is 17th in the class, is ahead of Shyam by 6 ranks, Shyam being 7 ranks ahead of Sudin.

II. Suketu is 26 ranks ahead of Sudin and Shyamala is 6 ranks behind Sudin while Savita stands exactly in the middle of Shyamala and Suketu in ranks, her rank being 17.

Directions (Qs.91-95) : Rearrange the following six sentences (A), (B), (C), (D) and (F) in the proper sequence to form a meaningful paragraph, then answer the questions given below them.

(A) The group desired to enhance the learning experience in schools with an interactive digital medium that could be used within and outside the class-room

(B) Then the teacher can act on the downloaded data rather than collect it from each and every student and thereby save his time and effort.

(C) Eductor, decided the group of engineers, all alumni of the Indain Institute of technology, when the founded Edutor Technologies in August 2009.

(D) They can even take tests and submit them digitally using the same tablets and the teachers in turn can download the tests using the company's cloud services.

(E) With this desire they created a solution that digitzes school textbooks and other learning materials so that students no longer need to carry as many books to school and back as before, but can access their study material on their touch-screen tablets.

(F) A mechanic works on motors and an accountant has his computer. Likewise, if a student has to work on a machine or device, what should it be called?

91. Which of the following sentences should be the **FIRST** after rearrangement?

(a) F (b) D
(c) A (d) C
(e) E

92. Which of the following sentences should be the **THIRD** after rearrangement?

(a) A (b) B
(c) D (d) E
(e) F

93. Which of the following sentences should be the **SIXTH (LAST)** after rearrangement?

(a) A (b) F
(c) E (d) B
(e) D

94. Which of the following sentences should be the **FOURTH** after rearrangement?

(a) A (b) F
(c) E (d) B
(e) D

95. Which of the following sentences should be the **FIFTH** after rearrangement?

(a) A (b) D
(c) C (d) E
(e) F

Directions (Qs. 96-100) : In these questions the symbols @. #, $, % and ★ are used with different meanings as follow.

'A @ B ' means 'A is not smaller then B'.
'A # B ' means 'A is neither smaller than nor equal to B'.
'A $ B' means 'A is neither greater than nor smaller than B'.
'A % B' means 'A is not greater than B'.
'A ★ B' means 'A is neither greater than nor equal to B'.

Now in each of the following questions assuming the given statements to be true, find out which of the conclusion I, II, III given below them is/are definitely true and mark your answer accordingly.

96. Statements: V $ Y, Y @ Z, Z % X, X # T

Conclusions:

I. T # Z II. X # Y
III. Z ★ Y

(a) None follows (b) Only I follows
(c) II and III follow (d) I and III follow
(e) Only III follows

97. Statements: R @ J, J % F, F ★ E, E % M

Conclusions:

I. M # J II. F % M
III. M ★ R

(a) Only I follows (b) Only II follows
(c) Only III follows (d) I and II follow
(e) All follow

98. Statements: H#R, R@L, L ★ W, W%F

Conclusions:

I. H # J II. F # L
III. H $ F

(a) Only I follows (b) I and II follow
(c) II and III follow (d) Either I or II follows
(e) All follow

99. Statements: M # K, M $ F, F % Q, Q ★ H

Conclusions:

I. H # K
II. Q # K
III. Q @ M

(a) I and II follow (b) Either I or II follows
(c) All follow (d) II and III follow
(e) None of the above

100. Statements: D ★ Q, Q $ L, L # T, T % H

Conclusions:

I. D ★ L
II. L @ H
III. H # L

(a) Only I follows (b) I and II follow
(c) Either II or III follows (d) All follow
(e) None follow

Directions (Qs. 101-105) : Given an input line the machine arranges the words and numbers in steps in a systematic manner as illustrated below:

Input line 59 dress fine shine 32 66 72 offer
Step I 72 56 dress fine shine 32 66 offer
Step II 72 shine 56 dress fine 32 66 offer
Step III 72 shine 66 56 dress fine 32 offer
Step IV 72 shine 66 offer 56 dress fine 32
Step V 72 shine 66 offer 56 fine dress 32
Step VI 72 shine 66 offer 56 fine 32 dress
STEP VI is the last step and the output in Step VI is the final output.

As per the rules followed in the above steps, find out in each of the following questions the appropriate step for the given input.

101. Step IV of an input is '62 sound 56 sleep roam present 33 49'. What will be the input definitely?
(a) Sound 62 sleep 56 roam present 33 49
(b) Sleep sound 62 56 roam present 33 49
(c) 62 Sound sleep 56 roam present 33 49
(d) Cannot be determined
(e) None of the above

102. Which of the following will be the third step for input 'jockey firm 36 43 growth chart 22 45 ?
(a) 45 jockey 43 growth firm 36 chart 22
(b) 45 jockey 43 firm growth 36 chart 22
(c) 45 jockey 43 growth 36 firm chart 22
(d) 45 jockey 43 firm 36 growth chart 22
(e) None of the above

103. Step II of an input is '53' window 42 50 door lock key 36'. How many more steps will be required to complete the arrangement?
(a) Three (b) Four
(c) Five (d) Six
(e) None of these

104. What will be the fifth step of an input whose first step is '85 journey train 36 54 daily 28 mansion'?
(a) 85 train 54 mansion 28 journey daily 36
(b) 85 train 54 mansion journey 36 daily 28
(c) 85 train 54 mansion 36 journey daily 28
(d) There is no such step
(e) None of the above

105. Which step will be the last step for an input whose second step is '63' Sour 18 56 grapes healthy 32 rise'?
(a) IV (b) V
(c) VIII (d) VII
(e) None of these

106. Which word/number will be sixth from right in step fifth whose second step is '63 Sour 18 56 grapes healthy 32 rise'?
(a) Rise (b) 56
(c) Sour (d) 32
(e) 18

107. There were 42 students in a hostel. Due to the admission of 13 new studenets, the expenses of the mess increase by ₹ 31 per day while the average expenditure per head diminished by ₹ 3. What was the original expenditure of the mass?
(a) ₹633.23 (b) ₹583.3
(c) ₹623.3 (d) ₹632
(e) None of these

108. A bag contains 5 red and 4 green balls and another bag contains 3 red and 7 black balls. If a ball is drawn from each bag. Find the probability that both are of different colours.
(a) $\frac{47}{90}$ (b) $\frac{5}{6}$
(c) $\frac{7}{18}$ (d) $\frac{2}{15}$
(e) None of these

109. The probability of getting 10 in a single throw of three fair dice is
(a) $\frac{1}{6}$ (b) $\frac{1}{8}$
(c) $\frac{1}{9}$ (d) None of these
(e) None of these

110. A circle with radius 2 is placed against a right angle. Another smaller circle is also placed as shown in the adjoining figure. What is the radius of the smaller circle?

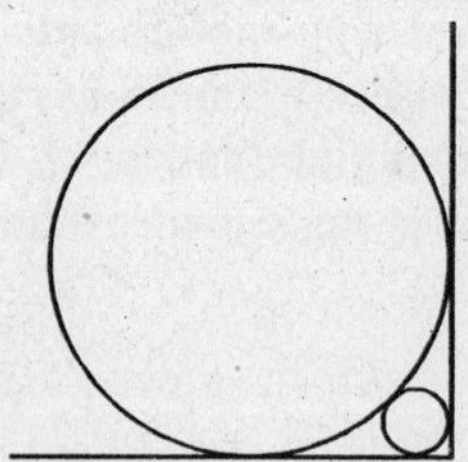

(a) $3-2\sqrt{2}$ (b) $4-2\sqrt{2}$
(c) $7-4\sqrt{2}$ (d) $6-4\sqrt{2}$
(e) None of these

Directions (Qs. 111-115): In each of the questions given below which one of the five Answer Figures on the right should come after the Problem Figures on the left, if the sequence were continued?

PROBLEM FIGURES

111.

□ S △ E C ☆ O B K L	☆ C E △ S □ L O B K	O △ B □ K L C ☆ E S	B ☆ K E C S O △ □ L	△ E □ S L O ☆ B K C

ANSWER FIGURES

(a)	(b)	(c)	(d)	(e)
B S K O C ☆ E △ □ L	O □ S L E △ C ☆ B K	L O S □ △ E C ☆ B K	O L S □ E △ C ☆ B K	□ B ☆ K L C △ E S O

112.

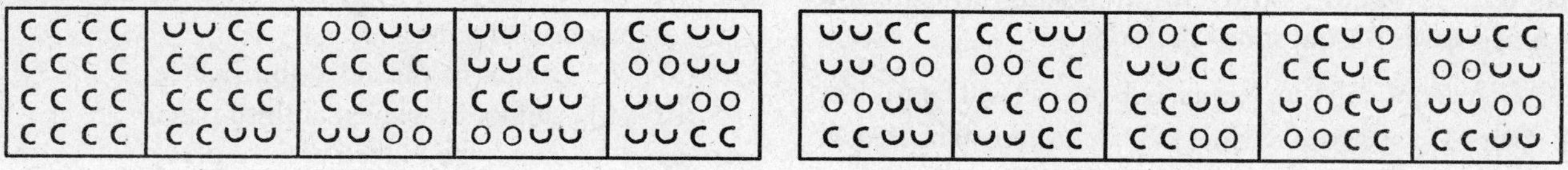

(a) (b) (c) (d) (e)

113.

(a) (b) (c) (d) (e)

114.

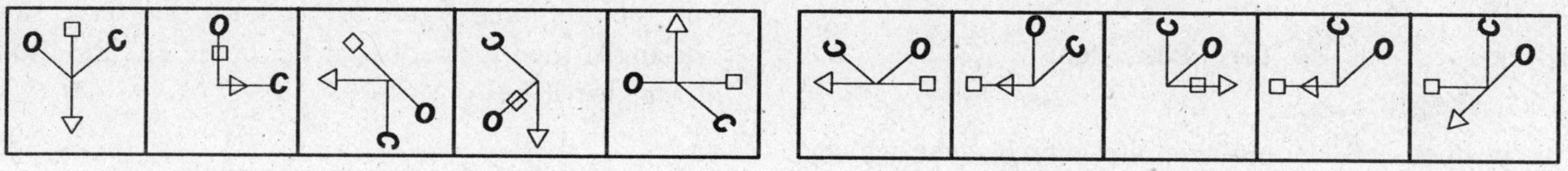

(a) (b) (c) (d) (e)

115.

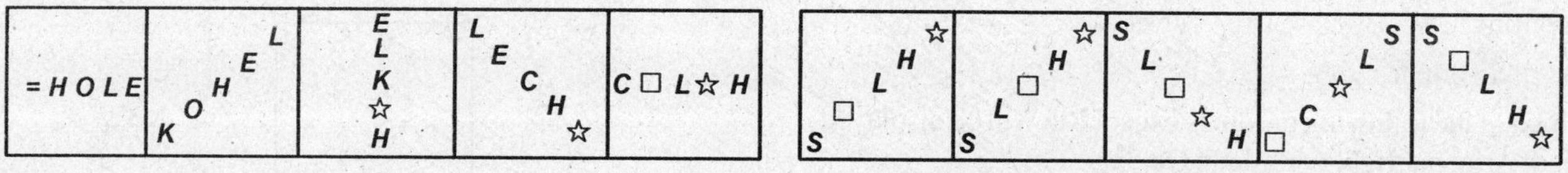

(a) (b) (c) (d) (e)

Directions (Qs. 116-118) : Choose the word which best expresses the closest meaning of the given word.

116. APOLITICAL
- (a) Antipolitical
- (b) Terrorist
- (c) Not interested in politics
- (d) Subversive
- (e) None of these

117. CANDOUR
- (a) Enthusiasm (b) Openness
- (c) Freedom (d) Intimacy
- (e) None of these

118. TRIVIAL
- (a) Significant (b) Momentous
- (c) Unimportant (d) Critical
- (e) None of these

Directions (Qs. 119-120) : Choose the word which best expresses the opposite meaning of the given word.

119. ELAN
- (a) Brashness (b) Dignity
- (c) Composure (d) Nervousness
- (e) None of these

120. IRASCIBLE
- (a) Kind (b) Friendly
- (c) Roguish (d) Clever
- (e) None of these

Directions (121-125) : Which phrase should replace the phrase given in bold in the sentence to make it grammatically correct? If the sentence is correct as it is given, then mark 'No correction required' as your answer.

121. We asked her **that how she got** time to write all these books.
- (a) that how did she got
- (b) that how she was getting
- (c) how did she get
- (d) how she got
- (e) No correction required

122. Studies in the past have shown that those who limit their activity span during the day in winters are **more likely to** suffer from depression.
- (a) more likely for (b) mostly likely to
- (c) most likely for (d) most likeliest for
- (c) No correction required

123. In some cases, factors like low salary, lack of growth prospects and lack of motivation **compel all employee** to look for a change.
- (a) compel those employees
- (b) compelling all employees
- (c) compelling the employee
- (d) compel employees
- (e) No correction required

124. Living with compassion and contributing to others lives **would helping us** add happiness to our lives as well.
- (a) will helping us (b) will help us
- (c) would helped them (d) will helped us
- (e) No correction required

125. The **easiest way for** prevent stress caused by work or home pressures is to indulge in high levels of physical activity.
- (a) easily way to (b) easier ways for
- (c) easiest way to (d) easier way from
- (e) No correction required

Directions (Qs. 126-128) : Study the following information carefully and answer the questions that follow :

Six products – Ariel, Vivel, Rin, Nirma, Gillette Gel and Pepsodent – are to be placed in six display windows' of a shop numbered 1-6 from left to right of a shopper standing outside the shop. As per the company requirements, Rin and Ariel should be displayed next to each other, but Ariel should be at least three windows away from Nirma. Pepsodent is preferred to be kept between Gillette Gel and Rin but away from Vivel at least by two windows. Vivel cannot be displayed next to Rin for the reasons of mixed-product identity. Also Vivel cannot be displayed in window 1.

126. Which of the following products is displayed left to Ariel?

(a) Vivel (b) Nirma
(c) Rin (d) Pepsodent
(e) Giuette gel

127. If the positions of Rin and Ariel are interchanged, which item will be displayed in window 5?

(a) Ariel (b) Nirma
(c) Rin (d) Vivel
(e) Pepsodent

128. Which of the following products except Rin will be displayed left of Ariel but right of Gillette Gel?

(a) Vivel (b) Rin
(c) Pepsodent (d) Nirma
(e) None of these

Directions (Qs. 129-132) : Study the following information carefully and answer the questions that follow :

In a club, combinations of five out of the eight songs P, Q, R, S, T, U, V and W are to be played by a DJ on a daily basis. On any one day, except for the first day of a month, only three of the songs must be the ones that were played on the previous day. The song combinations must also satisfy the following conditions :

(i) If song "P" is to be played on a day, song "V" cannot be played.
(ii) If song "Q" is to be played on a day, "T" must be one of the songs to be played after "Q".
(iii) If "R" is to be played on a day, "V" must be one of the songs to be Played after "R".
(iv) The last song to be played on any day must be either "S" or "U".

129. Which of the following could be the combination of songs to be played on the first day of a month ?

(a) P, R, V, S, U (b) Q, S, R, V, U
(c) T, U, R, V, S (d) U, Q, S, T, W
(e) None of these

130. If the songs "R" and "W" are to be played on the first day, which of the following could be the other songs to be played on that day ?

(a) P, T, U (b) Q, S, V
(c) T, S, V (d) Q, T, V
(e) None of these

131. Which of the following is TRUE of any day's valid combination of songs ?

(a) "P" cannot be played at third place
(b) "Q" cannot be played at third place
(c) "T" cannot be played at third place
(d) "U" cannot be played at fourth place
(e) None of these

132. If song "R" is played at third place in a sequence, which of the following cannot be the second song to be played in that sequence ?

(a) Q (b) S
(c) T (d) U
(e) None of these

133. If the length of diagonals DF, AG and CE of the cube shown in the adjoining figure are equal to the three sides of a triangle, then the radius of the circle circumscribing that triangle will be

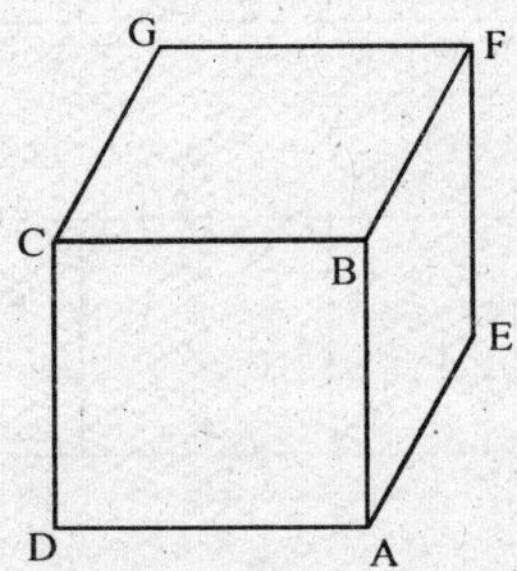

(a) equal to the side of the cube
(b) $\sqrt{3}$ times the side of the cube
(c) $\frac{1}{\sqrt{3}}$ times the side of the cube
(d) impossible to find from the given information
(e) None of these

134. A square is inscribed in a circle which is inscribed in an equilateral triangle. If one side of the triangle is 'a', find the area of the square.

(a) $\frac{a^2}{3}$ (b) $\frac{a^2}{6}$
(c) $\frac{3a^2}{8}$ (d) $\frac{\pi a^2}{12}$
(e) None of these

135. Find the area of the shaded region if ΔABC is an equilateral triangle of side 6 cm.

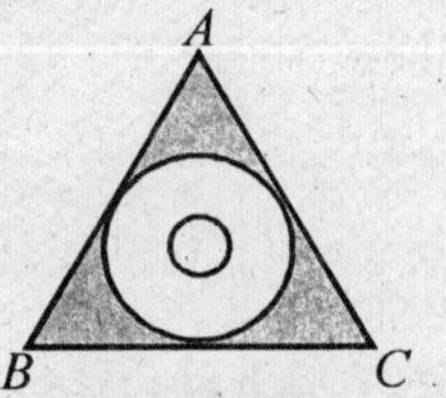

(a) 6.15 cm. (b) 5.15 cm.
(c) 4 cm. (d) 3.12 cm.
(e) None of these

Directions (Qs. 136-138) : Attempt these questions based on the information given against each :

136. Choose the option that best captures the essence of the text given below :

Some decisions will be fairly obvious - "no-brainers." Your bank account is low, but you have a two week vacation coming up and you want to get away to some place warm to relax with your family. Will you accept your in-laws' offer of free use of their Florida beachfront condo ? Sure. You like your employer and feel ready to move forward in your career. Will you step in for your boss for three weeks while she attends a professional development course? Of course

A. Some decisions are obvious under certain circumstances. You may, for example, readily accept a relative's offer of free holiday accommodation. Or step in for your boss when she is away.

B. Some decisions are no brainers. You need not think when making them. Examples are condo offers from in-laws and job offers from bosses when your bank account is low or boss is away.

C. Easy decisions are called "no-brainers" because they do not require any cerebral activity. Examples such as accepting free holiday accommodation abound in our lives.

D. Accepting an offer from in-laws when you are short on funds and want a holiday is a no-brainer. Another no-brainer is taking the boss's job when she is away.

(a) A (b) B
(c) C (d) D
(e) None of these

137. Choose the option that best captures the essence of the text given below :

Physically, inertia is a feeling that you just can't move; mentally, it is a sluggish mind. Even if you try to be sensitive, if your mind is sluggish, you just don't feel anything intensely. You may even see a tragedy enacted in front of your eyes and not be able to respond meaningfully. You may see one person exploiting another, one group persecuting another, and not be able to get angry. Your energy is frozen. You are not deliberately refusing to act; you just don't have the capacity.

A. Inertia makes your body and mind sluggish. They become insensitive to tragedies, exploitation, and persecution because it freezes your energy and decapacitates it.

B. When you have inertia you don't act although you see one person exploiting another or one group persecuting another. You don't get angry because you are incapable.

C. Inertia is of two types – physical and mental. Physical inertia restricts bodily movements. Mental inertia prevents mental response to events enacted in front of your eyes.

D. Physical inertia stops your body from moving; mental inertia freezes your energy, and stop your mind from responding meaningfully to events, even tragedies, in front of you.

(a) A (b) B
(c) C (d) D
(e) None of these

138. Choose the option that best captures the essence of the text given below :

Try before you buy We use this memorable saying to urge you to experience the consequences of an alternative before you choose it, whenever this is feasible . If you are considering buying a van after having always owned sedans, rent one for a week or borrow a friend's. By experiencing the consequences first hand, they become more meaningful. In addition, you are likely to identify consequences you had not even thought of before. May be you will discover that it is difficult to park the van in your small parking space at work, but that, on the other hand , your elderly father has a much easier time getting in and out of it

A. If you are planning to buy a van after being used to sedans, borrow a van or rent it and try it before deciding to buy it. Then you may realize that parking a van is difficult while it is easier for your elderly father to get in and out of it.

B. Before choosing an alternative, experience its consequences if feasible. If, for example, you want to change from sedans to a van, try one before buying it. You will discover aspects you may never have thought of.

C. Always try before you buy anything. You are bound to discover many consequences. One of the consequences of going in for a van is that it is more difficult to park than sedans at the office car park.

D. We urge you to try products such as vans before buying them. Then you can experience consequences you have not thought of such as parking problems. But your father may find vans more comfortable than cars.

(a) A (b) B
(c) C (d) D
(e) None of these

Directions (Qs. 139) : Go through the caselets below and answer the questions that follow :

139. Goodricke Group Ltd is planning to give top priority to core competence of production and marketing of tea in 2007. The company intends to increase the production of orthodox varieties of tea. Goodricke is planning to invest Rs. 10 crore to modernise the factories. The company has announced a net profit of Rs. 5.49 crore for 2006 as against Rs. 3.76 crore in 2005.

Which of the following can be deduced from the caselet?

(a) Core competence can be used for furthering company's interests.

(b) Production and marketing is core competence of Goodricke Group.

(c) Increase in production of existing products enhances core competence.

(d) Core competence leads to modernisation.

(e) None of these

140. I have been studying it, consciously and subconsciously, for forty years and I still find men unaccountable; people I know intimately can surprise me by some action of which I never thought them capable or by the discovery of some trait exhibit a side of themselves that I never even suspected. The idea in this sentence can be best summarised as

(a) Men are inconsistent and therefore one should not be confident even about one's closest friends.
(b) Men are unpredictable, one can never tell what they will do next, hence one should be very careful in one's dealings.
(c) No matter how closely you know somebody there still exists an unknown facet of his personality.
(d) If you know somebody still you cannot predict his behaviour.
(e) None of these

Directions (Qs.141-144) : Study the following information carefully and answer questions that follow :

The convenience of online shopping is what I like best about it. Where else can you shop even at midnight wearing your night suit? You do not have to wait in a line till the shop assistant is ready to help you with your purchases. It is much better experience as compared to going to a retail store. – A consumer's view.

141. Which of the following can be a **strong argument** in favour of retail store owners?

(a) Online shopping portals offer a great deal of discounts which retail stores offer only during the sale season.
(b) One can compare a variety of products online which cannot be done at retail stores.
(c) Many online shopping portals offer the 'cash on delivery' feature which is for those who are sceptical about online payments.
(d) Many consumers prefer shopping at retail stores which are nearer to their houses.
(e) In online shopping the customer may be deceived as he cannot touch the product he is paying for.

142. Which of the following can be **inferred** from the given information? *(An inference is something that is not directly stated but can be inferred from the given information)*

(a) One can shop online only at night.
(b) Those who are not comfortable using computers can never enjoy the experience of online shopping.
(c) All retail stores provide shopping assistants to each and every customer.
(d) The consumer whose view is presented has shopped at retailr stores as well as online.
(e) The consumer whose view is presented does not have any retail stores in her vicinity.

143. Read the following information carefully and answer the given question:

Many manufacturing companies are now shifting base to the rural areas of the country as there is a scarcity of space in urban areas. Analysts say that this shift will not have a huge impact on the prices of the products manufacutured by these companies as only about 30% consumers live in urban areas.

Which of the following may be **consequence** of the given information?

(a) The prices of such products will decrease drastically in the urban areas.
(b) People living in urban areas will not be allowed to work in such manufacturing companies.
(c) These manufacturing companies has set-ups in the urban areas before shifting base.
(d) Those who had already migrated to the urban areas will not shift back to rural areas.
(e) The number of people migrated from rural to urban areas in search of jobs may reduce.

144. Read the following information carefully and answer the given question:

'Pets are not allowed in the park premises' - A notice put up at the park entrance by the authority that is responsible for maintenance of the park.

Which of the following can be **an assumption** according to the given information? *(An assumption is something that is supposed or taken for granted)*

(a) At least some people who visit the park have pets.
(b) This is the only park which does not allow pets
(c) People who ignored this notice were fined
(d) There are more than one entrances to the park
(e) Many people have now stopped visiting the park

145. In a code language 'PROVIDE' is written as 'MULYFGB', then what will be code for 'BECAUSE' in same languages

(a) YZHDRVB (b) ZHYDRVB
(c) YHZDRVB (d) ZYDHVBR
(e) None of these

Directions (Qs.146-155): In the following passage there are blanks, each of which has been numbered. These numbers are printed below the passage and against each, five words/phrases are suggested, one of which fits the blank appropriately. Find out the appropriate word/phrase in each case.

There is a considerable amount of research about the factors that make a company innovate. So is it possible to create an environment **(146)** to innovation? This is a particularly pertinent **(147)** for India today. Massive problems in health, education etc. **(148)** be solved using a conventional approach but **(149)** creative and innovative solutions that can ensure radical change and **(150).** There are several factors in India's **(151).** Few countries have the rich diversity that India or its large, young population **(152).** While these **(153)** innovation policy interventions certain additional steps also required. These include **(154)** investment in research and development **(155)** the government and the private sector, easy transfer of technology form the academic world etc. To fulfill its promise of being prosperous and to be at the forefront, India must be innovative.

146. (a) stimuli (b) conducive
(c) incentive (d) facilitated
(e) impetus

147. (a) objective (b) controversy
(c) doubt (d) question
(e) inference

148. (a) cannot (b) possibly
(c) should (d) never
(e) must

149. (a) necessary (b) apply
(c) need (d) consider
(e) requires

150. (a) quantity (b) advantages
(c) increase (d) chaos
(e) growth

151. (a) challenges (b) praises
(c) favour (d) leverage
(e) esteem

152. (a) blessed (b) enjoys
(c) endows (d) prevails
(e) occurs

153. (a) aid (b) jeopardise
(c) promotes (d) endure
(e) cater

154. (a) acute (b) utilising
(c) restricting (d) inspiring
(e) increased

155. (a) both (b) besides
(c) combining (d) participating
(e) also

Directions (Qs. 156-157) : In each question, a statement is followed by three courses of action numbered I, II and III. Assume everything in the statement to be true. Decide which of the three given suggested courses of action logically follows for pursuing.

156. Statement :
The world will have to feed more than 10 billion people in the next century of whom half will be in Asia and will eat rice as their staple.

Courses of Action :

I. More funds should immediately be allocated for rice research to help ensure adequate supplies.
II. The people in Asia should be encouraged to change their food habit.
III. The rice should be grown in countries outside Asia to meet the demand.

(a) Only I and II follow
(b) Only II and III follow
(c) All follow
(d) None follows
(e) Only I and III follow

157. Statement :
If the faculty members also join the strike, then there is going to be a serious problem.

Courses of Action :

I. The faculty members should be persuaded not to go on strike.
II. Those faculty members who join the strike should be suspended.
III. The management should not worry about such small things

(a) None follows
(b) Only I follows
(c) Only I and II follow
(d) Only II and III follow
(e) All follow

158. A cylinder is circumscribed about a hemisphere and a cone is inscribed in the cylinder so as to have its vertex at the centre of one end, and the other end as its base. The volume of the cylinder, hemisphere and the cone are, respectively in the ratio :

(a) 2:3:2 (b) 3:2:1
(c) 3:1:2 (d) 1:2:3
(e) None of these

159. A right circular cone of height h is cut by a plane parallel to the base and at a distance h/3 from the base, then the volumes of the resulting cone and frustum are in the ratio

(a) 1:3 (b) 8:19
(c) 1:4 (d) 1:7
(e) None of these

160. Tap *A* can fill a tank in 20 hours, *B* in 25 hours but tap *C* can empty a full tank in 30 hours. Starting with *A*, followed by *B* and *C* each tap opens alternatively for one hour period till the tank gets filled up completely. In how many hour the tank will be filled up completely?

(a) $51\frac{11}{15}$ (b) $52\frac{2}{3}$
(c) $24\frac{4}{11}$ (d) $55\frac{2}{3}$
(e) None of these

Directions (Qs. 161-165) : Study the following table carefully and answer the questions given below it.

Fare in rupees for three different types of vehicles

Vehicle	Fare for distance upto					
	2 km	4 km	7 km	10 km	15 km	20 km
Type A	₹ 5.00	₹ 9.00	₹ 13.50	₹ 17.25	₹ 22.25	₹ 26.00
Type B	₹ 7.50	₹ 14.50	₹ 24.25	₹ 33.25	₹ 45.75	₹ 55.75
Type C	₹ 10.00	₹ 19.00	₹ 31.00	₹ 41.50	₹ 56.50	₹ 69.00

Note : Fare per km for intermittent distance is the same.

161. Shiv Kumar has to travel a distance of 15 kms in all. He decides to travel equal distance by each of the three types of vehicles. How much money is to be spent as fare?

(a) ₹51.75 (b) ₹47.50
(c) ₹47.25 (d) ₹51.25
(e) None of these

162. Ajit Singh wants to travel a distance of 15 kms. He starts his journey by Type A vehicle. After travelling 6 kms, he changes the vehicle to Type B for the remaining distance. How much money will he be spending in all?

(a) ₹42.25 (b) ₹36.75
(c) ₹40.25 (d) ₹42.75
(e) None of these

163. Mr X wants to travel a distance of 8 kms by Type A vehicle. How much more money will be required to be spent if he decides to travel by Type B vehicle instead of Type A?

(a) ₹16 (b) ₹12.50
(c) ₹14 (d) ₹13.50
(e) None of these

164. Rita hired a Type B vehicle for travelling a distance of 18 kms. After travelling 5 kms, she changed the vehicle to Type A. Again after travelling 8 kms by Type A vehicle, she changed the vehicle to Type C and completed her journey. How much money did she spend in all?

(a) ₹ 50 (b) ₹ 45.50
(c) ₹ 55 (d) ₹ 50.50
(e) None of these

165. Fare for 14th km by Type C vehicle is equal to the fare for which of the following?

(a) Type B – 11th km (b) Type B – 9th km
(c) Type A – 4th km (d) Type C – 8th km
(e) None of these

Directions (Qs. 166-170) : Study the following table to answer the given questions.

Number of students of different classes of a school playing different games.

Class → / Games ↓	XII	XI	X	IX	VIII	VII	VI
Chess	11	12	5	4	2	2	1
Cricket	38	40	12	17	25	18	20
Basket ball	11	9	7	6	0	0	0
Table Tennis	9	9	21	19	11	9	0
Football	40	27	18	19	12	16	14
Carrom	16	15	8	19	12	16	14
Tennis	8	9	11	5	6	0	0
Badminton	47	39	33	21	19	0	0

166. **Approximately** what per cent of Class VIII students play Cricket out of the total students playing Cricket?

(a) 13 (b) 4
(c) 25 (d) 15
(e) 17

167. What is the ratio of the students playing Football in Class XI to those in Class X?

(a) 1:2 (b) 2:5
(c) 2:3 (d) 3:2
(e) None of these

168. Which game is the most popular?

(a) Badminton (b) Football
(c) Carrom (d) Table Tennis
(e) Cricket

169. **Approximately** what per cent of Class X students play the Table Tennis out of the total Class X students playing the different given games?

(a) 20 (b) 21
(c) 27 (d) 26
(e) 18

170. Which game has ascending number of students from class IX to XII?

(a) Only Basketball (b) Only Badminton
(c) Chess and Badminton (d) No game
(e) None of these

Directions (Qs. 171-174) : Study the following information carefully and answer the questions that follow :

A scientist is trying to find a cure for the common cold using four ingredients. He can choose from the stable chemicals A, B and C and the unstable chemicals W, X, Y and Z, In order for the formula not to explode, there must be two stable chemicals in it Also, certain chemicals cannot be mixed because of their reaction together. Chemical B cannot be mixed with Chemical W. Chemical Y cannot be mixed with Chemical Z.

171. If the scientist calculated that Y is the most important chemical and must be used in the formula, which other ingredients must be a part of the cure?

(a) *A, B* and *Z* (b) *B, C* and *Z*
(c) *A, B* and *W* (d) *A, B* and *X*
(e) None of these

172. The scientist rejected chemical B because of its possible side effects but decided to use chemical Z. Which is a possible combination of the four ingredients in the formula?

(a) *A, W, Y* and *Z* (b) *A, C, W,* and *Z*
(c) *A, W, X* and *Z* (d) *A, X, Y* and *Z*
(e) None of these

173. Which of the following combinations of chemicals is impossible?

I. Using chemical *Y* and *W* together
II. Using chemical *B* and *C* together
III. Using chemical *W, X* and *Z* together

(a) III only (b) I and III only
(c) I only (d) II only
(e) None of these

174. Which of the following can never be true?

I. If chemical *C* is used, chemical *Z* is added
II. If chemical *A* is not used, chemical *W* is added
III. If chemical *C* is used, chemical *W* is added

(a) III only (b) (I) and (II) only
(c) (I), (II) and (III) (d) (II) only
(e) None of these

Directions (Qs. 175-177) : Study the following information carefully and answer the questions that follow :

Seven offices in an office building are to be painted. The offices, which are on one side of a hallway, are numbered consecutively. One to seven, from the front of the building to the back. Each office is to be painted one colour only according to the following conditions:

- Two offices must be painted white;
- Two offices must be painted blue
- Two offices must be painted green; and one office must be painted yellow'
- Two offices painted green must be next to each other
- Two offices painted blue cannot be next to each other
- The office painted yellow cannot be next to an office painted white
- Office 3 must be painted white

175. If office 4 is painted white and an Office that is painted green is next to an office that is painted white, which of the following must be true?
(a) Office 7 must be painted blue
(b) Office 6 must be painted white
(c) Office 6 must be painted blue
(d) Office 1 must be painted yellow
(e) None of these

176. If office 5 is painted white, which of the following could be true?
(a) Office 6 is painted blue
(b) Office 2 is painted yellow
(c) Office 4 is painted yellow
(d) Office 1 is painted blue
(e) None of these

177. Which of the following conditions, when combined with the original conditions, has the consequence of completely determining the colour that each office is painted?
(a) Office 6 must be painted blue
(b) Office 6 must be painted white
(c) Office 1 must be painted green
(d) Office 4 must be painted green
(e) None of these

Directions (Qs.178-180) : Below in each questions are given two statements (A) and (B). These statements may be either independent causes or may be effects of independent causes or a common cause. One of these statements may be the effect of the other statement. Read both the statements and decide which of the following answer choice correctly depicts the relationship between these two statements.

Mark answer (a) if statement (A) is the cause and statement (B) is its effect.

Mark answer (b) if statement (B) is the cause and statement (A) is its effect.

Mark answer (c) if both the statements (A) and (B) are independent causes.

Mark answer (d) if both the statements (A) and (B) are effects of independent causes.

Mark answer (e) if both the statements (A) and (B) are effects of some common cause.

178. (A) The local traders' association urged all its members to shut their establishments for two days and participate in the protest march.
(B) Government has recently cancelled licenses of many traders in the locality as they did not pay their taxes in time.

179. (A) Government has increased the procurement price of kharif crops by about ten per cent for the current year.
(B) Inadequate monsoon rainfall has created a drought like situation in many parts of the country.

180. (A) The Government has recently lifted ban on import of sugar for selling in the retail market.
(B) The prices of sugar in the retail market have stabilized after a considerable gap.

Directions (Qs. 181-185) : Study the following pie-chart carefully and answer the questions that follow :

Cost estimated by a family in renovation of their house

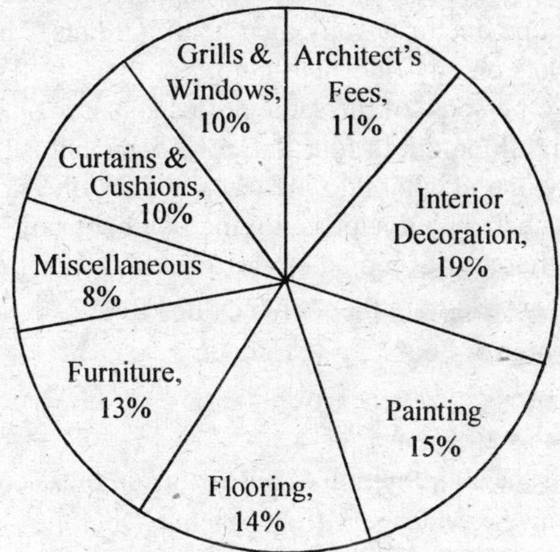

Total estimated cost is ₹1,20,000

181. What is the difference in the amount estimated by the family on interior decoration and that on architect's fees?
(a) ₹10,000 (b) ₹9,500
(c) ₹7,200 (d) ₹9,000
(e) None of these

182. During the process of renovation, the family actually incurred miscellaneous expenditure of ₹10,200. The miscellaneous expenditure incurred by the family is what percentage of the total estimated cost?
(a) 9.5% (b) 9%
(c) 8.5% (d) 10.5%
(e) None of these

183. Other than getting the discount of 12% on the estimated cost of furniture and the actual miscellaneous expenditure being ₹10,200 instead of the estimated one, the family's estimated cost is correct. What is the total amount spend by the family in renovating its house?
(a) ₹1,16,728 (b) ₹1,15,926
(c) ₹1,19,500 (d) ₹1,16,500
(e) None of these

184. What is the cost estimated by the family on painting and flooring together?
(a) ₹36,500 (b) ₹34,800
(c) ₹36,000 (d) ₹34,500
(e) None of these

185. The family gets a discount on furniture and pays 12% less than the estimated cost on furniture. What is the amount spent on furniture?
(a) ₹13,200 (b) ₹14,526
(c) ₹13,526 (d) ₹13,728
(e) None of these

Directions (Qs. 186-189) : Study the following information carefully and answer the questions that follow :

In a building there are thirteen flats on three floors— II, III and IV. Five flats are unoccupied. Three managers, two teachers, two lawyers and one doctor occupy the remaining flats. There are at least three flats on any floor and not more than six flats on any floor. No two persons of the same profession stay on any floor. On the second floor, out of four flats, one occupant is the lawyer and has only one neighbour. One teacher lives one floor below the other teacher. The doctor is not the neighbour of any of the lawyers. No flat is unoccupied on the third floor.

186. How many flats are there on the third floor?
(a) Three or Four (b) Four
(c) Five (d) Three
(e) None of these

187. What is the combination of occupants on the second floor?
(a) Lawyer, Manager (b) Teacher, Doctor
(c) Manager, Doctor (d) Manager, Teacher
(e) None of these

188. Who among the following is the neighbour of the other lawyer?
(a) Manager
(b) Teacher
(c) Both the Manager and the Teacher
(d) Data inadequate
(e) None of these

189. How many flats are occupied on the fourth floor?
(a) Two (b) Three
(c) Four (d) Data inadequate
(e) None of these

Directions (Qs. 190-195) : In each of these questions, a number series is given. In each series, only one number is wrong. Find out the wrong number.

190. 3601 3602 1803 604 154 36 12
(a) 3602 (b) 1803
(c) 604 (d) 154
(e) 36

191. 4 12 42 196 1005 6066 42511
(a) 12 (b) 42
(c) 1005 (d) 196
(e) 6066

192. 2 8 12 20 30 42 56
(a) 8 (b) 42
(c) 30 (d) 20
(e) 12

193. 32 16 24 65 210 945 5197.5
(a) 945 (b) 16
(c) 24 (d) 210
(e) 65

194. 7 13 25 49 97 194 385
(a) 13 (b) 49
(c) 97 (d) 194
(e) 25

195. 29, 37, 21, 43, 13, 53, 5
(a) 37 (b) 53
(c) 13 (d) 21
(e) 43

Directions (Qs. 196-200) : Study the following information carefully to answer the questions that follow :

There are two trains A and B. Both trains have four different types of coaches viz. General coaches, sleeper coaches, first class coaches and AC coaches. In train A, there are total 700 passengers. Train B has 30% more passengers than train A. 20% of the passengers of train A are in general coaches. One-fourth of the total number of passengers of train A are in AC coaches. 23% of the passengers of train A are in sleeper class coaches. Remaining passengers of train A are in first class coaches. Total number of passengers in AC coaches in both the trains together is 480. 30% of the number of passengers of train B is in sleeper class coaches, 10% of the total passengers of train B are in first class coaches. Remaining passengers of train B are in general class coaches.

196. What is the ratio of the number of passengers in first class coaches of train A to the number of passengers in sleeper class coaches of train B?
(a) 13 : 7 (b) 7 : 13
(c) 32 : 39 (d) Data inadequate
(e) None of these

197. What is the total number of passengers in the general coaches of train A and the AC coaches of train B together?
(a) 449 (b) 459
(c) 435 (d) 445
(e) None of these

198. What is the difference between the number of passengers in the AC coaches of train A and total number of passengers in sleeper class coaches and first class coaches together of train B?
(a) 199 (b) 178
(c) 187 (d) 179
(e) None of these

199. Total number of passengers in general class coaches in both the trains together is approximately. What percentage of total number of passengers in train B?
(a) 35 (b) 42
(c) 45 (d) 38
(e) 31

200. If cost of per ticket of first class coach ticket is ₹ 450, what total amount will be generated from first class coaches of train A?
(a) ₹ 100080 (b) ₹ 108000
(c) ₹ 100800 (d) ₹ 10800
(e) None of these

ANSWERS AND EXPLANATIONS

1. **(b)** (to) be [polite] → fa [so] (la)

she is [polite] → [so] me pa

(to) have manners → na (la) ma

2. **(b)**

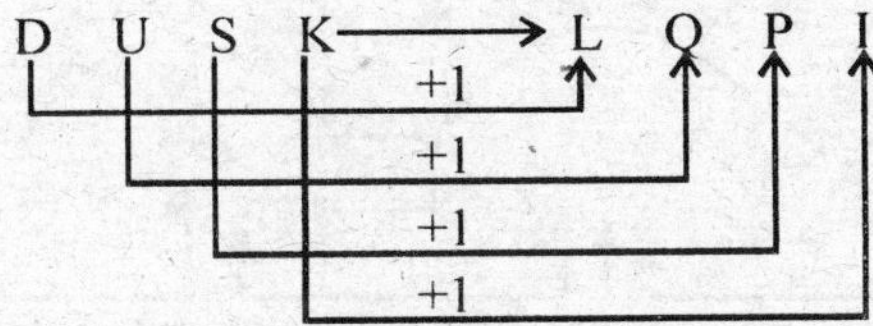

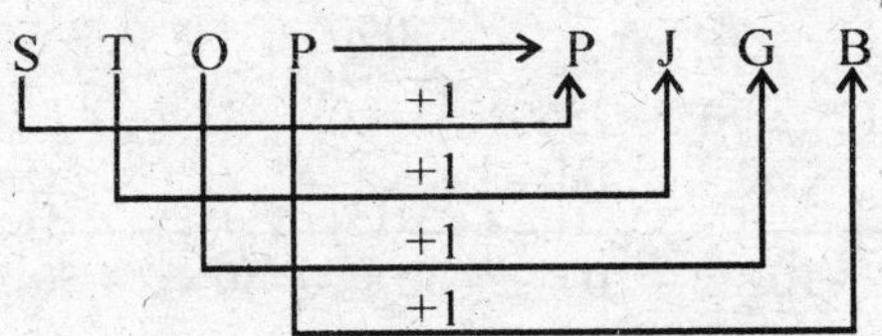

Similarly,

S T O P → P J G B (+1, +1, +1, +1)

3. **(c)** | Consonant | Consonant | Number |

Such combinations are : | DF1 | NP6 |

4. **(d)** | Letter | Number | Letter or Number |

Such combinations are:

| T4A | | F1U | | P6Q |

5. **(c)** | Vowel | Symbol |

Such combinations are:

| U# | | I© |

6. **(b)**

$R \xrightarrow{+2} T \xrightarrow{+2} A$

$9 \xrightarrow{+2} D \xrightarrow{+1} F$

$\# \xrightarrow{+2} @ \xrightarrow{+2} H$

$3 \xrightarrow{+2} V \xrightarrow{+2} 5$

$I \xrightarrow{+2} W \xrightarrow{+2} \star$

7. **(a)** Fourth to left of 12th from left means 8th from left.

7 R E T 4 A 9 % D F.

8th from left

8-10

Family Dramas (3)

- Social Message (2): Main Sati Hoon (10 PM), Detective Doom
- Adult content (1)

* The 3 family dramas are scheduled between 9.30 PM to 11 PM, with two shows with social message between 9.30 PM to 10.30 PM and one with adult content between 10.30 PM to 11 PM.

* The 2 news based programs are scheduled between 11 PM to 12 PM with the one having adult content is scheduled at 11.30 PM (Midnight Murders).

* So HIV and India is the other news based program and scheduled at 11 PM.

* Laugh a while is the third Family Drama with adult content and is scheduled at 10.30 PM.

8. **(d)** As discussed above.

9. **(c)** Detective Doom is a family drama with a social message and is scheduled at 9.30 PM. It do not have any adult content.

10. **(a)** HIV and India is scheduled between 11.00 PM to 11.30 PM.

11. **(b)** I. $12x^2 + 11x + 12 = 10x^2 + 22x$

$2x^2 - 11x + 12 = 0$

$2x^2 - 8x - 3x + 12 = 0$

$(x-4)(2x-3) = 0$

$x = 4, x = 3/2$

II. $13y^2 - 18y + 3 = 9y^2 - 10y$

$4y^2 - 8y + 3 = 0$

$4y^2 - 6y - 2y + 3 = 0$

$(2y-3)(2y-1) = 0$

$y = \frac{3}{2}, \frac{1}{2}$

$\therefore x \geq y$

12. **(c)** $\frac{18}{x^2} + \frac{6}{x} - \frac{12}{x^2} = \frac{8}{x^2}$

$\Rightarrow \frac{18 + 6x - 12}{x^2} = \frac{8}{x^2} \Rightarrow 6x + 6 = 8$

$\therefore x = \frac{2}{6} = 0.33$

II. $y^3 + 9.68 + 5.64 = 16.95$

$\Rightarrow y^3 = 16.95 - 15.32$

$\Rightarrow y^3 = 1.63 \Rightarrow y = \sqrt[3]{1.63}$

13. **(a)** I. $35x+70=0$

$\therefore \quad x=\frac{-70}{35}=-2$

II. $(81)^{1/4}y+(343)^{1/3}=0$

$\Rightarrow 3y+7=0 \Rightarrow 3y=-7$

$\therefore \quad y=-\frac{7}{3}=-233 \therefore x>y$

14. **(a)** I. $\frac{(2)^5+(11)^3}{6}=x^3$

$\Rightarrow \frac{32+1331}{6}=x^3 \Rightarrow \frac{1363}{6}=x^3$

$\therefore \quad x^3=227.167$

II. $4y^3=\frac{-589}{4}+5y^3 \Rightarrow \frac{589}{4}=y^3$

$\therefore \quad y^3=147.25 \therefore x>y$

15. **(d)** I. $x^{7/5} \div 9 = 169\,'\,x^{3/5}$

$\frac{x^{7/5}}{9}=\frac{169}{x^{3/5}}$

$\Rightarrow x^{10/5}=9\times 169 \Rightarrow x^2=9\times 169$

$x=\pm(3\times 13)=\pm 39$

II. $y^{1/4}\times y^{1/4}\times 7=\frac{273}{y^{1/2}}$

$y=\frac{273}{7}=39$

$x\le y$

16. **(c)** as per paragraph 1 A and C are correct, hence correct answer is (c)

17. **(c)** paragraph1 says (in line 13-14) that it is a myth... hence answer is (c)

18. **(c)** paragraph 1 – last few lines

19. **(a)** paragraph 2 , the 4th and 5th line explains this point.

20. **(b)** **21.** **(e)** **22.** **(d)** **23.** **(b)** **24.** **(a)**

25. **(c)**

Sol. (26 - 29)

	Mridul	Abhishek	Ranjan	Salil	Deepak	Pritam
Place	Chennai	Ahmedabad	Delhi	Bengaluru	Kolkata	Mumbai
Month	November	July	April	September	February	December
Brides	Ipsita	Veena	Hema	Jasmine	Geetika	Brinda

26. **(c)** Ranjan is Hema's Husband.

27. **(c)** Deepak's wedding took place in Kolkata.

28. **(d)** It's in the month of December.

29. **(a)** Salil's wedding was held in Bengaluru.

30. **(e)** New arrangement would be as follows:

K S 4 V 7 P 2 6 M 9

$\therefore$ Fourth element is V in the new arrangement.

31. **(e)** From element I to II the design rotates through 180°

32. **(b)** From element I to II the design is mirror image after being rotated through 90° clockwise.

33. **(c)** From element I to II the design is enclosed by another design.

34. **(e)** From element I to II the upper design encloses the lower design.

35. **(d)** From element I to II the design is divided into four equal parts and the lower left part becomes shaded.

36. **(e)**

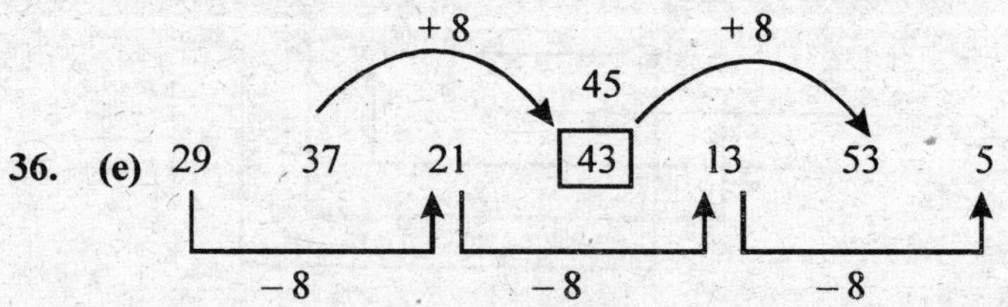

37. **(c)**

1090

150 290 560 1120 2140 4230 8400

– 10× 2 – 20 × 2 – 30 × 2 – 40 × 2 – 50× 2 – 60

38. **(c)** $\left(\frac{1500\times R_1\times 3}{100}\right)-\left(\frac{1500\times R_2\times 3}{100}\right)=13.50$

$\Rightarrow 4500(R_1-R_2)=1350 \Rightarrow R_1-R_2=\frac{1350}{4500}=0.3\%$

39. **(a)** Let the CP of the article be ₹ x.

Then, SP = ₹ $\frac{105x}{100}$

Now, new CP = ₹ $\frac{95x}{100}$ and new SP = $\frac{105x}{100}-1$

According to the question

$\frac{105x}{100}-1-\frac{95x}{100}=\frac{10\times 95x}{100\times 100}$

$\therefore \quad x=$ ₹ 200

40. **(d)** Let the average speed be x km/h.

and Total distance $=y$ km. Then,

$\frac{0.2}{10}y+\frac{0.6}{30}y+\frac{0.2}{20}y=\frac{y}{x}$

$\Rightarrow x=\frac{1}{0.05}=20\text{km/h}$

41. (d) The following changes occur in the subsequent figures:

(1) to (2) (2) to (3)

(3) to (4) (4) to (5)

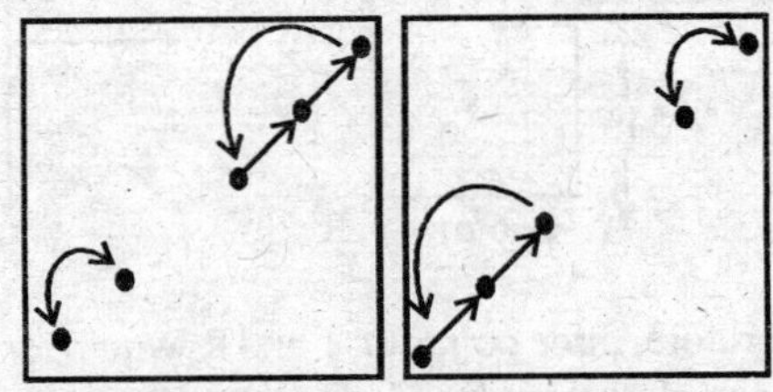

In Figure (4) the arrangement of designs would be as follows:)

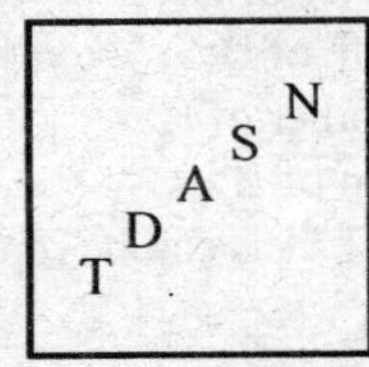

42. (e) The line segment with cross rotates respectively through 45°, 90°, 135°, 180° ... in clockwise direction.

43. (d) In each subsequent figure the designs move in clockwise direction and the number of designs at a particular position is fixed. Again, a new design appears at the lower right side. In figure (4), there should be design (L) in the place of circle at the lower right side.

44. (e) In the subsequent figures respectively one, tow, three, four ..., curves are inverted in a set order. In Figure (5) five curves have been inverted.

45. (e) Idiom **make a beeline for something** means : to go straight towards something / somebody as quickly as you can.

46. (a) Idiom **in the nick of time** means : at the very last moment; just in time before something bad happens.

47. (e) Idiom **on cloud nine** means : extremely happy.

48. (c)

49. (b) Idiom **rack your brain (s)** means : to think very hard or for a long time about something.

50. (b) According to question,

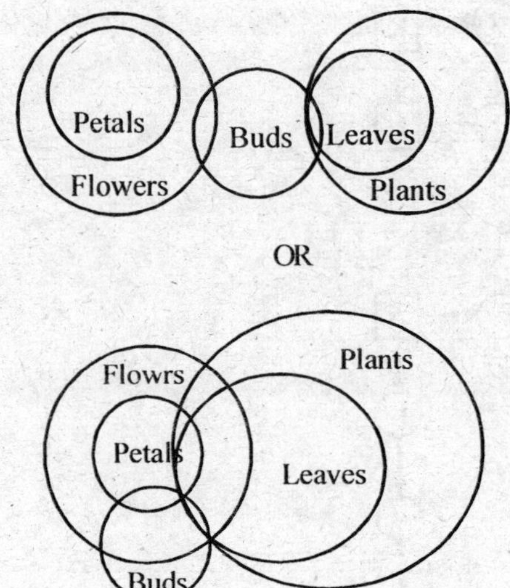

Conclusions I. false

II. false ⎤ or
III. false ⎦

Hence, only either II or III follows.

51. (d) According to question

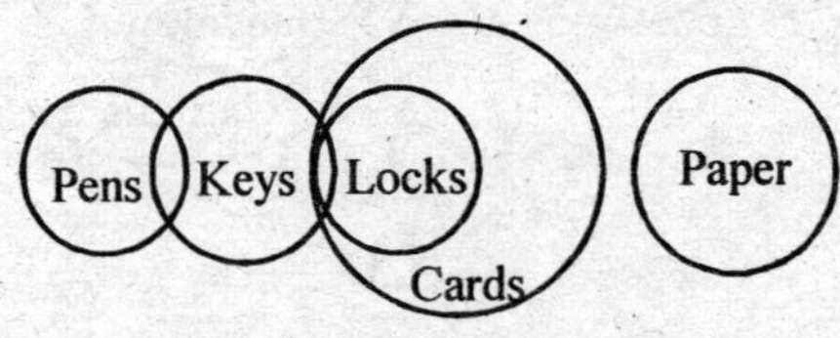

OR

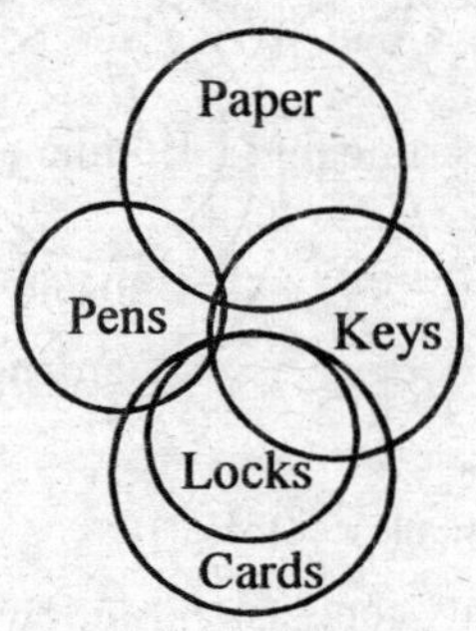

Conclusions I. True

II. True

III. True

Hence, All conclusions follow.

52. (e) According to question,

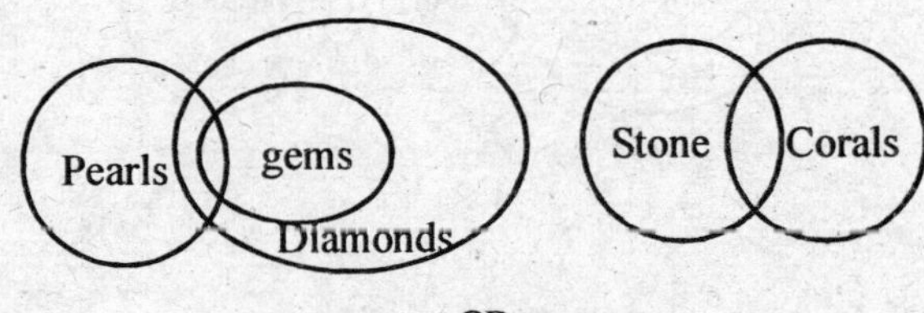

OR

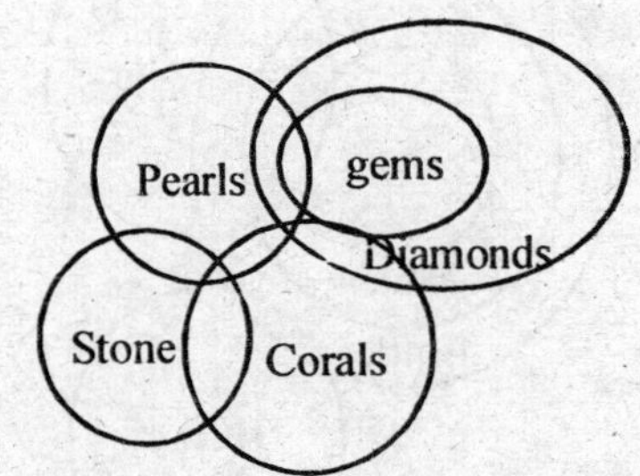

I. False ⎤
Conclusion II. True ⎥ or
III.False ⎦

Hence, only conclusions II and either I or III follow.

53. (a) According to question,

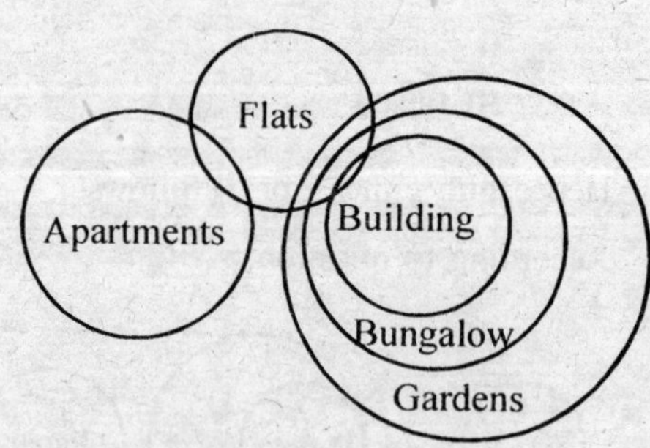

Or

Conclusions I. ✓, II. X, III. X

Hence, only conclusion I follows.

54. (c) According to question,

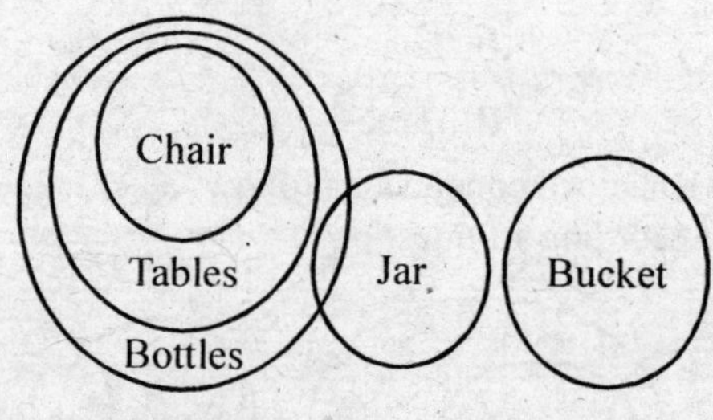

OR

Conclusions, I. ✓, II. ✓, III. ✓

Hence, All I, II and III follow.

55. (b)

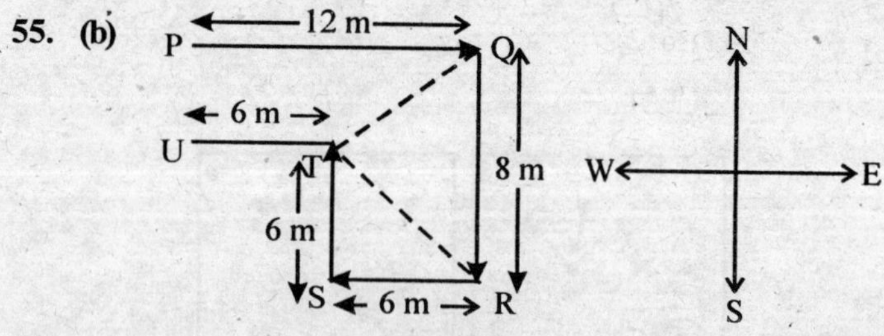

Therefore, three points Q, T and R, would form a triangle whose all the angles are less than 90°.

(56-60):

A + B ⇒ A is the father of B.

A × B ⇒ A is the sister of B.

A $ B ⇒ A is the wife of B.

A % B ⇒ A is the mother of B.

A ÷ B ⇒ A is the son of B.

56. (a) J ÷ P % H × T % L can be represented in diagram. As follows.

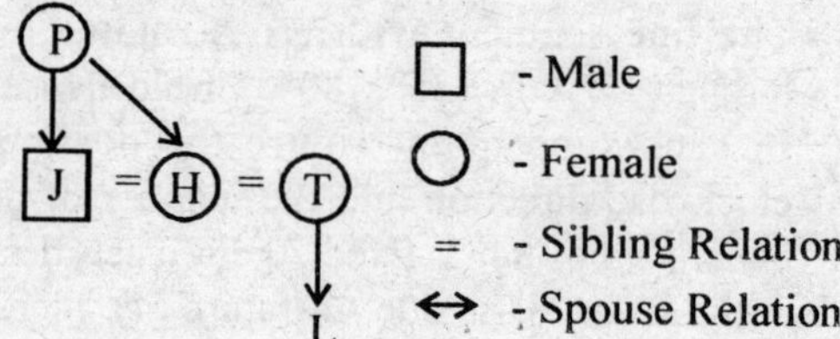

57. (b) L + R $ D + M × T

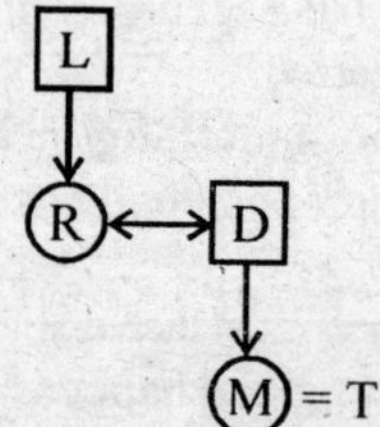

58. (b) I + T % J × L ÷ K

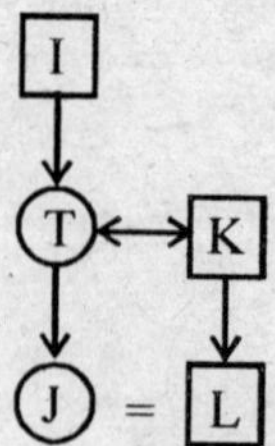

59. (d) W $ X + L + Y + T

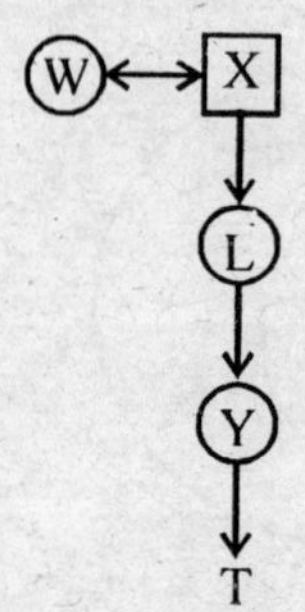

60. (d) R % T × P $ Q + V

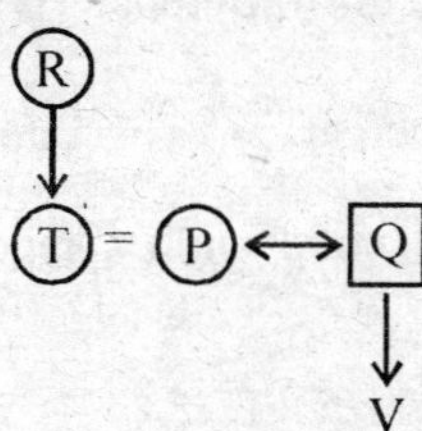

61. (d) In the subsequent figures two and three designs are inverted alternately. From problems Figure (1) to (2) the first and the second designs from the top interchange positions and the lowermost design moves to the middle position. From problem Figure (2) and (3) the lowermost design moves to the top and the second design from the top moves to the lowermost position while the third and the fourth designs interchange positions. From problem Figure (3) to (4) the top most and the lowermost designs interchange positions and the fourth design moves to the second position. From Problem Figure (4) to (5) the topmost design moves to the fourth position, the lowermost design moves to the topmost position while the second and the third designs interchange positions. Therefore, from problem Figure (5) to Answer Figure the third and the fourth designs would interchange positions and would be inverted, the lowermost design would move to the top position and the second design from the top would move to the lowermost position.

62. (a) The following changes occur in the subsequent figures:

(1) to (2) (2) to (3)

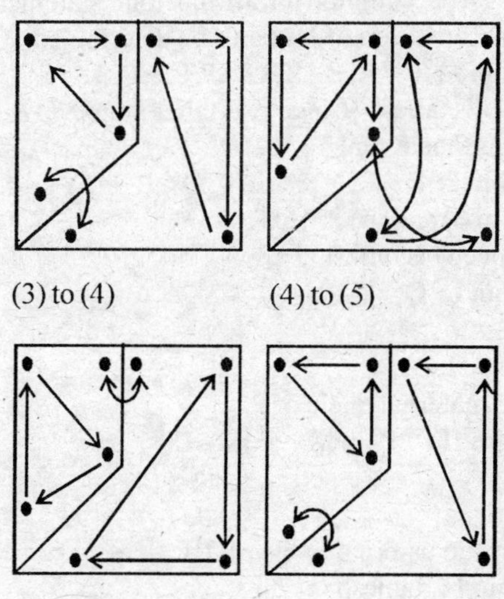

(3) to (4) (4) to (5)

(5) to (6)

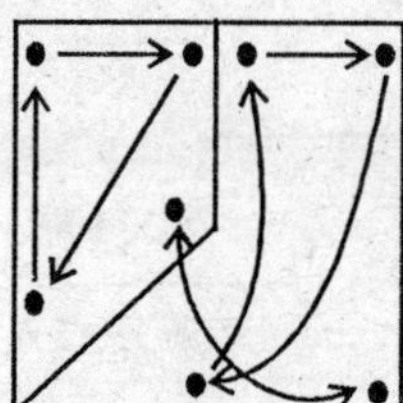

63. (d) From problem Figure (1) to (2) and from problem Figure (5) to Answer Figure the smaller square with four designs moves two steps in anticlockwise direction and the designs in each row interchange positions. The other three designs move two steps in clockwise direction.

64. (c) The following changes occur in the subsequent figures:

(1) to (2) (2) to (3)

(5) to (6)

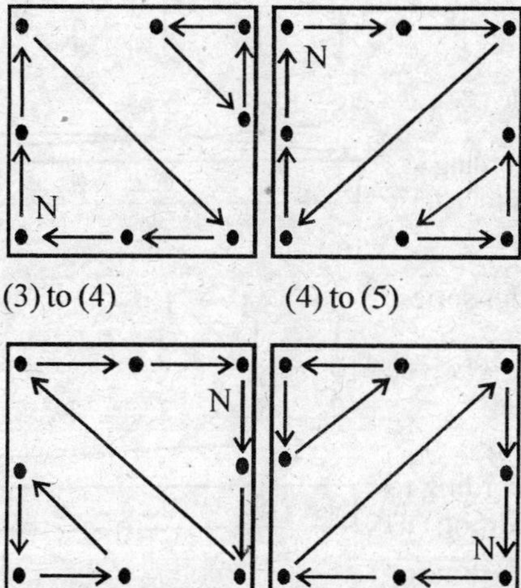

(3) to (4) (4) to (5)

65. (b) From problem Figure (1) to (2) the plane of designs rotates through 90° clockwise and the second and the fifth designs interchange positions. Similarly, the third and the fourth designs interchange positions. Similar changes occur from Problem Figure (3) to (4) and from problem figure (5) to Answer Figure.

66. (c) The central element interchanges place alternately with the element on either side and gets inverted while the third one is replaced by a new one. The whole figure rotates by 45° ACW in each step. The correct figure is

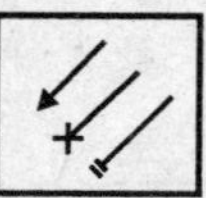

67. (a) The whole figure rotates by 45°, 90°, 135°, 180° ACW in subsequent steps. while the end elements interchange their places alternately on either end in subsequent steps.

68. (b) In each step the elements move one step downwards and towards right. A new element appears at the top-left position while the lower one is lost. The correct figure of (b) is

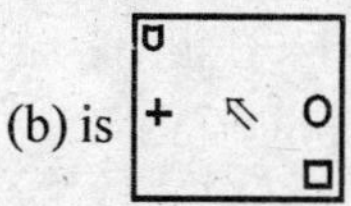

69. (e) The column of elements moves half-a-side from left to right. The central element interchanges alternately with upper and lower elements and the third element is placed at the lower end of the next column.

70. (c) In each step the similar corner elements move to middle of the sides while one of the middle elements moves to the centre. New elements appear at the corners. The correct figure of (c) is

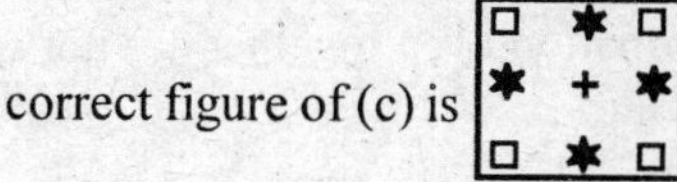

71. (d) **72.** (c) **73.** (a) **74.** (e) **75.** (a)

76. (a)

Letter series	E	R	W	H	K	A
Code	2	@	©	6	#	1
Code without condition	2	@	©	6	#	1

77. (e)

Letter series	M	P	E	K	D	U
Code	$	4	2	#	5	δ
According to condition (i)	δ	4	2	#	5	$

78. (d)

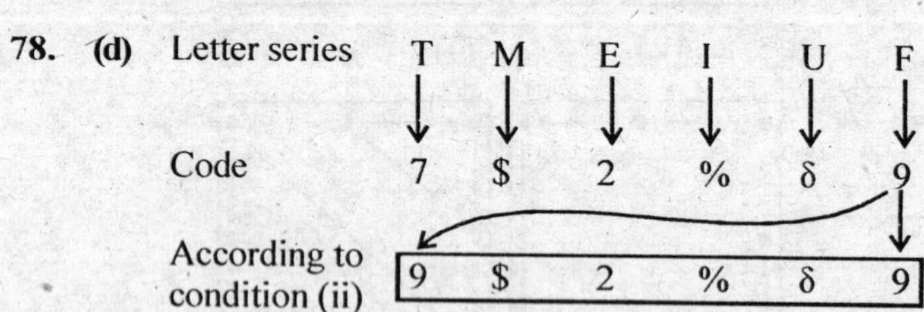

Letter series	T	M	E	I	U	F
Code	7	$	2	%	δ	9
According to condition (ii)	9	$	2	%	δ	9

79. (a)

Letter series	J	T	A	E	R	I
Code	3	7	1	2	@	%
According to condition (i)	%	7	1	2	@	3

80. (c)

Letter series	U	K	T	M	I	H
Code	δ	#	7	$	%	6
According to condition (iii)	★	#	7	$	%	★

81. (a) **From statement I,**

Ratio of the costs of first, second and third necklace is 6 : 5 : 7. Hence, the price of second necklace can be calculated.

82. (e) **From I:** Ratio of boys and girls = 3k : 4k

From II: No of girls – No of boys = 18

From I and II:

4k – 3k = 18 ∴ k = 18

∴ 4k + 3k = 18 × 7 = 126

83. (a) Only I alone is sufficient.

84. (d) To find out the cost of laying carpet we need (i) cost of carpet per square metre and, (ii) Area of the floor to be carpeted.

Both the information even together are not sufficient to fulfil our need.

85. (c) We know, if we have been given difference of Cl and SI during two years, then this difference (D) is equal to

$\frac{P \times r^2}{100^2}$ where P = Principal r = rate of interest

From I: We get the value of P and D. Hence,I alone is sufficient.

Again we know SI = $\frac{P \times R \times T}{100}$

where P = principal

R = rate of interest

T = time period

From II : We get value of P = x(say).

Then SI = x and T = $6\frac{2}{3}$ years

Hence, using the above formula we can get rate of interest from II alone also.

86. (d) **From I and II:** We get

D > B...(i)

K > W > M... (ii)

Still, we lack some clue as to whether B or M is the youngest. Hence, both statements I and II even together are not sufficient.

87. (d) **From I:** Na Ni Nok Ne → I will tell you ... (i)

Ni Nok Ne Nam → he will tell you ... (ii)

From (i) & (ii) Na → I and Nam = he

From II: Ni Ne Mo Nam → will he call you ... (iii) Ne Mok Sac Ni → how will you go ... (iv)

Ne Ni is common in all the four statements. Exact transformation of Ne can't be determined.

88. (c) **From I :** P > R, P > T, U > P, U > Q, U > S

→ U is tallest. [Since U is taller than P, Q & S and P is taller than R and T]

From II : R < U, P & Q...(i); Q > P ... (ii)

From (i) and (ii) R P Q U

Hence U is tallest.

89. (b) **From I :** Q(–)—N(+)—S

|

P(+) – L(–)

N is maternal uncle of P.

From II : (+) M – (+)K – L(–)

|

G (–)

M is the paternal uncle of P

90. (c) **From I :** Ramesh = 17th

∴ Shyam = (17 + 6 =) 23th

Sudin = (23 + 7 =) 30th

From II: Savita = 17th

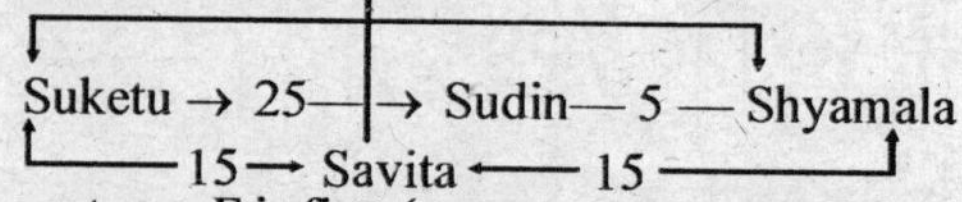

91. (a) sentence F is first (correct sequence- F,C,A,E,D,B)

92. (a) A is the third sentence

93. (d) sentence B will be the correct answer.

94. (c) E

95. (b) D

Sol. (Q. No. 96 to 100)

$\star \Rightarrow <$	$\# \Rightarrow >$	$@ \Rightarrow \geq$
$\% \Rightarrow \leq$	$\$ \Rightarrow =$	

96. (a) $V\$Y \Rightarrow V = Y$

$Y@Z \Rightarrow Y \geq Z$

$Z\%X \Rightarrow Z \leq X$

$X\#T \Rightarrow X > T$

From all above statements,

$V = Y \geq Z \leq X > T$

Conclusions I. $T\#Z \Rightarrow T > Z$ (False)

II. $X\#Y \Rightarrow X > Y$ (False)

III. $Z \star Y \Rightarrow Z < Y$ (False)

None follows.

97. (a) $R@J \Rightarrow R \geq J$

$J\%F \Rightarrow J \leq F$

$F \star E \Rightarrow F < E$

$E\%M \Rightarrow E \leq M$

From all above statements, $R \geq J \leq F < E \leq M$

Conclusions I: $M\#J \Rightarrow M > J$ (True)

II. $F\%M \Rightarrow F \leq M$ (False)

III. $M \star R \Rightarrow M < R$ (False)

Only (I) follows.

98. (b) $H\#R \Rightarrow H > R$

$R@L \Rightarrow R \geq L$

$L \star W \Rightarrow L < W$

$W\%F \Rightarrow W \leq F$

From all above statements, $H > R \geq L < W \leq F$

Conclusions I. $H\#L \Rightarrow H > L$ (True)

II. $F\#L \Rightarrow F > L$ (True)

III. $H\$F \Rightarrow H = F$ (False)

99. (c) $M\#K \Rightarrow M > K$

$M\$F \Rightarrow M = F$

$F\%Q \Rightarrow F \leq Q$

$Q \star H \Rightarrow Q < H$

From all above statements,

$K < M = F \leq Q < H$

Conclusions. I. $H\#K \Rightarrow H > K$ (True)

II. $Q\#K \Rightarrow Q > K$ (True)

III. $Q@M \Rightarrow Q \geq M$ (True)

So, all follow.

100. (a) $D \star Q \Rightarrow D < Q$

$Q\$L \Rightarrow Q = L$

$L\#T \Rightarrow L > T$

$T\%H \Rightarrow T \leq H$

From all above statemens,

$D < Q = L > T \leq H$

Conclusions. I. $D \star L \Rightarrow D < L$ (True)

II. $L@H \Rightarrow L \geq H$ (False)

III. $H\#L \Rightarrow H > L$ (False)

Only (I) and either (II) or (III) follow.

101. (d) Input cannot be determined.

102. (a) Input: Jockey firm 36 43 growth chart 22 45

Step I: 45 Jockey firm 36 43 growth chart 22

Step II: 45 Jockey 43 firm 36 growth chart 22

Step III: 45 Jockey 43 growth firm 36 chart 22.

103. (b) Step II 53 window 42 50 door lock key 36

Step III 53 window 50 42 door lock key 36

Step IV 53 window 50 lock 42 door lock key 36

Step V 53 window 50 lock 42 door lock key 36

Step VI 53 window 50 lock 42 door lock key 36

the step VI is the last step of the arrangement. Therefore four more steps are required to complete arrangement.

104. (c) Step I 85 journey train 36 54 daily 28 mansion

Step II 85 train journey 36 54 daily 28 mansion

Step III 85 train 54 journey 36 daily 28 mansion

Step IV 85 train 54 mansion journey 36 daily 28

Step V 85 train 54 mansion 36 journey daily 28

105. (e) Step II 63 sour 18 56 grapes healthy 32 rise

Step III 63 sour 56 18 grapes healthy 32 rise

Step IV 63 sour 56 rise 18 grapes healthy 32

Step V 63 sour 56 rise 32 18 grapes healthy

Step VI 63 sour 56 rise 32 healthy 18 grapes

So, the last step is step VI.

106. (b) As solved in Qs. 49. So, 56 is the sixth number from the right in step V.

107. (a) Let 'A' be the average expenditure. Then, according to question

$42A + 31 = 55(A - 3) \rightarrow 13A = 196 \rightarrow A = 196/13 = 15.07.$

Total expenditure original $= 15.07 \times 42 = 633.23$

108. (b)

5 Red + 4 Green	3 Red + 7 Black

The no. of ways in which two different coloured balls can be drawn are $G + R$, $R + B$, $G + B$.

$\therefore$ P (two different balls) = P(1st red and 2nd black) + P (1st green and 2nd red) + P (1st green and 2nd Black)

$$= \left(\frac{5}{9} \times \frac{7}{10}\right) + \left(\frac{4}{9} \times \frac{3}{10}\right) + \left(\frac{4}{9} \times \frac{7}{10}\right)$$

$$= \frac{35 + 12 + 28}{90} = \frac{75}{90} = \frac{5}{6}.$$

109. (b) With three dice the cases favourable for the event of getting 10 are

$$\left.\begin{matrix} 1+3+6 \\ 1+4+5 \\ 2+3+5 \end{matrix}\right\} \times 3! \quad \left.\begin{matrix} 2+2+6 \\ 2+4+4 \\ 3+3+4 \end{matrix}\right\} \times \frac{3!}{2!} \Rightarrow \text{Total of } 27.$$

Required probability $= \frac{27}{6^3} = \frac{1}{8}$

110. (d)

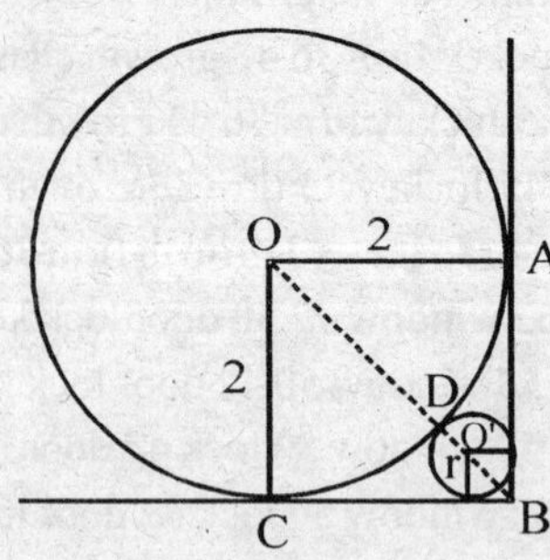

OABC is square with side = 2

$\therefore OB = \sqrt{2^2 + 2^2} = 2\sqrt{2}$

Let r be the radius of smaller circle

$OB = 2\sqrt{2} = OD + r + O'B = 2 + r + r\sqrt{2}$

$\Rightarrow r(\sqrt{2} + 1) = 2(\sqrt{2} - 1)$

$\Rightarrow r = \frac{2(\sqrt{2}-1)}{(\sqrt{2}+1)} = \frac{2(\sqrt{2}-1)^2}{2-1}$

$= 2(2 + 1 - 2\sqrt{2})$

$= 6 - 4\sqrt{2}$

111. (d) The shifting of the elements takes place in such a way that the change is completed in four steps. So the change from figure five to six will be similar to the change from figure one to figure two.

112. (a) In each step, two pairs of elements get changed, beginning from the upper left and lower right. The change takes place in three successive steps.

113. (c) The main design rotates respectively through 45° clockwise, 180° and 90° anticlockwise after every two figures. The shaded leaflet rotates through 45° clockwise, 90° clockwise, 135° clockwise, 45° anticlockwise and 90° anticlockwise.

114. (d) Watch the rotation of each element separetely. The triangel rotates by 90° ACW and 180°. The circle rotates 45°, 135°, 90° CW 45° CW ... 'C' rotates 45°, 90°, 135°, 180° CW.

115. (b) In each step elements interchange in pairs while one element beginning from one end is replaced by a new one. The line of orientation rotates by 45° ACW.

116. (c) 'A' when added as a prefix does not imply anti but an indifference or apathy e.g. 'amoral' and 'immoral' immoral means not moral while amoral is only someone who does not care about morals.

117. (b) Candour means frankness, Enthusiasm is excitement and Intimate is closeness or nearness.

118. (c) Trivial means insignificant or unimportant, momentous means for/of the moment, critical is someone who looks for faults.

119. (d) Elan means vigour or energy and enthusiasm, opposite of enthusiasm would be nervousness, composure means calmness, dignity is calm and serious manner while brashness is opposite to composure.

120. (c) Irascible is hot tempered, or someone who easily gets angry, roguish is playful, it is more clearly an antonym to hot tempered than friendly or even kind. Both words Irascible and roguish concern the temperament of a person, while others are about his nature.

121. (d) **122. (e)** **123. (d)** **124. (b)** **125. (c)**

For (Qs. 126 –128)

Here, alphabets A, V, R, N, G and P represent six products – Ariel, Vivel, Rin, Nirma, Gillette Gel and Pepsodent, respectively.

We conclude on two possible combinations. (i) ARPGNV and (ii) NGPRAV

126. (c) Since question is asked ".... left to Ariel (A)" Hence, only combination (ii) is true.

127. (c) If we interchange the position of Rin and Ariel, the item displayed in window 5 will be Rin.

128. (c) Except Rin, the product displayed left of Ariel but right of Gillette Gel is Pepsodent.

129. (c) (a) is obviously wrong for when P is played, then V cannot be played.

(b) is wrong because if Q is to be played, then T must also be played (after Q).

(c) does not contradict any of the conditions.

(d) is wrong because the last song must be either U or S.

So, (c) is correct.

130. (c) (a) If R is played then V must be played so, (a) is wrong

(b) If Q is played then T must be played so, (b) is wrong

(c) does not seem to contradict any condition given.

(d) U or S must be played everyday so, (d) is wrong.

131. (e) All the statements are false.

132. (a) If R is in the third position, then V must be in the fourth position as the last (fifth) is for U or S.

Now if Q is placed second, then T must be in either 3rd, 4th or 5th place which should be filled by R, V and (U or S) respectively. So, Q cannot be in the second place.

$\therefore$ (a) is correct.

133. (a) Let the side of the cube be 1. Then, diagonal $= \sqrt{3}$.

Now we have an equilateral triangle with side $\sqrt{3}$ and its altitude will be 3/2.

Circumradius = 2/3 × altitude = 2/3 × 3/2 = 1.

Thus, the radius of the circle circumscribing that triangle will be equal to the side of the cube.

134. (b)

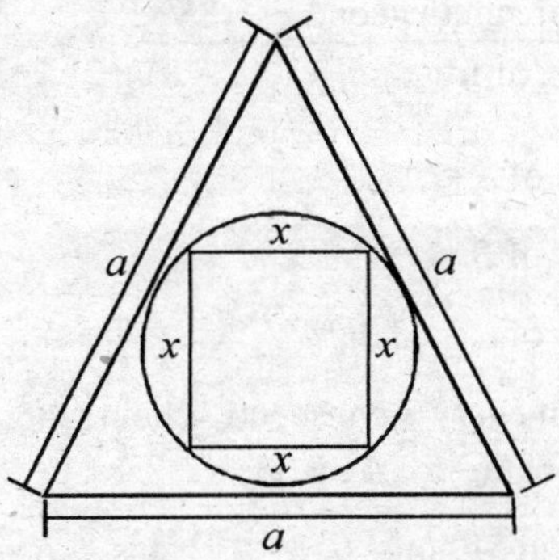

Radius of circle $R = \dfrac{\frac{\sqrt{3}}{4}}{\frac{3a}{2}} = \dfrac{\sqrt{3}}{6}a$

Diagonal of square = diameter of circle

$= 2.\dfrac{\sqrt{3}}{6}a$

$= \sqrt{2}x = \dfrac{\sqrt{3}}{3}a$

$x = \dfrac{\sqrt{3}}{3\sqrt{2}}a = \dfrac{\sqrt{6}}{6}a$

$\text{Area} = x^2 = \left[\dfrac{(\sqrt{6}a)}{6}\right]^2 = \dfrac{6}{36}a^2 = \dfrac{1}{6}a^2$

135. (a)

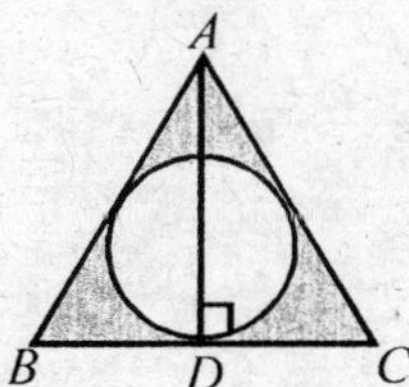

$\text{Height} = AD = \dfrac{\sqrt{3}}{2} \times \text{side} = \dfrac{\sqrt{3}}{2} \times 6 = 3\sqrt{3}$ cm

$\therefore$ Inradius $= \dfrac{1}{3} \times \text{height} = \dfrac{1}{3} \times 3\sqrt{3} = \sqrt{3}$ cm.

A(shaded region) = $A\,(\Delta\, ABC) - A$ (incircle)

$= \dfrac{\sqrt{3}}{4} \times (\text{side})^2 = \pi r^2$

$= \dfrac{\sqrt{3}}{4} \times 6 \times 6 - 3.14 \times \left(\sqrt{3}\right)^2$

$= 15.57 - 9.42 = 6.15$ cm.

136. (a) (a) comes across is the only reasonable option as the decisions to be taken in the passage are fairly obvious i.e. with a low bank account a free holiday offer may be taken up or if we are ready to move forward in our career then we can step in for the boss, when she is away. A is the most appropriate choice as its mentions that some decision are obvious under certain circumstances while other options.

137. (b) (b) is the correct choice because according to the passage having inertia means we are incapable of doing anything. Eventhough we may see one person exploiting another, or a group persecuting another.

138. (b) (b) is the only option as the passage clearly means to say that one should experience the consequences before choosing an alternative as then they become more meaningful. Also one can discover aspects one may not have ever thought of. Other options are more specifically about the van, whereas the point of the passage is to make a general statement about trying alternatives with van as an example.

139. (c) Option (c) which states "increase in production of existing products enhances core competence" is correct the reason being the company is planning to give priority to core competence and the only activity which can lead to it is increase in the production of orthodox varieties of tea.

140. (c) The author in the passage states that you are never able to totally know someone, as no matter how much you know them, you will be surprised by something they do or some trait they exhibit. This unpredictability always exists. Option (a) is incorrect because being unpredictable and being inconsistent are two different things. Option (b) is incorrect, because the author didn't mention that because of this unpredictability, one should be careful while dealing with others.

141. (c) In online shopping the customer may be deceived as he cannot touch the product he is paying for.

142. (d) The customer whose view is presented has shopped at retail stores as well as online.

143. (e) The number of people migrating from rural to urban areas in search of jobs may reduce.

144. (a) At least some people who visits the park have pets.

145. (c) As,

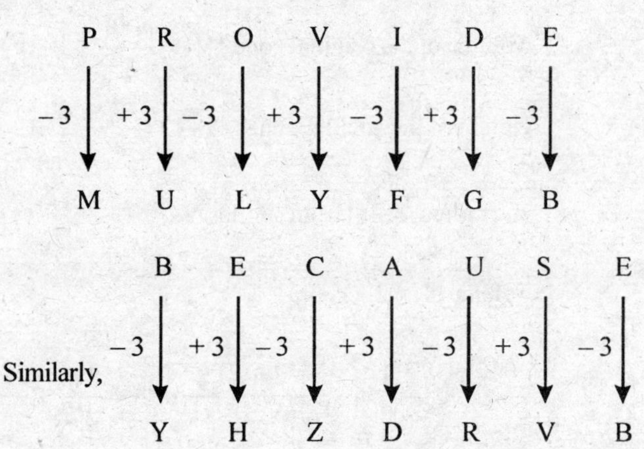

146. (b) conducive ; the other words do not fit in correctly

147. (d) question

148. (a) cannot fits correctly

149. (c) need

150. (e) growth

151. (c) favour

152. (b) enjoys

153. (a) aid is used correctly meaning facilitate

154. (e) increased

155. (a) both

156. (d) Eating habit of a society develops through centuries and is impossible to change, hence II can't be implemented. I and III will help address the growth in demand.

157. (c) Faculty members should be persuaded not to go on strike and an action against the members who join the strike should be taken.

158. (b) We have,
radius of the hemisphere = raidus of the cone
= height of the cone
= height of the cylinder = r (say)
Then, ratio of the volumes of cylinder, hemisphere and cone

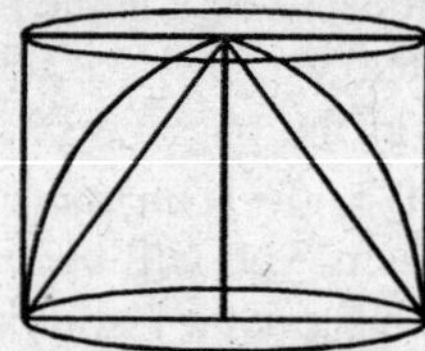

$$= \pi r^3 : \frac{2}{3}\pi r^3 : \frac{1}{3}\pi r^3 = 1 : \frac{2}{3} : \frac{1}{3} = 3:2:1$$

159. (b)

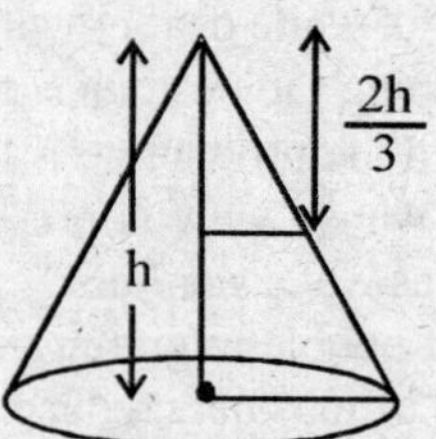

Volume of the original cone $'V' = \frac{\pi r^2 h}{3}$

Height of the smaller cone = 2h / 3

and radius $= \frac{2r}{3}$ (from similar Δ's)

Volume of smaller cone

$$= \frac{1}{3}\pi\left(\frac{2r}{3}\right)^2 \frac{2h}{3} = \frac{8}{81}\pi r^2 h = \frac{8V}{27}.$$

$$\frac{\text{Volume of smaller cone}}{\text{Volume of frustum}} = \frac{8V/27}{V - 8V/27} = \frac{8}{19}$$

160. (a) Efficiency of $A = 5\%$

Efficiency of $B = 4\%$

Efficiency of $C = -3.33\%$

It means in every 3 consecutive hours taps *A*, *B* and *C* can fill 5.66% (= 5 + 4 − 3.33).

Therefore in 51 hours (= 3 × 17) taps *A*, *B* and *C* can fill 96.33% (= 5.66 × 17)

∴ the remaining part i.e., 3.66% (= 100 − 96.33) can be filled up by *A* in $\frac{11}{15}$ hours $\left(= \frac{3.66}{5}\right)$, since it is now *A*'s turn.

Hence, the total time repuired $= 51 + \frac{11}{15} = 51\frac{11}{15}$

161. (d) Distance to be travelled by each type of vehicle

$$= \frac{15}{3} = 5 \text{ km}$$

Since, to travel 5 km by vehicle A, he will pay ₹ 9 for 4 km and for the next 1 km he will have to pay

₹ $= \frac{13.5 - 9.00}{(7-4)} \times 1$.

Similarly, for other cases.

Fare by A = ₹ $9 + \frac{13.50 - 9}{7 - 4} = 9 + 1.50 =$ ₹ 10.50

Fare by B $= 14.50 + \frac{24.25 - 14.50}{7 - 4}$

$= 14.50 + 3.25 = 17.75$

Fare by C $= 19 + \frac{31 - 19}{3} = 19 + 4 = 23$

Total fare = 10.50 + 17.75 + 23 = ₹ 51.25

162. (a) Fare by A $= 9 + \frac{4.50}{3} \times 2 =$ ₹ 12

Fare by B $= 24.25 + \frac{33.25 - 24.25}{3} \times 2 =$ ₹ 30.25

Total fare = 30.25 + 12 = ₹ 42.25

163. (b) Fare for 8 km by A $= 13.50 + \frac{17.25 - 13.50}{10 - 7}$

$= 13.50 + \frac{3.75}{3} = ₹\,14.75$

Fare by B $= 24.25 + \frac{33.25 - 24.25}{3} = ₹\,27.25$

Difference $= 27.25 - 14.75 = ₹\,12.50$

164. (e) Fare by B for 5 km $= 14.50 + 3.25 = ₹\,17.75$

Fare by A for 8 km $= 13.50 + \frac{17.25 - 13.50}{3}$

$= ₹\,14.75$

Fare by C for 5 km $= 19 + \frac{31 - 19}{3} = ₹\,23$

Total fare $= 17.75 + 14.75 + 23 = 55.50$

165. (b) Fare for 14th km by C $= \frac{56.50 - 41.50}{15 - 10} = ₹\,3$

Fare for 9th km by B $= \frac{33.25 - 24.25}{10 - 7} = ₹\,3$

166. (d) Total no. of students who play cricket
$= 38 + 40 + 12 + 17 + 25 + 18 + 20 = 170$

Reqd % $= \frac{25}{170} \times 100 \approx 15\%$

167. (d) Reqd ratio $= 27 : 18 = 3 : 2$

168. (e) Cricket

169. (e) Total Class X students who play different games = 115

Reqd % $= \frac{21}{115} \times 100 \approx 18\%$

170. (e) Basketball and Badminton are the two games which satisfy the conditions.

171. (d) Chemical *Y* has to be used.

⇓

Chemical *Z* cannot be used.

∴ Options (a) & (b) are ruled out

Also, chemicals *B* & *W* cannot be used with each other.

∴ Option (c) is ruled out

∴ Option (d) is the answer.

172. (b) Chemical *Z* is being used

⇓

Chemical *Y* cannot be used.

∴ Options (a) & (d) are ruled out

Option (c) is ruled out as the combination becomes unstable.

∴ Option (b) is the answer.

173. (a) III is impossible as the combination becomes unstable

∴ Option (a) is the answer.

174. (d) If Chemical A is not used, B and C have to be used. But then W cannot be used. Thus, (II) can never be true.

Sol. (175-177) :

Following information about 7 offices from front to back on one side of hallway.

- 2 offices are green.
- 2 offices are blue
- 2 offices are white
- 1 office is yellow
- The green offices are together
- The blue offices are never together.
- Office 3 is white
- The yellow office is not next to a white office.

175. (a) The two combinations possible with the 3rd and 4th offices painted white are given below. In both cases office 7 is painted blue.

7	blue	blue
6	green	yellow
5	green	blue
4	**white**	**white**
3	**white**	**white**
2	blue	green
1	yellow	green

176. (a) The possible combinations are :

7	green	yellow
6	green	blue
5	white	white
4	blue	blue
3	white	white
2	blue	green
1	yellow	green

So among the given options only (a) is possible.

177. (b)

	(a)	(b)	(c)	(d)
7		blue		
6	blue	white		
5		green		green
4		green		green
3	white	white	white	white
2		blue	green	
1		yellow	green	

In (a) the two green offices can be 1 & 2 or 4 & 5, both cases are possible, GGWWBBY; BWWGGBY etc. (from 1 to 7)

In (c) offices 1, 2 & 3 are fixed but 4 to 7 can have various options, viz WBYB, BWBY, BYBW, etc. (from 4 to 7)

In (d) offices 3, 4 & 5 are fixed but again multiple options are possible for the rest, viz. YBWGGBW, YBWGGWB, etc (from 1 to 7).

178. (b) It is clear that statement (B) is the cause and statement (A) is its effect.

179. (b) It is clear that statement (B) is the cause and statement (A) is its effect.

180. (a) It is clear that statement (A) is cause and statement (B) is its effect. If there is adequate supply in the retail market, the price would stabilise.

181. (c) Required difference

$$= \left(\frac{19-11}{100}\right) \times 120000 = 9600$$

182. (c) Required percentage

$$= \frac{10200}{120000} \times 100 = 8.5\%$$

183. (e) Estimated cost of furniture and miscellaneous expenditures

$$= \left(\frac{13+8}{100}\right) \times 120000 = 25200$$

Actual cost of furniture

$$= \frac{88}{100} \times \frac{13}{100} \times 120000 = 13728$$

Actual cost of furniture and miscellaneous expenditure

$$= 13728 + 10200 = 23928$$

Total expenditure of the family

$$= 120000 - 25200 + 23928 = 118728$$

184. (b) Required estimated cost

$$= \left(\frac{15+14}{100}\right) \times 120000 = 34800$$

185. (d) Amount spent on furniture

$$= \frac{88}{100} \times \frac{13}{100} \times 120000 = 13728$$

Sol. (186-189) :

Total Number of flats = 13; Unoccupied flats = 5

Occupied flats = 8

Number of flats on second floor = 4

Second floor comprises four flats. One occupant is lawyer and since he has only one neighbour, this implies that out of four flats on second floor, two are unoccupied.

Again, since no flat is unoccupied on the third floor, it implies that there are three unoccupied flats on floor IV.

Since there are at least three flats on any floor and no two same profession stay on any floor and the doctor is not the neighbour of any lawyer, then floor III comprises only three flats. Thus, floor IV comprises six flats (3 occupied + 3 unoccupied).

Since there are three managers and no two same profession stay on any floor, therefore, there will be a manager in each floor. Also there are only two occupant in second floor and one of them is lawyer, therefore, second occupant should be manager.

Again, since there are two teachers, there will be a teacher each on floors III and IV. Again, doctor can't be neighbour of a lawyer. Hence, the doctor and lawyer will not reside on same floor. Therefore, on floor III – either Doctor or Lawyer then,
on floor IV – either Lawyer or Doctor.

Floor	Total Flats	Occupied flats	Unoccupied flats	Occupants
II	4	2	2	Lawyer, Manager
III	3	3	0	Teacher, Manager, Lawyer or Doctor
IV	6	3	3	Teacher, Manager, Doctor or Lawyer

186. (d) Clearly, there are three flats.

187. (a) From above table that combination is Lawyer & Manager.

188. (c) Both the manager and the teacher are the neighbour of other lawyer.

189. (b) There are three flats occupied.

190. (d)

3601 3602 1803 604 ~~155~~ 154 36 12

$\div 1+1$ $\div 2+2$ $\div 3+3$ $\div 4+4$ $\div 5+5$ $\div 6+6$

154 is written in place of 155.

191. (b)

4 12 ~~45~~ 42 196 1005 6066 42511

$\times 2+(2)^2$ $\times 3+(3)^2$ $\times 4+(4)^2$ $\times 5+(5)^2$ $\times 6+(6)^2$ $\times 7+(7)^2$

42 is written in place of 45.

192. (a)

2 ~~6~~ 8 12 20 30 42 56

+ 4 + 6 + 8 + 10 + 12 + 14

8 is written in place of 6.

193. (e)

32 16 24 ~~60~~ 65 210 945 5197.5

× 0.5 × 1.5 × 2.5 × 3.5 × 4.5 × 5.5

65 is written in place of 60.

194. (d)

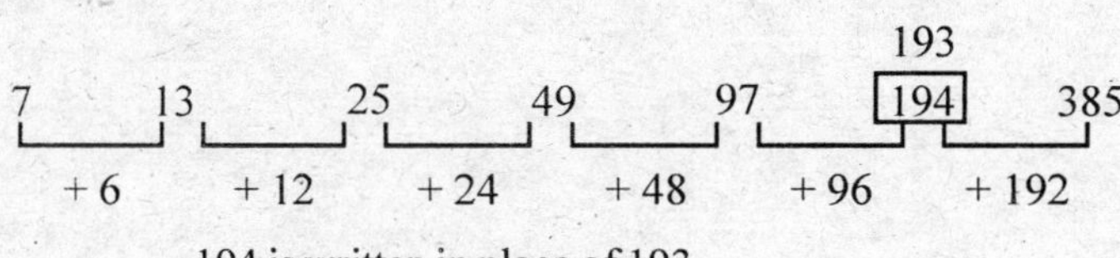

194 is written in place of 193

195. (e)

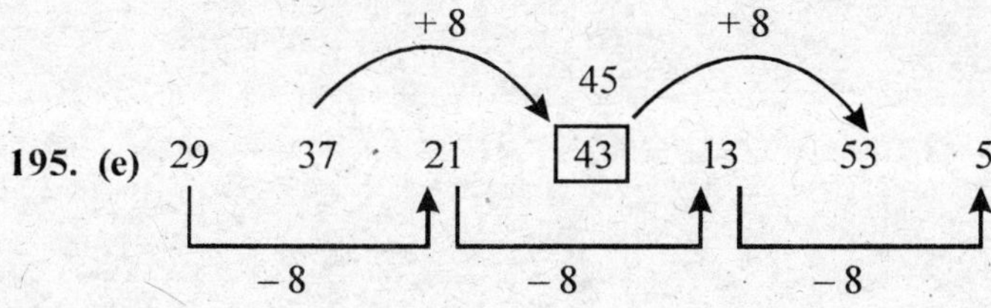

Sol. (196-200)

Number of Passengers in train A = 700

Number of Passenger in train B = 30% of 700 = 910

Coaches	General	Sleeper	First Class	AC	Total
Train A	140	161	224	175	700
Train B	241	273	91	305	910
Total	381	434	315	480	1610

196. (c) Number of passengers in first class coaches of train A = 224Number of passengers in sleeper class coaches of train B = 273

$\therefore$ Required ratio $= \frac{224}{273} = \frac{7 \times 32}{7 \times 39} = 32:39$

197. (d) Passengers in the general coaches of train A = 140

Passengers in the AC coaches of train B = 305

$\therefore$ Total = 140 + 305 = 445

198. (e) The number of passengers in AC coaches of train A = 175

Total number of passengers in sleeper class coaches and first class coaches together of train B

$= (273 + 91) = 364$

$\therefore$ Their difference = 364 – 175 = 189

199. (b) Passengers in general class coach of train A and train B = (140 + 241) = 381

Total number of passengers in train B = 910

$\therefore$ Required percentage $= \frac{381}{910} \times 100\% = 41.8\% \approx 42\%$

200. (c) The cost of per ticket of first class coach = ₹ 450

Number of Passenger in first class coaches of Train A = 224.

Total amount = 450 × 224 = ₹ 100800

SOLVED PAPER

(Based on Memory)

COMMON ENTRANCE TEST

MAHARASHTRA-CET MBA/MMS

11th MARCH 2012

1. In a certain code language 'how many goals scored' is written as '5 3 9 7'; 'many more matches' is written as '9 8 2'; and 'he scored five' is written as '1 6 3 '. How is 'goals' written in that code language?
(a) 5 (b) 7
(c) 5 or 7 (d) Data inadequate
(e) None of these

2. In a certain code TEMPORAL is written as OLDSMBSP. How is CONSIDER written in that code?
(a) RMNBSFEJ (b) BNMRSFEJ
(c) RMNBJEFS (d) TOPDQDCH
(e) None of these

3. How many meaningful English words can be made with the letters DLEI using each letter only once in each word?
(a) None (b) One
(c) Two (d) Three
(e) More than three

4. Among A, B, C, D and E, each having different weight, D is heavier than only A and C is lighter than B and E. Who among them is the heaviest?
(a) B (b) E
(c) C (d) Data inadequate
(e) None of these

5. Each odd digit in the number 5263187 is substituted by the next higher digit and each even digit is substituted by the previous lower digit and the digits so obtained are rearranged in ascending order, which of the following will be the third digit from the left end after the rearrangement?
(a) 2 (b) 4
(c) 5 (d) 6
(e) None of these

6. Pratap correctly remembers that his mother's birthday is before twentythird April but after nineteenth April, whereas his sister correctly remembers that their mother's birthday is not on or after twentysecond April. On which day in April is definitely their mother's birthday?
(a) Twentieth
(b) Twenty first
(c) Twentieth or twentyfirst
(d) Cannot be determined
(e) None of these

7. Ashok started walking towards South. After walking 50 metres he took a right turn and walked 30 metres. He then took a right turn and walked 100 metres. He again took a right turn and walked 30 metres and stopped. How far and in which direction was he from the starting point?
(a) 50 metres South (b) 150 metres North
(c) 180 metres East (d) 50 metres North
(e) None of these

8. If ÷ means +, – means ×, × means ÷ and + means –, then $15 - 8 \times 6 - 12 + 4 = ?$
(a) 20 (b) 28
(c) 8 (d) 2
(e) None of these

9. Town D is towards East of town F. Town B is towards North of town D. Town H is towards South of town B. Towards which direction is town H from town F?
(a) East (b) South-East
(c) North-East (d) Data inadequate
(e) None of these

10. How many such pairs of letters are there in the word SEARCHES each of which has as many letters between them in the word as in the English alphabet?
(a) None (b) One
(c) Two (d) Three
(e) More than three

Directions (Qs. 11 to 15): In each of the questions below are given four statements followed by four conclusions numbered I, II, III & IV. You have to take the given statements to be true even if they seem to be at variance with commonly known facts. Read all the conclusions and then decide which of the given conclusions logically follows from the given statements disregarding commonly known facts.

11. **Statements:** All cups are bottles. Some bottles are jugs.. No jug is plate. Some plates are tables.
Conclusions:
I. Some tables are bottles.
II. Some plates are cups.
III. No table is bottle.
IV. Some jugs are cups.
(a) Only I follows (b) Only II follows
(c) Only III follows (d) Only IV follows
(e) Only either 1 or III follows

12. **Statements:** Some chairs are handles. All handles are pots. All pots are mats. Some mats are buses.
Conclusions:
I. Some buses are handles.
II. Some mats are chairs.
III. No bus is a handle.
IV. Some mats are handles.
(a) Only I, II and IV follow
(b) Only II, III and IV follow
(c) Only either I or III and II follow
(d) Only either I or III and IV follow
(e) Only either I or III, II and IV follow

13. **Statements:** All birds are horses. All horses are tigers. Some tigers are lions. Some lions are monkeys.
Conclusions:
I. Some tigers are horses.
II. Some monkeys are birds.
III. Some tigers are birds.
IV. Some monkeys are horses.
(a) Only I and III follow
(b) Only I, II and III follow
(c) Only II, III and IV follow
(d) All I, II, III and IV follow
(e) None of these

14. **Statements:** Some benches are walls.
All walls are houses.
Some houses are jungles. All jungles are roads.
Conclusions:
I. Some roads are benches.
II. Some jungles are walls.
III. Some houses are benches.
IV. Some roads are houses.
(a) Only I and II follow
(b) Only I and III follow
(c) Only III and IV follow
(d) Only II, III and IV follow
(e) None of these

15. **Statements:**
Some sticks are lamps. Some flowers are lamps.
Some lamps are dresses. All dresses are shirts.
Conclusions:
I. Some shirts are sticks.
II. Some shirts are flowers.
III. Some flowers are sticks.
IV. Some dresses are sticks.
(a) None follows (b) Only I follows
(c) Only II follows (d) Only III follows
(e) Only IV follows

Directions (Qs. 16 to 20): Study the following information carefully and answer the questions given below:
A, B, C, D, E, F, G and H are eight employees of an organization working in three departments, viz Personnel, Administration and Marketing with not more than three of them in any department. Each of them has a different choice of sports from football, cricket, volleyball, badminton, lawn tennis, basketball, hockey and table tennis, not necessarily in the same order.

D works in Administration and does not like either football or cricket. F works in Personnel with only A, who likes table tennis. E and H do not work in the same department as D. C likes hockey and does not work in Marketing. G does not work in Administration and does not like either cricket or badminton. One of those who work in Administration likes football. The one who likes volleyball works in Personnel. None of those who work in Administration likes either badminton or lawn tennis. H does not like cricket.

16. Which of the following groups of employees work in Administration department?
(a) EGH (b) SAF
(c) BCD (d) BCD
(e) Data inadequate

17. In which department does E work?
(a) Personnel (b) Marketing
(c) Administration (d) Data inadequate
(e) None of these

18. Which of the following combinations of employee department favourite sport is correct?
(a) E - Administration - Cricket
(b) F - Personnel - Lawn Tennis
(c) H - Marketing - Lawn Tennis
(d) B - Administration - Table Tennis
(e) None of these

19. What is E's favourite sport?
(a) Cricket (b) Badminton
(c) Basketball (d) Lawn Tennis
(e) None of these

20. What is G's favourite sport?
(a) Cricket (b) Badminton
(c) Basketball (d) Lawn Tennis
(e) None of these

DIRECTIONS (Qs. 21 to 25): In the following questions, the symbols @, $, ★, # and δ are used with the following meaning as illustrated below:
P $ Q means 'P is not smaller than Q'.
P % Q means 'Pis neither smal ler than nor equal to Q'.
P # Q means 'P is neither greater than nor equal to Q'.
P δ Q means' P is neither greater than nor smal ler than Q'.
P ★ Q' means 'P is not greater than Q'.
Now in each of the following questions assuming the given statements to be true, find which of the four conclusions I, II, III and IV given below them is/are definitely true and give your answer accordingly.

21. **Statements:** H @ T, T#F, Fδ E, E★V
Conclusions:
I. V $ F
II. E@T
III. H@ V IV. T#V
(a) Only I, II and III are true
(b) Only I, II and IV are true
(c) Only II. Ill and IV are true
(d) Only I, III and IV are true
(e) All I, II, III and IV are true

22. **Statements:** D # R, R ★ K, K @ F, F $ J
Conclusions:
I. J # R **II.** J # K
III. R # F **IV.** K @ D
(a) Only I, II and III are true
(b) Only II, III and IV are true
(c) Only I, III and IV are true
(d) All I, II, III and IV are true
(e) None of these

23. **Statements:** N δ B, B $ W, W#H, H★M
Conclusions:
I. M @ W II. H@N
III. WδN IV. W#N
(a) Only I is true
(b) Only III is true
(c) Only IV is true
(d) Only either III or IV is true
(e) Only either III or IV and I are true

24. **Statements:** R★D, D$J, J#M, M@K
Conclusions:
I. K # J II. D@M
III. R# M IV. D@K
(a) None is true (b) Only I is true
(c) Only II is true (d) Only III is true
(e) Only IV is true

25. **Statements:** M $ K, K@N, N★ R, R# W
Conclusions:
I. W@K II. M$R
III. K @W IV. M@N
(a) Only I and II are true
(b) Only I. II and III are true
(c) Only III and IV are true
(d) Only II, III and IV are true
(e) None of these

DIRECTIONS (Qs. 26 to 30): Study the following information carefully and answer the questions given below. Following are the conditions for selecting Senior Manager-Credit in a bank.
The candidate must
(i) be a graduate in any discipline with at least 60 per cent marks.
(ii) have post-qualification work experience of at least ten years in the Advances Section of a bank,
(iii) be at least 30 years and not more than 40 years as on 1.4.2010.
(iv) have secured at least 40 per cent marks in the Group Discussion.
(v) have secured at least 50 per cent marks in the Interview.
In the case of a candidate who satisfies all the conditions EXCEPT
(A) at (i) above, but has secured at least 50 per cent marks in graduation and at least 60 percent marks in post-graduation in any discipline, the case is to be referred to the General Manager-Advances.
(B) at (ii) above, but has total post-qualification work experience of at least seven years, out of which at least three years as Manager-Credit in a bank, the case is to be referred to the Executive Director.

In each question below details of one candidate are given. You have to take one of the following courses of action based on the information provided and the conditions and subconditions given above and mark the number of that course of action as your answer. You are not to assume anything other than the information provided in each question. All these cases are given to you as on 01-04-2010.
(a) if the case is to be referred to the Executive Director.
(b) if the case is to be referred to the General Manager-Advances.
(c) if the data are inadequate to take a decision.
(d) if the candidate is not to be selected.
(e) if the candidate is to be selected.

26. Shobha Gupta has secured 50 per cent marks in the Interview and 40 percent marks in the Group Discussion. She has been working for the past eight years, out of which four years as Manager-Credit in a bank, after completing her BA degree with 60 per cent marks. She was born on 12th September 1978.

27. Rohan Maskare was born on 8th March 1974. He has been working in a bank for the past twelve years after completing his B Com degree with 70 per cent marks. He has secured 50 per cent marks in both the Group Discussion and the Interview.

28. Prakash Gokhale was born on 4th August 1977. He has secured 65 per cent marks in postgraduation and 58 per cent marks in graduation. He has been working for the past ten years in the Advances Department of a bank after completing his postgraduation. He has secured 45 percent marks in the Group Discussion and 50 per cent marks in the Interview.

29. Sudha Mehrotra has been working in the Advances Department of a bank for the past twelve .years after completing her B Com Degree with 60 per cent marks. She has secured 50 per cent marks in the Group Discussion and 40 per cent marks in the Interview. She was born on 15th February 1972.

30. Amit Narayan was born on 28th May 1974. He has been working in the Advances department of a bank for the past eleven years after completing his B Sc Degree with 65 per cent marks. He has secured 55 percent marks in the Group discussion and 50 per cent marks in the interview.

DIRECTIONS (Qs. 31 to 35): In each question below is given a statement followed by three courses of action numbered (A), (B) and (C). A course of action is a step or administrative decision to be taken for improvement, follow-up or further action in regard to the problem, policy, etc. On (he basis of the information given in the statement, you have to assume every thing in the statement to be true, then decide which of the suggested courses of action logically follow(s) for pursuing.

31. **Statement:** A heavy unseasonal downpour during the last two days has paralysed the normal life in the state in which five persons were killed but this has provided a huge relief to the problem of acute water crisis in the state
Courses of action:
(A) The state government should set up a committee to. review the alarming situation.
(B) The state government should immediately remove all the restrictions on use of potable water in all the major cities in the state.
(C) The state government should send relief supplies to all the affected areas in the state.
(a) None (b) Only (A)
(c) Only (B) and (C) (d) Only (C)
(e) All (A), (B), (C)

32. **Statement:** A large private bank has decided to retrench one-third of its employees in view of the huge losses incurred by it during the past three quarters.

Courses of action:

(A) The Govt should issue a notification to general public to immediately stop all transactions with the bank.

(B) The Govt should direct the bank to refrain from retrenching its employees.

(C) The Govt should ask the central bank of the country to initiate an enquiry into the bank's activities and submit its report.

(a) None (b) Only (A)
(c) Only (B) (d) Only (C)
(e) Only (A) and (C)

33. **Statement:** Many political activists have decided to stage demonstrations and block traffic movement in the city during peak hours to protest against the steep rise in prices of essential commodities.

Courses of action:

(A) The Govt should immediately ban all forms of agitations in the country.

(B) The police authority of the city should deploy additional forces all over.the city to help traffic movement in the city.

(C) The state administration should carry out preventive arrests of the known criminals staying in the city.

(a) Only (A) (b) Only (B)
(c) Only (C) (d) Only (A) and (B)
(e) None of these

34. **Statement:** The school dropout rate in many districts in the state has increased sharply during the last few years as the parents of these children make them work in the fields owned by others to earn enough for them to get at least one meal a day.

Courses of action:

(A) The Govt should put up a mechanism to provide foodgrains to the poor people in these districts through public distribution system to encourage the parents to send their wards to school.

(B) The Govt should close down some of these schools in the district and deploy the teachers of these schools to nearby schools and also ask remaining students to join these schools.

(C) Govt should issue arrest warrants for all the parents who force their children to work in fields instead of attending classes.

(a) Only (A) (b) Only (B)
(c) Only (C) (d) Only (A) and (B)
(e) None of these

35. **Statement:** One aspirant was killed due to stampede while participating in a recruitment drive of police constables.

Courses of action:

(A) The officials in charge of the recruitment process should immediately be suspended.

(B) A team of officials should be asked to find out the circumstances which led to the death of the aspirant and submit its report within a week.

(C) The Govt should ask the home department to stagger the number of aspirants over more number of days to avoid such incidents in future.

(a) Only (A) (b) Only (B)
(c) Only (C) (d) Only (B) and (C)
(e) None of these

36. **Effect:** Majority of the employees of the ailing organisation opted for voluntary retirement scheme and left the organisation with all their retirement benefits within a fortnight of launching the scheme. Which of the following can be a probable cause of the above effect ?

(a) The company has been making huge losses for the past five years and is unable to pay salary to its employees in time.

(b) The management of ttfe company made huge personal gains through unlawful activities.

(c) One of the competitors of the company went bankrupt last year.

(d) The company owns large tracts of land in the state which will fetch huge sum to its owners.

(e) None of these

37. **Statement:** Most of the companies in IT and ITES sectors in India have started hiring from engineering college campuses this year and are likely to recruit much more than yearly recruitment of the earlier years.

Which of the following substantiates the facts stated in the above statement?

(a) IT and ITES are the only sectors in India which are hiring from engineering college campuses.

(b) Govt has stepped up recruitment activities after a gap of five years.

(c) The IT and ITES companies have now decided to visit the engineering college campuses for tier-II cities in India as well.

(d) The availability of qualified engineers will substantially increase in the near future.

(e) None of these

38. **Cause:** The Govt has recently increased its taxes on petrol and diesel by about 10 per cent.

Which of the following can be a possible effect of the above cause?

(a) The petroleum companies will reduce the prices of petrol and diesel by about 10 per cent.

(b) The petroleum companies will increase the prices of petrol and diesel by about 10 per cent.

(c) The petroleum companies will increase the prices of petrol and diesel by about 5 per cent.

(d) The petrol pumps will stop selling petrol and diesel till the taxes are rolled back by the Govt.

(e) None of these

39. **Statement:** The Govt has decided to instruct the banks to open new branches in such a way that there is one branch of any of the banks in every village of population 1000 and above or a cluster of villages with population less than 1000 to provide banking services to all the citizens.
Which of the following will weaken the step taken by the Govt?
(a) The private sector banks in India have stepped up their branch expansion activities in rural India.
(b) Many Govt-owned banks have surplus manpower in its urban branches.
(c) All the banks, including those in private sector, will follow the Govt directive.
(d) Large number of branches of many Govt-owned banks in the rural areas are making huge losses every year due to lack of adequate business activities.
(e) None of these

DIRECTIONS (Qs. 40 to 42): Study the following information carefully and answer the questions given below:

The Centre reportedly wants to continue providing subsidy to consumers for cooking gas and kerosene for five more years. This is not good news from the point of view of reining in the fiscal deficit. Mounting subventions for subsidies means diversion of savings by the government from investment to consumption, raising the cost of capital in the process. The government must cut expenditure on subsidies to create more fiscal space for investments in both physical and social infrastructure. It should outline a plan for comprehensive reform in major subsidies including petroleum, food and fertilizers and set goal posts.

40. Which of the following is a conclusion which can be drawn from the facts stated in the above paragraph?
(a) Subsidy provided by the government under various heads to the citizen increases the cost of capital.
(b) Govt is unable to withdraw subsidies provided to various items.
(c) Govt subsidy on kerosene is purely a political decision.
(d) Govt does not have enough resources to continue providing subsidy on petroleum products.
(e) None of these

41. Which of the following is an inference which can be made from the facts stated in the above paragraph?
(a) India's fiscal deficit is negligible in comparison to other merging economies in the world.
(b) Subsidy on food and fertilizers are essential for the growth of Indian economy.
(c) Reform in financial sector will weaken India's position in the international arena.
(d) Gradual withdrawal of subsidy is essential for effectively managing fiscal deficit in India.
(e) None of these

42. Which of the following is an assumption which is implicit in the facts stated in the above paragraph?
(a) People in India may not be able to pay more for petroleum products.
(b) Many people in India are rich enough to buy petroleum products at market cost.
(c) Govt may not be able to create more infrastructural facilities if the present level of subsidy continues for a longer time.
(d) Govt of India has sought assistance from international financial organisations for its infrastructural projects.
(e) None of these

Directions (Qs. 43 to 45): Study the following information carefully and answer the questions given below:

Poverty measurement is an unsettled issue, both conceptually and methodologically. Since poverty is a process as well as an outcome, many come out of it while others may be falling into it. The net effect of these two parallel processes is a proportion commonly identified as the 'head count ratio', but these ratios hide the fundamental dynamism that characterises poverty in practice. The most recent poverty re-estimates by an expert group has also missed the crucial dynamism. In a study conducted on 13,000 households which represented the entire country in 1993-94 and again in 2004-05, it was found that in the ten-year period 18.2% rural population moved out of poverty whereas another 22.1 % fell into it over this period. This net increase of about four percentage points was seen to have a considerable variation across states and regions.

43. Which of the following is a conclusion which can be drawn from the facts stated in the above paragraph?
(a) Accurate estimates of number of people living below poverty line in India is possible to be made.
(b) Many expert groups in India are not interested to measure poverty objectively.
(c) Process of poverty measurement needs to take into account various factors to tackle its dynamic nature.
(d) People living below poverty line remain in that position for a very long time.
(e) None of these

44. Which of the following is an assumption which is implicit in the facts stated in the above paragraph?
(a) It may not be possible to have an accurate poverty measurement in India.
(b) Level of poverty in India is static over the years.
(c) Researchers avoid making conclusions on poverty measurement data in India.
(d) Govt of India has a mechanism to measure level of poverty effectively and accurately.
(e) None of these

45. Which of the following is an inference which can be made from the facts stated in the above paragraph?
(a) Poverty measurement tools in India are outdated.
(b) Increase in number of persons falling into poverty varies considerably across the country over a period of time.
(c) Govt of India has stopped measuring poverty-related studies.
(d) People living in rural areas are more susceptible to fall into poverty over a time.
(e) None of these

DIRECTIONS (Qs. 46 to 50): In each of the questions given below which one of the five answer figures on the right should come after the problem figures on the left, if the sequence were continued?

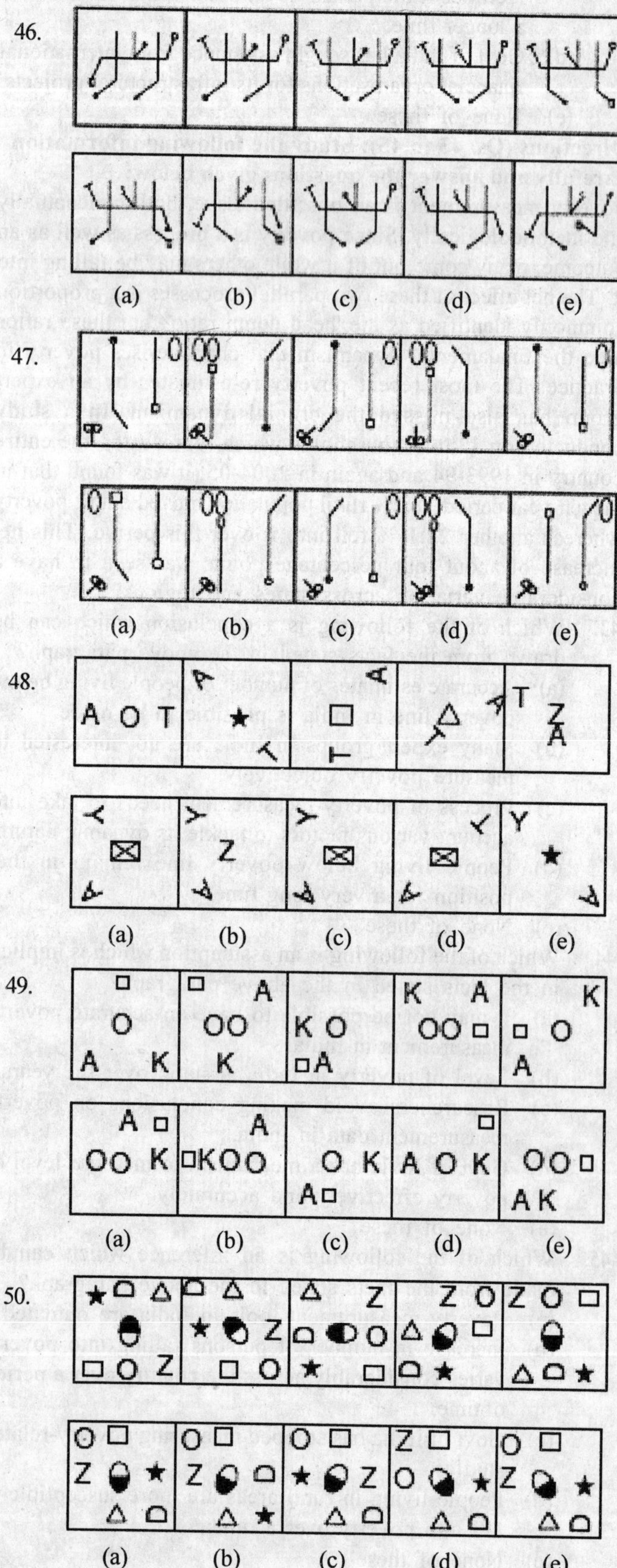

DIRECTIONS (Qs. 51 to 55) : Study the following table carefully to answer the questions that follow:

Number (N) of candidates (in lakhs) appearing for an entrance examination from six different states and the percentage (P) of candidates clearing the same over the years

State	A		B		C		D		E		E	
Year	N	P	N	P	N	P	N	P	N	P	N	P
2004	1.23	42	1.04	51	1.11	32	1.32	24	1.23	36	1.33	31
2005	1.05	43	1.12	62	1.07	47	1.15	49	1.18	55	1.24	24
2006	2.04	38	1.48	32	1.08	28	1.96	35	1.42	49	1.58	26
2007	1.98	41	2.07	43	1.19	30	1.88	46	1.36	47	1.79	29
2008	1.66	53	1.81	50	1.56	42	1.83	60	1.73	57	1.86	34
2009	1.57	39	1.73	36	1.64	52	2.01	56	1.69	55	1.95	37

51. What is the ratio of the total number of candidates clearing the entrance exam from State B in the year 2004 to that of those clearing the entrance exam from State C in the same year?
(a) 221:148 (b) 218:143
(c) 148:221 (d) 143:218
(e) None of these

52. In which year did the highest number of candidates clear the entrance exam from State D?
(a) 2008 (b) 2006
(c) 2009 (d) 2007
(e) None of these

53. What is the number of candidates not clearing the entrance exam from State A in the year 2007?
(a) 186820 (b) 11682
(c) 1868200 (d) 116820
(e) None of these

54. What is the total number of candidates clearing the entrance exam from States E and F together in the year 2006?
(a) 16160 (b) 110660
(c) 1.1066 (d) 1106600
(e) None of these

55. What is the average number of candidates appearing for the entrance exam from State D in the years 2007, 2008 and 2009 together?
(a) 186820 (b) 11682
(c) 1868200 (d) 116820
(e) None of these

DIRECTIONS (Qs. 56 to 60): Study the given information carefully and answer the questions that follow: An urn contains 6 red, 4 blue, 2 green and 3 yellow marbles.

56. If four marbles are picked at random, what is the probability that at least one is blue?
(a) 5/91 (b) 1/35
(c) 1/3 (d) 4/105
(e) None of these

57. If two marbles are picked at random, what is the probability that both are red?
(a) 5/91 (b) 1/35
(c) 1/3 (d) 4/105
(e) None of these

58. If three marbles are picked at random, what is the probability that two are blue and one is yellow?
(a) 5/91 (b) 1/35
(c) 1/3 (d) 4/105
(e) None of these

59. If four marbles are picked at random, what is the probability that one is green, two are blue and one is red?
(a) 24/455 (b) 13/35
(c) 11/15 (d) 7/91
(e) None of these

60. If two marbles are picked at random, what is the probability that either both are green or both are yellow?
(a) 5/91 (b) 1/35
(c) 1/3 (d) 4/105
(e) None of these

Directions (Qs. 61 to 65): Study the given pie-charts carefully to answer the questions that follow:

Break-up of number of employees working in different departments of an organisation, the number of males and the number of employees who recently go* promoted in each department.

Break-up of the employees working in different departments Total number of employees = 3,600 Employees working in different departments.

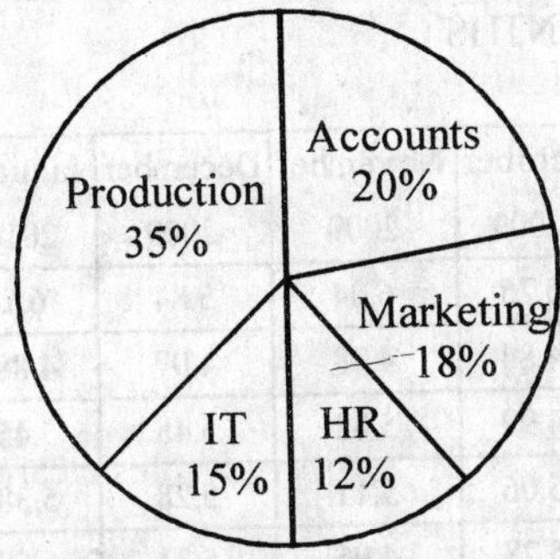

Break-up of the number of males in each department Total number of males in the organisation = 2.040 Break-up of the number of males working in each department

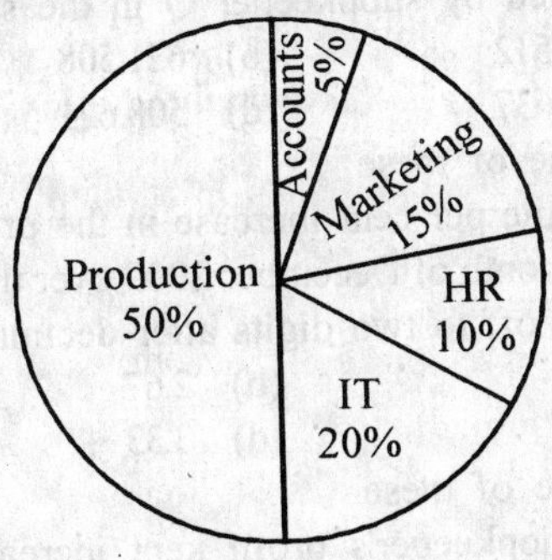

Break-up of the number of employees who recently got promoted in each department Total number of employees who got promoted = 1,200 Number of employees who recently got promoted from each department

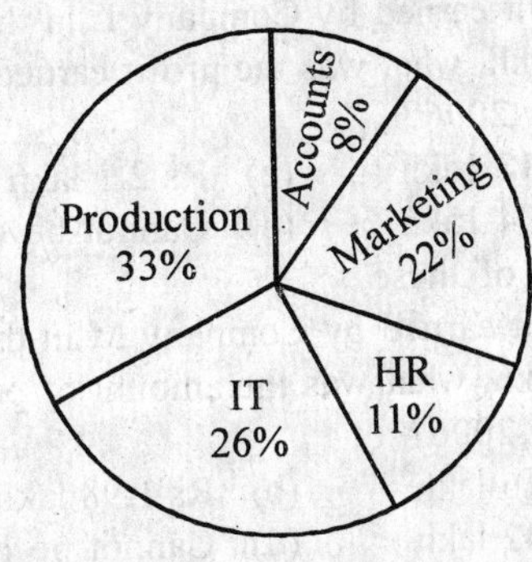

61. If half of the number of employees who got promoted from the IT department were males, what was the approximate percentage of males who got promoted from the IT department?
(a) 61 (b) 29
(c) 54 (d) 42
(e) 38

62. What is the total number of females working in the Production and Marketing departments together?
(a) 468 (b) 812
(c) 582 (d) 972
(e) None of these

63. How many females work in the Accounts department ?
(a) 618 (b) 592
(c) 566 (d) 624
(e) None of these

64. The total number of employees who got promoted from all the departments together was what per cent of the total number of employees working in all the departments together? (Rounded off to the nearest integer)
(a) 56 (b) 21
(c) 45 (d) 33
(e) 51

65. The number of employees who got promoted from the HR department was what per cent of the total number of employees working in that department? (rounded off to two digits after decimal)
(a) 36.18 (b) 30.56
(c) 47.22 (d) 28.16
(e) None of these

DIRECTIONS (Qs. 66 to 70): Study the graph carefully to answer the questions that follow. Percent rise in profit of two companies over the years

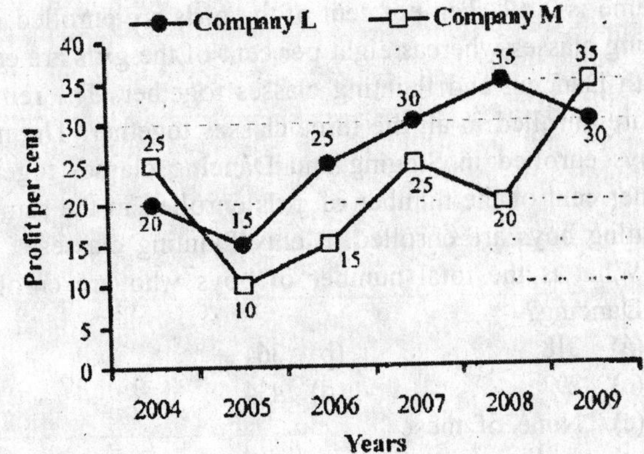

66. If the profit earned by Company L in the year 2005 was' Rs 1.84 lakh, what was the profit earned by the company in the year 2006?
(a) Rs 2.12 lakh (b) Rs 2.3 lakh
(c) Rs 2.04 lakh (d) Cannot be determined
(e) None of these

67. If the profit earned by Company M in the year 2008 was Rs 3.63 lakh, what was the amount of profit earned by it in the year 2006?
(a) Rs 2.16 lakh (b) Rs 1.98 lakh
(c) Rs 2.42 lakh (d) Cannot be determined
(e) None of these

68. What is the average per cent rise in the profit of Company L over all the years together appoximately?
(a) 1. 15 (b) 25
(c) 18 (d) 21
(e) None of these

69. Which of the following statements is TRUE with respect to the above graph?
(a) Company M made the highest profit in the year 2009.
(b) Company L made the least profit in the year 2005.
(c) The respective ratio of the profit earned by Company L to that by company M in the year 2006 was 6 : 5.
(d) Company L made the highest profit in the year 2008
(e) All are true

70. What is the percentage increase in per cent rise in profit of Company M in the year 2009 from the previous year?
(a) 25 (b) 15
(c) 50 (d) 75
(e) None of these

DIRECTIONS (Qs. 71 to 75): Study the information carefully to answer the questions that follow:

A school consisting of a total of 1560 students has boys and girls in the ratio of 7 : 5. All the students are enrolled in different types of hobby classes, viz Singing, Dancing and Painting. One-fifth of the boys are enrolled in only Dancing classes. Twenty per cent of the girls are enrolled in only Painting classes. Ten per cent of the boys are enrolled in only Singing classes. Twenty four per cent of the girls are enrolled in both Singing and Dancing classes together. The number of girls enrolled in only Singing classes is two hundred per cent of the boys enrolled in the same. One thirteenth of the boys are enrolled in all the three classes together. The ratio of boys enrolled in Dancing and Painting classes together to the girls enrolled in the same is 2 : 1. Ten per cent of the girls are enrolled in only Dancing classes whereas eight per cent of the girls are enrolled in both Dancing and Painting classes together. The remaining girls are enrolled in all the three classes together. The number of boys enrolled in Singing and Dancing classes together is fifty per cent of the number of girls enrolled in the same. The remaining boys are enrolled in only Painting classes.

71. What is the total number of boys who are enrolled in Dancing?
(a) 318 (b) 364
(c) 292 (d) 434
(e) None of these

72. Total number of girls enrolled in Singing is approximately what per cent of the total number of students in the school?
(a) 37 (b) 19
(c) 32 (d) 14
(e) 26

73. What is the total number of students enrolled in all the three classes together?
(a) 135 (b) 164
(c) 187 (d) 142
(e) None ofthese

74. Number of girls enrolled in only Dancing classes is what percent of the boys enrolled in the same? (rounded off to two digits after decimal)
(a) 38.67 (b) 35.71
(c) 41.83 (d) 28.62
(e) None ofthese

75. What is the ratio of the number of girls enrolled in only Painting classes to the number of boys enrolled in the same?
(a) 77:26 2) (b) 1 : 7 3
(c) 26:77 (d) 73:21
(e) None ofthese

DIRECTIONS (Qs. 76 to 80): Study the table carefully to answer the questions that follow:

PROFIT (IN Rs '000) MADE BY SIX DIFFERENT SHOPKEEPERS OVERTHE MONTHS

Month → Shopkeeper ↓	October 2009	November 2009	December 2009	January 2010	February 2010	March 2010
P	5.25	6.04	5.84	6.1	5.95	6.02
Q	4.84	4.28	4.97	4.88	5.04	5.12
R	4.99	5.82	5.48	5.45	5.68	5.36
S	5.06	5.11	5.28	5.38	5.44	5.59
T	5.28	4.96	5.31	5.69	4.93	5.72
U	5.94	6.23	5.87	6.07	6.19	6.23

76. What is the ratio of the profit earned by shopkeeper U in the months February 2010 and March 2010 together to that earned by shopkeeper Q in the same months?
(a) 637:512 (b) 621:508
(c) 512:637 (d) 508:621
(e) None of these

77. What is the per cent increase in the profit of shopkeeper S in the month of December 2009 over the previous month? (rounded off to two digits after decimal)
(a) 3.15 (b) 2.67
(c) 2.18 (d) 3.33
(e) None of these

78. Which shopkeeper's profit kept increasing continuously over the given months?
(a) R (b) Q
(c) T (d) U
(e) None of these

79. What is the difference in profit earned by shopkeeper T in January 2010 from the previous month?
    (a) Rs 640 (b) Rs 420
    (c) Rs380 (d) Rs 760
    (e) None of these
80. What was the average profit earned by shopkeeper R in the months of October 2009 and November 2009 together?
    (a) 5405 (b) 5040
    (c) 4825 (d) 4950
    (e) None of these

DIRECTIONS (Qs. 81 to 84): Study the given graph carefully to answer the questions that follow:

Number of days taken by three carpenters to finish making one piece each of four different items of furniture

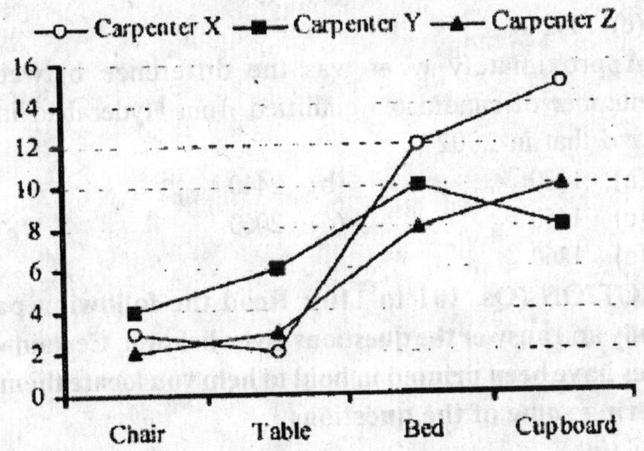

81. If Carpenter X and Carpenter Y were to make a chair together how many days would they take?
    (a) 1 day (b) 4 days
    (c) 3 days (d) 2 days
    (e) None of these
82. If Carpenter X, Y and Z were to make a table together how many days would they take?
    (a) 4 days (b) 3 days
    (c) 1 day (d) 2 days
    (e) None of these
83. What is the total number of days that Carpenter Z will take to make one piece each of all the four items together?
    (a) 32 days (b) 24 days
    (c) 1 1/59 day (d) 1 1/32 days
    (e) None of these
84. The radius of a circular field is equal to the side of a square field whose perimeter is 784 feet. What is the area of the circular field?
    (a) 107914 sq ft (b) 120736 sq ft
    (c) 107362 sq ft (d) 127306 sq ft
    (e) None of these
85. In how many different ways can the letters of the word 'STRESS' be arranged?
    (a) 360 (b) 240
    (c) 720 (d) 120
    (e) None of these

DIRECTIONS (Qs. 86 to 90): Study the given table carefully to answer the questions that follow: Number of people staying in five different localities and the percentage breakup of men, women and children in them

Locality	Total No. of People	Percentage		
		Men	Women	Children
F	5640	55	35	10
G	4850	34	44	22
H	5200	48	39	13
I	6020	65	25	10
J	4900	42	41	17

86. Total number of people staying in locality J forms approximately what per cent of the total number of people staying in locality F?
    (a) 81 (b) 72
    (c) 78 (d) 93
    (e) 87
87. What is the total number of children staying in localities H and I together?
    (a) 1287 (b) 1278
    (c) 1827 (d) 1728
    (e) None of these
88. The number of women staying in which locality is the highest?
    (a) H (b) J
    (c) F (d) G
    (e) None of these
89. What is the total number of men and children staying in locality I together?
    (a) 4115 (b) 4551
    (c) 4515 (d) 4155
    (e) None of these
90. What is the ratio of the number of men staying in locality F to the number of men staying in locality H?
    (a) 517:416 (b) 403:522
    (c) 416:517 (d) 522:403
    (e) None of these
91. The compound interest earned by Suresh on a certain amount at the end of two years at the rate of 8 p.c.p.a. wasRs 1,414.40. What was the total amount that Suresh got back at the end of two years in the form of principal plus interest earned?
    (a) Rs 9,414.40 (b) Rs 9,914.40
    (c) Rs 9,014.40 (d) Rs 8,914.40
    (e) None of these
92. The ratio of the present ages of a mother and daughter is 7 : 1. Four years ago the ratio of their ages was 19 : 1. What will be the mother's age four years from now?
    (a) 42 years (b) 38 years
    (c) 46 years (d) 36 years
    (e) None of these

93. Three friends J, K and L jog around a circular stadium and complete one round in 12, 18 and 20 seconds respectively. In how many minutes will all the three meet again at the starting point?
(a) 5 (b) 8
(c) 12 (d) 3
(e) None of these

94. 4 men can complete a piece of work in 2 days. 4 women can complete the same piece of work in 4 days whereas 5 children can complete the same piece of work in 4 days. If 2 men, 4 women and 10 children work together, in how many days can the work be completed?
(a) 1 day (b) 3 days
(c) 2 days (d) 4 days
(e) None of these

95. The speed of a boat when travelling downstream is 32 km/hr, whereas when travelling upstream it is 28 km/hr. What is the speed of the boat in still water?
(a) 27 km/hr (b) 29 km/hr
(c) 31 km/hr (d) Cannot be determined
(e) None of these

DIRECTIONS (Qs. 96 to 100): Study the following tables carefully and answer the questions given below:

Number of candidates appeared in a Competitive Examination from Five Centres over the Years Number

Centre → Year ↓	Mumabi	Delhi	Kolkata	Hyderabad	Chennai
2001	35145	65139	45192	51124	37346
2002	17264	58248	52314	50248	48932
2003	24800	63309	56469	52368	51406
2004	28316	70316	71253	54196	52315
2005	36503	69294	69632	58360	55492
2006	29129	59216	64178	48230	57365
2007	32438	61345	56304	49178	58492

Approximate percentages of Candidates qualified to appeared in the competitive examination from five centres over the years percentage

Mumabi	Delhi	Kolkata	Hyderabad	Chennai
12	24	18	17	9
10	28	12	21	12
15	21	23	25	10
11	27	19	24	8
13	23	16	23	13
14	20	21	19	11
16	19	24	20	14

96. In which of the following years was the difference in number of candidates appeared from Mumbai over the previous year the minimum?
(a) 2004 (b) 2006
(c) 2007 (d) 2002
(e) None of these

97. In which of the following years was the number of candidates qualified from Chennai the maximum among the given years?
(a) 2007 (b) 2006
(c) 2005 (d) 2003
(e) None of these

98. Approximately what was the total number of candidates qualified from Delhi in 2002 and 2006 together?
(a) 27250 (b) 25230
(c) 30150 (d) 28150
(e) 26250

99. Approximately how many candidates appearing from Kolkata in 2004 qualified in the competitive examination?
(a) 13230 (b) 13540
(c) 15130 (d) 15400
(e) 19240

100. Approximately what was the difference between the number of candidates qualified from Hyderabad in 2001 and that in 2002?
(a) 1680 (b) 2440
(c) 1450 (d) 2060
(e) 1860

DIRECTION (Qs. 101 to 110): Read the following passage carefully and answer the questions given below it. Certain words/ phrases have been printed in bold to help you locate them while answering some of the questions.

Governments have traditionally equated economic progress with steel mills and cement factories. While urban centers thrive and city dwellers get rich, hundreds of millions of farmers remain mired in poverty. However, fears of food shortages, a rethinking of antipoverty priorities and the crushing recession in 2008 arecausing a dramatic shift in world economic policy in favour of greater support for agriculture.

The last time when the world's farmers felt such love was in the 1970s. At that time, as food prices spiked, there was real concern that the world was facing a crisis in which the planet was simply unable to produce enough grain and meat for an expanding population. Governments across the developing world and international aid organisations **plowed** investment into agriculture in the early 1970s, while technological breakthroughs, like high-yield strains of important food crops, boosted production. The result was the Green Revolution and food production exploded.

But the Green Revolution became a victim of its own success. Food prices plunged by some 60% by the late 1980s from their peak in the mid- 1970s. Policymakers and aid workers turned their attention to the poor's other **pressing** needs, such as health care and education. Farming got **starved** of resources and investment. By 2004, aid directed at agriculture sank to 3.5% and "Agriculture lost its glitter." Also, as consumers in high-growth giants such as China and India became wealthier, they began eating more meat, so grain once used for human consumption got diverted to beef up livestock.

By early 2008, panicked buying by importing countries and restrictions **slapped** on grain exports by some big producers helped drive prices upto heights not seen for three decades. Making matters worse, land and resources got reallocated to produce cash crops such as biofuels and the result was that voluminous reserves of grain **evaporated**. Protestsbroke out across the emerging world and fierce food riots toppled governments.

This spurred global leaders into action. This made them aware that food security is one of the fundamental issues in the world that has to be dealt with in order to maintain administrative and political stability. This also spurred the U.S. which traditionally provisioned food aid from American grain surpluses to help needy nations, to move towards investing in farm sectors around the globe to boost productivity. This move helped countries become more productive for themselves and be in a better position to feed their own people.

Africa, which missed out on the first Green Revolution due to poor policy and limited resources, also witnessed a 'change'. Swayed by the success of East Asia, the primary poverty-fighting method favoured by many policymakers in Africa was to get farmers off their farms and into modern jobs in factories and urban centers. But that strategy proved to be highly insufficient. Income levels in the countryside badly trailed those in cities while the FAO estimated that the number of poor going hungry in 2009 reached an all time high at more than one billion.

In India on the other hand, with only 40% of its farmland irrigated, entire economic boom currently underway is held hostage by the unpredictable monsoon. With much of India's farming areas suffering from drought this year, the government will have a tough time meeting its economic growth targets. In a report, Goldman Sachs predicted that if this year too receives weak rains, it could cause agriculture to contract by 2% this fiscal year, making the government's 7% GDP-growth target look "a bit rich". Another green revolution is the need of the hour and to make it a reality, the global community still has much backbreaking farm work to do.

101. What is the author's main objective in writing the passage
 (a) Criticising developed countries for not bolstering economic growth in poor nations
 (b) Analysing the disadvantages of the Green Revolution
 (c) Persuading experts that a strong economy depends on industrialization and not agriculture
 (d) Making a case for the international society to engineer a second Green Revolution
 (e) Rationalising the faulty agriculture policies of emerging countries

102. Which of the following is an adverse impact of the Green Revolution ?
 (a) Unchecked crop yields resulted in large tracts of land becoming barren
 (b) Withdrawal of fiscal impetus from agriculture to other sectors
 (c) Farmers began soliciting government subsidies for their produce
 (d) Farmers rioted as food prices fell so low that they could not make ends meet
 (e) None of these

103. What is the author trying to convey through the phrase "making the government's 7% GDP growth target look "a bit rich""?
 (a) India is unlikely to achieve the targeted growth rate
 (b) Allocation of funds to agriculture has raised India's chances of having a high GDP
 (c) Agricultural growth has artificially inflated India's GDP and such growth is not real
 (d) India is likely to rave one of the highest GDP growth rates
 (e) A large portion of India's GDP is contributed by agriculture

104. Which of the following factors was/were responsible for the neglect of the farming sector after the green revolution?
 (A) Steel and cement sectors generated more revenue for the government as compared to agriculture.
 (B) Large scale protests against favouring agriculture at the cost of other important sectors such as education and healthcare.
 (C) Attention of policy makers and aid organizations was diverted from agriculture to other sectors.
 (a) None (b) Only (C)
 (c) Only (B) & (C) (d) Only (A) & (B)
 (e) All (A), (B) & (C)

105. What prompted leaders throughout the world to take action to boost the agriculture sector in 2008?
 (a) Coercive tactics by the U.S. which restricted food aid to poor nations
 (b) The realization of the link between food security and political stability
 (c) Awareness that performance in agriculture is necessary in order to achieve the targeted GDP
 (d) Reports that high-growth countries like China and India were boosting their agriculture sectors to capture the international markets
 (e) Their desire to influence developing nations to slow down their industrial development.

106. What motivated the U.S. to focus on investing in agriculture across the globe ?
 (a) To make developing countries become more reliant on U.S. aid
 (b) To ensure grain surpluses so that the U.S. had no need to import food
 (c) To make those countries more self sufficient to whom it previously provided food
 (d) To establish itself in the market before the high-growth giants such as India and China could establish themselves
 (e) None of these

107. What impact did the economic recession of 2008 have on agriculture ?
(a) Governments equated economic stability with industrial development and shifted away from agriculture
(b) Lack of implementation of several innovative agriculture programmes owing to shortage of funds
(c) It prompted increased investment and interest in agriculture
(d) The GDP as targeted by India was never achieved because of losses in agriculture
(e) None of these

108. What encouraged African policymakers to focus on urban jobs ?
(a) Misapprehension that it would alleviate poverty as it did in other countries
(b) Rural development outstripped urban development in many parts of Africa
(c) Breaking out of protests in the country and the fear that the government would topple
(d) Blind imitation of western models of development
(e) None of these

109. Which of the following had contributed to exorbitant food prices in 2008 ?
(A) Hoarding of food stocks by local wholesalers which inadvertently created a food shortage.
(B) Export of foodgrains was reduced by large producers.
(C) Diverting resources from cultivation of foodgrains to that of more profitable crops.
(a) None (b) Only (C)
(c) Only (B) (d) All (A), (B) & (C)
(e) Only (B) & (C)

110. Which of the following is true about the state of agriculture in India at present ?
(A) Of all the sectors, agriculture needs the highest allocation of funds.
(B) Contribution of agriculture to India's GDP this year would depend greatly upon the monsoon rains.
(C) As India is one of the high-growth countries, it has s jrplus food reserves to export to other nations.
(a) Only (A) and (C) (b) Only (C)
(c) Only (B) (d) Only (B) and (C)
(e) None of these

DIRECTION (Qs. 111 to 113): Choose the word/group of words which is most similar it meaning to the word printed in bold as used in the passage.

111. STARVED
(a) Deprived (b) Disadvantaged
(c) Hungry (d) Fasting
(e) Emaciated

112. SLAPPED
(a) Beaten (b) Imposed
(c) Withdrawn (d) Avoided
(e) Persuaded

113. PLOWED
(a) Cultivated (b) Bulldozed
(c) Recovered (d) Instilled
(e) Withdrew

DIRECTION (Qs. 114 and 115): Choose the word/phrase which is most opposite in meaning to the word printed in bold as used in the passage.

114. PRESSING
(a) Unpopular (b) Undemanding
(c) Unobtrusive (d) Unsuitable
(e) Unimportant

115. EVAPORATED
(a) Absorbed (b) Accelerated
(c) Grew (d) Plunged
(e) Mismanaged

DIRECTION (Qs. 116 to 120): Which of the phrases (a), (b), (c) and (d) given below each statement should be placed in the blank space provided so as to make a meaningful and grammatically correct sentence? If none of the sentences is appropriate, mark (e) i.e. 'None of these' as the answer.

116. Refuting the rationale behind frequent agitations for formation of separate States, a recent report
(a) proved that such agitations result in loss of governmental property
(b) indicated that the formation of small states does not necessarily improve the economy
(c) suggested that only large scale agitations have been effective in bringing out desired change in the past
(d) recommended dividing large States into smaller ones to improve governance
(e) None of these

117. Overlooking the fact that water scarcity intensifies during summer,
(a) the government issued guidelines to all builders to limit their consumption to acceptable limits
(b) provision for rainwater harvesting has been made to aid irrigation in drought prone areas
(c) the water table did not improve even after receiving normal monsoon in the current year
(d) many residential areas continue to use swimming pools, wasting large quantities of water
(e) None of these

118. He has lost most of his life's earning in the stock market but
(a) He still seems to be leading his life luxuriously and extravagantly
(b) he could not save enough to repay his enormous debts
(c) stock market is not a safe option to invest money unless done with caution
(d) experts have been suggesting to avoid investments in stock market because of its unpredictable nature
(e) None of these

119. Achieving equality for women is not only a laudable goal,
(a) political reforms are also neglected preventing women from entering legislatures and positions of power
(b) the problem is also deep rooted in the society and supported by it
(c) their empowerment is purposefully hampered by people with vested interests in all sections of the society
(d) it is also equally difficult to achieve and maintain for a long term
(e) None of these

120. ______ or else they would not keep electing him year after year.
(a) The party leader gave a strong message to the mayor for improving his political style
(b) Owing to numerous scandals against the mayor, he was told to resign from the post immed iately
(c) The mayor threatened the residents against filing a complaint against him
(d) The residents must really be impressed with the political style of their mayor
(e) None of these

DIRECTION (Qs. 121 to 125):: Each question below has two blanks, each blank indicating that something has been omitted. Choose the set of words for each blank that best fits the meaning of the sentence as a whole.

121. Drawing attention to the pitfalls of______solely on Uranium as a fuel for nuclear reactors, Indian scientists warned that Uranium will not last for long and thus research on Thorium as its____ must be revived.
(a) using, substitute
(b) believing, replacement
(c) depending, reserve
(d) reckoning, option
(e) relying, alternative

122. In an effort to provide______ for higher education to all, most of the universities have been providing education without adequate infrastructure, thus churning out ______ graduates every year.
(a) chances, fresh
(b) platform, capable
(c) opportunities, unemployable
(d) prospects, eligible
(e) policy, incompetent

123. The move to allow dumping of mercury _____ an outcry from residents of the area who _____ that high levels of mercury will affect their health and destroy ecologically sensitive forest area.
(a) resulted, insist
(b) provoked, fear
(c) incited, determined
(d) activated, accept
(e) angered, believe

124. _______ has been taken against some wholesale drug dealers for dealing in surgical items without a valid license and maintaining a stock of _____ drugs.
(a) Note, overwhelming
(b) Step, impressive
(c) Execution, outdated
(d) Action, expired
(e) Lawsuit, invalid

125. Even as the _____ else where in the world are struggling to come out of recession, Indian consumers are splurging on consumer goods and to _____ this growth, companies are investing heavily in various sectors.
(a) economies, meet
(b) countries, inhibit
(c) governments, measure
(d) nations, inflict
(e) companies, counter

DIRECTION (Qs. 126 to 130): Rearrange the following sentences (A), (B), (C), (D), (E) and (F) to make a meaningful paragraph and then answer the questions which follow

(A) While these disadvantages of bio fuels are serious, they are the only alternate energy source of the future and the sooner we find solutions to these problems the faster we will be able to solve the problems are now facing with gasoline.
(B) This fuel can also help to stimulate jobs locally since they are also much safer to handle thaw" gasoline and can thus have the potential to turnaround a global economy.
(C) These include dependence on fossil fuels for the machinery required to produce biofuel which ends up polluting as much as the burning of fossil fuels on roads and exorbitant cost of biofuels which makes it very difficult for the common man to switch to this option.
(D) This turnaround can potentially help to bring world peace and end the need to depend on foreign countries for energy requirements.
(E) Biofuels are made from plant sources and since these sources are available in abundance and can be reproduced on a massive scale they form an energy source that is potentially unlimited.
(F) However everything is not as green with the biofuels as it seems as there are numerous disadvantages involved which at times overshadow their positive impact.

126. Which of the following sentence should be the FIFTH after rearrangement ?
(a) A (b) B
(c) C (d) E
(e) F

127. Which of the following sentence should be the THIRD after rearrangement ?
(a) A (b) B
(c) C (d) D
(e) E

128. Which of the following sentence should be the FIRST after rearrangement ?
(a) A (b) B
(c) C (d) D
(e) E

129. Which of the following sentence should be the SIXTH (LAST) after rearrangement ?
(a) A (b) C
(c) D (d) E
(e) F

130. Which of the following sentence should be the SECOND after rearrangement ?
(a) A (b) B
(c) D (d) E
(e) F

DIRECTION (Qs. 131 to 135): Which of the phrases (a), (b), (c) and (d) given below each statement should replace the phrase printed in bold in the sentence to make it grammatically correct ? If the sentence is correct as it is given and 'No correction is required', mark (e) as the answer.

131. Soon after the Tsunami had killed thousands of people along the coasts of southern India, parliament psssas a bill that proposed to set up an institutional mechanism to respond promptly to natural disasters.
   (a) passed a bill that proposed
   (b) passes a bill with purpose
   (c) pass a bill proposing
   (d) passed a bill which propose
   (e) No correction required
132. Denial of wages forced scientists and teachers at the agriculture universities throughout the country to go on strike, crippling crucial research that could help the state of agriculture in the country.
   (a) from going on strike
   (b) which went on strike
   (c) on going for a strike
   (d) for going to strike
   (e) No correction required
133. In an attempt to boost their profits many edible oil producing companies have been engaging themselves in propaganda against commonly used oils and. promoting exotic and expensive varieties of oils as more healthier options.
   (a) as most healthiest options
   (b) as less healthy option
   (c) as a healthier option
   (d) as much healthiest option
   (e) No correction required
134. Thanks to numerous government initiatives, rural masses which was earlier unaware of the luxuries of urban ways of living are now connected to the same lifestyle.
   (a) who was earlier unaware
   (b) which were earlier aware
   (c) who were earlier conversant
   (d) who were earlier unaware
   (e) No correction required
135. Over the last few months, while most industries are busy in restructuring operations, cutting costs and firing, the Indian pharmaceutical and healthcare industry was adding manpower and giving salary hikes.
   (a) as many industries are
   (b) while most industries were
   (c) while many industries is
   (d) where many industries were
   (e) No correction required

DIRECTION (Qs. 136 to 145): In the following passage there are blanks, each of which]'as been numbered. These numbers are printed below the passage and against each, five words/ phrases are suggested, one of which fits the blank appropriately. Find out the appropriate word/ phrase in each case.

There is a considerable amount of research about the factors that make a company innovate. So is it possible to create an environment (136) to innovation? This is a particularly pertinent (137) for India today. Massive problems in health, education etc. (138) be solved using a conventional approach but (139) creative and innovative solutions that can ensure radical change and (140). There are several factors in India's (141). Few countries have the rich diversity that India or its large, young population (142). While these (143) innovation policy interventions certain additional steps are also required. These include (144) investment in research and development by (145) the government and the private sector, easy transfer of technology from the academic world etc. To fulfill its promise of beng prosperous and to be at the forefront, India must be innovative.

136. (a) stimuli (b) conducive (c) incentive (d) facilitated (e) impetus
137. (a) objective (b) controversy (c) doubt (d) question (e) inference
138. (a) cannot (b) possibly (c) should (d) never (e) must
139. (a) necessary (b) apply (c) need (d) consider (e) requires
140. (a) quantity (b) advantages (c) increase (d) chaos (e) growth
141. (a) challenges (b) praises (c) favour (d) leverage (e) esteem
142. (a) blessed (b) enjoys (c) endows (d) prevails (e) occurs
143. (a) aid (b) jeopardise (c) promotes (d) endure (e) cater
144. (a) acute (b) utilising (c) restricting (d) inspiring (e) increased
145. (a) both (b) besides (c) combining (d) participating (e) a

DIRECTION (Qs. 146 to 150): In each of the following questions four words are given of which two words are most nearly the same or opposite in meaning. Find the two words which are most nearly the same or opposite in meaning and indicate the number of the correct letter combination, by darkening the appropriate oval in your answer sheet.

146. (A) consent (B) nascent
   (C) emerging (D) insecure
   (a) A–C (b) B–D
   (c) B–C (d) A–D
   (e) A–B
147. (A) elated (B) eccentric
   (C) explicit (D) abnormal
   (a) A–B (b) B–D
   (c) A–C (d) A–D
   (e) D–C

148. (A) abundance (B) incomparable
(C) projection (D) plethora
(a) A–C (b) A–B
(c) C–D (d) B–D
(e) A–D

149. (A) purposefully (B) inaccurately
(C) inadvertently (D) unchangeably
(a) A–C (b) A–B
(c) B–C (d) B–D
(e) A–D

150. (A) germane (B) generate
(C) reliable (D) irrelevant
(a) B–D (b) B–C
(c) A–B (d) C–D
(e) A–D

DIRECTIONS (Qs. 151-155): Study the following pie-charts and table to answer these questions.

State wise Details of the adult population of a country

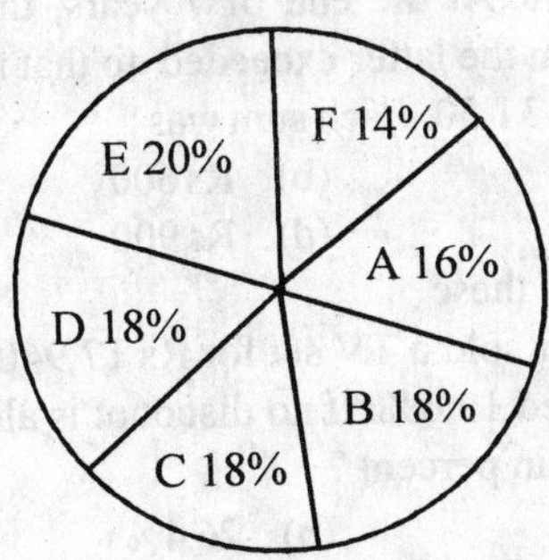

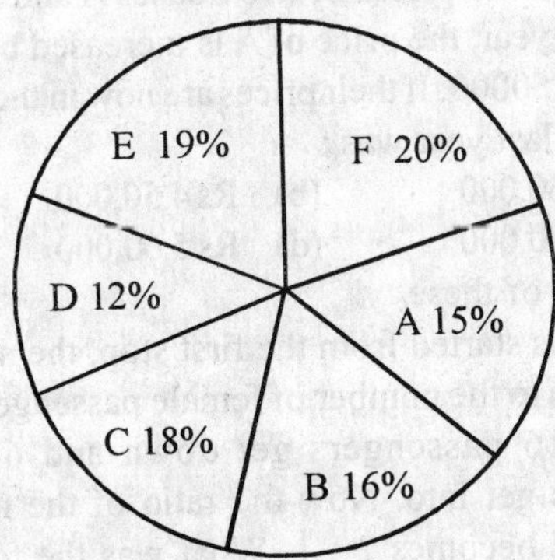

Male Female (M : F) Ratio

State	Graduate & Above M : F	Upto XII Std Pass M : F
A	7 : 5	7 : 9
B	5 : 3	3 : 5
C	5 : 4	4 : 5
D	9 : 8	7 : 7
E	9 : 7	9 : 10
F	4 : 3	3 : 2

151. What is the difference between the Graduate male population and XII Std male population from State 'A'?
(a) 24,000 (b) 14,000
(c) 28,000 (d) 36,000
(e) None of these

152. The Std XII male population of State C is what per cent of the total Std XII population of all the states together?
(a) 8% (b) 12%
(c) 11% (d) 9%
(e) None of these

153. Total Graduate population of State F is what per cent of the total Std XII population of State A?
(a) 56 (b) 72
(c) 68 (d) 76
(e) None of these

154. What is the ratio of the total Graduate and Std XII male population of State A to the total Graduate and Std XII female population of that State?
(a) 215:216 (b) 214:215
(c) 217:215 (d) 215:217
(e) None of these

155. What is the ratio of the total Graduate population of State D to the total Std XII population of that State?
(a) 17:16 (b) 16:17
(c) 64: 51 (d) 51:64
(e) None of these

DIRECTIONS (Qs. 156-160): Study the following pie-chart carefully to answer these questions.

Total number of passengers = 8500

Percentage of passengers

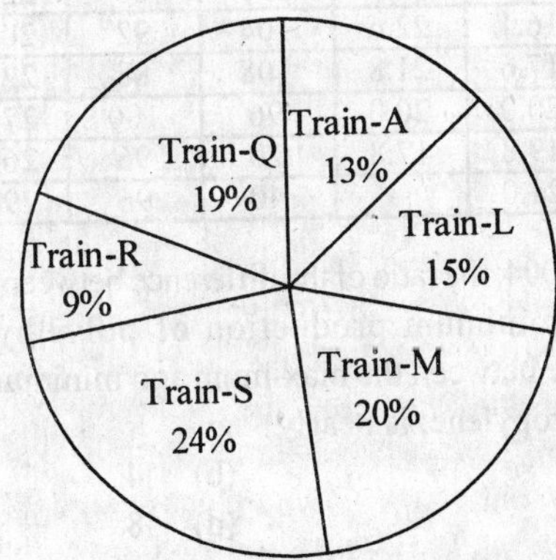

156. What was the **approximate** average number of passenger in Train-S, Train-M and Train-L together?
(a) 1521 (b) 1641
(c) 1651 (d) 1671
(e) 1691

157. If in Train-R 34 per cent of the passengers are females and 26 per cent are children, what is the number of males in that train?
(a) 306 (b) 316
(c) 308 (d) 318
(e) None of these

158. The number of passengers in Train-Q is approximately what percentage of the total number of passengers to Train-A and Train-R?
(a) 90 (b) 70
(c) 75 (d) 80
(e) 86

159. Which train has the second highest number of passengers?
(a) A (b) Q
(c) S (d) M
(e) L

160. How many more per cent (approximately) number of passengers are there in Train-M as compared to the number of passengers in Train-L?
(a) 29 (b) 49
(c) 43 (d) 33
(e) 39

DIRECTIONS (Qs. 161-165) : Study the table below to answer the questions that follow :

PRODUCTION OF PLASTIC MATERIAL

Month	Polypropylene ('000 tonnes)		Polyethylene ('000 tonnes)		Nylon ('000 tonnes)	
	2003-2004	2004-2005	2003-2004	2004-2005	2003-2004	2004-2005
March	17.6	20.8	104	40	3150	2900
April	16.4	20.6	100	88	3050	2850
May	16.0	21.4	80	96	3000	2900
June	15.4	19.2	88	80	2520	2800
July	16.0	19.2	90	84	2600	2700
August	16.6	21.4	94	80	2650	2750
September	16.4	20.8	98	84	2500	2650
October	17.8	23.0	100	80	2200	3000
November	16.4	22.6	104	92	2000	2950
December	17.6	21.8	108	88	2250	3000
January	20.0	20.0	96	100	2750	2350
February	19.8	17.8	20	96	2600	2250
March	21.0	–	40	96	2900	–

161. In 2003-2004, the ratio of the difference between the maximum and the minimum production of polyethylene, to the difference between the maximum and minimum production of polypropylene, is nearly
(a) 15 (b) 14
(c) 16 (d) 18
(e) None of these

162. The ratio of the maximum production of polyethylene in 2004-2005 to the minimum production of polyethylene in 2003-2004 is
(a) 5 (b) 4.8
(c) 5.4 (d) 4.2
(e) None of these

163. The maximum number of times the production in 2003-2004 equals the production in 2004-2005 is for which product?
(a) Polyethylene (b) Polypropylene
(c) Nylon (d) None of these
(e) None of these

164. For polyethylene, the production in 2003-2004 is greater than the production in 2004-2005 for how many months ?
(a) 5 (b) 8
(c) 10 (d) 9
(e) None of these

165. The difference between the minimum production of polypropylene in 2004-2005 and the minimum production of polypropylene in 2003-2004 is how many times the difference in July's production of polyethylene (of the two Years)?
(a) 2 times (b) 3 times
(c) equal (d) 0.4 times
(e) None of these

166. In a family, a couple has a son and a daughter. The age of the father is three times of his daughter and the age of the son is half of his mother. The wife is nine years younger to her husband and the brother is seven years older than his sister. What is the age of the mother?
(a) 40 years (b) 50 years
(c) 45 years (d) 60 years
(e) None of these

167. Two equal sums of money were invested, one at 4% and the other at 4.5%. At the end of 7 years, the simple interest received from the latter exceeded to that received from the former by Rs 31.50. Each sum was :
(a) Rs 1,200 (b) Rs 600
(c) Rs 750 (d) Rs 900
(e) None of these

168. A shopkeeper sold a TV set for Rs 17,940 on a discount of 8% and gained 19.6%. If no discount is allowed, then what will be his gain percent ?
(a) 25% (b) 26.4%
(c) 32.8 % (d) 30%
(e) None of these

169. The ratio of the prices of two houses A and B was 4 : 5 last year. This year, the price of A is increased by 25% and that of B by Rs 50000. If their prices are now in the ratio 9 : 10, the price of A last year was :
(a) Rs 3,60,000 (b) Rs 4,50,000
(c) Rs 4,80,000 (d) Rs 5,00,000
(e) None of these

170. When a bus started from the first stop, the number of male passengers to the number of female passengers was 3 : 1. At the stop 16 passengers get down and 6 more female passengers get into. Now the ratio of the male to female passengers becomes 2 : 1. What was the total number of passengers in the bus when it started from the first stop?
(a) 64 (b) 48
(c) 54 (d) 72
(e) None of these

171. One year ago, a mother was 4 times older to her son. After 6 years, her age becomes more than double her son's age by 5 years. The present ratio of their age will be :
(a) 13 : 12 (b) 3 : 1
(c) 11 : 3 (d) 25 : 7
(e) None of these

172. A and B are two alloys of gold and copper prepared by mixing metals in the ratio 7 : 2 and 7 : 11 respectively. If equal quantities of the alloys are melted to form a third alloy C, the ratio of gold and copper in C will be

(a) 7:5 (b) 5:9
(c) 5:7 (d) 9:5
(e) None of these

173. A train starts from Delhi at 6 : 00 AM and reaches Ambala Cantt at 10 AM. The other train starts from Ambala Cantt at 8 AM and reaches Delhi at 11:30 PM. If the distance between Delhi and Ambala Cantt. is 200 km, then at what time did the two trains meet each other ?

(a) 8:56 AM (b) 8:46 AM
(c) 7:56 AM (d) 8:30 AM
(e) None of these

174. If the length and width of a rectangular garden plot were each increased by 20 per cent, then what would be the per cent increase in the area of the plot ?

(a) 25% (b) 24%
(c) 36% (d) 44%
(e) None of these

175. A track is in the form of a ring whose inner circumference is 352 m and the outer circumference is 396 m. The width of the track is :

(a) 44 m (b) 14 m
(c) 22 m (d) 7 m
(e) None of these

176. PQRS is a diameter of a circle whose radius is r. The lengths of PQ, QR and RS are equal. Semi-circles are drawn on PQ and QS to create the shaded figure below :

The perimeter of the shaded figure is :

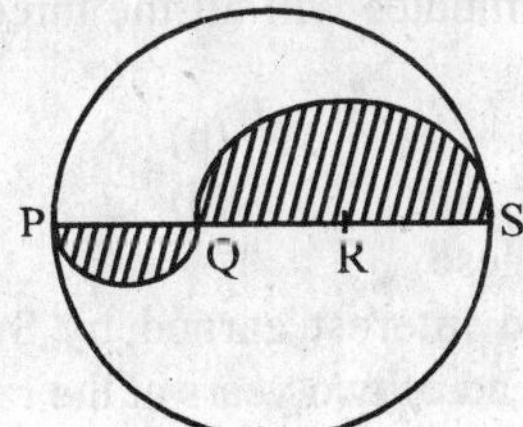

(a) πr (b) $\frac{4\pi r}{3}$
(c) $\frac{5\pi r}{3}$ (d) $\frac{3\pi r}{2}$
(e) None of these

DIRECTIONS (Qs. 177 - 184) : Staff employed in a UNESCO office in Paris are represented by four intersecting circles as in the given diagram. Each circle represents people who can read and write English, French, Spanish and Russian. Strength of people in each circle is also shown alongside. Study the diagram to answer the questions that follow.

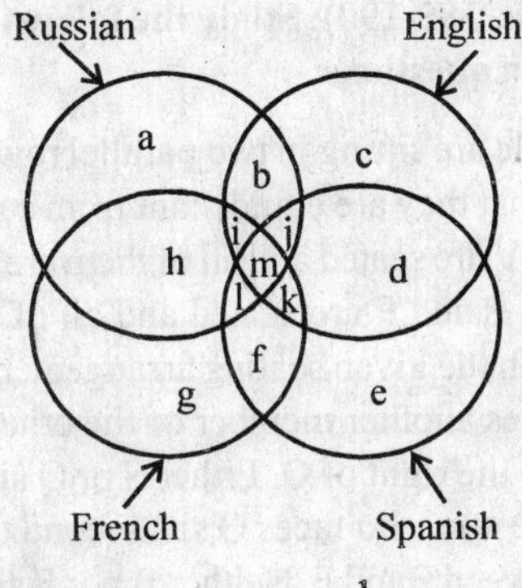

$a = 40 \quad c = 2a \quad e = \frac{1}{2}a \quad g = 2E$

177. People who can read and write English, French and Spanish are represented by :

(a) a (b) d
(c) k (d) f
(e) None of these

178. People who can read and write all the four languages are represented by :

(a) j (b) m
(c) l (d) k
(e) None of these

179. People who can read and write all the language except Spanish, are represented by :

(a) k (b) g
(c) b (d) i
(e) None of these

180. People who cannot read and write Russian, English and French, are represented by :

(a) l (b) j
(c) h (d) e
(e) None of these

181. People who cannot read and write Spanish and French but are conversant with English and Russian are represented by :

(a) b (b) j
(c) m (d) k
(e) None of these

182. Which of the following languages is known by the maximum number of people as per the diagram?

(a) Spanish only (b) French only
(c) English only (d) Russian only
(e) None of these

183. How many people know only Spanish ?

(a) 10 (b) 20
(c) 40 (d) 60
(e) None of these

184. How many people can read and write any one language except French ?

(a) 100 (b) 160
(c) 140 (d) 120
(e) None of these

DIRECTIONS (Qs. 185-190): Study the following information to answer the given questions:

Twelve people are sitting in two parallel rows containing six people each such that they are equidistant from each other. In row 1: P, Q, R, S, T and V are seated and all of them are facing South. In row 2: A, B, C, D, E and F are seated and all of them are facing North. Therefore, in the given seating arrangement, each member seated in a row faces another member of the other row.

S sits third to the right of Q. Either S or Q sits at an extreme end of the line. The one who faces Q sits second to the right of E. Two people sit between Band F. Neither B nor F sits at an extreme end of the line. The immediate neighbour of B faces the person who sits third to the left of P. R and T are immediate neighbours. C sits second to the left of A. T does not face the immediate neighbour of D.

185. Who amongst the following sit at the extreme ends of the rows?
(a) S, D (b) Q, A
(c) V,C (d) P, D
(e) Q, F

186. Who amongst the following faces S?
(a) A (b) B
(c) C (d) D
(e) F

187. How many persons are seated between V and R?
(a) One (b) Two
(c) Three (d) Four
(e) None of these

188. P is related to A in the same way as S is related to B based on the given arrangement. Which of the following is T related to, following the same pattern?
(a) C (b) D
(c) E (d) F
(e) Cannot be determined

189. Which of the following is true regarding T?
(a) F faces T.
(b) V is an immediate neighbour of T.
(c) F faces the one who is second to the right of T.
(d) T sits at one of the extreme ends of the line.
(e) Q sits second to the right of T.

190. Four of the following five are alike in a certain way based on the given arrangement and so form a group. Which is the one that does not belong to that group?
(a) A-T (b) B-T
(c) F-P (d) C-V
(e) E-Q

DIRECTIONS (Qs. 191-197): Study the following information carefully and answer the given questions.

Nine friends A, B, C, D, E, F, G, H and K are sitting around a circle facing the centre. A sits second to left of D. K sits third to right of F. Neither K nor F is an immediate neighbour of A or D. G and H are immediate neighbours of each other. E sits third to right of H. B is not an immediate neighbor of F.

191. What is the position of F with respect to the position of B ?
(a) Second to the right (b) Third to the left
(c) Second to the left (d) Third to the right
(e) Sixthtotheright

192. Who amongst the following is an immediate neighbour of H ?
(a) C (b) B
(c) K (d) F
(e) A

193. Starting from A, if all the friends are made to sit in the alphabetical order in clockwise direction, the positons of how many (except A) will remain unchanged ?
(a) None (b) One
(c) Two (d) Three
(e) Four

194. H is related to C and B is related to E in a certain way. To whom amongst the following is G related following the same pattern ?
(a) F (b) H
(c) C (d) A
(e) D

195. What will come in place of the question mark ?
DC DB DF DA
(a) DG (b) DE
(c) DH (d) DK
(e) Either DK or DE

196. Who sits third to the left of A?
(a) H (b) G
(c) C (d) F
(e) B

197. Which of the following pairs represents the immediate neighbours of C?
(a) FH (b) AB
(c) BD (d) EK
(e) DF

198. Three friends J, K and L jog around a circular stadium and complete one round in 12, 18 and 20 seconds respectively. In how many minutes will all the three meet again at the starting point?
(a) 5 (b) 8
(c) 12 (d) 3
(e) None of these

199. The compound interest earned by Suresh on a certain amount at the end of two years at the rate of 8 p.c.p.a. was ₹1,414.40. What was the total amount that Suresh got back at the end of two years in the form of principal plus interest earned?
(a) ₹9,414.40 (b) ₹9,914.40
(c) ₹9,014.40 (d) ₹8,914.40
(e) None of these

200. A men can complete a piece of work in 2 days. 4 women can complete the same piece of work in 4 days whereas 5 children can complete the same piece of work in 4 days. If 2 men, 4 women and 10 children work together, in how many days can the work be completed?
(a) 1 day (b) 3 days
(c) 2 days (d) 4 days
(e) None of these

ANSWERS AND EXPLANATIONS

1. (c) How many goals scored → 5397 ...(1)
Many more matches → 982 ...(2)
He scored five → 163 ...(3)
From (1) & (2)
Many → 9
From (1) & (3)
scored → 3
∴ goals can be 5 or 7.

2. (a)
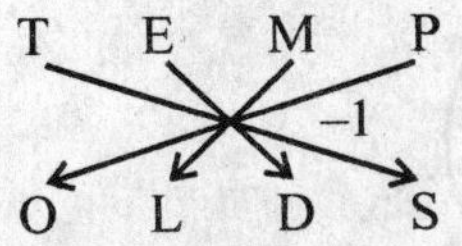

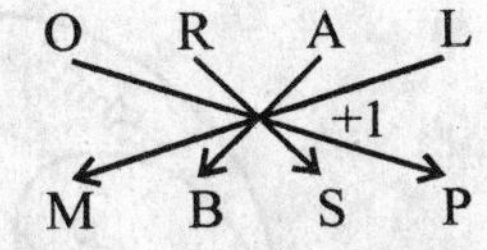

and
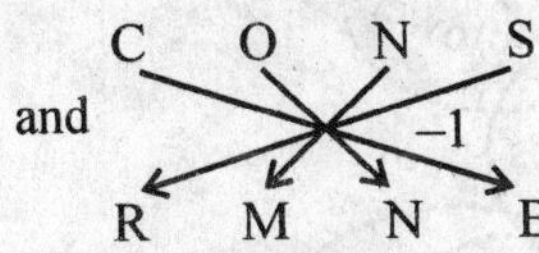

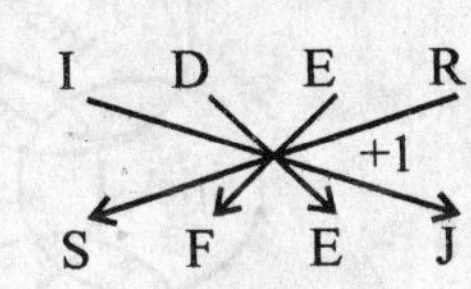

3. (c) Three; LIED, DIEL, IDLE

4. (d) According to question
D > A
B/E > C
Now B/E > C > D > A
From above we can't determine that which one is heaviest.
Therefore, Data indadequate.

5. (b)
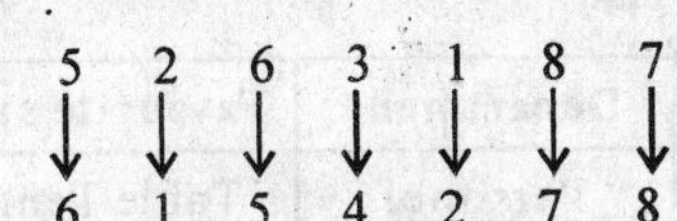

1 < 2 < 4 < 5 < 6 < 7 < 8

6. (c) According to Pratap his mother's birthday may be on 20th, 21st or 22nd April.
According to Pratap's sister their mother's birthday may be form 1st April to 21st April.
common Dates ⇒ 20th and 21st.

7. (d)
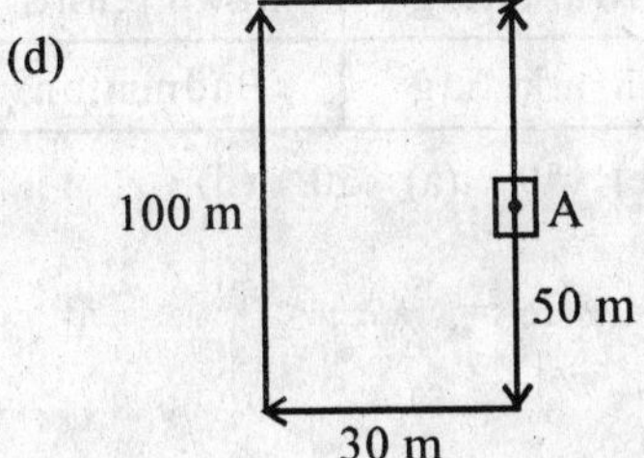

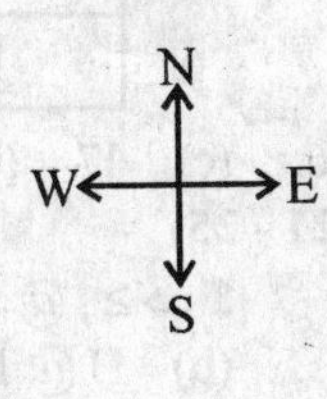

Required Distance ⇒ 100 – 50 = 50 m
Direction ⇒ North

8. (b) $15 - 8 \times 6 - 12 + 4 = ?$
$15 \times 8 \div 6 + 12 - 4 = ?$
$20 + 12 - 4 = ?$
$28 = ?$

9. (d)
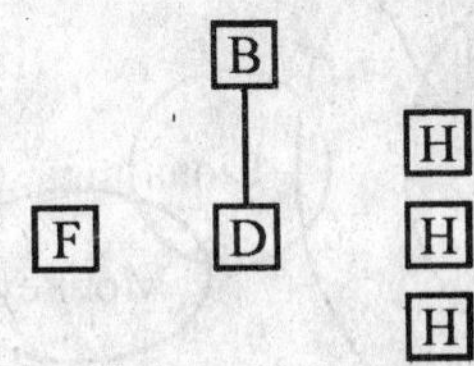

The position of town H is not specifically mentioned.

10. (d)
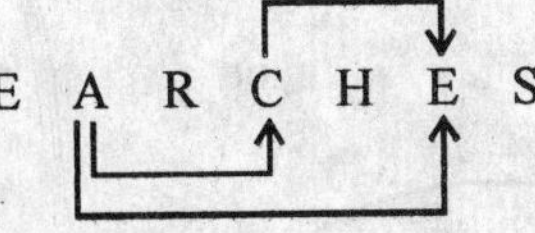

11. (e)
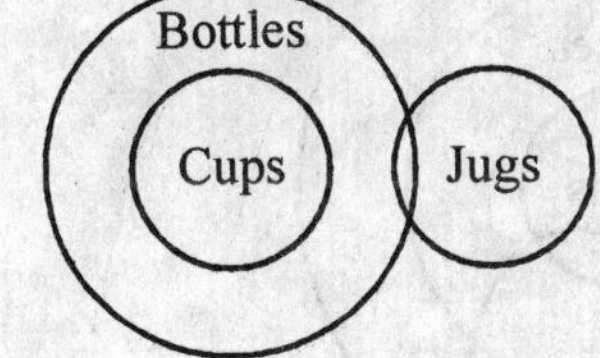

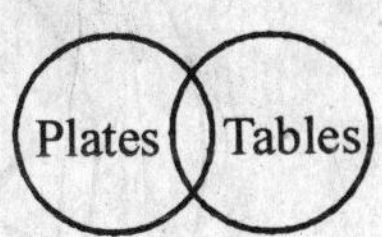

or

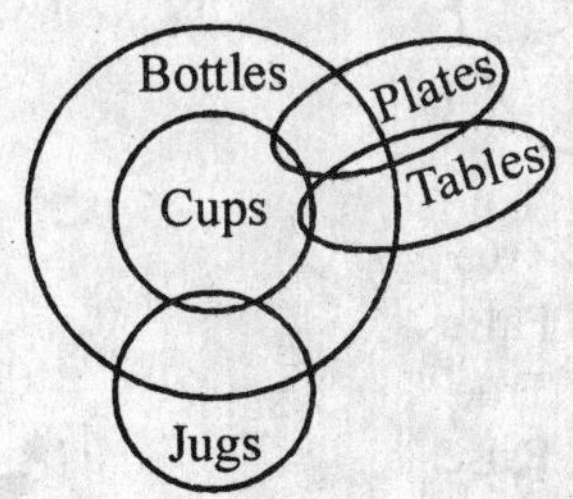

∴ Either I or III follows.

12. (c)
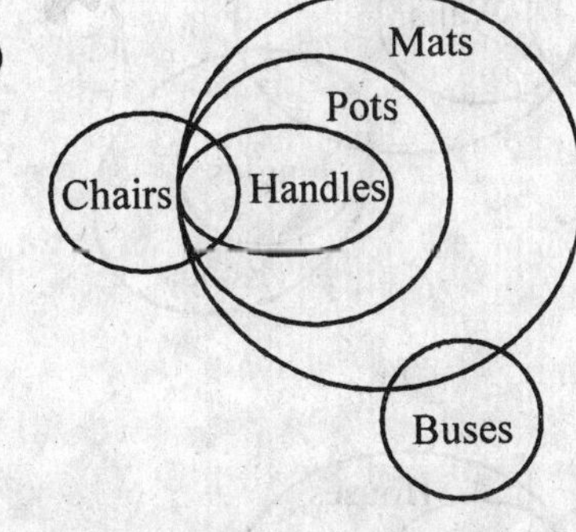

or

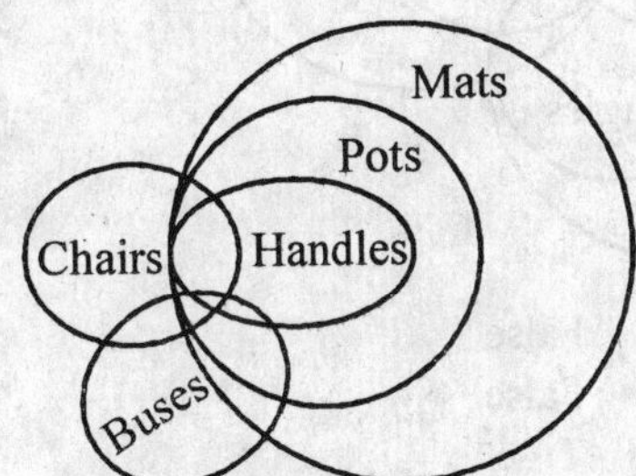

13. (a)

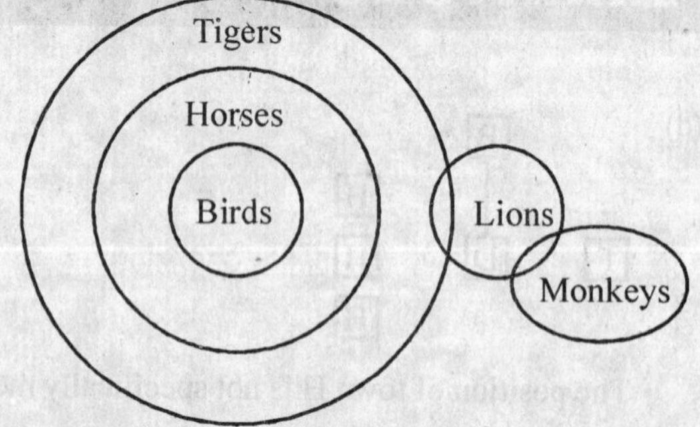

or

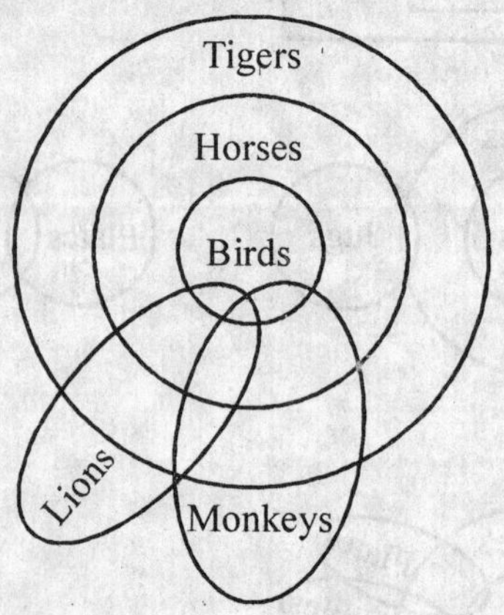

Conclusion I : True
II : False
III : True
IV : False

14. (c)

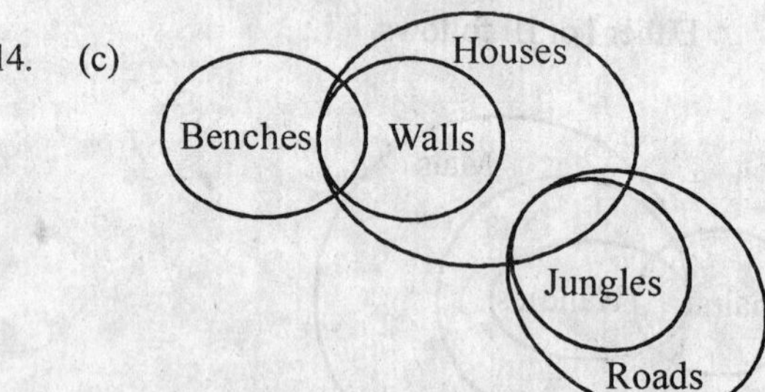

or

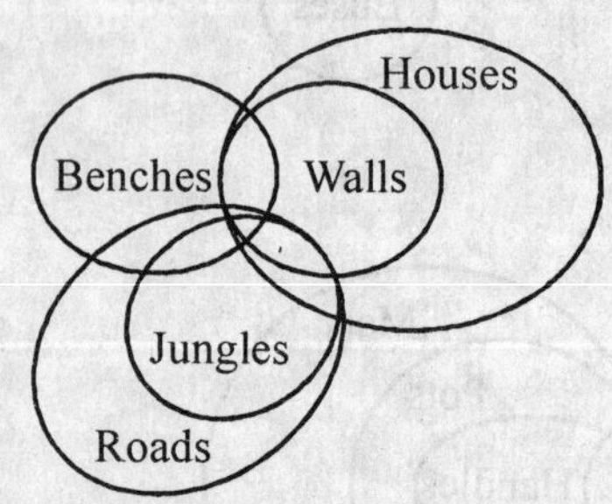

Conclusion I : False
II : False
III : True
IV : True

15. (a)

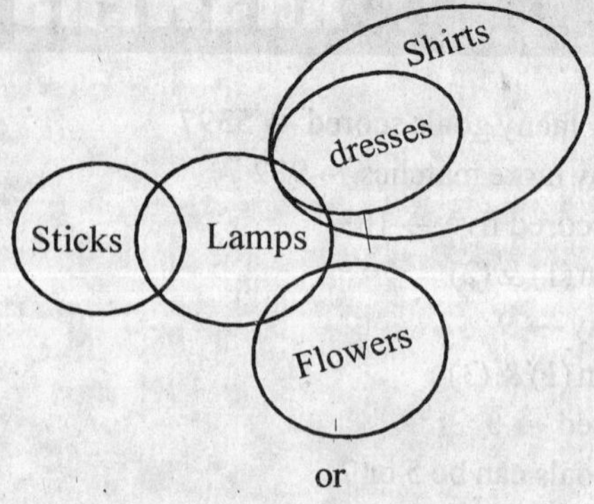

or

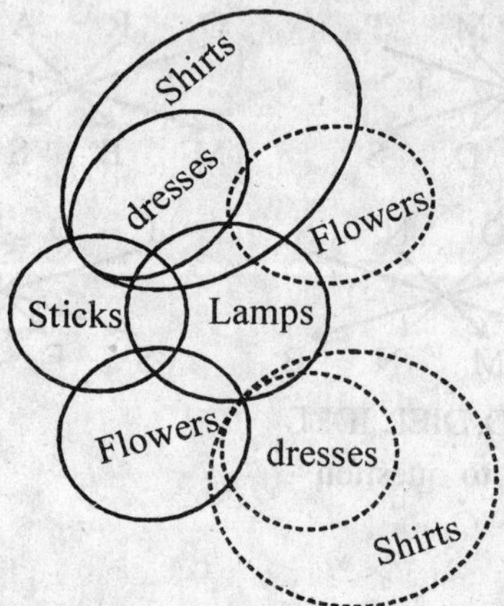

Conclusion I : False
II : False
III : False
IV : False

(16 - 20)

Employee	Department	Favourite sport
A	Personel	Table Tennis
B	Administration	Foot ball
C	Administration	Hockey
D	Administration	Basketball
E	Marketing	Cricket
F	Personnel	Volley ball
G	Marketing	Lawn tennis
H	Marketing	Badminton

16. (c) 17. (b) 18. (e) 19. (a) 20. (d)

(21 - 25)

$\$ \Rightarrow \geq$, $@ \Rightarrow >$, $\# \Rightarrow <$, $\delta \Rightarrow =$, $\bigstar \Rightarrow \leq$

21. (b) $H @ T \Rightarrow H > T$

$T \# F \Rightarrow T < F$

$F \delta E \Rightarrow F = E$

$E \bigstar V \Rightarrow E \leq V$

$\therefore H > T < F = E \leq V$

Conclusions

I. $V \$ F \Rightarrow V \geq F$: True

II. $E @ T \Rightarrow E > T$: True

III. $H @ V \Rightarrow H > V$: Not true

IV. $T \# V \Rightarrow T < V$: True

22. (e) $D \# R \Rightarrow D < R$

$R \bigstar K \Rightarrow R \leq K$

$K @ F \Rightarrow K > F$

$F \$ J \Rightarrow F \geq J$

Therefore, $D < R \leq K > F \geq J$

Conclusions

I. $J \# R \Rightarrow J < R$: False

II. $J \# K \Rightarrow J < K$: True

III. $R \# F \Rightarrow R < K$: False

IV. $K @ D \Rightarrow K > D$: True

23. (c) $N \delta B \Rightarrow N = B$

$B \$ W \Rightarrow B \geq W$

$W \# H \Rightarrow W < H$

$H \bigstar M \Rightarrow H \leq M$

Therefore, $N = B \geq W < H \leq M$

Conclusions

I: $M @ W \Rightarrow M > W$: True

II: $H @ N \Rightarrow H > N$: False

III: $W \delta N \Rightarrow W = N$; Not true

IV: $W \# N \Rightarrow W < N$: Not true

W is either smaller or equal to N. Therefore either III or IV is true.

24. (a) $R \bigstar D \Rightarrow R \leq D$

$D \$ J \Rightarrow D \geq J$

$J \# M \Rightarrow J < M$

$M @ K \Rightarrow M > K$

Therefore, $R \leq D \geq J < M > K$

Conclusions

I. $K \# J \Rightarrow K < J$: Not true

II. $D @ M \Rightarrow D > M$: Not true

III. $R \# M \Rightarrow R < M$: Not true

IV. $D @ K \Rightarrow D > K$: Not true

25. (e) $M \$ K \Rightarrow M \geq K$

$K @ N \Rightarrow K > N$

$N \bigstar R \Rightarrow N \leq R$

$R \# W \Rightarrow R < M$

Therefore, $M \geq K > N \leq R < W$

Conclusions,

I. $W @ K \Rightarrow W > K$: Not true

II. $M \$ R \Rightarrow M \geq R$: Not true

III. $K @ W \Rightarrow K > W$: Not true

IV. $M @ N \Rightarrow M > N$: Not true

(26-30)

Q. No.	Candidate	Conditions							Answers
		(i) or A		(ii) or B		(iii)	(iv)	(v)	
26.	Shobha	✓	–	–	✓	✓	✓	✓	(a)
27.	Rohan	✓	–			✓	✓	✓	(c)
28.	Prakash	–	✓	✓	–	✓	✓	✓	(b)
29.	Sudha	✓	–	✓	–	✓	✓	×	(d)
30.	Amit	✓	–	✓	–	✓	✓	✓	(e)

31. (d) 32. (a) 33. (b) 34. (a) 35. (d)

36. (a) The company has been making huge losses for the past five years and is unable to pay salary to its employees in time.

37. (c) 38. (b) 39. (d) 40. (a) 41. (d) 42. (c)

43. (c) 44. (a) 45. (b)

46. (d) In each subsequent figure one smaller design rotates through 90° clockwise or anticlockwise and it is replaced with a new design.

47. (b) In subsequent figures the design (♈) rotates through 45° and 90° anticlockwise respectively in alternarte manner. As far as the pattern of other designs is concerned the problem is based on the rule (1) = (5) and hence (2) = (6).

48. (c) The design (A) moves one - half and one step in clockwise direction alternately after being related through 45° anticlockwise while design (T) moves one-half step in clockwise direction after being rotated through 45° anticlockwise and the central design is replaced with new design in each subsequent figure.

49. (a) In the subsequent figures the square moves respectively one-half, one, one and a half, two.....step(s) in anticlockwise direction, the design (A) moves along diagonal while the design (K) moves one-half and one step in clockwise direction alternately. The number of circles is the same in alternate figures.

50. (e) In each next figure central design rotates througth 45° anticlockwise and all other designs move one-half step in anticlockwise direction.

51. (a) Total no. of candidates clearing the entrance exam from state B in 2004 $= \dfrac{1.04 \times 51}{100} = 221$

No. of candidates clearing the entrance exam from state C in 2004 $= \dfrac{1.11 \times 32}{100} = 148$

$\therefore$ Required Ratio $= 221 : 148$

52. (c) No. of candidates clearing the exam form state D :

Year 2004 = 3168

2005 = 5635

2006 = 6860

2007 = 8648

2008 = 10980

2009 = 11256

53. (d) No. of candidates not clearing the entrance exam from state A in 2007 $= \left(\dfrac{1.98 \times 59}{100}\right) L = 116820$

54. (b) No. of candidates clearing the exam from state E & F together in 2006 $= \left(\dfrac{1.42 \times 49}{100} + \dfrac{1.58 \times 26}{100}\right)$ Lakhs

$= 110660$

55. (e) Average no. of candidates appearing for the exam from state D in year 2007, 2008 & 2009

$$= \left(\frac{1.88 + 1.83 + 2.01}{3}\right) \text{Lakhs} = 190666.67$$

56. (e) Total possible outcomes for 4 marbles out of 15 marbles $= 15_{C_4} = 1365$

When no marbles is blue, then selution is out of 11 marbles $= 11_{C_4} = 330$

$$\therefore \text{Req. probability} = 1 - \frac{330}{1365} = 1 - \frac{22}{91} = \frac{69}{91}$$

57. (e) Total possible outcome $= 15_{C_2} = 105$

Selection of 2 marbles out of 6 red $= 6_{C_2} = 15$

$$\text{Required Probability} = \frac{15}{105} = \frac{1}{7}$$

58. (e) Total possible outcome $= 15_{C_3} = 455$

Outcome for two blue and one yellow marbles

$= 4_{C_2} \times 3_{C_1} = 18$

$$\therefore \text{Required Probability} = \frac{18}{455}$$

59. (a) Total possible outcome $= 15_{C_4} = 1365$

Outcome for one green, two blue & one red marbles

$= 2_{C_1} \times 4_{C_2} \times 6_{C_1} = 72$

$$\therefore \text{Req. Probability} = \frac{72}{1365} = \frac{24}{455}$$

60. (d) Total possible outcomes $= 15_{C_2} = 105$

Outcome for either two green or two yellow marbles

$= 2_{C_2} + 3_{C_2} = 1 + 3 = 4$

$$\therefore \text{Req. Probability} = \frac{4}{105}$$

61. (e) No. of male employees in IT depdartment

$$= \frac{2040 \times 20}{100} = 408$$

No. of promoted male employees in IT departement

$$= \frac{1}{2}\left(1200 \times \frac{26}{100}\right) = 156$$

$$\therefore \text{Req. percentage} = \frac{156}{408} \times 100 = 38\%$$

62. (c) No. of female employees in production department

$$= \left(\frac{3600 \times 35}{100} - \frac{2040 \times 50}{100}\right) = 240$$

No. of female employees in marketing department

$$= \left(\frac{3600 \times 18}{100} - \frac{2040 \times 15}{100}\right) = 342$$

$\therefore$ Req. no. of employees $= 240 + 342 = 582$

63. (a) No. of female employees in accounts department

$$= \left(\frac{3600 \times 20}{100} - \frac{2040 \times 5}{100}\right) = 618$$

64. (d) Req. percentage $= \frac{1200}{3600} \times 100 = 33\%$

65. (b) Total no. of employees in HR department

$$= \frac{3600 \times 12}{100} = 432$$

No. of promoted employees in HR department

$$= \frac{1200 \times 11}{100} = 132$$

$$\therefore \text{Req. percentage} = \frac{132}{432} \times 100 = 30.56\%$$

66. (b) Profit of company L in the year 2006

$$= \left(\frac{1.84 \times 125}{100}\right) \text{Lakhs} = 2.3 \text{ Lakhs}$$

67. (c) Profit of company M in the year 2006

$$= \left(3.63 \times \frac{100}{120} \times \frac{100}{125}\right) \text{Lakhs} = 2.42 \text{ Lakhs}$$

68. (b) Average percentage rise in profit of company L over the year $= \frac{20 + 15 + 25 + 30 + 35 + 30}{6} = 25\frac{5}{6}\% \approx 25\%$

69. (a) From the graph it is clear that company M made the highest profit in the year 2009.

70. (d) Req. percentage $= \frac{35 - 20}{20} \times 100 = 75\%$

Calculations (71 - 75) :

Total no. of boys $= \frac{1560 \times 7}{12} = 910$

Only ir dancing $= \frac{1}{5} \times 910 = 182$

Only in singing $= 91$

Singing, dancing and Painting $= 910 \times \frac{1}{13} = 70$

Dancing and Painting $= 104$

Singing and dancing $= \frac{156}{2} = 78$

Only in painting = 385

Total no. of girls = 1560 − 910 = 650

Only in painting = $\frac{650}{5} = 130$

Singing and dancing = $\frac{650 \times 24}{100} = 156$

Only in singing = 2 × 91 = 182

Only in dancing = 65

Dancing and painting = $\frac{650 \times 8}{100} = 52$

Dancing, singing and painting = 65

71. (d) Total no. of boys enrolled in dancing class = 182 + 70 + 104 + 78 = 434

72. (e) No. of girls enrolled in singing class = 156 + 182 + 65 = 403

$\therefore$ Req. percentage = $\frac{403}{1560} \times 100 = 26$

73. (a) Req. No. of students = 70 + 65 = 135

74. (b) Req. percentage = $\frac{65}{182} \times 100 = 35.71$

75. (c) Req. Ratio = 130 : 385 = 26 : 77

76. (b) Req. ratio = (6.19 + 6.23) : (5.04 + 5.12) = 621 : 508

77. (d) Req. percentage increase = $\frac{5.28 - 5.11}{5.11} \times 100 = 3.33$

78. (e) Shopkeeper 'S' kept increasing his profit continuously.

79. (c) Req. different in profit = (5.69 − 5.31) = 380

80. (a) Req. average profit = $\left(\frac{4.99 + 5.82}{2}\right) = 5405$

81. (e) Part of the chair prepared by x and y in 1 day

$= \frac{1}{2} + \frac{1}{4} = \frac{3}{4}$

Hence, 1 chair will be prepared in $\frac{4}{3}$ days.

82. (c) Part of the table prepared by x, y and z in 1 day

$= \frac{1}{3} + \frac{1}{6} + \frac{1}{2} = 1$

Hence : The table will be completed in 1 day.

83. (a) Req. no. of days = 3 + 2 + 12 + 15 = 32

84. (b) Radius of the circular field = side of the square

$= \frac{784}{4} = 196$ feet

$\therefore$ Area of the circular field

$= \pi r^2 = \frac{22}{7} \times 196 \times 196$

= 120736 sq. feet.

85. (d) The no. of letters in the word 'STRESS' is six of which 's' comes thrice.

$\therefore$ Req. no. of arrangements = $\frac{6!}{3!} = 120.$

86. (e) Req. percentage = $\frac{4900}{5640} \times 100 \approx 87\%$

87. (b) No. of children in the localities H & I

$= \frac{5200 \times 13}{100} + \frac{6020 \times 10}{100} = 1278$

88. (d) No. of women :

Locality F = $\frac{5640 \times 35}{100} = 1974$

Locality G = $\frac{4850 \times 44}{100} = 2134$

Locality H = $\frac{5200 \times 39}{100} = 2028$

Locality I = $\frac{6020 \times 25}{100} = 1505$

Locality J = $\frac{4900 \times 41}{100} = 2009$

89. (c) No. of men and children in Locality

I = $\frac{6020 \times 75}{100} = 4515$

90. (a) Req. ratio = $\frac{5640 \times 55}{100} : \frac{5200 \times 48}{100} = 517 : 416$

91. (b) $CI = P\left[\left(1 + \frac{R}{100}\right)^T - 1\right]$

$1414.40 = P\left[\left(1 + \frac{8}{100}\right)^2 - 1\right]$

$1414.40 = P \times \left[\left(\frac{27}{25}\right)^2 - 1\right]$

$P = \frac{1414.40 \times 625}{104} = \text{Rs } 8500$

$\therefore$ Amount = 8500 + 1414.40 = Rs. 9914.40

92. (c) Let the ages of the mother and daughter be 7x and x years

$\therefore$ Four years ago

$\frac{7x - 4}{x - 4} = \frac{19}{1}$

$19x - 76 = 7x - 4$

$x = 6$

$\therefore$ Mother's age after 4 years = 7x + 4 = 7 × 6 + 4 = 46 years

93. (d) Req. time = LCM of (12, 18 and 20 seconds.)
180 seconds = 3 minutes

94. (a) 4×2 men $\equiv 4 \times 4$ women $\equiv 20$ chiildren
2 men = 4 women = 5 children
$\therefore$ 2 men + 4 women + 10 children = 20 children
$\therefore M_1 D_1 = M_2 D_2$
$5 \times 4 = 20 \times D_2 \Rightarrow D_2 = 1$ day

95. (e) Speed of boat in still water = $\frac{1}{2}$ (Rate downstream + Rate upstream)
$= \frac{1}{2}(32 + 28) = 30$ km/h.

96. (c) Diff. in 2003 = 24800 − 17264 = 7536
in 2004 = 28316 − 24800 = 3516
in 2005 = 36503 − 28316 = 8187
in 2007 = 32438 − 29129 = 3309

97. (a) No. of candidates passed from chennai

Year 2003 = $\frac{51406 \times 10}{100} = 5140.6 \approx 5141$

Year 2004 = $\frac{52315 \times 8}{100} = 4185.20 \approx 4185$

Year 2005 = $\frac{55492 \times 13}{100} = 7213.96 \approx 7214$

Year 2006 = $\frac{57365 \times 11}{100} = 6310.15 \approx 6310$

Year 2007 = $\frac{58492 \times 14}{100} = 8188.8 \approx 8189$

98. (d) No. of candidates passed from Delhi in 2002 and 2006
$= \frac{58248 \times 28}{100} + \frac{59216 \times 20}{100} = 16309 + 11843 \approx 28150$

99. (b) Req. no. of passed candidates = $\frac{71253 \times 19}{100} \approx 13540$

100. (e) Req. difference = $\frac{50248 \times 21}{100} - \frac{51124 \times 17}{100}$
$= 10551 - 8691 \approx 1860.$

101. (d)
102. (b)
103. (c)
104. (b) Only (c)
105. (b) The realization of the link between food security and political stability.
106. (c) To make those countries more self sufficient to whom it previously provided food.
107. (c) It prompted increased investment and interest in agriculture.
108. (a) Misapprehension that it would alleviate poverty as it did in other countries.
109. (e) Only (b) and (c).
110. (c) Only (b)
111. (a) The meaning of the word **Starve (Verb)** as used in the passage is : keep deprived of : to not give something that is needed.
Hence, the words **starved** and **deprived** are synonymous.
112. (b) The meaning of the word **Slap (Verb)** as used in the passage is : impose : to order especially in a sudden or an unfair way, that something must happen or somebody must do something.
Hence, the words **slapped** and **imposed** are synonymous.
113. (a) The meaning of the word **Plow (Verb)** as used in the passage is : to invest a large amount of money in a company or project : to cultivate.
Hence, the words **plowed** and **cultivated** are synonymous.
114. (b) The meaning of the word **Pressing (Adjective)** as used in the passage is : urgent, serous, insistent, needing to be dealt with immediatley.
Hence, the words **pressing** and **undemanding** are antonymous.
115. (c) The meaning of the word **Evaporate (Verb)** as used in the passage is : to disappear, especially by gradually becoming less and less.
Hence, the words **evaporated** and **grew** are antonymous.
116. (c) Suggested that only large scale agitations have been effective in bringing out desired change in the past.
117. (d) many residential areas continue to use swimming pools, wasting large quantities of water.
118. (a) He still seems to be leading his life luxuriously and extravagantly.
119. (e) None of these
120. (d) The residents must really be impressed with the political style of their mayor.
121. (e) relying, alternative
122. (c) opportunities, unemployable
123. (b) provoked, fear
124. (d) Action, expired
125. (a) economies, meet
126. (c) C
127. (b) B
128. (e) E
129. (a) A
130. (c) D
131. (a) The event shows past time Hence simple past or 'passed a bill that proposed' will be a correct usage.
132. (e) No correction required
133. (c) In comparison between two things, Comparative Degree is used. Use of double comparatives is not proper.

Hence, 'as a healthier option' should be used.

134. (d) For living beings Relative Pronoun 'who' is used. Hence, who were earlier unaware will be a correct usage.

135. (b) The event shows past time. Hence 'while most industries were' should be used.

136. (b) conducive

137. (d) question

138. (a) cannot

139. (c) need

140. (e) growth

141. (c) favour

142. (b) enjoys

143. (a) aid

144. (e) increased

145. (a) both

146. (c) The word **Nascent (Adjective)** means : beginning to exist : not yet fully developed.
The words **nascent** and **emerging** are synonymous.

147. (b) The word **Eccentric (Adjective)** means : considered by other people to be strange or unusual.
The words **eccentric** and **abnormal** are synonymous.

148. (e) The word **Plethora (Noun)** means : an amount that is greater than is needed ; excess. The word **Abundance (Noun)** means : a large quantity that is more than enough.

149. (a) The word **inadvertently (Adverb)** means : unintentionally ; without intending to : by accidnet. The words **purposefully** and **inadvertently** are antonymous.

150. (a) The word **Germane (Adjective)** means : connected with something in an important or appropriate way : relevant. The words **germane** and **irrelevant** are antonymous.

151. (b) Reqd difference

$$= 24 \times 10^5 \times 16\% \times \frac{7}{12} - 32 \times 10^5 \times 15\% \times \frac{7}{16}$$

$$= 224000 - 210000 = 14000$$

152. (a) Reqd % $\dfrac{\frac{4}{9} \times 18\% \times 24}{32} \times 100 = 8\%$

153. (e) Reqd % $\dfrac{14\% \text{ of } 24}{15\% \text{ of } 32} \times 100 = 70\%$

154. (c) Reqd ratio

$$A \rightarrow \frac{(\text{graduate} + \text{XII})\text{ male}}{(\text{graduate} + \text{XII})\text{ female}}$$

$$\frac{24 \times 16\% \times \frac{7}{12} + 32 \times 15\% \times \frac{7}{16}}{24 \times 16\% \times \frac{5}{12} + 32 \times 15\% \times \frac{9}{16}} = 217 : 215$$

155. (a) Reqd ratio $= 24 \times 17 : 32 \times 12$

156. (d) Required average number of passengers

$$= \frac{1}{3}[(24 + 20 + 15)\% \text{ of } 8500]$$

$$= \frac{1}{3} \times \frac{8500 \times 59}{100} \approx 1671$$

157. (a) Number of passengers in Train R $= \dfrac{8500 \times 9}{100} = 765$

$\therefore$ Number of males $= (100 - 34 - 26)\%$ of 765

$$= \frac{765 \times 40}{100} = 306$$

158. (e) Required per cent $= \dfrac{19}{(13+9)} \times 100 \approx 86$

159. (d) It is clear from the pie - chart

160. (d) Required per cent $= \dfrac{20 - 15}{15} \times 100 \approx 33$

161. (c) Difference between maximum and minimum production of polypropylene $= 21.0 - 15.4 = 5.6$
Difference between maximum and minimum production of polyethylene $= 108 - 20 = 88$

$\therefore$ The ratio $= \dfrac{88}{5.6} = 15.7 \approx 16$.

162. (a) Maximum productions of polyethylene in 2004-05 $= 100$
Minimum production of polyethylene in 2003-04 $= 20$

$\therefore$ Ratio $= \dfrac{100}{20} = 5$.

163. (b) Polypropylene is the product for which we see in the given data, that the production in 2003-04 equals production in 2004-05 for the maximum number (1) of times.

164. (d) For polyethylene the production in 2003-04 is greater than 2004-05 in 9 months.

165. (d) Minimum production of Polypropylene in 2004-05 $= 17.8$
Minimum production of Polypropylene in 2003-04 $= 15.4$
Difference $= 2.4$
Difference in July's production of polyethylene $= 90 - 84 = 6$

Ratio $= \dfrac{2.4}{6} = 0.4$ times.

166. (d) Suppose husband's age be H years.
Then wife's age $W = H - 9$

Son's age $S = \dfrac{H - 9}{2}$

Daughter's age $D = \dfrac{H}{3}$

According to question,

$$\frac{H}{3}+7=\frac{H-9}{2} \Rightarrow \quad 2H+42=3H-27$$

$$\Rightarrow H=42+27=69$$

$$\therefore\ W=60.$$

But conventional method like this will take time to solve the problem. Easier way is to solve through options. For example take the middle option. Selecting middle option is best strategy as it indicates towards possible answer. Moreover, a closer look reveals that 40+9 is not divisible by 3 and same is applicable for 50+9. Divisibility by 3 is desirable as husband's age is 3 times that of the daughter. This leaves options (c) and (d). Solving through option (c).

45+9 = 54 H.

D = 18
S = 22.5 → Difference is 4.5 years, so this is incorrect.

Solving through option (d) matches all conditions.

167. (d) Let each sum be Rs x. Then

Difference of S.I. = Rs 31.50

$$\frac{x\times 4\frac{1}{2}\times 7}{100}-\frac{x\times 4\times 7}{100}=31.50$$

$$\text{or}\quad \frac{7x}{100}\times\frac{1}{2}=\frac{63}{2}\quad \text{or}\quad x=\text{Rs }900$$

168. (d) SP = Rs 17940; Discount = 8%

$$\therefore\ \text{Marked price}=\frac{17940}{0.92}=\text{Rs }19500$$

Gain = 19.6%

$$\therefore\ CP=\frac{17940}{1.196}=\text{Rs }15000$$

New SP without discount = Rs 19500

Gain = (19500 – 15000) = Rs 4500

$$\text{Gain\%}=\frac{4500}{15000}\times 100=30\%$$

169. (a) Let the prices of two houses A and B be Rs $4x$ and Rs $5x$, respectively for the last year.

Then, the prices of A this year = Rs $(1.25\times 4x)$ and that of B = Rs $(5x+50{,}000)$

This year, Ratio of their prices = 9 : 10

$$\therefore\quad \frac{1.25\times 4x}{5x+50{,}000}=\frac{9}{10}$$

$$\Rightarrow 50x-45x=450000 \Rightarrow 5x=4{,}50{,}000$$

$$\Rightarrow x=90{,}000$$

Hence, the price of A last year was $4x$ = Rs 3,60,000

170. (a) Let initially, the number of males and females in the bus be 3x and x, respectively.

$\therefore$ Total no. of passengers = 4x

At the first stop, the number of male passengers

$$=(4x-16)\times\frac{3}{4}=3x-12$$

$$\text{and female passengers}=(4x-16)\times\frac{1}{4}+6=x+2$$

$$\text{Now, }\frac{3x-12}{x+2}=\frac{2}{1} \Rightarrow 3x-12=2x+4 \Rightarrow x=16$$

Hence, the total numbers of passengers, initially $=16\times 4=64$

171. (d) Let the present age of mother be x years and present age of Son be y years.

$\therefore$ According to the Question :

$(x-1)=4(y-1)$ ....(1)

and $(x+6)=5+2(y+6)$ ...(2)

Equation (1) and (2) gives us

$x-1=4y-4 \Rightarrow x-4y=-3 \Rightarrow x=-3+4y$ ...(3)

and $x+6=5+2y+12 \Rightarrow x-2y=11$

$\Rightarrow x=11+2y$ ...(4)

Equating equation (3) and (4), we get

$-3+4y=11+2y$

$\Rightarrow 2y=14 \Rightarrow y=7$ and $x=25$

Hence, Ratio of their present age = x : y = 25 : 7

172. (a) Quality of gold in alloy A $=\frac{7}{9}$

Quantity of gold in Alloy B $=\frac{7}{18}$

Let the quantity of gold in alloy C = g

<u>According to rule of alligatioin.</u>

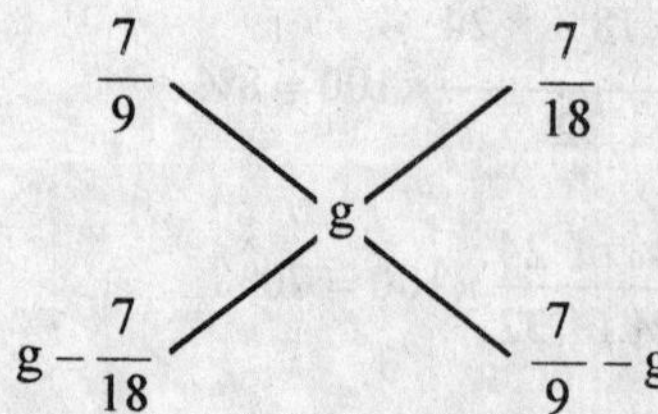

According to condition of problems

$$g-\frac{7}{18}=\frac{7}{9}-g \Rightarrow 2g=\frac{7}{9}+\frac{7}{18}$$

$$\Rightarrow g=\frac{7}{12}$$

Ratio of gold and copper = 7 : 12 – 7 = 7 : 5

173. (a) Speed of first train = 50 km/hr.

Speed of second train = $\frac{400}{7}$ km/hr.

At 8:00 AM distance between two trains is 100 kms.
Relative velocity

$$= 50 + \frac{400}{7} = \frac{350+400}{7} = \frac{750}{7} \text{ km/h}$$

Time taken $= \frac{100 \times 7}{750} \times 60 = 56$ min. Hence, the two trains meet each other at 8:56 AM.

174. (d) Let the length and breadth be 10 units each. Then, original area = 100 square units.
Now, new length = 12 units and new width = 12 units
New area = 12 × 12 = 144 square units.

$$\therefore \% \text{ increase in area} = \frac{144-100}{100} \times 100 = 44\%$$

Alternative :

$$\left(\frac{20}{100} + \frac{20}{100} + \frac{20 \times 20}{100 \times 100}\right) \times 100\%$$

$$= \left(\frac{1}{5} + \frac{1}{5} + \frac{1}{25}\right) \times 100\%$$

$$= \frac{11}{25} \times 100\% = 44\% \text{ increase}$$

175. (d) Let the inner radius be r_1 and the outer radius be r_2.

Then, $2\pi r_1 = 352 \Rightarrow r_1 = \frac{352}{2\pi}$

Again, $2\pi r_2 = 396 \Rightarrow r_2 = \frac{396}{2\pi}$

Width of the track

$$= (r_2 - r_1) = \frac{396-352}{2\pi} = \frac{44 \times 7}{2 \times 22} = 7\text{m}$$

176. (a) $PS = \text{Diameter} = 2r$

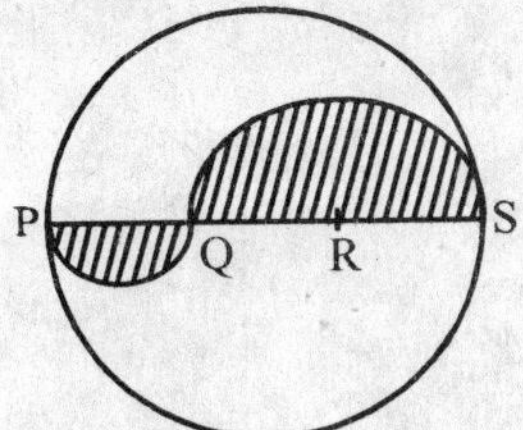

Therefore, $PQ = QR = RS = \frac{2r}{3}$

Perimeter of the shaded region

$$= \overline{PQ} + \overline{QS} = \frac{1}{2}\left(2\pi \times \frac{r}{3}\right) + \frac{1}{2}\left(2\pi \times \frac{2r}{3}\right)$$

$$= \frac{\pi r}{3} + \frac{2\pi r}{3} = \pi r$$

177. (c) The region k represents those who can read and write french, English and Spanish.

178. (b) The region m is common to all the circles. Hence, it represents all those who can read and write all the four languages.

179. (d) The region i represents all those who can read and write all the four languages except Spanish.

180. (d) The region e represents the people who cannot read and write Russian, English and French.

181. (a) b is the common region representing all those who conversant English and Russian but not French and Spanish.

182. (c) We have, a = 40, c = 2a = 80

$$e = \frac{1}{2}a = 20, \quad g = 2e = 20$$

Thus, according to the diagram English is known by the maximum number of people.

183. (b) The region e represents all those who know Spanish and e = 20.

184. (c) The no. of people who can read and write any one language except french = a + c + e = 40 + 80 + 20 = 140.

(185-190) :

Row 1. ↓ P V S T R Q
Row 2. ↑ C F A E B D

185. (d) 186. (a) 187. (b)
188. (b) 189. (c)
190. (e) There is a difference of one in all the rest.

(191-197) :

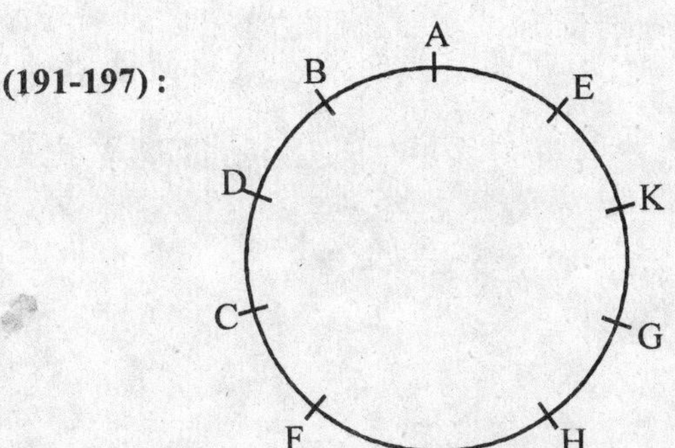

191. (d) F is third to the right of B.
192. (d) F and G are immediate neighbours of H.

193. (b)

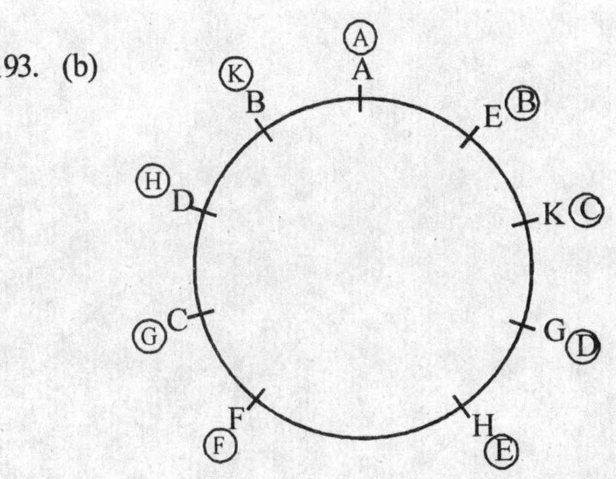

194. (a) H is second to the right of C.
B is second to the right of E.
G is second to the right of F.

195. (c) DC, DE $\Rightarrow$ Immediate neighbours of D.
DF, DA $\Rightarrow$ F is second to the right of D.
A is second to the right of D.
Therefore, ? = DH
H is third to the right of D.

196. (b) G sits third to the left of A.

197. (e) Immediate neighbours of C are D and F.

198. (d) J, K and L will meet again at the starting point after LCM of 12, 18 & 20.
LCM of 12, 18 & 20 = 180 seconds = 3 min

199. (a) Required $P\left[\left(1+\frac{8}{100}\right)^2-1\right]=1414.4$

P = Principal

$\Rightarrow P\left[\frac{729}{625}-1\right]=1414.4$

$\Rightarrow 1414.4\times\frac{625}{104}=8500$

Total amount to be returned
= 8500 + 1414.4 = ₹9914.14

200. (a) 2 man can do in 4 days
4 women can do in 4 days
10 children can do in 2 days
2m + 4w + 10c can do in

$\frac{(4\times4)+(4\times2)+(4\times2)}{4\times4\times2}=1$ day.

SOLVED PAPER (Based on Memory) COMMON ENTRANCE TEST

MAHARASHTRA-CET MBA/MMS 27th FEB. 2011

1. Typically, the entrepreneur is seen as an individual who owns and operates a small business. But, simply to own and operates a small business — or even a big business — does not make someone an entrepreneur. If this person is a true entrepreneur, then new products are being created, new ways of providing services are being implemented.
Which of the following conclusions can best be drawn from the above passage?
(a) An owner of a large business may be an entrepreneur.
(b) Someone who develops an enterprise may be considered an entrepreneur.
(c) Entrepreneurs do not own and operate small businesses.
(d) Entrepreneurs are the main actors in economic growth.
(e) Entrepreneurs are inventors.

DIRECTIONS (Qs. 2 - 5) : In each of the questions below there is an inference, which is based on the given passage. Examine each inference separately in the context of the passage and decide upon its degree of truth or falsity. Mark your answer as :
(a) if you think the inference is 'definitely true';
(b) if you think the inference is probably true' though not definitely true in the light of the facts given;
(c) if you think the 'data is inadequate' i.e., from the facts given, you cannot say whether the inference is likely to be true or false;
(d) if you think the inference is 'definitely false'.
(e) None of these

The reforms are aimed at having an impact over a wide cross-section of the economy. With improvements and greater efficiency in mobilising and allocating resources, the basis will become stronger for promoting economic growth and development. The reforms aim at increasing efficiency of the financial sector and the range of financial services available within the economy. The introduction of bank capital adequacy and accounting standards, together with improvement in the regulation and supervision of financial institutions and capital market, is aimed at installing greater public confidence, ensuring safety and soundness of the financial system, bringing about greater transparency and accountability in operations and encouraging overall increased resources, mobilisation within the economy.

2. Prior to reforms, the banking sector was running inefficiently although resource allocation was efficient.
3. Bank capital adequacy was not in operation before reforms.
4. Public confidence has some connection with resource mobilisation.
5. The economic reforms have aimed only at the financial sector.

DIRECTIONS (Q.6-10) : In each of the following questions two rows of numbers are given. The resultant number in each row is to be worked out separately based on the following rules and the questions below the rows of numbers are to be answered. The operations of numbers progress from left to right.

Rules :
(i) If a two-digit odd number is followed by a two-digit odd number they are to be added.
(ii) If a two-digit even number is followed by a two-digit odd number which is a perfect square, the even number is to be subtracted from the odd number.
(iii) If a three-digit number is followed by a two-digit number the first number is to be divided by the second number.
(iv) If a prime number is followed by an even number the two are to be added.
(v) If an even number is followed by another even number the two are to be multiplied.

6. 23 15 12
X 24 49
If X is the resultant of the first row, what is the resultant of the second row?
(a) 24 (b) 25
(c) 28 (d) 22
(e) None of these

7. 37 12 21
38 81 14
What is the difference between the resultants of the two rows?
(a) 23 (b) 32
(c) 13 (d) 18
(c) None of these

8. 16 8 32
132 11 X^2
If X is the resultant of the first row, what is the resultant of the second row?
(a) 192 (b) 128
(c) 132 (d) 144
(e) None of these

9. 345 23 X
45 17 81
If X is the resultant of the second row, what is the resultant of the first row?
(a) 285 (b) 33
(c) 135 (d) 34
(e) None of these

10. 12 28 84
37 22 18
What is the sum of resultants of the two rows?
(a) 77 (b) 87
(c) 84 (d) 72
(e) None of these

DIRECTIONS (Qs. 11-17) : Read the following passage carefully and answer the questions given below it.

In a disarmingly frank talk at the Indian Merchants Chamber in Mumbai, the Japanese Ambassador in India dwelt at length on issues that exercise the minds of Japanese investors when they consider investment proposals in India. Raising the question "What comparative advantages does India offer as an investment market ?", he said though labour in India is expensive, wage-levels are offset by productivity level to a large extent.

Acknowledging that the vastness of the Indian market is a great inducement for investment in manufacturing industry, he wondered if it was justifiable to provide that overseas termittance of profit in foreign exchange be fully covered by exchange earnings as had been done. Significantly, on the eve of the Prime Minister's visit to Japan, the government delinked profits repatriation from exports, meeting this demand.

The Ambassador said foreign investors needed to be assured of the continuity and consistency of the liberalisation policy and the fact that new measures had been put into force by means of administrative notifications without amending government laws acted as a damper.

The Ambassador pleaded for speedy formulation of the exit policy and pointed to the highly restrictive control by the government on disinvestment by foreign partner in joint ventures in India.

While it is all too easy to dismiss critical comment on conditions in India contemptuously, there can be little doubt that if foreign investment is to be wooed assiduously, we will have to meet exacting international standards and cater at least partially to what we may consider the idiosyncrasies of our foreign collaborators. The Japanese too have passed through a stage in the fifties when their products were derided as sub-standard and shoddy. That they have come out of that ordeal of fire to emerge as an economic superpower speaks a much of their doggedness to pursue goals against all odds acceptable standards.

There is no gainsaying that the paste record of Japanese investment is a poor benchmark for future expectations.

11. The author has appreciated the Japanese for their
    (a) quality of products manufactured in the fifties.
    (b) passing through an ordeal.
    (c) perseverance in raising quality of products.
    (d) future expectations.
    (e) None of these

12. According to the Japanese Ambassador, which of the following motivates the foreign investors to invest in Indian manufacturing industry?
    (a) very large scope of Indian market
    (b) overseas remittance of profit in foreign exchange
    (c) assurance of continuity of the liberalisation policy
    (d) high productivity levels
    (e) None of these

13. The purpose of the author in writing this passage seems to be to
    (a) discourage foreign investment in India.
    (b) critically examine Indian investment environment.
    (c) paint a rosy picture of India's trade and commerce.
    (d) criticize government's liberalization policy.
    (e) raise the expectations of foreign investors.

14. According to the Japanese Ambassador, India offers a comparative advantage to foreign investors in terms of
    (a) inexpensive labour
    (b) abysmally low wage levels
    (c) higher productivity
    (d) skilled workforce
    (e) None of these

15. For seeking more and more foreign investment, the author suggests that we should
    (a) satisfy fully the whims of our foreign collaborators.
    (b) dismiss all critical comments on Indian conditions.
    (c) link profit repatriations to exports.
    (d) raise the quality of product to match international standards.
    (e) None of these

16. From the passage it can be inferred that the author is
    (a) a political commentator.
    (b) a secretary of the Japanese Ambassador.
    (c) a Japanese investor.
    (d) an Indian investor.
    (e) None of these

17. Which of the following statement(s) is/are true about the critical comments on investment conditions in India?
    A. These comments are difficult to be countered.
    B. These comments are received from various international quarters.
    C. These comments are based more on biases than on facts.

    (a) Only C (b) Only B
    (c) Only A (d) A & B only
    (e) A & C only

18. Eight chairs are numbered form 1 to 8. Two women and three men wish to occupy one chair each. First the women chose the chairs from amongst the chairs marked 1 to 4. Then the men selected the chairs from amongst the remaining chairs marked 5 to 8. The number of all possible arrangements is :
    (a) ${}^4C_3 \times {}^4C_4$ (b) ${}^4P_2 \times {}^4P_3$
    (c) ${}^4C_3 \times {}^4P_3$ (d) ${}^4C_2 \times {}^4C_3$
    (e) None of these

19. The circumference of a circular ground is 88 m. A strip of land, 3 m wide, inside and along circumference of the ground is to be levelled. What is the budgeted expenditure if the levelling cost is ₹ 7 per square m?
    (a) ₹ 1,050 (b) ₹ 1,125
    (c) ₹ 1,325 (d) ₹ 1,650
    (e) None of these

20. A rectangular courtyard, 3.78 m long and 5.25 m broad, is to be paved exactly with square tiles, all of the same size. The largest size of such a tile and the number of tiles required to pave it is:
(a) 430 (b) 440
(c) 450 (d) 460
(e) None of these

DIRECTIONS (Qs. 21 to 23) : In these questions, a question is followed by two statements labelled I and II, choose
(a) if statement I is sufficient to answer the question asked, but statement II by itself is not sufficient to answer the question;
(b) if statement II by itself is sufficient to answer the question, but statement I alone is not sufficient to answer the question;
(c) if both the statements I and II together are sufficient to answer the question but neither statement by itself is sufficient to answer the question and
(d) if the two statements, even when taken together, are not sufficient to answer the question.

21. Is the sum of x and y an odd number ?
I. x and y are two different prime numbers.
II. The product of x and y is an even number.

22. Is the integer x divisible by 3 ?
I. The last digit in x is 3.
II. $x + 5$ is divisible by 6.

23. The sum of the 6th and 15th terms of an arithmetic progression is equal to the sum of 7th, 10th and 12th terms of the same progression. Which term of the series should necessarily be equal to zero ?
(a) 10th (b) 8th
(c) 1st (d) None of these

DIRECTIONS (Q. 24-25) : Fashion has become one of the largest fads among the youth. The amount of time wastage and expenditure on fashion is very large. What bothers, however, is the fact that fashion is here to stay despite countless arguments against it. What is required, therefore, is that strong efforts should be made in order to displace the excessive craze of fashion from the minds of today's youth.

24. Which of the following statements finds the least support by the argument made by the author in the given paragraph?
(a) Youngsters should be motivated to do constructive business rather than wasting time on fashion.
(b) The world of fashion being glamorous and glittery attracts people towards itself.
(c) Following the latest fashion increases the self-efficacy of people, thus increasing their overall mental abilities.
(d) Many universities have implemented a dress code to put a check on the increasing fad amongst the youth which was affecting their grades.
(e) None of these

25. Which of the following can be inferred from the given paragraph?
(a) The author has made strong efforts to wipe out fashion from the minds of youth.
(b) Steps need to be taken in order to control the growing fad of fashion amongst the youth.
(c) The author is upset with the shift of fashion from the traditional ethnic wear to western outfits.
(d) Fashion world is responsible for lack of creativity among the youth.
(e) None of these

DIRECTIONS (Q. 26-27) : The government cannot afford to compartmentalise education. It has to be emphasised that any country which does not have a good university education will never be listed as an independent country and will never be able to progress. Only countries prepared to tolerate a second-rate and subjugate status in the world would neglect higher education. If India has had any position in the comity of nations in the past, it was only because it had a better higher education than many of its Asian counterparts. This clear emphasis on higher education, however, does not imply that it should be supported and developed at the cost of primary and secondary education.

26. Which of the following best explains the main idea of the paragraph?
(a) The government has made a wrong move in compartmentalising education.
(b) To highlight the superiority of India in higher education as comapred to the rest of the world.
(c) To emphasise more on primary education rather than higher education.
(d) Higher education is important for the growth of a country.
(e) None of these

27. Which of the following is the most likely title of the bigger passage (having the same main idea as that of the given paragraph) in which this paragraph might have appeared?
(a) Education–a fundamental right of every child.
(b) Indian education–an unfortunate neglect of primary education.
(c) Lack of higher education opportunities in India.
(d) A comparison of higher education in Inidia with that of the west.
(e) Importance of higher education in the growth of a country.

DIRECTIONS (Qs. 28-33) : Read the following passage carefully and answer the questions given below it.

Politicians and generals talk of military strategies and manouvres but something completely different is needed. Stability will come only when economic opportunities **exist**, when youth can find jobs and support formilies rather than seeking their livelihood in violence. Peace can only be achieved with a withdrawal of foreign troops, sanctions and peacekeepeers and the arrival of jobs, productive farms and factories, healthcare and schools. Repeatedly, the **fragile** peace in impoverished countries has broken down because of the lack of economic follow-up. Despite promises of aid, the actual record of international aid to post-war reconstruction is **deficient**.

Once the war ends, agencies involved in post-war relief efforts fail to understand how to start or restart economic development in a low income setting. They **squander** time, surplus aid funds and opportunities because they are not familiar with local conditions and do not understand their point of view. There are distinct phases of outside help to end a conflict. In the first phase focus is on providing food, water, shelter and medicine to refugees, i.e., humanitarian. In the second, emphasis is on the refugees returning home while in the last phase long-term investments and strengthening of courts is the main focus. However, once a conflict is over, aid agencies sanctioned by the World Bank send study groups instead of requisite personnel. There is a gap of several years before moving from humanitarian relief to economic development. By the time such help arrives the war has restarted. It is possible to restart economic development through targeted "quick impact" initiatives. Most economies in post-conflict countries are based on agriculture. Providing free packages of seeds, fertilizers and low-cost equipment quickly will ensure that former soldiers will return to their farms and establish their livelihood. But the window of opportunity closes quickly and one has to implement these measures almost immediately.

28. Which of the following is a reason why post-conflict reconstruction efforts have failed?
(a) Aid organizations do not understand issues from the perspective of the poor.
(b) Rapid economic development in low-income countries.
(c) World Bank studies are not valid.
(d) International aid organizations become too involved in reconstruction effots.
(e) None of these

29. Where does the problem lie in implementing post-war relief measures?
(a) Aid agencies fail to study the situation.
(b) Economic development measures are too rapid.
(c) Focus on economic development not humanitarian aid.
(d) Lack of funds to implement programmes.
(e) Lack of essential and qualified personnel.

30. According to the author, how can political stability be achieved?
(a) Increasing the number of foreign troops in areas of conflict.
(b) Depending more on foreign aid.
(c) Following recommendations given by the World Bank.
(d) Providing economic opportunities.
(e) None of these

31. Which of the following is NOT TRUE in the context of the passage?
(a) Focus in the first phase of a war is on providing humanitarian aid.
(b) Sanctions are not a means to ensure peace.
(c) Adequate time must be taken to plan and implement quick impact strategies.
(d) Providing employment to the younger generation will prevent wars.
(e) Focus on delivering justice through courts should be in the last phase of conflict aid.

32. How can economic development be restarted in an impoverished country?
(a) Long-term studies should be commissioned.
(b) Retaining soldiers in the army to ensure law and order.
(c) Restrict number of aid agencies to avoid waste.
(d) Focusing on agricultural initiatives.
(e) Deploying peacekeepers in the country.

33. What is the benefit of "quick impact" aid?
(a) Soldiers earn income from the army and their farms.
(b) Providing alternate livelihood to soldiers before war can restart.
(c) Free land is given to soldiers.
(d) Price of equipment is low.
(e) None of these

DIRECTIONS (Q. 34-39) : In the following questions two equations numbered I and II are given. You have to solve both equations and give answer

(a) if $x > y$ (b) if $x \geq y$
(c) if $x < y$ (d) $x \leq y$
(e) if $x = y$ or the relationship cannot be established

34. I. $x^2 - 7x + 10 = 0$ II. $y^2 + 11y + 10 = 0$
35. I. $x^2 + 28x + 192 = 0$ II. $y^2 + 16y + 48 = 0$
36. I. $2x - 3y = -3.5$ II. $3x - 2y = -6.5$
37. I. $x^2 + 8x + 15 = 0$ II. $y^2 + 11y + 30 = 0$
38. I. $x = \sqrt{3136}$ II. $y^2 = 3136$
39. I. $x = \sqrt{7921}$ II. $y = \sqrt[3]{704969}$

DIRECTIONS (Qs. 40- 44) : In the diagram below the circle stands for the 'educated', square for the 'hardworking, triangle for the 'urban' and the rectangle for the 'honest' people. Different regions in the diagram are numbered from 1 to 12. Study the diagram carefully and then answer the questions that follow:

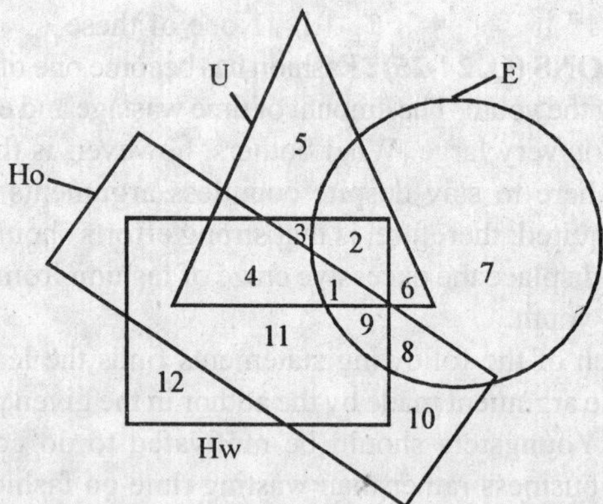

40. People who are urban, educated and hardworking and honest are represented by
(a) 8 (b) 1
(c) 2 (d) 9
(e) None of these

41. Hardworking people, who are uneducated, dishonest and are urban, are represented by
(a) 2 (b) 4
(c) 9 (d) 3
(e) None of these

42. Hardworking, non-urban people who are neither educated nor honest are indicated by
(a) 10 (b) 12
(c) 11 (d) 9
(e) None of these

43. In the above diagram, which of the following statements is true ?
   (a) All educated people are urban.
   (b) Uneducated people are either honest or hardworking.
   (c) Some honest people are also hardworking and are educated.
   (d) No person is urban, educated, honest and hardworking.
   (e) None of these

44. Region 4 is best described as consisting of
   (a) People who are uneducated, urban, hardworking and dishonest
   (b) People who are urban, hardworking, honest and educated
   (c) People who are uneducated, urban, honest and hardworking
   (d) People who are non-urban, honest, uneducated and hardworking.
   (e) None of these

DIRECTIONS (Q. 45-57) : Read the following passage carefully and answer the questions given below it. Certain words are given in bold to help you locate them while answering some of the questions.

The wakeup call that China represents to India is not limited to its showpiece urban centres of that New Delhi hopes India will experience the benefits that the Olympic games have brought to Beijing. More **pertinent** is the comparison of the agricultural sectors of the two countries. Why and how has China managed to outstrip India in agriculture when 25 years ago the two countries were on par on most parameters? Both have traditionally been agrarian economies and over half their populations continue to depend on the land for their livelihood. With large populations and histories of famine. India and China share **concern** on issues such as food security. However, while India's agricultural sector is projected to grow by about 2.5 per cent this year–a slide from the previous year's growth–China's has been steadily growing at between 4 per cent and 5 per cent over the last fifteen years. The widest divergence between India and China is in the profitable horticultural sector with the production of fruits and vegetables in China leaping from 60 million tonnes in 1980 compared to India's 55 million tonnes at the same time, to 450 million tonnes in 2003 ahead of India's corresponding 135 million tonnes. China's added advantage lies in the more diversified composition of its agricultural sector with animal husbandry and fisheries which account for close to 45 per cent of growth compared to 30 per cent of India.

According to the latest report by the Economic Advisory Council, the traditional excuses for India's substandard performance in the farm sector are inadequate since India is placed favourably when compared to China in terms of quantity of arable land, average farm size, farm mechanisation, etc. The reasons for China having uotperformed India are three fold: technological improvements accruing from research and development (China has over 1,000 R and D centres **devoted** to agriculture), investment in rural infrastructure and an increasingly liberalised agricultural policy moving away from self-sufficiency to leveragin gthe competitive advantage with a focus on "efficiency as much as equity". Investment in rural infrastructure, roads storage facilities, marketing facilities are also crucial but government support in India has mainly been through subsidies, not investment. There has been much debate about subsidies and their utility; the opposing view being that subsidies are against the market reforms and distort the market as well as reduce resource efficiency. In contrast to the 2,046 applications for the registration of new plant varieties in China over the past few years, data reveals that despite India having the largest number of agricultural scientists in the world India's current research track record is abysmal, equivalent to what China achieved in the 1980s. Far from developing new strains, the number of field crop varieties fell by 50 per cent between 1997 and 2001 despite the fact that there was sharp and **sustained** increase in funding. One reason is that majority of the budget is eaten up by staff salaries with only 3 per cent being allotted for research. In contrast, most agricultural research centres in China must use Central government funding purely for research. Funds relating to salaries and other administrative incidentals must be generated by the centres themselves. The centres and scientists are thus encouraged to engage in joint ventures with private sector companies to form commercial signoffs from their research. In fact, research staff are now being hired on a contract basis with pay based on performance and salaries raised proportionately for those who perform well. India needs to learn from China's example and adopt a **pragmatic** approach if it has to meet its targets of the Eleventh Five Year Plan.

45. What has been the major area of difference in the development of the agricultural sectors of India and China?
   (a) Quantity of arable land in China is far greater than in India.
   (b) Food security is not a concern for China as the country is basically self-sufficient.
   (c) China has experienced substantial growth in production in allied agricultural activities like horticulture.
   (d) India's agricultural sector is too diversified so it is difficult to channel funds for development.
   (e) None of these

46. Which of the following is/are area/s in which China has not outdone India?
   (A) Development of urban infrastructure
   (B) Activities allied to agriculture like animal husbandry
   (C) Successful bids for international sporting events
   (a) None (b) Only (B)
   (c) Only (A) (d) Both (A) and (C)
   (e) None of these

47. Which of the following is NOT TRUE in the context of the passage?
    (a) Agricultural status of China and India was equivalent a quarter of a century ago.
    (b) India's current economic growth rate is half that of China.
    (c) China is traditionally an agrarian economy.
    (d) Agricultural research in India is inadequate.
    (e) India's current agricultural growth rate has fallen from the previous year.
48. How are Chinese agricultural research facilities governed?
    (a) Salaries of staff are linked to performance and this hampers productive research.
    (b) Their funding comes from the government alone to prevent private comapnies from manipulating the direction of their research.
    (c) A fixed proportion of governmetn grants is allotted to be utilised for administrative incidentals which cannot be exceeded.
    (d) Research staff even those on contract are entitled to increments for good performance.
    (e) None of these
49. Which of the following is an advantage that India holds over China with respect to the agricultural sector?
    (a) Lack of diversification of the agricultural sector
    (b) Superior technology and farming practices
    (c) Greater prevalence of farm mechanisation
    (d) Provision of fertilizer and power subsidies
    (e) Abundant research generated by their scientists
50. Why was there a drop in development of new crop varieties for five years from 1997?
    (a) Government funding for research fell during that period.
    (b) Funds were diverted during this period to agricultural mechanisation.
    (c) The private sector was not allowed to fund research.
    (d) A large number of agricultural scientists left India for better opportunities abroad during this period.
    (e) None of these
51. What argument has been posed against implementation of subsidies?
    (A) Subsidies sacrifice equity for efficiency.
    (B) Subsidies hamper efficient resource utilisation.
    (C) Subsidies reduce private sector investment and involvement in agriculture.
    (a) Both (A) and (B) (b) Only (B)
    (c) Both (B) and (C) (d) Only (A)
    (e) None of these
52. Which of the following is not responsible for China's successful transformation of its agricultural sector?
    (A) Change in philosophy from self-sufficiency to competitiveness and efficiency
    (B) Greater allocation for subsidies
    (C) Increased investment in marketing and distribution networks
    (a) Only (B) (b) Both (B) and (C)
    (c) Both (A) and (C) (d) All (B) and (C)
    (e) None of these

DIRECTIONS (Q. 53-55: Choose the word which is most nearly the SAME in meaning as the word printed in bold as used in the passage

53. **concern**
    (a) importance (b) regret
    (c) business (d) anxiety
    (e) emphasis
54. **pertinent**
    (a) intense (b) sizeable
    (c) practical (d) visible
    (e) significant
55. **devaoted**
    (a) surrendered (b) dedicated
    (c) established (d) staunch
    (e) dependent

DIRECTIONS (Q. 56-57): Choose the word which is most OPPOSITE in meaning as the word printed in bold as used in the passage

56. **sustained**
    (a) intermittent (b) discouraged
    (c) habitual (d) defeated
    (e) restrained
57. **pragmatic**
    (a) faithful (b) unwilling
    (c) idealistic (d) practical
    (e) inexperienced
58. Given, $n = 1 + x$, where x is the product of four consecutive integers. Then which of the following is true ?
    A. n is an odd integer
    B. n is prime.
    C. n is a perfect square
    (a) Both A and C are correct.
    (b) Both A and B are correct.
    (c) Only A is correct
    (d) Only C is correct
    (e) None of these
59. Two equal sums were borrowed at 8% simple interest per annum for 2 years and 3 years, respectively. The difference in the interests was ₹ 56. The sum borrowed were :
    (a) ₹690 (b) ₹700
    (c) ₹740 (d) ₹780
    (e) None of these
60. An alloy contains copper and zinc in the ratio 5 : 3 and another alloy contains copper and tin in the ratio 8 : 5. If equal weights of both the alloys are melted together, then the weight of tin in the resulting alloy per unit will be:
    (a) $\frac{26}{5}$ (b) $\frac{5}{26}$
    (c) $\frac{7}{40}$ (d) $\frac{40}{7}$
    (e) None of these

61. A and B enter into a partnership with ₹. 50,000 and ₹. 60,000 respectively. C joins them after x months contributing ₹ 70,000 and B leaves x months before the end of the year. If they share the profit in the ratio of 20 : 18: 21, then find the value of x.
(a) 6 (b) 3
(c) 9 (d) 8
(e) None of these

62. The average age of an adult class is 40 years. 12 new students with an average age of 32 years join the class, thereby decreasing the average by 4 years. The original strength of the class was
(a) 12 (b) 11
(c) 10 (d) 15
(e) None of these

63. The diameter of a cycle wheel is 70 cm. A cyclist takes 30 hours to reach a destination at the speed of 22 km/h. How many revolutions will the wheel make during this journey?
(a) 3 million (b) 3 lakhs
(c) 4 lakhs (d) 2 lakhs
(e) None of these

64. If the radius of a circle is increased by 100%, then the area of the circle increases by :
(a) 100% (b) 200%
(c) 300% (d) 400%
(e) None of these

65. A worker is paid ₹ 56 for 35 hour in a week. Up to 40 hours, he is paid at the normal rate and on overtime, 1.5 times the normal. How many hours did he work to get ₹ 88 ?
(a) 48 hours (b) 50 hours
(c) 58 hours (d) 55 hours
(e) None of these

66. The weight of an empty bottle is 20% of the weight of bottle when filled with some liquid. Some of the liquid has been removed. Then the bottle, along with the remaining liquid, weighed half of the original weight. What fractional part of the liquid has been removed?
(a) $\frac{3}{5}$ (b) $\frac{1}{9}$
(c) $\frac{2}{5}$ (d) $\frac{1}{8}$
(e) None these

DIRECTIONS (Q. 67-71) : The first figure in the first unit of the problem figures bears a certain relationship to the second figure. Similarly, one of the figures in the answer figures bears the same relationship to the second figure in the second unit of the problem figures. You are therefore to locate the figure which would fit in the question mark.

67.
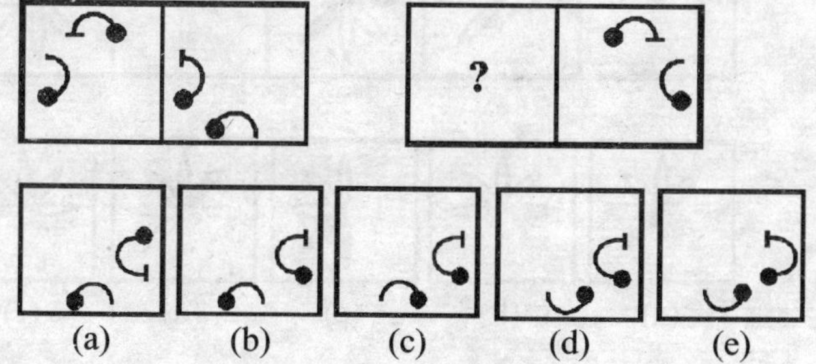

68.
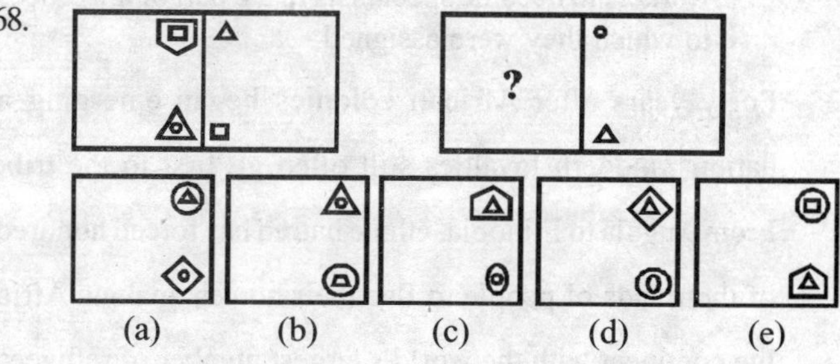

69.
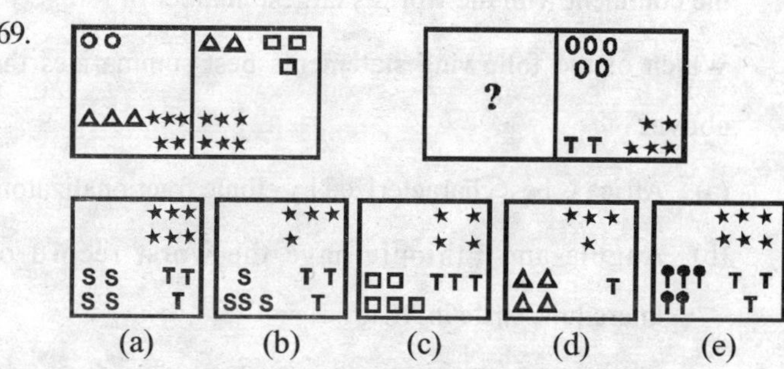

70.
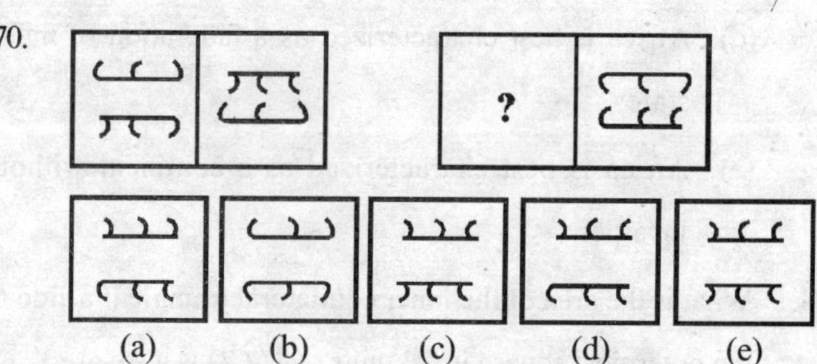

71.
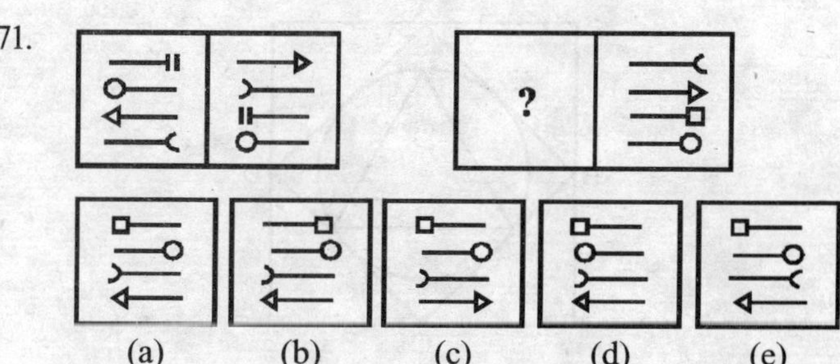

72. Pioneers of the motor-car industry realized that if they were going to meet the growing demand for their product, they had to adapt the labor force used in the productive process. Instead of many men working to complete all the stages of one car at a time, they assigned defined tasks to each man which they would repeat on every car.
Which of the following can be concluded from the passage?
(a) Early motor car manufacturers intended to increase productivity by applying the principle of division of labor.
(b) The car workers became disgruntled because they were assigned monotonous, repetitive tasks on the assembly line.
(c) Economies of scale enabled early motor companies to expand.
(d) A bad worker would perform the same task badly on each car, leading to many more rejects.

(e) The new production process enabled certain car workers to become specialists in the part of the process to which they were assigned.

73. Forty years after African colonies began emerging as nations, modern loyalties still often go first to the tribe. From Angola to Ethiopia, ethnic hatred has forced hundreds of thousands of people to flee their homes, making Africa the continent with the world's largest number of refugees. Which of the following statements best summarizes the above?

(a) Africa is best characterized by ethnic fractionalizaton.

(b) Angola and Ethiopia have the worst record of interethnic strife in Africa.

(c) Continued warfare has made Africa a nation of refugees.

(d) Africa is best characterized as a federation of many states.

(e) Africa is best characterized as a continent without loyalties.

74. What is the area of the inner equilateral triangle if a side of the outermost square is '*a*' units? (*ABCD* is a square.)

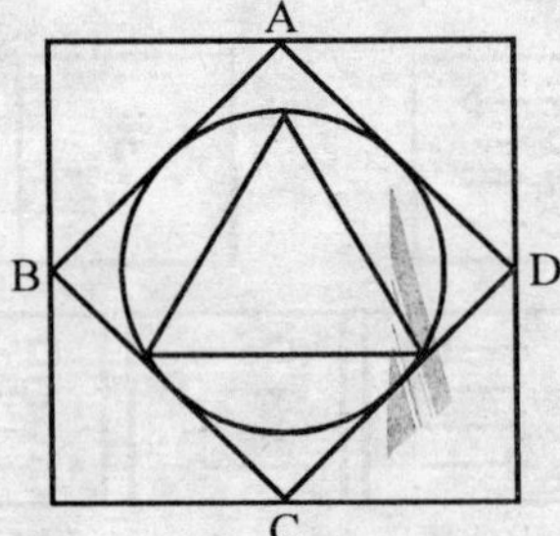

(a) $\frac{3\sqrt{3}a^2}{32}$ sq. units (b) $\frac{3\sqrt{3}a^2}{64}$ sq. units

(c) $\frac{5\sqrt{3}a^2}{32}$ sq. units (d) None

(e) None of these

75. In the figure below, *ABCD* is a square with side 10 cm. *BPD* is an arc of a circle with centre *C*. *BQD* is an arc of a circle with centre *A*. What is the area of the shaded region ?

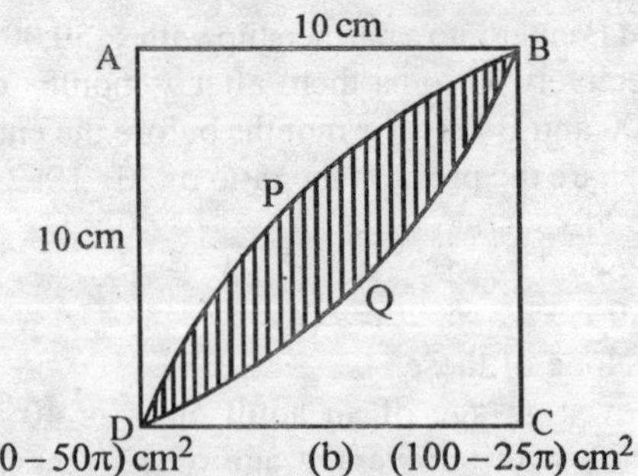

(a) $(100-50\pi)$ cm^2 (b) $(100-25\pi)$ cm^2

(c) $(50\pi-100)$ cm^2 (d) $(25\pi-100)$ cm^2

(e) None of these

76. A right-angled triangle has a hypotenuse of 13 cm and one side as 12 cm. Its area is :

(a) 30 cm^2 (b) 39 cm^2

(c) 80 cm^2 (d) 78 cm^2

(e) None of these

77. A tree breaks due to storm and the broken part bends so that the top of the tree first touches the ground, making an angle of 30° with the horizontal. The distance from the foot of the tree to the point where the top touches the ground is 10 m. The height of the tree is :

(a) $10(\sqrt{3}+1)$m (b) $10\sqrt{3}$m

(c) $10(\sqrt{3}-1)$ m (d) $\frac{10}{\sqrt{3}}$ m

(e) None of these

DIRECTIONS (Q. 78-82) : In each of the questions given below which one of th efive answer figures on the righ tshould come after the problem figures on the left if the sequence were continued?

78.

79.

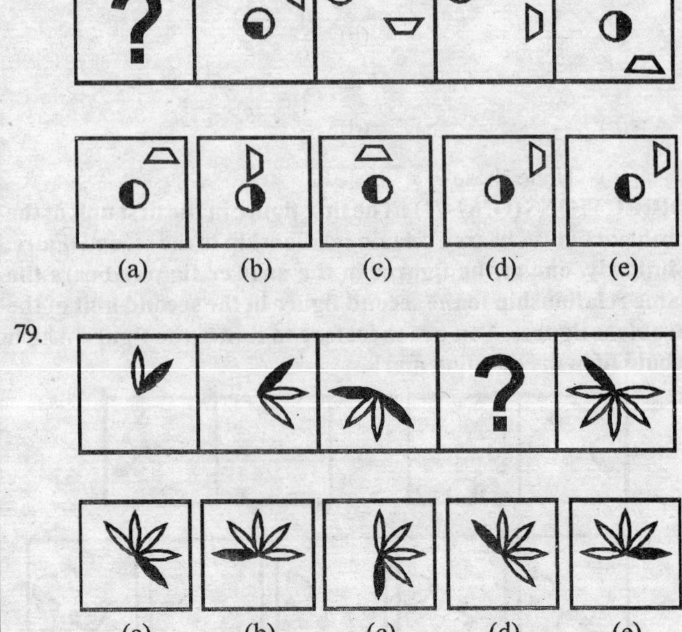

80.

(a) (b) (c) (d) (e)

81.

(a) (b) (c) (d) (e)

82.

(a) (b) (c) (d) (e)

DIRECTIONS (Q. 83-92): In the following passage there are blanks, each of which has been numbered. These numbers are printed below the passage and against each, five words are suggested, one of which fits the blank appropriately. Find out the appropriate word in each case.

(**83**) a country needs money for a development project, what can it do? It can (**84**) to the World Bank or Asian Development Bank for aid. A country with a foreign currency problem can ask the International Monetary Fund for (**85**). However, (**86**) there is no way out for a country which has shortage of food. The country cannot (**87**) import the food if it is rare like pulses which are grown only by a few countries in such cases the problem is more (**88**).

This situation has led experts to suggest the (**89**) of establishing a World Agricultural Bank. The food situation today is serious since production is not keeping (**90**) with demand. The World Agricultural Bank can therefore be established by member-countries who have to (**91**) both capital as well as surplus food to the Bank. The stocks would form a corpus which would be used to assist members in (**92**) of distress.

83. (a) Though (b) Supposed (c) Unless (d) That (e) When
84. (a) appeals (b) go (c) approach (d) solicit (e) requests
85. (a) backing (b) helping (c) solution (d) assistants (e) relieve
86. (a) simply (b) during (c) fact (d) presently (e) while
87. (a) attempt (b) yet (c) even (d) try (e) start
88. (a) address (b) acute (c) declined (d) achievable (e) prohibited
89. (a) object (b) implementation (c) knowledge (d) advice (e) idea
90. (a) up (b) ahead (c) paced (d) line (e) tune
91. (a) demand (b) share (c) benefit (d) contribute (e) fund
92. (a) controls (b) combats (c) times (d) needs (e) areas

DIRECTIONS (Qs. 93 to 97) : Study the data presented in the following graph to answer the questions :

MONTHLY EXPENDITURE OF A FIRM FROM JANUARY TO JULY DURING THE YEARS 1997, 1998, 1999

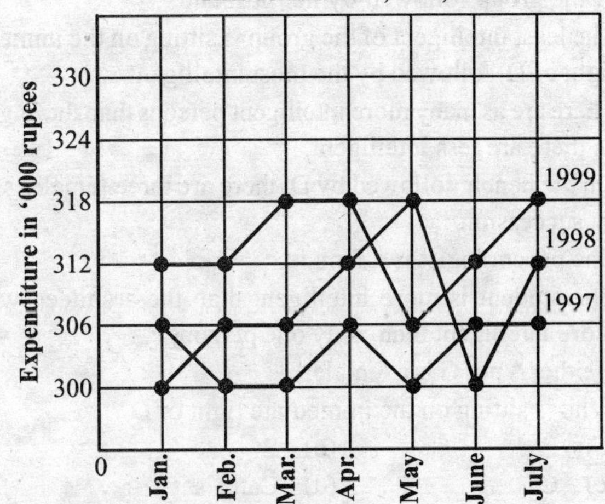

93. What is the total expenditure during the period under review (7 months) in 1997 ?
(a) ₹21, 07, 000 (b) ₹96, 07, 000
(c) ₹21, 54, 000 (d) ₹21, 24, 000
(e) None of these

94. What total expenditure has been made during the year 1997 and 1998 in the period covered in the graph ?
(a) ₹24, 87, 000 (b) ₹2, 70, 000
(c) ₹48, 27, 000 (d) ₹42, 78, 000
(e) None of these

95. What is the average monthly expenditure during the year 1999 covering the period shown in the graph ?
(a) ₹2, 75, 000 (b) ₹2, 70, 000
(c) ₹3, 14, 000 (d) ₹2, 47, 000
(e) None of these

96. Which month has been the least expensive during 1999 ?
(a) June (b) April
(c) May (d) July
(e) None of these

97. The expenditure in April 1999 was.....higher than that of corresponding period in 1998.
(a) 1.5% (b) 2%
(c) 2.5% (d) 0.94%
(e) None of these

DIRECTIONS (Qs. 98-102) : Read the information given below and answer the questions that follow:

(i) There is a group of seven persons A, B, C, D, E, F and G.
(ii) There are four males, three females, two married couples and three unmarried persons in the group.
(iii) The seven persons are seated in a row on the bench.
(iv) Their professions are : engineer, teacher, doctor, psychologist, businessman, architect and student.
(v) B is not married and another person, the psychologist, is the most intelligent.
(vi) The engineer is married to the teacher, who is the least intelligent of the group.
(vii) D is an architect. He is sitting on the leftmost corner.
(viii) The student is sitting on the rightmost corner of the bench.
(ix) The doctor is married to C. C is the second most intelligent of the group followed by her husband.
(x) The least intelligent of the group is sitting on the immediate right of D, followed by the most intelligent.
(xi) There are as many more intelligent persons than the engineer as there are less intelligent.
(xii) On the bench, followed by D, there are three females sitting in succession.
(xiii) The psychologist is a female.
(xiv) The student is more intelligent than the architect, who is more intelligent than only one person, F.
(xv) Neither A nor G is a female.

98. Who is sitting on the immediate right of D ?
(a) F (b) E
(c) C (d) Can't say
(e) None of these

99. Which two are sitting together ?
(a) D and E (b) E and A
(c) Teacher and businessman
(d) Engineer and doctor
(e) None of these

100. The engineer is not more intelligent than :
(a) student (b) architect
(c) teacher (d) businessman
(e) None of these

101. Which of these cannot be a married couple ?
(a) A-F (b) A-C
(c) G-F (d) None of these
(e) D-E

102. Which of these represents the correct order of intelligence (in the decreasing sequence)?
(a) EBF (b) CDF
(c) ECB (d) BCE
(e) None of these

DIRECTIONS (Qs. 103-105) : Four of the following five are alike in a certain way and so form a group. Which is the one that does not belong to the group?

103.
(a) understand (b) comprehend
(c) learn (d) restate
(e) recognize

104.
(a) cornea (b) skin
(c) iris (d) pupil
(e) sclera

105.
(a) triangle (b) cylinder
(c) sphere (d) cube
(e) cone

DIRECTIONS (Qs. 106 - 108): In each of these questions a set of 3 or 4 sentences which convey an idea is given. Of these, one or two is/are suppressed. To fill up the spaces of the suppressed sentence(s) two possible fillers as (A) and (B) are given. Find out which one, two or none can fill up the space for the suppressed sentence(s) to make the paragraph meaningful and select your answer accordingly.

Caution: While marking your answer please also consider the sequence of the sentences if both the sentences are required to fill up the spaces.

106. As far as aircraft maintenance procedures are concerned, they are rigorous. (.............). Such cases may end-up in disastrous results, though exceptionally.
A. All problems are immediately corrected on almost every occasion.
B. Only due to urgency or want of aircraft for substitution, certain ones are overlooked.
(a) A and B (b) B and A
(c) A only (d) B only
(e) None of these

107. The interrogation lasted for about nine full working days. (.............). The judge observed that he was impressed with the outcome as the involvement of the accused in the crime was crystal clear.
A. Hardly anything worth the name came out of such a marathon interrogation.

B. The prosecution lawyer, though in vain, had relentlessly applied all his wit to expose the accused.

(a) A and B (b) B and A
(c) A only (d) None
(e) None of these

108. There is no doubt that we must be fair and honest in all our dealings. (.........). What you really are is less important than what you are perceived by people around you.

A. It means that perception assumes greater importance than reality.

B. But even more important is how you are perceived by others.

(a) A and B (b) B and A
(c) A only (d) B only
(e) None of these

Directions (Q. 109-113) : In each of th efollowing questions, a related pair of figures is followed by five numbered pairs of figures. Select the pair that has a relationship similar to that in the unnumbered pair. The best answer is to be selected from a group of fairly close choices.

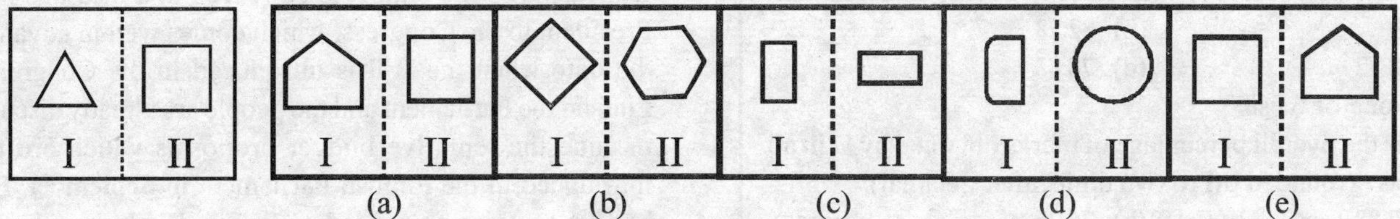

In this question element II of unnumbered figure is related to the element I of the figure in a certain way. Element II has one side more than the element I. The pair in the figure No. 5 has the same relationship. Therefore, (e) is the answer. Now solve the following questions.

109.

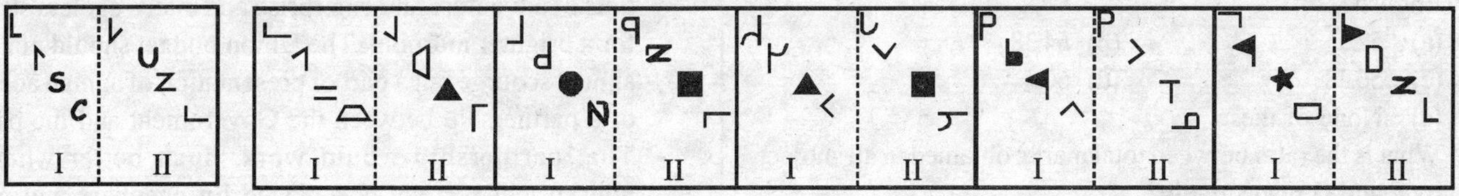

I II | I II | I II | I II | I II | I II
(a) (b) (c) (d) (e)

110.

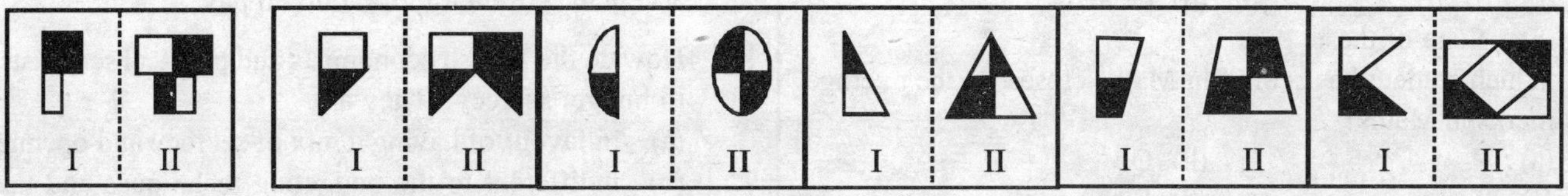

I II | I II | I II | I II | I II | I II
(a) (b) (c) (d) (e)

111.

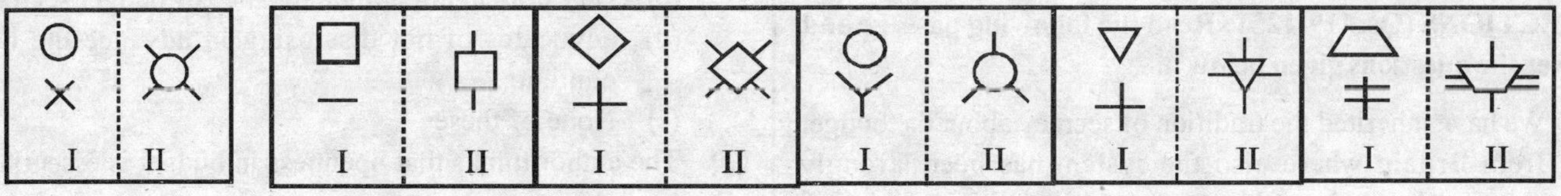

I II | I II | I II | I II | I II | I II
(a) (b) (c) (d) (e)

112.

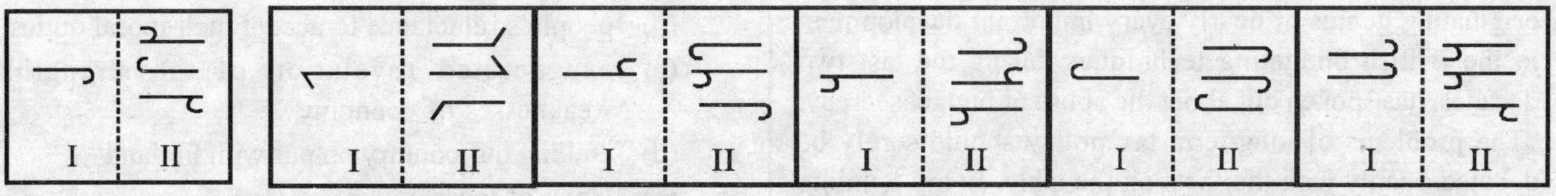

I II | I II | I II | I II | I II | I II
(a) (b) (c) (d) (e)

113.

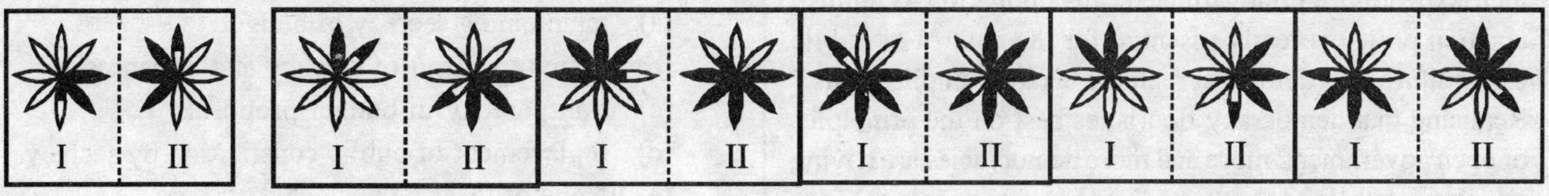

I II | I II | I II | I II | I II | I II
(a) (b) (c) (d) (e)

DIRECTIONS (Q. 114-118): Study the following table carefully to answer these questions.

Subject → Student ↓	Marks obtained out of					
	History (75)	Geography (75)	Science (120)	Maths (150)	English (80)	Hindi (60)
P	45	53	100	117	50	45
Q	56	58	96	132	46	0
T	48	60	112	120	52	42
D	62	67	88	108	48	34
G	66	55	92	140	60	32
F	54	64	108	116	53	40

114. What is the average percentage of marks obtained by all the students in Science? (rounded off to two digits after decimal)
(a) 99 (b) 82.78
(c) 88.72 (d) 78.88
(e) None of these

115. What is the overall percentage of marks obtained by D in all subjects? (rounded off to two digits after decimal)
(a) 72.88 (b) 76.28
(c) 73.17 (d) 72.68
(e) None of these

116. What are the average marks obtained by all students in English?
(a) 52.5 (b) 64.38
(c) 56.38 (d) 60.5
(e) None of these

117. What is the ratio between total marks obtained in all subjects by F and G respectively?
(a) 87:89 (b) 89:87
(c) 67:69 (d) 69:67
(e) None of these

118. Which student has scored in Maths closest to the average marks in Maths?
(a) P (b) Q
(c) T (d) F
(e) None of these

DIRECTIONS (Qs. 119-125) : Read the following passage and answer the questions given below it.

We have inherited the tradition of secrecy about the budget from Britain where also the system has been strongly attacked by eminent economists and political scientists including Peter Jay. Sir Richard Clarke, who was the originating genius of nearly every important development in the British budgeting techniques during the last two decades, has spoken out about the abuse of budget secrecy: "The problems of long-term tax policy should surely be debated openly with the facts on the table. In my opinion, all governments should have just the same duty to publish their expenditure policy. Indeed, this obligation to publish taxation policy is really essential for the control of public expenditure in order to get realistic taxation implications." Realising that democracy flourishes best on the principles of open government, more and more democracies are having an open public debate on budget proposals before introducing the appropriate Bill in the legislature. In the United States the budget is conveyed in a message by the President to the Congress, which comes well in advance of the date when the Bill is introduced in the Congress. In Finland the Parliament and the people are already discussing in June the tentative budget proposals which are to be introduced in the Finnish Parliament in September. Every budget contains a cartload of figures in black and white - but the dark figures represent the myriad lights and shades of India's life, the contrasting tones of poverty and wealth, and of bread so dear and flesh and blood so cheap, the deep tints of adventure and enterprise and man's ageless struggle for a brighter morning. The Union budget should not be an annual scourge but a part of presentation of annual accounts of a partnership between the Government and the people. That partnership would work much better when the nonsensical secrecy is replaced by openness and public consultations, resulting in fair laws and the people's acceptance of their moral duty to pay.

119. How do the British economists and political scientists react to budget secrecy? They are
(a) in favour of having a mix of secrecy and openness.
(b) indifferent to the budgeting techniques and taxation policies.
(c) very critical about maintenance of budget secrecy.
(d) advocates of not disclosing in advance the budget contents.
(e) None of these

120. The author thinks that openness in budget is essential as it leads to
(a) prevention of tax implications
(b) people's reluctance to accept their moral duties
(c) exaggerated revelation of the strengths and weaknesses of economy
(d) making our country on par with Finland
(e) None of these

121. The author seems to be in favour of
(a) maintaining secrecy of budget
(b) judicious blend of secrecy and openness
(c) transparency in budget proposals
(d) replacement of public constitution by secrecy
(e) None of these

122. Which of the following statements is definitely TRUE in the context of the passage?
   (a) The British Government has been religiously maintaining budget secrecy.
   (b) Budget secrecy is likely to lead to corrupt practices.
   (c) Consulting unjustifiable taxes with public helps make them accept those taxes.
   (d) There should be no control on public expenditure in democratic condition.
   (e) None of these

123. Sir Richard Clarke seems to deserve the credit for
   (a) transformation in the British budgetary techniques.
   (b) maintenance of secrecy of the British budget.
   (c) detection of abuse of transparency in budget.
   (d) bringing down the tax load on British people.
   (e) None of these

124. From the contents of the passage, it can be inferred that the author is
   (a) authoritarian in his approach.
   (b) a democratic person.
   (c) unaware of India's recent economic developments.
   (d) a conservative person.
   (e) None of these

125. For making the budget realistic, the Government should
   (a) refrain from making public the proposed provisions before finalisation.
   (b) discuss it secretly within themselves.
   (c) encourage the public to send in their suggestions.
   (d) consult the public, defend their own plans and accept public suggestions.
   (e) None of these

Directions (Qs. 126 - 130) : Read the following information carefully to answer the questions that follow.

In a car exhibition, seven cars of seven different companies, viz. Cadillac, Ambassador, Fiat, Maruti, Mercedes, Bedfort and Fargo were displayed in a row, facing east such that

(A) Cadiallac car was to the immediate right of Fargo.
(B) Fargo was fourth to the right of Fiat.
(C) Maruti was between Ambassador and Bedford.
(D) Fiat, which was the third to the left of Ambassador car was at one of the ends.

126. Which of the following was the correct position of the Mercedes ?
   (a) Immediate right to Cadillac
   (b) Immediate left to Bedford
   (c) Between Bedford and Fargo
   (d) Fourth of the right of Maruti
   (e) None of these

127. Which of the following is definitely true ?
   (a) Fargo car is between Ambassador and Fiat
   (b) Cadillac is to the immediate left of Mercedes
   (c) Fargo is to the immediate right of cardillac
   (d) None of these
   (e) None

128. Which cars are on the immediate either sides of the Cadillac car ?
   (a) Ambassador and Maruti
   (b) Maruti and fiat
   (c) Fiat and Mercedes
   (d) Mercedes and Fargo
   (e) None of these

129. Which of the following is definitely true ?
   (a) Maruti is to the immediate left of Ambassador.
   (b) Bedford is to the immediate left of Fiat.
   (c) Bedford is at one of the ends.
   (d) Fiat is second to the right of Maruti.
   (e) None of these

130. Which of the following groups of cars is to the right of Ambassador car ?
   (a) Cadillac, Fargo and Maruti
   (b) Maruti, Bedford and Fiat
   (c) Mercedes, Cardillac and Fargo
   (d) Bedford, Cadillac and Fargo
   (e) None of these

DIRECTIONS (Qs. 131-132) : Six products U, V, W, X, Y and Z are to be placed in display windows of a shop. There are six display windows – numbered 1, 2, 3, 4, 5, 6 and one product is to be put in one window. Moreover, U cannot be immediately to the left or immediately to the right of V. W must be immediately to the left of X. Z cannot be in window number 6.

131. Which of the following products cannot be placed in window no. 1 ?
   (a) U (b) V
   (c) W (d) X
   (e) None of these

132. If X is placed in window no. 3, then W must be placed in which window ?
   (a) 1 (b) 2
   (c) 4 (d) 5
   (e) None of these

Directions (Q.133-137) : In each of the questions given below which one of the five answer figures on the right should come after the problem figures on the left, if the sequenc were continued?

133.

(a) (b) (c) (d) (e)

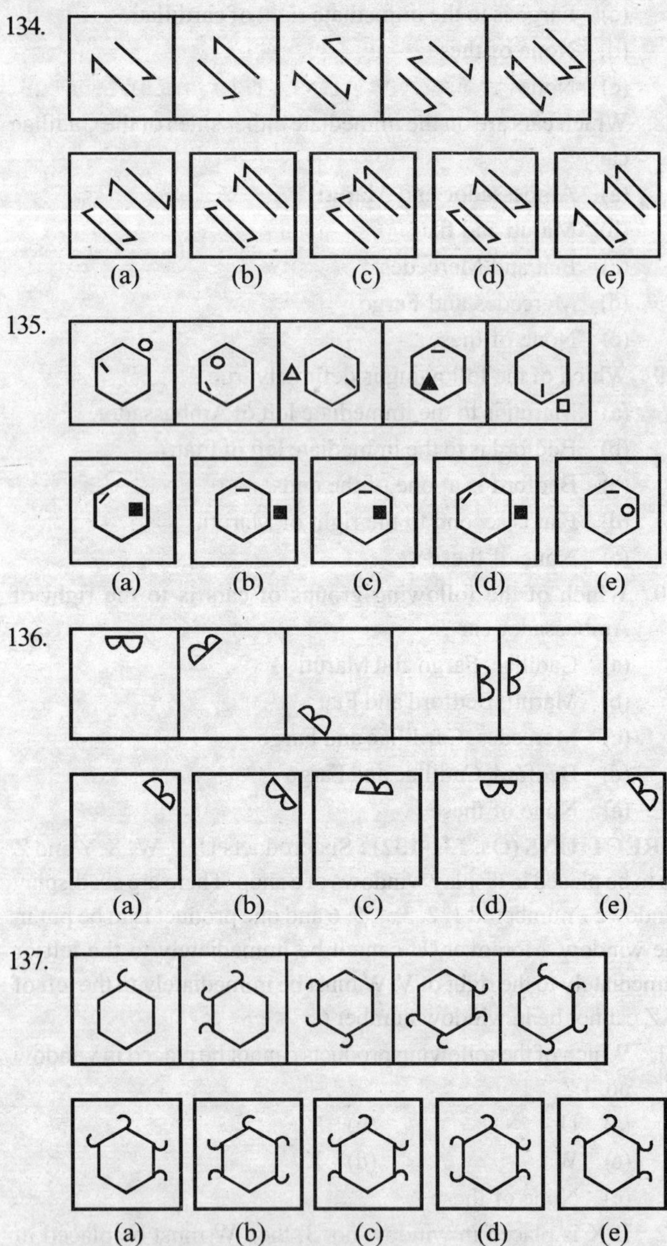

138. In the past, to run for one's country in the Olympics was the ultimate achievement of any athlete. Nowadays, an athlete's motives are more and more influenced by financial gain, and consequently we do not see our best athletes in the Olympics, which is still only for amateurs.

Which of the following will most weaken the above conclusion?

(a) The publicity and fame that can be achieved by competing in the Olympics makes athletes more "marketable" by agents and potential sponsors, while allowing the athletes to retain their amateur status.

(b) The winning of a race is not an important as participating.

(c) There is a widely held belief that our best Olympic athletes already receive enough in terms of promotion and sponsorship.

(d) It has been suggested that professional athletes should be allowed to compete in the games.

(e) Athletics as an entertainment is like any other entertainment job and deserves a financial reward.

139. Farmers in the North have observed that heavy frost is usually preceded by a full moon. They are convinced that the full moon somehow generates the frost.

Which of the following, if true, would weaken the farmers conviction?

(a) The temperature must fall below 10 degrees Celsius (50 degrees Fahrenheit) for frost to occur.

(b) Absence of a cloud cover cools the ground which causes frost.

(c) Farmers are superstitious.

(d) No one has proven that the moon causes frost.

(e) Farmers are not experts in meteorology.

DIRECTIONS (Qs. 140 - 142) : The human civilization stands on an edge of destiny.

It lies today on the mercy of nuclear weapons, which have the power to destroy us completely lest controlled wisely. In such a crisis situation, it is important to develop sensitivity towards the basic values of life. It includes an explicit realisation that that humans swim in an ocean where they must swim together and sink together. At this juncture, a single rotten fish would damage the ocean as a whole. Man cannot afford to tamper with his loyalty to peace and international understanding, which is the only ways to deal with the situation. Anyone who does so, dooms the entire past, present and the future of the human civilisation.

140. What, according to the author, should be done to avoid the destruction of life by nuclear weapons?

(a) Ban the use of nuclear weapons throughout the world

(b) Enforce stricter laws and boycotts against the nations using nuclear weapons

(c) Generate more awareness regarding the harm of using nuclear weapons

(d) Work towards international harmony and understanding

(e) None of these

141. Which of the following can be inferred from the given paragraph?

(A) Nuclear war,m one day or the other is poised to end the human civilisation.

(B) It is is not possible for the countries to exist in unison regardless of what happens in other countries.

(C) Unless all the nuclear weapons on earth are destroyed, peace cannot be restored.

(a) Only A (b) Only B

(c) Only B and C (d) Only A and C

(e) None of these

142. A pill that can induce abortions in pregnant women has become available in France. The drug, RU 486, has proved more than 95% effective in tests conducted by a scientific team in Paris. The drug is an anti–hormone which disrupts pregnancy by blocking the implantation of a fertilized egg in the wall of the uterus. In France, the pill will be available to women who are 49 days late in their menstrual cycle. The company that manufactures the pill, Roussel Uclaf, states, however, that the pill is not a "morning after" pill for use as a contraceptive.

Which of the following statements can be correctly deduced from the text above?

(a) The drug RU486 is a new type of contraceptive.
(b) The drug RU486 blocks egg production.
(c) The drug RU486 can be used to terminate pregnancy.
(d) The drug RU486 will replace conventional abortion techniques.
(e) The drug RU486 will only be available in France.

DIRECTIONS (Q. 143-144):

Although an eco-friendly process and one of the main ways to save the environment, recycling is not gaining pace in the industry. The process of recycling undergoes many processes. First is collecting and sorting of garbage. This requires a lot of manpower and tools which are expensive. Another disadvantage of recycling which makes it unviable is that for the manufacturers, economically, the recycled material is not highly demanded since its quality is not as good as the original material. So if the marketing of recycled goods is not worthwhile, then the whole process of recycling cannot be economically efficient. Recycled products face other disadvantages as well, such as short self life, less durability, etc.

143. The author has listed the disadvantages of recycling to

(a) explain the reason why recycling is not a popular option besides having various positive effects on the environment.
(b) give arguments to support the stopping of the process of recycling completely.
(c) predict the effects of stoppage of recycling on the environment.
(d) show that there are better options than recycling available for utilization.
(e) None of these

144. Why is the marketing of recycled products not worthwhile, according to the author?.

(A) The original products are being sold at a much lower price as compared to the recycled products.

(B) The overall effect of recycling on the environment is detrimental rather than beneficial.

(C) It does not give appropriate economic returns since recycled products lack demand in the market.

(a) Only A (b) Both B and C
(c) Only C (d) Both A and B
(e) None of these

DIRECTIONS (Qs. 145 - 146) : Read the relationships given below to answer the questions that follow.

Archana is elder than Suman. Arti is elder than Archana but younger than Kusum. Kusum is elder than Suman. Suman is younger than Arti and Gita is the eldest.

145. Who is the youngest ?

(a) Archana (b) Suman
(c) Arti (d) Kusum
(e) None of these

146. Age wise, who is in the middle ?

(a) Suman (b) Archna
(c) Arti (d) Kusum
(e) None of these

DIRECTIONS (Q. 147-151) : Study the following Tabale carefully and answer the questions given below :

The annual income of 6 persons over the years (in lacs)

Year	Persons					
	Harish	Indira	Jasmeet	Kiran	Lalita	Manish
2001	1.44	1.45	2.00	1.68	1.8	2.50
2002	1.50	1.56	2.12	1.74	1.92	2.61
2003	1.56	1.64	2.25	1.92	2.00	2.68
2004	1.62	1.70	2.30	2.00	2.11	2.73
2005	1.68	1.84	2.33	2.05	2.18	2.80
2006	1.73	1.95	2.40	2.17	2.20	2.85

147. In the year 2002 who among the given people got the highest increase (in percentage) in their annual salary from the previous year?

(a) Manish (b) Harish
(c) Lalita (d) Indira
(e) Kiran

148. What is the **approximate** per cent increase in the annual income of Kiran in the year 2004 from that of the previous year?

(a) 5.5 (b) 6
(c) 4 (d) 7
(e) 2.5

149. What is the **approximate** average annual income of Harish over the given years?

(a) ₹ 1.622 lacs (b) ₹ 1.88 lacs
(c) ₹ 2.588 lacks (d) ₹ 1.562 lacs
(e) ₹ 1.588 lacs

150. The average annual income earned by Indira over the given years is **approximately** what per cent of the average income earned by Jasmeet over the given years?

(a) 10.15 (b) 75.50
(c) 13.44 (d) 24.50
(e) 71.25

151. What is the ratio of the annual income of Indira to that of Manish in the year 2005?
(a) 23 : 35 (b) 23 : 37
(c) 32 : 35 (d) 43 : 70
(e) 33 : 53

DIRECTIONS (Q. 152-155) : Study the following information carefully to answer these questions.

Eight friends P, R, T, V, W, J, F and K are sitting around a circle facing the centre. T is third to the right of F and second to the left of W, P and R are not neighbours of W, R is third to the right of K, J is between W and K.

152. Which of the following is the correct position of T with respect to K's position?
(a) Second to the left
(b) Third to the left
(c) Third to the right
(d) Second to the right
(e) None of these

153. Which of the following pairs is the neighbour of J ?
(a) RP (b) FJ
(c) VT (d) JW
(e) WK

154. Who is to the immediate right of F?
(a) J (b) P
(c) R (d) V
(e) None of these

155. Which of the following is the correct position of V?
(a) Second to the left of R
(b) Between T and P
(c) To the immediate right of W
(d) To the immediate left of W
(e) None of these

156. A and B start walking in opposite directions. A covers 3 km and B covers 4 km. Then A turns right and walks 4 km while B turns left and walks 3 km. How far is each from the starting point ?
(a) 5 km (b) 4 km
(c) 10 km (d) 8 km
(e) None of these

157. A set of eight candidates A, B, C, D, E, F, G and H are being interviewed by two panels of interviewers : Panel I and Pannel II – from 9.30 to 10.50 on a particular day. Each panel will spend about 10 minutes per candidate and at no time during the interview process will a panel be without any candidate. The original schedule of interviews for the eight candidates are given in the following table :

Candidates	Panel – I Time	Panel – II Time
A	9:30 to 9:40	10:10 to 10:20
B	9:40 to 9:50	10:20 to 10:30
C	9:50 to 10:00	10:30 to 10:40
D	10:00 to 10:10	10:40 to 10:50
E	10:10 to 10:20	9:30 to 9:40
F	10:20 to 10:30	9:40 to 9:50
G	10:30 to 10:40	9:50 to 10:00
H	10:40 to 10:50	10:00 to 10:10

Due to requests from the candidates, the interview schedule was altered for several candidates. The alternations were made in such a way that whenever a change was made, the time schedule for both the panels of a particular candidate was exchanged in entirety with the time schedule of another candidate. The following alterations were made :

I. A's place was taken by G.
II. A in turn was accommodated in C's place.
III. C in turn was accommodated in E's place.
IV. E took H's place.
V. H took G's place

If G and A had to leave together, then how much time did any of them has to wait?
(a) A has to wait 10 minutes
(b) G has to wait 20 minutes
(c) G has to wait 30 minutes
(d) A has to wait 20 minutes
(e) None of these

DIRECTIONS (Q. 158-160) : Each of the questions below consists of a question and three statements numbered I, II and III given below it. You have to decide the data provided in which of the statements are sufficient to answer the question. Choose your answer accordingly.

158. Among P, T, J, F and L who scored the highest?
I. P scored less than J and F.
II. T scored more than F but less than L.
III. J has not scored the highest.
(a) Only I and II
(b) Only I and III
(c) Only II and either I or III
(d) Only I and either II or III
(e) All I, II and III

159. Pillar 'P' is in which direction with respect to pillar 'Q'?
   I. Pillar 'M' is to the East of pillar T, which is to the South of pillar 'Q'.
   II. Pillar 'P' is to the North of pillar 'M'.
   III. Pillar 'R' is to the North of pillar 'P' and to the East of pillar 'Q'.
   (a) Only I and II
   (b) Only I and III
   (c) Only II and either I or III
   (d) Only III
   (e) All I, II and III

160. What is the code for 'adequate' in a code language?
   I. In the code language, 'rainfall is adequate' is written as 'vo al ji'.
   II. In the code language, 'food is adequate' is written as 'vo ji fa'.
   III. In the code language, 'food is delicious' is written as 'fa vo re'.
   (a) Only I and III
   (b) Only II and III
   (c) Only I and II
   (d) All I, II and III
   (e) None of these

DIRECTIONS (Q. 161-165) : Read each sentence to find out whether there is any error in it. The error, if any, will be in one part of the sentence. The number of that part is the answer. If there is no error, the answer is (e). (Ignore errors of punctuation, if any.)

161. The ongoing merger among (a) /the two companies will/ (b) have an adverse/ (c) impact on consumers. (d) No error (e)

162. It is evident that/ (a) the banking sector has underwent/ (b) tremendous changes during/ (c) the past two decades. (d) No error (e)

163. According to the consultant/ (a) a more detail analysis of/ (b) customer needs / (c) and product pricing is required. (d) No error (e)

164. Over the next five years / (a) the government needs to invest/ (b) at less 350 billion dollars/ (c) in rural infrastructure. (d) No error (e)

165. The lack of no funds / (a) has resulted in several / (b) delays in launching our / (c) new product in India. (d) No error (e)

DIRECTIONS (Qs. 166 - 170) : Read the following information and answer the questions that follow :

In a certain code language, 481 means Sky is blue. 246 means Sea is deep and 698 means Sea looks blue.

166. What number is the code for 'sky' ?
   (a) 4 (b) 8
   (c) 1 (d) 3
   (e) None of these

167. What number is the code for 'is' ?
   (a) 8 (b) 1
   (c) 4 (d) 2
   (e) None of these

168. What number is the code for 'looks' ?
   (a) 4 (b) 8
   (c) 6 (d) 9
   (e) None of these

169. What number is the code for 'sea' ?
   (a) 2 (b) 8
   (c) 6 (d) 4
   (e) None of these

170. What number is the code for 'blue' ?
   (a) 8 (b) 6
   (c) 1 (d) 9
   (e) None of these

DIRECTIONS (Q. 171-175): In each of the questions given below which one of the five answer figures on the right should come after the problem figures on the left, if the sequence were continued?

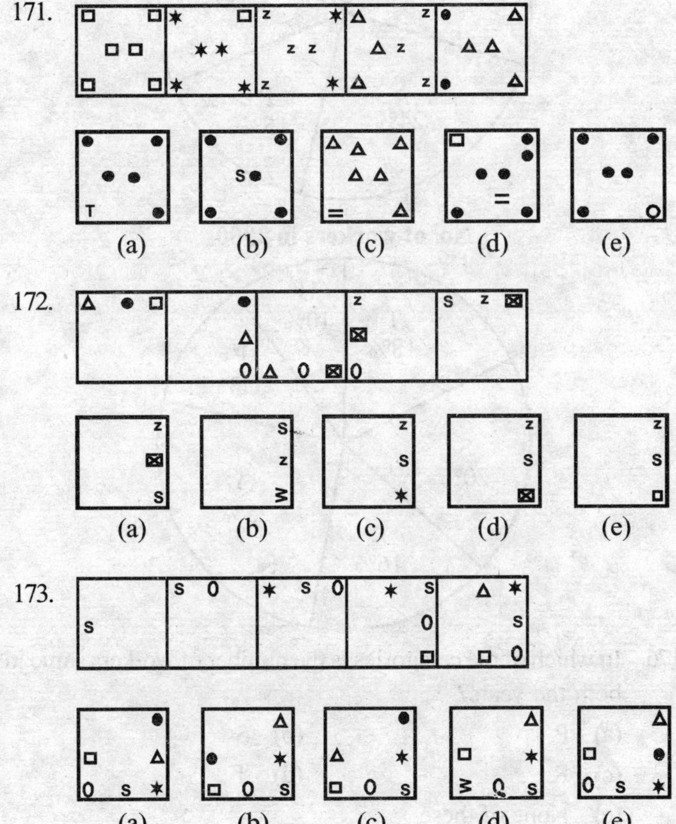

171.

172.

173.

174.

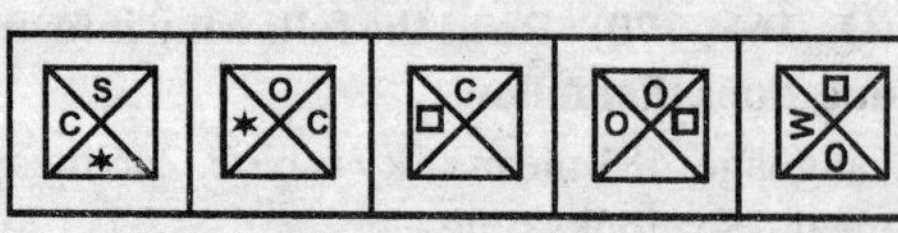

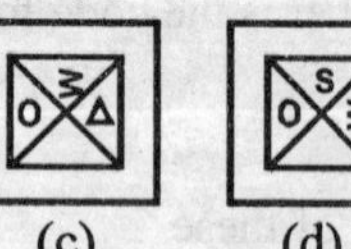

(a) (b) (c) (d) (e)

175.

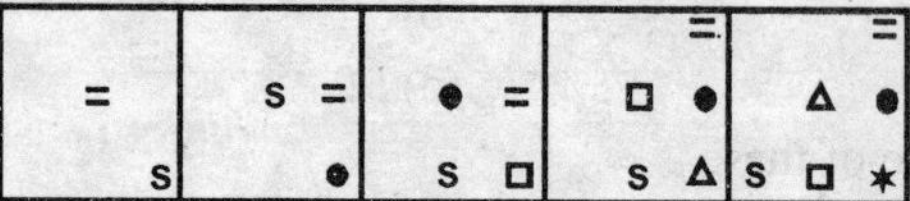

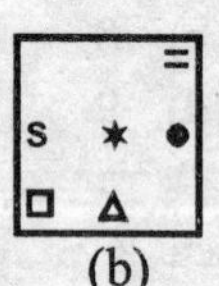
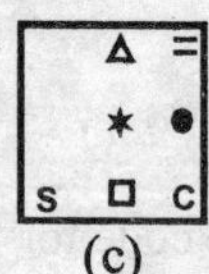
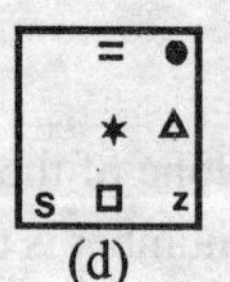
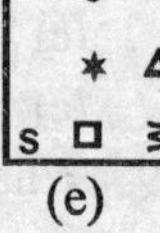

(a) (b) (c) (d) (e)

DIRECTIONS (Qs. 176-180) : Study the following graphs which show the number of workers of different categories of a factory for two different years. The total number of workers in 1998 was 2000 and in 2000 was 2400

No. of workers in 1998

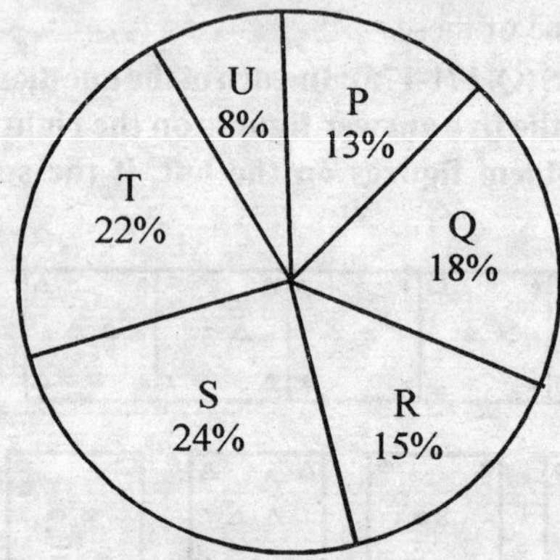

No. of workers in 2000

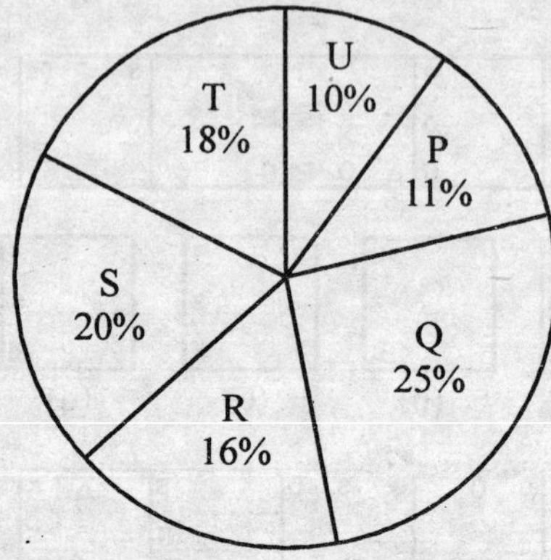

176. In which of the categories is the number of workers same in both the years?

(a) P (b) S
(c) R (d) T
(e) None of these

177. Find the percentage increase in the number of workers in category U in 2000 :

(a) 25% (b) $33\frac{1}{3}\%$
(c) 50% (d) $66\frac{2}{3}\%$
(e) None of these

178. What is the total number of increased workers for the categories in which the number of workers has been increased?

(a) 468 (b) 382
(c) 408 (d) 168
(e) None of these

179. Which categories have shown decrease in the number of workers from 1998 to 2000?

(a) P (b) Q
(c) R (d) T
(e) None of these

180. Find the maximum difference between the number of workers of any two categories taken together for any one year and that of any two for the other year.

(a) 660 (b) 416
(c) 636 (d) 502
(e) None of these

DIRECTIONS (Qs. 181-185): In a certain instruction system the different computation processes are written as follows :

(a) '$x * y, \lambda z$ 'means 'z is multiplied by the sum of x and y'.
(b) 'x \$ y % z' means 'y is subtracted from x and the resultant is divided by z'.
(c) '$x \# y \uparrow z$' means 'x is subtracted form the product of y and z'.
(d) 'x @ y © z' means 'x is added to the resultant when y is divided by z'.

In each of the questions below, a set of instruction sequences is given. You are required to find out the outcome which should come in place of the question mark (?) in each of the given sets of sequence.

181. (i) $14 \# 5 \uparrow 7 = m$
(ii) 12 @ m © 4 = ?

(a) 19 (b) $9\frac{1}{3}$
(c) 28 (d) Cannot be determined
(e) None of these

182. (i) 120 \$ 40 % 8
(ii) t @ ? © 5 = 40

(a) 100 (b) 150
(c) 200 (d) 160
(e) None of these

183. (i) $48 \# 12 \uparrow 8 = b$
(ii) $b * 8 \lambda 5 = ?$

(a) 200 (b) 240
(c) 260 (d) 280
(e) None of these

183. (i) $9 * 5 \lambda 15 = n$
(ii) $n \$ 20 \% 8 = ?$

(a) 8 (b) 40
(c) 5 (d) 13
(e) None of these

185. (i) $26 @ 45 © 9 = k$
(ii) $k * 14 \lambda 4 = ?$

(a) 120 (b) 45
(c) 49 (d) 87
(e) None of these

DIRECTIONS (Qs. 186 to 192) : A word arrangement machine, when given a particular input, rearranges it following a particular rule. The following is the illustration of the input and the steps of arrangement:

Input : *Punjabi music has rhythm and lively beat.*
Step I : *music Punjabi has rhythm and lively beat.*
Step II : *music and Punjabi has rhythm lively beat .*
Step III : *music and Punjabi rhythm has lively beat.*
Step IV : *music and Punjabi rhythm has beat lively.*
Step V : *is the last step of this input.*

Now, study the logic and answer the questions that follow:

186. What would be the penultimate step for the following input?

Input: *Kaho Naa Pyaar Hai is slowly fading*

(a) *Naa fading Hai Kaho Pyaar is slowly.*
(b) *Naa fading Kaho Pyaar Hai is slowly*
(c) *Naa Kaho Pyaar Hai is slowly fading.*
(d) *Naa fading Kaho Pyaar Hai slowly is.*

187. If step IV of an input is *'scripted are himself both films Amit by'*, which of the following would be step I of that input?

(a) *scripted are himself both films by Amit*
(b) *scripted are both films by Amit himself*
(c) *scripted both films are by Amit himself*
(d) *Can't be determined*

188. **Input:** *I am full confidence about my abilities.*

What will be the fourth step for this input?

(a) *confidence I full am abilities about my*
(b) *confidence I full am about my abilities*
(c) *confidence I am full about my abilities*
(d) *No such step*

189. Which of the following will be last step for the input given below?

Input: *Fashion no longer hold as much interest.*

(a) *hold much Fashion no as longer interest.*
(b) *hold much Fashion no longer interest as.*
(c) *hold much Fashion no longer as interest.*
(d) *hold much no Fashion longer as interest.*

190. How many steps will be required to get the final output from the following input?

Input: *She danced dandia on beats for him*

(a) IV (b) V (c) III (d) VI

191. If step I of an input is '*had remember the poisonous look Minakshi cast*' what step would be 'had the Minakshi look remember poisonous cast'?

(a) VII (b) III (c) VI (d) None of these

192. If step II is '*Puja and wish congratulations heartiest Deepawali for*', which of the following would be the input?

(a) *Heartiest congratulations and wish for Deepawali Puja*
(b) *Heartiest Deepawali for and puja wish congratulations*
(c) *Heartiest Deepawali for puja and wish congratulations*
(d) *Can't be determined*

193. Raman is 9th from downwards in a class of 31 students. What will be his position from upwards?

(a) 21st (b) 22nd
(c) 23rd (d) 24th

DIRECTIONS (Q. 194-198) : Study the following information carefully to answer the questions given below it.

Seven professionals A, B, C, D, E, F and G are practising their professions in different cities Chennai, Bangalore, Hyderabad, Mumbai, Ahmedabad, Jaipur and Bhubaneshwar, not necessarily in the same order. Each has a different profession-Doctor, Engineer, Pharmacist, Lawyer, Counsellor, Professor and Artist, not necessarily in the same order.

A is a Pharmacist and practises in Bhubaneshwar. D practises in Bangalore but is not a Doctor or an Artist. The one who practises in Hyderabad is a Professor. G is a Counsellor and does not practise in Mumbai or Chennai. E is a Lawyer and practises in Ahmedabad. F practises in Chennai but is not an artist. C practises in Mumbai.

194. What is D's profession?

(a) Doctor (b) Professor
(c) Engineer (d) Cannot be determined
(e) None of these

195. Who is the Professor?
(a) B (b) C
(c) D (d) E
(e) None of these

196. Which of the following combinations of profession and place is correct?
(a) Pharmacist-Jaipur (b) Engineer-Chennai
(c) Doctor-Bangalore (d) Artist-Mumbai
(e) None of these

197. Which of the following persons works in Jaipur?
(a) B (b) G
(c) C (d) B or G
(e) None of these

198. Who is the Doctor?
(a) D (b) B
(c) C (d) B or C
(e) None of these

199. If it is possible to make only one meaningful word from the third, the sixth, the ninth and the tenth letters of the word PARENTHESIS, using each letter only once, last letter of the word is your answer. If no such word can be formed your answer is X and if more than one such word can be formed your answer is Y.
(a) R (b) T
(c) S (d) Y
(e) X

200. Which of the given chioces will come in place of question mark?

Celsius : Temperature : : Meter : ____ ?
(a) Kilogram (b) Second
(c) Darkness (d) Depthness
(e) None of these

❑❑❑

ANSWERS AND EXPLANATIONS

1. (b) Answer (b) is the best choice. Note the cue word "then" before "new products" and "new ways." An entrepreneur is one who creates or implements change, not necessarily an inventor, as in answer (e). Answer (a) is true (the owner of a large business may be an entrepreneur), but it is not the best conclusion that can be drawn from the passage. It is a necessary but insufficient condition. Note that the text states that to own a small or large business does not make someone an entrepreneur. Answer (c) is not supported by the passage, and not enough information is given to conclude answer (d)
2. (b) As the passage does not mention a thing about efficiency, it is difficult to assess, earlier banks were efficient or not. But talk of greater transparency and accountability in banking operations indicates about need of improvement.
3. (a) Sentence 4 indicates towards this.
4. (b) Sentence 4 talks about aims at increasing public confidence. But no parameter of public confidence is given.
5. (d) First sentence talks about wide cross-section of economy.

For (Qs. 6-10) : Let R_n denote the resultant of the nth row.

6. (e) $X = R_1 = 23\ 15\ 12$
   $= 38\ \ 12$ [applying Rule (i)]
   $= 456$ [applying Rule (v)]
   Now, $R_2 = X\,24\ 49$
   $= 456\ 24\ 49$
   $= 19\ \ 49$ [applying Rule (iii)]
   $= 68$ [applying Rule (i)]
7. (c) $R_1 = 37\ 12\ 21$
   $= 49\ 21$ [applying Rule (iv)]
   $= 70$ [applying Rule (i)]
   $R_2 = 38\ 81\ 14$
   $= 43\ 14$ [applying Rule (ii)]
   $= 57$ [applying Rule (iv)]
   $\therefore\ R_1 - R_2 = 70 - 57 = 13$
8. (a) $X = R_1 = 16\ 8\ 32$
   $= 128\ 32$ [applying Rule (v)]
   $= 4$ [applying Rule (iii)]
   $\therefore\ X^2 = 16$
   Now, $R_1 = 132\ \ 11\ X^2$
   $= 132\ 11\ 16$
   $= 12\ 16$ [applying Rule (iii)]
   $= 192$ [applying Rule (v)]
9. (d) $X = R_2 = 45\ 17\ 81$
   $= 62\ 81$ [applying Rule (i)]
   $= 19$ [applying Rule (ii)]
   Now, $R_1 = 345\ 23\ X$
   $= 345\ 23\ 19$
   $= 15\ 19$ [applying Rule (iii)]
   $= 34$ [applying Rule (i)]
10. (e) $R_1 = 12\ 28\ 84$
    $= 336\ 84$ [applying Rule (v)]
    $= 4$ [applying Rule (iii)]
    $R_2 = 37\ 22\ 18$
    $= 59\ 18$ [applying Rule (iv)]
    $= 77$ [applying Rule (iv) again]
11. (c) The meaning is implied in the last sentence.
12. (a) The Japanese ambassador acknowledges that the vastness of the Indian market is a great inducement for investment in the manufacturing industry.
13. (b) The author describes the Indian investment scenario in toto. He presents a comparative analysis regarding foreign investment in India.
14. (e) Comparatively though labour is inexpensive in India, but at the same time productivity is not high. Therefore, it cannot be cited as an advantage here.
15. (d) If foreign investment is to be wooed assiduously, we will have to meet exacting international standards.
16. (a) The author is a political commentator because he talks about the government policy and makes various proposals regarding foreign investment in India.
17. (b) The passage reflects the views of the Japanese ambassador who also talks about the problems faced by foreign investors in India.
18. (b) The number of arrangements of choosing the chairs numbered from 1 to 4 by the two women = ${}^4P_2$
    Similarly, for men, number of arrangements = ${}^4P_3$
    $\therefore$ Required no. of ways $= {}^4P_2 \times {}^4P_3$
19. (d) Radius of circular ground $= \dfrac{88}{2\pi} = 14$ m
    Area of strip of land $= \pi\left(14^2 - 11^2\right) = 75\pi$
    Cost $= 75\pi \times 7 =$ ₹ 1650
20. (c) The largest size of the tile
    = H.C.F. of 3.78 and 5.25
    $= \dfrac{\text{H.C.F. of } 378 \text{ and } 525}{\text{L.C.M. of } 100 \text{ and } 100} = \dfrac{21}{100} = 0.21\text{ m}$
    $\therefore$ Number of tiles required to pave the rectangular yard
    $= \dfrac{3.78 \times 5.25}{0.21 \times 0.21} = 18 \times 25 = 450$
21. (c) Since the sum of two different prime numbers may be odd or even, if we take those two different prime number which product is an even number, then we can find that x and y will be odd.

22. (b) Statement I : There are many numbers with last digit 3 are not divisible by 3. Hence, statement (I) is not sufficient to answer the question.
Statement II : $x+5$ is divisible by 6.
Now, 12, 18, 24, 30 ..... are also divisible by 6 but 7, 13, 19, 25 .... are not divisible by x.
Hence, this statement satisfies to answer the question.

23. (b) Let the first term and common difference of the AP be a and d, respectively.
Now, $(a+5d)+(a+14d)$
$= (a+6d)+(a+9d)+(a+11d)$
or $2a+19d = 3a+26d$
or $a+7d=0$
i.e. 8th term is 0.

24. (c) 3 goes in the opposite direction: it talks about the utility of fashion whereas the author does not talk of fashion approvingly.

25. (b) Read the last sentence of the paragraph.

26. (d) All others are either distorted or partial reading of the paragraph.

27. (e) This is what we have arrived at in the question above.

28. (a) Read the first two sentences of the second para.

29. (e) Aid agencies send study groups instead of requisite personnel.

30. (d) Stability will come only when economic opportunities exist.

31. (c) Too much time can't be taken as "the window of opportunity closes quickly".

32. (d) Since, most economies in post-conflict countries are based on agriculture.

33. (b) Read the third para carefully.

34. (a) I $\Rightarrow (x-5)(x-2)=0 \Rightarrow x=2, 5$
II $\Rightarrow (y+10)(y+1)=0 \Rightarrow y=-1, -10$
Therefore $x>y$

35. (d) I $\Rightarrow (x+12)(x+16)=0$
$\Rightarrow x=-12, -16$
II $\Rightarrow (x+4)(y+12)=0$
$\Rightarrow y=-4, -12$
Therefore $y \geq x$.

36. (c) Solving (I) & (II), we get
$x=-2.5$ and
$y=-0.5$ $\therefore y>x$.

37. (b) I $\Rightarrow (x+3)(x+5) \Rightarrow x=-3, -5$
II $\Rightarrow (y+5)(y+6) \Rightarrow y=-5, -6$
Therefore $x \geq y$.

38. (b) I $\Rightarrow x=\sqrt{3136}=56$
II $\Rightarrow y=\pm\sqrt{3136}=56, -56$
Therefore $x \geq y$.

39. (c) I $\Rightarrow x=81$
II. $\Rightarrow y=89$
Therefore $x<y$.
Note : $x=\sqrt{7921}$ gives only +ve value.
Do not confuse it with $x^2=7921$. In this case, when we find value of x, then $x=\pm 81$.
But $x=\sqrt{7921}$ means only +ve value is given.

40. (b) 1 represents the common region in all the figures.

41. (d) The region represented by 3 is the required region.

42. (b) Region 12 represents hardworking, non-urban people who are neither educated nor honest.

43. (c) (a) It is not true as the regions represented by 7, 8 and 9 donot fall in U but they fall in E.
(b) It is also not true as the region represented by 5

44. (c) The region 4 does not fall in the circle but it falls in all the three other geometrical figures.

45. (c) The widest divergence between India and China is the profitable horticultural sector.............China's added advantage lies in the more diversified composition of its agricultural sector.......

46. (a) In all of these China has outdone India.

47. (b) The passage talks only about agricultural growth rate, not economic growth in general.

48. (e) None of these is fully true.

49. (c) India is placed favourably when compared to china in terms of quantity of arable land, average farm size, farm mechanisation, etc.

50. (e) Majority of the budget is eaten up by staff salaries with only 3 per cent being allotted for research.

51. (c) There has been much debate about subsidies and their utility; the opposing view being that subsidies are gainst the amrket reforms and distort the market as well as reduce resource efficiency.

52. (a) China has concentrated on investment rather than on subsidies.

53. (d) anxiety

54. (e) significant

55. (b) dedicated

56. (a) intermittent

57. (c) idealistic

58. (a) Let $x=1\times2\times3\times4=24$
Therefore, $n=1+24=25=$ odd
Clearly, n is an odd integer and a perfect square.
This is true for all values of x (product of any four consecutive integers).

59. (b) Let the sum be ₹ x
Now, $56=\dfrac{x\times8\times(3-2)}{100} \Rightarrow x=₹700$

60. (b) The first type of alloy does not contain tin. Second type alloy contains tin. Therefore, quantity of tin in 2 units of the resulting alloy $=\dfrac{5}{13}$
$\Rightarrow$ Quantity of tin in 1 unit of the resulting alloy
$=\dfrac{\frac{5}{13}}{2}=\dfrac{5}{26}$

61. (b) According to the given information

$$\frac{50,000\times12}{60,000\times(12-x)}=\frac{20}{18}\Rightarrow\frac{50,000\times12\times18}{60,000\times20}=12-x$$

$\therefore$ x = 3 months

62. (a) Let the original strength of the class = x

$$\therefore \quad \frac{x\times40+12\times32}{x+12}=40-4$$

$$\Rightarrow 40x+384=36x+432\Rightarrow 40x-36x=432-384$$

$\therefore \quad x=12$

63. (b) Circumference of the wheel

$$=2\pi r=2\times\frac{22}{7}\times35=220\text{ cm}$$

Number of revolutions made by the wheel during the journey $=\frac{2200000\times30}{220}$ (22 km = 2200000 cm)

$= 300000 = 3$ lakhs

64. (c) Let the radius of the circle be 10 units, then its area = $\pi(10)^2=100\pi$ sq. units

New radius = 20 units, then new area

$=\pi(20)^2=400\pi$ sq. units

% increase in area $=\frac{\pi(400-100)}{100\pi}\times100=300\%$

65. (b) Let the worker worked for (40 + x) hours.

Now, $\frac{56}{35}\times40+\frac{x\times1.5\times56}{35}=88$ or $2.4x=24$

$\Rightarrow x=10$ hours

The worker worked for (40 + 10) = 50 hours

66. (e) Let the weight of the filled bottle be 100 g. Then, the weight of the empty bottle is 20 g.

Let x gm liquid removed

Now, $100-x=\frac{100}{2}\Rightarrow x=50$

Required ratio $=\frac{50}{100}=\frac{1}{2}$

67. (c) From fig II to I : The arc with dash rotates by 90° ACW while the other arc rotates by 90° ACW and gets inverted. Both the elements shift one side CW.

68. (d) From fig II to I : The elements shift diagonally. The upper-left gets enlarged and a new element appears inside while the lower-left remains the same size and a new element with more number of sides appears outside it.

69. (b) From fig II to I : The elements shift one side ACW. The number of one group increases by one and the number of the other group decreases by one. One of the groups is replaced by new elements while its number decreases by one.

70. (e) From fig II to I : The end arcs of the upper and the left arc of the lower figure get inverted and both the figures get inverted on their base.

71. (a) From fig II to I : The first and the third, and the second and the fourth elements, from top interchange places and get inverted, except the second from top.

72. (a) Choice (a) sums up the conclusion of the passage and is thus the appropriate answer. It combines the intention of the car manufacturers–to produce more cars–with the choosen method, dividing labour into component tasks. Choice (b) may have been a further outcome of implementing this policy, but the passage does not comment on this; therefore, (b) is not appropriate. Choice (c) mentions another direction in which the car manufacturers may have moved, i.e., opening larger plants, etc. and this process may have been assisted by what is discussed in the passage but again this cannot be concluded from the passage. So, (c) is also inappropriate.

Choices (d) and (e) are both concomitant with the division of labour process – (d), a disadvantage, and (e), and advantage-but neither of them can be inferred from the passage and therefore are inappropriate.

73. (a) Ethno fractionalization is characteristic of a continent with many tribes that are ethnically different. Statement (b) is flawed; Angola and Ethiopia are not given as worst-case examples. Alternatives (d) and (e) are not true. Alternative (c) is the second best summarization, even though warfare is at most inferred.

74. (d)

We have, $BD \parallel EF$ and $BD=2EF$

Now, $EF=\frac{1}{2}\times a \quad (\because BD=a)$

Area of the equilateral triangle GEF

$$=\frac{\sqrt{3}}{4}\left(\frac{1}{2}a\right)^2=\frac{\sqrt{3}}{4}\times\frac{1}{4}a^2=\frac{\sqrt{3}}{16}a^2\text{ sq. units}$$

Hence, none of the given options is the correct.

75. (c) Area of section $BQDAB$ = Area of the sector $BPDCB$

$$\frac{1}{4}\pi r^2=\frac{1}{4}\pi(10)^2=25\pi\, cm^2$$

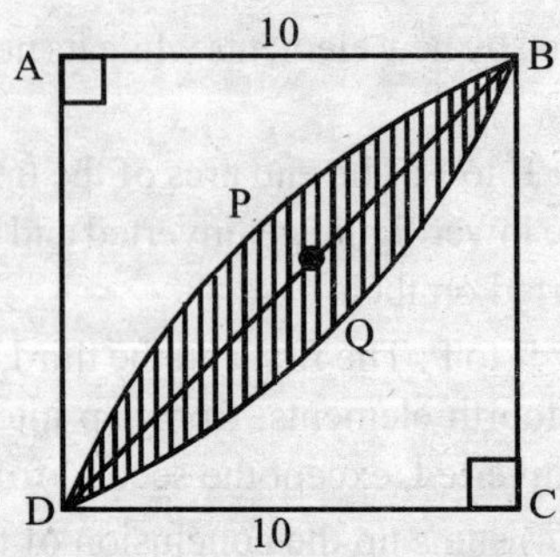

Area of $\Delta ABD = \frac{1}{2} \times 10 \times 10 = 50 \text{ cm}^2$

Area of the shaded portion below the diagonal BD

$= (25\pi - 50) \text{ cm}^2$

Area of the total shaded portion $= 2(25\pi - 50)$

$= (50\pi - 100) \text{ cm}^2$

76. (a) $PQ = \sqrt{(13)^2 - (12)^2} = \sqrt{169 - 144} = \sqrt{25} = 5 \text{ cm}$

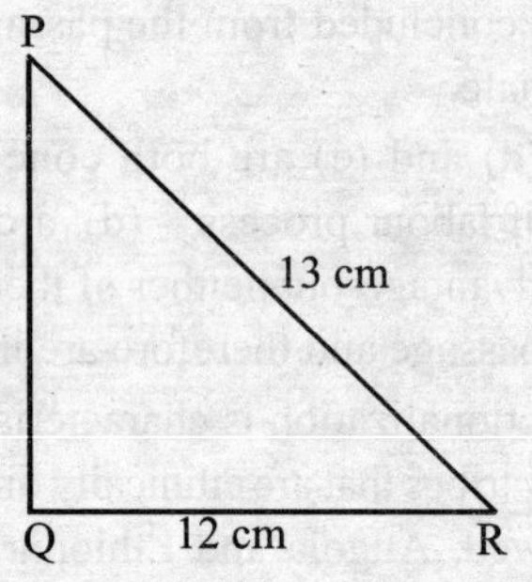

$\therefore$ Area of the right $\Delta PQR = \frac{1}{2} \times 12 \times 5 = 30 \text{ cm}^2$

77. (b) $\tan 30° = \frac{BD}{10} \Rightarrow BD = \frac{10}{\sqrt{3}}$

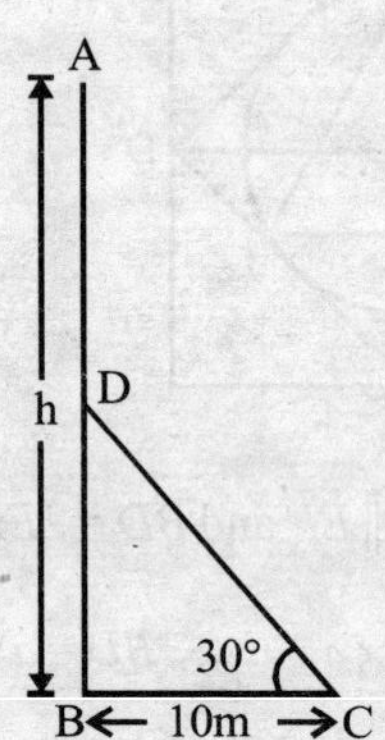

Now, $CD^2 = (10)^2 + \left(\frac{10}{\sqrt{3}}\right)^2$

or $CD^2 = 100 + \frac{100}{3} = \frac{400}{3} \Rightarrow CD = \frac{20}{\sqrt{3}}$

Height of the tree $= BD + AD$

$= BD + CD = \frac{10}{\sqrt{3}} + \frac{20}{\sqrt{3}} = \frac{30}{\sqrt{3}} = 10\sqrt{3}$ m

78. (a) In each step the quadrilateral rotates by 90° ACW while it shifts half a side CW alternately.

79. (b) The whole figure rotates by 45°, 90°, 135°, 180°,.......CW in subsequent steps. While a petal is added on the CW side in each step. The shaded petal changes side in each step.

80. (a) In each step the elements shift one step ACW while one of the elements is replaced by a new one in ACW order.

81. (a) The whole figure rotates by 90°, 135°, 180°, ...CW in subsequent steps. A petal is added on the CW side while the shading shifts from one side to the other to each step.

82. (e) In the first step the upper and the left elements interchange places, so do the lower and the right while the element coming to the left is replaced. In the next step the upper and the right and the lower and the left interchange places.

83. (e)	84. (b)	85.	(a)
86. (d)	87. (c)	88.	(b)
89. (e)	90. (a)	91.	(d)
92. (c)			

93. (d) Total expenditure

$= 306 + 300 + 300 + 306 + 300 + 306 + 306$

$=$ ₹ 2124 thousands

94. (d) Total expenditure in the year 1998

$= 300 + 306 + 306 + 312 + 318 + 300 + 312$

$=$ ₹ 2154 thousands

Total expenditure in 1997 and 1998

$= 2124 + 2154 = 4278$ thousands

95. (c) Average monthly expenditure in year 1999

$= \frac{312 + 312 + 318 + 318 + 306 + 312 + 318}{7}$

$= \frac{2196}{7} = 313.714$ thousands $\approx$ ₹ 3,14,000

96. (c) In the year 1999, the least expenses of Rs 306 thousands is in the month of May.

97. (b) Expenditure in April 1998 = 312 thousands

Expenditure in April 1999 = 318 thousands

Required % $= \frac{6}{312} \times 100 = 1.92 \approx 2\%$

For Qs. 98-102.

Always make schematic representation in these type of queston and then solve as follows.

Sitting sequence

M	F	F	F	M	M	M
(1)	(2)	(3)	(4)	(5)	(6)	(7)
D	F Teacher	Psychologist	C	Dr	⇌ Er	Stu

Intelligence Rank

(1)	(2)	(3)	(4)	(5)	(6)	(7)
Psyc	C ↓ B. Man	Dr	Er	Stu	Arch D	F ↓ Teacher

98. (a) 99. (d) 100. (d)
101. (d) 102. (b)
103. (d) All others are related to sence organe.
104. (b) All others are parts of eye.
105. (a) All others are three dimensional figures.
106. (a) A continues talking about the quality of aircraft maintenance. Further B has to follow, as the last sentence of the para says, 'such cases', which refers to the case given in B.
107. (d) None of A and B can be accomodated. As per the last sentence of the given para the involvement of the accused was crystal clear, which is not the case in A and B.
108. (d) Only B can be accomodated. A can not be included of what has been said in the opening sentence. But B is include as it is in line with the closing sentence.
109. (b) The upper element rotates by 90° CW, gets inverted vertically and moves to the lower position. The second from upper get vertically inverted and moves to upper position. The lower one rotates by 90° ACW and moves to second from upper while the second from lower is replaced by a new one.
110. (c) The mirror image of the figure is added to the LHS with a different shading.
111. (d) The line segments of the lower element are attached to the upper element.
112. (b) The middle and the upper elements are 180°-rotated forms of the first while the lower is the same. The attached part changes its direction in the upper and the lower elements.
113. (b) The whole figure rotates by 135° CW and one extra petal is added to its CW side and the shading of the half-shaded petal is changed.
114. (b) Total marks obtained by all the students in Science

$$= \frac{100}{120} \times (100 + 96 + 112 + 88 + 92 + 108)$$

$$= \frac{100}{120} \times 596 = 82.77 = 82.78 \text{ (approx)}$$

115. (e) Total marks obtained by D in all subjects

$$\frac{62\times4}{3} + \frac{67\times4}{3} + \frac{88\times10}{12} + \frac{108\times2}{3} + \frac{48\times5}{4} + \frac{34\times5}{3}$$

$$= 82.66 + 89.11 + 73.30 + 72 + 60 + 56.66$$

$$= \frac{433.73}{6} = 72.28\%$$

116. (b) Avg. marks obtained by all students in English

$$= \frac{\frac{100}{80} \times (50 + 46 + 52 + 48 + 60 + 53)}{6}$$

$$= \frac{386.25}{6} = 64.375 = 64.38 \text{ (approx)}.$$

117. (a) Total marks obtained in all subjects by F = 54 + 64 + 108 + 116 + 53 + 40 = 435
total marks obtained in all subjects by G = 66 + 55 + 92 + 140 + 60 + 32 = 445

$$\text{Required ratio} = \frac{435}{445} = 87 : 89$$

118. (c) Avg. marks in Maths

$$= \frac{733}{6} = 122 \text{ (approx)}.$$

119. (c) Eminent British economists and political scientists have strongly attacked the tradition of budget secrecy.
120. (e) It leads to the control of public expenditure in order to set realistic taxation implications.
121. (b) He has presented the example of both the open budget system and the secret budget system, practised by various countries and has looked into all their aspects.
122. (c) Detection of abuse transparency in budget.
123. (a) Sir Richard Clarke was the originating genius of nearly every important development in the British budgeting techniques during the last two decades.
124. (a) Authouritarian in his approach.
125. (d) An open public debate on budget proposals should be held before introducing the appropriate bill.

For Q. 126 to 130 :

The seven cars can be arranged in a row as follows:

Fiat	Bedfort	Maruti	Ambasador	Fargo	Cardiallac	Marcedes

126. (a) Clearly, Mercedes is exactly at the immediate right of Cadillac.
127. (b) Only the option (b) gives a definitely true statemtent.
128. (d) Clearly, in the above position chart, mercedes is to the immediate right of Cadiallac while Fargo is to the immediate left of it.
129. (a) Only the statement in option (a) is true.
130. (c) As we see above, Fargo, Cadillac and Mercedes are to the right of Ambassador car.
131. (d) As W is to be placed immediately to the left of X, we cannot place X in window 1.

132. (b) Clearly, W must be placed in window no. 2 as dictated by the restrictions.

133. (d) In each subsequent step the element shifts one step CW while a new element appears on its ACW side.

134. (b) In alternate steps a new arrow is added while the existing arrows get inverted in each step.

135. (c) The smaller element shifts one step ACW and goes inside and outside in subsequent steps. The line inside shifts one, two, three......steps in subsequent steps.

136. (a) The element shifts half, one, one and a-half, two, two-and-a-half sides ACW in subsequent steps while it rotates by 135°, 90°, 45°, 0°, – 45° CW in subsequent steps and gets inverted on its base in alternate steps.

137. (c) The whole figure rotates by 135° and 45° ACW alternately. While the two facing arcs shift one and two steps in subsequent steps.

138. (a) It is fact that athletes can attract sponsorship and make money and that participation in the Olympics can aid this process. On the basis that it is true that athletes are more and more attracted by the profit motive the conclusion that the best athletes do not compete in the Olympics is weakened. Therefore, (a) is the appropriate answer. Alternative (b) is an oft-stated maxim, but in this case, it is not relevant to the argument. The fact that people believe that amateur athletes are receiving adequate alternative remuneration does not bear on the argument for allowing genuine professional athletes into the games. So, (c) is inappropriate. Choice (d) comes close to weakening the argument, because if professional (as well as amateur) athletes were allowed to compete, presuming the partticipants were selected on merit, then the best athletes would be seen. However, it has only been a suggestion, perhaps in the part, (in which case it was not adopted) or in the future (in which case its adoption is not certain). Choice (e) represents an opinion that might or might not be held by the writer, but, whether or not the author agrees, it does not weaken the argument; therefore, (e) is inappropriate.

139. (b) The argument represents a fallacy in causality. Absence of cloud cover enables the moon to be seen. And, it is the absence of cloud cover–not a full moon–that causes the ground to cool and produce frost. Answer choice (a) may be a necessary but insufficient condition for frost to occur; that is, there may be an absence of frost even below 10 degrees Celsius. Farmers may be superstitious, but there is nothing in the statement that links superstition with the farmers' conviction (alternative (c). Alternative (d) is inappropriate because, even if true, it could not change the farmers' convictions. Farmers do not have to be experts in meteorology (e) to hold a conviction.

140. (d) Read the third and fourth senteces together.

141. (a) (a) follows from the first two sentences of the paragraph. (b) is absurd. (c) is not hinted at.

142. (c) Statement (a) cannot be deduced from the text. It is an untrue statement: a contraceptive is something that can prevent conception, and the drug discussed here does not prevent conception. Therefore, (a) is an incorrect choice. Statement (b) is also an untrue statement. The drug is reported to block egg implantation, not egg production. There is nothing in the paragraph concerning the drug's effectiveness, side effects, benefits, or dangers as compared to other abortion techniques, so there is no basis from which the reader can deduce or infer that the new drug will replace conventional abortion techniques. So (d) is not appropriate. Although the drug has been manufactured and tested in France, there is no indication that its use will be limited to that country alone, so statement (e) is not valid. The statement in (c) is the only limited statement that can be deduced from the text–that the drug RU486 can be used to unduce abortion, thus terminating pregnancy.

143. (e) Don't go for 1 because it could be correct only if we substitute "in spite of" for "besides".

144. (c) Read the fifth and sixth sentences of the paragraph.

For (Qs. 145 & 146) :

The age wise order is as follows :

Gita > Kusum > Arti > Archana > Suman

145. (b) 146. (c)

147. (d) Look at the data given in the table very cerefully. The highest increase in annual income from 2001 to 2002 is witnessed in Indira's annual income.

148. (c) Required per cent increase

$$= \frac{(2.00 - 1.92)}{1.92} \times 100 = 4.16\%$$

149. (e) Required average annual income (in lacs)

$$= \frac{(1.44 + 1.50 + 1.56 + 1.62 + 1.68 + 1.73)}{6}$$

$$= \frac{9.53}{6} \approx 1.588$$

150. (b) Required per cent

$$= \frac{\dfrac{1.45 + 1.56 + 1.64 + 1.70 + 1.84 + 1.95}{6}}{\dfrac{2.00 + 2.12 + 2.25 + 2.30 + 2.33 + 2.40}{6}} \times 100$$

$$= \frac{1.45 + 1.56 + 1.64 + 1.70 + 1.84 + 1.95}{2.00 + 2.12 + 2.25 + 2.30 + 2.33 + 2.40} \times 100$$

$$= \frac{10.14}{13.4} \times 100 \approx 75.67\%$$

151. (a) Required ratio $= \frac{1.84}{2.80} = 23 : 35$

For (Qs.152-155) : From the first two statements we obtain the following figure:

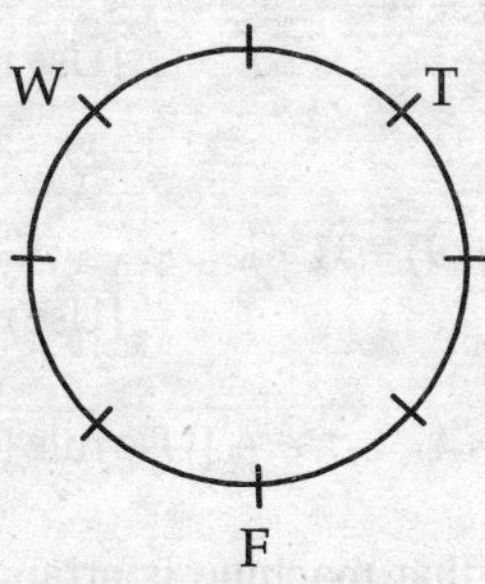

Again J is between W and K. Hence,

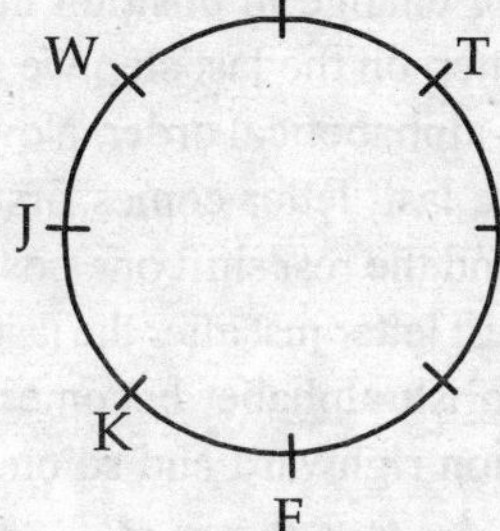

Now, R is third to the right of K. Again, P is not a neighbour of W. So he will occupy the second remaining vacancy while V will be come the neighbour of W. Hence, the final figure will be as follows :

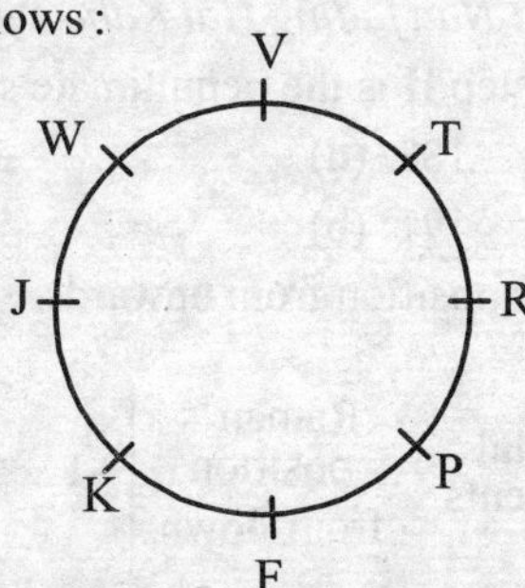

152. (e) T is opposite K. Hence he can be called either fourth to th eleft or fourth to the right.
153. (e)
154. (b)
155. (d)
156. (a) Here, O is the starting point.

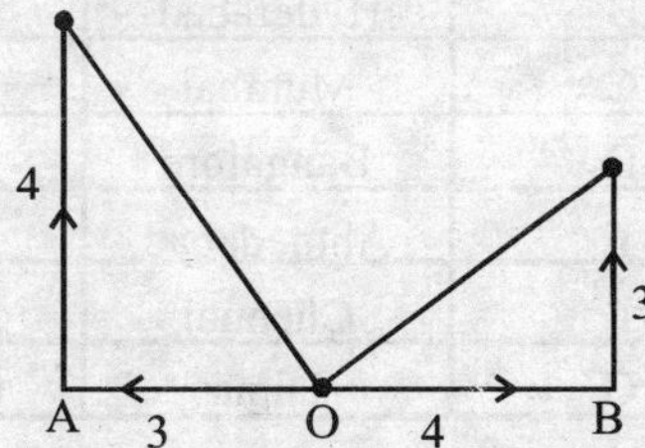

Both A and B are $\sqrt{3^2+4^2}$ = 5 km from the starting point.

157. (b) G finishes at 10:20 and A finishes at 10:40. Hence G would have to wait for 20 minutes.
158. (e) **From I and II:** We get
L > T > F > P
J > P
From I, II and III : We get
L > T > F > P
L > J > P
Hence, 'L' scored the highest.
159. (d) From III : We get

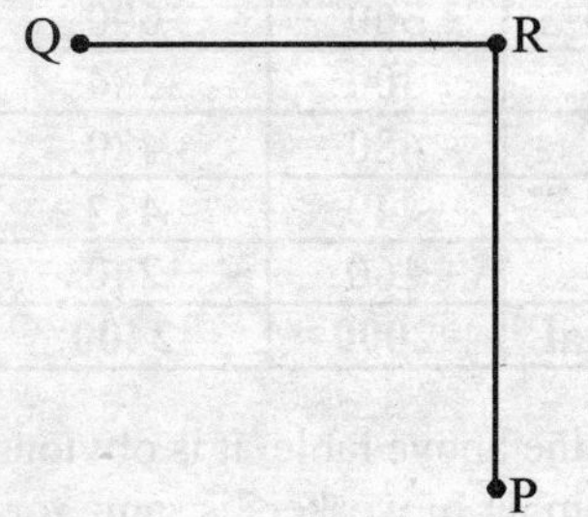

It is obvious from the positions of 'P' and 'Q' that the pillar 'P' is to the North-East of the pillar 'Q'.

160. (b) From II and III : We get
food is adequate ⇒ vo ji fa ...(i)
food is delicious ⇒ fa vo re ...(ii)
From (i) and (ii), we get 'vo fa' is the code of 'food is', hence the code for 'adequate' is 'ji'.
161. (a) Substitute between for among
162 (b) Substitute undergone
163. (b) Substitute detailed
164. (c) Substitute at least
165. (a) Delete no.

For Qs.166-170.

'481' means 'sky is blue' ..... (i)
'246' means 'sea is deep' .... (ii)
'698' means 'sea looks blue' ... (iii)
(i) and (ii) ⇒ '4' means 'is'
(ii) and (iii) ⇒ '6' means 'sea'.
∴ From (ii), '2' means 'deep.'
(i) and (iii) ⇒ '8' means 'blue'.
∴ From (iii), '9' means 'looks'
and from (i) '1' means 'sky'

166. (c) 167. (c) 168. (d) 169. (c) 170. (a)
171. (a) In subsequent steps 5, 4, 3, 2, 1 elements are replaced in a set order.
172. (c) In alternate steps the middle and CW-end elements shift half-a side CW. The ACW-end and the middle elements shift one-and-a-half sides CW while the third one is replaced by a new one. The new element appears alternately on CW and ACW ends.
173. (b) In each step the elements shift half-a-side. CW while a new element is added alternately at CW and ACW ends.
174. (e) In each step the middle element shifts to the opposite side. One of the remaining elements is replaced alternately on CW and ACW ends.
175. (d) In each step a new element appears at lower-right and in the subsequent step it shifts to the centre. The central element shifts alternatively to middle-right and lower-middle.

For (Qs. 176-180)

The data given in the two pie charts can be summarized as follows :

	1998	2000
P	260	264
Q	360	600
R	300	384
S	480	480
T	440	432
U	160	240
Total	**2000**	**2400**

176. (b) From the above table, it is obvious that in category S, the number of workers is same for both the years.

177. (c) % increase in number of workers in category U in 2000

$= \dfrac{240-160}{160} \times 100 = 50\%.$

178. (c) Increase in P = 4
Increase in Q = 240
Increase in R = 84
Increase in S = 0
Increase in U = 80
Total Increase = 408.

179. (d) From the above table, it is obvious that there is a decrease only in category T.

180. (a) The required difference
$=(600+480)-(160+260)=660.$

For (Qs. 181-185) :

Here (a) $x * y \lambda z$ means $9x + y) \times x$
(b) $x \$ y \% z$ means $(x - y) \div z$
(c) $x \# y * z$ means $(y \times z) - x$
(d) $x @ y © z$ means $x + (y \div z)$

181. (a) We have
(i) $(6 \times 7) - 14 = 28 = m$
$\therefore m = 28$ [Use rule (c)]
Now,
(ii) $12 + (28 \div 4) = 19$
$\therefore ? = 19$ [Use rule (d)]

182. (b) We have
(i) $(120-40) \div 8 = 10 = t$ [Use rule (b)]
$\therefore t = 10$
Now,
(ii) $10 + (? \div 5) = 40$
or $? \div 5 = 40 - 10$ [Use rule (d)]
or $? = (40 - 10) \times 5 = 150$

183. (d) We have
(i) $(12 \times 8) - 48 = 48 = b$
$\therefore b = 48$ [Use rule (c)]
Now,
(ii) $(48+8) \times 5$
56×5 [Use rule (a)]
$= 280$

184. (e) We have
(i) $(9+5) \times 15 = 210 = n$ [Use rule (a)]
$\therefore n = 210$
Now,
(ii) $(210-20) \div 8$
$= 190 \div 8$ [Use rule (b)]
$= 23.75$

185. (e) We have
(i) $26 + (45 \div 9) = 31 = k$
$\therefore k = 31$ [Use rule (d)]
Now,
(ii) $(31+14) \times 4$ [Use rule (a)]
$= 180$

186-192. It is clear that machine is arranging the words of the input neither on the basis of no. of letters in each word nor alphabetical nor change in position in a fixed pattern. But after a keen watch on the last step we find that last letter of each word is in alphabetical order. Now, it can be found that the word whose last, letter comes first in English alphabet becomes first and the rest shift one position rightward. Now the word with last letter just after the last letter of the arranged word as in English alphabet becomes second and the rest shift one position righward and so on.

186. (b) **Input :** *Kaho Naa Pyaar Hai is slowly fading.*
Step I: *Naa Kaho Pyaar Hai is slowly fading.*
Step II: *Naa fading Kaho Pyaar Hai is slowly.*
Step III: *Naa fading Hai Kaho Pyaar is slowly.*
Hence, step II is the penultimate step.

187. (d) 188. (d) 189. (c)
190. (a) 191. (b) 192. (d)

193. (c) Raman's position from upwards

$$= \left[\text{Total students} - \text{Raman's position from down} \right] + 1$$

$= [31 - 9] + 1 = 23$rd

194-198:

Professional	City	Profession
A	Bhubaneshwar	Pharmacist
B	Hyderabad	Professor
C	Mumbai	Artist
D	Bangalore	Engineer
E	Ahmedabad	Lawyer
F	Chennai	Doctor
G	Jaipur	Councellor

194. (c) 195. (a)
196. (d) 197. (b)
198. (e)

199. (a) The desired letters are R, T, S and I. The only meaningful word that can be formed from these letters is STIR.

200. (d) As we measure temperature from celsius similaraly from meter we measure Depthness.

SOLVED PAPER
(Based on Memory)
COMMON ENTRANCE TEST

MAHARASHTRA-CET MBA/MMS 21st FEB. 2010

1. The door of Aditya's house faces the East. From the back side of his house, he walks straight 50 meters, then turns to the right and walks 50 metres again. Finally, he turns towards left and stops after walking 25 metres. Now, Aditya is in which direction from the starting point?
(a) South-east (b) North-east
(c) South-west (d) North-west
(e) None of these

2. If it is possible to make a meaningful word with the third, fifth, eighth and tenth letters of the word DISTRIBUTE, which of the following will be the third letter of that word? If no such word can be made, give 'X' as the answer and if more than one such words can be made, give 'M' as the answer.
(a) S (b) R
(c) E (d) X
(e) M

3. If a meaningful word beginning with B can be formed from HACEB, then the fourth letter of that word is your answer. If no such word can be formed, then your answer is (e) i.e., None of these.
(a) A (b) C
(c) E (d) H
(e) None of these

4. In the following question, varius terms of an alphabet series are given with one term missing as shown by (?). Choose the missing terms out of the given alternatives.
ADVENTURE, DVENTURE, DVENTUR, ?, VENTU
(a) DVENT (b) VENTURE
(c) VENTUR (d) DVENTU
(e) None of these

5. In a certain code language, CREATIVE is written as BDSBFUJS. How is TRIANGLE written in that code?
(a) BHSSFKHM (b) BHSSMHHF
(c) BSHSFHKM (d) BSSHFMKH
(e) None of these

6. On a shelf six volumes are placed side-by-side labelled A, B, C, D, E and F. B, C, E, F have green covers while others have yellow covers. A, D, B are new volumes while the rest are old volumes. A, C, B are law reports while the rest are medical exacts. Which two volumes are old medical extracts and have green covers?
(a) B and C (b) C and D
(c) C and E (d) E and F
(e) None of these

7. In the following questions a letter-number series is given with one term missing as shown by (?). Choose the missing term out of the given alternatives.
Q 1 F, S2E, U6D, W21C, ?
(a) Y 44 B (b) Y 66 B
(c) Y 88 B (d) Z 88 B
(e) None of these

Directions (Qs. 8-10) : Read the following data and use it for answering the questions that follow:

Six people A, B, C, D, E and F live on a six storey building, each on one floor. The following statements describe where they stay.
(1) B lives on floor 6.
(2) A is equally far from C and E
(3) F is an engineer.
(4) D is two floors above F.
(5) C does not live next to an engineer.

8. If statement 5 is disregarded, which floor does A stay on?
(a) 5 (b) 4
(c) 3 (d) 1
(e) 6

9. Which of the following is not true?
(a) F is not next to D
(b) C lives between B and D
(c) E lives on floor 2
(d) B is on floor 6
(e) All of the above are correct.

10. If condition 5 is invalid, how many types of arrangements are possible?
(a) 2 (b) 3
(c) 1 (d) 5
(e) None of these

Directions (Q. 11-15) : What approximate value will come in place of the question-mark (?) in the following questions ?

11. $175 \times 28 + 275 \times 27.98 = ?$
(a) 11800 (b) 12600
(c) 12800 (d) 11600
(e) 12200

12. $324.995 \times 15.98 \div 4.002 + 36.88 = ?$
(a) 1300 (b) 1230
(c) 1440 (d) 1380
(e) 1340

13. $1164 \times 128 \div 8.008 + 969.007 = ?$
(a) 18800 (b) 19000
(c) 19600 (d) 19200
(e) 18600

14. $\sqrt{624.98} + \sqrt{729.25} = ?$

(a) 58 (b) 56
(c) 52 (d) 63
(e) 61

15. 69.008% of 699.998 + 32.99% of 399.999 = ?

(a) 615 (b) 645
(c) 675 (d) 715
(e) 725

Directions (16-30) : Read the following passage carefully and answer the questions given below it. Certain words have been printed in bold to help you locate them while answering the questions.

The United States is the main pole of attraction for foreign skilled workers; 40% of its foreign-born adult population have tertiary level education. Since the early 1990s, some 900, 000 highly skilled professionals, mainly IT workers from India, China, Russia and a few OECD countries (including Canada, the UK and Germany) have migrated to the United States under the H1B temporary visa programme. The United States also takes in 32% of all foreign students studying in the OECD countries. Indeed, higher education is an important channel for US firms recruiting highly skilled migrants; some 25% of H1B visa holders in 1999 were previously students enrolled at US universities.

But the United States is not the only magnet. Canada also attracts talent and, despite its modest loss of skilled migrants to the US, is in fact, a net importer of human capital. Skilled migration to Germany and France has been lower in recent history, but these countries have now implemented policies to attract foreign students, researchers and IT workers. In 2000, Germany launched a sort of "green-card" scheme to recruit 20,000 foreign IT specialists and by the end of the following year had recruited half that number, mainly from eastern Europe. In addition, dynamic Asian economies like Singapore are trying to plug shortages in IT workers through immigration from neighbouring Malaysia or even China. Even if the current economic slump has reduced global demand for IT and other specialty workers, foreign talent remains in demand.

The costs and benefits of the brain drain and circulation of talent are hotly debated. International mobility of skilled workers can generate global benefits by improving knowledge flows and **satisfying** the demand for skills. The contribution of foreign skilled workers to economic growth and achievement in host countries, in particular to research, innovation and entrepreneurship, is increasingly recognised-witness the number of foreign-born US Nobel Prize winners or creators of global high-tech companies, such as Intel or eBay, and other successful start-ups. It is important to **distinguish** between emigrants from OECD countries and those from developing countries.

The risk of a brain drain damaging rich countries is arguably lower, but it does exist. Canada may well lose skilled workers to the United States and import skilled human capital from other countries. However, the quality of the two-way flow is **key**, though it is difficult to calculate whether the loss of a top genetics researcher at a public lab can be compensated for by the arrival of even several hundred IT specialists. But as skilled migration between advanced countries is often temporary, there may be a double gain from the circulation of the highly skilled: first from the overseas experience acquired by their genetics researcher, and second from the constant inflow of skilled workers.

In sending countries in the developing world, the challenge is greater. For these countries, **capturing** benefits mostly depends on attracting back skilled emigrants and providing opportunities for them to use their new technological competencies. Returnees also can bring valuable management experience, entrepreneurial skills and access to global networks. They may even bring venture capital. But this is looking on the bright side.

Mostly, the problems caused by the brain drain in poorer sending countries are great. Migrants from developing countries are generally more likely to stay in the host country than migrants from advanced countries. Survey evidence on the share of foreign PhD graduates in science and technology who stay abroad show that 79% of 1990-91 doctoral recipients from India and 88% of those from China were still working in the United States in 1995. In contrast, only 11% of Koreans and 15% of Japanese who earned science and engineering (S&E) doctorates from US universities in 1990-91 were working in the United States in 1995. In the longer term, however, return flows of people and capital may not only offset some **potential** negative effects of international migration but also constitute an economic development strategy in its own right. In Chinese Taipei, for example, half of all the companies emerging from that economy's largest science park, Hsinchu, were started by returnees from the United States. And in China, the Ministry of Science and Technology estimates that returning overseas students started most Internet-based ventures.

The **harsh** reality is that only a handful of countries have been successful in luring their talented emigrés back home. The International Organization for Migration (IOM) estimates that some 300,000 professionals from the African continent live and work in Europe and North America. By some estimates, up to a third of R&D professionals from the developing world are believed to reside in the OECD area. While there are often media reports of successful Indian entrepreneurs in the United States who establish branches or even firms in India only a small number actually return; in 2000, it was estimated that some 1,500 highly qualified Indians returned from the United States, although more than 30 times that number depart each year.

The relative success of Chinese Taipei, Korea and Ireland in fostering return migration has been attributed to the opening of their economies and policies to foster domestic investments in innovation and R&D. Developing countries with some infrastructure in R&D, like India, are more likely to attract the return of migrants, as well as money and business contacts. "Scientific diaspora" and "immigrant entrepreneur networks" can also help sending countries capture benefits and know-how from emigrants overseas. Grass roots initiatives in South Africa and Latin America have been developed to link researchers abroad to networks in their home countries. Indian professionals in the US have been the primary drivers of knowledge and capital flows to India. The Indian government has contributed to the emergence of these private networks through legislative and tax rules that encourage remittances and investment from Indians abroad. The diaspora idea has been put to work by advanced countries too, like Switzerland, whose online network, Swiss-List.com was established to encourage networking among Swiss scientists in the US and to foster contacts with peers in Switzerland.

Governments can do quite a lot to address the causes of the brain drain. Science and technology policies are **key** in this regard. Developing centres of excellence for scientific research and framing the conditions for innovation and hightech entrepreneurship can make a country **attractive** to highly skilled workers, both from within the country and from outside. China has recently launched a project to develop 100 universities into world-class institutions that not only provide higher education training, but also academic employment and research opportunities.

In the OECD, the UK government plans to increase the salaries of post-doctorates by 25% and increase funding for the hiring of university professors. In France, some 7,000 teaching-researcher posts have been created since 1997 to retain talent and encourage the return of post-doctorates working abroad. The European Commission is looking to improve the attractiveness of the European research area and has doubled the amount of funding devoted to human resources in the Sixth Research Framework Programme to € 1.8 billion.

16. Which of the following can be inferred from the passage?
    1. 'Brain drain' should be transformed 'brain bank'
    2. The risk of brain drain damaging only developed countries.
    3. Brain drain in poorer countries are great.

    (a) Only 1 (b) Only 2
    (c) Only 3 (d) 1 and 2 only
    (e) 1 and 3 only

17. Which of the following is/are true in the context of the passage?
    1. OECD countries are also facing skill migration problems.
    2. Skill migration problem only affects developing and transition economics.
    3. The risk of brain drain is real.

    (a) Only 1 (b) Only 2
    (c) Only 3 (d) 2 and 3 only
    (e) All 1, 2 and 3

18. According to the passage, migration from the advance countries
    (1) are generally for stay in the host country
    (2) are only for higher education
    (3) is arguably lower but it does not exist

    (a) Only 1 (b) Only 2
    (c) Only 3 (d) 1 and 3 only
    (e) 2 and 3 only.

19. According to the passage skilled migration between OECD countries
    1. may be a double gain
    2. is more harmful than that of developing countries
    3. is often temporary

    (a) Only 1 (b) Only 2
    (c) Only 3 (d) 1 and 3
    (e) 2 and 3

20. What is the meaning of the term 'OECD' as used in the passage?
    (a) An organisation that encourages trade and economic growth.
    (b) An organisation of economically developed countries
    (c) An organisation of excellence and developed countries
    (d) An organisation of talented emigres countries.
    (e) None of these

21. Which of the following statements is/are true in the context of the passage?
    1. Higher education is an important channel for US firms recruiting highly skilled migrants.
    2. In 2000, Germany launched a sort of green-card scheme to recruit 20,000 foreign IT specialists
    3. Only 33% of R&D Professionals from the developing word are believed to reside in the OECD area.

    (a) Only 1 (b) Only 2
    (c) Only 3 (d) 1 and 3
    (e) All 1, 2 and 3

22. According to passage, which of the following encourage(s) in growth of skilled migration ?
    1. Higher salaries
    2. Developed science and technology and R&D unit.
    3. Academic employment and research opportunities.

    (a) Only 1 (b) Only 2
    (c) Only 3 (d) 2 and 3 only
    (e) All 1, 2 and 3

23. Select the most appropriate title among the options given below:
    (a) Brain drain : old myth, new realities
    (b) Global skilled workers
    (c) Brain drain : winners and losers
    (d) Brain drain : what government can do
    (e) The risk of brain drain

Directions (Qs. 24 - 27) : Choose the word/group of words which is most nearly the SAME in meaning as the word given in bold in the passage.

24. POTENTIAL
(a) Possible (b) Promise
(c) Capability (d) Capacity
(e) Undeveloped

25. CAPTURING
(a) Arrest (b) Invade
(c) Attract (d) Encapsulate
(e) Seize

26. HARSH
(a) Barbarous (b) Unfriendly
(c) Brassy (d) Rough
(e) Brutal

27. DISTINGUISH
(a) Separate (b) Perceive
(c) Distinction (d) Discriminate
(e) Set apart

Directions (Qs. 28-30) : Choose the word which is most OPPOSITE in meaning of the word given in bold as given in the passage.

28. KEY
(a) Peripheral (b) Basis
(c) Centre (d) Foundation
(e) Clue

29. ATTRACTIVE
(a) Ugly (b) Uninviling
(c) Appealing (d) Delightful
(e) Repulsion

30. SATISFYING
(a) Completion (b) Unavailable
(c) Discounted (d) Enjoyable
(e) Rewarding

Directions (Qs. 31-35) : Read the following passage carefully and answer the questions given below it:

A, B, C, D, E, F, G and H are sitting around a circular table, facing the centre. A sits third to the left of C and second to the right of E. B sits second to the right of D who is not an immediate neighbour of E. H sits second to the left of F, G is not an immediate neighbour of D.

31. Which of the following pairs has only one person sitting between them, if the counting is done in clockwise direction?
(a) F, G (b) H, G
(c) H, C (d) H, B
(e) None of these

32. Who sits third to the right of E?
(a) D (b) G
(c) F (d) B
(e) None of these

33. What is the position of G with respect to A's position?
(a) Immediately to the right
(b) Second to the left
(c) Third to the right
(d) Third to the left
(e) Fourth to the right

34. Who sits between E and A?
(a) F (b) D
(c) G (d) B
(e) None of these

35. Starting from A's position, if all the eight are arranged in alphabetical order in clockwise direction, the sitting position of how many members (excluding A) would remain unchanged?
(a) None (b) One
(c) Two (d) Three
(e) Four

Directions (Qs. 36-40) : In each of the following question, in four out of the five figures, element I is related to element II in the same particular way. Find out the figure in which the element I is not so related to element II.

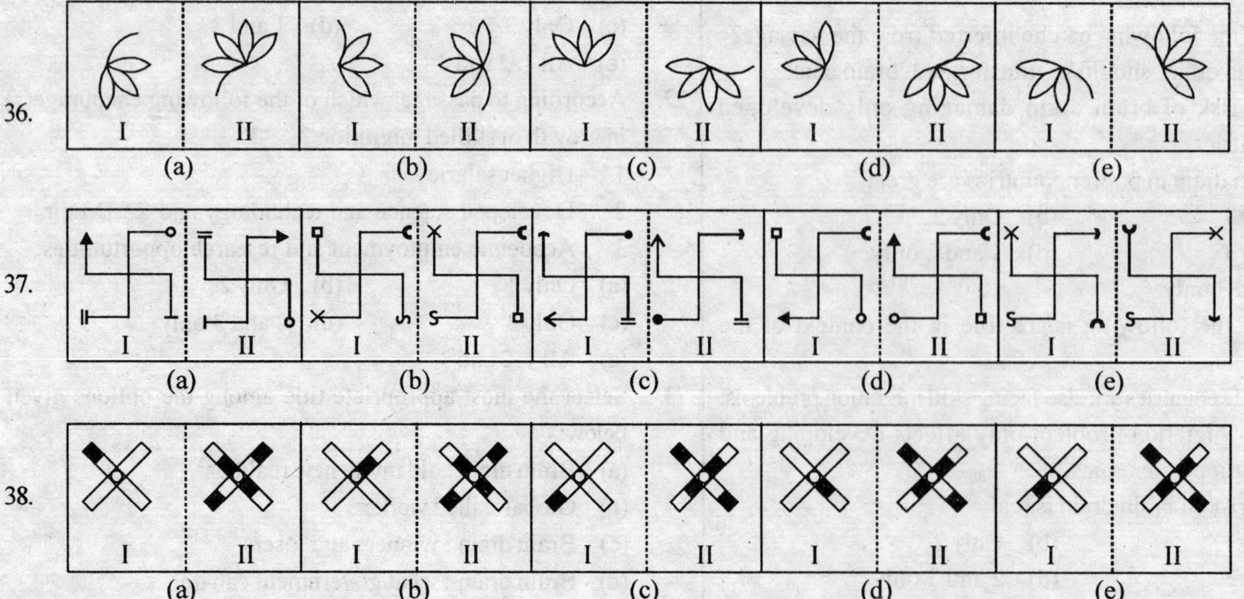

39.
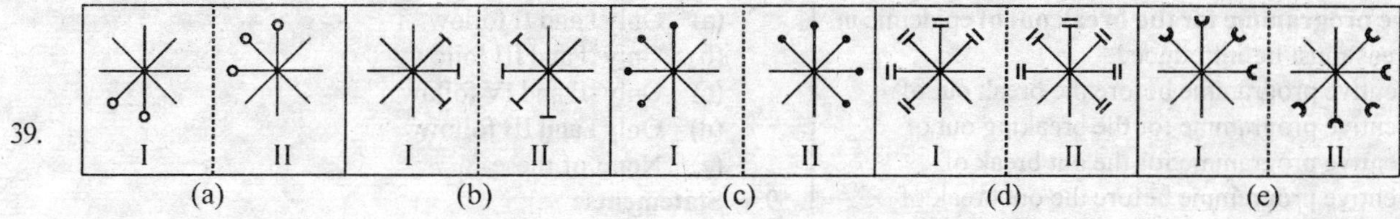

40.
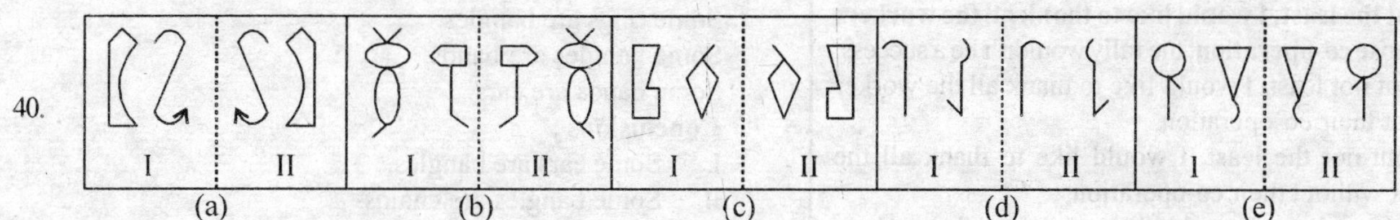

Directions (Q. 41-45) : What approximate value will come in place of the question-mark (?) in the following questions ? (You are not expected to calculate the exact value.)

41. $(35.95)^2 - (24.001)^2 = ?$
(a) 680 (b) 700
(c) 720 (d) 740
(e) 730

42. 75% of 230 – ? = 64% of 249
(a) 14 (b) 17
(c) 22 (d) 18
(e) 20

43. $(24.99)^2 + (31.05)^2 = (?)^2$
(a) 45 (b) 36
(c) 32 (d) 30
(e) 40

44. $367.85 \div 22.95 \times 14.99 = ?$
(a) 280 (b) 240
(c) 260 (d) 220
(e) 290

45. $5687.285 + 4872.35 \div 12 = ?$
(a) 5995 (b) 5905
(c) 6025 (d) 6095
(e) 6295

Directions (Qs. 46-50) : In each of the following questions, there are seven figures, the first and last of which are unnumbered and the remaining are numbered as (a), (b), (c), (d) and (e). These seven figures form a series. However, one of the five numbered figures does not fit into the series. The number of that figure is the answer.

46.
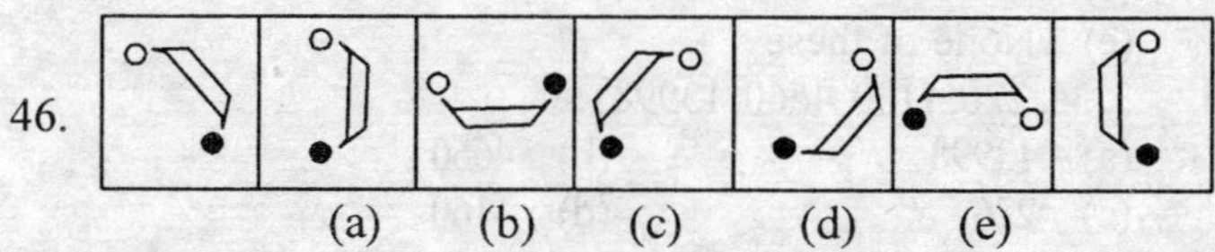

47.
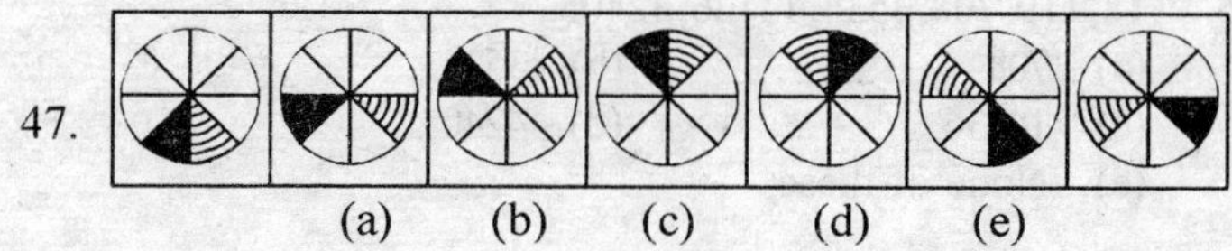

48.
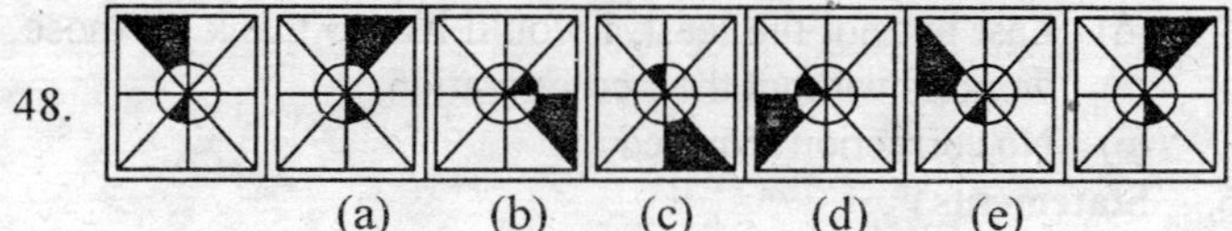

49.
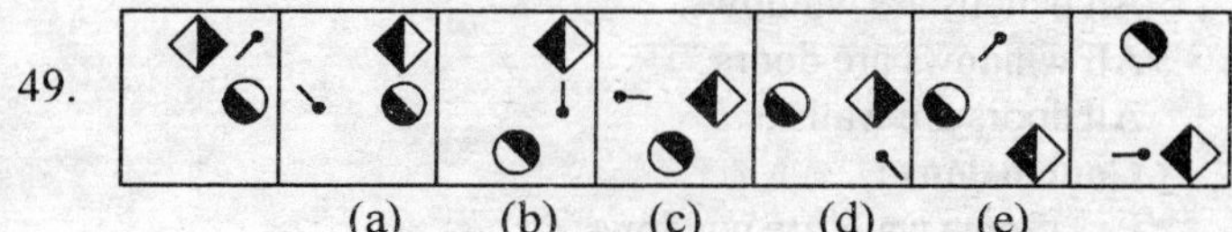

50.
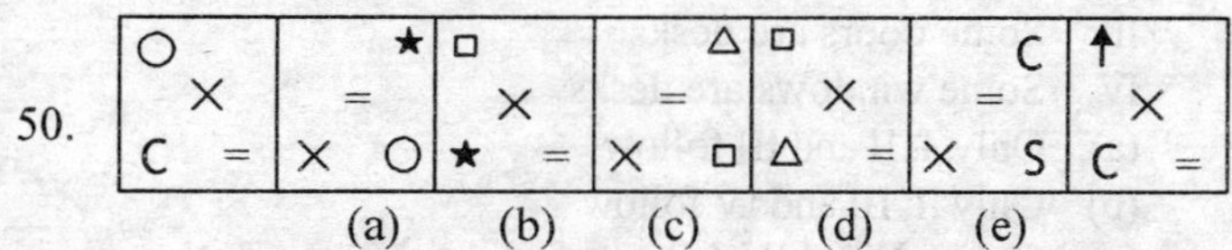

Directions (Qs. 51-55) : Read each of the following sentences, some part of the whole sentence is given bold. Below each sentence is given five ways of phrasing the bold given part. Select the answer from among the choices which produces the most effective sentence, one that is clear and exact. If there is no error in the bold given part (e) is the answer.

51. That was the record that **make me sit up and take notice** of Neil Hannon.
(a) made me sit up and take notice
(b) had made me sit up and take notice
(c) has made me sit up and take notice
(d) sit up and take notice
(e) No correction required

52. mistakes that **catch up with** him when he ran for President.
(a) caught up in (b) caught up with
(c) caught up on (d) caught up at
(e) No correction required

53. When I told her about breaking the window, **she goes through the roof**.
(a) she went through the roof
(b) she went via the roof
(c) she went through roof
(d) she went with roof
(e) No correction required

54. **A preventive programme for the break out of** epidemic in quake-hit areas must be introduced.
(a) A preventive programme before the break out of
(b) A preventive programme for the breaking out of
(c) A preventive programme for the out break of
(d) A preventive programme before the out break of
(e) No correction required

55. **Last but not the least, I would like to thank all the workers without whose co-operation,** the rally wouldn't be a success.
(a) Last but not least, I would like to thank all the worker without their co-operation.
(b) Last but not the least, I would like to thank all the worker without their co-operation,
(c) Last but not least, I would like to thank all the workers without whose co-operation,
(d) Last but not the least, I would like to thank all those workers without their co-operation,
(e) No correction required

56. **Statements :**
All desks are pencils.
All pencils are windows.
All windows are doors.
All doors are walls.
Conclusions :
I. Some walls are windows
II. All desks are doors
III. Some doors are desks
IV. Some windows are desks
(a) Only, I, II and III follow
(b) Only II, III and IV follow
(c) Only I, II and IV follow
(d) Only I, II and IV follow
(e) None of these

57. **Statements :**
Some boxes are tablets.
Some tablets are toys.
All toys are jungles.
Some jungles are trees.
Conclusions :
I. Some trees are tablets.
II. Some tablets are jungles.
III. Some jungles are toys.
IV. Some toys are boxes.
(a) None follows
(b) Only I follows
(c) Only II follows
(d) Only II and III follow
(e) Only IV follows

58. **Statements :**
All blades are trains.
Some trains are rods.
All rods are papers.
Some papers are windows.
Conclusions :
I. Some windows are blades.
II. Some papers are trains.
III. Some trains are blades.
IV. Some papers are blades.
(a) Only I and II follow
(b) Only II and III follow
(c) Only III and IV follow
(d) Only I and III follow
(e) None of these

59. **Statements :**
Some chains are rings.
Some rings are bangles.
Some bangles are hands.
Some hands are ears.
Conclusions :
I. Some ears are bangles.
II. Some bangles are chains.
III. Some hands are rings.
IV. No chain is bangle.
(a) None follows
(b) Only II follows
(c) Only IV follows
(d) Only either II or IV follows
(e) Only III follows

60. **Statements :**
All books are cards.
Some cards are benches.
All benches are chairs.
Some chairs are tables.
Conclusions :
I. Some chairs are cards.
II. Some tables are chairs.
III. Some cards are books.
IV. Some chairs are benches.
(a) Only II, III and IV follow
(b) Only I, II and III follow
(c) Only I, III and IV follow
(d) All follow
(e) None of these

Directions (Qs. 61–65) : In the following number series only one number is Wrong. Find out the Wrong number.

61. 1, 4, 27, 256, 3125, 46658
(a) 46658 (b) 4
(c) 27 (d) 3125
(e) None of these

62. 18000, 3600, 720, 142.2, 28.8, 5.76
(a) 28.8 (b) 3600
(c) 5.76 (d) 142.2
(e) None of these

63. 12, 237, 406, 527, 604, 657
(a) 237 (b) 406
(c) 527 (d) 657
(e) None of these

64. 3, 35, 226, 1160, 4660, 13998
(a) 13998 (b) 4660
(c) 226 (d) 1160
(e) None of these

65. 18, 119, 708, 3534, 14136, 42405
(a) 708 (b) 3534
(c) 14136 (d) 42405
(e) None of these

Directions (Qs. 66-75) : In each of the following questions, there is a set of four figures labelled A, B, C and D called the Problem Set followed by a set of five other figures labelled (a), (b), (c), (d) and (e) called the Answer Set. One figure of problem set contains a question mark. Select a suitable figure from the Answer Set which will substitute this question mark so that a series is formed by the figures A, B, C and D taken in order. The number of the selected figure is the answer.

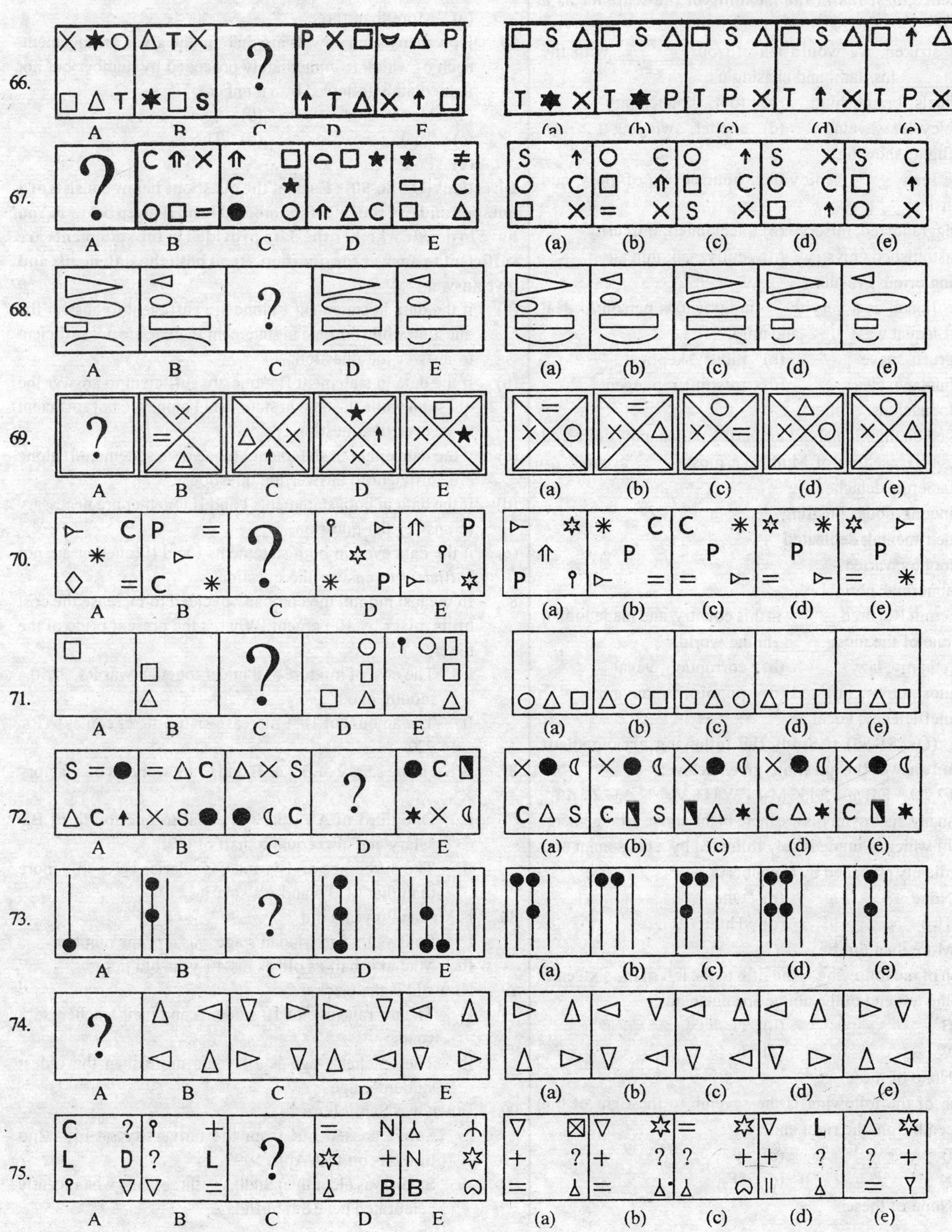

Directions (Q. 76-80) : Each of the sentences below has one or more blank spaces. Each blank indicating that a word has been omitted. Beneath each sentence five words or set of words are given. Choose the one word or set of words, which, when inserted in the sentence, best fits in the meaning of the sentence as a whole.

76. Panic striken, we would take to our ______, with the mali______ his lathi and chasing us.
(a) heels; brandishing (b) foot; threatening
(c) bicycle; waveing (d) shelter; swinging
(e) flight; showing

77. I have seen______, enjoy their hour or two of glory, and vanish into______.
(a) aggrandized; misery (b) acclaimed; obscurity
(c) astonished; mystry (d) enlivened; thin air
(e) inglorious; vacuum

78. While Jinnah as a very______and taciturn person to deal with, Liaquat was______and mild.
(a) gruff; suave (b) pious; skeptical
(c) humane; clear (d) trustful; repungent
(e) loquacious; explicit

79. I walked on thinking about his earthy philosophy, delivered in the______setting of Mumbai's most______avenue.
(a) baneful; detached
(b) incongruous; bustling
(c) detrimental; dedicated
(d) motley; varied
(e) abnormal; normal

80. The permit Raj bred______in this country, and made Indian state one of the most______in the world.
(a) lethargy; lazy (b) corruption; venal
(c) mosquitoes; infested (d) jingoism; chauvinist
(e) inefficiency; vocal

Directions (Qs. 81-85) : Study the following arrangement carefully and answer the questions given below :

R % E 5 D 2 # 9 A F B @ J 3 I K M 4 1 W U 8 V © N ★ G Z δ 6 7

81. How many such symbols are there in the above arrangement, each of which is immediately followed by a consonant and immediately preceded by a number?
(a) None (b) One
(c) Two (d) Three
(e) More than three

82. Which of the following is the fifth to the left of the sixteenth from the left end of the above arrangement?
(a) B (b) U
(c) W (d) N
(e) None of these

83. Which of the following is the seventh to the right of the fourteenth from the right end?
(a) B (b) #
(c) N (d) U
(e) None of these

84. How many such consonant are there in the above arrangement, each of which is immediately preceded by a number and immediately followed by a letter?
(a) None (b) One
(c) Two (d) Three
(e) More than three

85. How many such vowels are there in the given arrangement, each of which is immediately proceded by number but not immediately followed by a number?
(a) None (b) One
(c) Two (d) Three
(e) Four

Directions (Qs. 86-90) : Each of the questions below consists of a question and two statements numbered I and II given below it. You have to decide whether the data provided in the statements are sufficient to answer the question. Read both the statements and give answer

(a) if the data in statement I alone are sufficient to answer the question while the data in statement II alone are not sufficient to answer the question.
(b) if the data in statement II alone are sufficient to answer the question while the data in statement I alone are not sufficient to answer the question.
(c) if the data either in statement I alone or in statement II alone are sufficient to answer the question.
(d) if the data in both statements I and II together are necessary to answer the question.
(e) if the data even in both statements I and II together are not sufficient to answer the question.

86. In the last month, the company decided to increase the cost of its mixer by 10 percent. What is the present price of the mixer?
I. The cost of mixture and juicer together was Rs. 2850 a month ago.
II. The amount of 10% increase on the mixer comes to Rs. 220.

87. What is the salary of B ? A, B and C are workers of a factory X.
I. One third of A's salary is equal to one-fourth of B's salary and also equal to half of C's.
II. The difference of B's and C's salaries is Rs. 400 more than that of B's and A's salaries.

88. Is Madan 20 years old ?
I. Four years ago Madan's age was a prime number.
II. Madan is half as old as his 46-year-old father.

89. How old is the teacher ?
I. The average age of 10 students and their teacher is 25 years.
II. The teacher's age is 10 years more than the oldest student's age.

90. When was Samir born ?
I. Samir passed out from the university on his 22nd birthday on 16th April 1999.
II. Samir was elder than Sudha by three years who recently celebrated her 18th birthday.

Directions (Q. 91-95) : Rearrange the following six sentences (1), (2), (3), (4), (5) and (6) in the proper sequence to form a meaningful paragraph, then answer the questions given below them.

(1) It gives peace of mind that counters stress well.
(2) It was there before and it is there now.
(3) This can be achieved through meditation.
(4) Stress is definitely present in everybody's life.
(5) And, it is very likely, that it will be there in future, too.
(6) In such a situation, what best we can do is control the stress.

91. Which of the following would be the FIRST statement after rearrangement ?
(a) 1 (b) 2
(c) 3 (d) 4
(e) 5

92. Which of the following would be the LAST (SIXTH) statement after rearrangement ?
(a) 1 (b) 2
(c) 3 (d) 4
(e) 5

93. Which of the following would be the SECOND statement after rearrangement ?
(a) 1 (b) 2
(c) 3 (d) 4
(e) 5

94. Which of the following would be the FOURTH statement after rearrangement ?
(a) 1 (b) 2
(c) 3 (d) 4
(e) 6

95. Which of the following would be the FIFTH statement after rearrangement ?
(a) 1 (b) 2
(c) 3 (d) 4
(e) 5

Directions (Qs. 96-100) : In each question below is given a letter group followed by four combinations of digits/ symbols lettered (a), (b), (c) and (d). You have to find out which of the combination correctly represents the group of letters based of the following coding system and the conditions that follow and mark the letter of the combination as your answer. If none of the combinations correctly represents the group of letters, mark (e) i.e., 'None of these' as your answer.

Letter :	P	M	A	D	E	J	I	T	Q	U	O	F	H	W	B
Digit/ Symbol :	6	$	7	1	%	2	δ	8	3	©	4	@	9	5	★

Conditions :

(i) If the first letter is a consonant and the last letter is a vowel, their codes are to be interchanged.

(ii) If the first letter is a vowel and the last letter is a consonant, both are to be coded as the code for the last letter.

(iii) If both the first and the last letters are consonants, both are to be coded as '#'

96. OHBWDFT
(a) 89★51@4 (b) 49★51@8
(c) 89★51@8 (d) 49★51@4
(e) None of these

97. AHBWMPE
(a) 79★5$6% (b) 79★5$67
(c) #9★5$6# (d) %9★5$67
(e) None of these

98. FEPWBUH
(a) @%65★©9 (b) #%65★©#
(c) 9%65★©@ (d) 9%65★©9
(e) None of these

99. HOPDAMI
(a) 94617$9 (b) δ4617$δ
(c) 94617$δ (d) δ4671$9
(e) None of these

100. UAQFJPE
(a) ©73@26% (b) %73@26©
(c) %73@26% (d) ©73@26©
(e) None of these

Directions (Qs. 101-105) : Study the following information carefully and answer the given questions :

A word and number arrangement machine when given an input line of words and numbers rearranges them following a particular rule in each step. The following is an illustration of input and rearrangement.

Input : 51 pour 32 start now 23 46 house
Step I : 23 51 pour 32 start now 46 house
Step II : 23 start 51 pour 32 now 46 house
Step III : 23 start 32 51 pour now 46 house
Step IV : 23 start 32 pour 51 now 46 house
Step V : 23 start 32 pour 46 51 now house
Step VI : 23 start 32 pour 46 now 51 house
and VI is the last step of the rearrangement.

As per the rules followed in the above steps, find out in each of the following questions the appropriate step for the given input.

101. **Step II of an input is :**
18 task bear cold dish 81 63 31
How many more steps will be required to complete the rearrangement?
(a) Three (b) Four
(c) Five (d) Six
(e) None of these

102. **Input :**
72 59 37 go for picnic 24 journey
How many steps will take to complete the rearrangement?
(a) Three (b) Four
(c) Five (d) Six
(e) None of these

103. **Input :**
nice flower 34 12 costly height 41 56
Which of the following will be step III?
(a) 12 nice 34 height flower costly 41 56
(b) 12 nice 34 height 41 flower costly 56
(c) 12 nice 34 flower costly height 41 56
(d) 12 nice flower 34 costly height 41 56
(e) None of these

104. **Step II of an inputs is**
16 victory 19 36 53 store lake town
Which of the following will be step V?
(a) 16 victory 19 town store 36 53 lake
(b) 16 victory 19 town 36 store 53 lake
(c) 16 victory 19 town 36 53 store lake
(d) There will be no such step
(e) None of these

105. **Input :**
milk pot 18 24 over goal 36 53
Which of the following steps will be the last but one ?
(a) VI (b) V
(c) VII (d) VIII
(e) None of these

106. A train 108 m long moving at a speed of 50 km/hr crosses a train 112 m long coming from the opposite direction in 6 seconds. The speed of the second train is
(a) 48 km/hr (b) 54 km/hr
(c) 66 km/hr (d) 82 km/hr
(e) None of these

107. Two numbers are in the ratio 5 : 4 and their difference is 10. What is the larger number ?
(a) 30 (b) 40
(c) 50 (d) 60
(e) None of these

108. A finance company declares that, at a certain compound interest rate, a sum of money deposited by anyone will become 8 times in three years. If the same amount is deposited at the same compound rate of interest, then in how many year will it become 16 times ?
(a) 5 years (b) 4 years
(c) 6 years (d) 7 years
(e) None of these

109. The age of a man is 3 times that of his son. 15 years ago, the man was 9 times as old his son. What will be the age of the man after 15 years?
(a) 45 years (b) 60 years
(c) 75 years (d) 65 years
(e) None of these

110. Ten different letters of an alphabet are given. Words with 5 letters are formed from these given letters. Then the number of words which have at least one letter repeated is :
(a) 69760 (b) 30240
(c) 99748 (d) 45100
(e) None of these

Directions (Qs. 111-120) : In each of the questions given below which one of the five answer figures on the right should come after the problem figures on the left, if the sequence were continued?

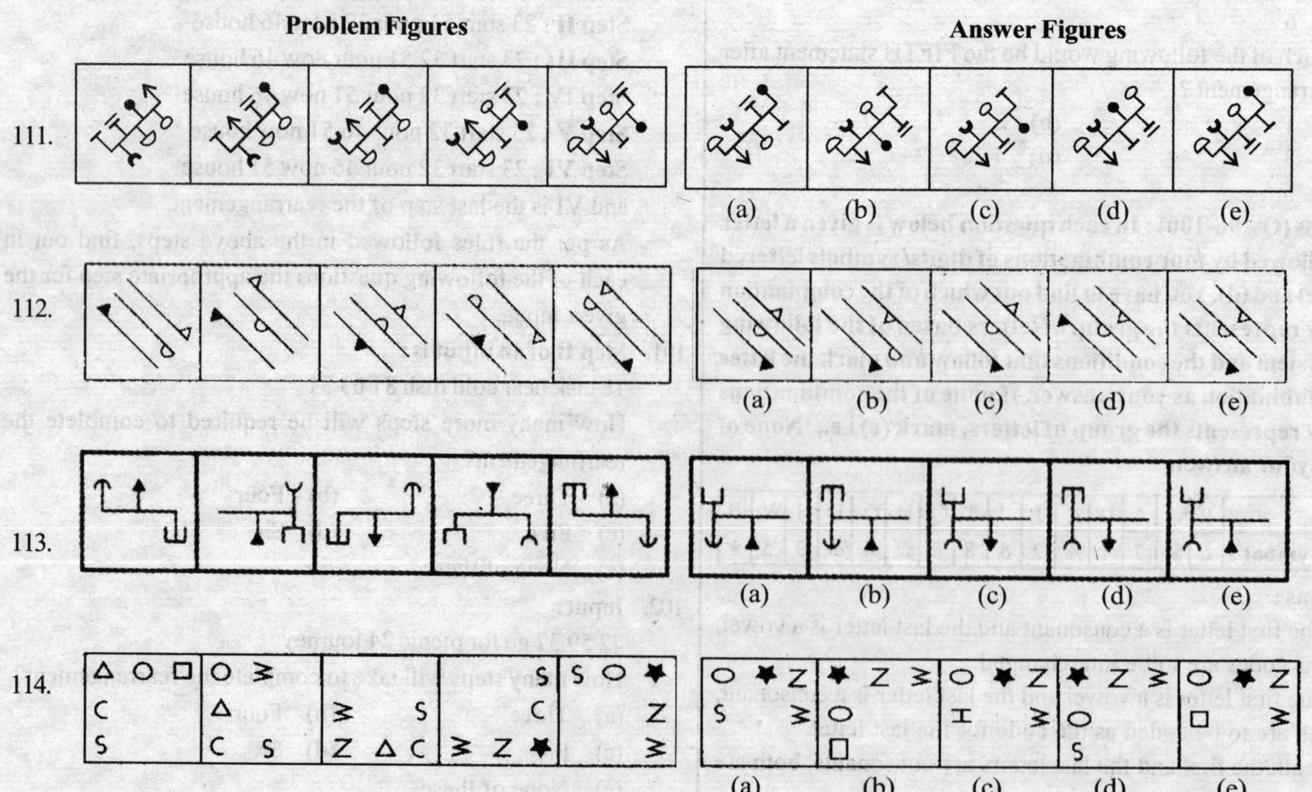

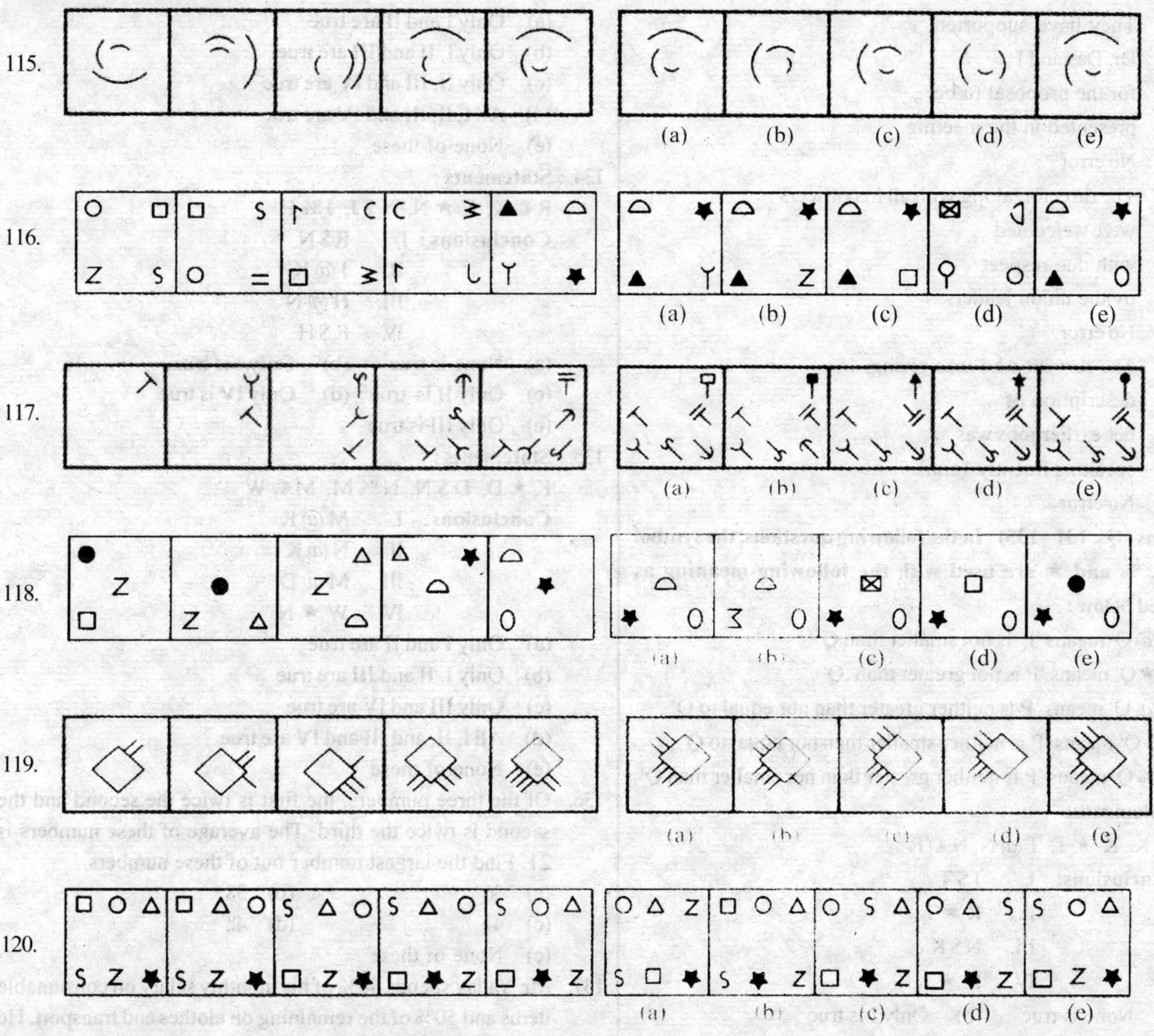

Directions (Q. 121-130) : Read each sentence to find out whether there is any grammatical error in it. The error if any will be in one part of the sentence, the number of that part will be the answer. If there is no error, mark (E), as the answer. (Ignore errors of punctuation, if any.)

121. (a) The recent election campaign
(b) has been one of
(c) the most noisiest campaigns in
(d) the last decade (e) No error

122. (a) Inspite of the best governmental efforts
(b) emission of greenhouse gases
(c) and noxious chemicals
(d) remain a cause of worry
(e) No error

123. (a) The rate of metabolism of
(b) a body is comparatively lowest when
(c) it is at rest and is
(d) thus optimum for examination.
(e) No error

124. (a) The recently imposed dress code
(b) in the university has enraged
(c) the student who will be going
(d) on strike since tomorrow.
(e) No error

125. (a) Changed social setting
(b) demands the schools to teach
(c) moral and social values
(d) among with the academic skills.
(e) No error

126. (a) He slipped on
(b) the break-even floor
(c) and looked around
(d) for support.
(e) No error

127. (a) You cannot force me
(b) to do all your jobs
(c) unless you do not
(d) give advance notice.
(e) No error

128. (a) They have supported
(b) Dr. Das and I
(c) for the proposal to be
(d) presented in the meeting.
(e) No error

129. (a) The director, along with all his officers
(b) were welcomed
(c) with due respect
(d) by the union leaders.
(e) No error

130. (a) The servant who was giving
(b) description of
(c) her earlier jobs was
(d) speaking fluently Tamil.
(e) No error

Directions (Qs. 131 –135) : In the following questions, the symbol @, ©, $, % and ★ are used with the following meaning as illustrated below :

'P @ Q' means 'P is not smaller than Q'.

'P ★Q' means 'P is not greater than Q'.

'P @ Q' means 'P is neither greater than nor equal to Q'.

'P $ Q' means 'P is neither smaller than nor equal to Q'.

'P % Q' means 'P is neither greater than nor smaller than Q'.

131. **Statements :**
J $ K, K ★ T, T @ N, N © R
Conclusions: I. J $ T
II. R ★ T
III. N $ K
IV. R ★ K
(a) None is true (b) Only I is true
(c) Only II is true (d) Only III is true
(e) Only IV is true

132. **Statements :**
F % W, W © R, R @ M, M $ D
Conclusions: I. D @ R
II. M $ F
III. R @ D
IV. R ★ F
(a) None is true (b) Only I is true
(c) Only II is true (d) Only IV is true
(e) Only III is true

133. **Statements :**
H @ B, B ★ E, V © E, W $ V
Conclusions: I. W $ E
II. H @ E
III. H @ V
IV. W $ B
(a) Only I and II are true
(b) Only I, II and III are true
(c) Only II, III and IV are true
(d) All I, II, III and IV are true
(e) None of these

134. **Statements :**
R © K, K ★ N, N $ J, J % H
Conclusions : I. R $ N
II. J @ K
III. H @ N
IV. R $ H
(a) None is true (b) Only I is true
(c) Only II is true (d) Only IV is true
(e) Only III is true

135. **Statements :**
K ★ D, D $ N, N % M, M © W
Conclusions: I. M @ K
II. N @ K
III. M @ D
IV. W ★ N
(a) Only I and II are true
(b) Only I, II and III are true
(c) Only III and IV are true
(d) All I, II, and III and IV are true
(e) None of these

136. Of the three numbers, the first is twice the second and the second is twice the third. The average of these numbers is 21. Find the largest number out of these numbers.
(a) 36 (b) 38
(c) 47 (d) 48
(e) None of these

137. Mr. Yadav spends 60% of his monthly salary on consumable items and 50% of the remaining on clothes and transport. He saves the remaining amount. If his savings at the end of the year were Rs 48,456, how much amount per month would he have spent on clothes and transport ?
(a) Rs 8,076 (b) Rs 4,038
(c) Rs 9691.20 (d) Rs 4845.60
(e) None of these

138. Two numbers are in the ratio 2 : 3. If eight is added to both the numbers, then the ratio becomes 3 : 4. The numbers are:
(a) 15 and 20 (b) 16 and 24
(c) 13 and 17 (d) 17 and 9
(e) None of these

139. A trader marks his goods at such a price that he can deduct 15% for cash and yet make 20% profit. Find the marked price of an item which costs him Rs 90 :
(a) Rs $135\frac{11}{13}$ (b) Rs $105\frac{3}{21}$
(c) Rs $127\frac{1}{17}$ (d) Rs $95\frac{1}{21}$
(e) None of these

140. The ratio between the circumference and area of a circle of radius 5 cm. is

(a) 2:5 (b) 2:25
(c) 1:5 (d) 5:2
(e) None of these

Directions : (Qs. 141-150) Read the following information carefully and answer the questions given below.

Following are the conditions for admitting students in an MBA college :

The student must

(i) have secured at least 80 per cent aggregate marks in XII Std. in Commerce stream or B.Com degree .

(ii) have secured an average of at least 90 per cent marks in Accounts, Business Studies and Economics in XII Std. Exam.

(iii) pay Rs. 1,20,000 at the time of admission.

(iv) be at least 17 years old as on 1st September, 2002.

However, in the case of a candidate who fulfils all the criteria EXCEPT

(A) at (ii) above, completed Cost Accountancy or Chartered Accountancy then refer to Dean.

(B) at (iii) above, but can pay at least Rs. 1,00,000, at the time of admission and the rest amount within 6 months be referred to the Chairman, Admission.

Based on the above criteria and information provided below, make a decision in each case. You are not to assume anything. If the data given are not enough to take a decision mark your answer as 'data inadequate'. These cases are given to you as on 1.9.2002. Give answer.

(a) if the student is not to be admitted.
(b) if the student is to be admitted.
(c) if the case is to be referred to the Dean.
(d) if the case is to be referred to the Chairman, Admission.
(e) if the data are inadequate to take decision.

141. Anup Shrivastava has passed XII Std. Exam in Commerce stream with 95 per cent aggregate marks. He was born on December 2, 1984. He has secured 90 per cent average marks in Accounts, Business Studies and Economics. He can pay Rs. 1,20,000 at the time of admission.

142. Sudha Malhotra has secured an average of 95 per cent marks in Accounts, Business Studies and Economics. She has secured 75 per cent aggregate marks in XII Std. Exam in Commerce stream. She can pay Rs. 1,20,000 at the time of admission. She is 18 years old.

143. Ashok Khera has secured 80 per cent marks in B.Com degree. He can pay Rs. 1,00,000 at the time of admission and rest amount within 6 months. He has secured 90 per cent average marks in Accounts, Business Studies and Economics.

144. Usha Nadkarni was 16 years old as on January 5, 2000. She can pay Rs. 1,20,000 at the time of admission. She has secured 80 per cent average marks in Accounts, Business Studies and Economics. She has completed Cost Accountancy.

145. Vibha Gadre has secured 90 per cent aggregate marks in XII Std. Exam in Commerce stream and 95 per cent average marks in Accounts, Business Studies and Economics. She was born on April 25, 1984. She can pay Rs. 1,00,000 at the time of admission.

146. Arun Sharma was born on August 17, 1983. He can pay Rs. 1,20,000 at the time of admission. He has secured 85 per cent aggregate marks in XII Std. Exam in Commerce stream and also 85 per cent average marks in Accounts, Business Studies and Economics.

147. Vimal Kar has secured 75 per cent aggregate marks in XII Std. Exam in Commerce stream and 80 percent marks in B.Com degree. He can pay Rs. 1,10,000 at the time of admission. He was born on April 12, 1984. He has secured 92 per cent average marks in Accounts, Business Studies and Economics.

148. Anand Upadhyaya was born on September 20, 1984. He has secured 92 per cent aggregate marks in XII Std. Exam in Commerce stream and also 92 per cent average marks in Accounts, Business Studies and Economics. He can pay Rs. 1,1,20,000 at the time of admission.

149. Usha Khanna has secured 90 per cent aggregate marks in XII Std. Exam in Commerce stream. She has secured 95 per cent average marks in Accounts, Business Studies and Economics. She can pay Rs. 1,20,000 at the time of admission. She was born on February 20, 1983.

150. Karan Thapar was born on July 15, 1982. He can pay Rs. 1,20,000 at the time of admission. He has secured 89 per cent average marks in Accounts, Business Studies and Economics. He has completed Chartered Accountancy.

Directions (151-160) : In the following passage, there are blanks. Each of which has been numbered. These numbers are printed below the passage and against each, five words are suggested, one of which fit the blank appropriately. Find out the appropriate word in each case.

Rising seas, caused by global warming, have for the first time washed an inhabited island off the face of the Earth. The __151__ of Lohachara island, in India's part of the Sundarbans where the Ganges and the Brahmaputra rivers empty into the Bay of Bengal, marks the __152__ when one of the most __153__ predictions of environmentalists and climate scientists has started coming true.

Current sea level rise projections could be underestimating the impact of human-induced climate change on the world's oceans, scientists suggest. By __154__ surface temperatures against sea level rise, the team found that levels could rise by 59% more than current __155__.

Geologists have discovered underwater deposits of hydrates icy deposits of frozen methane gas at far __156__ depths under the ocean floor than expected. The finding suggests that, in a globally __157__ world, the hydrates could __158__ suddenly and release their gas into the atmosphere, thus __159__ the planet even more.

World sea level keep __160__ for more than 1,000 years even if government manage to slow a projected surge in temperatures this century blamed on greenhouse gases, a draft U.N. climate report says.

151. (a) obliteration (b) eradication
     (c) effect (d) destroy
     (e) efface
152. (a) instant (b) moment
     (c) importance (d) significance
     (e) concern
153. (a) unrepentant (b) penitent
     (c) apologetic (d) sorry
     (e) contrite
154. (a) planning (b) schemering
     (c) plotting (d) conspiring
     (e) raising
155. (a) record (b) forecast
     (c) level (d) estimate
     (e) key
156. (a) shallower (b) superficial
     (c) empty (d) profound
     (e) deep
157. (a) chilled (b) cooled
     (c) heated (d) sunny
     (e) warmed
158. (a) melt (b) affect
     (c) defrost (d) dissolve
     (e) fade
159. (a) heating (b) cooling
     (c) melting (d) warming
     (e) raising
160. (a) sensitive (b) rising
     (c) constant (d) decreasing
     (e) affecting

Directions (Qs. 161-165) : A statment is given followed by three courses of action. A course of action is taken for improvement, follow-up etc. Read the statement carefully and pick the correct answer choice.

161. **Statement :** Inefficient batting by frontline batsmen caused the team to mess up things in the last series.

     Causes of Action :

     I. The bowlers should be sent in the beginning and the frontline batsmen towards the end.

     II. The frontline batsmen should be asked to concentrate on their practice.

     III. A fresh crop of batsmen should replace the existing ones.

     (a) Only I and II follow
     (b) Only III follows
     (c) Only I follows
     (d) Only II follows
     (e) None follows

162. **Statement : Although strict vigilance by the police has brought down the rate of night crimes, daylight robberies and chain-snatching etc. have only increased.**

     Courses of action :

     I. The police should be asked to stop its vigilance programme during nights.

     II. The police should be given powers to kill criminals involved in day light robberies and chain-snatching.

     III. The police should be directed to reorient its strategy so that daylight crimes are not ignored.

     (a) I and II follow (b) Only III follows
     (c) Only I follows (d) II and III follow
     (e) I and III follow

163. **Statement :** The recent landmark decision in which the court has put a ban on the plying of thousands of diesel buses that have not converted to CNG, has created a great problem to commuters in city X.

     Courses of action :

     I. The government should make it mandatory for private vehicles to ferry passengers at a charge in city X.

     II. The government should draw up a contingency plan to tackle the transport problem in the city.

     III. The government should appear to the court to allow it to phase out diesel buses gradually.

     (a) Only I follows (b) Only II follows
     (c) Only I and II follow (d) All follow
     (e) None of these

164. **Statement :** The Company 'X' has rejected first lot of valves supplied by Company 'A' and has cancelled its entire huge order quoting use of inferior-quality material and poor craftsmanship.

Courses of action :

I. The Company 'A' needs to investigate functioning of its purchase, production and quality control departments.

II. The Company 'A' should inspect all the valves rejected by Company 'X'

III. The Company 'A' should inform Company 'X' that steps have been taken for improvement and renegotiate schedule of supply.

(a) Only I and II (b) Only II
(c) All I, II and III (d) II and either I or III
(e) None of these

165. **Statement :**

The vehicular traffic has increased so much in the recent past that it takes at least two hours to travel between the city and the airport during peak hours.

Courses of Action :

I. Non-airport bound vehicles should not be allowed to ply on the road connecting the city and the airport.

II. The load of vehicular traffic should be diverted through various link roads during peak hours.

III. The departure and arrival of flights should be regulated so as to avoid congestion during peak hours.

(a) Only I follows (b) Only I and II follow
(c) Only II follows (d) All follow
(e) None follows

Directions (Qs. 166 to 170) : Study the table carefully to answer the questions that follow :

Number of Students (in thousands) Appearing (A) for a Competitive exam from six different Management Institutes A, B, C, D, E and F and Percentage passing (P) the exam in years 2002 – 2007.

Year	2002		2003		2004		2005		2006		2007	
Institute	A	%P	A	%P	A	%P	A	%P	A	%P	A	%P
A	2.3	11	4.2	21	3.5	12	2.0	22	1.8	14	1.2	17
B	3.5	14	3.6	16	3.4	11	1.3	15	2.3	16	2.1	18
C	1.8	23	2.8	13	2.9	16	4.5	24	2.3	23	3.9	20
D	2.9	18	2.8	15	1.6	20	3.2	20	3.3	16	4.0	19
E	4.4	17	3.2	23	1.9	16	1.5	18	3.1	18	2.7	14
F	3.2	21	3.0	14	4.0	14	2.6	11	3.8	19	2.3	13

A = Appeared % P = Percentage passing

166. What is the total number of students passing in the exam from Institute B in the year 2002 and 2003 together?

(a) 1206 (b) 1500
(c) 1146 (d) 1066
(e) None of these

167. What is the respective ratio of number of students passing in the exam from Institute C in the year 2004 to those passing in the exam from Institute E in the year 2007 ?

(a) 232 : 189 (b) 117 : 248
(c) 248 : 117 (d) 189 : 232
(e) None of these

168. Which Institute has the highest number of students appearing for the exam in all the years together?

(a) D (b) E
(c) F (d) C
(e) None of these

169. What is the total number of students passing in the exam in the year 2005 from all Institutes together?

(a) 2836 (b) 2911
(c) 2624 (d) 2543
(e) None of these

170. The number of students passing is in the exam from Institute D in the year 2006 is which percent of the total number of students appearing from all Institute together in that year ? (rounded off to two digit after decimal)

(a) 4.12 (b) 2.86
(c) 4.07 (d) 3.18
(e) None of these

Directions (Qs. 171-175) : Given below are pairs of events 'A' and 'B'. You have to read both the events 'A' and 'B' and decide their nature of relationship. You have to assume that the information given in 'A' and 'B' is true and you will not assume anything beyond the given information in deciding the answer. Mark answer:

(a) If 'A' is the effect and 'B' is its immediate and principal cause.
(b) If 'A' is the immediate and principal cause and 'B' is its effect.
(c) If 'A' is an effect but 'B' is not its immediate and principal cause.
(d) If 'B' is an effect but 'A' is not its immediate and principal cause.
(e) None of these

171. **Event (A)** : The revised entry fee for internationally known Taj Mahal monument has been increased by Rs 50 and Rs 500 for Indians and foreigners respectively.

Event (B) : There has been adequate increase in the number of foreign tourists visiting India in view of the improved infrastructure facilities.

172. **Event (A)** : Due to mechanisation the life of human beings is becoming more comfortable in urban areas.
Event (B) : Life is becoming insecure in urban area.

173. **Event (A)** : India is today gearing to become a leading producer and exporter of a range of minerals.
Event (B) : India is endowed with rich mineral resources.

174. **Event (A)** : The high-profile criminal was arrested and put behind bars.
Event (B) : The cops made more than adequate security arrangements in Jail.

175. **Event (A)** : The sale of cars has dropped in the state X since last Monday.
Event (B) : The state 'X' has suspended registration of cars which do not conform to the emission norms stipulated recently.

Directions (Q. 176-180) : Study the graph carefully to answer the questions that follow-

Number of students in different specializations of a college.

Specialization	Number of Students
HR	225
Marketing	275
IT	200
Finance	175
Production	375
Merchandising	350

Ratio of male and female students.

Specialization	Male	Female
HR	9	16
Marketing	3	2
IT	9	31
Finance	2	3
Production	11	4
Merchandising	4	3

176. What is the total number of Males studying in all specializations together ?
(a) 755 (b) 925
(c) 836 (d) 784
(e) None of these

177. What is the number of Females studying in the HR specialization ?
(a) 158 (b) 128
(c) 136 (d) 144
(e) None of these

178. What is the respective ratio of total number of students studying in the specialization production to those studying in the Merchandising specialization ?
(a) 15 : 14 (b) 8 : 7
(c) 14 : 15 (d) 7 : 8
(e) None of these

179. In which specialization are the lowest number of Females studying ?
(a) Marketing (b) Production
(c) HR (d) Finance
(e) None of these

180. What is the total number of students from all specialization together in the college ?
(a) 1500 (b) 1575
(c) 1525 (d) 1625
(e) None of these

Directions (Qs. 181–183) : Each of the questions below is based on the following passage. Read the passage to choose the best answer.

Passage : If a person reads a lot, he will increase his vocabulary. So, the passage to choose the best answer.

181. The argument is based on the **assumption(s)**.
A. Strong vocabulary is important for writing and speaking.
B. People should read books containing unfamiliar words.
C. The books to be read should be entertaining.
(a) A only (b) B only
(c) C only (d) A, B and C
(e) A and B only

182. Which one of the following would **weaken** the argument?
(a) Educated people can express their thoughts better.
(b) The style of a person is coloured by the style of the author he reads.
(c) Only a well read person can make proper use of the English language.
(d) Those who passed vocabulary tests could not write well.
(e) None of these

183. Which of the following will **strengthen** the argument?
A. Slow readers cannot do well in competitive examinations.
B. Everyone must study in an English medium school.
C. In order to become a good speaker in English, one must increase one's vocabulary.
(a) A only (b) B only
(c) C only (d) A and B only
(e) A, B and C

Directions (Q. 184-188) : Study the following graph carefully and answer the questions given below it.

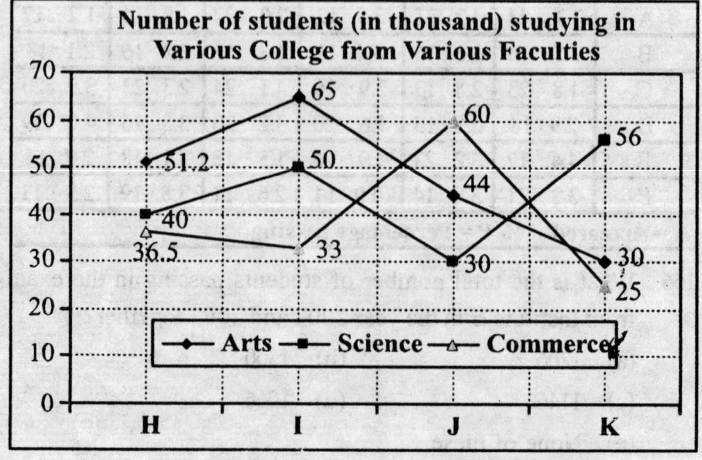

184. What is the difference between the total number of students studying in college H and those studying in college K ?
(a) 16100 (b) 15800
(c) 16300 (d) 16700
(e) None of these

185. What is the total number of students studying in all the colleges together ?
(a) 520900 (b) 520700
(c) 610200 (d) 510800
(e) None of these

186. What is the respective ratio of the students from the faculty of Science from colleges H and I together to the students from the same faculty from colleges J and K together ?
(a) 43 : 45 (b) 41 : 43
(c) 45 : 43 (d) 43 : 41
(e) None of these

187. The number of students from the faculty of Science from college I are approximately what per cent of the total number of students studying in that college ?
(a) 34 (b) 37
(c) 29 (d) 31
(e) 39

188. What is the average number of students from the faculty of Commerce from all the colleges together ?
(a) 36825 (b) 38655
(c) 35625 (d) 36585
(e) None of is these

Directions (Qs. 189& 190) : Use the statement given below to answer the questions that follow.

All good athletes want to win and all athletes who want to win, eat a well-balanced diet; therefore, all athletes who do not eat a well-balanced diet are bad athletes.

189. If assumptions of the argument above are true, then which of the following statements must be true?
(a) No athlete who does not eat a well-balanced diet is a good athlete.
(b) No bad athlete wants to win.
(c) Every athlete who eats a well-balaned diet is a good athlete.
(d) All athletes who want to win are good athletes.
(e) None of these

190. Which of the following, if true, would refute the assumptions of the arguments above ?
(a) Bob, the accountant, eats a well-balanced diet, but he is not a good athlete.
(b) Ann wants to win, but she is not a good athlete.
(c) All the players on the Burros baseball team eat a well-balanced diet.
(d) Cindy, the basketball star, does not eat a well-balanced diet, but she is a good athelete.
(e) None of these

Directions (Qs. 191 to 195) : The following bar chart shows the production of mobile phones by three different companies P, Q and R for different years. Study this chart to answer the questions that follow.

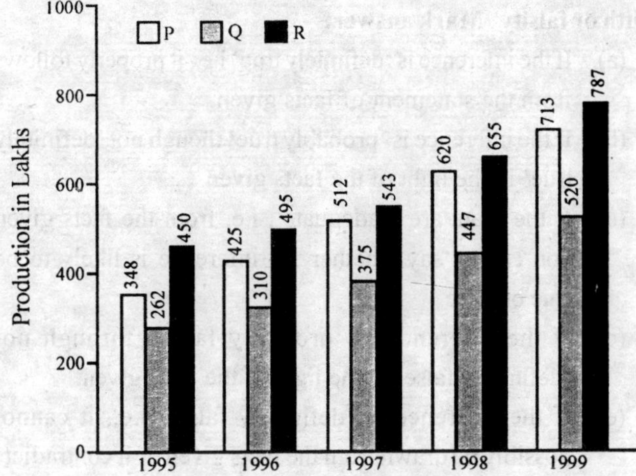

191. Considering the production of each company separately, in how many instances, is the percentage increase in the production of mobile phone over the previous year's production greater than 20% ?
(a) 4 (b) 6
(c) 5 (d) 7
(e) None of these

192. The annual percentage increase in the total production of mobile phone from 1995 to 1999 was :
(a) 24.08% (b) 23.12%
(c) 22.64% (d) 20%
(e) None of these

193. In 1996, 15% of the urban population and 8% of the rural population used mobile phone. If the total population in 1996 is 1.1 billion, then what is the urban population in million? (Assume that one mobile phone is used by a single person.)
(a) 600 (b) 0.6
(c) 500 (d) 0.5
(e) None of these

194. If the ratio of the average cost to the customer of each mobile phone of the companies P, Q and R is 2 : 4 : 3, then what is the percentage increase in the total revenue of the mobile phone produced in the years 1997 to 1999. (Assume that the cost of the mobile phone remained the same.)
(a) 39.89% (b) 40.53%
(c) 42.64% (d) 41.27%
(e) None of these

195. Over the five-year period, the percentage increase in production was maximum for:
(a) P (b) Q
(c) R (d) Cannot be determined
(e) Both P and Q

Directions (Qs.196-200) : Below is given a passage followed by several possible inferences which can be drawn from the facts stated in the passage. You have to examine each inference separately in the context of the passage and decide upon its degree of truth or falsity . Mark answer:

(a) If the inference is 'definitely true' i.e., it properly follows from the statement of facts given.

(b) If the inference is 'probably true' though not 'definitely true' in the light of the facts given.

(c) If the 'data are inadequate', i.e. from the facts given you cannot say whether the inference is likely to be true or false.

(d) If the inference is 'probably false', through not 'definitely false' in the light of the facts given.

(e) If the inference is 'definitely false', i.e., it cannot possibly be drawn from the facts given or it contradicts the given facts.

Hurdles imposed in the path of foreign investors by regulations must be removed if the country wants to attract quality foreign investment. Particularly, when foreign institutional investors no longer seem very enamoured by the Indian story. Although the foreign exchange reserve does not face the risk of falling to the levels of early 1990, the country should create an environment to attract more long term investments instead of just portpolio inflows or hot money. Essentially a diluted version of Regulation issued in 1998 with its requirement that foreign partners with JVs set up in India prior to 2005 must obtain a green light from the domestic partner to set up another similar venture has the potential to be misused. Further, the foreign partner is also required to obtain prior approval from the government before a new venture in the same area of business as the existing one is set up.

196. **Foreign investors are keen to invest in long term projects in India in the current scenario.**
197. **Many countries in the Asian continent have foreign investor friendly guidelines.**
198. **India's foreign exchange reserve in early 1990s was much below the current level.**
199. **India needs to tighten its norms for granting foreign investments to key sectors.**
200. **Foreign direct investment in India is mainly short-term investment.**

❑❑❑

ANSWERS AND EXPLANATIONS

1. (d) Since Aditya's house faces towards East and he walks from backside of his house, it means that he starts walking towards West. Thus, the movements of Aditya are as shown in Fig. (A to B, B to C, C to D).

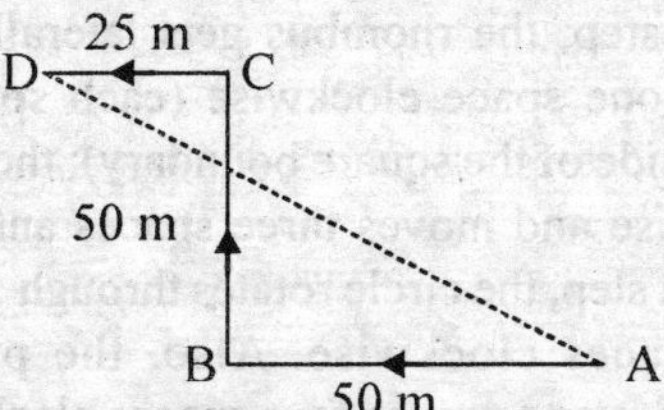

Clearly, Aditya's final position is D which is to the North-west of the starting point A.

2. (b) The third, fifth, eighth and tenth letters of the word DISTRIBUTE are S, R, U and E respectively. The word formed is SURE and its third letter is R.

3. (b) The word formed is BEACH. Clearly, the fourth letter is C.

4. (c) One letter from the beginning and one from the end of a term are removed, one by one, in alternate steps.

5. (a) The letters in the first half and second half of the word are written in the reverse order and then in the group of letters so obtained, the first, third, fifth and seventh letters and each moved one step forward while the second, fourth, sixth and eighth letters are each moved one step backward to get the code. Thus, we have:

TRIANGLE → TRIA/NGLE → AIRT/ELGN → BHSSFKHM

6. (d)

	Green cover	Yellow cover	New volume	Old volume	Reports	Medical extracts
A		✓	✓		✓	
B	✓		✓		✓	
C	✓			✓	✓	
D		✓	✓			✓
E	✓			✓		✓
F	✓			✓		✓

Clearly, E and F are old volumes which have green covers and are medical extract.

7. (c) 1st letter : $Q \xrightarrow{+2} S \xrightarrow{+2} U \xrightarrow{+2} W \xrightarrow{+2} \textcircled{Y}$

Middle number :

$1 \xrightarrow{\times1+1} 2 \xrightarrow{\times2+2} 6 \xrightarrow{\times3+3} 21 \xrightarrow{\times4+4} \textcircled{88}$

3rd letter :

$F \xrightarrow{-1} E \xrightarrow{-1} D \xrightarrow{-1} C \xrightarrow{-1} \textcircled{B}$

For (Qs. 8-10)

The given information can be tabulated as below:

Floor	1	2	3	4	5	6
Person	E	F	A	D	C	B

8. (c) 9. (c) 10. (c)

11. (b) $? \approx 175 \times 28 + 275 \times 28$
$= 28(175 + 275)$
$= 28 \times 450$
≈ 12600

12. (e) $? \approx 325 \times 16 \div 4 + 37$
$= 325 \times 4 + 37$
$= 1300 + 37$
$= 1337$
≈ 1340

13. (c) $? \approx 1164 \times 128 \div 8 + 969$
$= 1164 \times 16 + 969$
$= 18624 + 969$
$= 19593$
≈ 19600

14. (c) $? \approx \sqrt{625} + \sqrt{729}$
$= 25 + 27 = 52$

15. (a) $? \approx \frac{69}{100}$ of $700 + \frac{33}{100}$ of 400
$= 483 + 132$
$= 615$

16. (e) Refer to the 1st and 2nd sentence of 3rd para.

17. (e) In the context of the passage, all of the given statements are correct.

18. (c) In the light of the facts given, only statement 3 is true.

19. (d) In the light of the passage only statement 1 and 3 are true.

20. (a) Organisation for economic cooperation and development.

21. (e) All of the given statements are true.

22. (e) All of the given statements are true.

23. (a) In the light of passage, option (a) is the most appropriate title.

24. (a) 25. (c) 26. (b) 27. (e)
28. (a) 29. (b) 30. (c) 31. (b)
32. (c) 33. (d) 34. (e) 35. (a)

For (Qs. 31-35)

The given information can be shown as below:

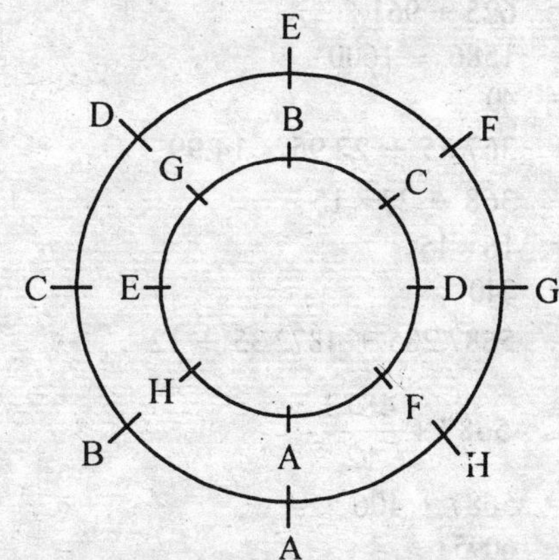

31. (c) 32. (c) 33. (d)
34. (e) H sits between E and A
35. (a)

36. (c) From figures I and II, the group of leaves is rotating 135° anticlockwise, one leaf is increasing and the half-leaf is reversing on the other side. The two figures of option (c) do not follow this pattern.

37. (a) From figures I to II, the designs on the ends of the main design (卐) interchange their positons in the following manner: 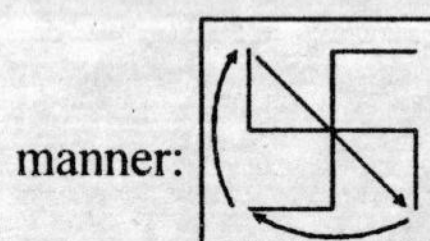
The two figures of option (a) do not follow this pattern.

38. (e) From figures I to II, the shaded portion in the rectangles move from outside to inside and from inside to outside the main design. The shaded portion appears in all the four rectangles, in the rectangles in opposite direction, the shaded portion is in the same side and in the adjacent rectangles on the other side. Two figures of option (e) do not follow this pattern of change.

39. (a) From figures I to II, the designs on the lines rotate leaving one line in the anticlockwise direction, simultaneously one design increases ahead of them in the same direction. (a) does not follow this pattern.

40. (d) In all other figures, the two figures are mirror images, *i.e.*, one is the mirror image of the other.

41. (c)
$$
\begin{aligned}
? &= (35.95)^2 - (24.001)^2 \\
&\approx (36)^2 - (24)^2 \\
&= (36+24)(36-24) \\
&= 60 \times 12 \\
&= 720
\end{aligned}
$$

42. (a)
$$
\begin{aligned}
\because \frac{75}{100} \text{ of } 230 - ? &= \frac{64}{100} \text{ of } 249 \\
\therefore ? &= 172.5 - 159.36 \\
&= 13.14 \\
&\approx 14
\end{aligned}
$$

43. (e)
$$
\begin{aligned}
\because (?)^2 &= (24.99)^2 + (31.05)^2 \\
&= (25)^2 + (31)^2 \\
&= 625 + 961 \\
&= 1586 \approx 1600 \\
\therefore ? &= 40
\end{aligned}
$$

44. (b)
$$
\begin{aligned}
? &= 367.85 \div 22.95 \times 14.99 \\
&\approx 368 \div 23 \times 15 \\
&= 16 \times 15 \\
&= 240
\end{aligned}
$$

45. (d)
$$
\begin{aligned}
? &= 5687.285 + 4872.35 \div 12 \\
&\approx 5687 + \frac{4872}{12} \\
&= 5687 + 406 \\
&\approx 6095
\end{aligned}
$$

46. (e) The complete figure rotates sequentially through 45° clockwise, 90° clockwise, 135° clockwise, 180° clockwise, ... The two circles at the ends interchange positions in every second step.

47. (e) The dark shading moves one space clockwise and the curved line shading moves one space anticlockwise in each step. In Fig. (e) the dark shading has moved three spaces clockwise instead of one.

48. (a) The inner shading moves two spaces anticlockwise and one space anticlockwise alternately while the outer shading moves one space clockwise and two spaces clockwise alternately.

49. (c) In one step, the rhombus gets laterally inverted and moves one space clockwise (each space is equal to half-a-side of the square boundary); the pin rotates 90° clockwise and moves three spaces anticlockwise . In the next step, the circle rotates through 180° and moves two spaces clockwise. Also, the pin rotates 45° clockwise and moves four spaces clockwise.

50. (d) The elements move in the sequences 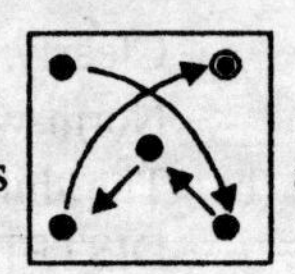 and 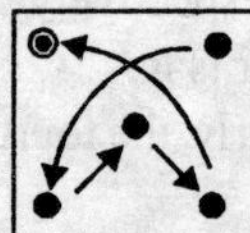 alternately. Also, in each step, the element that reaches the encircled position gets replaced by a new element. In Fig. (d) the square must be replaced by the element 'S'.

51. (a) Make me sit up and take notice means 'make **somebody** sit up and take notice'

52. (b) Caught up with means 'to have unpleasant consequences for, especially after a period of quiesence'

53. (a) Went through the roof means 'to become extremely angry'

54. (d) Corrects the misuse of phrasal verb for noun. 'Breakout' is a phrasal verb meaning 'to start or appear suddenly' while ' out break' is a noun meaning 'sudden appearence. A preposition or an article is used before a noun, not a verb. Use preposition 'before' in place of 'for' because a preventive measure is taken before the appearance of epidemic.

55. (c) Corrects the idiomatic error. 'Last but not least' is an idiom which means 'last but not less important than others'.

56. (e)

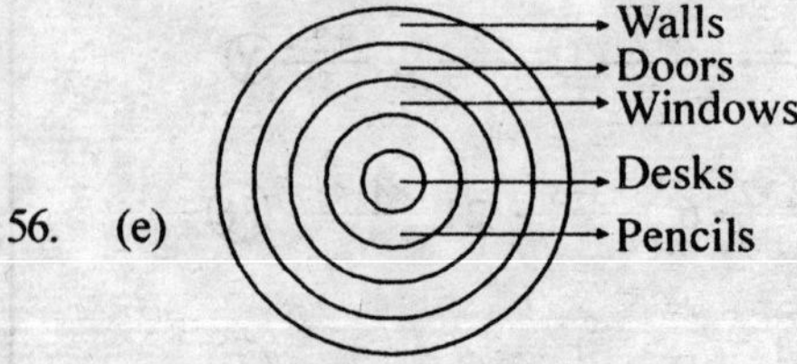

57. (d)

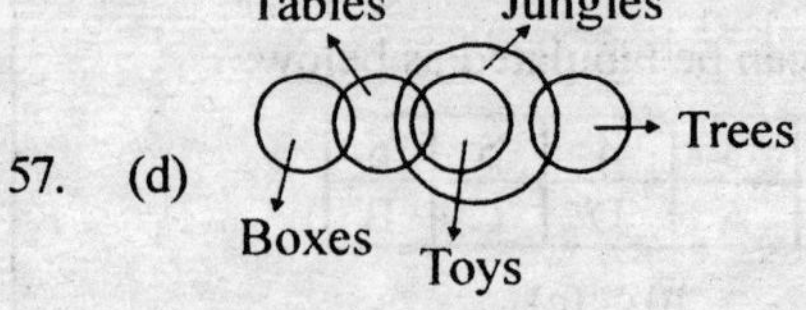

Or

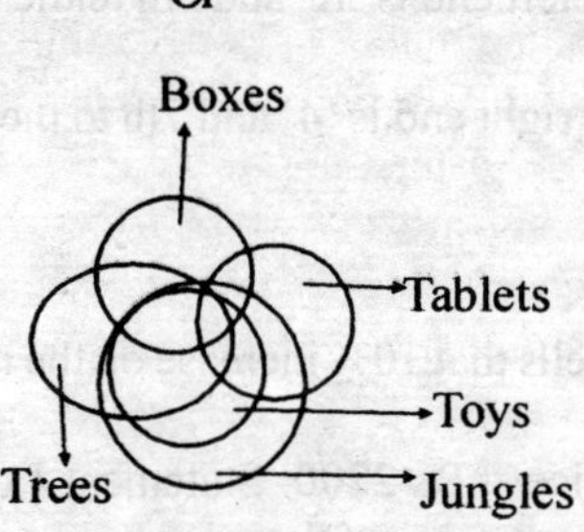

58. (b)

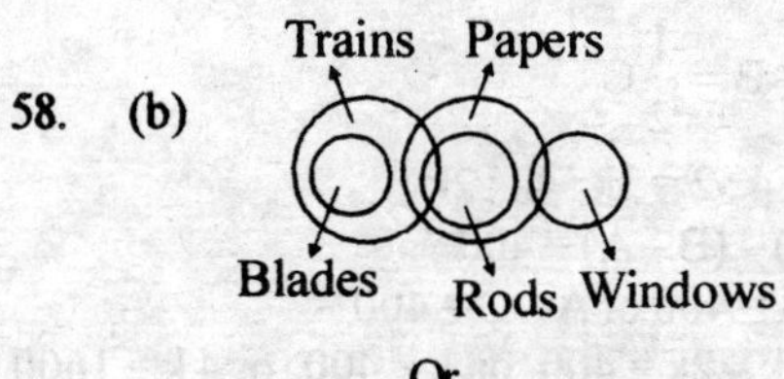

Or

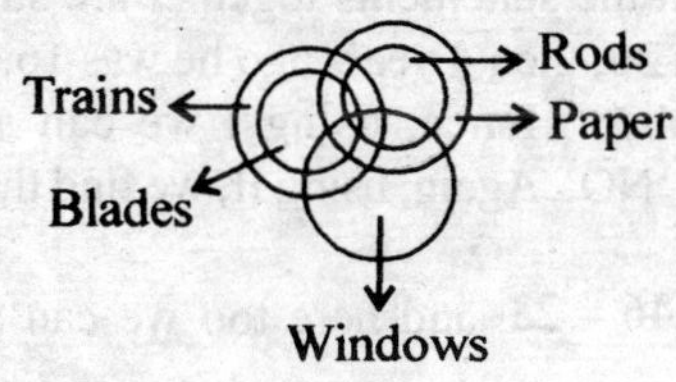

59. (d)

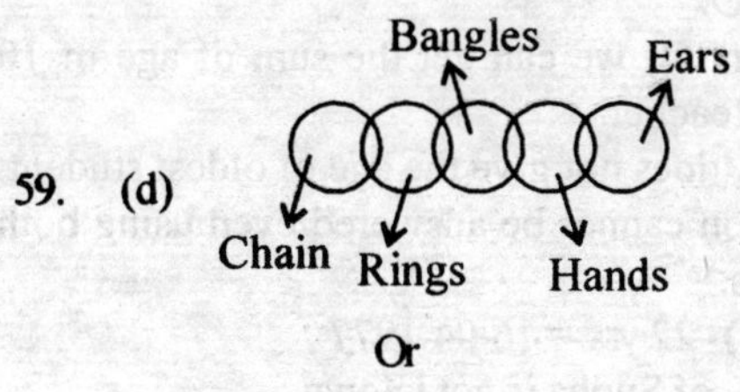

Or

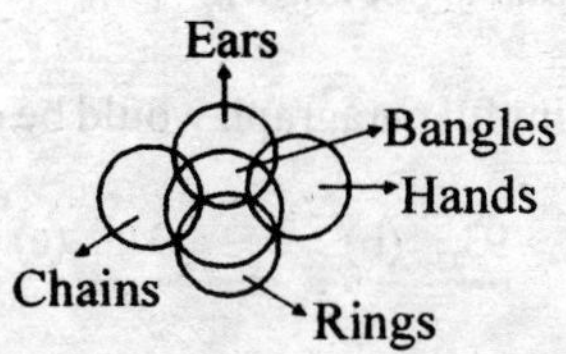

60. (d)

Books Chairs

Cards Benches Tables

61. (a)

[46656]

1 4 27 256 3125 46658

$(1)^1$ $(2)^2$ $(3)^3$ $(4)^4$ $(5)^5$ $(6)^6$

$\because$ Correct number $= (6)^6 = 46656$

$\therefore$ Wrong number $= 46658$

62. (d)

[144]

18000 3600 720 142.2 28.8 5.76

$\div 5$ $\div 5$ $\div 5$ $\div 5$ $\div 5$

$\because$ Correct number $= 720 \div 5 = 144$

$\therefore$ Wrong number $= 142.2$

63. (e)

[608]

12 237 406 527 604 657

$+15^2$ $+13^2$ $+11^2$ $+9^2$ $+7^2$

$\because$ Correct number $= 527 + 9^2 = 608$

$\therefore$ Wrong number $= 604$

64. (c)

[228]

3 35 226 1160 4660 13998

$\times7+7\times2$ $\times6+6\times3$ $\times5+5\times4$ $\times4+4\times5$ $\times3+3\times6$

$\because$ Correct number $= 35 \times 6 + 6 \times 3 = 210 + 18 = 228$

$\therefore$ Wrong number $= 226$

65. (b)

[3535]

18 119 708 3534 14136 42405

$\times7-7$ $\times6-6$ $\times5-5$ $\times4-4$ $\times3-3$

$\because$ Correct number $= 708 \times 5 - 5 = 3540 - 5$
$= 3535$

$\therefore$ Wrong number $= 3534$

66. (c) In each step, all the symbols move in the sequence

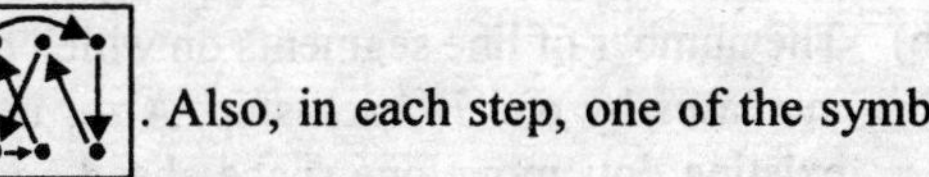

. Also, in each step, one of the symbols gets repalced by a new symbol and this replacement goes on in an anticlockwise sequence, *i.e.* lower-right, lower-middle, lower-left, upper-left, upper-middle, ...

67. (a) In the first step, the symbols move in the sequence

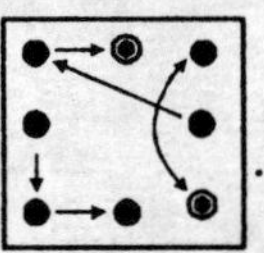

. In each subsequent step, the symbols move in the sequence obtained by rotating the previous sequence through 90° clockwise. Also, in each step, the symbols that reach the encircled position get replaced by new symbols.

68. (e) In the first step, the lowermost element remains unchanged while the other three elements change their sizes (large elements get reduced in size and small unchanged while the other three elements change their sizes. In the third step, the second element remains unchanged while the other three elements change their sizes. In the fourth step, the third element remains unchanged while the other three elements change their sizes. Also, whenever, the arc changes its size, it gets vertically inverted and whenever the triangle changes its size, it gets laterally inverted.

69. (a) In the first step, the symbols move in the sequence

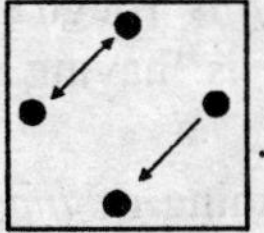

. In each subsequent step, the symbols move in the sequence obtained by rotating the previous sequence through 90° anticlockwise. Also, in each one of the first two steps, the symbol that reaches the lower position, gets replaced by a new symbol and in each one of the next two steps, the symbol that reaches the upper position, gets replaced by a new symbol.

70. (d) In each step, the symbols move in the sequence

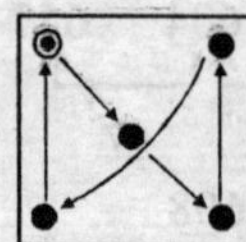

and the symbol that reaches the encircled position gets replaced by a new symbol.

71. (c) In each step, all the existing elements move one space anticlockwise; a new element is added at the anticlockwise-end and the two elements at the clockwise-end interchange positions.

72. (d) In each step, all the symbols move in the sequence

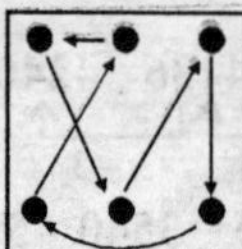

. Also, in each step, one of the symbols gets replaced by a new symbol and this replacement goes on in an anticlockwise sequence, *i.e.* lower-left, lower-middle, lower-right, upper-right, upper-middle,...

73. (b) The number of line segments on which the dots move, increases by one in each step. Also, in one step, the existing dots move one space ahead and a new dot is added to the figure and in the next step, the existing dots move one space ahead. The path of the dots is as shown below:

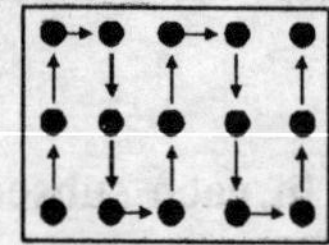

74. (e) The upper-left and the lower-left triangles rotate 90° anticlockwise and 180° alternately while the other two triangles (upper-right and lower-right) rotate 90° clockwise and 180° alternately.

75. (b) In each step, the symbols move in the sequence

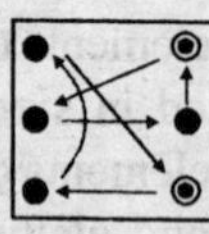

and the symbols that reach the encircled positions get replaced by new symbols.

76. (a) heels - brandishing. Meaning of *brandishing* is waveing in order to threaten because of anger and excitement.

77. (b) acclaimed - obscurity. Meaning of *acclaimed* is 'publicly praised'. Meaning of *obscurity* is 'the state of not being well known'.

78. (a) gruff - suave. Meaning of *gruff* is 'rough and abrupt in manners'. Meaning of *suave* is 'having a confident, smooth and elegant manners'.

79. (b) incongruous - bustling. Meaning of *incongruous* is 'out of place, strange because not in harmony with the surroundings'. Meaning of *bustling* is 'noisy and full of activity (of a place).

80. (b) corruption - venal. Meaning of *venal* is 'corrupt and dishonest; taking money illegally for work'.

81. (a) There is no any symbol.

82. (a) 16th from the left end is 'K' and 5th to the left of 'K' is 'B'.

83. (c) 14th from the right end is '4' and 7th to the right of it is 'N'.

84. (b) 1 W U

85. (c) 9 A F and 3 I K

86. (a) Statement II tells that 10% increase on the mixer comes to be Rs 220.

∴ Present Price = Rs 2200. Statement I does not tell about the present price of the mixer.

87. (d) From I : $\frac{1}{3}A = \frac{1}{4}B = \frac{1}{2}C$

or, A : B : C = 3 : 4 : 2 = 3k : 4k : 2k

From II : (B – C) – (B – A) = 400

or B – C – B + A = 400 or A – C = 400

From I and II : 3k – 2k = 400 or k = 400 or 4 k = 1600

Hence, both the statements together are sufficient.

88. (c) If Madan is 20, then 4 years ago he was 16. 16 is not a prime number. Hence, using I we can answer the question as 'NO'. Again, using II, we find that Madan's age is $\frac{1}{2} \times 46 = 23$ and here too we can answer the question as NO.

89. (e) From statement (I) we can get the sum of age of 10 students and teacher

Statement (II), does not give the age of oldest student. Hence, question cannot be answered even using both the statements.

90. (a) I : (16-04-1999) - 22 yrs. = 16-04-1977

II : The D.O.B. of Sudha is not known.

For (Qs. 91-95) :

Proper sequence to form a meaningful paragraph would be 4, 2, 5, 6, 3, 1.

91. (d) 92. (a) 93. (b) 94. (e)

95. (c)

96. (c) 89★51@8

97. (a) 79★5$6%

98. (b) #%65★©#

99. (e) δ4617$9

100. (a) ©73@26%

101. (c) **Step II** : 18 task bear cold dish 81 63 31

Step III : 18 task 31 bear cold dish 81 63

Step IV : 18 task 31 dish bear cold 81 63

Step V : 18 task 31 dish 63 bear cold 81

Step VI : 18 task 31 dish 63 cold bear 81

Step VII : 18 task 31 dish 63 cold 81 bear

Hence, 5 more steps will be required to complete the rearrangement.

102. (d) **Input** : 72 59 37 go for picnic 24 journey

Step I : 24 72 59 37 go for picnic journey

Step II : 24 picnic 72 59 37 go for journey

Step III : 24 picnic 37 72 59 go for journey

Step IV : 24 picnic 37 journey 72 59 go for

Step V : 24 picnic 37 journey 59 72 go for

Step VI : 24 picnic 37 journey 59 go 72 for

Hence, VI steps will be required to complete the rearrangement.

103. (a) **Input** : nice flower 34 12 costly height 41 56.
Step I : 12 nice flower 34 costly height 41 56.
Step II : 12 nice 34 flower costly height 41 56.
Step III : 12 nice 34 height flower costly 41 56.

104. (d) **Step II** : 16 victory 19 36 53 store lake town
Step III : 16 victory 19 town 36 53 store lake
Step IV : 16 victory 19 town 36 store 53 lake
There is no V step.

105. (b) **Input** : milk pot 18 24 over goal 36 53
Step I : 18 milk pot 24 over goal 36 53
Step II : 18 pot milk 24 over goal 36 53
Step III : 18 pot 24 milk over goal 36 53
Step IV : 18 pot 24 over milk goal 36 53
Step V : 18 pot 24 over 36 milk goal 53
Step VI : 18 pot 24 over 36 milk 53 goal
The last step is VI.
Hence, the prelast step is V.

106. (d) Let the speed of the second train be x km/h
The relative speed = (50 + x) km/h
These trains will cross each other in a time equivalent of covering a distance equal to 108 + 112, i.e. 220 meters in 6 seconds, running speed of (50 + x) km/h

$$\therefore \frac{1}{50+x} \times \frac{220}{1000} = \frac{6}{3600} \Rightarrow x = 82$$

∴ The speed of the second train = 82 km/hr.

107. (c) Let the numbers be $5x$ and $4x$.
Now, difference of numbers = 10
i.e. $5x - 4x = 10 \Rightarrow x = 10$
∴ Larger number = $10 \times 5 = 50$

108. (b) Given $8P = P\left(1+\frac{r}{100}\right)^3$
Where P = Principal amount,
r = Compound interest rate
$\Rightarrow r = 100\%$
∴ Let the time in which the principal amount becomes 16 times be n

Then $16P = P\left(1+\frac{r}{100}\right)^n$

$\Rightarrow 16 = 2^n \Rightarrow n = 4$ yrs.

109. (c) Let the present age of the father and son be x and y years, respectively.
Then, we have $x = 3y$ ... (i)
and $(x-15) = 9(y-15)$ or $x - 15 = 9y - 135$
or $x - 9y = -120$ ... (ii)
From (i) and (ii), $x = 60$ years
Age of the father after 15 years = 60 + 15 = 75 years

110. (a) No. of words which have at least one letter repeated = total no. of words – total no. of words in which no letter is repeated
$= 10^5 - {}^{10}P_5$
$= 100000 - 10 \times 9 \times 8 \times 7 \times 6$
$= 100000 - 30240 = 69760$

111. (b) In each subsequent figure the designs change their positions in the following manner on the main design:

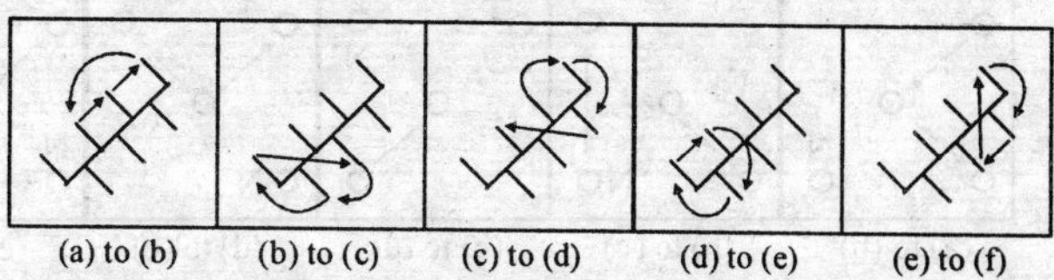

(a) to (b) (b) to (c) (c) to (d) (d) to (e) (e) to (f)

112. (e) In each subsequent figure the designs formed on the three diagonal lines form after shifting and reversing as follows :

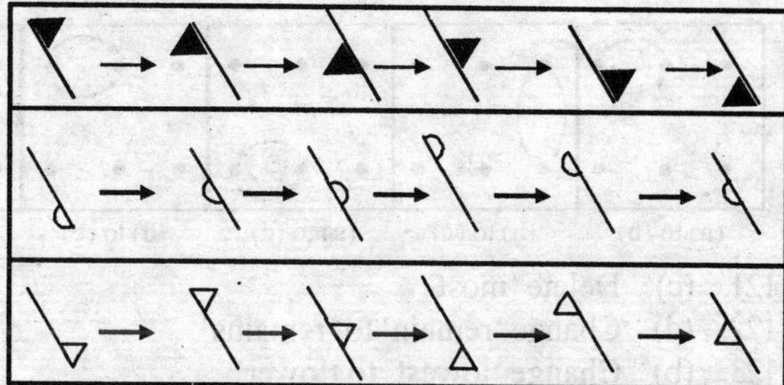

113. (e) In each subsequent figure, the changes occur in the following manner:
'↑' remains at the centre, twice upwards and twice downward and '▲' reverses in each next step.
'↑' remains twice at a position, twice at the left-hand upwards, twice at the right-hand upwards, twice at right-hand downwards, and '∩' reverses in each next step.
'⊥' also remains twice at the right-hand downwards, twice at the left-hand downwards, twice at the left-hand upward and '␣' reverses in each next step.

114. (c) In each subsequent figure, the designs shift half side anticlockwise first and then one side anticlockwise respectively and a new design forms one by one from back side each time then forward side respectively.

115. (c) The smallest arc twice remains unchanged on its position and then shifts one hand anticlockwise. The middle arc shifts one hand clockwise in each step, while the biggest arc twice remains unchanged on its position and then rotates anticlockwise.

116. (e) In each subsequent figure, the designs shift as follows and a new design forms at the place of N:

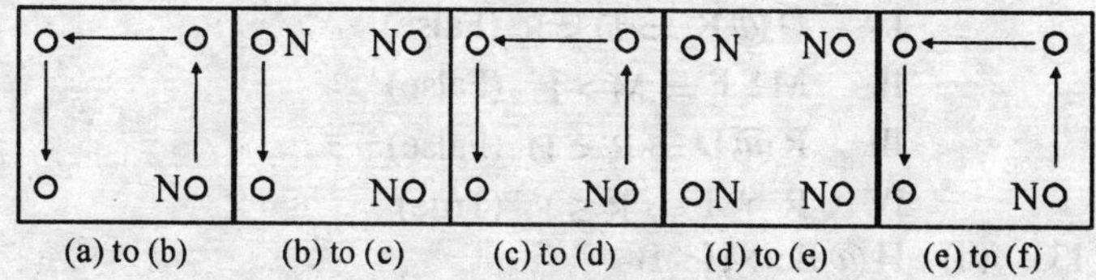

(a) to (b) (b) to (c) (c) to (d) (d) to (e) (e) to (f)

117. (d) In each next figure, the designs shift one place downwards and one new design appears at the back first, third and fifth designs rotate 90° anticlockwise in each step. While second and fourth designs rotate 90° clockwise. If this process continues, (d) will be the answer figure.

118. (b) In each subsequent figure, the designs shift as follows and a new design forms at the place of N:

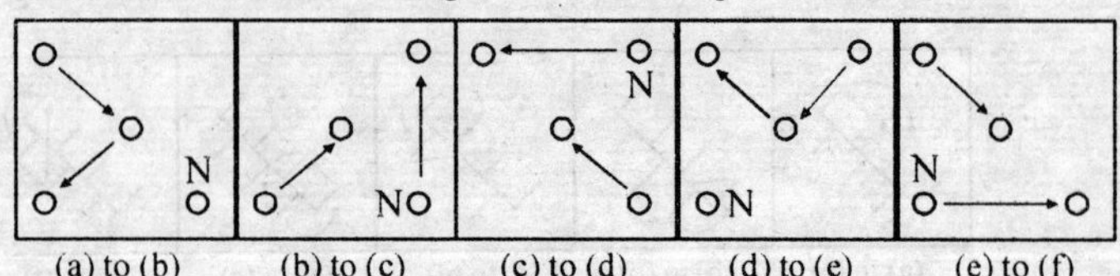

(a) to (b) (b) to (c) (c) to (d) (d) to (e) (e) to (f)

119. (a) In each subsequent figure, the lines on the sides of the square shift clockwise and one line increases. Hence, (a) will be the answer figure.

120. (b) In each subsequent figure, the designs shift as follows:

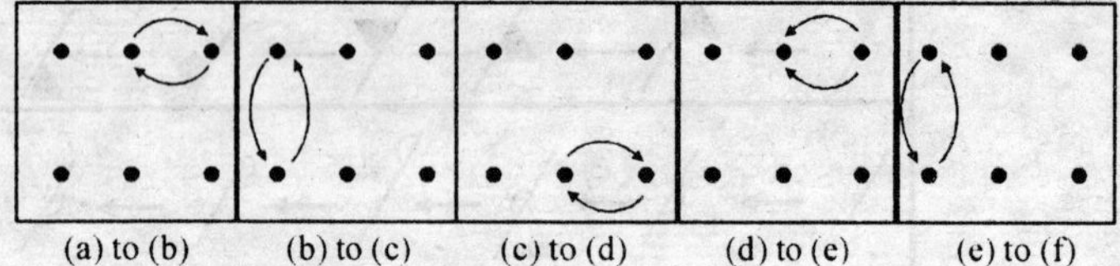
(a) to (b) (b) to (c) (c) to (d) (d) to (e) (e) to (f)

121. (c) Delete 'most'
122. (d) Change 'remain' to 'remains'
123. (b) Change 'lowest' to 'lower'
124. (d) Change 'since' to 'from'
125. (d) Delete 'with'.
126. (a) Insert 'down' after 'slipped'.
127. (c) Delete 'do not' after 'you'. 'unless' itself is negative, the use of negative 'do not' is therefore incorrect.
128. (b) Change 'I' to 'me'
129. (b) Change 'were' to 'was'. Singular verb should be used since the subject the 'The director' is singular.
130. (d) Change 'fluently' to 'fluent'.
131. (d) $J\$K \Rightarrow J > K$
$K \bigstar T \Rightarrow K \le T$
$T @ N \Rightarrow T < N$
and $N © R \Rightarrow N \ge R$
$\therefore J > K \le T < N \ge R$
I. $J\$T \Rightarrow J > T$ (False)
II. $R \bigstar T \Rightarrow R \le T$ (False)
III. $N\$K \Rightarrow N > K$ (True)
IV. $R \bigstar K \Rightarrow R \le K$ (False)

132. (d) $F \% W \Rightarrow F = W$
$W © R \Rightarrow W \ge R$
$R @ M \Rightarrow R < M$
and $M\$D \Rightarrow M > D$
$\therefore F = W \ge R < M > D$
I. $D @ R \Rightarrow D < R$ (False)
II. $M\$F \Rightarrow M > F$ (False)
III. $R @ D \Rightarrow R < D$ (False)
IV. $R \bigstar F \Rightarrow R \le F$ (True)

133. (d) $H @ B \Rightarrow H < B$
$B \bigstar E \Rightarrow B \le E$
$V © E \Rightarrow V \ge E$
and $W\$V \Rightarrow W > V$
$\therefore H < B \le E \le V < W$
I. $W\$E \Rightarrow W > E$ (True)
II. $H @ E \Rightarrow H < E$ (True)
III. $H @ V \Rightarrow H < V$ (True)
IV. $W\$B \Rightarrow W > B$ (True)

134. (e) $R © K \Rightarrow R \ge K$
$K \bigstar N \Rightarrow K \le N$
$N\$J \Rightarrow N > J$
and $J \% H \Rightarrow J = H$
$\therefore R \ge K \le N > J = H$
I. $R\$N \Rightarrow R > N$ (False)
II. $J @ K \Rightarrow L < K$ (False)
III. $H @ N \Rightarrow H < N$ (True)
IV. $R\$H \Rightarrow R > H$ (False)

135. (c) $K \bigstar D \Rightarrow K \le D$
$D\$N \Rightarrow D > N$
$N \% M \Rightarrow N = M$
and $M © W \Rightarrow M \ge W$
$\therefore K \le D > N = M \ge W$
I. $M @ K \Rightarrow M < K$ (False)
II. $N @ K \Rightarrow N < K$ (False)
III. $M @ D \Rightarrow M < D$ (True)
IV. $W \bigstar N \Rightarrow W \le N$ (True)

136. (a) Let the numbers be x, y and z.
According to the question :

$$x = 2y \text{ and } y = 2z \Rightarrow z = \frac{y}{2}$$

$$\therefore \text{Average} = \frac{2y + y + \frac{y}{2}}{3} = 21 \Rightarrow \frac{7y}{6} = 21 \Rightarrow y = 18$$

i.e. Numbers are 36, 18 and 9.
The largest number is 36.

137. (b) Monthly saving of Mr. Yadav $= \frac{48456}{12} = \text{Rs } 4038$
% of salary spent on consumable items = 60%
remaining % = 40
% spent on clothes and transport = 50% of 40 = 20
Thus % monthly savings = 20
Thus, % of saving
= % of salary spent on transport and clothes
Required amount = Rs 4038.

138. (b) Let the numbers be 2x and 3x. ($\because$ Ratio = 2 : 3)
Now, according to the question $\frac{2x+8}{3x+8} = \frac{3}{4}$
$\Rightarrow 8x + 32 = 9x + 24 \Rightarrow x = 8$
$\Rightarrow$ Numbers are 16 and 24.

139. (c) $SP = \frac{(100+20)}{100} \times 90 = \text{Rs } 108$

$$\therefore \text{Marked price} = \frac{108}{0.85} = \text{Rs } 127.05 \equiv 127\frac{1}{17}$$

140. (a) $2\pi \times 5 : \pi.5^2 \Rightarrow 2 : 5$

For 141-150 :

Q. No.	i	ii/(A)	iii/(B)	iv	Ans.
141.	√	√	√	√	(b)
142.	×	√	√	√	(a)
143.	√	√	(√)	–	(e)
144.	√	(√)	√	√	(c)
145.	√	√	(√)	√	(d)
146.	√	×	√	√	(a)
147.	√	√	(√)	√	(d)
148.	√	√	√	√	(b)
149.	√	√	√	√	(b)
150.	√	(√)	√	√	(c)

Not to be admitted ⇒ (a)

i+ii+iii+iv ⇒ (b)

i+(A)+iii+iv ⇒ (c)

i+ii+(B)+iv ⇒ (d)

Data inadequate ⇒ (e)

151. (a) 152. (b) 153. (c) 154. (c)
155. (b) 156. (a) 157. (e) 158. (a)
159. (d) 160. (b)

161. (d) I is a bizarre solution : do we expect the lower-order batsmen to tackle the new ball in the opening overs? II is a desirable course of action because practice is supposed to improve one's performance. III again is being over-optimistic. We can't expect the entire lot of inexperienced batsmen to perform better than all the established ones.

162. (b) I does not follow because stopping vigilance would be foolish thing to do. A better solution could be to reduce vigilance during nights a little and reinforce daylight vigilance as III suggests. Killing criminals is equivalent to giving punishment and this is an area for the judiciary, not for the police. So II does not follow.

163. (e) I does not follow because of the word 'mandatory'. II and III are advisable because they will reduce problem.

164. (c) As in the statement it is mentioned 'rejection due to inferior-quality material and poor craftsmanship', it is well known that purchase department is responsible for purchasing the inferior quality material. Again production department is responsible for improper inspection. Hence investigation is compulsory for all the department. Hence I follows. II follows because claim of company 'X' may be wrong. III follows because relationship with a previous client should always be kept up.

165. (c) The best option in this case is to divert the load of vehicular traffic through various link roads during peak hours.

166. (d) Students passing from Institute B in

$$2002 = 3500 \times \frac{14}{100} = 490$$

Students passing from Institute B in

$$2003 = 3600 \times \frac{16}{100} = 576$$

So, students passing from Institute B in year 2002 and 2003 together $= 490 + 576 = 1066$.

167. (a) Students passing in 2004 from Institute

$$C = 2900 \times \frac{16}{100} = 464$$

Students passing in 2007 from Institute

$$E = 2700 \times \frac{14}{100} = 378$$

$$\text{Their ratio} = \frac{464}{378} = \frac{232}{189}.$$

168. (c) Students appearing from defferent Institutes are:

Institute

A: $2300 + 4200 + 3500 + 2000 + 1800 + 1200 = 15000$

B: $3500 + 3600 + 3400 + 1300 + 2300 + 2100 = 16200$

C: $1800 + 2800 + 2900 + 4500 + 2300 + 3900 = 18200$

D: $2900 + 2800 + 1600 + 3200 + 3300 + 4000 = 17800$

E: $4400 + 3200 + 1900 + 1500 + 3100 + 2700 = 16800$

F: $3200 + 3000 + 4000 + 2600 + 3800 + 2300 = 18900$

169. (b) Student passing in 2005 from all Institutes together.

$$\text{Institute A} = 2000 \times \frac{22}{100} = 440$$

$$B = 1300 \times \frac{15}{100} = 195$$

$$C = 4500 \times \frac{24}{100} = 1080$$

$$D = 3200 \times \frac{20}{100} = 640$$

$$E = 1500 \times \frac{18}{100} = 270$$

$$F = 2600 \times \frac{11}{1000} = 286$$

Total = 2911

170. (d) Student passing in 2006 examination from Institute

$$D = 3300 \times \frac{16}{100} = 528$$

Total students appearing in 2006 from all Institutes $= 1800 + 2300 + 2300 + 3300 + 3100 + 3800 = 16600$

$$\text{Per cent} = \frac{528}{16600} = 3.18$$

171. (c) There may be several causes for the increment in entry fee in the Taj Mahal. Event (B) may be one of the causes. It is also possible that the hike in maintenance cost is the other cause of this increment.

172. (d) Insecurity is a long-run impact of this habit of too much comfort. Comfort leads to a distaning from follow beings. And this loneliness later results in insecurity.

173. (c) Event (A) is the effect but event (B) is not its immediate and principal cause because to get the above outcome proper use of rich mineral resources is equally important.

174. (b) The security arrangements were made to check the high-profile criminal from escaping.

175. (a) If less cars are allowed, the sale is bound to drop.

176. (c) Required number
$= 81 + 165 + 45 + 70 + 275 + 200$
$= 836$

177. (d) No. of Females in H. R. specialization
$= \frac{225 \times 16}{(9+16)} = 144$

178. (a) Required ratio $= \frac{375}{350}$
$= 15:14$

179. (b) No. of females in H.R.
$= \frac{16}{25} \times 225 = 144$
No. of females in marketing
$= \frac{2}{5} \times 275 = 110$
No. of females in I. T.
$= \frac{31}{40} \times 200 = 155$
No. of females in Finance
$= \frac{3}{5} \times 175 = 105$
No. of females in Production
$= \frac{4}{15} \times 375$
$=$ **100** (Lowest)
and No. of females in Merchandising
$= \frac{3}{7} \times 350 = 150$

180. (e) Required number
$= 225 + 275 + 200 + 175 + 375 + 350$
$= 1600$

181. (a) In the light of the passage only assumption A is implicit. Hence option (a) is the correct option.

182. (d) Assumption (d) weakens the argument.

183. (c) Clearly assumption (c) is in support of the argument given in the passage.

184. (d) Required difference
$= [(51.2+40+36.5)-(30+56+25)]$ thousand
$= (127.7-111)$ thousand
$= 16.7$ thousand
$= 16700$

185. (b) Total number of students
$= [51.2+40+36.5+65+50+33+44+30+60+30+56+25]$ thousand
$= (127.7 + 148 + 134 + 111)$ thousands
$= 520.7$ thousand
$= 520700$

186. (c) Required ratio $= \frac{(40+50)}{(30+56)}$
$= \frac{90}{86} = 45:43$

187. (a) Required % $= \frac{50 \times 100}{148}\%$
$= 33.78\%$
$\approx 34\%$

188. (e) Required average number
$= \frac{36.5+33+60+25}{4}$ thousand
$= \frac{154.5}{4}$ thousand
$= 38625$

189. (a) Clearly, (a) is a valid conclusion.

190. (d) Clearly (d) refused the arguments in the statement.

191. (b) Percentage increase in the production of mobile phone for the three companies :
For company P, in
$1996 = \frac{425-348}{348} \times 100 = 22.13\%$
$1997 = \frac{512-425}{425} \times 100 = 20.47\%$
$1998 = \frac{620-512}{512} \times 100 = 21.09\%$
$1999 = \frac{713-620}{620} \times 100 = 15\%$
For company Q, in
$1996 = \frac{310-262}{262} \times 100 = 18.32\%$
$1997 = \frac{375-310}{310} \times 100 = 20.97\%$
$1998 = \frac{447-375}{375} \times 100 = 19.2\%$

$$1999 = \frac{520-447}{447} \times 100 = 16.33\%$$

For company R, in

$$1996 = \frac{495-450}{450} \times 100 < 20\%$$

$$1997 = \frac{543-495}{495} \times 100 < 20\%$$

$$1998 = \frac{655-543}{543} \times 100 = 20.62\%$$

$$1999 = \frac{787-655}{655} \times 100 = 20.15\%$$

So, we get in all 6 instances in which production of mobile phone over the previous year's production is greater than 20%.

192. (c) Annual % increase from 1995 to 1996

$$= \frac{960}{1060} \times 100 \times \frac{1}{4} = \frac{90.57}{4} = 22.64\%$$

193. (c) Total population in 1996 = 1.1 billion = 1,100,000,000
Total production of mobile phone in 1996
$= 425 + 310 + 495 = 1230$ lakhs = 1,23,000,000
Let the urban population be U.
Then rural population would be 1,100,000,000 – U
Now, 15% of U + 8% of (1,100,000,000 – U) = 123,000,000
$\Rightarrow$ U = 500,000,000 = 500 million.

194. (d) Number of mobile phone produced by P, Q, R in 1997 and 1999 (in lakhs)

Company / Year	P	Q	R
1997	512	375	543
1999	713	520	787

Let the cost price of the companies P, Q, R be Rs 2K, Rs. 4K and Rs 3K, respectively.
Therefore,
Total revenue collected in 1997
$= 512 \times 2K + 375 \times 4K + 543 \times 3K = 4153\,K$
and the total revenue collected in 1999
$= 713 \times 2K + 520 \times 4K + 787 \times 3K = 5867\,K$
% increase in revenue from 1997 to 1999

$$= \frac{1714K}{4153K} \times 100 = 41.27\%$$

195. (a) % Increase for P $= \frac{713-348}{348} \times 100 = 104.89\%$

% Increase for Q $= \frac{520-262}{262} \times 100 = 98.47\%$

% Increase for R $= \frac{787-450}{450} \times 100 = 74.88\%$

Clearly, the % increase in production is maximum for the company P over the five year period.

196. (e) The statement is 'definitely false'. It is clear from the passage that foreign institutional investors no longer seem very enamoured by the Indian story.

197. (c) Data are 'inadequate'. The passage nowhere talks about many Asian countries.

198. (a) The statement is 'definitely true' as mentioned in 3rd and 4th sentence that Indian forex does not face the risk of falling to the levels of early 1990.

199. (d) In the light of the facts given in the passage, inference is probably false.

200. (b) In the light of facts given in the passage the inference is probably true.

MAHARASHTRA COMMON ENTRANCE TEST
15th FEBRUARY 2009
SOLVED PAPER
(Based on Memory)

1. Five friends A, B, C, D and E are standing in a row facing South but not necessarily in the same order. Only B is between A and E. C is immediate right to E, and D is immediate left to A. On the basis of above information, which of the following statements is **definitely true** ?
   (a) B is to the right of E
   (b) A is second to the left of C
   (c) D is third to the left of E
   (d) B is to the left of A
   (e) None of these
2. If the sentence "you must go early to catch the train" is coded as "early catch train must to go the you", what will be code for the sentence "morning exercise will help you to keep fit" ?
   (a) help to fit you exercise will keep morning
   (b) help to fit exercise you will keep morning
   (c) will help to fit you exercise keep morning
   (d) will fit to exercise you help keep morning
   (e) None of these
3. In a certain code language the word 'DIPLOMA' is written as 'FERHQIC'. How will the word 'FOREIGN' be written in that code ?
   (a) HJTAKCP (b) HKTALCP
   (c) HKTAKCP (d) HKTAKBP
   (e) None of these
4. A B C D E F G H I J K L M N O P Q R S T U V W X Y Z
   Four of the following five letter groups of the English alphabet given above are alike in a certain way and so form a group. On the basis of their position in English alphabet, which is the one that does not belong to the group ?
   (a) DKG (b) FMI
   (c) MTP (d) JQM
   (e) HOL
5. How many pairs of letters are there in the word EXPLOSION which have as many letters between them as in the English alphabet ?
   (a) One (b) Two
   (c) Three (d) Four
   (e) None of these
6. If only the consonants in the word MEAT are changed in such a way that each of them becomes the next letter in the English alphabet and the remaining letters are kept unchanged, then how many meaningful words can be formed with the new set of letters using each leter only once in a word ?
   (a) None (b) Two
   (c) Three (d) One
   (e) None of these
7. How many meaningful words can be formed by replacing only the consonants in the word BREAK by the next letter in the English alphabet and keeping the vowels unchanged?
   (a) None (b) One
   (c) Two (d) Three
   (e) More than three
8. In a certain code language 'CREATIVE' is written as 'BDSBFUJS'. How is 'TRIANGLE' written in that code ?
   (a) BSHSFHKM (b) BHSSMHHF
   (c) BSSHFMKH (d) BHSSFKHM
   (e) None of these
9. In a row of girls, Rita and Monika occupy the ninth place from the right end and tenth place from the left end respectively. If they interchange their places, Rita and Monika occupy seventeenth place from the right and eighteenth place from the left, respectively. How many girls are there in the row?
   (a) 25 (b) 26
   (c) 27 (d) Data inadequate
   (e) None of these
10. In a certain code language 'Ka Bi Pu Ya' means 'You are very intelligent'; 'Ya Lo Ka Wo' means 'They seem very intelligent'; 'La Pu Le' means 'You can see' and 'Sun Pun Yun Ya' means 'how intelligent she is', In that language, which of the following words mean 'are'?
   (a) Ka (b) Bi
   (c) Ya (d) Pu
   (e) None of these

DIRECTIONS (Qs. 11-15) : *Answer the questions based on the information given below :*

In a basket, 5 red, 3 white and 8 blue pencils are kept, three pencils are drawn at random, then

11. Find the probability that each pencil is of different colour.
   (a) $\frac{14}{3}$ (b) $\frac{3}{14}$
   (c) $\frac{5}{14}$ (d) $\frac{9}{11}$
   (e) None of these
12. Find the probability that the two pencil is blue and one white colour.
   (a) $\frac{4}{15}$ (b) $\frac{20}{3}$
   (c) $\frac{3}{20}$ (d) $\frac{8}{17}$
   (e) None of these

13. Find the probability that the all pencil is of red colour.
(a) $\frac{1}{56}$ (b) $\frac{1}{54}$
(c) $\frac{16}{5}$ (d) $\frac{5}{16}$
(e) None of these

14. How many ways committee of four people can be chosen from 7 ?
(a) 760 (b) 840
(c) 320 (d) 850
(e) None of these

15. In how many ways 9 people are accomodate 4 chair ?
(a) 3205 (b) 3025
(c) 3024 (d) 3022
(e) None of these

DIRECTIONS (Qs. 16-20) : *Each of the following series consists of seven figures, two of which at the ends are unlettered. One of the five lettered figures does not fit into the series. Find out the figure.*

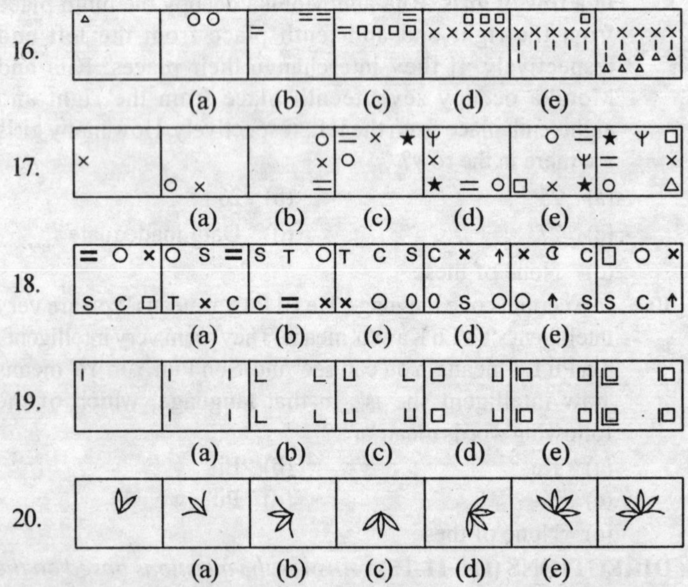

DIRECTIONS (Qs. 21-15) : *What* ***approximate*** *value should come in place of the question mark (?) in the following equation ? (you are not expected to calculate the exact value).*

21. $11.593 \times 31.118 \times 24.924 = ?$
(a) 8990 (b) 8989
(c) 8991.4 (d) 8971.5
(e) None of these

22. $9938 \div 92 \div 9 = ?$
(a) 12 (b) 14
(c) 25 (d) 18
(e) None of these

23. Cube root of 750000 = ?
(a) 90.85 (b) 90.87
(c) 99 (d) 90
(e) None of these

24. $158.25 \times 4.6 + 21\%$ of $847 + ? = 950.93$
(a) 35 (b) 40
(c) 25 (d) 50
(e) 45

25. $248.251 \div 12.62 \times 20.52 = ?$
(a) 400 (b) 450
(c) 600 (d) 350
(e) 375

DIRECTIONS (Qs. 26-30) : *Each of these questions has a sentence with a bold part. Choose the best option to replace the bold part.*

26. Panchayati Raj institutions are now **entrusted upon the execution of all rural upliftment schemes and programs** in India.
(a) entrusted with the execution of all rural upliftment schemes and programs
(b) entrusted with the execution of all rural uplift schemes and programs
(c) entrusted upon the execution of all rural upliftment schemes and programs
(d) entrusted within the execution for all rural upliftment programs and schemes.
(e) None of these

27. **Reared in a village where computers and the internet were objects of curiosity,** Murty today hardly gives a thought to the immense possibilities that the internet revolution has thrown open to him.
(a) reared in a village where computers and the internet were objects of curiosity.
(b) curious to know that computers and the internet were objects of curiosity in the village he was reared up.
(c) being reared in the village where the computers and the internet are objects of curiosity.
(d) reared in a village where computers and the internet were an object of curiousness.
(e) None of these

28. Armed with the talents of a high intellect, **an actor with extra-ordinary gifts and an ingenious criminal,** Charles Sobhraj played an overbearing role in the sensationalisation of crime during the later part of the 20th century in the Indian sub-continent.
(a) an actor with extra-ordinary gifts and an ingenious criminal.
(b) an ingenious actor and an extra-ordinarily gifted criminal.
(c) a gifted actor and an ingeniously criminal.
(d) an extra-ordinarily gifted actor and an ingenious criminal.
(e) None of these

29. In the fall of 1996, the Indian government **dispatched samples of the cells of the militants to those four US scientists, who were only the Americans authorized to test them.**
(a) dispatched samples of the cells of the militants to those four US scientists, who were only the Americans authorized to test them.
(b) dispatched samples of the militant's cells to those four US scientists, the only Americans authorized to test them.
(c) dispatched samples of the cells of militants to those four US scientists who were authorized to test them.
(d) dispatch the samples of the cells of the militants to those four US scientists, who were the only Americans authorized to test them.
(e) None of these

30. To prepare himself, he subjected himself to two weeks of total abstinence and intensive training in the open fields of Panipat, **climbing the hills nearby 30 times, spend nights in the open and to test to see** how long he could hold out without food.
   (a) climbing the hills nearby 30 times, spend nights in the open and to test to see
   (b) climbed the hills nearby 30 times, spending nights in the open and tested to see
   (c) spending nights in the open by climbing the hills near by 30 times and tested for seeing
   (d) climbing the hills nearby 30 times, spending nights in the open and testing to see
   (e) None of these

DIRECTIONS (Qs. 31-35) : *Find out the next number.*

31. 2, 11, 27, 52, 88, 137, ?
   (a) 201 (b) 308
   (c) 406 (d) 278
   (e) None of these

32. 405, 135, 54, 27, 18, ?
   (a) 35 (b) 18
   (c) 27 (d) 36
   (e) None of these

33. 18, 32, 58, 108, 206, 400, ?
   (a) 402 (b) 386
   (c) 406 (d) 786
   (e) None of these

34. 1 3 6 11 20 37 ?
   (a) 72 (b) 70
   (c) 91 (d) 49
   (e) 36

35. 2 11 27 113 561 3369 ?
   (a) 23581 (b) 5921
   (c) 2457 (d) 3281
   (e) 3369

DIRECTIONS (Qs. 36-40) : *The second figure in the first unit of the problem figures bears a certain relationship to the first figure. Similarly, the second figure in the second unit of the problem figures bears the same relationship with which one of the five answer figures ? That answer figure should replace the question mark.*

36.

37.

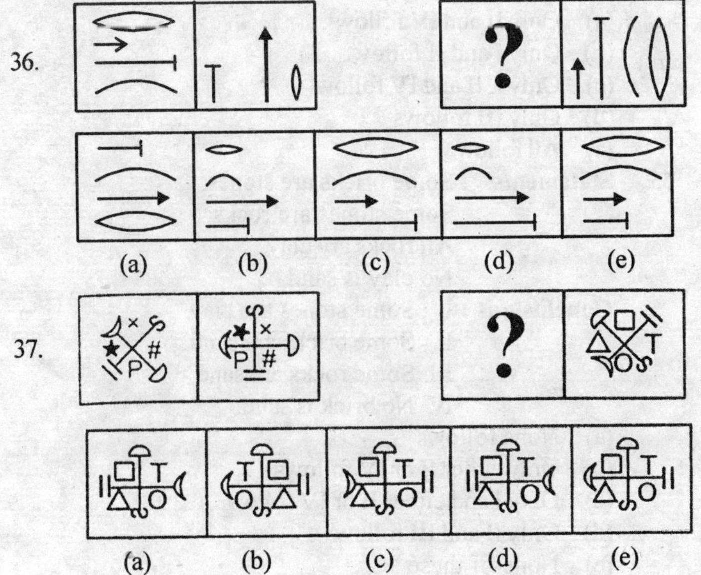

38.

39.

40.

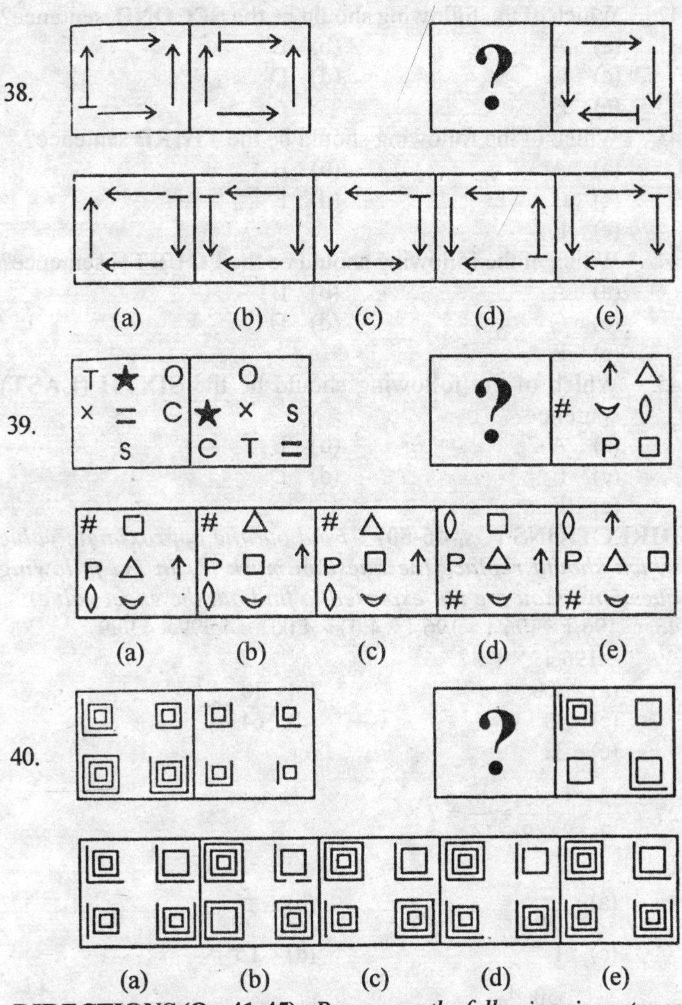

DIRECTIONS (Qs. 41-45) : *Rearrange the following six sentences (A), (B), (C), (D), (E) and (F) in the proper sequence to form a meaningful paragraph, then answer the questions given below them.*

A. All human beings are aware of the existence of a power greater than that of the mortals- the name given to such a power by indiviuals is an outcome of birth, education and choice

B. This power provides an anchor in times of adversity, difficulty and trouble.

C. Industrial organisations also contribute to the veneration of this power by participating in activities such as religious ceremonies and festivities organized by the employees.

D. Their other philanthrophic contributions include the construction and maintenance of religious place such as temples or gurudwaras.

E. Logically, therefore such a power should be remembered in good times also.

F. The top management/ managers should participate in all such events, irrespective of their

41. Which of the following should be the **FIRST** sentence?
   (a) A (b) B
   (c) F (d) D
   (e) E

42. Which of the following should be the **SECOND** sentence?
(a) A (b) B
(c) C (d) D
(e) E

43. Which of the following should be the **THIRD** sentence?
(a) A (b) B
(c) C (d) F
(e) E

44. Which of the following should be the **FOURTH** sentence?
(a) A (b) B
(c) C (d) D
(e) E

45. Which of the following should be the **SIXTH (LAST)** sentence?
(a) A (b) B
(c) E (d) D
(e) F

DIRECTIONS (Qs. 46-50) : *Find out the **approximate** value which should replace the question mark (?) in the following questions. (You are not expected to find out the exact value).*

46. $196.1 \times 196.1 \times 196.1 \times 4.01 \times 4.001 \times 4.999 \times 4.999 = 196.1^3 \times 4 \times ?$
(a) 100 (b) 16
(c) 10 (d) 64
(e) 32

47. $\frac{2}{7} \times \frac{1}{8} + \frac{3}{7} \div \frac{6}{14} = ?$
(a) $\frac{2}{56}$ (b) $\frac{3}{56}$
(c) 1 (d) 2.5
(e) $\frac{50}{60}$

48. $10.1^{2.01} + 2.9^{3.001} = ?$
(a) 130 (b) 160
(c) 115 (d) 147
(e) None of these

49. $\sqrt{1999.9997} = 4.76 \times ?$
(a) 11 (b) 45
(c) 49 (d) 6
(e) 9

50. $23\% \text{ of } 4011 + \frac{1}{7} \text{ of } 5555 = ?$
(a) 7000 (b) 1900
(c) 9022 (d) 1700
(e) 1450

DIRECTIONS (Qs. 51-55) : *In each of the questions below are given four statements followed by four conclusions numbered I, II, III and IV. You have to take the given statements to be true even if they seem to be at variance from commonly known facts. Read all the conclusions and then decide which of the given conclusions logically follows from the given statements disregarding commonly known facts.*

51. **Statements** : Some pens are stands.
Some stands are containers.
All containers are boxes.
All boxes are drawers.

Conclusions : I. Some boxes are stands.
II. Some drawers are stands.
III. Some drawers are containers.
IV. Some boxes are pens.
(a) Only I and II follow
(b) Only II and III follow
(c) Only I, II and III follow
(d) All follow
(e) None of these

52. **Statements** : All paints are colours.
Some colours are brands.
Some brands are certificates.
All certificates are degrees.

Conclusions : I. Some brands are degrees.
II. Some certificates are colours.
III. Some colours are paints.
IV. No paint is degree.
(a) None follows (b) Only I follows
(c) Only III follows (d) Only either I or II follows
(e) None of these

53. **Statements** : Some files are covers.
All covers are keys.
All keys are locks.
Some locks are doors.

Conclusions : I. Some doors are keys.
II. Some doors are covers.
III. All keys are covers.
IV. Some doors are files.
(a) None follows (b) Only I follows
(c) Only II follows (d) Only II and III follow
(e) None of these

54. **Statements** : Some desks are chairs.
All chairs are tables.
All tables are computers.
All computers are phones.

Conclusions : I. Some phones are desks.
II. Some computers are chairs.
III. All tables are phones.
IV. Some desks are tables.
(a) Only II and IV follow
(b) Only I and II follow
(c) Only I, II and IV follow
(d) Only III follows
(e) All follow

55. **Statements** : Some bricks are stones.
Some stones are rocks.
All rocks are clay.
No clay is sand.

Conclusions : I. Some stones are clay.
II. Some bricks are sand.
III. Some rocks are sand.
IV. No brick is sand.
(a) None follows
(b) Only either II or IV follows
(c) Only I and either II or IV follow
(d) Only II and III follow
(e) None of these

DIRECTIONS (Qs. 56-60) : *In each of the following questions in four out of the five figures, element I is related to element II in the same particular way. Find out the figure in which element I is not so related to element II.*

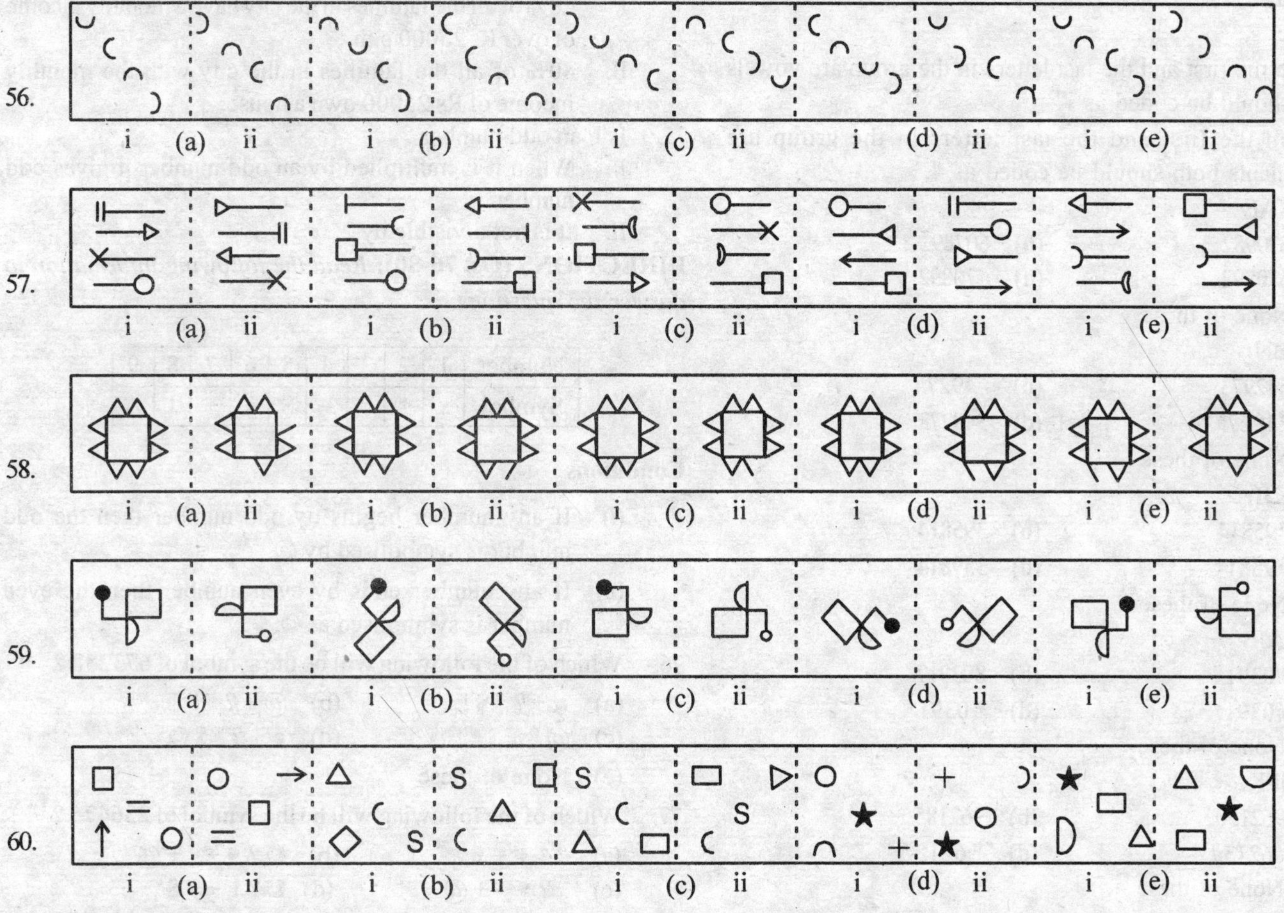

DIRECTIONS for (Qs. 61- 65) : *Five incomplete sentences are given. You have to obtain correct option from among 10 incomplete sentences /words common options to complete the question statements.*

A. to eat quickly and cheaply
C. having used for
B. is because their
D. even if
E. eating quickly
F. has
G has been used for
H. of their
I. in spite of
J. with

61. Fast food restaurants have become popular because many working people want ....
(a) Only 'A' (b) Only 'B'
(c) Both 'A' and 'B' (d) Only 'C'
(e) None of these

62. Encounters between people from different countries can result in misunderstandings .... different conceptions about space.
(a) Only 'C' (b) Only 'H'
(c) Both 'C' and 'D' (d) Only 'J'
(e) None of these

63. *Oscillatoria* are one of the few plants that can move about .... a wavy, gliding motion.
(a) Only 'D' (b) Only 'E'
(c) Both 'E' and 'F' (d) Only 'J'
(e) None of these

64. Vitamin E cream, a moisturising emollient, ... maintaining soft, healthy looking skin.
(a) Only 'F' (b) Only 'G'
(c) Both 'G' and 'C' (d) Only 'I'
(e) None of these

65. Many people in Delhi celebrated Diwali in a grand way .... the high prices.
(a) Only 'I' (b) Only 'J'
(c) Both 'I' and 'J' (d) Only 'A'
(e) None of these

DIRECTIONS (Qs. 66-70) : *Study the following letters and their corresponding digit codes followed by certain conditions of coding and answer the questions given below them by finding out which of the digit combinations given in (a), (b), (c) and (d) is the coded form of the letter groups given in each question and mark your answers accordingly. If none of the coded form represents the letter group mark answer as (e), i.e. None of these.*

Letter :	P	N	A	J	I	R	E	B	U	K
Digit :	5	3	9	1	4	6	2	7	0	8

Conditions :

(1) If both the first and the last letters in the group are vowels both should be coded as ∗.

(2) If both the first and the last letters in the group are consonants both should be coded as #.

66. RBUKAE
(a) 670982 (b) 607892
(c) 670892 (d) #70892
(e) None of these

67. PIAEBN
(a) 542973 (b) #4927#
(c) *4927* (d) 549273
(e) None of these

68. NAPKJI
(a) *95814 (b) 395814
(c) *9581* (d) 359814
(e) None of these

69. KUNAJB
(a) #0391# (b) 803917
(c) #0391* (d) * 0391*
(e) None of these

70. AREJPK
(a) 962150 (b) 962185
(c) #6215# (d) * 6215 *
(e) None of these

DIRECTIONS (Qs. 71-75) : *Each of the items below has a question followed by two statements labelled as I and II. Use the data given in the statements I and II together with other information to decide whether these statements are sufficient to answer the given question.* ***Mark your answer as*** *:*

(a) if you can get the answer from statement I alone but not from II alone;
(b) if you can get the answer from I alone but not from II alone;
(c) if you can get the answer from both the statements I and II together but not from I alone or II alone and
(d) if you cannot get the answer from the statements I and II together and need more data.
(e) if you can get the answer from either statement I or II alone.

71. How many families in Jammu city own exactly two cars?
I. 150 families in Jammu city own at least one car.
II. 45 families in Jammu city own at least three cars.

72. Ashok and Pawan are standing together on a sunny day Ashok's shadow is 10 feet long. Pawan's shadow is 9 feet long. How tall is Pawan ?
I. Ashok is 6 feet tall.
II. Ashok is standing 2 feet away from Pawan.

73. How far is it from town P to Q ? Town R is 30 km from town P.
I. It is 20 km from town Q to town R.
II. There is a railway line between town P and town Q.

74. What percentage of families in a city have monthly income of Rs 25000 and own a house ?
I. 28% of all the families in the city have a monthly income of over Rs 25000 p.m.
II. 40% of all the families in the city with the monthly income of Rs 25000 own a house.

75. Is b an odd number ?
I. When it is multiplied by an odd number it gives odd number.
II. It is not divisible by 2.

DIRECTIONS (Qs. 76-80): *Read the following information to answer the questions:*

Number	1	2	3	4	5	6	7	8	9
Symbol	x	*	?	÷	$	•	+	!	Δ

Conditions :

(i) If any number begins by odd number then the odd number is symbolised by @.

(ii) If any number ends by even number then the even number is symbolised as ©.

76. Which of the following will be the symbol of 673258 ?
(a) • + ? * $! (b) @ + ? * !
(c) @ ? + $ * ! (d) • + ? * $ ©
(e) None of these

77. Which of the following will be the symbol of 236475 ?
(a) ? * • ÷ x (b) © ? • ÷ + @
(c) x ? • ÷ + @ (d) © ? 1 ÷ + $
(e) None of these

78. Which of the following will be the symbol of 846721?
(a) © ÷ • + * x (b) ! ÷ © ? • + @
(c) ! ÷ • + * x (d) © ÷ • + * x
(e) None of these

79. Which of the following will be the symbol of 178524?
(a) @ + ! $ *© (b) x + ! $ ©
(c) @ + !$ * ÷ (d) * + ! $ ÷
(e) None of these

80. Which of the following will be the symbol of 25486 ?
(a) *$ ÷ Δ (b) *$ ÷ !©
(c) ©$ ÷ !• (d) *$! ÷ •
(e) None of these

DIRECTIONS (Qs. 81 - 85) : *A sentence with two blanks is followed by four alternatives. Select the most appropriate alternative to fill up these blanks most meaningfully.*

81. To a greater or lesser degree all the civilised countries of the world are made up of small class of rulers, ..., and of a large class of subjects, ...
(a) formed by a small minority, who are uncivilized
(b) powerfully corrupt, pointless crusaders
(c) corrupted by too much power, corrupted by too much passive obedience
(d) who are ruled, who ruled.
(e) None of these

82. Though one eye is kept firmly on the............, the company now also promotes .... contemporary art.
(a) present, experimental
(b) future, popular
(c) present, popular (d) market, popular
(e) None of these

83. Indian intellectuals may boast, if they are so inclined, of being .... to the most elitist among the intellectual .... of the world.
(a) subordinate, traditions
(b) heirs, cliques
(c) ancestors, societies
(d) heir, traditions
(e) None of these

84. The Internet is a medium where users have nearly ....choices and .... constraints about where to go and what to do.
(a) unbalanced, nonexistent
(b) embarrassing, no
(c) unlimited, minimal (d) choking, shocking
(e) None of these

85. If you are ....you tend to respond to stressful situations, in a calm, secure, steady and .... way.
(a) resilient, rational (b) obdurate, manageable
(c) propitious, stable (d) delectable, flexible
(e) None of these

DIRECTIONS (Qs. 86 - 90) : *Study the following graph and answer accordingly :*

The following graph shows the construction of house (in lakhs) for various income groups.

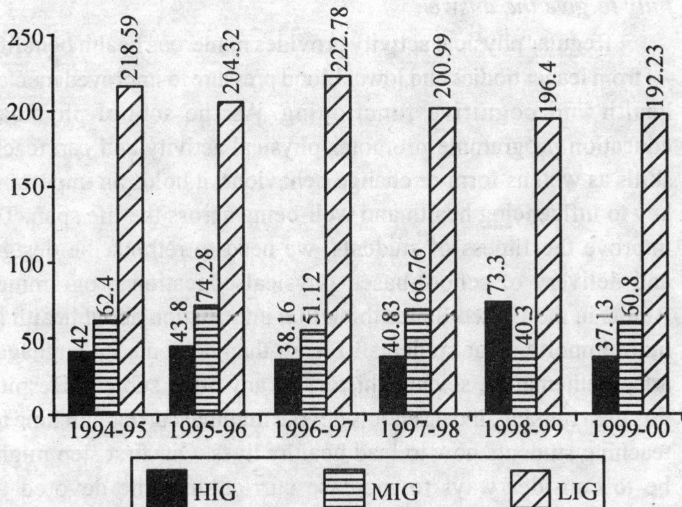

86. What per cent of houses constructed for MIG in 1998-99 ?
(a) 23% (b) 12%
(c) 14% (d) 11%
(e) None of these

87. The total constructions in 1999-00 was what per cent less than that in the year 1995-96 ?
(a) 10% (b) 12%
(c) 14% (d) 15%
(e) None of these

88. What is the ratio of minimum and maximum constructions by any of the three income groups in any of the years?
(a) 1 : 2 (b) 1 : 3
(c) 1 : 6 (d) 2 : 5
(e) None of these

89. Find the percentage increase in the MIG from 1994-95 to 1997-98.
(a) 9% (b) 5%
(c) 7% (d) 11%
(e) 8.5%

90. In which of the following years the MIG constructions less than the HIG constructions ?
(a) 1999-00 (b) 1998-99
(c) 1995-96 (d) 1997-98
(e) None of these

DIRECTIONS (Qs. 91-95) : *In these questions the symbols @, #, ★, $ and used with different meanings as follows :*

'A @ B' means 'A is not greater than B'
'A # B' means 'A is neither greater than nor equal to B'.
'A ★ B' means 'A is not smaller than B'.
'A $ B' means 'A is neither smaller than nor equal to B'.
'A © B' means 'A is neither greater than nor smaller than B'.

Now in each of the following questions assuming the given statements to be true, find out which of the conclusions I, II, III given below them is/are **definitely true** and mark your answer accordingly.

91. **Statements** : H $ K, K© R, R @ J, J # F
Conclusions : I. R # H
II. F $ H
III. H $ J
(a) Only I and II are true (b) Only I is true
(c) Only II is true (d) Only II and III are true
(e) All are true

92. **Statements** : L @ M, M ★ P, M # D, D $ F
Conclusions : I. L @ P
II. P @ D
III. M © F
(a) Only I is true
(b) Only III is true
(c) Only either I or III is true
(d) Only I and II are true
(e) None is true

93. **Statements** : T @ V, V # Q, Q © L, L ★ M
Conclusions : I. M @ Q
II. T @ L
III. T # L
(a) Only I is true (b) Only II is true
(c) Only III is true (d) Only I and III are true
(e) None of these

94. **Statements** : J ★ E, D @ E, E $ K, K © T
Conclusions : I. J $ D
II. J ★ D
III. E $ T
(a) None is true (b) Only II and III are true
(c) Only I and III are true (d) All are true
(e) None of these

95. **Statements** : H @ I, I # L, L ★ A, A $ Q
Conclusions : I. H # L
II. H ★ L
III. Q # H
(a) Only I is true
(b) Only I and II are true
(c) Only III and either I or II are true
(d) Only either I or II is true
(e) None is true

DIRECTIONS(Qs. 96-100) : *In the following questions, each word in capital letters is followed by three words lettered by A, B and C. Choose the word(s) which is/are similar in meaning from the options given below :*

96. HIATUS
A. Atrocious B. Dominance C. Gap
(a) Only 'A' (b) Both 'A' and 'B'
(c) Only 'C' (d) All 'A', 'B' and 'C'
(e) None of these

97. DENOUEMENT
A. Outcome B. Eschew C. Character
(a) Only 'A' (b) Both 'A' and 'B'
(c) Only 'C' (d) All 'A', 'B' and 'C'
(e) None of these

98. FOMENT
A. Vex B. Waste C. Instigate
(a) Only 'A' (b) Both 'A' and 'B'
(c) Only 'C' (d) All 'A', 'B' and 'C'
(e) None of these

99. GRIT
A. Level B. Courage C. Grease
(a) Only 'A' (b) Both 'A' and 'B'
(c) Only 'C' (d) All 'A', 'B' and 'C'
(e) None of these

100. OMINOUS
A. Threatening B. Powerful C. Ubiquitous
(a) Only 'A' (b) Both 'A' and 'B'
(c) Only 'C' (d) All 'A', 'B' and 'C'
(e) None of these

DIRECTIONS (Qs. 101-105) : *In each of the following questions a number series is given. After the series a number is given followed by (a), (b), (c), (d) and (e). You have to complete the series starting with the number given and following the sequence of the original series. Answer the questions that follow the series.*

101. 5 6 16 57 244 1245
2 (1) (2) (3) (4) (5)
What will come in place of (4) ?
(a) 46 (b) 39
(c) 156 (d) 173
(e) None of these

102. 3 5 9 17 33 65
7 (1) (2) (3) (4) (5)
What will come in place of (4) ?
(a) 95 (b) 51
(c) 99 (d) 49
(e) None of these

103. 7 4 5 9 20 52.5
3 (1) (2) (3) (4) (5)
What will come in place of (3) ?
(a) 4.5 (b) 2
(c) 6 (d) 7
(e) None of these

104. 3 10 32 111 460 2315
2 (1) (2) (3) (4) (5)
What will come in place of (2) ?
(a) 29 (b) 30
(c) 26 (d) 28
(e) None of these

105. 5 8 6 10 7 12
7 (1) (2) (3) (4) (5)
What will come in place of (4) ?
(a) 14 (b) 16
(c) 9 (d) 11
(e) None of these

DIRECTIONS (Qs. 106-110) : *Read the following passage carefully to give the answer.*

Regular physical activity provides numerous health benefits — from leaner bodies and lower blood pressure to improved mental health and cognitive functioning. As the school physical education programme promotes physical activity and can teach skills as well as form or change behaviour, it holds an important key to influencing health and well-being across the life span. To improve the fitness of students, we need to rethink the design and delivery of school-based physical education programme. Adults in the United States think that information about health is more important for students to learn than contents in language, arts, mathematics, science, history or any other subject. Despite this high ranking, most schools devote minimal curriculum time to teaching students how to lead healthy lives. Our first step might be to consider ways to increase curriculum time devoted to physical education. In addition, schools need to thoughtfully analyse the design and delivery of school physical education programme to ensure that they are engaging, developmentally appropriate, inclusive and instructionally powerful.

106. According to this passage, regular physical activity is needed to :
(a) control one's blood pressure
(b) lose one's weight
(c) improve one's cognitive skill
(d) improve one's physical as well as mental health
(e) None of these

107. In order to tone up the physical education programme :
(a) it should be made compulsory at school
(b) an assessment of the existing programme should be made
(c) a committee should be set up in every school
(d) the programme should be reoriented and implemented
(e) None of these

108. According to American, health education is more important than teaching :
(a) social sciences (b) liberal arts
(c) any subject (d) natural sciences
(e) None of these

109. The author wants the reoriented physical education programme to be :
(a) given minimal curriculum time
(b) very comprehensive
(c) relevant to the modern society
(d) thoughtful
(e) None of these

110. In order to improve the physical education programme, we should first of all :
(a) allot more time to the teaching and learning of physical activity
(b) decide on the number of activities to be taught
(c) employ qualified instructors
(d) increase the teaching load of instructors
(e) None of these

DIRECTIONS (Qs. 111-115) : *The graph below gives the percentage of students passed over the period shown. Study the graph carefully and answer accordingly.*

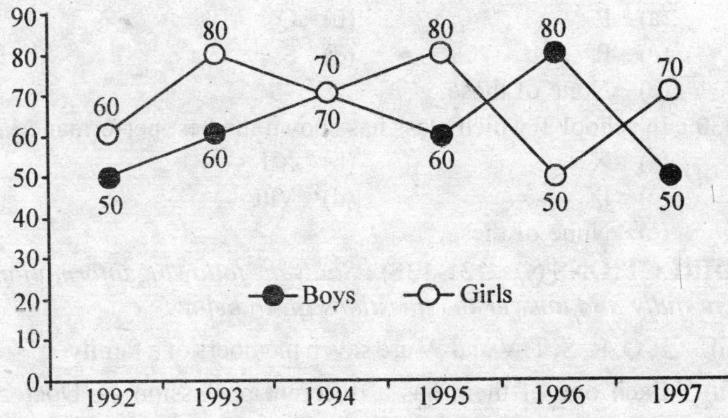

111. What is the overall percentage of failed boys over the period shown ?
(a) $61\frac{2}{3}$ (b) 35
(c) $35\frac{1}{3}$ (d) $38\frac{1}{3}$
(e) None of these

112. In which of the following years did the performance of girls improve the maximum as compared to the previous year ?
(a) 1992 (b) 1993
(c) 1997 (d) 1996
(e) None of these

113. For how many times was there a paired rise or fall in the per cent age of successfull boys and girls ?
(a) Nil (b) 1
(c) 2 (d) 3
(e) None of these

114. For how many years was there a paired rise or fall in the percentage of boys and girls passed over the period shown ?
(a) Nil (b) 1
(c) 2 (d) 3
(e) None of these

115. What is the ratio of the average of failed girls and that of failed boys ?
(a) 17:21 (b) 23:19
(c) 21:17 (d) 7:8
(e) None of these

DIRECTIONS (Qs. 116-120) : *Answer these questions based on the information given.*

Five boys Amit, Suresh, Vishnu, Ujjwal and Rakesh are sitting in a row facing South. Five girls Alka, Jyoti, Veena, Prabha and Nayan are sitting in front of them in a row, each one facing one of them. All these are not necessarily in the same serial order. Vishnu is facing Veena, Suresh and Rakesh are not facing Prabha. Amit is at one of the ends. Nayan is fourth to the right of Alka and is facing Rakesh. Jyoti is between Alka and Veena.

116. Which pair occupies the middle position of the rows?
(a) Rakesh, Nayan (b) Suresh, Prabha
(c) Veena, Vishnu (d) Ujjwal, Jyoti
(e) None of these

117. Who is facing Jyoti?
(a) Ujjwal (b) Amit
(c) Amit or Ujjwal (d) Suresh
(e) None of these

118. Which of the following pairs are sitting diagonally opposite?
(a) Rakesh, Alka (b) Amit, Alka
(c) Nayan, Rakesh (d) Suresh, Nayan
(e) None of these

119. Which of the following is Prabha's position?
(a) Between Jyoti and Nayan
(b) Immediate left of Nayan
(c) Facing Suresh
(d) Second to the right of Alka
(e) None of these

120. Which of the following is Suresh's position ?
(a) Between Amit and Vishnu
(b) Right of Ujjwal
(c) Left of Rakesh
(d) Between Vishnu and Rakesh
(e) None of these

DIRECTIONS (Qs. 121-125) : *In each of the following problems, a related pair of figures is given followed by five numbered pairs of figures. Select a pair that has a relationship similar to that in the original pair.*

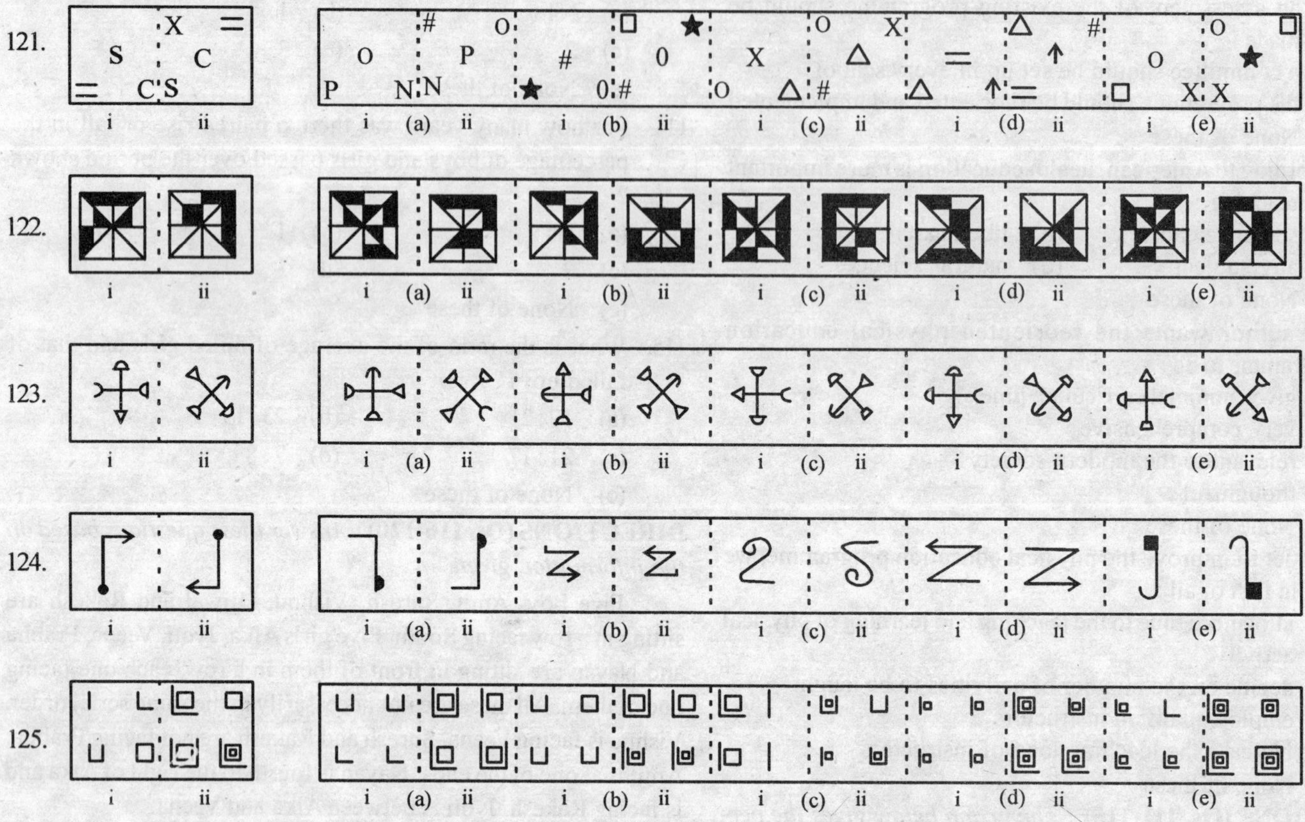

DIRECTIONS (Qs. 126-130) : *Study the following table carefully and answer accordingly. The table shows the no. of passed and failed students of the different schools P, Q, R, S, T and U in the different classes.*

	P		Q		R		S		T		U	
	Pa	Fa	Pa	Fa	Pa	Fa	Pa	Fa	Pa	Fa	Pa	Fa
VIII	460	240	260	400	500	250	400	500	300	140	360	440
IX	440	250	280	380	520	200	200	250	500	240	340	460
X	475	245	300	300	510	200	250	150	530	240	365	435
XI	500	200	320	280	480	240	300	160	500	245	375	425
XII	560	220	350	240	440	260	320	170	525	255	430	370

126. Find the percentage of total failed students in class X.
(a) 59.5 (b) 60.5
(c) 40.5 (d) 39.25
(e) None of these

127. What is the different in the average no. of passed students of P and that of T ?
(a) 18 (b) 16
(c) 14 (d) 15
(e) None of these

128. Which school has shown the worst performance ?
(a) Q (b) S
(c) U (d) Data inadequate
(e) None of these

129. Which shcool has the same average no. of passed and failed students in each class ?
(a) P (b) Q
(c) R (d) S
(e) None of these

130. In school T which class has shown the best performance ?
(a) X (b) XII
(c) IX (d) VIII
(e) None of these

DIRECTIONS (Qs. 131-135) : *Study the following information carefully and answer the questions given below:*

(i) P, Q, R, S, T, V and W are seven members of a family.

(ii) Each one of them has a different profession — Doctor, Teacher, Lawyer, Engineer, Architect, Chartered Accountant and Banker — and their incomes are different.

(iii) There are two married couples in the group.

(iv) R is the Doctor and earns more than the Engineer and the Lawyer.

(v) T is married to the Chartered Accountant and she earns the least.

(vi) No lady is either Lawyer or Engineer.

(vii) Q, the Teacher, earns less than P, and Banker W is married to Q and he earns more than S and P.

(viii) V is not the Lawyer. The Chartered Accountant earns less than the Lawyer but more than the Banker.

131. Who earns the maximum in the family?
(a) V (b) W
(c) R (d) S
(e) None of these

132. Which of the following is a pair of married couple?
(a) RT (b) VT
(c) QT (d) WQ
(e) None of these

133. What is P's position from the top when they are arranged in descending order of their incomes?
(a) Second (b) Fourth
(c) Third (d) First
(e) None of these

134. At least how many male members are there in the family?
(a) Two (b) Three
(c) Four (d) Five
(e) None of these

135. What is the profession of V ?
(a) Engineer
(b) Chartered Accountant
(c) Engineer or Chartered Accountant
(d) Data inadequate
(e) None of these

DIRECTIONS (Qs. 136-140) : *Answer based on the following passage. Choose the most appropriate option from the alternative given the each question.*

Since times immemorial people have been communicating with each other verbally or nonverbally. No one can live in society without communicating. It may be in the form of silence. There are some expressions of emotions, like happiness, sadness, fear, and anger which are considered to be universal.

In today's competitive world, it has become essential that one must have skills in more than one area. A person might possess a number of good qualities necessary for dealing with various problems of daily lives, but lack of effective communication might make the task difficult. Whether it is a corporate world, academic world or social world, the ability to communicate effectively has become a need today. Communication can make or break a relationship, begin or end a war. Perhaps, this is the most important thing, we do in our lives. It is said that motivation is very important, if a person wants to achieve something in life. How can people be motivated ? It's again through communication only. A person might achieve in life many thing, if he/she knows the art and science of communication.

In this context, it is said that culture has a great impact on communication. In fact, culture is communication and communication is culture. When we talk about Indian culture, it is observed that people are very context sensitive. One has to be very cautious about the time and the context of communication, in order to make communication more effective.

Gender and communication is another important area, which has drawn the attention of scholars. Whereas many scholars are of the opinion that men and women differ in their communication styles, some scholars have found no significant difference. Are women better communicators than men ? It is a question of debate. Perhaps, it may be due to the biology or socialization process or both. The researchers will strive to find out a suitable answer to this.

Who does not like a smiling face and friendly and warm communication ? Whether it is boss or subordinate, teacher or student, husband or wife, father or son, everyone needs to develop skills in communication. This will not only help in getting accomplishment of difficult tasks done, but also will give a peace of mind which ultimately may lead to a successful and meaningful life.

136. The author focusses primarily on
(a) gender and communication
(b) culture and communication
(c) communication skills
(d) Biological influence
(e) None of these

137. It can be inferred from the passage that
(a) women are better communicators
(b) men are better communicators
(c) both are equally good communicators
(d) communication skills need to be developed
(e) None of these

138. According to the passage
(a) in Indian culture people are not context sensitive
(b) indian people are very context sensitive
(c) women are very context sensitive
(d) either (a) aor (b)
(e) None of these

139. Which of the following alternatives is closest in meaning to "communication style" ?
(a) communication type
(b) interaction type
(c) way of interacting
(d) both (a) and (c)
(e) None of these

140. According to the passage, it can be inferred that
(a) motivation is necessary
(b) onc gets motivated through communication
(c) motivation is necessary for good communication
(d) motivation is needed for a successful life
(e) None of these

DIRECTIONS (Qs. 141-145) : *In each of the following questions a question is followed by three statements. Study the question and the statements and decide the information given in which of the statements is/are necessary to answer the question ?*

141. What is the staff strength of Company 'X' ?
I. Male and female employees are in the ratio of 2 : 3 respectively
II. Of the officer employees 80% are males.
III. Total number of officers is 132.
(a) I and III only (b) II and either III or I only
(c) All I, II and III (d) Any two of the three
(e) None of these

142. Find three positive consecutive even numbers.
   I. The average of four consecutive even numbers starting from the last of the given numbers is 17.
   II. The difference of the highest and the lowest number is 4.
   III. The sum of the squares of the three numbers is 440.
   (a) I alone is sufficient
   (b) III is sufficient
   (c) I and II are sufficient
   (d) Either I or III is sufficient
   (e) None of these

143. Sonu's income is how much more than Monu's?
   I. Sonu's income is 30% less than her husband's whose provident fund deduction at the rate of 5% is Rs. 975 per month.
   II. Monu spends 30% of her income on house rent, 15% of which is electricity bill.
   III. Sonu's expenditure on house rent is Rs. 4,500 more than that of the Monu's.
   (a) Only II and III are sufficient
   (b) Any two statements are sufficient
   (c) Only I and III are sufficient
   (d) Even all together are not sufficient
   (e) None of these

144. Find out the share of B out of the combined share of A, B and C of Rs. 946.
   I. The share of A is 2/9 of the combined share of B and C.
   II. The share of B is 3/19 of the combined share of A and C.
   III. The share of C is 2.143 times the combined share of B and A.
   (a) Only statements I and III are sufficient
   (b) Only statement II is sufficient
   (c) Any two statements are sufficient
   (d) Either statements I and III together or II alone is sufficient.
   (e) None of these

145. Mohan is 6 years older than Sohan. What will be the sum of their present ages ?
   I. After 6 years, the ratio of their age will be 6 : 5.
   II. The ratio of their present ages is 5 : 4.
   III. 6 years ago, the ratio of their ages was 4 : 3.
   (a) Only II is sufficient
   (b) Only I is sufficient
   (c) Only I and III together are sufficient.
   (d) Any one of I, II and III is sufficient.
   (e) None of these

DIRECTIONS (Q. 146-150) : *In each of these questions, a statement is followed by two courses of action numbered I and II. Assume everything in the statement to be true, and decide which of the suggested course(s) of action logically follow(s) for pursuing. Mark answer as :*
(a) If only I follows
(b) If either I or II follows
(c) If only II follows
(d) If neither I nor II follows
(e) None of these

146. **Statement :** There has been significant drop in the water level of all the lakes supplying water to the city.
   Courses of action :
   I. The water supply authority should impose a partial cut in supply to tackle the situation.
   II. The government should appeal to all the residents through mass media for minimum use of water.

147. **Statement :** A large number of people visiting India from country 'X' has been tested positive for carrying viruses of a killer disease.
   Courses of action :
   I. The Government of India should immediately put a complete ban on people coming to India from country 'X' including those Indians who are settled in country 'X'.
   II. The Government of India should immediately set-up detection centres at all its airports and seaports to identify and quarantine those who are tested positive.

148. **Statement :** The prices of foodgrains and vegetables have substantially increased due to prolonged strike call given by the truck owners association.
   Courses of action :
   I. The government should immediately make alternative arrangement to ensure adequate supply of foodgrains and vegetables in the market.
   II. The government should take steps to cancel the licences of all vehicles belonging to the association.

149. **Statement :** There have been an unprecedented increase in the number of requests for berths in most of the long distance trains during the current holiday season.
   Courses of action :
   I. The railway authority should immediately increase the capacity in each of these trains by attaching additional coaches.
   II. The people seeking accommodation should be advised to make their travel plan after the holiday

150. **Statement :** While laying pipes for one of the utility companies a huge fire broke out due to damage done to the gas pipeline.
   Courses of action :
   I. All the licences of the utility company should immediately be suspended pending enquiry into the incidence.
   II. People residing in the area should be advised to stay indoors to avoid burn injuries.

DIRECTIONS (Qs.151-155) : *Study the following table to answer the given questions.*

Number of students of different classes of a school playing different games.

Games ↓ Class →	XII	XI	X	IX	VIII	VII	VI
Chess	11	12	5	4	2	2	1
Cricket	38	40	12	17	25	18	20
Basketball	11	9	7	6	0	0	0
Table Tennis	9	9	21	19	11	9	0
Football	40	27	18	19	12	16	14
Carrom	16	15	8	19	12	16	14
Tennis	8	9	11	5	6	0	0
Badminton	47	39	33	21	19	0	0

151. **Approximately** what percent of class VIII students play Cricket out of the total students playing Cricket ?
(a) 13 (b) 4
(c) 25 (d) 15
(e) 17

152. What is the ratio of the students playing football in Class XI to those in Class X ?
(a) 1 : 2 (b) 2 : 5
(c) 2 : 3 (d) 3 : 2
(e) None of these

153. Which game is the most popular ?
(a) Badminton (b) Football
(c) Carrom (d) Table Tennis
(e) Cricket

154. **Approximately** what per cent of Class X students play Table Tennis out of the total Class X students playing the different given games ?
(a) 20 (b) 21
(c) 27 (d) 26
(e) 18

155. Which game has ascending number of students from class IX to XII ?
(a) Only Basketball
(b) Only Badminton
(c) Chess and Badminton
(d) No game
(e) None of these

DIRECTIONS (Qs. 156-160) : *Read the following passage carefully to give the answer.*

Compact discs (CDs)' have revolutionised the music industry with their surprisingly realistic sound. The six-inch discs look like thin plastic sandwiches with aluminium at the centre. They have digitally recorded material that is read by laser beams, so the sound has none of the crackling of vinyl records. CDs are also virtually indestructible, and they are lighter and smaller than conventional records. Since their introduction, CDs have become more affordable and widely available. In fact, they are now sold in electronics and video stores that didn't formerly carry records or cassettes.

There has been a phenomenal growth in the sale of CDs. Sales climbed dramatically during the second half of the 1980s. In the 1990s sales have been even greater. CDs have all but replaced records in stores and, in spite of their being less affordable than cassettes, they continue to gain in popularity.

156. The main appeal of CDs is their:
(a) price (b) size
(c) availability (d) sound
(e) None of these

157. The word 'revolutionised' as used in line 1 could best be replaced by :
(a) changed (b) fought
(c) surprised (d) marked
(e) None of these

158. The author refers to CDs as 'sandwiches' because they:
(a) are light (b) are small
(c) are layered (d) don't crackle
(e) None of these

159. According to tile passage, which one of the following is true?
(a) New kinds of stores are selling CDs
(b) CDs are available as cassettes
(c) Stores are selling more CDs than cassettes
(d) Stores are losing money on their cassettes
(e) None of these

160. The author's main purpose is to :
(a) tell how CDs are made
(b) discuss the growth of CDs
(c) compare CDs to sandwiches
(d) describe the stores that sell CDs
(e) None of these

DIRECTIONS (Qs. 161-165) : *Each of the following question s consists of unmarked figures followed by five figures marked (a), (b), (c), (d) and (e). Select a figure from the marked figures which will continue the series established by the unmarked figures.*

161. Problem Figures :

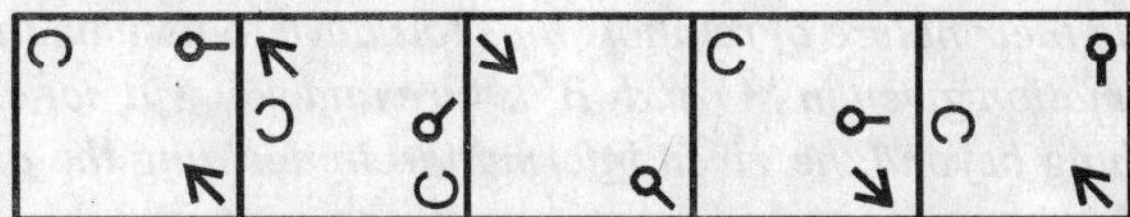

Answer Figures :

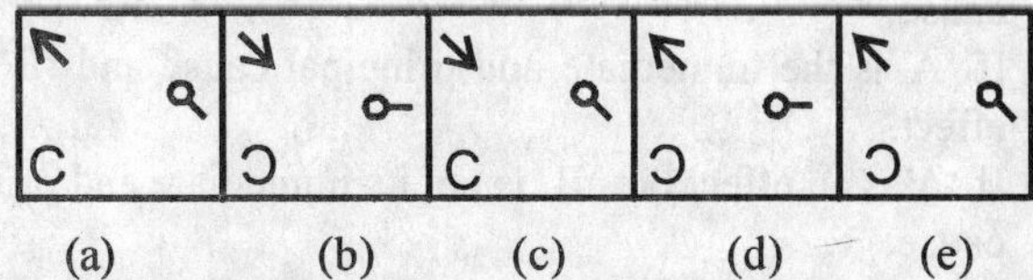

(a) (b) (c) (d) (e)

162. Problem Figures :

O X | = □ = X O X O | ★ □ O O X = | X = □ O ★ ↑

Answer Figures :

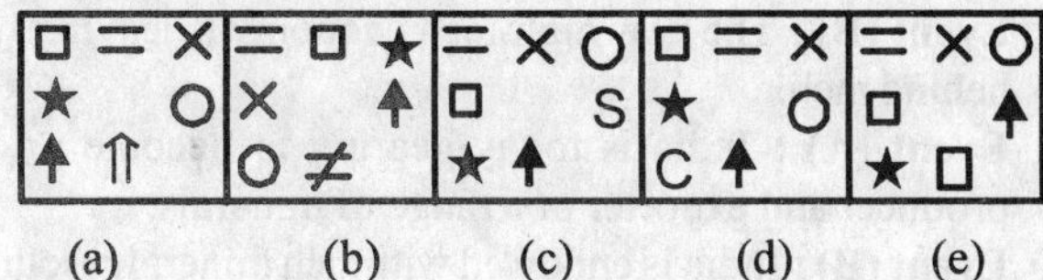

(a) (b) (c) (d) (e)

163. Problem Figures :

Answer Figures :

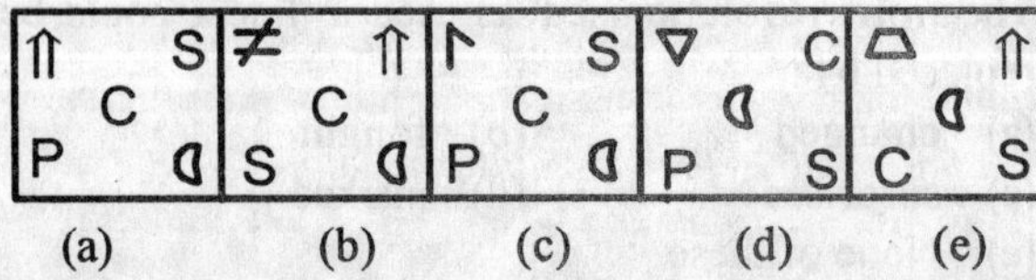

(a) (b) (c) (d) (e)

164. Problem Figures :

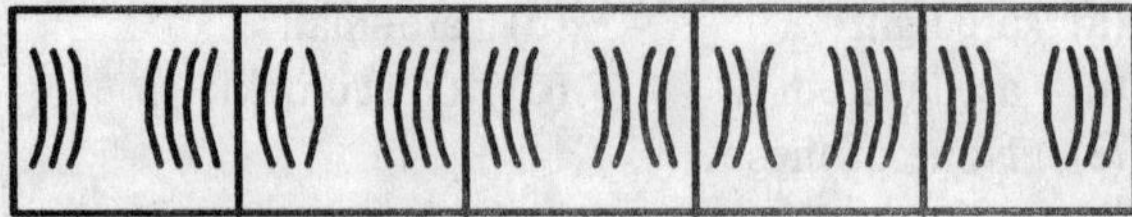

Answer Figures :

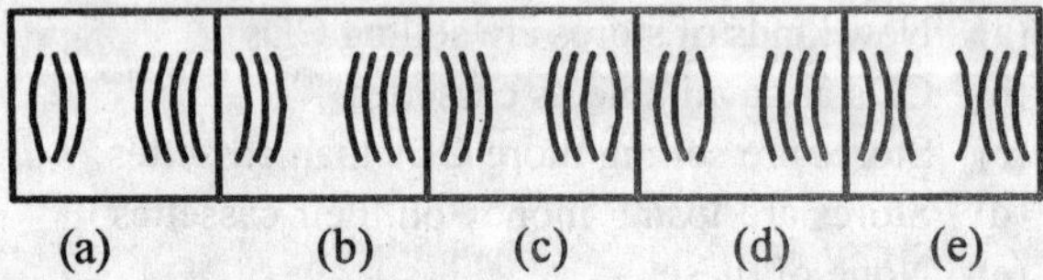

(a) (b) (c) (d) (e)

165. Problem Figures :

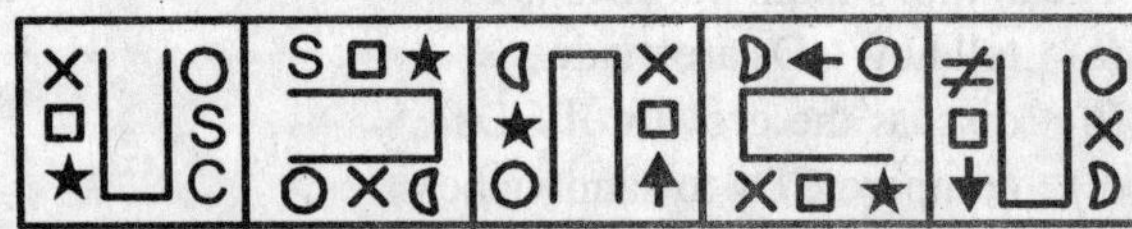

Answer Figures :

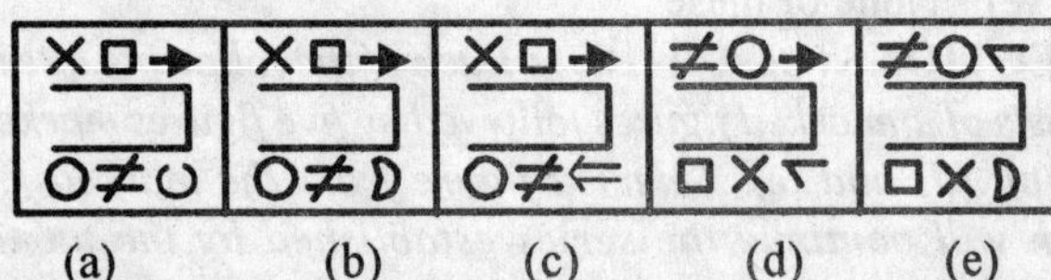

(a) (b) (c) (d) (e)

DIRECTIONS (Qs. 166-170) : *Given below are pairs of events 'A' and 'B'. You have to read both the events 'A' and 'B' and decide their nature of relationship. You have to assume that the information given in 'A' and 'B' is ture and you will not assume anything beyond the given information in deciding the answer.*

Mark answer :

(a) If 'A' is the effect and 'B' is the immediate and principal cause.
(b) If 'A' is the immediate and principal cause and 'B' is its effect.
(c) If 'A' is an effect but 'B' is not its immediate and principal cause.
(d) If 'B' is an effect but 'A' is not its immediate and principal cause.
(e) None of these.

166. **Event (A) :** Women have achieved parity with men in obtaining four-year college degrees and are more likely to work in managerial and professional careers today than 20 years ago.
Event (B) : The new high-tech economy is leaving women behind men.

167. **Event (A) :** India is today gearing to become a leading producer and exporter of a range of minerals.
Event (B) : India is endowed with rich mineral resources.

168. **Event (A) :** Parliament gave nod to Tobacco Control Bill last week.
Event (B) : Non-smokers no longer have to be victims of passive smoking.

169. **Event (A) :** The people of state X have claimed that vegetables like *parwal* and *kakora* are treated with malachite green to make them look fresh.
Event (B) : The officials of Food Adulteration Department has started collecting samples of vegetables from suspicious places in state X.

170. **Event (A) :** According to an NGO report, there are high levels of pesticides in Coca Cola, Pepsi, and other aerated drinks.
Event (B) : Members of Parliament have demanded for a ban on the supply of aerated drinks in the Parliament.

DIRECTIONS (Qs. 171-180) : *Read the following information carefully and answer the questions given below.*

Following are the conditions for admitting students in an engineering college :

The student must

(i) have secured at least 80 per cent aggregate marks in XII Std. Exam in Science stream.
(ii) have secured an average of at least 90 per cent marks in Physics, Chemistry and Mathematics in XII Std. Exam.
(iii) pay Rs 20,000 at the time of admission.
(iv) be at least 17 years old as on 1st September, 2002. However, in the case of a candidate who fulfils all the criteria except
  (A) at (ii) above, but has secured 95 percent aggregate marks, be referred to the Principal.
  (B) at (iii) above, but can pay at least Rs 15,000, be referred to the Chairman, Admission.

Based on the above criteria and information provided below, make a decision in each case. You are not to assume anything. If the data given are not enough to take a decision, mark your answer as 'data inadequate'. These cases are given to you as on 1.9.2002. Give answer :

(a) if the student is to be admitted.
(b) if the student is not to be admitted.
(c) if the case is to be referred to the Principal.
(d) if the case is to be referred to the Chairman Admission.
(e) if the data are inadequate to take decision.

171. Anup Shrivastava has passed XII Std. Exam in Science stream with 95 percent aggregate marks. He was born on December 2, 1984. He has secured 90 percent average marks in Physics, Chemistry and Mathematics. He can pay Rs 20,000 at the time of admission.

172. Sudha Malhotra has secured an average of 95 percent marks in Physics, Chemistry and Mathematics. She has secured 75 percent aggregate marks in XII Std. Exam in Science stream. She can pay Rs 20,000 at the time of admission. She is 18 years old.

173. Ashok Khera has secured 80 percent marks in XII Std. Exam in Science stream. He can pay Rs 15,000 at the time of admission. He has secured 90 percent average marks in Physics, Chemistry and Mathematics.

174. Usha Nadkarni was 16 years old as on January 5, 2000. She can pay Rs 20,000 at the time of admission. She has secured 80 percent average marks in Physics, Chemistry and Mathematics. Her aggregate marks in XII Std. Exam in Science stream is 96 per cent.

175. Vibha Gadre has secured 90 per cent aggregate marks in XII Std. Exam in Science stream and 95 per cent average marks in Physics, Chemistry and Mathematics. She was born on April 25, 1984. She can pay Rs 15,000 at the time of admission.
176. Arun Sharma was born on August 17, 1983. He can pay Rs 20,000 at the time of admission. He has secured 85 per cent aggregate marks in XII Std. Exam in Science stream and also 85 per cent average marks in Physics, Chemistry and Mathematics.
177. Vimal Kar has secured 95 per cent aggregate marks in XII Std. Exam in Science stream. He can pay Rs 16,000 at the time of admission. He was born on April 12, 1984. He has secured 92 per cent average marks in Physics, Chemistry and Mathematics.
178. Anand Upadhyaya was born on September 20, 1984. He has secured 92 per cent aggregate marks in XII Std. Exam in Science stream and also 92 per cent average marks in Physics, Chemistry and Mathematics. He can pay Rs 20,000 at the time of admission.
179. Usha Khanna has secured 90 per cent aggregate marks in XII Std. Exam in Science stream. She has secured 95 per cent average marks in Physics, Chemistry and Mathematics. She can pay Rs 20,000 at the time of admission. She was born on February 20, 1983.
180. Karan Thapar was born on July 15, 1982. He can pay Rs 20,000 at the time of admission. He has secured 89 per cent average marks in Physics, Chemistry and Mathematics. He has secured 96 per cent aggregate marks in XII Std. Exam in Science stream.

DIRECTIONS (Qs. 181-185) : *The first figure in the first unit of the problem figures bears a certain relationship to the second figure. Similarly, one of the figures in the answer figures bears the same relationship to the second figure in the second unit of the problem figures. You are therefore to locate the figure which would replace the question mark.*

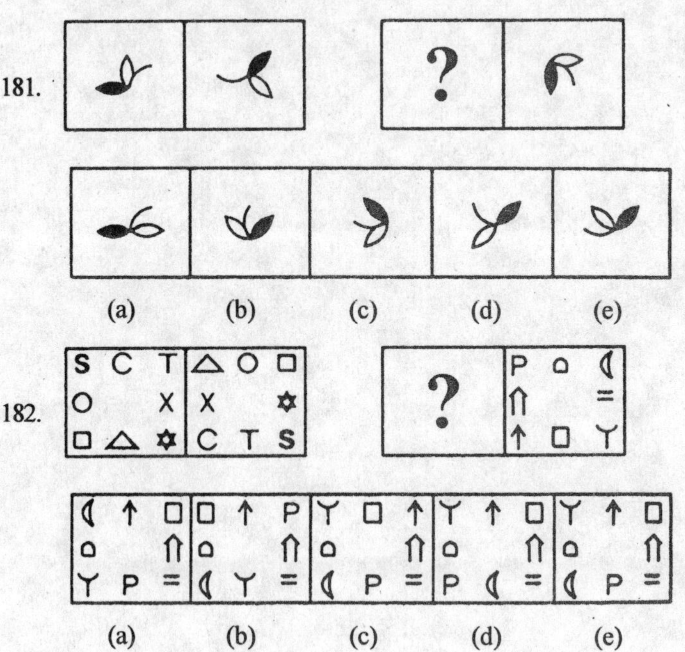

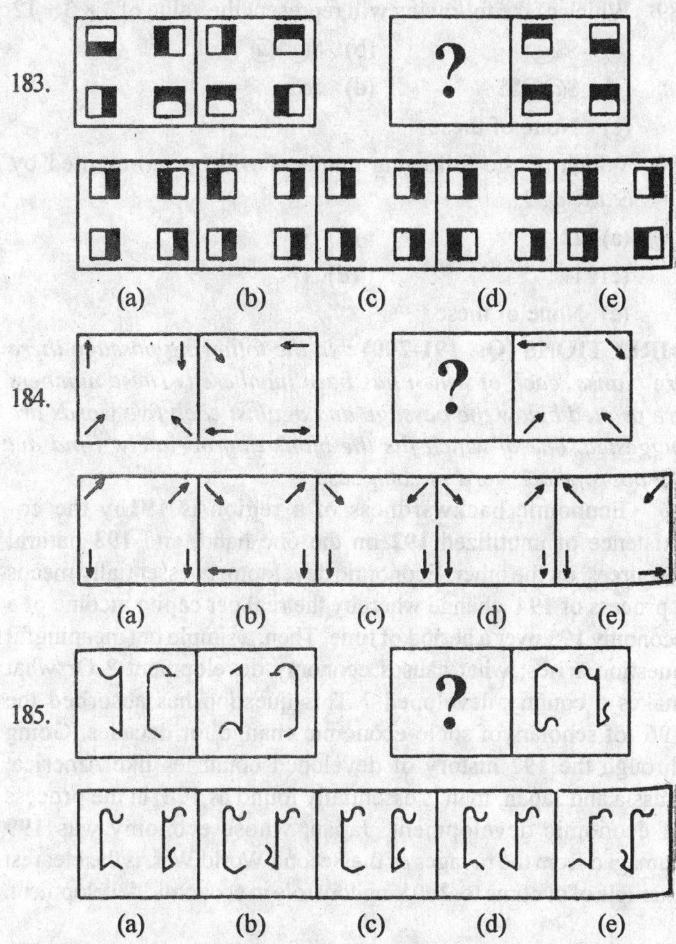

DIRECTIONS (Qs. 186 - 190) : *Study the following information and answer the questions given below:*

In a certain code, the symbol for 0 (zero) is @ and for 1 is $. There are no other symbols for all other numbers greater than one. The numbers greater than 1 are to be written only by using the two symbols given above. The value of the symbol for 1, doubles itself every time it shifts one place to the left. Study the following example:

'0' is written as @ '1' is written as $
'2' is written as $@ '3' is written as $$
'4' is written as $@@ and so on

186. Which of the following will represent 11?
(a) $@$$ (b) @$$@
(c) $$@@ (d) $@$@@
(e) None of these
187. Which of the following will represent 8?
(a) $$@@ (b) @$$@
(c) $$@@ (d) @@$$
(e) None of these
188. Which of the following numbers will be represented by $$@$?
(a) 8 (b) 11
(c) 13 (d) 12
(e) None of these

189. Which of the following will represent the value of 3 × 3 + 1?
(a) $$@$ (b) $@$@
(c) $@@$$ (d) $$$
(e) None of these

190. Which of the following numbers will be represented by $@@@$?
(a) 22 (b) 31
(c) 14 (d) 17
(e) None of these

DIRECTIONS (Qs. 191-200) : *In the following passage there are blanks, each of which has been numbered. These numbers are printed below the passage and against each five words are suggested, one of which fits the blank appropriately. Find out the appropriate word in each case.*

Economic backwardness of a region is **191**by the co-existence of unutilized **192** on the one hand, and **193** natural resources, on the other. Economic development essentially means a process of **194** change whereby the real per capita income of a economy **195** over a period of time. Then, a simple but meaningful question arises; what causes economy development ? Or what makes a country developed ? This question has absorbed the **196** of scholars of socio-economic change for decades. Going through the **197** history of developed countries like America, Russia and Japan, man is essentially found as **198** in the process of economic development. Japan, whose economy was **199** damaged from the ravages of the Second World War, is the clearest example of our time to **200** kingdom role in economic development.

191. (a) developed (b) cured
(c) improved (d) enhanced
(e) characterised

192. (a) sources (b) finances
(c) funds (d) manpower
(e) industries

193. (a) exhaustive (b) unexploited
(c) abundant (d) indefinite
(e) unreliable

194. (a) upward (b) drastic
(c) negligible (d) incredible
(e) sudden

195. (a) diminishes (b) degenerates
(c) increases (d) succumbs
(e) stabilizes

196. (a) plans (b) attempts
(c) attention (d) resources
(e) strategy

197. (a) existing (b) glorious
(c) ancient (d) economic
(e) discouraging

198. (a) pivotal (b) neutral
(c) insignificant (d) enchanted
(e) vicious

199. (a) increasingly (b) always
(c) gradually (d) deliberately
(e) badly

200. (a) enlighten (b) validate
(c) negate (d) underestimate
(e) belittle

ANSWERS WITH EXPLANATIONS

1. (c) D A B E C
2. (b) you must go early to catch the train
   1 2 3 4 5 6 7 8
   early catch train must to go the you
   4 6 8 2 5 3 7 1
   Similarly, morning exercise will help you to keep fit
   1 2 3 4 5 6 7 8
   4 6 8 2 5 3 7 1
   help to fit exercise you will keep morning
3. (c) As $D \xrightarrow{+2} F$, $I \xrightarrow{-4} E$, $P \xrightarrow{+2} R$, $L \xrightarrow{-4} H$, $O \xrightarrow{+2} Q$, $M \xrightarrow{-4} I$, $A \xrightarrow{+2} C$
   Similarly, $F \xrightarrow{+2} H$, $O \xrightarrow{-4} K$, $R \xrightarrow{+2} T$, $E \xrightarrow{-4} A$, $I \xrightarrow{+2} K$, $G \xrightarrow{-4} C$, $N \xrightarrow{+2} P$
   Hence, FOREIGN is coded as HKTAKCP.
4. (e) In all others, the sequence is that of +7 and –4 respectively.
5. (c) E X P L O S I O N
6. (a) The new set of letters are :
   N, E, A, U. Hence no meaningful word can be made.
7. (c) Here letters are : B, R, E, A and K. When the consonants are replaced by the next letter then we have C, S, E, A and L to form words. These words are as follows :
   1. SCALE 2. LACES
8. (d) C R E A T I V E
   When the letters in both the halves are reversed, we get

   A E R C E V I T
   +1 –1 +1 –1 +1 –1 +1 –1
   B D S B F U J S

   Next, the letters have been written as one place forward and one place backward alternately.
   Similarly, TRIANGLE is coded as follows :

   T R I A N G L E
   A I R T E L G N
   +1 –1 +1 –1 +1 –1 +1 –1
   B H S S F K H M

   Hence, code for TRIANGLE is BHSSFKHM.
9. (b) Total no. of girls = I Position + II position – 1
   = 10 + 17 – 1 or 9 +18 – 1 = 26.
10. (b) From first 2 sentences 'Ka Ya' means 'very intelligent'. From 1st and 3rd sentences 'Pu' means 'you'
    ∴ In first sentence 'are' means 'Bi'
11. (b) $\frac{{}^5C_1 \times {}^3C_1 \times {}^8C_1}{{}^{5+3+8}C_3} = \frac{5 \times 3 \times 8}{{}^{16}C_3} = \frac{5 \times 3 \times 8}{\frac{16!}{13! \times 3!}}$
    $= \frac{5 \times 3 \times 8 \times 13! \times 3!}{16!} = \frac{3}{14}$
12. (c) $\frac{{}^8C_2 \times {}^3C_1}{{}^{16}C_3} = \frac{\frac{8 \times 7}{2} \times 3}{\frac{16 \times 15 \times 14}{6}} = \frac{3}{20}$
13. (a) $\frac{{}^5C_3}{{}^{16}C_3} = \frac{\frac{5 \times 4 \times 3}{3 \times 2}}{\frac{16 \times 15 \times 14}{3 \times 2}} = \frac{1}{56}$
14. (b) ${}^7C_4 = 7 \times 6 \times 5 \times 4 = 840$
15. (c) We choose 4 people from 9 in ${}^9C_4$ ways. Then they are sitted on the chair in 4! ways.
    ∴ Required no. of ways $= {}^9C_4 \times 4! = 9 \times 8 \times 7 \times 6 = 3024$
16. (c) In subsequent steps 2, 3, 4, 5 ... elements are added while two elements are lost in each step except in fig. 1 where only one is lost (there is only one pre-existing element).
17. (e) 'X' moves one side anticlockwise and a new element is added to its clockwise element to 'X' shifts to anticlockwise side while others move half-a-side anticlockwise.
18. (b) Elements move from 1 to 3 → 8 → 9 → 7 → 2 → 1 in each step while one of the elements beginning from the lower left is replaced by a new one in anticlockwise direction. In fig 2 the lower middle should have been replaced.
19. (d) 3 and 4 line segments are added in alternate steps.
20. (e) The whole figure rotates by 45° anticlockwise in each step. In one step one arc is lost from clockwise side and one is added in anticlockwise side while in the next step two arcs forming a petal are added.
21. (a) $? = 11.593 \times 31.118 \times 24.224$
    $= 11.6 \times 31 \times 25$
    $= 8990$
22. (a) $? = 9938 \div 92 \div 9 = 12$
23. (d) $? = \sqrt[3]{750000} = \sqrt[3]{(90.85)^3} = 90$
24. (e) $158.25 \times 4.6 + 21\%$ of $847 + ? = 950.93$
    $158.25 \times 4.6 + 177.9 + ? = 950$
    $728 + 177 + ? = 950$
    $905 + ? = 950$
    $\therefore ? = 950 - 905 = 45$
25. (a) $248.251 \div 12.62 \times 20.52 = ?$
    $\therefore ? \approx 240 \div 12 \times 20 = 20 \times 20 = 400$
26. (a) 'Entrusted upon' (c) and 'entrusted' within (d) do not fit here as when you are 'entrusted with' (a) some thing you are given its responsibility, like what Panchayatas are there for.

27. (a) The given sentence is correct, so option (a) is the answer which repeats the underline sentence.

28. (d) 'an extra-ordinarily gifted actor and an ingenious criminal' is the right option. Ingenious can not be used with an actor.

29. (d) 'only the' is the wrong usage and shall be replaced with 'the only'. (b) is wrong as when those .... Who is the right usage. (c) is wrong as 'the' is missing before militants.

30. (d) The 4th statement is correct as it uses the same form of the verbs in a single sentence – climbing, spending and testing. (c) changes the meaning of the sentence.

31. (a) 2 11 27 52 88 137 **201**
+9 +16 +25 +36 +49 +64

32. (b) 432 135 54 27 18 18
−297 −81 −27 −9 −0
−216 −54 −18 −9

33. (d) 18 32 58 108 206 400 786
+14 +26 +50 +98 +194 +386
+12 +24 +48 +96 +192

34. (b) 1 3 6 11 20 39 70
Here $1 \times 2 + 1 = 3$; $3 \times 2 + 0 = 6$; $6 \times 2 - 1 = 11$;
$11 \times 2 - 2 = 20$; $20 \times 2 - 3 = 37$; $37 \times 2 - 4 = 70$

35. (a) 2 11 27 113 561 3369 23581
Here $2 \times 2 + 7 = 11$; $11 \times 3 - 6 = 27$;
$27 \times 4 + 5 = 113$; $113 \times 5 - 4 = 561$;
$561 \times 6 + 3 = 3369$; $3369 \times 7 - 2 = 23581$

36. (b) **From fig. II to I :** The first from RHS becomes the first from LHS. The second from RHS becomes the second from LHS and two LHS elements shift to RHS. Then the whole figure rotates by 90° clockwise. The bigger becomes smaller and vice versa.

37. (e) **From fig. II to I :** The main figure rotates by 45° clockwisewhile the adjacent smaller elements move one step anticlockwise. The semilunar part of the main figure gets laterally inverted.

38. (a) **From fig. II to I :** The arrows move one side anticlockwise while the arrows reaching upper and lower positions reverse their directions.

39. (a) From fig II to I : whole group of designs is inverted. After invertion movement of designs is shown as follows :

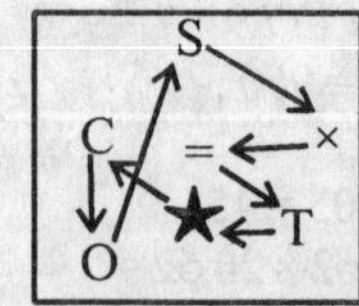

40. (c) **From fig. II to I :** Beginning from the upper right in anticlockwise direction, 2, 3, 5 and 6 bars are added respectively forming concentric squares.

For Qs. (41-45) : The arrangement ABECDF is correct.
A is the opening sentence of the paragraph . This is followed by B, E, C and D and then F is the last sentence of the given paragraph.

41. (a) 42. (b) 43. (e) 44. (c) 45. (e)

46. (a) $196.1 \times 196.1 \times 196.1 \times 4.01 \times 4.01 \times 4.001 \times 4.999 \times 4.999$
$= (196.1)^3 \times 4 \times ?$
or $4 \times ? = 4.01 \times 4.001 \times 4.999 \times 4.999$ or $? = 4 \times 5 \times 5 = 100$

47. (c) $? = \frac{2}{7} \times \frac{1}{8} + \frac{3}{7} \times \frac{14}{6} = \frac{1}{28} + 1 = 1\frac{1}{28} = 1$

48. (a) $? = (10.1)^{2.01} + (2.9)^{3.001} = (10)^2 + (3)^3 = 100 + 27 = 130$

49. (e) $4.76 \times ? = \sqrt{1999.9997}$
$4.76 \times ? = 44.72$ or $? = 9$

50. (d) $? = 23\%$ of $4011 + \frac{1}{7}$ of $5555 = 922.53 \div 79357 = 1700$

51. (c)

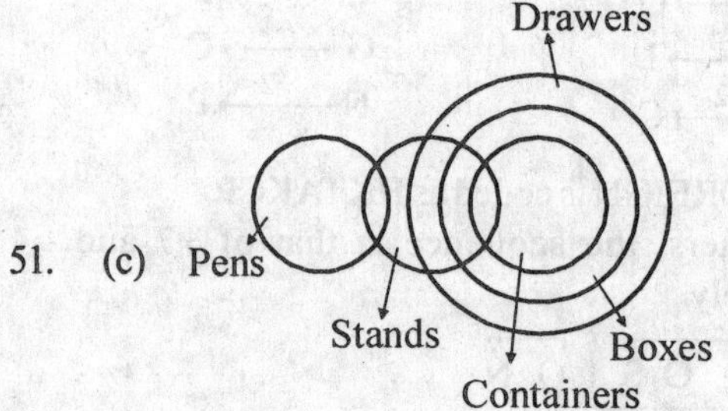

Or

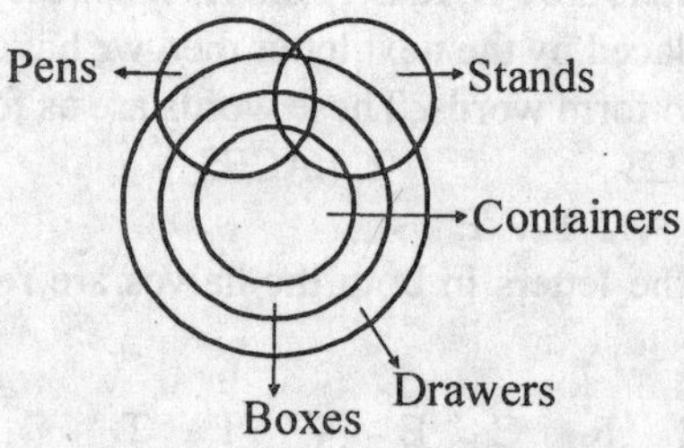

52. (e)

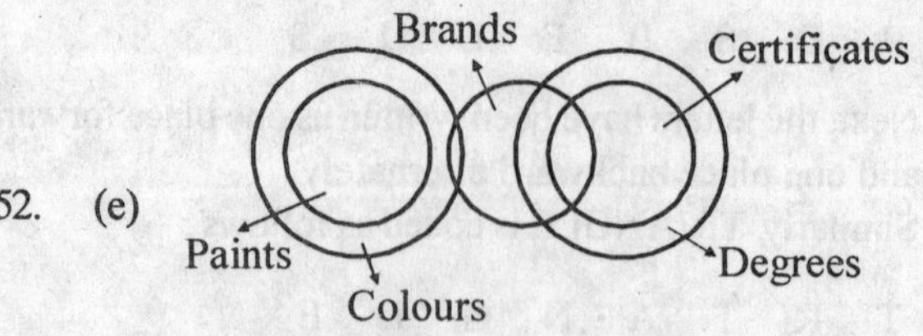

Or

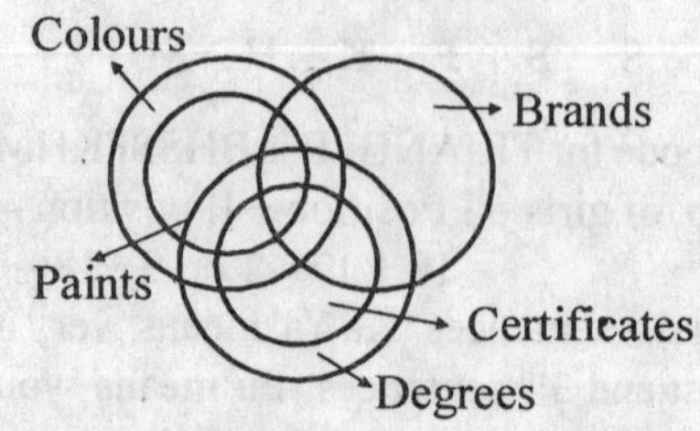

53. (a)

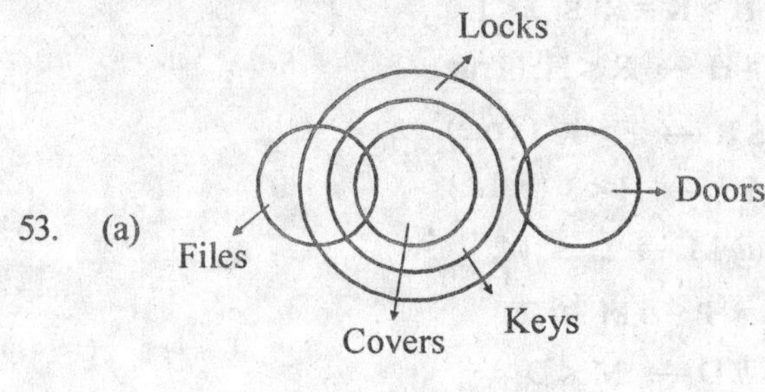

Or

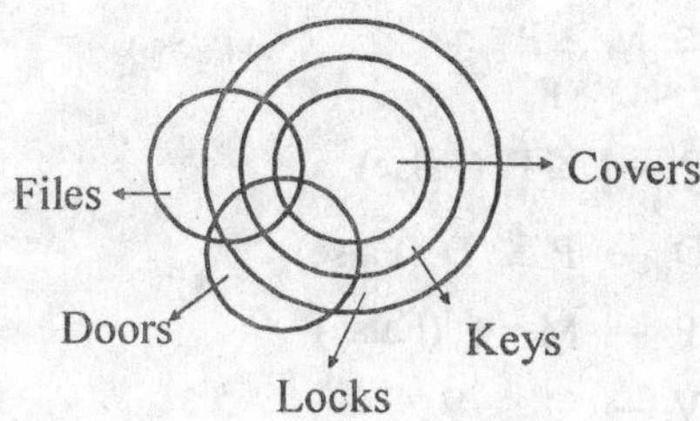

54. (e)

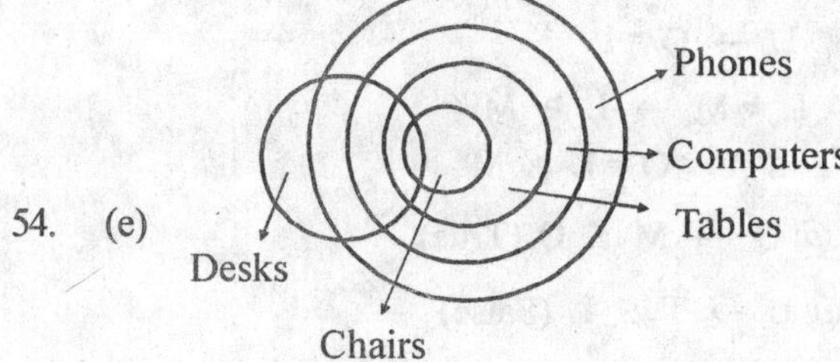

55. (c)

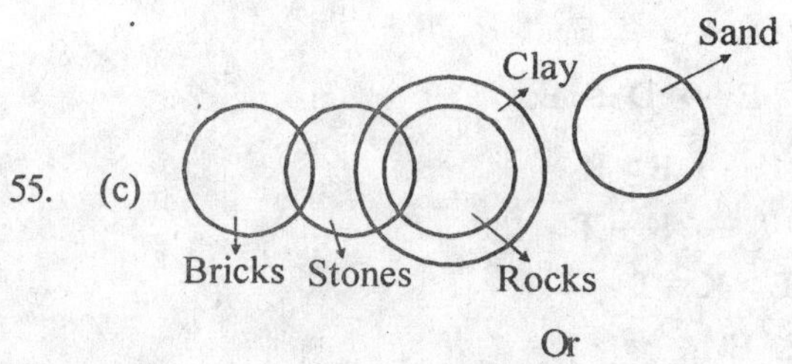

Or

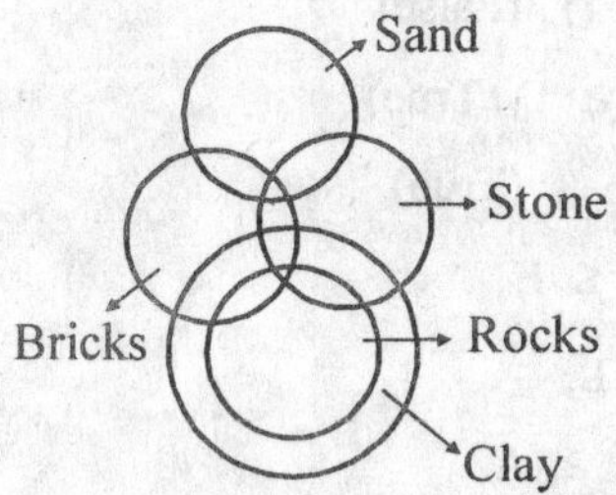

56. (a) In other figures elements on the ends rotate by 90° anticlockwise while the elements in between them rotate by 90° clockwise.

57. (e) The upper three elements move one step downwards and get inverted while a new element appears at the uppermost position.

58. (a) One line segment is lost in all other figures whereas in fig 1 three line segments are lost.

59. (c) The figure rotates by 90° clockwise and gets inverted on its axis. The circle gets unshaded.

60. (b) The lower-right moves to top-left, the top-left to centre, centre to lower-left. The loser-left moves to top-right and rotates by 90° clockwise.

61. (a) 'Want' is usually followed by the to + verb form and not verb + ing form.

62. (b) 'Because' cannot be used as the conjunction in the sentence as it should be followed by 'of', i.e., 'of their' is the most appropriate use.

63. (d) What is required to fill the gap is not an auxillary verb but a preposition

64. (b) It is a sentence without a subject, the object 'Vitamin E cream' is the subject, so it is in passive form, thus 'has been used' will be the correct usage.

65. (a) Since the two parts separated by the gap are of opposite in meaning. The part after the gap is not a complete sentence (the prices were high)

66. (c) RBUKAE → 670892

67. (b) PIAEBN → #4927#

68. (b) NAPKJI → 395814

69. (a) KUNAJB → #0391#

70. (e) AREJPK → 962158

71. (d) Since data about families who own two cars is not given then, we cannot answer the question with the help of both statements.

72. (a) From statement I we can get the ratio of Ashok's height and his shadow's height, so we can get the Pawan's height.
Hence, statement (I) alone is sufficient to answer the question.

73. (d) Since the direction of P and Q is not given, so, distance between Q and P cannot be calculated even when we use both the statements.

74. (c) From statement I, we can get the percentage of families whose monthly income is 25000 p.m. From statement I and II, we can get the percentage of families in a city have monthly income of 25000 and own a house.
Hence, (I) and (II) both, are required to answer the question.

75. (e) Statement I is sufficient to give answer as the product of two odd numbers always gives odd number. Statement II is also sufficient to give answer as odd number is never divided by 2

76. (d)

6	7	3	2	5	8
↓	↓	↓	↓	↓	↓
●	+	?	*	$	©

As '8' is the end-number, its symbol will change according to rule (ii).

77. (e)

2	3	6	4	7	5
↓	↓	↓	↓	↓	↓
*	?	●	÷	+	$

78. (c) 8 4 6 7 2 1
$\downarrow \downarrow \downarrow \downarrow \downarrow \downarrow$
! ÷ ● + * x

79. (a) 1 7 8 5 2 4
$\downarrow \downarrow \downarrow \downarrow \downarrow \downarrow$
@ + ! $ * ©

80. (b) 2 5 4 8 6
$\downarrow \downarrow \downarrow \downarrow \downarrow$
* $ ÷ ! ©

81. (c) In the context of the passage, (c) seems to be the most appropriate option.

82. (b) Clearly the first blank has to be future. As the company keeps an eye on the future and promotes popular contemporary art.

83. (c) Indian intellectuals can not be the ancestors. They can be heir (a person who inherits or is entitled to inherit the rank, title, position, etc., of another). Heirs is a wrong word.

84. (c) 'Unlimited choices' and 'minimal constraints' are the right usage.

85. (a) Resilient means recovering readily from illness, depression, adversity, or the like; buoyant. Obdurate means unmoved by persuasion, pity, or tender feelings; stubborn; unyielding. Propitious means presenting favourable conditions; favourable. Delectable means delightful; highly pleasing; enjoyable.

86. (e) Reqd. % $= \frac{40.3}{310} \times 100 = 13\%$

87. (a) Total construction in 1999-00
$= 37.13 + 60.8 + 192.23 = 290.16$
Total construction in 1995-96
$= 43.80 + 74.28 + 204.32 = 322.40$
Reqd. % $= \frac{322.40 - 290.16}{322.40} \times 100 = 10\%$

88. (c) Minimum constructions
$= 37.13$
Maximum constructions
$= 222.78$
Ratio $= 37.13 : 222.78 = 1 : 6$

89. (c) Percentage increase $= \frac{66.76 - 62.40}{62.40} \times 100 = 7\%$

90. (b) In 1998-99, the MIG construction is less than the HIG construction.

91. (a) H$K $\rightarrow$ H > K,
K©R $\rightarrow$ K = R
R@J $\rightarrow$ R ≤ J
and J#F $\rightarrow$ J<F
$\therefore$ H > K = R ≤ J < F
I. R # H $\rightarrow$ R < H (True)
II. F $ R $\rightarrow$ F > R (True)
III. H $ J $\rightarrow$ H < J (False)

92. (e) L @ M $\rightarrow$ L ≤ M,
M ★ P $\rightarrow$ M ≥ P,
M # D $\rightarrow$ M < D
and D $ F $\rightarrow$ D < F
$\therefore$ L ≤ M ≥ P
and M < D > F
I. L @ P $\rightarrow$ L ≤ P (False)
II. P @ D $\rightarrow$ P ≤ D (False)
III. M © F $\rightarrow$ M = F (False)

93. (d) T @ V $\rightarrow$ T ≤ V,
V # Q $\rightarrow$ V < Q,
Q © L $\rightarrow$ Q = L
and L ★ M $\rightarrow$ L ≥ M
$\therefore$ T ≤ V < Q = L ≥ M
I. M @ Q $\rightarrow$ M ≤ Q (True)
II. T @ L $\rightarrow$ T ≤ L (False)
III. T # L $\rightarrow$ T < L (True)

94. (b) J ★ E $\rightarrow$ J ≥ E,
D @ E $\rightarrow$ D ≤ E,
E $ K $\rightarrow$ E > K
and K © T $\rightarrow$ K = T
$\therefore$ J ≥ E > K = T
and D ≤ E
I. J $ D $\rightarrow$ J > D (False)
II. J ★ D $\rightarrow$ J ≥ D (True)
III. E $ T $\rightarrow$ E > T (True)

95. (a) H @ I $\rightarrow$ H ≤ I,
I # L $\rightarrow$ I < L,
L ★ A $\rightarrow$ L ≥ A
and A $ Q $\rightarrow$ A > Q
$\therefore$ H ≤ I < L ≥ A > Q
I. H # L $\rightarrow$ H < L (True)
II. H ★ L $\rightarrow$ H ≥ L (False)
III. Q # H $\rightarrow$ Q < H (False)

96. (c) **Hiatus** is a break or a **gap** in a process, atrocious is bad and crude, while dominance is extreme and forceful influence.

97. (a) **Denouement** is the final part of a drama or a story, i.e. the **outcome**, eschew is to avoid doing something bad.

98. (c) **Foment** is to stir up, and **instigate** means to initiate or stir up and vex is annoyed.

99. (e) **Grit** is a sense of determination to face a difficult condition i. e., courage.

100. (a) **Ominous** is a sign of something bad in future, threat is a warning for future, ubiquitous is something that is found.

101. (e) Ans = 172. The series is $\times 1 + 1^2, \times 2 + 2^2, \times 3 + 3^2, ...$

102. (e) Ans = 97. The series is ×2-1 in each term.

103. (c) The series is ×0.5 + 0.5, ×1 + 1, ×1.5 + 1.5, ×2 + 2, ...

104. (b) The series is $3 \times 1 + 7 \times 1 = 10$,
$0 \times 2 + 6 \times 2 = 32, 32 \times 3 + 5 \times 3 = 111$,
$111 \times 4 + 4 \times 4 = 460, 460 \times 5 + 3 \times 5 = 2315, ...$

105. (c) The series is $\times 2 - 2, + 2 \div 2, \times 2 - 2, + 2 \div 2, ...$

106. (d) According to this passage, regular physical activity is needed to improve one's physical as well as mental health

107. (d) In order to tone up the physical education programme the programme should be reoriented and implemented

108. (c) According to American, health education is more important than teaching any subject

109. (d) The author wants the reoriented physical education programme to be thoughtful

110. (a) In order to improve the physical education programme, we should first of all allot more time to the teaching and learning of physical activity

111. (d) Overall percentage of passed boys

$$= \frac{50+60+70+80+50}{6} = 61\frac{2}{3}$$

∴ Overall percentage of failed boys

$$= 100 - 61\frac{2}{3} = 38\frac{1}{3}$$

112. (c) For 1997, the improvement is

$$\frac{70-50}{50} \times 100\% = 40\%$$

For 1993, the improvement is

$$\frac{80-60}{60} \times 100\% = 33\frac{1}{3}\%$$

So, the desired year is 1997.

113. (d) For the years 1993, 1995 and 1997 the gap is constant.

114. (b) Only for the year 1993 we observe a paired rise in the percentage of boys as well as of girls.

115. (e) Average of percentage of passed girls

$$= \frac{60+80+70+80+50+70}{6} = \frac{410}{6} = 68\frac{1}{3}$$

∴ Average of percentage of failed girls

$$= 100 - 68\frac{2}{3} = 31\frac{2}{3}$$

From the solution of above questions

Average percentage of failed boys $= 38\frac{1}{3}$

$$\therefore \text{ Reqd ratio} = 31\frac{2}{3} : 38\frac{1}{3} = 95 : 115 = 19 : 23$$

For (Qs. 116-120):

The given information can be tabulated as below

Boys	Amit	Suresh	Vishnu	Ujjwal	Rakesh
Girls	Alka	Jyoti	Veena	Prabha	Nayan

116. (c) 117. (d) 118. (a) 119. (b)

120. (a)

121. (b) The anticlockwise-end element moves to centre. The central element moves to clockwise corner while clockwise-end element moves two sides clockwise and a nw element appears at its anticlockwise corner.

122. (a) The inner shaded parts get combined. So do the outer ones but their number remains unchanged.

123. (d) The whole figure rotates by 135° clockwise while arrow head and arc get reversed.

124. (d) The whole figure rotates by 180°.

125. (e) Four, five, two and six line segments are added to lower left, upper left, upper left and lower right elements respectively to form conentric squares.

126. (d) Total failed students in class X = 245 + 300 + 200 + 150 + 240 + 435 = 1570

And total no. of students = (475 + 245 =)720 + 600 + 710 + 400 + 770 + 800 = 4000

$$\therefore \text{ Reqd. percentage} = \frac{1570}{4000} \times 100 = 39.25$$

127. (b) Reqd. difference $= \frac{1}{5}\{(460 - 300) + (440 - 500) + (475 - 530) + (500 - 500) + (560 - 525)\}$

$$= \frac{1}{5}(160 - 60 - 55 + 0 + 35) = \frac{1}{5} \times 80 = 16$$

128. (c) The school which will show the maximum percentage of failed students will be the desired school.

By visual inspection we see that the no. of failed students for Q and U are higher than the others. So, we simply test the percentage of failed students for these two schools (you can find out the percentage of the same for other schools and verify the conclusion below yourself).

For Q it is $\frac{1600}{(1510+1600=)3110} \times 100$

= slightly greater than $\frac{1600}{3000} \times 100 = \frac{100}{2} = 50$

and less than $\frac{1600}{3000} \times 100$, i.e., 53.3

For U it is

$$\frac{2130}{(1870+2130=4000)} \times 100 = \frac{213}{4} = 53.25$$

Clearly, the percentage of failed students for U is higher than Q. Hence, U is the desired school.

129. (e) We see that total no. of students of U in each class is the same and so, U has the same desired average no.

130. (a) The result may be obtained by getting the highest value of the ratio of passed and failed students of certain class.

Clearly, $\frac{500}{240} > \frac{500}{245}$ (comparing the denominators)

And $\frac{530}{240} > \frac{500}{240}$ (comparing the numer)

Also, $\frac{530}{240} > \frac{525}{255}$ (comparing both)

Let us now compare $\frac{300}{140} (\approx 2.14)$ and $\frac{530}{240} (\approx 2.21)$

Obviously $\frac{530}{240}$ (class X) is the greatest.

Hence, class X has shown best performance.

For (Qs. 131-135):

Here persons are: P, Q, R, S, T, V and W
Professions are: Doctor, Teacher, Lawyer, Engineer, Architect, Chartered Accountant and Banker.
From clues (iv) and (vii), we get R is the doctor. W is a male Q is a female and she is a teacher. P is the Banker.
Now, from clues (v) and (vi), we get T is a female. She is not Chartered Accountant. She is neither Lawyer nor Engineer. Obviously, T is an architect.
Thus, S, V and W are Lawyer, Engineer or Chartered Accountant. But, from clue (viii), V is not the Lawyer. This implies V is either Engineer or Chartered Accountant. And W is not a Chartered Accountant (clue vii and v). Now, let us arrange the names of the persons according to their incomes. Assign numerics 1 to 7 according to descending order of incomes.
From clue (v), T occupies seventh position.
From clues (iv), (v), (vii) and (viii) we get

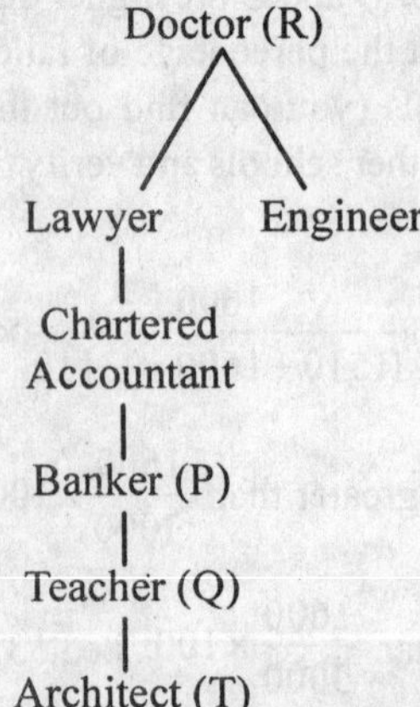

The above information does not give a clear picture. The only thing (about the positions of the person) which can be said with certainty is that R occupies the first position and T occupies the seventh position. Position of Engineer may be and position from 2 to 6.
The married couples are: 1. WQ and 2. T and V or S.

	Person						
Prof ↓	P	$Q_{(-)}$	R	$S_{(+)}$	$T_{(-)}$	$V_{(+)}$	$W_{(+)}$
Doc	×	×	✓	×	×	×	×
Tea (–)	×	✓	×	×	×	×	×
Law (+)	×	×	×	—	×	×	—
Eng (+)	×	×	×	—	×	—	—
Arch (–)	×	×	×	×	✓	×	×
CA (+)	×	×	×	—	×	—	×
Banker	✓	×	×	×	×	×	×

131. (c) 132. (d)

133. (e) (Fourth or Fifth)

134. (b) We do not know about sex of the doctor and the banker. But, on the basis of sex of the lawyer, the engineer and the chartered accountant we can conclude at least three males exist in the group.

135. (c)

136. (c) The passage is about communication skills.

137. (d) "the ability to communicate effectively has become a need today."

138. (e) All the choices provided are wrong

139. (c) Style means way of interacting.

140. (b) "How can people be motivated ? It's again through communication only."

141. (e) Question cannot be answered even with the information in all the three statements.

142. (d) We can find the even numbers as 10, 12 and 14 with the help of either statement I or III.

143. (d) It is not possible to find the value of Sonu's income and hence it is not possible to find the difference between Sonu and Monu's Salary.

144. (b) Since we have to find share of B so we can easily calculate for the statement B.
∴ Statement II is sufficient.

145. (d) It is possible to find the ages of Mohan and Sohan by all the three statement individually.
(Mohan's age is 30 and Sohan's 24 using any of I, II and III)

146. (b) Either I or II can be advised. Water supply authority must partial cut in supply to tackle the situation or appeal to all residents for minimum use of water.

147. (c) I is not advisable because from this decision virus negative person would be also affected. II will be the right action to tackle the situation.

148. (a) It is duty of government to make alternative arrangement. So, I is advisable. II is not advisable because it will be extreme action and against of fundamental right.

149. (a) Increased capacity of train will be helpful to tackle the situation, so it is advisable. II is not advisable, what is meaning of this advise for those people who want to utilise holiday. Hence only I follows.

150. (c) I cannot be advised because it can be created problem to continue supply of gas. II is advisable because it will be helpful to save life.

151. (d) Total no. of students who play cricket
$= 38 + 40 + 12 + 17 + 25 + 18 + 20 = 170$

Reqd. % $= \frac{25}{170} \times 100 \approx 15\%$

152. (d) Reqd. ratio $= 27 : 18 = 3 : 2$

153. (e) Cricket is the most popular game.

154. (e) Total Class X students who play different games = 115

Reqd. % $= \frac{21}{115} \times 100 \approx 18\%$

155. (e) Basketball and Badminton are the two games which satisfy the conditions.

156. (d) The fist line of the passage tells us that the main appeal of CDs is their "suspiciously realistic sound.

157. (a) This synonym question can be done through elimination. 'Revolution' is usually done to bring about change so (a) should be the right answer. But we must confirm other options also it cannot be (b) because in the sense of passage 'revolution is not used as a 'fight', (c) is also incorrect, so is (d), so (a) is the right answer.

158. (c) 'Sandwiches' means between two things. CDs have aluminium between two layers of plastic so CDs are call sandwiches because they are layered and not because of their size or weight.

159. (a) (b), (d) and (d) are incorrect statement the passage does not suggest either (c) or (d) and (b) is factually incorrect, thus these 3 options can be eliminated. (a) is the right answer as suggested by the last line of the first paragraph.

160. (b) (a), (c) and (d) are all mentioned in the passage but they do not receive any emphasis or special attention. The author's main concern remains to discuss the growth of CDs, which includes all other options.

161. (e) In each step, element 'C' rotates by 90° and shifts one step downwards. The arrow shifts diagonally and rotates by 180° alternately. The pin rotates by 45° anticlockwise and 90° clockwise alternately while it shifts one step downwards in each step.

162. (a) The clockwise-end element shifts one side and half-a-side clockwise while the other elements are arranged in reverse order. A new element is added in each step once on anticlockwise end and next on clockwise end.

163. (c) One of the corner elements shifts to centre. The central element shifts to anticlockwise corner. The anticlockwise-corner elements shift diagonally while the third one is replaced by a new one. This change goes on in anticlockwise order.

164. (b) Two, three, four, two ... arcs are inverted in subsequent steps.

165. (c) The main figure rotates by 90° anticlockwise. The circle and the square shift from one side to another in each step while the others shift one step anticlockwise. One and two new elements appear in alternate steps in place of the square and the circle.

166. (e) The two are independent events contradicting each other.

167. (c) Event (A) is the effect but event (B) is not its immediate and principal cause because to get the above outcome proper use of rich mineral resources is equally important.

168. (b) It is the parliament's nod to Tobacco Control Bill, which gave the non-smokers a new horizon.

169. (b) Event (B) is the effect and event (A) is the immediate and principal cause behind it. The move taken by the Food and Adulteration Department is the result of the claim made by the people.

170. (b) Once again, event (A)is the immediate and principal cause of event (B). The demand sought by the parliamentarians is due to the report revealed by the NGO.

For (Qs. 171-180):

Q. No.	i	ii/A	iii/B	iv	Ans.
171	√	√	√	√	(a)
172	×	√	√	√	(b)
173	√	√	(√)	–	(e)
174	√	(√)	√	√	(c)
175	√	√	(√)	√	(d)
176	√	×	√	√	(b)
177	√	√	(√)	√	(d)
178	√	√	√	√	(a)
179	√	√	√	√	(a)
180	√	(√)	√	√	(e)

i + ii + iii + iv ⇒ (a)
i + A + iii + iv ⇒ (c)
i + ii + B + iv ⇒ (d)
Data inadequate ⇒ (e)
Not to be admitted ⇒ (b)

181. (e) **From fig. II to I :** The petals rotate by 135°anticlockwise while the arc rotates by 135°clockwise.

182. (e) **From fig. II to I :** The elements move from position 1 to 8 → 3 → 7 → 2 → 4 → 6 → 9 → 1.

183. (c) **From fig. II to I :** The upper right square rotates by 90° anticlockwise while the other three rotate by 90° clockwise.

184. (d) **From fig. II to I :** The upper left and the lower right rotate by 135° anticlockwise. The lower left rotates by 135° clockwise while the upper right rotates by 90° anticlockwise.

185. (b) **From fig. II to I :** The left element gets vertically unverted while the right one gets laterally inverted.

For(Qs. 186 -190)

The following are the questions on the conversion of decimal number system into binary number system and vice versa.

186. (a)

2	11	remainder
2	5	1
2	2	1
	1	0

$\therefore (11)_{10} = (1011)_2 = \$@\$\$$

187. (e) $(8)_{10} = (1000)_2 = \$@@@$

188. (c) $\$\$@\$ = (1101)_2$

To convert binary number into decimal number start coming from the right, starting with zero (0).

Now $\begin{matrix} 1 & 1 & 0 & 1 \\ 3 & 2 & 1 & 0 \end{matrix}$

$\therefore\ 1\times 2^3 + 1\times 2^2 + 0\times 2^1 + 1\times 2^0 = 8+4+0+1 = (13)_{10}$

189. (b) $3\times 3 + 1 = (10)_9 = (1010)_2 = \$@\$@$

190. (d) $\$@@@\$ = (10001)_2 = (17)_9$

191. (e) 192. (d) 193. (b) 194. (b)

195. (c) 196. (c) 197. (d) 198. (a)

199. (e) 200. (b)

MAHARASHTRA COMMON ENTRANCE TEST
17th FEBRUARY 2008
SOLVED PAPER
(Based on Memory)

1. In a certain code GOAL is written as AGLO and BEAR is written as ABRE. How is SEND written in that code?
(a) NSDE (b) NDES
(c) DENS (d) SNED
(e) None of these

2. 'MP' is related to 'OR' and 'DG' is related to 'FI' in the same way as 'RU' is related to
(a) TX (b) TW
(c) TY (d) UW
(e) None of these

3. In a certain code language 'Ne Pe Le' mean 'what is this'. 'Bo Le Se' means 'is that okay' and 'Se Ni Di' means 'that was easy'. What is the code for 'okay' in that code language?
(a) Le (b) Se
(c) Ne (d) Ni
(e) None of these

4. How many such pairs of letters are there in the word CREDITABLE each of which has as many letters between them as they have in English alphabet?
(a) One (b) Two
(c) Three (d) Four
(e) More than four

5. In a certain code 'PRISM' is written as 'OSHTL' and 'RUBLE' is written as 'QVAMD'. How will 'WHORL' be written in that code?
(a) XIPSM (b) XGNOK
(c) UINSK (d) EGPQM
(e) VINSK

6. If + means –, – means ÷, ÷ means × and × means +, what is the value of $125 - 5 \times 10 \div 13 + 28 = ?$
(a) 129 (b) 127
(c) 149.15 (d) 150
(e) None of these

7. In a row of boys facing North, Amit is 5th to the left of Ashok. Alok is 3rd to the right of Amit. Vilas is 3rd to the left of Ashok. Which of the following describes the position of Vilas?
(a) To the immediate right to Amit
(b) To the immediate left to Alok
(c) To the immediate right to Alok
(d) 3rd to the right of Amit
(e) None of these

8. In a certain code language BROUGHT is written as EOMXDKQ, how is SITTING be written is this code language?
(a) PMQQMPC (b) PMQQPMC
(c) PMMQQPC (d) BMQQPPC
(e) None of these

9. The financial markets of which of the following countries were badly affected by sub prime crisis?
(a) Russia (b) Brazil
(c) UK (d) USA
(e) None of these

10. Which of the following countries in the world is the highest consumer of gold?
(a) USA (b) Bangladesh
(c) Russia (d) India
(e) None of these

Directions (Qs. 11-15) : In each of the questions below a group of letters are given followed by four groups of digits/symbol combinations numbered (a) (b), (c) and (d). Letters are to be coded as per the codes and conditions given below. You have to find out which of the combinations (a), (b) , (c) and (d) is correct and indicate your answer accordingly. If none of the four represents the correct code, mark (e) i.e. 'None of these' as your answer.

Letter	: B H S N T O A K R I E U G
Digit/ Symbol Code	: 6 8 1 # 5 2 $ 3 9 @ 4 7 %

Conditions :

(i) If the first as well as last letter is vowel, both are to be Coded as 'O'.
(ii) If the first letter is a vowel and the last letter is consonant, both are to be coded as 'Z'.
(iii) If the first letter is a consonant and the last letter is vowel. both are to be coded as '*'.

11. ONSIRT
(a) 2#1@95 (b) Z#@195
(c) Z#19@Z (d) Z#1@95
(e) None of these

12. KIUBSR
(a) O@76129 (b) O@7610
(c) 3@7691 (d) 3@6719
(e) None of these

13. BKAEUG
(a) 03$470 (b) 63$470
(c) 03$47% (d) 63$47%
(e) None of these

14. STOKGA
(a) 1523%$ (b) 1523%*
(c) *523%* (d) *523%$
(e) None of these

15. ORHSNU
(a) O98#17 (b) O981#O
(c) 298#10 (d) 2981#7
(e) None of these

16. Who is the Uncle of V ? If
(I) T is the Brother of P
(II) R is the Daughter of P
(III) M is the Sister of T and
(IV) V is the Brother of R
(a) M (b) T
(c) P (d) Either M or T
(e) None of these

17. P is the brother of Q and R, S is R's mother, T is P' s father. Which of the following statements cannot be said to be definitely true?
(a) T is Q's father (b) T is S's husband
(c) P is S's son (d) S is A' s brother
(e) Q is E's son

18. How many 7s are there in the following sequence which are immediately preceded by 4 but not immediately followed by 2 ?
4 7 2 7 2 3 5 9 7 4 7 5 2 4 7 9 4 7 8 4 7 1
(a) 1 (b) 2
(c) 3 (d) 4
(e) More than 4

19. If it is decided to write every alternate letter of the English alphabet always small starting with B onwards, and, all other letters always in capital, which of the following is the correct way of writing 'WEDNESDAY' ?
(a) WeDNesDay (b) WEdnESdAy
(c) wEDNESDAY (d) WEdNESdAy
(e) None of these

20. A man said to a woman. Your only brother's sister is my mother'. How is the woman related to the man's grandmother on his mother's side?
(a) Sister (b) Sister-in- law
(c) Daughter (d) Mother-in-law
(e) None of these

21. Following question is based on the informations given below.
(i) Six boys are sitting around a circle facing the centre.
(ii) P is to the immediate left of S.
(iii) J is between A and B.
(iv) H is between P and A.
If S and B exchange their positions, who will be to the immediate right of B ?
(a) Cannot be determined
(b) A
(c) J
(d) P
(e) None of these

22. P is father of G, A is sister of C, D is uncle of A, C is brother of G and G is father of B. Who is uncle of B ?
(a) D (b) P
(c) C (d) Cannot be determined
(e) None of these

23. In a certain code language 'ew xa hu de' means 'she is eating apples', 'ew po va' means 'she sells toys' and 'ut li de' means 'I like apples'. Which words in the language mean 'she and apples'?
(a) ut and de (b) ew and de
(c) de and po (d) xa and ew
(e) None of these

24. In a certain code CHETAN is written as FEHQDK. How is SUNDER written in that code ?
(a) VRQAHO (b) PXKGHO
(c) VRQABU (d) PXKGBU
(e) None of these

25. Two letters in the word ROUBLE have as many letters between them in the word as in the English alphabet. Which one of the two comes earlier in the alphabet?
(a) U (b) E
(c) R (d) L
(e) None of these

26. H is shorter than J. P is taller than H. A is taller than J but shorter than D. J is taller than P. Who among them will be in the middle if they stand in a row according to height?
(a) H (b) P
(c) J (d) D
(e) A

Directions (Qs. 27-28) : In each question, a related pair of words is followed by five lettered pairs of words. Select the numbered pair that has a relationship similar to that in the original pair.

27. Resignation : Office
(a) Appointment : Interview
(b) Abdication : Throne
(c) Illness : Hospital
(d) Moisture : Rain
(e) Competition : Game

28. Bunch : Key
(a) Players : Team
(b) Beehive : Bee
(c) Examination : Subject
(d) Bouquet : Flower
(e) Hound : Pack

29. Pointing at Preeti, Vivek said, 'Her father is the son of my mother's sister'. How is Vivek related to Preeti?
(a) Nephew (b) Brother
(c) Cousin (d) Grand-father
(e) None of these

30. If it is possible to make only one meaningful word from the second, the third, the seventh and the tenth letters of the word FRIGHTENED, what will be the third letter of that word? If it is possible to make more than one such word your answer is M and if it is not possible to make any meaningful word your answer is N.
(a) D (b) I
(c) R (d) M
(e) N

Directions (Qs. 31-35) : The first figure in the first unit of the problem figures bears a certain relationship to the second figure. Similarly one of the figures in the answer figures bears the same relationship to the second figure in the second unit of the problem figures. You are therefore to locate the figure which would fit in the question mark.

31. **Problem Figures**

Answer figures

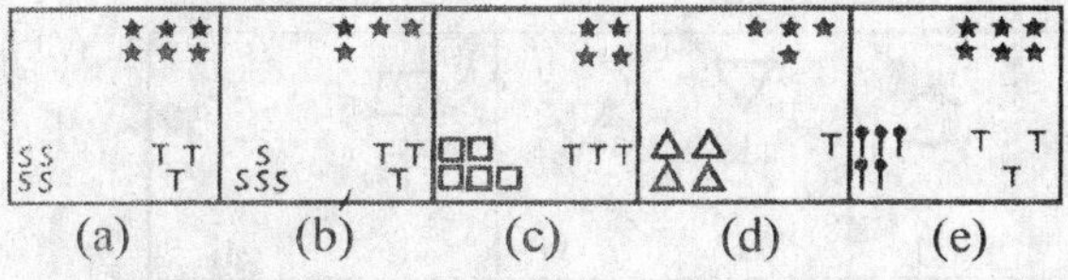

32. **Problem Figures**

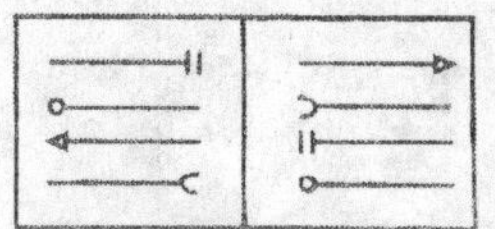

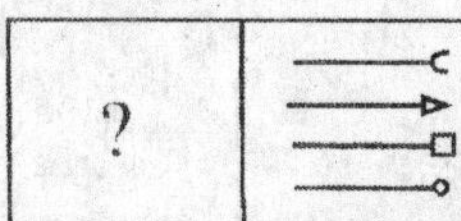

Answer figures

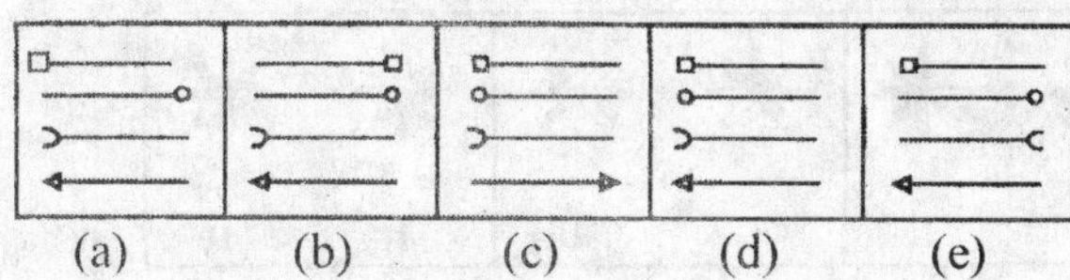

33. **Problem Figures**

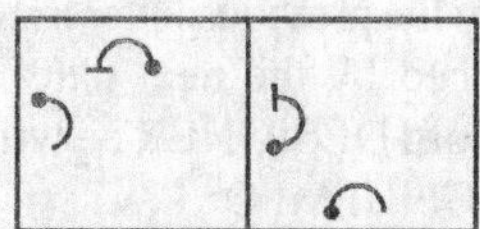

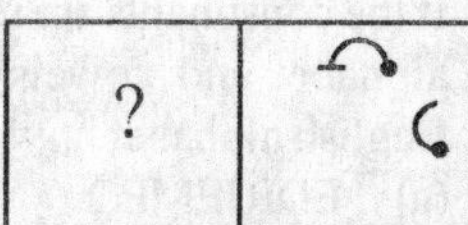

Answer figures

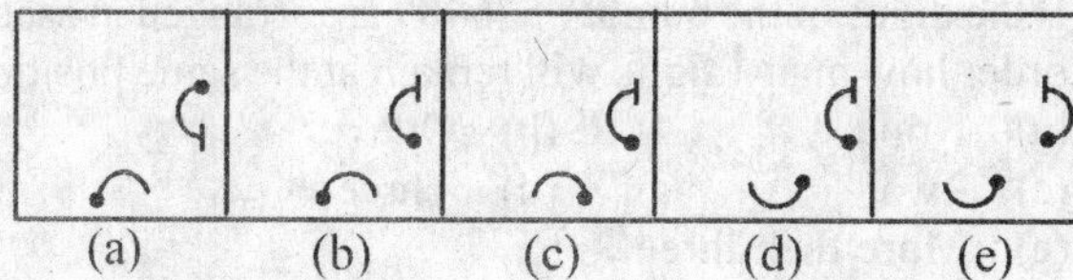

34. **Problem Figures**

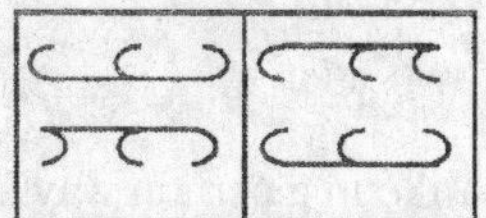

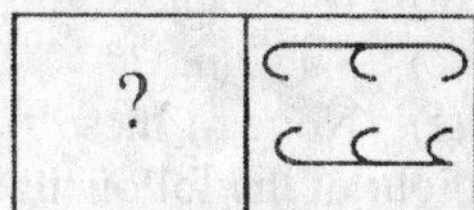

Answer figures

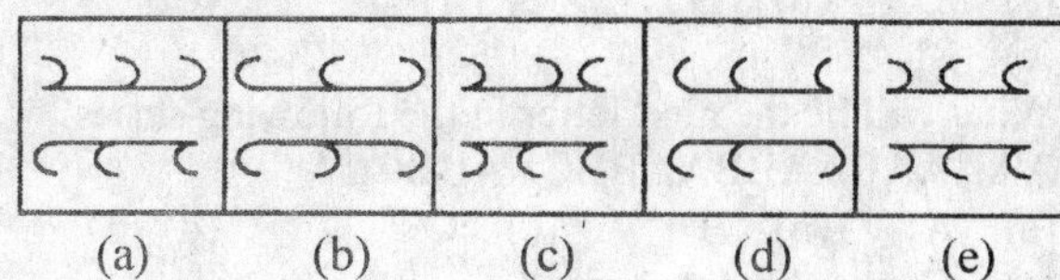

35. **Problem figures**

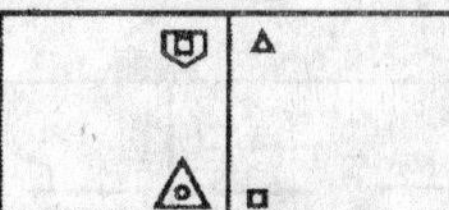

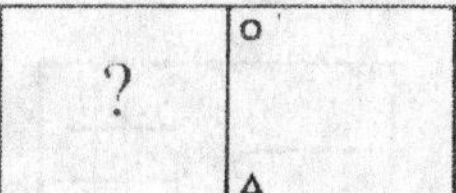

Answer figures

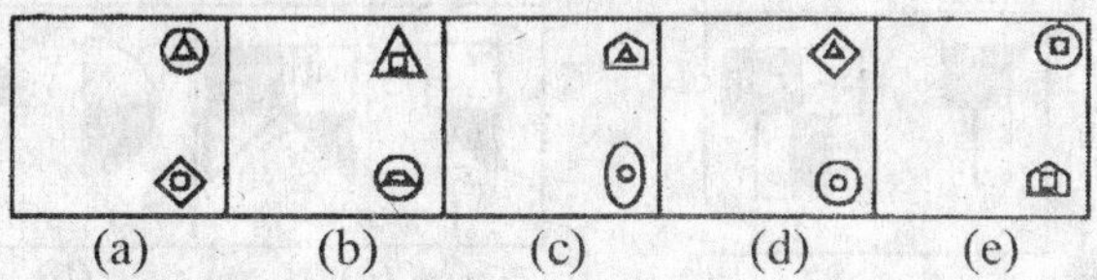

Directions (Qs. 36-40): Below is given a passage followed by several possible inferences numbered from 36 to 40 which can be drawn from the facts stated in the passage. You have to examine each inference separately in the context of the passage and decide upon its degree of truth or falsity. Marks answer

(a) if you think the inference is 'definitely true' i.e. it property follows from the statement of facts given;
(b) if you think the inference is 'probably true' though not 'definitely true', in the light of the facts given;
(c) if you think the data are inadequate i.e. from the facts given you cannot say whether the inference is likely to be true of false;
(d) if you think the inference is 'probably false' though not ' definitely false' in the light of the facts given
(e) if you think the inference is 'definitely false' i.e. it cannot possibly be drawn from the facts given or it contradicts the given facts.

Now, read the following passage and the inferences given below them and mark your answers on the separate answer sheet.

The serious accident in which a person was run down by a car yesterday has again focused attention on the most unsatisfactory state of street lighting. No one expects side roads to be provided with the same standard of lighting as a main road, but unless the council is prepared to make good its promise as regards road lighting, it will only be a question of time before there are further and perhaps fatal accidents.

36. It seems that the council has promised to improve the state of lighting on side roads.

37. Several accidents have so far taken place because of unsatisfactory lighting.

38. The accident that occurred was fatal.

39. The accident occurred at night.

40. There will not be a single accident on roads if they are satisfactorily illuminated.

Directions (Qs. 41-45) : In each of the following questions, a related pair of figures is followed is by five lettered pairs of figures. Select the pair that has a relationship similar to that in the unlettered pair. The best answer is to be selected from a group of fairly close choices.

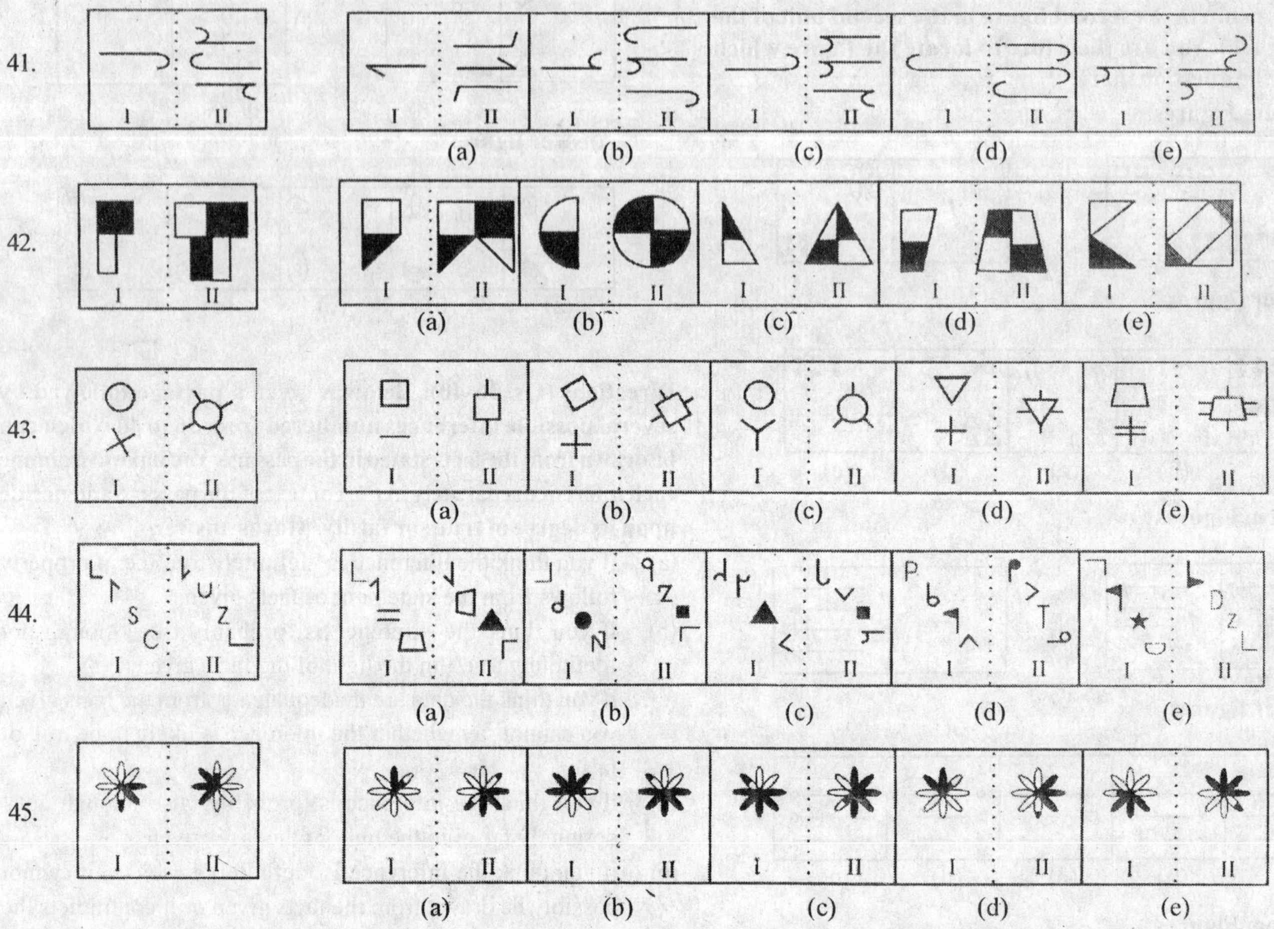

Directions (Qs. 46-50) : In the following questions, two equations numbered I and II are given. You have to solve both the equations and

Give answer

(a) if $X > Y$

(b) if $X \geq Y$

(c) if $X < Y$

(d) if $X \leq Y$

(e) if $X = Y$ or the relationship cannot be established.

46. I. $X = \sqrt{1369}$

II. $(Y)^2 = 1369$

47. I. $X^2 + 9X + 20 = 0$

II. $Y^2 + 7Y + 12 = 0$

48. I. $X^2 + 2Y - 11.5 = 0$

II. $4Y + 2X = 23$

49. I. $X^2 + 11X + 28 = 0$

II. $Y^2 + 15Y + 56 = 0$

50. I. $2X - 4Y = 12$

II. $4X - 2Y = 0$

51. If the consonants are replaced by the previous letter in English alphabet and vowels are replaced by the next letter in the English alphabet how will the word DESIGNER be written?

(a) EDRJEMFQ (b) CFRJFMFQ
(c) CDRJFMFQ (d) CFRJHMFQ
(e) None of these

52. If the digits of the number 576489 are arranged in ascending order how many digits will remain at the same position?

(a) None (b) One
(c) Two (d) Three
(e) More than three

53. In a certain code RIDE is written as % # $ @ and TAIL is written as © *#D, how is DATE written in that code ?

(a) D # © @ (b) D * © @
(c) $ # © @ (d) $ © * @
(e) None of these

54. Four of the following five are alike in a certain way and so form a group. Which is the one that does not belong to the group?

(a) 85 (b) 79 (c) 71 (d) 73
(e) 83

55. What will be the next letter in the following series?

AAAAABAABBAABBCAABBCCA

(a) A (b) B (c) C (d) D
(e) Cannot be determined

Directions (Qs. 56-60) : These questions are based on the following letter/ number/symbol arrangement. Study it carefully and answer the questions.

3 B E 4 # W 9 A 2 J K * 1 5 U Q R 7 F @ H I 6 $ V

56. How many such numbers are there, each of which is immediately preceded by a vowel but not immediately followed by a consonant ?
(a) None (b) One
(c) Two (d) Three
(e) More than three

57. 6I : E4 :: A9 : ?
(a) 7F (b) F@
(c) R7 (d) 7R
(e) None of these

58. How many such symbols are there in the above arrangement, each of which is immediately preceded by a consonant and immediately followed by a number ?
(a) None (b) One
(c) Two (d) Three
(e) More than three

59. Which element is sixth to the right of eleventh from the right end ?
(a) # (b) @
(c) 1 (d) H
(e) None of these

60. Four of the following five are alike in a certain way on the basis of their positions in the above arrangement and so form a group. Which is the one that does not belong to the group?
(a) W 9 # (b) B E 3
(c) 2 J A (d) H I @
(e) R Q 7

Directions (Qs. 61-65): In each of the questions given below which one of the five answer figures on the bottom should come after the problem figures on the top, if the sequence were continued?

61. **Problem Figures**

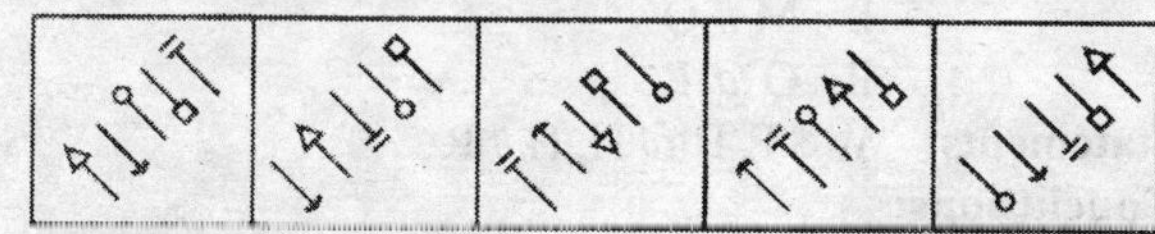

Answer Figures

(a) (b) (c) (d) (e)

62. **Problem Figures**

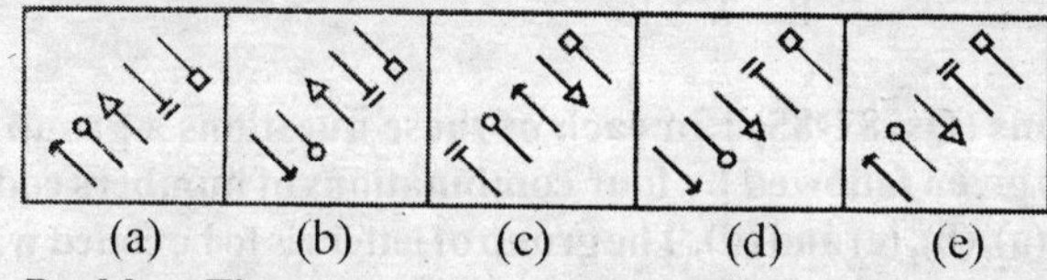

Answer Figures

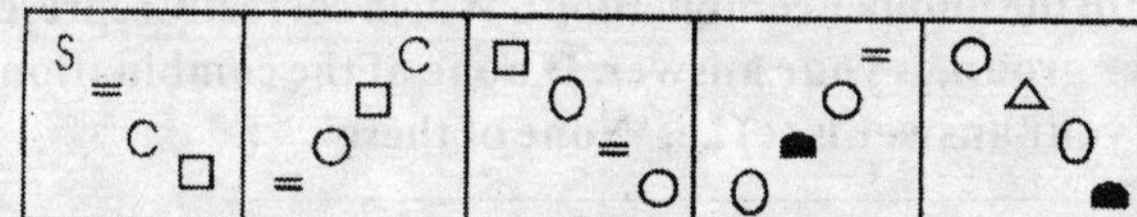

(a) (b) (c) (d) (e)

63. **Problem Figures**

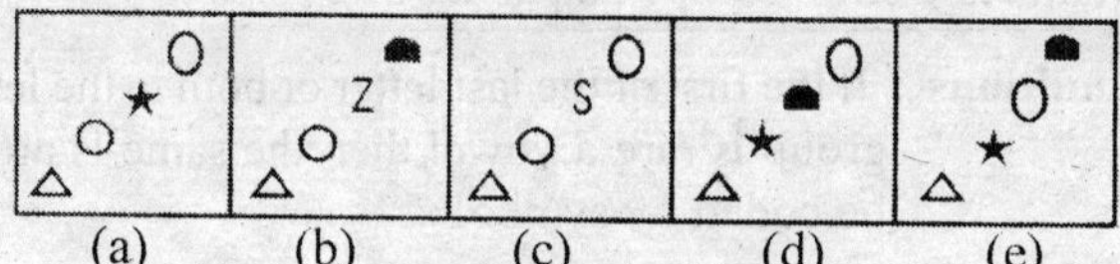

Answer Figures

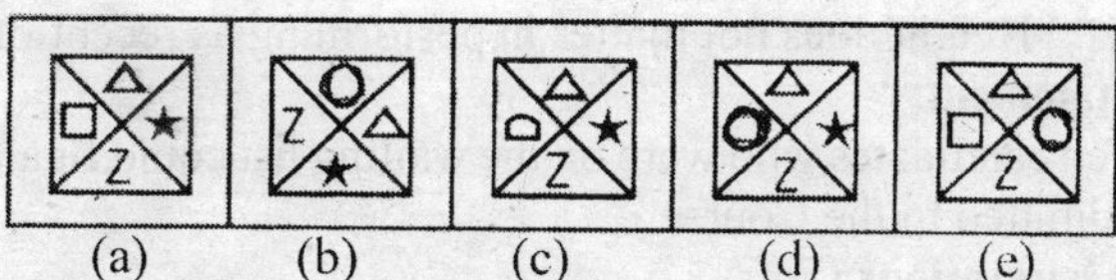

(a) (b) (c) (d) (e)

64. **Problem Figures**

Answer Figures

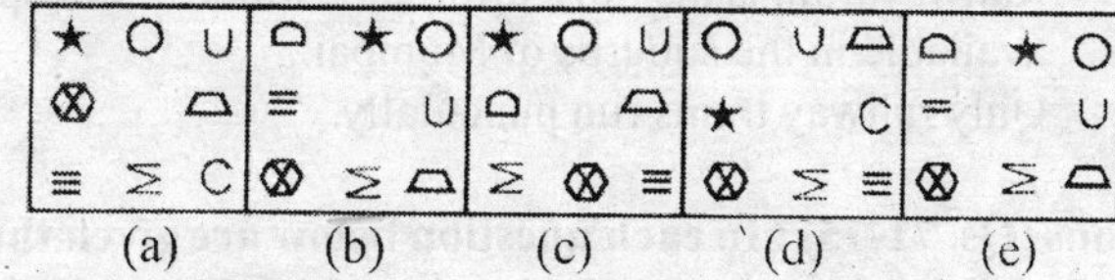

(a) (b) (c) (d) (e)

65. **Problem Figures**

Answer Figures

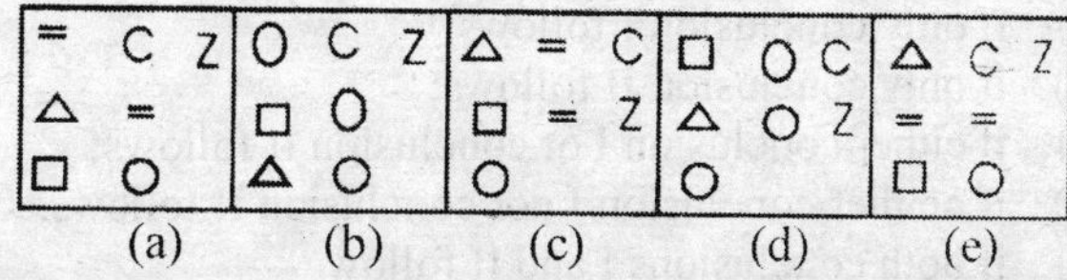

(a) (b) (c) (d) (e)

Directions (Qs. 66-70) : In each question below is given a statement followed by two assumptions numbered I and II. An assumption is something supposed or taken for granted. You have to consider the statement and the following assumptions and decide which of the assumptions is implicit in the statement. Give answer
(a) if only assumption I is implicit;
(b) if only assumption II is implicit;
(c) if either I or II is implicit;
(d) if neither I nor II is implicit;
(e) if both I and II are implicit.

66. **Statement:**
These mangoes are too cheap to be good.
Assumptions:
I. When the mango crop is abundant, the prices go down.
II. The lower the selling price, the inferior is the quality of the commodity.

67. **Statement:**
Although more amenities have been provided the fares have not been raised.
Assumptions :
I. Fares are dependent on amenities provided.
II. Fares are independent of amenities provided.

68. **Statement:**
Wanted unmarried, presentable, matriculate girls between 19 and 22 able to spear fluently in English to be trained as receptionists.
Assumptions:
I. Fluency in English is a pre-requisite for good performance as receptionist.
II. Height does not matter in performing as receptionist.

69. **Statement:**
Ten candidates who were on the waiting list could finally be admitted to the Course.
Assumptions :
I. Wait listed candidates do not ordinarily get admission.
II. A large number of candidates were on the waiting list.

70. **Statement:**
In Mumbai railway trains are indispensable for people in the suburbs to reach their places of work on time.
Assumptions:
I. Railway train is the most affordable mode of transport available in the suburbs of Mumbai.
II. Only railway trains run punctually.

Directions (Qs. 71-75) : In each question below are given three statements followed by two conclusions numbered I and II . You have to take the three given statements to be true even if they seem to be at variance from commonly known facts and then decide which of the given conclusions logically follow(s) from the three given statements, disregarding commonly known facts. Then decide which of the answers (a), (b), (c), (d) and (e) is correct answer and indicate it on the answersheet. Given answer
(a) if only conclusion I follows;
(b) if only conclusion II follows;
(c) if either conclusion I or conclusion II follows;
(d) if neither conclusion I nor conclusion II follows;
(e) if both conclusions I and II follow.

71. **Statement:**
Some phones are cells. All cells are batteries. Some batteries are tools.
Conclusions:
I. Some tools are cells.
II. Some batteries are phones.

72. **Statements:**
All numbers are letters. Some letters are words. Some words are symbols.
Conclusions:
I. Some symbols are letters.
II. Some words are numbers.

73. **Statements:**
All keys are cards. All cards are locks . No keys are doors.
Conclusions:
I. No lock is door
II. Some locks are doors.

74. **Statements:**
Some stars are plants. Some plants are trees. All trees are flowers.
Conclusions:
I. Some flowers are plants.
II. Some flowers are stars.

75. **Statements:**
Some books are papers. All papers are files. All files are records.
Conclusions:
I. Some records are books
II. Some files are papers.

Directions (Qs. 76 - 80) : In these questions symbols #, @, $, *, % are to be used with different meanings as follows:
'A # B' means 'A is neither smaller than nor equal to B'.
'A @ B' means 'A is smaller than B'.
'A $ B' means 'A is not greater than B'
'A * B' means ' A is not smaller than B'.
'A % B' means 'A is neither smaller than nor greater than B'.
In each question, three statements showing relationships have been given, which are followed by two conclusions I & II. Assuming that the given statements are true, find out which conclusion(s) is/are definitely true.
Mark answer
(a) if only conclusion I is true;
(b) if only conclusion II is true;
(c) if either conclusion I or II is true;
(d) if neither I nor II is true and
(e) if both concuIsions I and II are true.

76. **Statements:** T @ J, J * M, M $ B
Conclusions:
I. T # M
II. J $ B

77. **Statements:** R# F, F @ K, K $ V
Conclusions :
I. R # V
II. V # F

78. **Statements:** E @ A, A % F, F $ Q
Conclusions :
I. E @ Q
II. Q * A

79. **Statements:** L # M, M % D, D * Q
Conclusions:
I. M # Q
II. Q @ L

80. **Statements:** W $ F, F @ H, H # R
Conclusions:
I. W # R
II. W $ R

Directions (Qs. 81-85) : In each of these questions a group of letters is given followed by four combinations of numbers codes lettered (a), (b), (c) and (d). The group of letters is to be coded with the numbers codes and the condition given below. The 'serial number of the number combination'. Which correctly represents the letter group, is your answer. If none of the combinations is correct your answer is (e) i.e, 'None of these'.

Letters	D	J	K	Q	H	V	N	E	B	A
Numbers Codes	3	9	7	6	4	8	2	1	5	0

Conditions : If the first or the last letter or both in the letter group is /are a vowel then the same is/are to be coded by symbol #.

81. EHNDJV
(a) #42389 (b) 142398
(c) #42398 (d) 14239#
(e) None of these

82. KQDJNH
(a) 763942 (b) 736924
(c) #36924 (d) #63924
(e) None of these

83. AJNVQE
(a) #9286# (b) 09286#
(c) #92861 (d) 092861
(e) None of these

84. QHJVND
(a) 648923 (b) 649823
(c) #49823 (d) 64892#
(e) None of these

85. JKEDHA
(a) 97#34# (b) 971340
(c) 971430 (d) 97134#
(e) None of these

Directions (Qs. 86-90) : Each of the questions below consists of a question and two statements numbered I and II given below it. You have to decide whether the data provided in the statements are sufficient to answer the question. Read both the statements and give answer

(a) if the data in Statement I alone are sufficient to answer the question, while the data in Statement II alone are not sufficient to answer the question;
(b) if the data in Statement II alone are sufficient to answer the question, while the data in Statement I alone are not sufficient to answer the question;
(c) if the data in Statement I alone or in Statement II alone are sufficient to answer the question;
(d) if the data in both the Statements I and II are not sufficient to answer the question;
(e) if the data in both the Statements I and II together are necessary to answer the question.

86. How is P related to Q'?
Statements:
I. Mother of P is daughter of R
II. R is sister of Q

87. Among five friends A, B, C, D and E who is the youngest?
Statements:
I. B and D are older than C and E
II. C is older than only E

88. Tower R is in which direction with respect to Q?
Statements:
I. M is to the East of Q and to the North of R.
II. L is to the West of R and to the South of Q.

89. How many children are there in the row of children facing North?
Statements:
I. Kavitha is twelth from the left end of the row and is seventh to the right of Nisha.
II. Nisha is twentieth from the right end of the row.

90. How many sons does 'D' have ?
Statements:
I. R is the only sister of T and M who are sons of D.
II. T and M are only brothers of R who is daughter of D.

Directions (Qs. 91-95) : In each of these questions there are two sets of figures. The figures on the top are problem figures (four figures and one question marked space) and those on the bottom are answer figures indicated by lettters (a) (b) (c) (d) and (e). A series is established if one of the five answer figures is placed at the 'question-marked space." Question figures from a series if they change from left to right according to some rule. The letter of the answer figure which should be placed in the question-marked space is the answer. All the five figures i.e. four problem, figures and one answer figure placed in the question-marked space should be considered as forming the series.

91. **Problem Figures**

Answer Figures

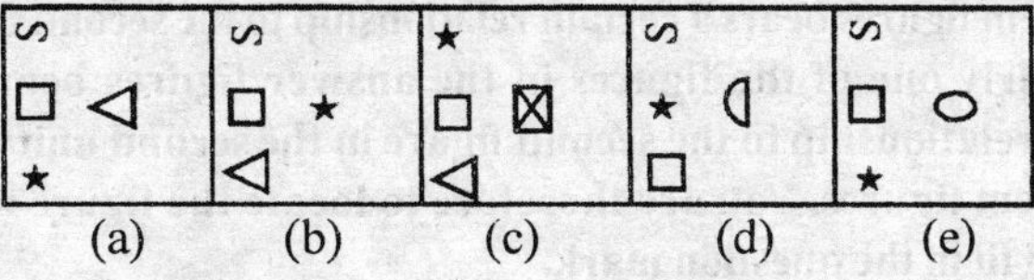

(a) (b) (c) (d) (e)

92. **Problem Figures**

Answer Figures

(a) (b) (c) (d) (e)

93. **Problem Figures**

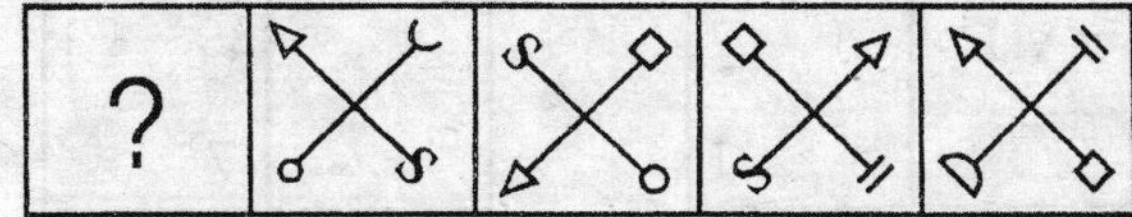

Answer Figures

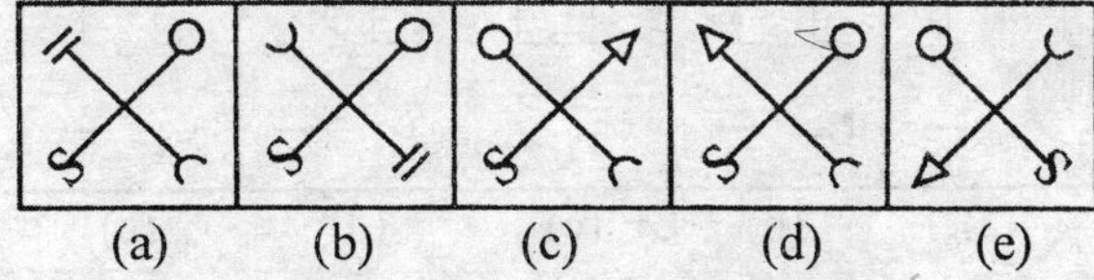

(a) (b) (c) (d) (e)

94. **Problem Figures**

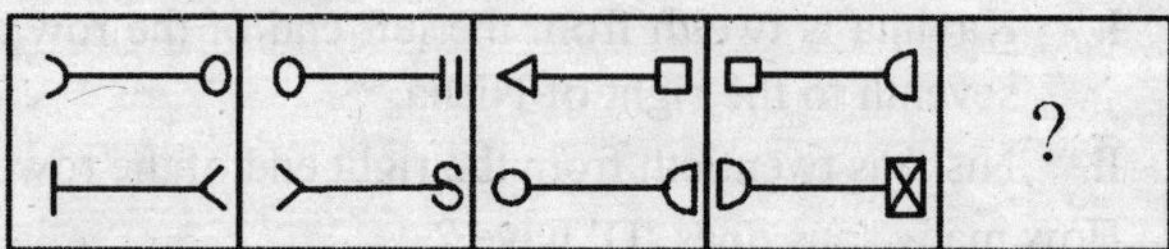

Answer Figures

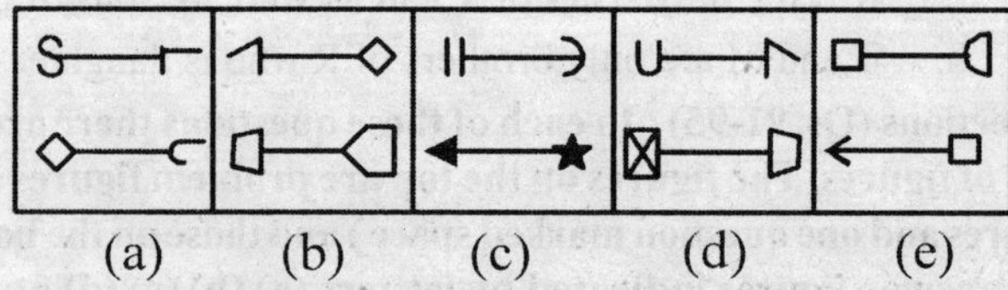

(a) (b) (c) (d) (e)

95. **Problem Figures**

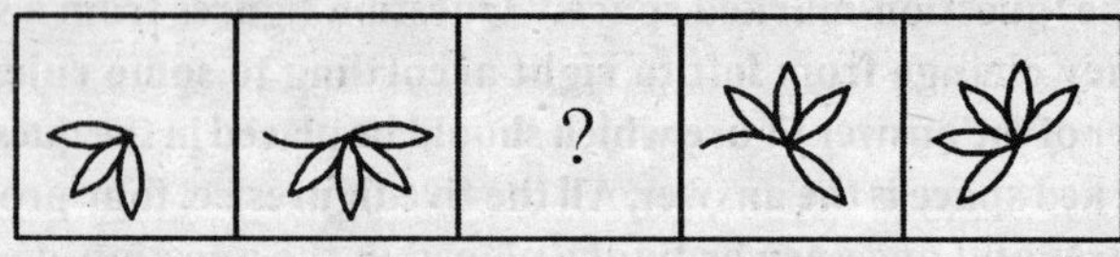

Answer Figures

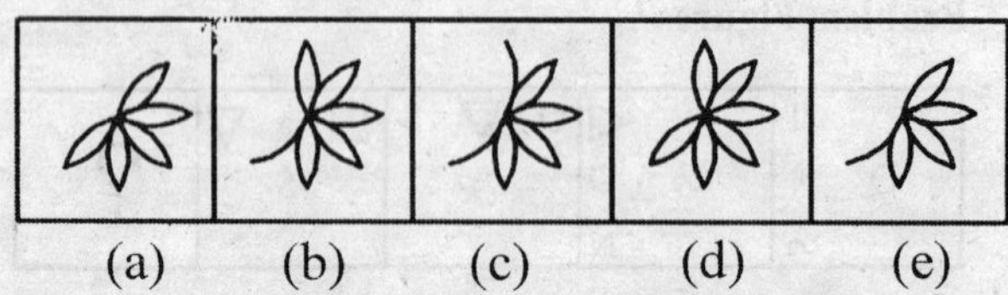

(a) (b) (c) (d) (e)

Directions (Qs. 96-100) : The first figure in the first unit of the problem figures bears a certain relationship to the second figure. Similarly one of the figures in the answer figures bears the same relationship to the second figure in the second unit of the problem figures. You are therefore to locate the figure which would fit in the question mark.

96. **Problem Figures**

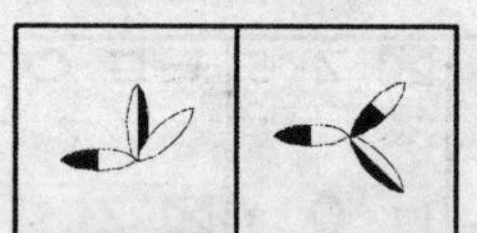

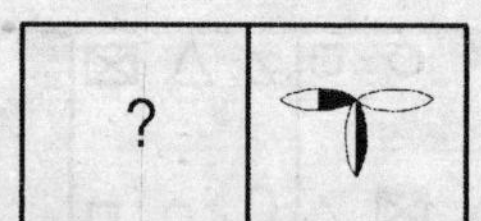

Answer Figures

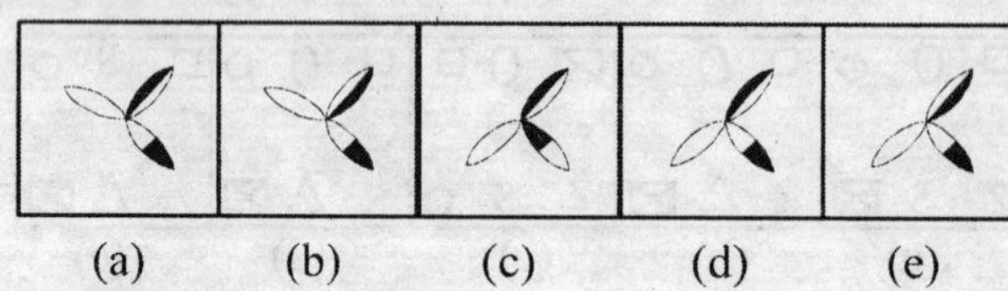

(a) (b) (c) (d) (e)

97. **Problem Figures**

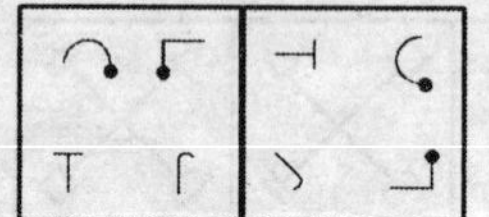

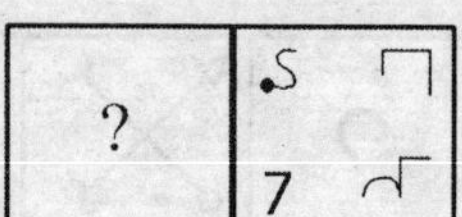

Answer Figures

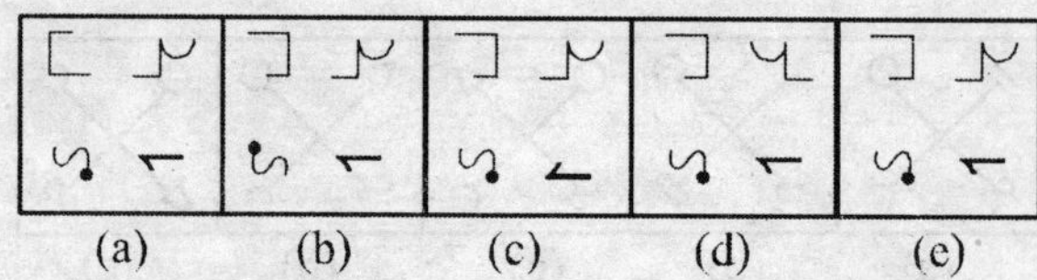

(a) (b) (c) (d) (e)

98. **Problem Figures**

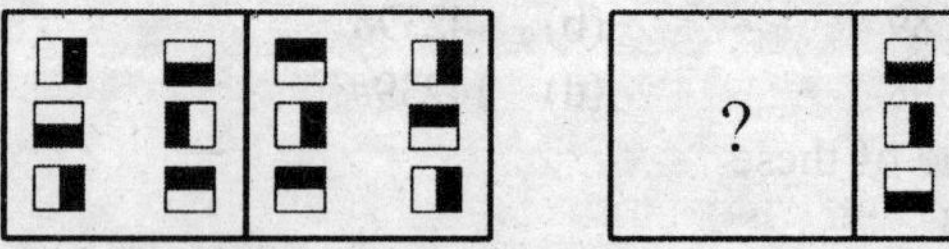

Answer Figures

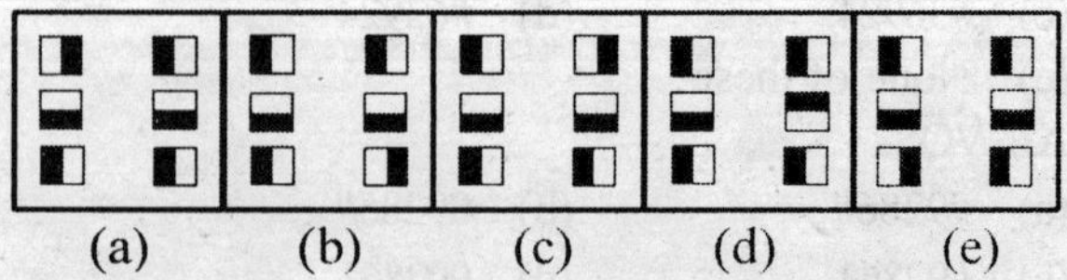

(a) (b) (c) (d) (e)

99. **Problem Figures**

Answer Figures

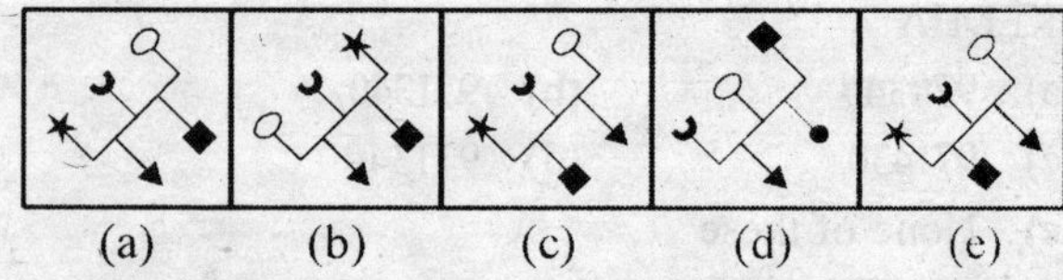

(a) (b) (c) (d) (e)

100. **Problem Figures**

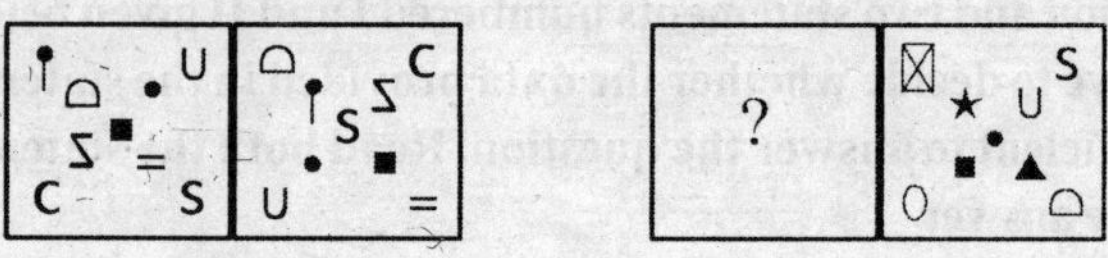

Answer Figures

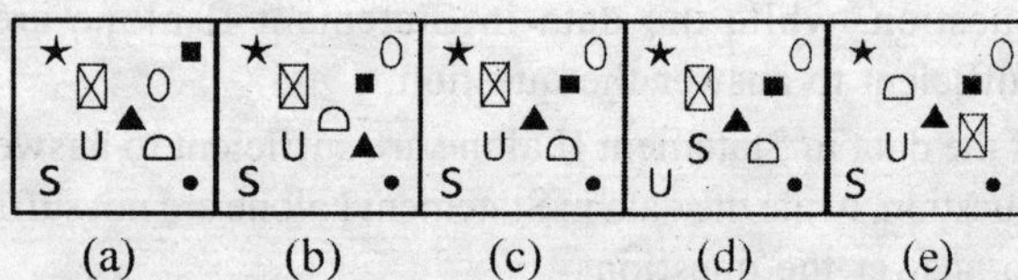

(a) (b) (c) (d) (e)

Directions (Qs. 101- 105) Read the following passage carefully and answer the questions given below it.

Seven officers A, B, C, D, E, F and G travel to different places- Delhi, Kolkata, Hyderabad, Bangalore, Pune, Tirupati and Ahmedabad.

Each of them is working in different departments — Accounts, Personal, Marketing, HR, Computers, PR and Security. The order of persons, places and departments is not necessarily the same.

B travels to Delhi and works in Personnel department. C goes to Hyderabad but does not work in Accounts or Computers. E does not travel to Kolkata or Tirupati and works in HR. F goes to Ahmedabad and works in Marketing. G works in Security department but does not go to Kolkata or Bangalore. A goes to Tirupati, The one goes to Kolkata does not work in Accounts.

101. G goes to which place?
(a) Tirupati (b) Ahmedabad
(c) Delhi (d) Pune
(e) None of these

102. Who works in Accounts department?
(a) B (b) C
(c) D (d) C or D
(e) None of these

103. C works in which department?
(a) Computers (b) Accounts
(c) PR (d) Cannot be determined
(e) None of these

104. Who works in Computer department?
(a) D (b) C
(c) A (d) G
(e) None of these

105. Who goes to Bangalore?
(a) D (b) E
(c) F (d) D or E
(e) None of these

Directions (Qs. 106-110) : In each of the questions given below which one of the answer figures on the right should come after the problem figures on the left, if the sequence were continued?

106. **Problem Figures**

Answer Figures

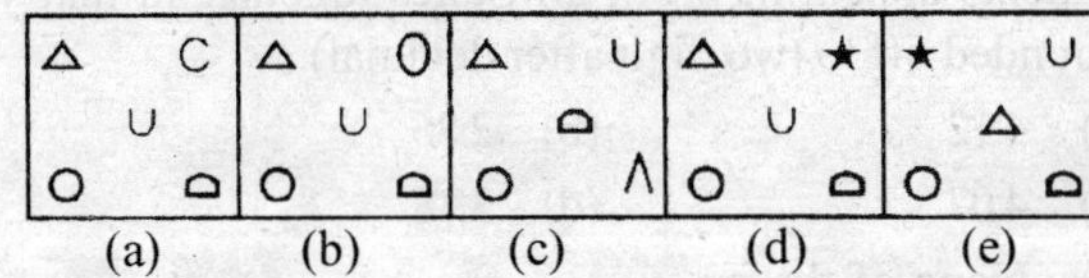

(a) (b) (c) (d) (e)

107. **Problem Figures**

Answer Figures

(a) (b) (c) (d) (e)

108. **Problem Figures**

Answer Figures

(a) (b) (c) (d) (e)

109. **Problem Figures**

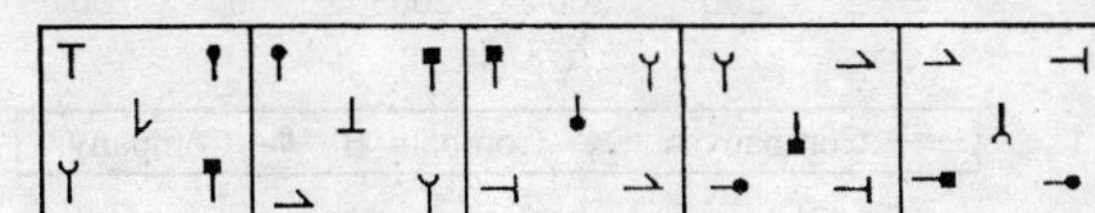

Answer Figures

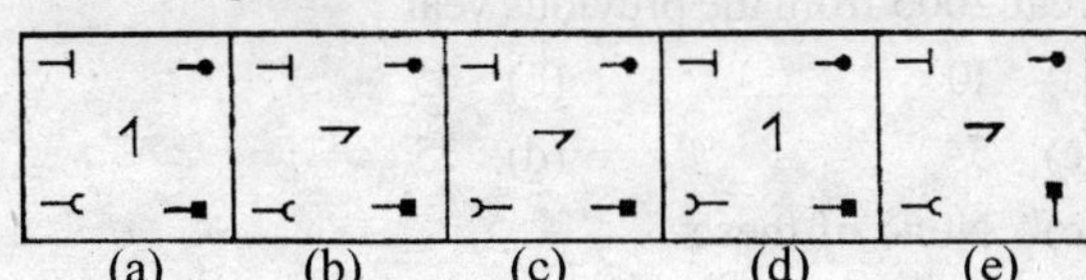

(a) (b) (c) (d) (e)

110. **Problem Figures**

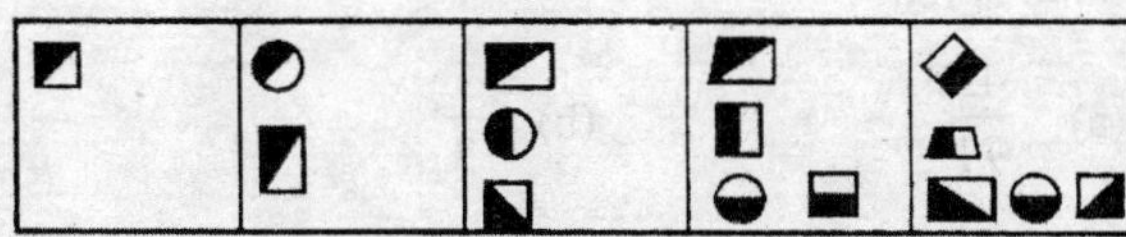

Answer Figures

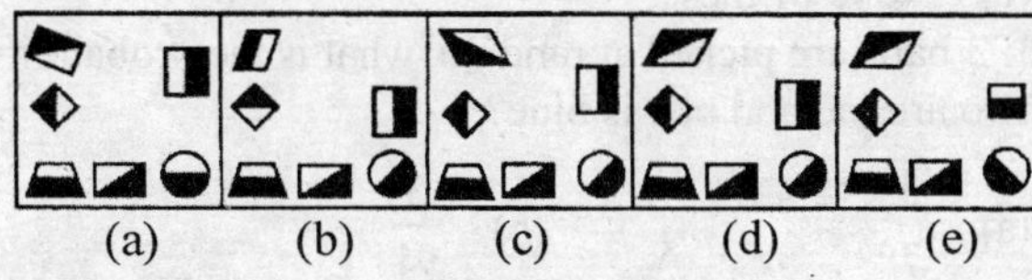

(a) (b) (c) (d) (e)

Directions (Qs. 111 to 115): What should come in place of the question mark (?) in the following questions?

111. $|\sqrt{10609}| \times |\sqrt{7938.81}| = ?$
(a) 9177.3 (b) 81973.
(c) 8553.3 (d) 8682.7
(e) None of these

112. $\left[\left[(13)^2\right]^3\right]^? = 2197$
(a) –3 (b) $\frac{1}{3}$
(c) $\frac{1}{2}$ (d) –4
(e) None of these

113. 18.4% of 656 + 12.7% of 864 = ?
(a) 252.623 (b) 230.432
(c) 210.284 (d) 246.182
(e) None of these

114. $(98.4)^2 + (33.6)^2 = ?$
(a) 10811.52 (b) 18011.52
(c) 10921.25 (d) 19021.25
(e) None of these

115. 8959 ÷ ? ÷ 4 ÷ 5 = 26.35
(a) 15 (b) 13
(c) 11 (d) 17
(e) None of these

Directions (Qs. 116 to 120): Study the information carefully and answer the questions that follow:

A basket contains 2 blue, 4 red, 3 green and 5 black balls.

116. If 3 balls are picked at random, what is the probability that either all are red or all are green?
(a) $\frac{9}{14}$ (b) $\frac{6}{91}$
(c) $\frac{5}{364}$ (d) $\frac{14}{91}$
(e) None of these

117. If 2 balls are picked at random, what is the probability that none is red?

(a) $\frac{45}{91}$ (b) $\frac{1}{7}$

(c) $\frac{5}{14}$ (d) $\frac{9}{14}$

(e) None of these

118. If 3 balls are picked at random, what is the probability that two are red and one is blue?

(a) $\frac{3}{7}$ (b) $\frac{3}{91}$

(c) $\frac{5}{100}$ (d) $\frac{3}{70}$

(e) None of these

119. If 4 balls are picked at random, what is the probability that either 2 are blue and 2 are red or 2 are green and 2 are black?

(a) $\frac{14}{91}$ (b) $\frac{3}{182}$

(c) $\frac{3}{14}$ (d) $\frac{36}{91}$

(e) None of these

120. If 4 balls are picked at random, what is the probability that all are black?

(a) $\frac{2}{7}$ (b) $\frac{3}{7}$

(c) $\frac{4}{1001}$ (d) $\frac{6}{1001}$

(e) None of these

Directions (Qs. 121 to 125): Study the table carefully to answer the questions that follow:

Number of Students (in thousands) Appearing (A) for a Competitive exam from Six different States and Percentage passing (P) the exam the years

Year	2002		2003		2004		2005		2006		2007	
States	A	%P	A	%P	A	%P	A	%P	A	%P	A	%P
A	2.3	11	4.2	21	3.5	12	2.0	22	1.8	14	1.2	17
B	3.5	14	3.6	16	3.4	11	1.3	15	2.3	16	2.1	18
C	1.8	23	2.8	13	2.9	16	4.5	24	2.3	23	3.9	20
D	2.9	18	2.8	15	1.6	20	3.2	20	3.3	16	4.0	19
E	4.4	17	3.2	23	1.9	16	1.5	18	3.1	18	2.7	14
F	3.2	21	3.0	14	4.0	14	2.6	11	3.8	19	2.3	13

A = Appeared % P = Percentage passing

121. What is the total number of students passing in the exam from State B in the year 2002 and 2003 together?

(a) 1206 (b) 1068

(c) 1146 (d) 1226

(e) None of these

122. What is the respective ratio of number of students passing in the exam from Stae C in the year 2004 to those passing in the exam from State E in the year 2007 ?

(a) 232 : 189 (b) 117 : 248

(c) 248 : 117 (d) 189 : 232

(e) None of these

123. Which State has the highest number of students appearing for the exam in all the years together?

(a) D (b) E

(c) F (d) C

(e) None of these

124. What is the total number of students passing in the exam in the year 2005 from all states together?

(a) 2836 (b) 2911

(c) 2624 (d) 2543

(e) None of these

125. The number of students passing is in the exam from State D in the year 2006 is which percent of the total number of students appearing from all States together in that year ? (rounded off to two digit after decimal)

(a) 4.12 (b) 2.86

(c) 4.07 (d) 3.18

(e) None of these

Directions (Qs. 126 to 130): Study the graph carefully to answer the questions that follow :

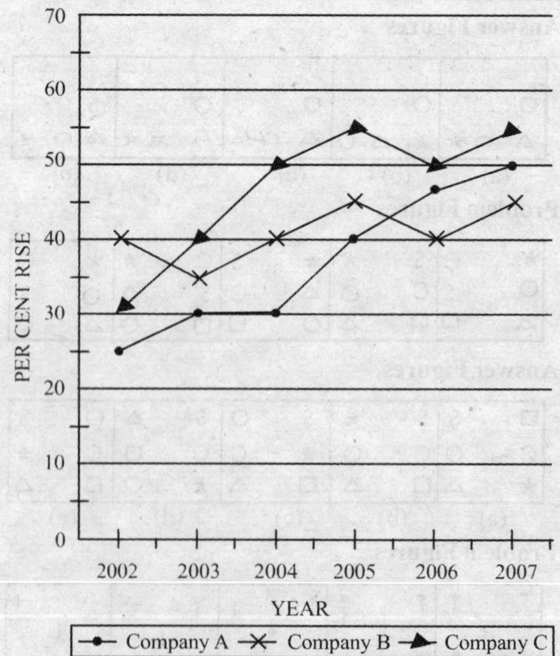

126. What is the percent increase in Profit of Company C in the year 2005 from the previous year ?

(a) 10 (b) 45

(c) 5 (d) 25

(e) None of these

127. Which of the following statements is **true** with respect to the graph.
(a) Company C made the highest profit in the year 2005.
(b) The profit made by Company A in the year 2003 and 2004 was the same.
(c) Average profit made by Company B over the years is more than the average profit made by Company A over the years.
(d) Per cent increase in profit of Company B in the year 2003 was less than its per cent increase in profit in the year 2002.
(e) None of these

128. What is the per cent increase in profit of Company C in the year 2004 from the previous year?
(a) 25 (b) 10
(c) 15 (d) 20
(e) None of these

129. What is the **approximate** average of the per cent increase in Profit of Company A ever the years?
(a) 22 (b) 37
(c) 48 (d) 26
(e) 42

130. If the profit of Company B in the year 2006 was Rs 3.22 lakhs, what was its profit in the year 2005 ?
(a) Rs 3.1 lakhs (b) Rs 3.08 lakhs
(c) Rs 2.3 lakhs (d) Rs 2.94 lakhs
(e) None of these

Directions (Qs. 131 to 135) : What approximate value should come in place of the question mark (?) in the following questions? (You are not expected to calculate the exact value).

131. $\sqrt[3]{860000} = ?$
(a) 75 (b) 80
(c) 110 (d) 125
(e) 95

132. $1\frac{5}{8}+5\frac{1}{3}+2\frac{2}{5}=?$
(a) 15 (b) 4
(c) 19 (d) 9
(e) 21

133. $8769 \div 82 \div 4 = ?$
(a) 27 (b) 44
(c) 429 (d) 12
(e) 512

134. $?\% \text{ of } 45.999 \times 16\% \text{ of } 83.006 = 116.073$
(a) 6 (b) 24
(c) 19 (d) 30
(e) 11

135. $12.998 \times 27.059 \times 17.999 = ?$
(a) 6020 (b) 6330
(c) 6800 (d) 6540
(e) 6150

Directions (Qs. 136 to 140): Study the table carefully to answer the questions that follow:

Number of Males (M) and Females (F) woking in different Departments of different Organisations

Department	HR		Accounts		IT		Marketing		Production		R&D	
Organisations	M	F	M	F	M	F	M	F	M	F	M	F
P	28	36	43	32	33	36	22	25	44	11	42	40
Q	25	28	32	20	38	36	23	20	48	8	38	40
R	26	34	40	21	30	32	18	16	53	12	36	39
S	22	26	35	20	49	46	26	15	58	10	34	38
T	18	24	36	16	50	48	24	21	56	12	38	32
U	20	32	30	28	45	48	28	19	52	15	40	29

136. Number of males working in the Accounts department of Organisation Q form what per cent of the total number of people working in that Organisation from all departments together?
(a) 9 (b) 15
(c) 4 (d) 19
(e) None of these

137. What is the respective ratio of total number of females working in the HR and Production departments of Organisation R to the total number of females working in the IT and R & D departments of organisation?
(a) 18:23 (b) 42:23
(c) 21:43 (d) 23:18
(e) None of these

138. What is the total number of people working in the IT and Production department of Organisation U?
(a) 186 (b) 128
(c) 160 (d) 153
(e) None of these

139. What is the average number of males working in the Marketing department of all organisations together ?
(a) $26\frac{1}{3}$ (b) $27\frac{1}{2}$
(c) $20\frac{1}{3}$ (d) $23\frac{1}{2}$
(e) None of these

140. Which organisation has the highest number of females working in it from all departments together?
(a) S (b) P
(c) U (d) R
(e) None of these

141. What will be the circumference of a circle with area equal to 98.56 sq. m?
(a) 32.4 m. (b) 48.2 m.
(c) 56.4 m. (d) Cannot be determined
(e) None of these

142. What will be the compound interest accrued on an amount of Rs 2,750 @ 14 p.c.p.a at the end of 3 years?
(a) Rs 1,254.115 (b) Rs 1,626.182
(c) Rs 1,324.246 (d) Rs 1,452.184
(e) None of these

143. A 280 metres long train crosses a platform thrice its length in 50 seconds. What is the speed of the train in kms./ hr.?

(a) 82.38 (b) 80.64
(c) 60.48 (d) 64.86
(e) None of these

144. In how many different ways can letters of the word "TEENAGE' be arranged ?

(a) 840 (b) 5040
(c) 1680 (d) 2520
(e) None of these

145. 24 men can complete a piece of work in 16 days and 18 women can complete the same work in 32 days. 12 men and 6 women work together for 16 days. If the remaining work was to be completed in 2 days, how many additional men would be required besides 12 men and 6 women?

(a) 16 (b) 64
(c) 24 (d) 48
(e) None of these

Directions (Qs. 146 to 150) : Study the graph carefully to answer the questions that follow:

Number of men, women and children in six different colonies

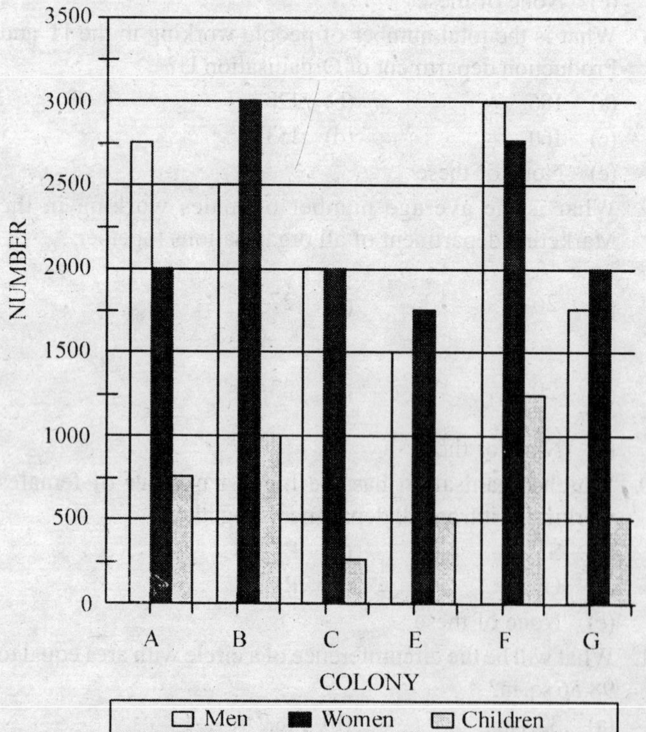

146. What is the difference between the total number of men and the total number of women from all colonies together ?

(a) 250 (b) 0
(c) 100 (d) 50
(e) None of these

147. What is the average number of children from all colonies together ?

(a) $708\frac{1}{3}$ (b) $622\frac{1}{2}$
(c) $683\frac{1}{3}$ (d) $712\frac{1}{2}$
(e) None of these

148. Total number of members from Colony F form **approximately** what per cent of the total number of members from all colonies together ?

(a) 22 (b) 8
(c) 13 (d) 29
(e) 36

149. What is the respective ratio of number of men to the number of women of Colony E?

(a) 8 : 3 (b) 13 : 11
(c) 6 : 5 (d) 7 : 6
(e) None of these

150. Number of children from Colony B form what per cent of the total number of members of that Colony? (rounded off to two digits after decimal)

(a) 14.26 (b) 13.19
(c) 12.64 (d) 15.38
(e) 14.83

Directions (Qs. 151 to 160) : Read each sentence to find out whether there is any grammatical error in it. The error, if any, will be in one part of the sentence. The number of that part is the answer. If there is no error, the answer is (e) i.e. 'No error', (ignore the errors of punctuation, if any).

151. Industrial accidents/ (a) usually result into / (b) negligence, ignorance/ (c) or carelessness (d) No error (e)

152. Some people are like /(a) to do a lot of social work /(b) even though they are poor/(c) and lack resource /(d) No error (e)

153. Some men/(a) have conveniently believe /(b) that women are inferior to / (c) men in respect of abilities (d) No error (e)

154. His equalities include /(a) the ability to take/ (b) right and / (c) quickly decisions . (d)/ No error (e)

155. If you want to /(a) ensure prompt service /(b) please be contacted to us/ (c) at your earlier convenience. / (d) No error (e)

156. They founded / (a) this institution for /(b) the welfare of the poor/ (c) and the disable people (d)/ No error (e)

157. He asked me/(a) what had my total investments /(b) during the/(c) last five years. (d)/ No error. (e)

158. He takes the /(a) prescribed medicine regularly / (b) and that is how/ (c) he has succeed to control his ailment . (d) No error (e)

159. We should take/ (a) regular exercises /(b) to keep ourself / (c) fit and active (d)/ No error (e)

160. Each time you /(a) reach this spot, / (b) go back and /(c) start your next (d)/ round again. (d)/ No error (e).

Directions (Qs. 161 to 175) : Which of the phrases (a), (b) and (c) given below each sentence should replace the phrase given in bold in the following sentence to make the sentence grammatically correct if it has an error in it? If none of the three phrases can correct the sentence, mark (d) i.e. 'None of these' as the answer. If the sentence is correct as it is and no correction is required, mark (e) i.e. 'No correction required' as the answer.

161. The honourable court **had taken a leniency view** because the accused had no previous criminal record.
(a) had viewed leniency
(b) had taken a leniency viewing
(c) had taken a lenient view
(d) None of these
(e) No correction required

162. Maintaining global peace is our **self-made commitment** to the word.
(a) self-making commitment
(b) self-made committee
(c) made of self-commitment
(d) None of these
(e) No correction required

163. The dinner party hosted by the President at the club was shifted to **an undisclosed location**.
(a) a locality undisclosing
(b) a undisclosing location
(c) an undisclose location
(d) None of these
(e) No correction required

164. The government should launch such projects which **should reversible** the destructive cycle of flood and drought.
(a) should have reversible
(b) should be reverse
(c) should have been reverse
(d) None of these
(e) No correction required

165. A committee comprising eminent experts from various fields **were setting up.**
(a) was set up (b) were being set up
(c) was setting up (d) none of these
(e) No correction required

166. Our foreign exchange reserves **have been increased substantial**.
(a) have been increased substantially
(b) have increased substantially
(c) have substantially increasing
(d) None of these
(e) No correction required

167. The key to a **competitive economy is** its investment regime.
(a) competition economy is
(b) competing economist lays
(c) economy competition was
(d) None of these
(e) No correction required

168. Driving a car in jammed traffic **require extraordinary patience** – especially when other drivers are not disciplined.
(a) required extraordinary patient
(b) requires extraordinary patience
(c) requiring extraordinary patience
(d) None of these
(e) No correction required

169. Chinese army possesses highly sophisticated simulators on **which their soldiers are training.**
(a) which their soldiers training on
(b) on which their soldiers have trains
(c) which their soldiers do train
(d) None of these
(e) No correction required

170. Every novel activity **will be likely to face** resistance from vested interests.
(a) is likely to face
(b) will be likely facing
(c) would be like facing
(d) None of these
(e) No correction required

171. We observed that traders were not primarily **dedicated with art of selling**.
(a) dedicated to the art of
(b) dedicated by the art of
(c) dedicated in the art by
(d) None of these
(e) No correction required

172. It **is become equally clear** that campaign against smoking will have little success until people realize its importance.
(a) has become equal and clear
(b) has become equally clear
(c) has become clearly equal
(d) None of these
(e) No correction required

173. Once the event is over, many people **claimed credit for success** but disown the responsibility for failure.
(a) claim credit of success
(b) claim credit for success
(c) claiming credit for success
(d) None of these
(e) No correction required

174. People **should be have their own** mechanism to guard against the activities of unscrupulous elements.
(a) shall be have their own
(b) should be having its own
(c) should have owning its
(d) None of these
(e) No correction required

175. The **real wonder is that** the artisans while constructing the Ajanta Caves possessed only the simplest hand tools.
(a) really wonder is that
(b) really wonderful is that
(c) real wonderful is that
(d) None of these
(e) No correction required

DIRECTIONS (Qs. 176 to 190) : Read the following passage carefully and answer the questions given below it. Certain words have been printed in bold to help you locate them while answering some of the questions.

The Prime Minister's recent trip to Nigeria, the first bilateral prime ministerial visit to Africa since Jawaharlal Nehur's 45 years ago, recalls a long neglected Indian obligation. "It is up to Asia to help Africa to the best of her ability," Nehru told the Bandung Conference in 1955, "because we are sister continents. "The Prime Minister's proposed strategic partnership with African nations might at last make good that 52-year old promise and also, perhaps, challenge China's expedient diplomacy.

In the intervening years, the West's **sanctimonious** boycott of many African regimes - after nearly a century of extreme colonial exploitation – left the continent in the grip of oppressive rulers looking for new political sponsors, arms-sellers and trading partners. Not only was it an **abdication** of the developed world's responsibility to the world's least developed region, sanctions actually compounded the sufferings of poorer Africans. The Darfur killings continue and there is no mellowing of Robert Mugabe's repression in Zimbabwe.

A bandoned by the West Africa looked elsewhere. Beijing filled the vacuum by eagerly embracing dangerous and unsavoury regimes in its search for oil and other minerals. China demonstrated its influence by playing host to 48 out of 53 African leaders a year ago in a jamboree that was historic as well as historical. Historic because China has succeeded in becoming the pre-eminent outside power in Africa and its second biggest trading partner. Historical because modern Chinese diplomacy draws on the Middle kingdom's ancient formula; the tribute system. It was how the son of Heaven brought those nations whom the Celestial Empire called "barbarians' into his imperial trading and , through it, cultural and political system.

Contemporary China's economic **penetration** of Africa also heralds a new era of cultural and political ties though the Chinese foreign ministry repeatedly assure the world that "our cooperation is not designed to be against or **preclude** any third party." This is untrue in a world of finite resources. Once the Chinese are established in a country, no one else gets a foothold. Myanmar, where India failed to obtain the desired gas concessions, is a prime example. Aware that the hunt for energy is a zero-sum game, China's leadership courts African leaders with regular visits and substantial grants.

After decades of neglect – Vajpayee's Africa visit over a decade ago was to attend a Commonwealth Summit– India will have to move cautiously but quickly if it is to break China's monopoly. Along with investing in Africa's human capital, ,China has outlined a strategic investment plan to build three to five trade economic cooperation zones in Africa by 2009 to boost trade, which is expected to tap \$40 billion this year. That could double to \$30 billion by 2010 on the back of an insatiable demand for natural resources to feed China's **booming** economy.

176. What was Jawaharlal Nehru's consideration for helping African nations?
(a) The people in the continent were extremely backward
(b) The Bandung Conference was held in Afrcan Continent
(c) African Continent is emotionally related to Asian Continent
(d) Nehru had promised the British rulers to help Africa after independence
(e) The West had exploited African people

177. The example of Myanmar given by the author proves
(a) that when China patronizes a country it does not allow other nations to enter
(b) India's foresight to feed its growing hunger for energy
(c) Myanmar's political acumen to have symbiosis with China
(d) that a country's political wisdom does not necessarily establish economic stability
(e) None of these

178. Which of the following is the author's suggestion to India to break the Chinese monopoly?
(a) Move away cautiously but quickly from the African nations
(b) Arrange P. M's regular visits to African countries
(c) Outline a strategic plan of investment in the African countries
(d) Plan for an increased economic help to African countries
(e) None of these

179. From the contents of the passage, it can be inferred that the author's views are
(a) in favour of India gaining an edge over China
(b) against India's entering into a competition with China
(c) in favour of not making any investment in African countries
(d) appreciate of oppressive and barbaric African rulers
(e) None of these

180. The author considers the claims of the Chinese Foreign Ministry regarding third party as
(a) just and worthy of trust
(b) true but slightly exaggerated
(c) too exorbitant to be true
(d) an underestimate of the quality and quantity of their help
(e) None of these

181. Which of the following best explains the term " Middle kingdom's ancient formula"?
(a) Rendering free hand for political, cultural & commercial upliftment
(b) Influencing the underdeveloped countries through apparently patronizing policy
(c) Referring the underdeveloped folks as barbarians and mistreating them
(d) Becoming pre-eminent outside power and thus ruling over them
(e) None of these

182. Which of the following was/were the reason(s) for the backwardness of African Nations?
(1) Mistreatment by the alien rulers
(2) Tyrannical leaders governing the gullible masses
(3) Exploitation and neglect by Western countries
(a) (1) and (2) only (b) (2) and (3) only
(d) (1) and (3) only (d) None of these
(e) All the three

183. Why did African countries explore help from countries other than the Western countries?
(a) The Western countries had turned a blind eye to the African countries
(b) The Western countries were not able to maintain their own economy
(c) Other countries like China were ready to extend help without expecting returns.
(d) The flow of help from Western countries was only of a lopsided nature
(e) None of these

184. China's substantial grants to African countries are an act of
(a) China's modern policy of rendering social service on humanitarian considerations
(b) stepping up its campaign of universal brotherhood among nations
(c) rendering selfless service to certain underdeveloped countries to beat the western countries.
(d) calculated selfish motive to fulfill its energy needs
(e) None of these

DIRECTIONS (Qs. 185 to 187) : Choose the word which is most OPPOSITE in meaning of the word given in bold as used in the passage.

185. Contemporary
(a) Fashionable (b) Modern
(c) Current (d) Existing
(e) Old

186. booming
(a) striving (b) sounding
(c) failing (d) thriving
(e) degrading

187. preclude
(a) disqualify (b) permit
(c) prevent (d) pre-empt
(e) include

DIRECTIONS (Qs. 188 to 190) : Choose the word which is most nearly the SAME in meaning as the word given in bold as used in the passage.

188. sanctimonious
(a) permissive (b) incongruent
(c) poetic (d) holy
(e) scrupulous

189. abdication
(a) abandonment (b) obligation
(c) instigation (d) addiction
(e) spiritualization

190. penetration
(a) infiltration (b) entry
(c) piercing (d) access
(e) breaking

DIRECTIONS (Qs. 191 to 200) : In the following passage, there are blanks, each of which has been numbered. These numbers are printed below the passage and against each, five words are suggested, one of which fits the blank appropriately. Find out the appropriate word in each case.

The (191) of evil, as well as the approach to dealing with evil is (192) in Eastern and Western religious traditions and culture. The East (193) that it is God's job to deal with evil. The individual has (194) to do with it; he can only party. It is the God who will take action to oust evil from our midst. In certain religions there are specific deities responsible for (195) evil forces. So the power of prayer is appreciated; (196) needs only to pray and deities will take care.

The Eastern approach will doubtless seem (197) if not completely incomprehensible in the West (198) there is a much more action-oriented approach to dealing with evil. It is viewed as the (199) of the individual to take action against evil and to deal (200).

191. (a) concept (b) interaction
(c) sublimation (d) influence
(e) remedy

192. (a) similar (b) illogical
(c) different (d) analogous
(e) potential

193. (a) declines (b) describes
(c) suspects (d) ignores
(e) believes

194. (a) everything (b) nothing
(c) lot (d) responsibility
(e) hesitation

195. (a) invoking (b) stabilizing
(c) mobilizing (d) counteracting
(e) instigating

196. (a) one (b) which
(c) who (d) he
(c) deity

197. (a) reasonable (b) emotional
(c) rationalistic (d) realistic
(e) odd

198. (a) though (b) because
(c) where (d) as
(e) when

199. (a) monopoly (b) prerogative
(c) right (d) responsibility
(e) desire

200. (a) regularly (b) firmly
(c) haphazardly (d) politely
(e) decently

ANSWERS WITH EXPLANATIONS

1. (a) As ... And,

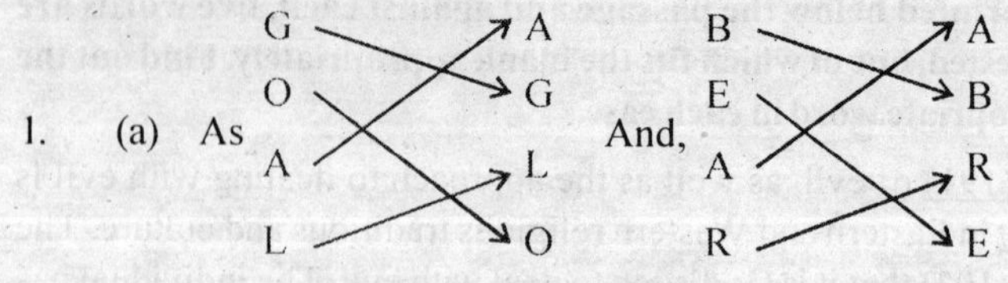

Similarly

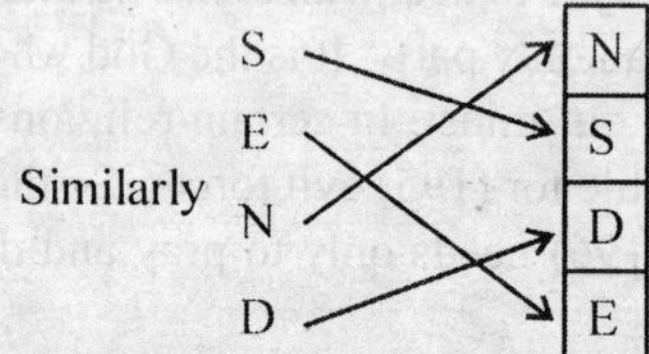

2. (b) M P and D G

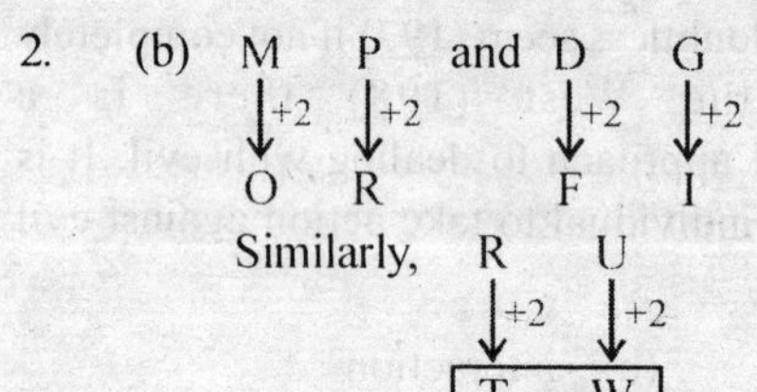

3. (e)

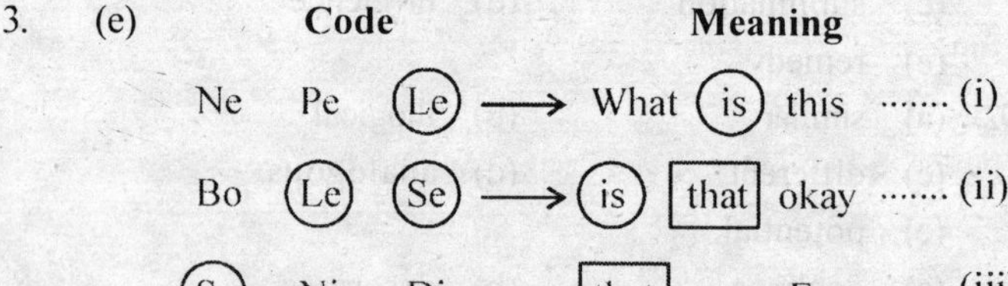

From (ii) Bo means 'okay'.

4. (c) Between C and E one gap and one letter (R). Between E and D no gap, so no letter. Between A and B, no gap, so no letter.

C R E D I T A B L E

5. (e) As, And,

P $\xrightarrow{-1}$ O   R $\xrightarrow{-1}$ Q

R $\xrightarrow{+1}$ S   U $\xrightarrow{+1}$ V

I $\xrightarrow{-1}$ H   B $\xrightarrow{-1}$ A

S $\xrightarrow{+1}$ T   L $\xrightarrow{+1}$ M

M $\xrightarrow{-1}$ L   E $\xrightarrow{-1}$ D

Similarly,

W $\xrightarrow{-1}$ V

H $\xrightarrow{+1}$ I

O $\xrightarrow{-1}$ N

R $\xrightarrow{+1}$ S

L $\xrightarrow{-1}$ K

6. (b) $125 - 5 \times 10 \div 13 + 28 = ?$

$\Rightarrow 125 \div 5 + 10 \times 13 - 28 = ?$

$\Rightarrow 25 + 130 - 28 = ?$

$\Rightarrow ? = 127$

7. (b)

Amit		Vilas	Alok		Ashok

N

8. (e) As,

B $\xrightarrow{+3}$ E

R $\xrightarrow{-3}$ O

O $\xrightarrow{-2}$ M

U $\xrightarrow{+3}$ X

G $\xrightarrow{-3}$ D

H $\xrightarrow{+3}$ K

T $\xrightarrow{-3}$ Q

Similarly,

S $\xrightarrow{+3}$ V

I $\xrightarrow{-3}$ F

T $\xrightarrow{-2}$ R

T $\xrightarrow{+3}$ W

I $\xrightarrow{-3}$ F

N $\xrightarrow{+3}$ Q

G $\xrightarrow{-3}$ D

9. (d)

10. (d)

11. (c)

Letter	O	N	S	I	R	T
Code	Z	#	1	@	9	Z

Condition (ii) is applied.

12. (e)

Letter	K	I	U	B	S	R
Code	3	@	7	6	1	9

13. (d)

Letter	B	K	A	E	U	G
Code	6	3	$	4	7	%

14. (c)

Letter	S	T	O	K	G	A
Code	*	5	2	3	%	*

Condition (iii) is applied.

15. (b)

Letter	O	R	H	S	N	U
Code	O	9	8	1	#	O

Condition (i) is applied.

16. (b)

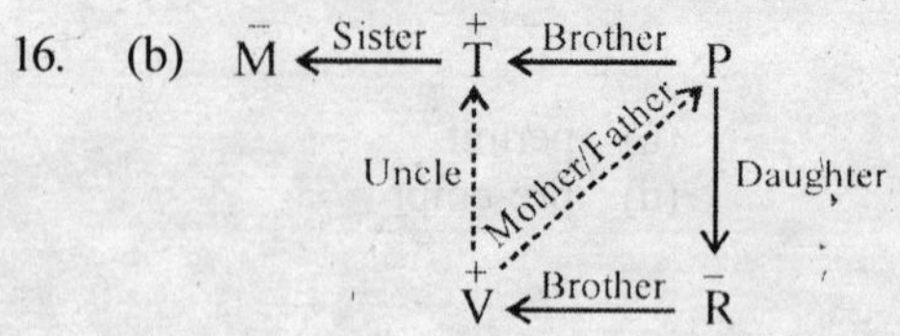

17. (d,e)

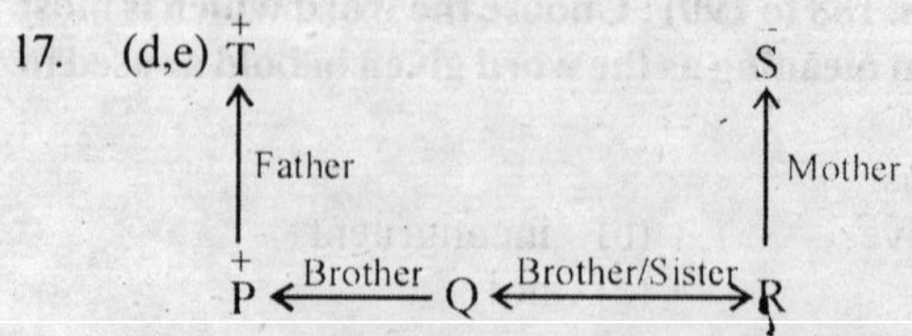

No information is given about A and E. The gender of S is female. So, S can't be A's brother. Similarly, Q is son of T and S.

18. (d) 4 7 2 7 2 3 5 9 7 4 [7] 5 2 4 [7] 9 4 [7] 7 8 4 [7] 1

19. (b) According to given conditions, every letters at the even places will be written in small and letters at the odd place will be written in capital letters.

Hence,

W —23rd place→ W

E —5th place→ E

D —4th place→ d

N —14th place→ n

E —5th place→ E

S —19th place→ S

D —4th place→ d

A —1st place→ A

Y —25th place→ Y

20. (c)

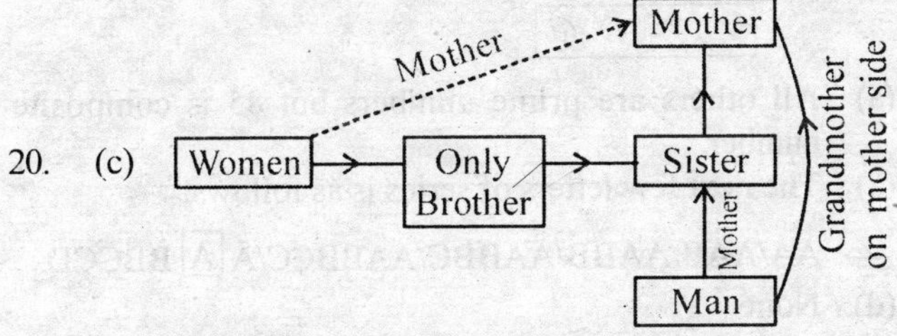

21. (e)

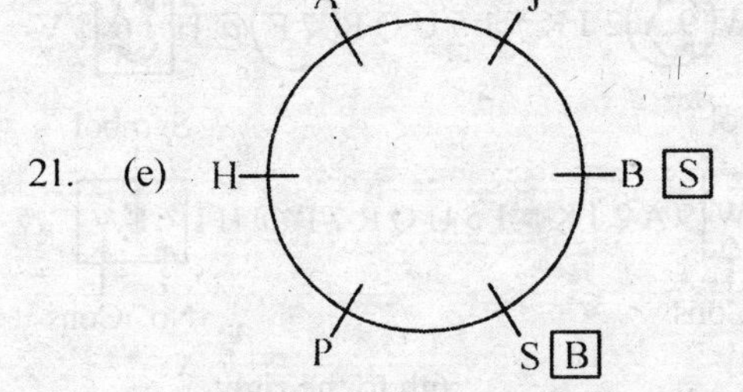

If S and B exchange their positions, S will be to the immediate right of B.

22. (c)

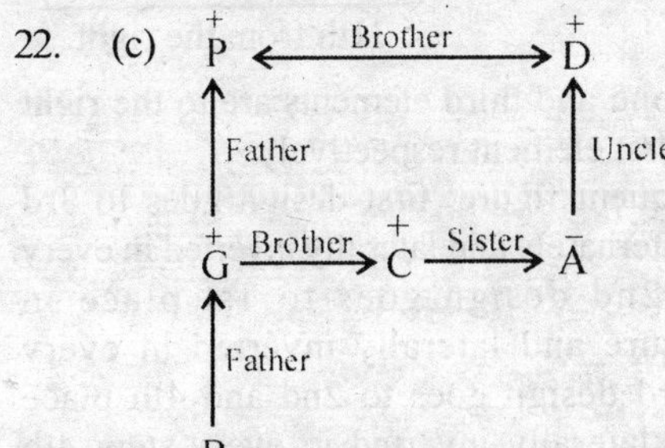

23. (b)

Code		Meaning	
(ew) xa his [de]	→	(She) is eating [apples]	....(i)
(ew) po va	→	(She) sells toys	....(ii)
ut li [de]	→	I like [apples]	....(iii)

From (i), she apples ⇒ ew de

24. (a) As, Similarly,

As,	Similarly,
C —(+3)→ F	S —(+3)→ V
H —(−3)→ E	U —(−3)→ R
E —(+3)→ H	N —(+3)→ Q
T —(−3)→ Q	D —(−3)→ A
A —(+3)→ D	E —(+3)→ H
N —(−3)→ K	R —(−3)→ O

25. (d) R O U B L E

L comes before O in the alphabet.

26. (c) According to height, row is as follows:
H P J A D
So, J stands in the middle.

27. (b) Giving up job from office is called resignation. Similarly giving up the position of being king or queen or throne is called abdication.

28. (d) Group of keys is called bunch. Similarly group of flowers is called bouquet.

29. (e)

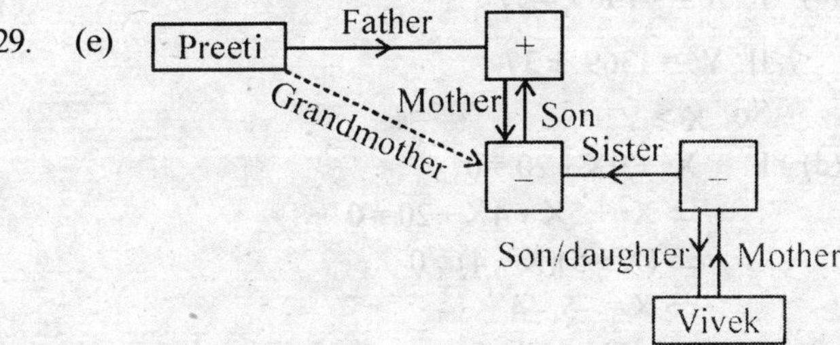

It is clear that Vivek is the son/daughter (since sex of Vivek is not clear) of Preeti's grandmother's sister. So, Vivek is uncle of Preeti.

30. (d) Letters : R, I, E, D
Word : RIDE, DIRE

31. (b) From the problem figure II to I, every group of designs moves 90° anticlockwise and every group of designs reduced or added by one. One group of designs changes into new one. Similarly, answer figure (b) would fit in the question mark.

32. (a) From problem figure II to I, first and third designs interchange their positions and reversed. Second and fourth design also interchange their position and only second design reversed. Similarly answer figure (a) would fit in the question mark.

33. (a) From problem figure II to I, both design move 90° clockwise. ⟩ rotates 90° anti-clockwise and ⌒ rotates 270° anti-clockwise.

34. (d) From problem figure II to I, both designs rotates horizontally and one curve moves in opposite directiŏn.

35. (d) From problem figure II to I triangle and square move 180° clockwise and a pentagon covers to square and a circle appears inside the triangle. Similarly answer figure (d) would fit in the question mark.

36. (a) 'But unless the council is prepared to make good its promis as regards road lighting'. From this sentence the inference is definitely true.

37. (e) 'It will only be question of time before there are further and perhaps fatal accident.' From this sentence the inference is definitely false.
38. (b) A person was run down in the accident. So it seems fatal.
39. (b) Although the time of accident is not given in the passage but the tenor of the passage suggests it happened at night.
40. (c) We can assume nothing about this inference from the passage.
41. (b) Relationship in option (b) is similar to question figure.
42. (c) The figure in section II is obtained by adding same figure but laterally inverted in left side of section I. The black portion is reversed in newly added portion.
43. (d) The figure in section II is obtained when lower design in section I is overlapped by upper design.
44. (b) Figure in option (b) is most similar to the problem figure.
45. (e) Relationship in option (e) is similar to question figure.
46. (b) I. $X = \sqrt{1369} = 37$

II. $Y^2 = 1369 \pm 37$

So, $X \geq Y$

47. (d) I. $X^2 + 9X + 20 = 0$

$\Rightarrow X^2 + 5X + 4X + 20 = 0$

$\Rightarrow (X + 5)(X + 4) = 0$

$\Rightarrow X = -5, -4$

II. $Y^2 + 7Y + 12 = 0$

$\Rightarrow Y^2 + 4Y + 3Y + 12 = 0$

$\Rightarrow (Y + 4)(Y + 3) = 0$

$\Rightarrow Y = -4, -3 = 0$

[$X = -4$ and $Y = -4 \Rightarrow X = Y$

$X = -5$ and $Y = -3 \Rightarrow X < Y$]

So, $X \leq Y$

48. (e) I. $X + 2Y - 11.5 = 0$

$\Rightarrow X + 2Y = 11.5$

II. $2X + 4Y = 23$

There are infinite solution.

No relation can be established between X and Y.

49. (b) I. $X^2 + 11X + 28 = 0$

$\Rightarrow X^2 + 7X + 4X + 28 = 0$

$\Rightarrow (X + 7)(X + 4) = 0$

$\Rightarrow X = -7, -4$

II. $Y^2 + 15Y + 56 = 0$

$\Rightarrow Y^2 + 8Y + 7X + 56 = 0$

$\Rightarrow (Y + 8)(Y + 7) = 0$

$\Rightarrow Y = -8, -7$

So, $X \geq Y$

50. (a) I. $2X - 4Y = 12$

II. $4X - 2Y = 0$

$X = -2, Y = -4$

So, $X > Y$

51. (b)

D	E	S	I	G	N	E	R
(Con)	(Vow)	(Con)	(Vow)	(Con)	(Con)	(Vow)	(Con)
↓ −1	↓ +1	↓ −1	↓ +1	↓ −1	↓ −1	↓ +1	↓ −1
C	F	R	J	F	M	F	Q

52. (d)

Number:	5	7	[6]	4	[8]	[9]
Re-arranged:	4	5	[6]	7	[8]	[9]

So, 6, 8 and 9 remain at the same position.

53. (e) R I D E and T A I L

↓ ↓ ↓ ↓ ↓ ↓ ↓ ↓

% # $ @ © * # D

So, D A T E

↓ ↓ ↓ ↓

$ * © @

54. (a) All others are prime numbers but 85 is composite number.
55. (a) The next few letters of series is as follows:

AA/AAB/AABB/AABBC/AABBCC/A [A] BBCCD

56. (d) None
57. (a)

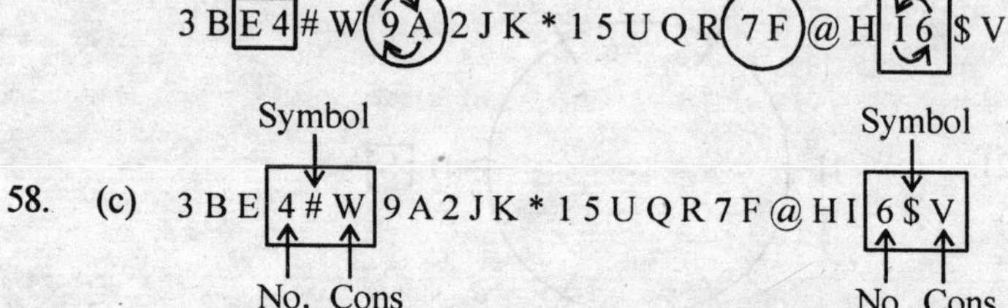

58. (c) 3 B E 4 # W 9 A 2 J K * 1 5 U Q R 7 F @ H I 6 $ V

No. Cons   No. Cons

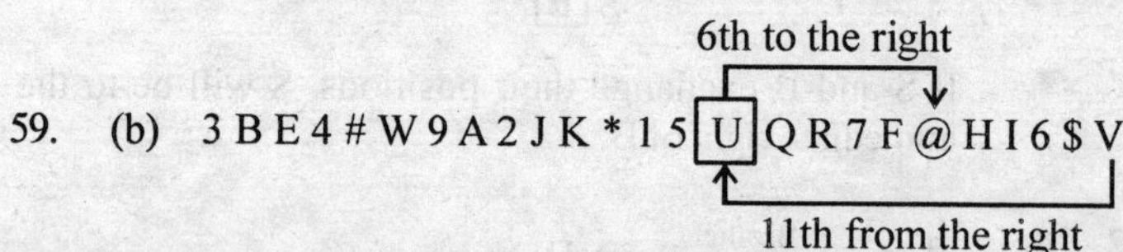

59. (b)

60. (e) In all other second and third elements are to the right and left of the first element respectively.
61. (d) In every subsequent figure, first design goes to 3rd and 2nd place alternately and laterally inverted in every second step. 2nd design goes to 1st place in subsequent figure and laterally inverted in every second step. 3rd design goes to 2nd and 4th place alternately and laterally inverted in every step. 4th design goes to 5th and 3rd place alternately and laterally inverted in every 2nd step.
62. (d) The 1st design replaced by a new one in 3rd and 2nd place alternately. The 2nd design becomes 4th and 1st design subsequently. The 3rd design becomes 1st and 4th design. The 4th design becomes 2nd and 3rd alternately.
63. (c) Every design rotates 90° and 180° alternately in subsequent figure and one figure replaced by new one.
64. (c) Every design rotates 90°, 90° and 45° anti-clockwise respectively and one new design is added in every next step. One previous design replaced by new one.

65. (a) One new pair of designs appear in every subsequent figure as follows

One previous design omitted in every subsequent figure. Design 'O' moves $\frac{1}{2}$ and 1; 'Z' moves $1\frac{1}{2}$ and 1; '□' moves $\frac{1}{2}$ and 1; 'c' moves $1\frac{1}{2}$ and 1; '△' moves $\frac{1}{2}$ and 1 respectively in every subsequent figure.

66. (b) We cannot assume anything about the factors affecting lower prices of mango from the statement. So assumption I is not implicit. Assumption II is clearly implicit in the statement.

67. (a) The author clearly assumes I while making statement, that is why the emphasis is on amenities.

68. (a) It is clear that assumption I is implicit in the statement. Assumption II does not make any sense.

69. (d) From the given statement we cannot assume any given assumption.

70. (d) The emphasis is on time not affordability. So assumption I is not implicit in the statement. Assumption II is also not implicit because of the word 'only'.

71. (b)

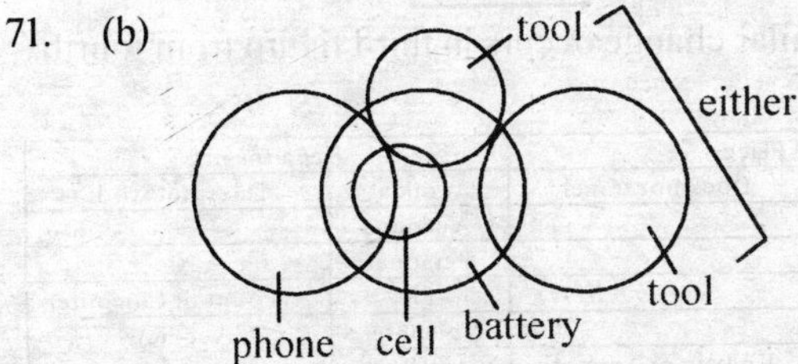

I. ×　　II. ✓

72. (d)

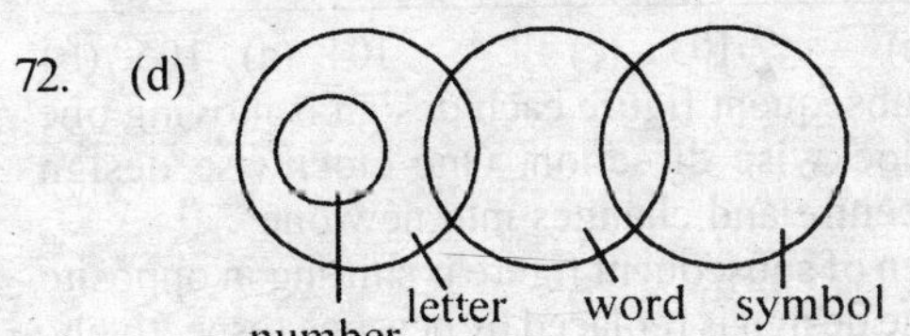

I. ×
II. ×

73. (c)

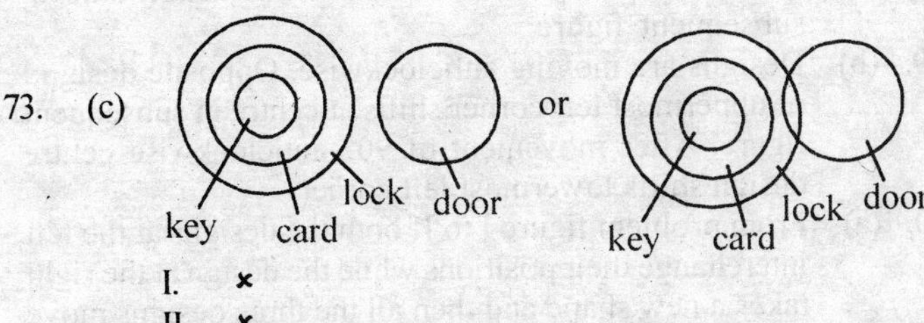

I. ×
II. ×

But I and II are complementary pairs. So either I or II follows.

I. ×　　II. ×

74. (a)

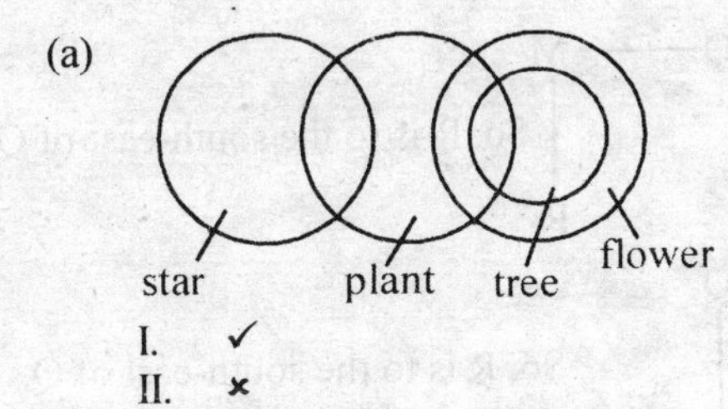

I. ✓
II. ×

75. (e)

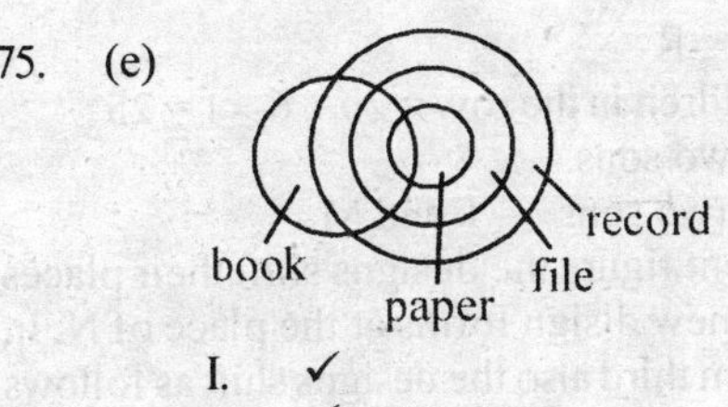

I. ✓
II. ✓

76. (d) $T < J,\ J \geq M,\ M \leq B$
No relation between T and M, and J and B.
So neither I nor II is true.

77. (b) $R > F,\ F < K,\ K \leq V$
No relation between R and V. So conclusion I is not true.
But $V \geq K > F$ or $V > F$
So, conclusion II is true.

78. (a) $E < A,\ A = F,\ F \leq Q$
Combining all, $Q \geq F = A > E$ or $E < Q$ and $Q \geq A$
So, only conclusion I is true.

79. (b) $L > M,\ M = D,\ D \geq Q$
Combining all, $L > M = D \geq Q$ or $M \geq Q$ and $Q < L$.
So, only conclusion II is true.

80. (c) $W \leq F,\ F < H,\ H > R$
Although no direct relation between W and R but I and II together show all three probable relations. Hence either I or II is true.

81. (c)

Letter	E	H	N	D	J	V
Code	#	4	2	3	9	8

Since 1st letter is vowel then $E \rightarrow \#$

82. (e)

Letter	K	Q	D	J	N	H
Code	7	6	3	9	2	4

83. (a)

Letter	A	J	N	V	Q	E
Code	#	9	2	8	6	#

Since both 1st and last letters are vowel then $A \rightarrow \#$

84. (b)

Letter	Q	H	J	V	N	D
Code	6	4	9	8	2	3

85. (d)

Letter	J	K	E	D	H	A
Code	9	7	1	3	4	#

Since last letter is vowel then $A \rightarrow \#$

86. (d) P's sex can't be determined even after joining the two statements.

87. (b) **From II :** C is older than only E. It means E is the youngest.

88. (c) **From I :** Q ——— M

So, R is to the south-east of Q.

R

From II : Q

So, R is to the south-east of Q.

L ——— R

89. (e) **I + II :** No of children in the row = 20 + 6 – 1 = 25

90. (c) **From I :** D has two sons.

From II : D has two sons — T and M.

91. (e) In each subsequent figure the designs shift their places as follows and a new disign forms at the place of N. In second figure from third also the designs shift as follows after shifting one side anticlockwise –

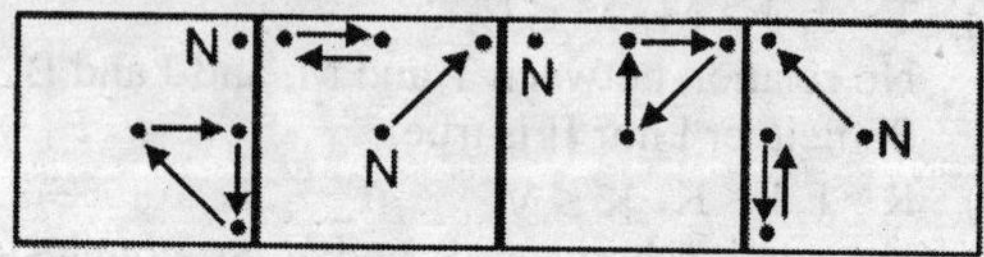

92. (a) In each subsequent figure the designs shift as follows and a new design forms at the place of N

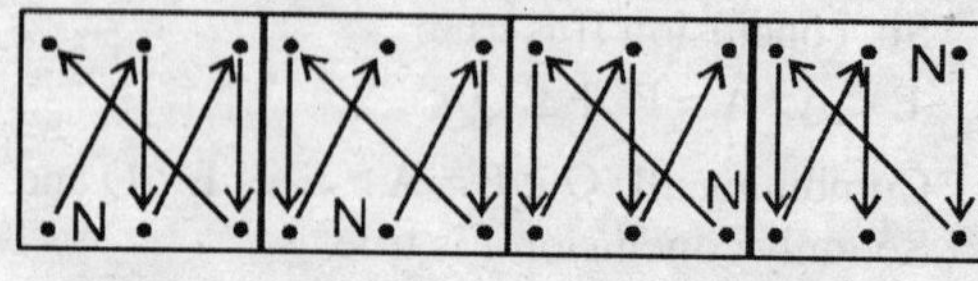

(1) to (2) (2) to (3) (3) to (4) (4) to (5)

93. (a) In each subsequent figure the designs shift as follows and a new design forms at the place of N

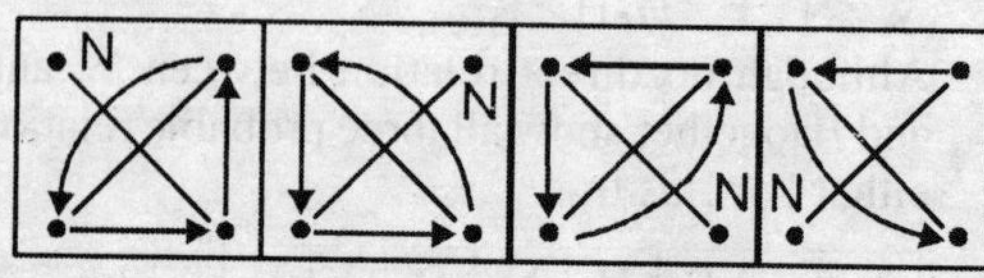

(1) to (2) (2) to (3) (3) to (4) (4) to (5)

94. (b) In second figure from first the right side both designs on the upper and lower straight line come on the left same line and new designs form on the both right side ends. Now all four new designs form on the lines in the third figure and in fourth figure, from third the above changing sequence becomes continue. So four designs of all ends of the line form new in the fifth figure.

95. (c) In each subsequent figure 2 and $1\frac{1}{2}$ leaves form new respectively in the anticlockwise forward direction and $\frac{1}{2}$, 1, $1\frac{1}{2}$ and 2 leaves become missed in the same direction backward side.

96. (d) In first figure from second the leaves form as follows with shaded part and rotation...

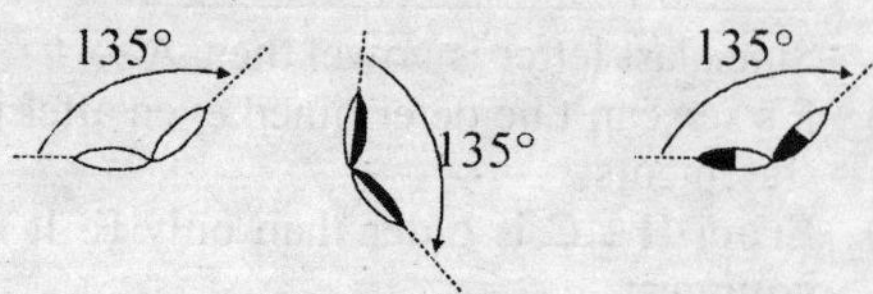

The similar change becomes in third figure from fourth.

97. (e) In first figure from second the upper right design reverses after rotating 90° clockwise, the upper left design rotates 90° anticlockwise, the lower right design rotates 180° anticlockwise and the lower left design rotates 135° anticlockwise. These all designs shift one side anticlockwise with this change also. The similar change occurs in third figure from fourth.

98. (b) In first figure from second the designs form after rotating 90° clockwise or anticlockwise as follows and the similar change occurs in the third figure from fourth also ...

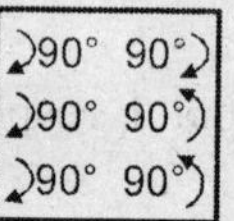

99. (a) In first figure from second the main design rotates 90°clockwise and the formed designs on it shift as follows and a new design forms at the place of N

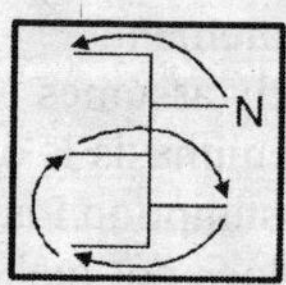

The similar change occurs in third figure from fourth also.

100. (c) In first figure from second the designs shift as follows:

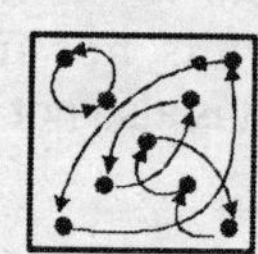

The similar change occurs in third figure from fourth.

For (Qs. 101-105):

Officers	Places		Departments	
	Goes to	Does not travel	Work in	Does not work
A	Tirupati		Account	
B	Delhi		Personal	
C	Hyderabad		PR	Account or Computer
D	Kolkata		Computer	Account
E	Bangalore	Kolkata or Tirupati	HR	
F	Ahmedabad		Marketing	
G	Pune	Kolkata or Bangalore	Security	

101. (d) 102. (e) 103. (c) 104. (a) 105. (b)

106. (d) In every subsequent figure each design is moving one arm anticlockwise direction. One clockwise design comes in centre and changes into new one.

107. (e) Each design of subsequent figure is shifting in opposite arm and one design is replaced by new one respectively.

108. (b) Left side designs goes to right side in every subsequent figure. Upper and lower two designs of right side exchange their positions and to shift in left side in subsequent figure.

109. (b) Designs are moving anticlockwise. Opposite designd of uppermost left corner shifts at centre in subsequent figure. After movement of 90° anticlockwise centre design shifts lowermost left corner.

110. (a) From problem figure I to II both the designs at the left interchange their positions while the design at the right takes a new shape and then all the three designs move clockwise through 90°. From problem figure III to IV both the designs at the left interchange their position while the design at the right takes a new shape and then all the three designs move anticlockwise through 90°. The same order is repeated.

111. (a) $|\sqrt{10609}| \times |\sqrt{7938.81}|$

$\sqrt{10609} = 103$, by division method, as below:

$$\begin{array}{r|l} & 103 \\ 10 & \overline{1}\overline{06}\overline{09} \\ & 100 \\ 203 & \ \ 609 \\ & \ \ 609 \\ & \ \ \ \ 0 \end{array}$$

Also,, $\sqrt{7938.81} = 89.1$, by division method, as below:

$$\begin{array}{r|l} & 89.1 \\ 8 & 79\overline{38}.\overline{81} \\ & 64 \\ 169 & 1538 \\ & 1521 \\ 1781 & \ \ 1781 \\ & \ \ 1781 \\ & \ \ \ \ 0 \end{array}$$

Hence $103 \times 89.1 = 9177.3$

112. (c) Let x be there in place of question mark.

So, $\left[\left[(13)^2\right]^3\right]^x = 2197 \Rightarrow \left[(169)^3\right]^x = 2197$

$4826809^x = 2197$, taking $\log_{10}$ on both the sides

$x \log_{10}(4826809) = \log_{10} 2197$

$\Rightarrow x \times 6.68366 = 3.34183$

$\Rightarrow x = \frac{1}{2}$

113. (b) 18.4% of $656 + 12.7\%$ of $864 = 0.184 \times 656 + 0.127 \times 864$
$= 120.704 + 109.728 = 230.432$

114. (a) $(98.4)^2 + (33.6)^2 = 9682.56 + 1128.96 = 10811.52$

115. (d) Let there be x in place of question mark

So, $\frac{8959}{x \times 4 \times 5} = 26.35 \Rightarrow x = \frac{8959}{26.35 \times 20} = 17$

116. (c) There are $2 + 4 + 3 + 5 = 14$ balls.
Total possible selection of 3 balls out of $14 = {}^{14}C_3$

$= \frac{14 \times 13 \times 12}{3!} = 28 \times 13$

P(3 red or 3 green) $= \frac{{}^4C_3}{{}^{14}C_3} + \frac{{}^3C_3}{{}^{14}C_3}$

$= \frac{4}{28 \times 13} + \frac{1}{28 \times 13} = \frac{5}{364}$

117. (a) Total number of balls are 14. There are 4 red balls and 10 non-red balls.

Total selection possible is ${}^{14}C_2 = \frac{14 \times 13}{21} = 91$.

Possible selection for non-red balls are

${}^{10}C_2 = \frac{10 \times 9}{21} = 45$.

So, probability that non of the two balls, pecket-up is red $= \frac{{}^{10}C_2}{{}^{14}C_2} = \frac{45}{91}$.

118. (b) Total number of balls are 14, 4 balls are red and 2 are blue. Hence for selecting 2 red balls and 1 blue balls, possibilities are ${}^4C_2 \times {}^2C_1$ out of ${}^{14}C_3$ selections.
So, probability (2 red and 1blue)

$$= \frac{{}^4C_2 \times {}^2C_1}{{}^{14}C_3} = \frac{\frac{4 \times 3}{2} \times 2}{\frac{14 \times 13 \times 12}{3!}} = \frac{12}{14 \times 13 \times 2} = \frac{3}{91}$$

119. (e) Total number of balls = 14, red = 4 blue =2, green =3, black =5

P{(2 blue and 2 red) or (2 green and 2 black)}

$$= \frac{{}^2C_2 \times {}^4C_2}{{}^{14}C_4} + \frac{{}^3C_2 \times {}^5C_2}{{}^{14}C_4}$$

$$= \frac{1 \times 6 + 3 \times 10}{\frac{14 \times 13 \times 12 \times 11}{4 \times 3 \times 2}} = \frac{36}{13 \times 7 \times 11} = \frac{36}{1001}$$

120. (e) Total number of balls = 14, Number of black balls = 5
So, the probability of picking 4 black balls =

$\frac{{}^5C_4}{{}^{14}C_4} = \frac{5}{\frac{14 \times 13 \times 12 \times 11}{4 \times 3 \times 2}} = \frac{5}{1001}$ which matches none except choice (e).

121. (e) Students passing from State B in 2002

$= 3500 \times \frac{14}{100} = 490$

Students passing from State B in 2003

$= 3600 \times \frac{16}{100} = 576$

So, students passing from State B in year 2002 and 2003 together $= 490 + 576 = 1066$.

122. (a) Students passing in 2004 from State C

$= 2900 \times \frac{16}{100} = 464$

Students passing in 2007 from State E

$= 2700 \times \frac{14}{100} = 378$

Their ratio $= \frac{464}{378} = \frac{232}{189}$

123. (c) Students appearing from defferent state are:

State A : $2300 + 4200 + 3500 + 2000 + 1800 + 1200 = 15000$
B : $3500 + 3600 + 3400 + 1300 + 2300 + 2100 = 16200$
C: $1800 + 2800 + 2900 + 4500 + 2300 + 3900 = 18200$
D: $2900 + 2800 + 1600 + 3200 + 3300 + 4000 = 17800$
E: $4400 + 3200 + 1900 + 1500 + 3100 + 2700 = 16800$
F: $3200 + 3000 + 4000 + 2600 + 3800 + 2300 = 18900$

124. (b) Student passing in 2005 from all states together.

State A $= 2000 \times \frac{22}{100} = 440$

$B = 1300 \times \frac{15}{100} = 195$

$C = 4500 \times \frac{24}{100} = 1080$

$D = 3200 \times \frac{20}{100} = 640$

$E = 1500 \times \frac{18}{100} = 270$

$F = 2600 \times \frac{11}{1000} = 286$

Total = 2911

125. (d) Student passing in 2006 examination from State D

$= 3300 \times \frac{16}{100} = 528$

Total students appearing in 2006 from all states
$= 1800 + 2300 + 2300 + 3300 + 3100 + 3800 = 16600$

Per cent $= \frac{528}{16600} = 3.18$

126. (a) Per cent increase $= \frac{55-50}{50} \times 100 = 10\%$.

127. (d) Company C has not made the highest profit in 2005. Also average profit made by company A in 2003 and 2004 was not the same. Average profit made by company B over the years is not more than the average profit made by compnay A over the years. But per cent increase in profit of compnay B in 2003 was less than that in year 2002.

128. (a) Per cent increase in 2004 from previous year

$= \frac{50-40}{40} \times 100 = \frac{10}{0.4} = 25\%$

129. (b) Approximate average of per cent increase in profit of company A over the years

$= \frac{25+30+30+40+45+50}{6} = 36.66 \simeq 37\%$

130. (e) Profit is 2006 was 3.22 lakhs:
Per cent rise in profit in 2005 was 45%.
Let amount of profit in 2005 be x.
Profit rise in 2006 are 40% and profit amount = 3.22

So, profit per cent rise was $\frac{40-45}{45} \times 100 = -11.1\%$

The fall in profit was 11.1%
So, profit in 2006 was 88.9% of that in 2005.
So, $0.889 \times x = 3.22, x = 3.62$ lakhs.
This figure is not matching with figure given in any of the options, (a) to (d).

131. (e) Let x be there in the question mark.

So, $\sqrt[3]{860000} = x \Rightarrow x^3 = 860000$

Taking $\log_{10}$ on boths the sides $3\log_{10} x = 5.9345$
$\log x = 1.9782$, Taking antilog we get $x \simeq 95$
[$\log x$ is nearly 2 so, x will be near to but less than 100]

132. (d) $1\frac{5}{8} + 5\frac{1}{3} + 2\frac{2}{5} = \frac{13}{8} + \frac{16}{3} + \frac{12}{5}$

$= \frac{15 \times 13 + 40 \times 16 + 12 \times 24}{120} = \frac{195 + 640 + 288}{120}$

$= \frac{1123}{120} \simeq 9.35$ which is near to 9.

133. (a) $8769 \div 82 \div 4 = \frac{8769}{4 \times 82} = \frac{8769}{328}$, value of this lies between 25 to 30. So the given option (a) mathces it.

134. (c) Let x be there in place of question mark so, $x\%$ of $45.999 \times 16\%$ of $83.006 = 116.073$.

We take $\frac{x}{100} \times 46 \times \frac{16}{100} \times 83 = 116$

$x \times 0.46 \times 13.28 = 116$

or $x \times 6.11 = 116 \Rightarrow x \simeq 19$.

135. (b) $12.998 \times 27.059 \times 17.999$
Can be taken as near to $13 \times 27 \times 18 \simeq 6318$
This figure is close to figure given in option (b).

136. (a) Total number of males working in Account Deptt. of organisation Q = 32
Total number of people working in Organisation
$Q = 25 + 28 + 32 + 20 + 38 + 36 + 23 + 20 + 48 + 8 + 38 + 40 = 356$

Per cent of male of Account Deptt. to the total

$= \frac{32}{356} \times 100 \simeq 9\%$

137. (e) For Organisation R : Female working in HR and Production = 34 + 12 = 46. Female working in IT and R & D = 32 + 39 = 71

So, required ratio $= \frac{46}{71}$ which is not matching with any figure given in the option (a) to (d).

138. (c) Total number of people working in IT and Production Deptt. of Organisation U :
$45 + 48 + 52 + 15 = 93 + 67 = 160$

139. (d) Average no. of males working together in organisation in Marketing Deptt.

$= \frac{22+23+18+26+24+28}{6} = \frac{141}{6} = 23\frac{1}{2}$

140. (b) Females working in different organisation
$P = 36 + 32 + 36 + 25 + 11 + 40 = 180$
$Q = 28 + 20 + 36 + 20 + 8 + 40 = 152$
$R = 34 + 21 + 32 + 16 + 12 + 39 = 154$
$S = 26 + 20 + 46 + 15 + 10 + 38 = 155$
$T = 24 + 16 + 48 + 21 + 12 + 32 = 153$
$U = 32 + 28 + 48 + 19 + 15 + 29 = 171$
Organisation P has highest number of female working.

141. (e) Area of the circle $= \pi r^2 = 98.56$

$\Rightarrow r^2 = \frac{28.56}{\pi} = \frac{98.56}{22} \times 7 = 31.36 \Rightarrow r = 5.6$

Circumference of circle $= 2\pi r = 5.6 \times 2 \times \frac{22}{7} = 35.20$ cm

142. (c) Principal amount = Rs 2750; Interest rate = 14% p.a.

Compound interest, $= 2750\left(1 + \frac{14}{100}\right)^3 - 2750$

So, C.I $= 2750\left[\left(\frac{114}{100}\right)^3 - 1\right] = 2750\left[\frac{1481544}{1000000} - 1\right]$

$$\Rightarrow \text{C.I} = 2750\left[\frac{481544}{1000000}\right] = \text{Rs.}1324.246$$

143. (b) From the given problem length of the platform $= 280 \times 3 = 840$ metre.
Train travels $840 + 280 = 1120$ metre to cross the platform and takes 50 seconds,

$$\text{So, speed} = \frac{1120}{50} = 22.4\,\text{m/sec} = \frac{22.4}{1000} \times 3600$$

$$= 80.64\,\text{km/hr}$$

144. (a) Letters of word TEENAGE has 7 letter in which E is repeated thrice. So, the number of ways are

$$\frac{7!}{3!} = \frac{7 \times 6 \times 5 \times 4 \times 3!}{3!} = 840$$

145. (d) 24 men in 16 days do 1 work

1 man in 1 day can do $\frac{1}{24 \times 16}$ work

18 women in 32 days can do 1 work

so, 1 women in 1day can do $\frac{1}{18 \times 32}$ work

12 men and 6 women work for 16 days,

$$\text{so work done} = \frac{12 \times 16}{24 \times 16} + \frac{6 \times 16}{18 \times 32}$$

$$= \frac{1}{2} + \frac{1}{6} = \frac{4}{6} = \frac{2}{3} \text{ work.}$$

Work remaining $= \frac{1}{3}$ work.

Work to be completed in 2 days, so let x men be employed.

$$\text{So, } \frac{(12 + x) \times 2}{24 \times 16} + \frac{6 \times 2}{18 \times 32} = \frac{1}{3}$$

$$\Rightarrow \frac{12 + x}{12 \times 16} + \frac{1}{48} = \frac{1}{3}$$

$$\Rightarrow \frac{12 + x}{12 \times 16} = \frac{1}{3} - \frac{1}{48} = \frac{15}{48}$$

$$\Rightarrow 12 + x = \frac{12 \times 16 \times 15}{48} = 60$$

$$\Rightarrow x = 48$$

146. (b)

Colonies	Men	Women	Deff:
A	2750	2000	750
B	2500	3000	–500
C	2250	2250	0
E	1500	1750	–250
F	3000	2750	250
G	1750	2000	–250
	13750	13750	0

So the defference = 0

147. (a) Total children $= 750 + 1000 + 250 + 500 + 1250 + 500 = 4250$

$$\text{Average} = \frac{4250}{6} = \frac{2125}{3} = 708\frac{1}{3}$$

148. (a) Total number of members from colony
$F = 3000 + 2750 + 1250 = 7000$
Total number from all colonies $= 13750 + 13750 + 4250 = 31750$
Per centage of member of colony F to total

$$= \frac{7000}{31750} \times 100 \simeq 22\%$$

149. (e) Number of man of colony E = 1500,
Number of woman of colony E = 1750

$$\text{Required ratio} = \frac{1500}{1750} = \frac{30}{35} = \frac{6}{7}$$

This does not match figure given in choice (a) to (b).

150. (d) Number of children, Colony B = 1000,
Total members of Colony B $= 2500 + 3000 + 1000 = 6500$
The per centage of children to total member

$$= \frac{1000 \times 100}{6500} = 15.38$$

151. (b) The error lies in the second part of the sentence because the industrial accidents always result 'due to' or 'out of' negligence, ignorance etc. They do not result into negligence or carelessness. The later part of sentence includes causes of accidents not the results.

152. (a) The error lies in first part of the sentence because 'are' is not supposed to be used, the first part can be written in simple present tense form which is 'some people like to do ....

153. (b) The error lies in the 2nd part of the sentence as in the sentence it is being talking about majority of men who believe that women are inferior. The correct grammatical form would be some men have conveniently believed.

154. (d) The error lies in the 4th part of the sentence. The word 'quickly' is not the correct form of adjective to be used with word decisions. The correct form would be right and quick decisions.

155. (c) The error lies in the 3rd part of the sentence. The subject verb agreement in sentence is not correct.

156. (d) The error is in the 4th part . The word 'disabled' would be used because they are talking about the welfare of poor and disabled people which includes majority of people who face under this category not a particular individual.

157. (b) The error is in the second part when we inquire about something once a period of time we use the 'had been' form so the correct form would be "He asked me what had been my total investments........."

158. (c) The error lies in the 3rd part. Instead of 'how' the word 'why' would be used because in the sentence the reason is being given as to 'why' he has succeeded to control his ailment.

159. (a) The error is in the first part of the sentence.

160. (e) This sentence is grammatically correct as the subject verb arrangement is proper.

161. (c) 'Leniency' is not the grammatically correct word to be used the correct word is lenient and the only answer choice which uses this word is option (c).

162. (e) The sentence is grammatically correct so no correction is required.

163 (e) The sentence is correct, so no correction is required.

164. (d) None of the given answer choices fit in correctly as some or the other grammatical error is present. The correct form of sentence would be "The government should launch such projects which should reverse the

distractive cycle of flood and drought !"

165. (a) Only the first answer choice fits correctly because the sentence is in the past tense where the action 'that is of setting up the committee' is already over.

166. (b) The correct answer choice is (b) because it expresses that the action is complete, i.e. our foreign exchange reserves have increased substantially. The sentence is the form of present perfect tense the 1st answer choice would have fit in if the action would have begun in past and still continued, i.e present perfect continuous tense.

167. (e) The sentence is grammatically correct and no correction is required .

168. (d) None of the given answer choices fit in correctly.

169. (d) None of the given answer choice fit correctly in the sentence.

170. (a) Only the answer choice (a) fits correctly because the sentence is simple present tense and if 'will be or would be' is used it becomes a sentence which uses future tense.

171. (a) The word dedicated cannot be used with 'by' 'in' and 'with', grammatically it can only be used with word 'to' something.

172. (b) The sentence is an illustration of present perfect tense so it should use 'has' in place of 'is' because after reading the sentence it becomes clear as to what will be the consequences of the campaign .

173. (b) The second answer choice fits correctly because the 'ed' form of word claim cannot be used.

174. (d) None of the given answer choices fit in correctly. The correct grammatical form of sentence will be 'People should have their own mechanism ....'.

175. (e) The sentence is grammatically correct and no correction is required.

176. (c) "It is up to Asia to help Africa to the best of her ability "Nehru told the Bandung conference in 1955, " because we are sister continents." These statements explain that African continent is emotionally related to Asian continent.

177. (a) Once the Chinese are established in a country, no one else gets a foothold. Mayanmar, where India failed to obtain the desired gas concessions, is a prime example. These lines explain China's monopoly.

178. (e) None of the answer choices are author's suggestion to India to break the Chinese monopoly. In the passage the author only says that India will have to move cautiously but quickly if it is to break Chinese monopoly.

179. (a) Every where in the passage we find author favours India gaining an edge over China. Author throughout the passage is highlighting China's own prospective while they are helping the African's.

180. (e) According to the passage the Chinese foreign ministry repeatedly assure the world that "our co-operation is not designed to be against or preclude any third party". None of the answer choices matches author's consideration because the claimes of China's foreign ministry are totally untrue.

181. (b) The terms " Middle kingdom's ancient formula" is used in the passage in context of China helping the African nations, embracing their dangerous regimes, influencing the under developed countries through apparently patronizing policies.

182. (e) All the reasons are responsible for the backwardness of African Nations — The West's sanctimonious boycott of African regimes – after nearly a century of colonial exploitation — left the continent in the grip of oppressive rulers . These lines from passage explains the answer.

183. (a) African countries explore help from countries other than that the western countries.

184. (d) China's selfis motive is highlighted in the following lines of the passage "Beijing filled the vacuum by eagerly embracing dangerous and unsavory regions in its search for oil and other minerals."

185. (e) The word contemporary means something which is presently in fashion so the opposite is old.

186. (e) The word booming means to grow, develop or progress rapidly, so the opposite would be degrading means to reduce to lower rank.

187. (e) The word preclude means to exclude from something which is the opposite of word include which means to involve.

188. (e) The word sanctimonious means making a hypocritical show of religion, devotion etc. which is similar to word scrupulous which means showing a strict regard for what one considers right .

189. (a) The word abdication means the act or state of abdicating or renunciation, it means to relinquish power or responsibility formally which is similar to word abandonment which means to leave completely or finally.

190. (b) The word penetration means the act or process of piercing or penetrating something which is similar to the word entry which means are act of entering or entrance.

191. (a) Out of the given answer choices the word concept fits because in the passage 'evil' is being talked as a thought.

192. (c) The two most probable answer choices here are similar and different, but the word different fits because as we read the passage we find that the approach of dealing with evil in east differs to that of west.

193. (e) The word believes fits because after reading we find that the east believes that its god's job to deal with evil, individual has nothing to do.

194. (b) The word nothing suits the best because in second half of sentence it's mentioned that he can only party means he is not capable of anything else. So the word 'nothing' fits the best.

195. (d) The word that fits is 'counteracting' — Now in this particular sentence of the extract its being said - that deities are responsible for checking evil forces and one can only pray and deities will take care.

196. (a) The word 'one' fits because here the individual is being talked about.

197. (e) The word odd fits beacuse of the difference between the eastern and western appraoch.

198. (c) The word 'where' fits because they are talking about the approach in west.

199. (d) The word responsibility fits because the accountability of the individual to take action.

200. (b) The word firmly fits because when a person takes an action it should not be likely to change and one should be steadfast.

MAHARASHTRA COMMON ENTRANCE TEST
25th FEBRUARY 2007
SOLVED PAPER
(Based on Memory)

1. Four of the following five are alike in a certain way and so form a group, which is the one that does not belong to the group?
(a) Door (b) Wall
(c) Window (d) Roof
(e) Concrete

2. 'Locker' is related to 'Jewellery' in the same way as 'Godown' is related to
(a) Storage (b) Grasim
(c) Garments (d) Goods
(e) Eatables

3. In a certain code DESK is written as # $ 52, RIDE is written as % 7#$. How is RISK written in that code?
(a) %725 (b) %752
(c) %7#2 (d) %7$#
(e) None of these

4. How many such pairs of letters are there in the word "INSTRUCTION" which have as many letters between them in the word as in the English alphabet?
(a) One (b) Two
(c) Three (d) Four
(e) None of these

5. If in a certain code 1578963 is written for PRIVATE and 2344903 is written for MESSAGE. What is written for SIEGE in that code?
(a) 54307 (b) 47343
(c) 34705 (d) 43230
(e) 47303

6. In a certain code language 15729 is written as AEGBI and 2346 is written as BCDF, then how will 23549 be written in that language?
(a) BCEDI (b) CEBDI
(c) CBEDI (d) ABEDI
(e) None of these

7. "BEGK" is related to "ADFJ" in the same way as the "PSVY" is related to
(a) ORUX (b) ROUX
(c) LOUT (d) LOOT
(e) None of these

Directions (Qs. 8-10): **In question 8 and 10 select the alternative which completes the series.**

8. WFB, TGD, QHG, ?
(a) NJK (b) NIJ
(c) OIK (d) NIK
(e) PJK

9. BMX, DNW, FOU, ?
(a) HPR (b) GPS
(c) HPT (d) MQS
(e) GHO

10. KORT : PJWO :: FINR : ?
(a) JCRN (b) JSMR
(c) KDSM (d) KCSM
(e) JRMR

DIRECTIONS (Qs. 11-15) : In each of the following questions select the one which is different from other three?

11. (a) 65 (b) 90
(c) 94 (d) 85
(e) 56

12. (a) GJM (b) EIL
(c) VXB (d) PSV
(e) MSP

13. (a) Hindustan (b) The Telegraph
(c) Outlook (c) Indian Express
(e) India Today

14. (a) Mars (b) Sun
(c) Saturn (d) Mercury
(e) Pluto

15. (a) EIK (b) NQT
(c) RVX (d) KOQ
(e) KIO

DIRECTIONS (Qs. 16-25): Study the following graph to answer the given questions.

Percentage increase in income I and expenditure (E) of companies A and B over the given years from the previous year

	Company A	Company B
Income in 1999	Rs. 10 crores	Rs. 20 crores
Expenditure in 1999	Rs. 5 crores	Rs. 10 crores

$$\text{Profit} = I - E;\ \%\ \text{Profit} = \frac{\text{Profit}}{E} \times 100$$

Percentage increase

90, 80, 70, 60, 50, 40, 30, 20, 10, 0

2000 2001 2002 2003 2004 2005

Expenditure of company A
Income of company A
Income of company B
Expenditure of company B

16. How much was the income of Company B in 2000?
(a) Rs 21 crores (b) Rs 25 crores
(c) Rs 26 crores (d) Cannot be determined
(e) None of these
17. How much was the expenditure of Company A in 1998?
(a) Rs 2.5 crores (b) Rs 1.5 crores
(c) Rs 6 crores (d) Cannot be determined
(e) None of these
18. Which year was the income of Company A around Rs 90 crores?
(a) 2004 (b) 2005
(c) 2003 (d) Cannot be determined
(e) None of these
19. How much is the per cent profit of Company A in 2000?
(a) 73.3 (b) 57.7
(c) 64.4 (d) Cannot be determined
(e) None of these
20. How much is the profit of Company B in 2001?
(a) Rs 14,27,50,000 (b) Rs 11,50,00,000
(c) Rs 8,45,00,000 (d) Cannot be determined
(e) None of these
21. How much is the income of Company A in 2002?
(a) Rs 18,20,00,000 (b) Rs. 31,62,50,000
(c) Rs 30,94,00,000 (d) Cannot be determined
(e) None of these
22. Which year was the income of Company B around Rs. 76 crores?
(a) 2003 (b) 2004
(c) 2005 (d) 2002 and 2003
(e) None of these
23. The income of Company A in 2001 is what per cent of that of 1999?
(a) $233\frac{1}{3}$ (b) 1261
(c) 182 (d) 150
(e) None of these
24. For Company B, what is the broad and approximate per cent profit in 2003?
(a) 175 (b) 180
(c) 320 (d) 140
(e) 240
25. Which of the following is NOT true?
(a) The expenditure of both the companies increased every year.
(b) In 2005, the profit of Company B was more than that of Company A.
(c) The per cent profit of Company B was more than that of Company A in each year from 2000 onwards.
(d) In 2002, the expenditure of Company B was, less than that of Company A.
(e) The expenditure of Company B was not the same for any of the two given years.

DIRECTIONS (Qs. 26-30): Rearrange the following six sentences (A), (B), (C), (D), (E) and (F) in the proper sequence to form a meaningful paragraph, then answer the questions given below them.

(A) Do the devices that make it possible to do so many things at once truly raise our productivity or merely help us spin our wheels faster?
(B) More important, they're exploring what can be done about it – how we can work smarter, live smarter and put our beloved gadgets back in their proper place, with us running them, not the other way around.
(C) The dinging digital devices that allow us to connect and communicate so readily also disrupt our work, our thoughts and what little is left of our private lives.
(D) They have begun to calculate the pluses, the minuses and the economic costs of the interrupted life – in dollars, productivity and dysfunction.
(E) What sort of toll is all this disruption and metnal channel switching taking on our ability to think clearly work effectively and function as healthy human beings?
(F) Over the past five years, psychologists, efficiency, experts and information-technology researchers have begun to explore those questions in detail.

26. Which of the following should be the **FIRST** sentence?
(a) A (b) B (c) C (d) D (e) E
27. Which of the following should be the **SECOND** sentence?
(a) A (b) B (c) C (d) D (e) E
28. Which of the following should be the **THIRD** sentence?
(a) A (b) B (c) C (d) D (e) F
29. Which of the following should be the **FIFTH** sentence?
(a) A (b) B (c) C (d) D (e) E
30. Which of the **following should** be the **SIXTH (LAST)** sentence?
(a) A (b) B (c) C (d) D (e) E

DIRECTIONS (Qs. 31-35): Which of the phrases (a), (b), (c) and (d) given below should replace the phrase given in bold in the following sentence to make the sentence grammatically meaningful and correct. If the sentence is correct as it is and no correction is required, mark (e) as the answer.

31. In any serious investigation, all points of suspicions **should check properly.**
(a) must check properly
(b) should be checked properly
(c) should properly check
(d) must properly check
(e) No correction required
32. The circumstances in which **succumbed below pressure,** are not known.
(a) succumbed below force
(b) was succumbed below pressure
(c) was succumbing below force
(d) succumbed to pressure
(e) No correction required
33. All human beings **are vulnerable to** greed and temptations.
(a) are vulnerable for
(b) have vulnerability of
(c) were vulnerable at
(d) have been vulnerable with
(e) No correction required

34. **How did the burglar got** into the bank is a mystery.
(a) How did the burglar get
(b) What did the burglar get
(c) How the burglar got
(d) Why did the burglar get
(e) No correction required

35. What most of the people think right cannot be **said to be necessary and** right?
(a) said to be necessarily
(b) said to be necessarily and
(c) necessarily said to be
(d) said necessary and to be
(e) no correction required

DIRECTIONS (QS. 36-40): In each of the following questions series begins with unnumbered figure on the extreme left. One and only one of the five numbered figures in the series does not fit into the series. The two unnumbered figures one each on the extreme left and the extreme right fit into the series. You have to take as many aspects into account as possible of the figures in the series and find out the one and only one of the five figures which does not fit into the series. The letter of that figure is the answer.

Study the following questions.

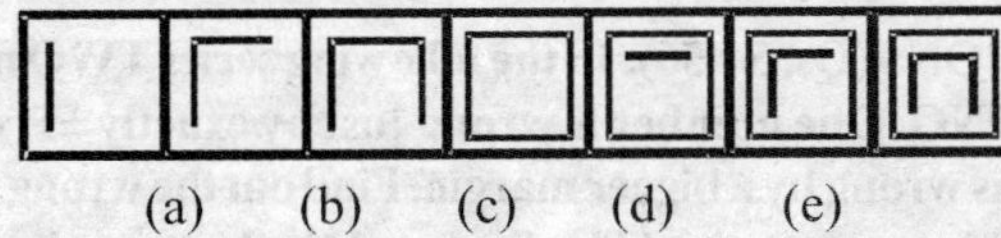

In this question the number of lines in the figures goes on increasing by one from left to right. If we go by this aspect of number of lines' only then there is no wrong figure in the series. But if we also consider these 'manner' in which the 'number of lines' in the figures goes on increasing from left to right we come to know that the figure No. (d) does **NOT** fit into the series. Therefore, (d) is the answer.

Now solve the following questions.

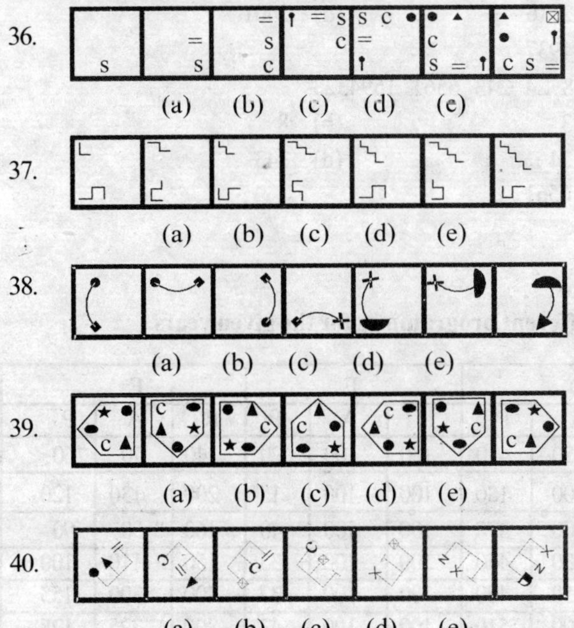

DIRECTIONS (QS. 41-45): Each of the questions below consists of a question and two statements numbered I and II are given below it. You have to decide whether the data provided in the statements are sufficient to answer the question. Read both the statements and give answer

(a) if the data in Statement I ALONE are sufficient to answer the question, while the data in Statement II alone are not sufficient to answer the question;
(b) if the data in Statement II ALONE are sufficient to answer the question, while the data in Statement I alone are not sufficient to answer the question;
(c) if the data in Statement I ALONE or in Statement II ALONE are sufficient to answer the question;
(d) if the data in BOTH the Statements I and II, are not sufficient to answer the question;
(e) if the data in both the Statements I and II TOGETHER are necessary to answer the question.

41. What is the code for 'sky' in the code language?
I. In a code language 'sky is clear' is written as '*de ra fa*'.
II. In the same code language 'make it clear' is written as '*de ga jo*'.

42. How is Mohan related to Divya?
I. Mohan is the only son of Divya's mother-in-law.
II. Rani is Mohan's only sister.

43. Village 'R' is in which direction with respect to village 'D'?
I. Village 'R' is to the north of village 'T' which is to the West of village 'F'.
II. Village 'D' is to the west of village 'T'.

44. How many children does 'M' have?
I. 'H' is the only daughter of 'X' who is wife of 'M'.
II. 'K' and 'J' are brothers of 'M'.

45. What is Sunil's rank from the top in a class of 25 students?
I. Sunil ranks three ranks above Sudhir who ranks 18th from the bottom.
II. Sunil's rank from the top is two ranks below Sheela who ranks 23rd from the bottom.

DIRECTIONS (Qs. 46-50): In each question below are three statements followed by three conclusions numbered I, II and III. You have to take the three given statements to be ture even if they seem to be at variance from commonly known facts and then decide which of the answers (a), (b), (c), (d) and (e) is the correct answer and indicate it on the answer sheet.

46. **Statements:** Some chairs are tables.
Some tables are drawers.
Conclusions: **I.** Some shelves are tables.
II. Some drawers are chairs.
III. Some shelves are drawers.
(a) Only I and III follow
(b) Only I and either II or III follow
(c) Only II and either I or III follow
(d) All I, II and III follow
(e) None of these

47. **Statements:** All trees are flowers.
Some flowers are leaves.
No leaf is bud
Conclusions: **I.** No bud is a flower.
II. Some buds are flowers.
III. Some leaves are trees.
(a) Only II and III follow
(b) Only III follows
(c) Only either I or II follows
(d) Either I or II and III follow
(e) None of these

48. **Statements:** All stones are rocks.
Some rocks are bricks.
Some bricks are cement.
Conclusions: **I.** Some cements are rocks.
II. Some bricks are stone
III. Some stones are cement.
(a) Only I and either II or III follow
(b) Only either II or III follows
(c) Only I and II follow
(d) All follow
(e) None of these

49. **Statements:** All flats are buildings.
All buildings are bungalows.
All bungalows are apartments.
Conclusions: **I.** Some apartments are flats.
II. All flats are bungalows.
III. Some bungalows are flats.
(a) None follows
(b) Only I and II follow
(c) Only II and III follow
(d) Only I and III follow
(e) All I, II and III follow

50. **Statements:** Some spectacles are lenses.
Some lenses are frames.
All frames are metals.
Conclusions: **I.** Some lenses are metals
II. Some metals are spectacles.
III. Some frames are spectacles.
(a) None follows
(b) Only I follows
(c) Only I and either II or III follow
(d) Only I and II follow
(e) None of these

51. When a bus stared from the first stop, the ratio of number of male passengers to the number of female passengers was 3 : 1. At the first stop, 16 passengers got down and 6 more female passengers got in. The ratio of the male to female passengers now became 2 : 1. What was the total number of passengers in the bus when it started from the first stop?
(a) 64 (b) 48
(c) 54 (d) 72
(e) None of these

52. A circular running path is 726 metres in circumference. Two men start from the same point and walk in opposite directions @ 3.75 km/hr and 4.5 km/hr respectively. When will they meet for the first time?
(a) After 5.5 minutes (b) After 6.0 minutes
(c) After 5.28 minutes (d) After 4.9 minutes
(e) None of these

53. If a solid sphere of radius 10 cm is moulded into 8 spherical solid balls of equal radius, then the surface area of each ball is
(a) $60\pi\ cm^2$ (b) $50\pi\ cm^2$
(c) $75\pi\ cm^2$ (d) $100\pi\ cm^2$
(e) None of these

DIRECTIONS (Qs. 54-56): In the following series TWO numbers are WRONG. One number is wrong just by exactly ±1, whereas the other is wrong by a bigger margin. Find out the wrong number with the bigger margin. (The first and the last numbers in the series are correct).

54. 1 8 32 65 125 216 343 512
(a) 8 (b) 32
(c) 65 (d) 216
(e) 343

55. 2500 2401 2116 1937 1764 1600 1444
(a) 1600 (b) 1764
(c) 2116 (d) 2401
(e) 1937

56. 1 3 8 24 243 6561 1594323
(a) 3 (b) 8
(c) 24 (d) 243
(e) 6561

Directions (Qs. 57-61): Study the following table to answer the given questions.
Number of candidates who registered (R), appeared (A) and passed (P) for different programmes for the given years.

Prog.	A			B			C			D			E			F		
Year	R	A	P	R	A	P	R	A	P	R	A	P	R	A	P	R	A	P
1900	500	500	400	100	100	50	50	45	20	900	450	420	100	100	20	140	70	60
2000	600	550	400	110	110	55	50	46	20	1000	500	180	100	100	15	200	130	120
2001	550	525	410	160	160	90	50	44	20	1300	600	370	100	100	40	160	90	90
2002	800	700	550	190	190	110	70	60	30	1900	800	440	100	100	35	150	110	100
2003	850	825	600	300	300	200	70	65	30	1800	750	460	100	100	37	400	300	155
2004	990	950	750	350	345	290	90	85	35	1600	800	510	100	100	42	300	225	128

57. For which programme there seems to be fixed number decided to pass for different years?
(a) A (b) B (c) C (d) D (e) E

58. In 2002, for Programme A, what is the percentage of passed over Registered?
(a) 78.57 (b) 87.50
(c) 78.09 (d) $68\frac{3}{4}$
(e) None of these

59. For Programme B, which year is the per cent increase in Registered from the previous year the maximum?
(a) 2003 (b) 2004
(c) 2002 (d) 2001
(e) None of these

60. How much is the difference in the number appeared and passed for Programme D for the given years?
(a) 1410 (b) 1500
(c) 1620 (d) 4600
(e) None of these

61. In 2003, which programme had the maximum per cent of passed over registered?
(a) A (b) B (c) C (d) D (e) E

62. In a school the ratio of boys and girls is 3 : 2 respectively. When 6 more girls join this ratio becomes 6 : 5. How many boys are there in the school?
(a) 24 (b) 30
(c) 42 (d) Cannot be determined
(e) None of these

63. If $x^2 - 7x = -12$, what is the value of x?
(a) −3 or −4 (b) 3 or 4
(c) 3 or −4 (d) Cannot be determined
(e) None of these

64. A boat running downstreams covers a distance of 10 kms in 2 hours. While coming back upstreams the boat takes 5 hours to cover the same distance. If the speed of the current is 1.5 kmph, what is the speed of the boat in still water?
(a) 2.5 kmph (b) 4.5 kmph
(c) 3.5 kmph (d) Cannot be determined
(e) None of these

65. An article when sold at Rs 4,500, incurred 10% loss. At what price should it be sold to earn 10% profit?
(a) Rs 5,000 (b) Rs 4,950
(c) Rs 5,445 (d) Rs 5,500
(e) None of these

DIRECTIONS (QS. 66-75): In each of the questions given below which one of the five answer figures should come after the problem figures, if the sequence were continued?

66. **Problem Figures**

Answer Figures

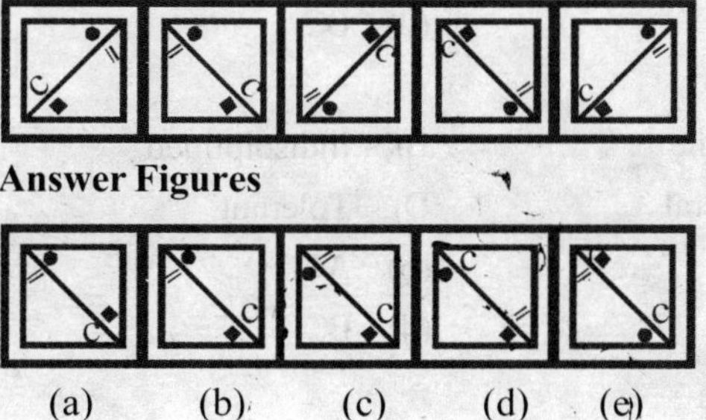

(a) (b) (c) (d) (e)

67. **Problem Figures**

= ? S X	X ? S =	= S ? X	X ? S =	= S ? X

Answer Figures

X ? S =	= ? S X	= ? S X	X S ? =	XS = ?
(a)	(b)	(c)	(d)	(e)

68. **Problem Figures**

α β γ	β α γ	β γ α	γ α β	γ α β

Answer Figures

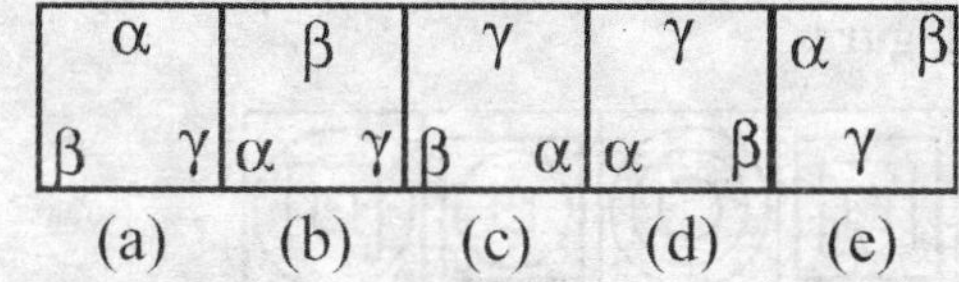

(a) (b) (c) (d) (e)

69. **Problem Figures**

< < <	> < <	> > <	> > >	< > >

Answer Figures

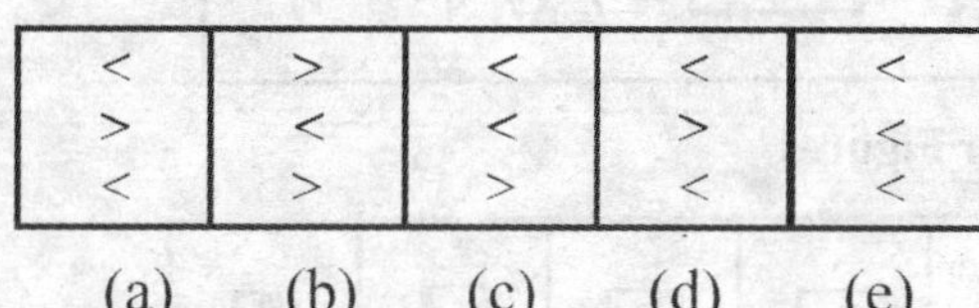

(a) (b) (c) (d) (e)

70. **Problem Figures**

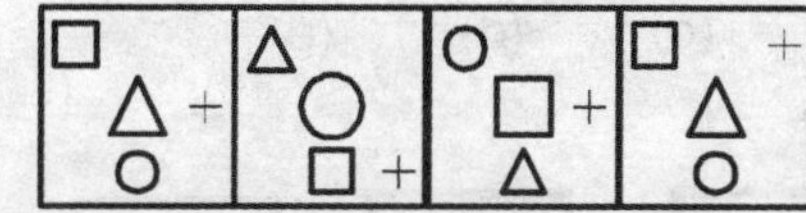

Answer Figures

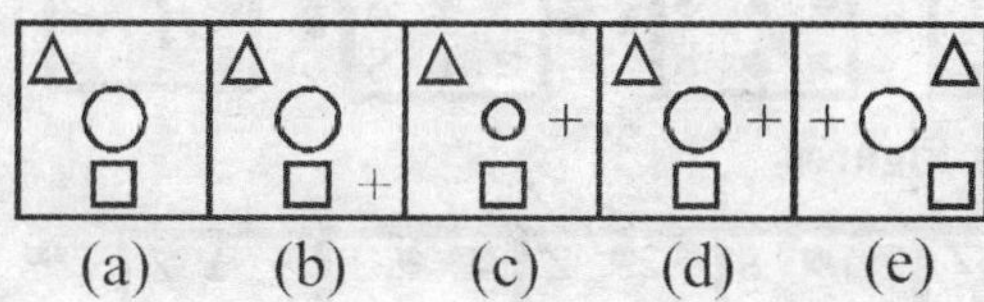

(a) (b) (c) (d) (e)

DIRECTIONS *(Qs 71 – 75)* **: Which Answer Figure is related to Problem Figure III in same way as Problem Figure II is related to Problem Figure I?**

71. **Problem Figures**

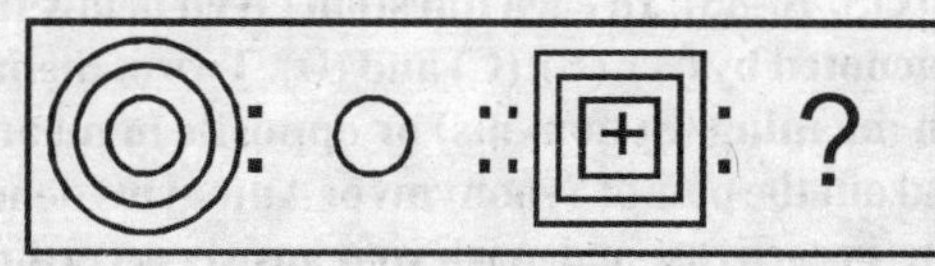

Answer Figures

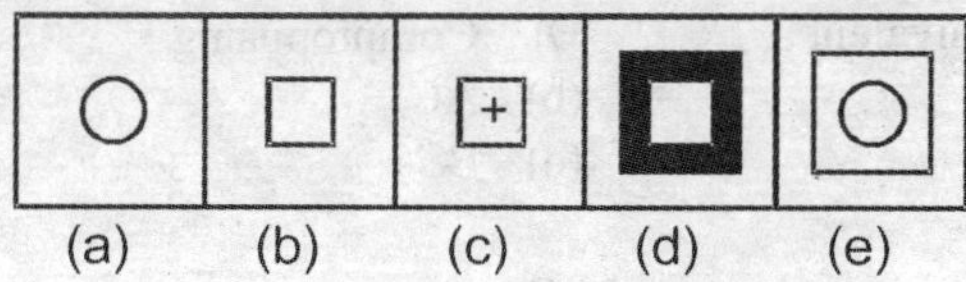

(a) (b) (c) (d) (e)

72. **Problem Figures**

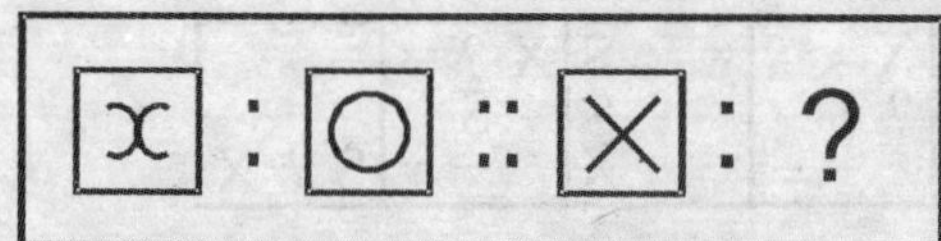

Answer Figures

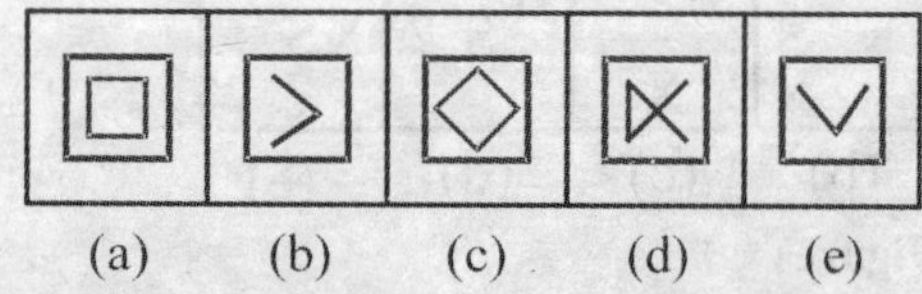

(a) (b) (c) (d) (e)

73. **Problem Figures**

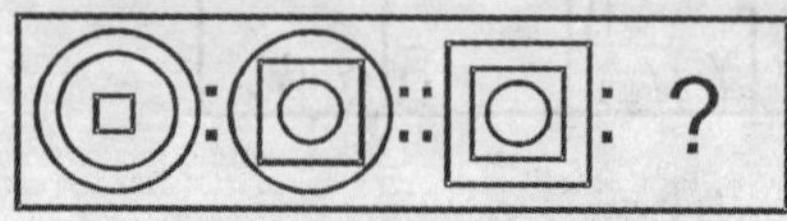

Answer Figures

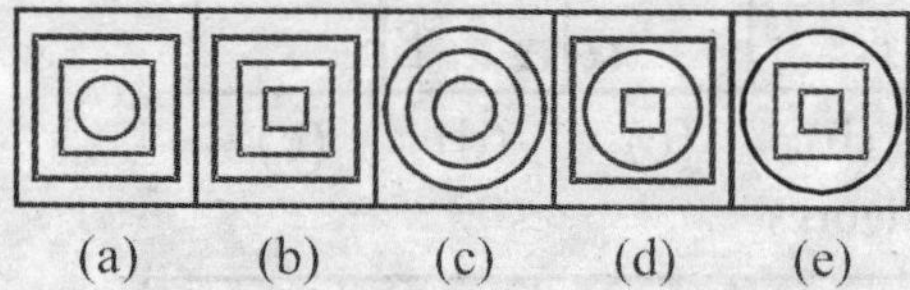

(a) (b) (c) (d) (e)

74. **Problem Figures**

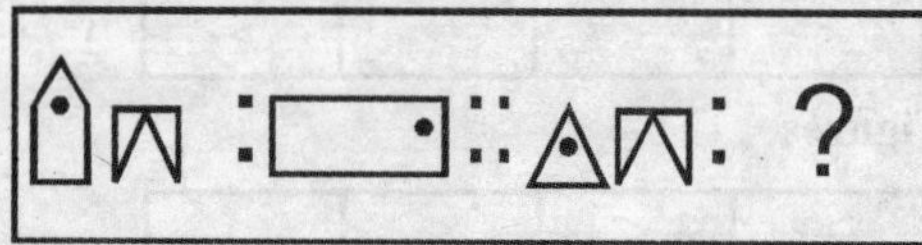

Answer Figures

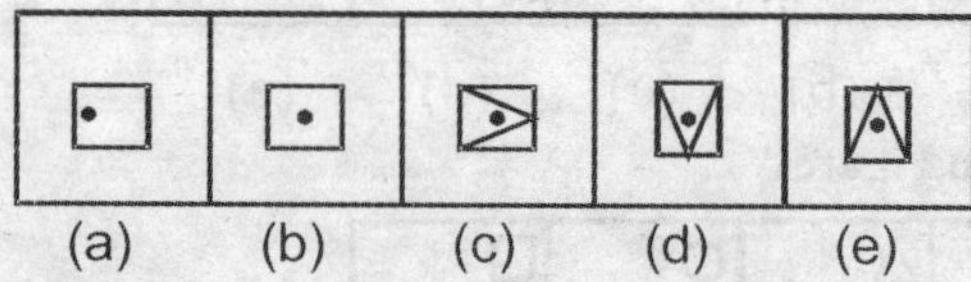

(a) (b) (c) (d) (e)

75. **Problem Figures**

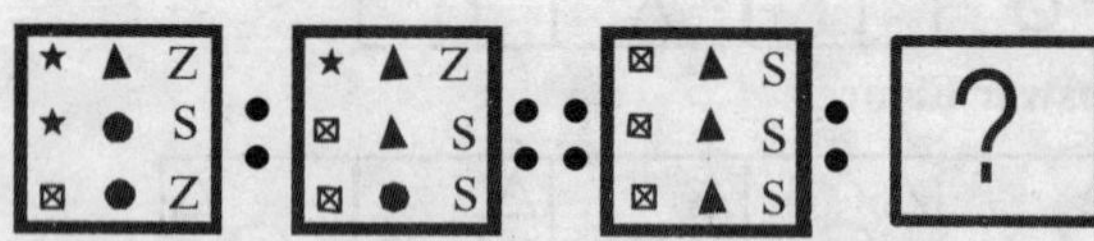

Answer Figures

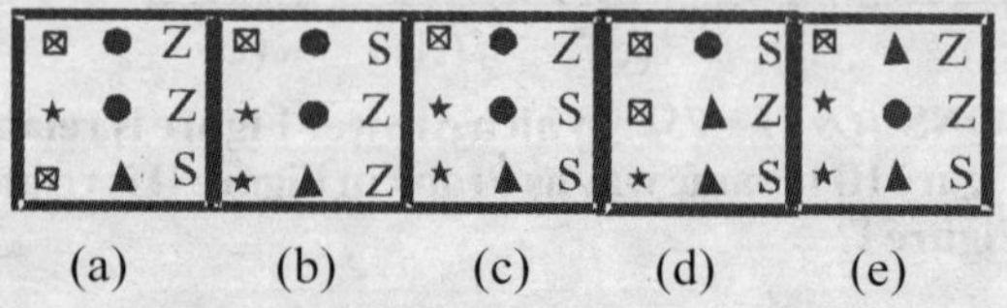

(a) (b) (c) (d) (e)

DIRECTIONS (QS. 76-85): In each question given below there are four words denoted by (A), (B), (C) and (D). Two of them are either similar in meaning (Synonyms) or opposite in meaning (Antonyms). Find out the pair of Synonyms or Antonyms denoted by AB, AC, AD etc. in each case and mark your answer accordingly.

76. A) Benevolent B) Malevolent
C) Equivalent D) Compromising
(a) AB (b) AC
(b) AD (d) BC
(e) CD

77. A) Irresponsible B) Ambitious
C) Unmotivated D) Unsympathetic
(a) AB (b) AC
(c) AD (d) BC
(e) CD

78. A) Reliance B) Offending
C) Unreasonable D) Dependence
(a) AB (b) AC
(c) AD (d) BC
(e) CD

79. A) Crafty B) Idle
C) Cunning D) Interacting
(a) AB (b) AC
(c) AD (d) BC
(e) CD

80. A) Decent B) Innocent
C) Guilty D) Adolescent
(a) AB (b) AC
(c) AD (d) BC
(e) CD

81. A) Notorious B) Luminous
C) Envious D) Jealous
(a) AB (b) AC
(c) AD (d) BC
(e) CD

82. A) Lively B) Sluggish
C) Boredom D) Heavy
(a) AB (b) AC
(c) AD (d) BC
(e) CD

83. A) Envisage B) Expect
C) Demand D) Foresee
(a) AB (b) AC
(c) AD (d) BC
(e) CD

84. A) Inspire B) Engrave
C) Stimulate D) Respond
(a) AB (b) AC
(c) AD (d) BC
(e) CD

85. A) Docile B) Indisciplined
C) Liberal D) Tolerant
(a) AB (b) AC
(c) AD (d) BC
(e) CD

DIRECTIONS (QS. 86-90): In the following questions, the symbols β, γ, ψ, α and δ are used with the following meanings.

P β Q means P is not smaller than Q.

P γ Q means P is neither greater than nor smaller than Q.

P ψ Q means P is not greater than Q.

P α Q means P is neither smaller than nor equal to Q.

P δ Q means P is neither greater than nor equal to Q.

Now in each of the following questions, assuming the given statements to be ture, find which of the two conclusions I and II given below them is/are definitely true. Give answer,

(a) if only conclusion I is true;
(b) if only conclusion II is true;
(c) if either I or II is true;
(d) if neither I nor II is true; and
(e) if both I and II are true.

86. **Statements:** M β N, H ψ Q, B β M
Conclusions: **I.** H γ M
II. Q γ N

87. **Statements:** C α B, L δ S, S ψ C
Conclusions: **I.** B α S
II. C α L

88. **Statements:** I β H, E α F, I γ F
Conclusions: **I.** E α I
II. H δ E

89. **Statements:** V γ O, R γ V, O β B
Conclusions: **I.** R γ R
II. R α B

90. **Statements:** L α U, T γ V, O β B.
Conclusions: **I.** T α W
II. U γ W

DIRECTIONS (QS. 91-95): Read the following information carefully and answer the questions given below.

Five Indian players Sachin, Bhutia, Leander, Anand and Gopichand are related with the advertisement of different products of different companies – Nike, Reebok, Pepsi, Coca Cola and Adidas , though not respectively. Sachin advertises neither for sports-wear nor for Rackets. Leander advertises for shoes but not by company Coca Cola. Pepsi and Adidas neither produces Diet Coke nor sports-wear. Gopichand advertises for the company. Nike but neither for mineral water nor for Diet coke. Bhutia and Anand advertises for Adidas and Pepsi, though not respectively. Coca Cola does not produce mineral water.

91. Sachin advertises for which company?
(a) Coca Cola (b) Adidas
(c) Pepsi (d) Data inadequate
(e) None of these

92. Mineral water is the product of which company?
(a) Nike (b) Coca Cola
(c) Pepsi (d) Data Inadequate
(e) None of these

93. Who advertises for the company Reebok?
(a) Sachin (b) Leander
(c) Gopichand (c) Data Inadequate
(e) None of these

94. Which of the following is definitely true?
(a) Leander-Shoes - Nike
(b) Sachin-Diet Coke-Coca Cola
(c) Sachin-Diet Coke-Coca cola
(d) Bhutia-Sportswear - Reebok
(e) None of these

95. Which of the following is definitely false?
(a) Leander-Nike-Shoes
(b) Anand - Pepsi-Mineral Water
(c) Bhutia-Adidas-Rackets
(d) Gopichand-Nike-Rackets
(e) None of these

DIRECTIONS (QS. 96-100): Study the following information to answer the given questions.

Some committees are to be formed from amongst 7 women Professors, 5 men Professors, 4 men Readers, 2 women Readers, 11 women Lecturers and 10 men Lecturers following the given conditions in each question. In how many different ways can it be done based on the conditions?

96. A committee of 10 in which there are 5 men and 5 women.
(a) ${}^{39}C_{10}$ (b) ${}^{19}C_5 \times {}^{20}C_5$
(c) ${}^{19}P_5 \times {}^{20}P_5$ (d) $\frac{{}^{19}P_5 \times {}^{20}P_5}{{}^{39}P_{10}}$
(e) None of these

97. A committee of 6 professors in which at least 2 men are there.
(a) 350 (e) 700
(c) 812 (d) 2450
(d) None of these

98. A committee of 25 in which all the lecturers are there. Remaining seats among Professors and Readers.
(a) 12650 (b) 3060
(c) 64260 (d) 6100
(e) None of these

99. A committee of 15 in which only Lecturers are there.
(a) 13650 (b) 352716
(c) 15504 (d) 54264
(e) None of these

100. A committee of 4 Professors in which equal number of men and women are there.
(a) 495 (b) 248
(c) 35 (d) 40
(e) None of these

DIRECTIONS (QS. 101-115): Read the following passage carefully and answer the questions given below it. Certain words / phrases have been printed in bold to help you locate them while answering some of the questions.

Amartya Sen wrote about the Indian tradition of skepticism and heterodoxy of opinion that led to high levels of intellectual argument. The power sector in India is a victim of this tradition at its worst. Instead of **forcefully** communicating, supporting and honestly and firmly implementing policies, people just debate them. It is argued that central undertakings produce power at lower tariffs and must therefore build most of the required extra capacities. This is a **delusion.** They no longer have access to low-cost government funds.

Uncertainty about payment remains a reason for the hesitation of private investment. They had to sell only to SEBs (State Electricity Boards). SEB balance sheets are cleaner after the "securitisation" of the Rs 40,000 crore or so owed by SEBs to central government undertakings, now shown as debt instruments. But state governments have not implemented agreed plans to ensure repayment when due. The current annual losses of around Rs 28,000 crore make repayment highly uncertain. The central undertakings that are their main suppliers have payment security because the government will come to their help. Private enterprises do not have such assurance and are concerned about payment security, that must be resolved.

By the late 1990s, improving the SEB finances was recognised as fundamental to power reform. **Unbundling** SEBs, working under corporate discipline and even privatisation and not vertically integrated state enterprises, are necessary for efficient and financially viable electricity enterprises. Since government will not **distance** itself from managing them, privatising is an option. The Delhi model has worked. But it receives no public support.

The Electricity Act 2003, the APRDP (Accelerated Power Reform and Development Programme) with its incentives and penalties, and the creation of independent regulatory commissions, were the means to bring about reforms to improve financial **viability** of power sector. Implementation has been half-hearted and results disappointing. The concurrent nature of electricity in the Constitution **impedes** power sector improvement. States are more responsive to populist pressures than the central government, and less inclined to take drastic action against electricity thieves.

Captive power would add significantly to capacity. However, captive generation, three years after the Act enabled it, has added little to capacity because rules for open access were delayed. Redefined captive generation avoids state vetoes on purchase or sale of electricity except to state electricity enterprises. Mandating open access on state-owned wires to power regardless of ownership and customer would encourage electricity trading. The Act recognised electricity trading as a separate activity. A surcharge on transmission charges will pay for cross-subsidies. These were to be eliminated in time. Rules for open access and the quantum of surcharge by each state commission (under broad principles defined by the central commission) have yet to be announced by some. The few who have announced the surcharge have kept it so high that no trading can take place.

101. The author thinks it appropriate to -
(a) discuss any policy in details and make it fool proof instead of implementing it hastily.
(b) follow Indian tradition meticulously as skepticism is essential for major decisions.
(c) divert our energies from fruitlessly contracting policies to supporting its implementation whole-heartedly.
(d) intellectual arguments and conceptualisation of every policy is definitely better than its enforcement.
(e) none of these

102. Why are the central undertakings not capable of generating power at low cost?
(a) Due to paucity of low-cost funds
(b) Due to their access to Government funds
(c) Due to their delusion about government funds
(d) Because of their extra capacities
(e) None of these

103. Which of the following is the reason for apathy of private investors in power sector?
(a) Their hesitation
(b) Uncertainly of their survival
(c) Cut-throat competition
(d) Lack of guarantee of timely returns
(e) None of these

104. What was the serious omission on the part of the State Government?
(a) Agreement for late recovery of dues
(b) Reluctance to repay to private investors as per agreed plan
(c) Non-implementation of recovery due to unplanned and haphazard polices
(d) Lack of assurance from private enterprises
(e) None of these

105. Which of the following is/are considered necessary for improving performance of electricity enterprises?
(A) Corporate work culture
(B) Privatisation
(C) Properly integrated state enterprises
(a) All the three (b) (A) and (B) only
(c) (A) and (C) only (d) (B) and (C) only
(e) None of these

106. The example of "Delhi Model" quoted by the author underlines his feelings of
A. happiness about its success.
B. unhappiness for lack of public support
C. disgust towards privatisation.
(a) (A) and (B) only
(b) (B) and (C) only
(c) (A) and (C) only
(d) All the three
(e) None of these

107. Which of the following was/were not considered as the instrument(s) to accomplish financial well-being of power sector?
(a) The Electricity Act 2003
(b) The APRDP with its incentives and penalties
(c) Setting up of independent regulatory commissions
(d) States vulnerability to populist pressures
(e) Taking drastic action against electricity thieves.

108. Why were the results of the power sector reforms NOT as had been anticipated?
(a) The means to bring about reforms were illconceived.
(b) The enforcement of the reform means was inadequate and apathetic.
(c) The Act and the reform measures were contradicting with each other.
(d) The incentives on the one hand and penalties on the other created dissatisfaction.
(e) None of these

109. What serious drawback of the states is pointed out by the author of the passage?
   (a) The incentives and penalties enforced by the states were disproportionately incomparable
   (b) The enforcement of the provisions of the acts was drastic and harsh
   (c) Their vulnerability to fall prey to populist pressures
   (d) Imposition of penalties were not judicious and incentives were not free from partiality.
   (e) None of these

DIRECTIONS (QS. 110-112): Choose the word or group of words which is most nearly the SAME in meaning as the word printed in bold.

110. **DISTANCE**
   (a) keep away (b) differentiate between
   (c) long for (d) have remoteness
   (e) advance along
111. **DELUSION**
   (a) proper understanding
   (b) wrong prediction
   (c) false belief
   (d) unkind propaganda
   (e) unrealistic optimism
112. **VIABILITY**
   (a) ability to reform (b) ability to meditate
   (c) power to bounce (d) ability to spend
   (e) capability to survive

DIRECTIONS (QS. 113-115): Choose the word or group of words which is most OPPOSITE in meaning of the word printed in bold.

113. **FORCEFULLY**
   (a) vehemently (b) meekly
   (c) dispassionately (d) neutrally
   (e) unlawfully
114. **IMPEDE**
   (a) interferes (b) grows
   (c) excels (d) promotes
   (e) exaggerates
115. **UNBUNDLING**
   (a) disorganising (b) reorienting
   (c) segregating (d) winding
   (e) integrating

DIRECTIONS (116-120): Study the following information carefully to answer these questions.

Seven friends M, T, K, Q, R, P and H have taken admissions in the three different engineering streams Electrical, Computers and Electronics. At least two students are admitted in each stream. Each one is in a different college A, B, C, D, E, F and G. The order of students stream and the college is not necessarily the same. K is the admitted to college C in Electronics. The one who studies in college A does not study Computers. M studies in college G but not Electrical or Computers. T and P study in the same stream but not in Electrical. H studies in college F in the same stream as K. Q studies in college B. T does not study in college E.

116. Who studies in college 'A'?
   (a) T (b) P
   (c) R (d) R or T
   (e) None of these
117. Three students study in which of the following streams?
   (a) Electrical (b) Electronics
   (c) Electrical or Electronics (d) Computers
   (e) Computers or Electronics
118. Which of the following combinations of student and the stream is **correct**?
   (a) R - Computers (b) Q - Electrical
   (c) T - Electrical (d) R - Electronics
   (e) None of these
119. The student studying in college 'G' studies in which stream?
   (a) Electrical (b) Computers
   (c) Electronics (d) Electrical or Electronics
   (e) Computers or Electrical
120. P studies in which college and stream?
   (a) A - Electrical (b) A - Electronics
   (c) D - Computers (d) E - Computers
   (e) None of these

DIRECTIONS (QS. 121-125): In each of the questions given below a group of digits is given followed by four combinations of letters/symbols. You have to find out which of the four combinations correctly represents the group of digits based on the letter/symbol codes and the conditions given below. If none of the four combinations represents the group of digits correctly, give (e) i.e. "None of these" as the answer.

Digit:	3	9	6	2	8	7	5	4	1
Symbol:	K	T	$	F	H	#	%	D	M

Conditions for the coding the group of digits:

1. If the first digit is odd and last digit is even, the codes for the first and the last digits are to be interchanged.
2. If the first as well as the last digit is even, both are to be coded by the code for last digit.
3. If the first as well as the last digit is odd, both are to be coded as 'X'.

121. 564923
   (a) %$DTFK (b) K$DTFK
   (c) X$DTFX (d) K$DTF%
   (e) None of these
122. 658247
   (a) $%HFD# (b) #%HFD$
   (c) %$HFD# (d) %#HFD$
   (e) None of these
123. 436958
   (a) DK$T%D (b) DK$T%H
   (c) HK$T%H (d) #%$HK#
   (e) None of these
124. 756834
   (a) #%$HKD (b) D%$HK#
   (c) D%$HKD (d) #%$HK#
   (e) None of these
125. 291378
   (a) FTMK#H (b) XTMK#X
   (c) HTMK#F (d) FTMK#F
   (e) None of these

DIRECTIONS (QS. 126-130): In each of these questions two equations I and II are given. Based on these, give answer

(a) if $x > y$
(b) if $x \geq y$
(c) if $y > x$
(d) if $y \geq x$
(e) either $x = y$ or the relationship between x and y cannot be established.

126. I. $Y = -5$ or 4.3
II. $x^2 = 18$

127. I. $x^2 + 5x + 6 = 0$
II. $y^2 + 11y + 30 = 0$

128. I. $x = \sqrt{64}$
II. $y = (-2)^3$

129. I. $153.5 = x$
II. $57.5 = y$

130. I. $y - x = z$
II. $zx - 1 = 0.0005$

DIRECTIONS (QS. 131 – 140): In each of these questions there are two sets of figures. The figures of the top are Problem Figures (four figures and one question-marked space) and those on bottom are Answer Figures indicated by (a), (b), (c), (d) and (e). A series is established if one of the five Answer Figures is placed at the "question-marked space". Question Figures form a series if they change from left to right according to some rule. The number of the Answer Figure which should be placed in the question-marked space is the answer. All the five figures i.e. four Problem Figures and one Answer Figure placed in the question-marked space should be considered as forming the series. Study the following questions.

Problem Figures

Answer Figures

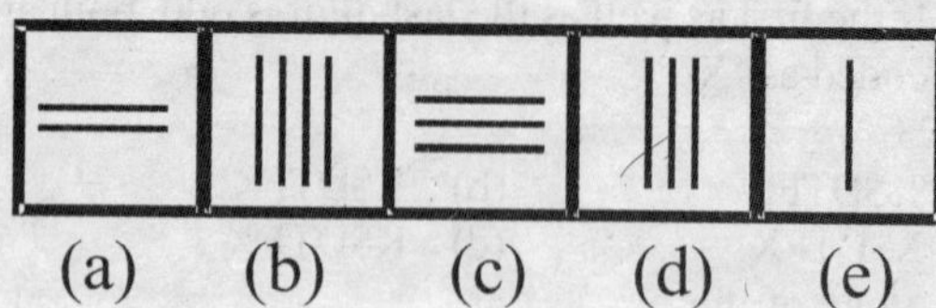

(a) (b) (c) (d) (e)

If we place the Answer Figure d in the question marked space it makes a series which indicates that one vertical line is added in each figure. So the answer is '(d)'. Note that if we go by only one aspect of number of lines Answer Figure (c) may also fit in. So you have to consider all different aspects.

131. **Problem Figures**

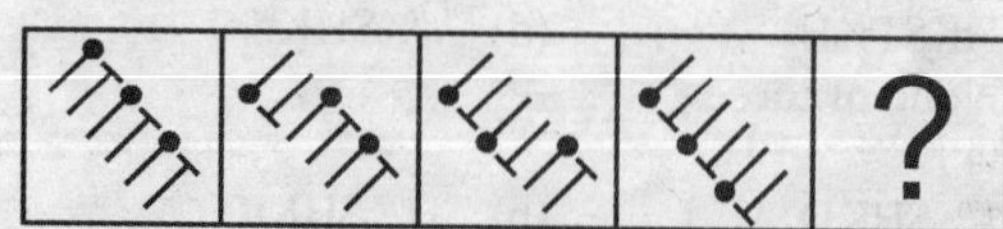

Answer Figures

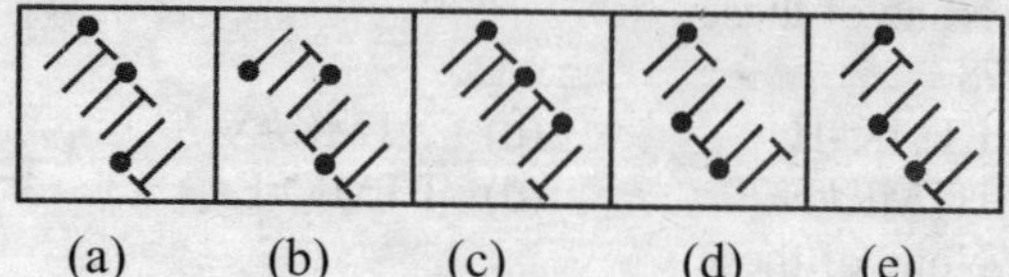

(a) (b) (c) (d) (e)

132. **Problem Figures**

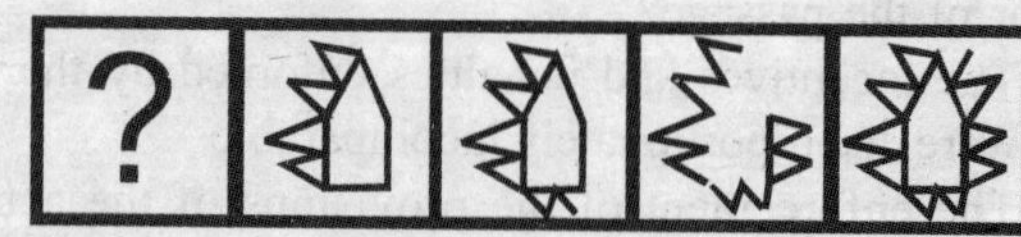

Answer Figures

(a) (b) (c) (d) (e)

133. **Problem Figures**

Answer Figures

(a) (b) (c) (d) (e)

134. **Problem Figures**

Answer Figures

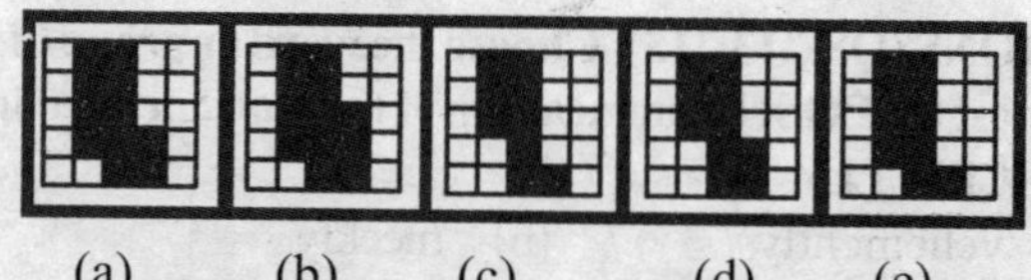

(a) (b) (c) (d) (e)

135. **Problem Figures**

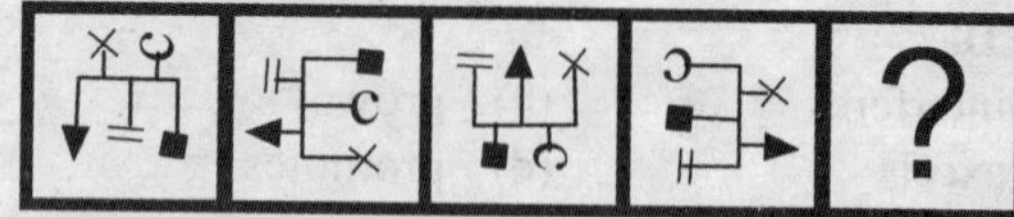

Answer Figures

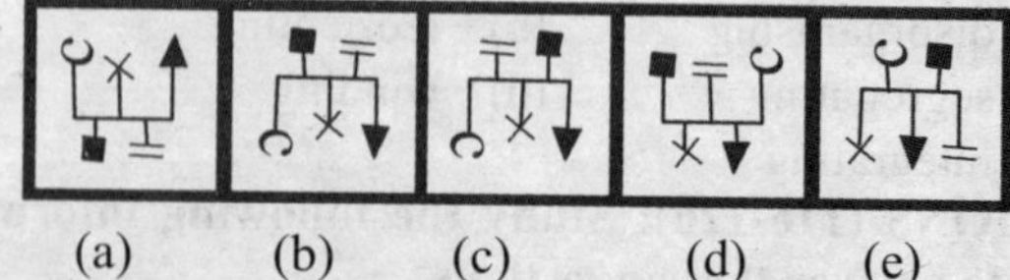

(a) (b) (c) (d) (e)

136. **Problem Figures**

Answer Figures

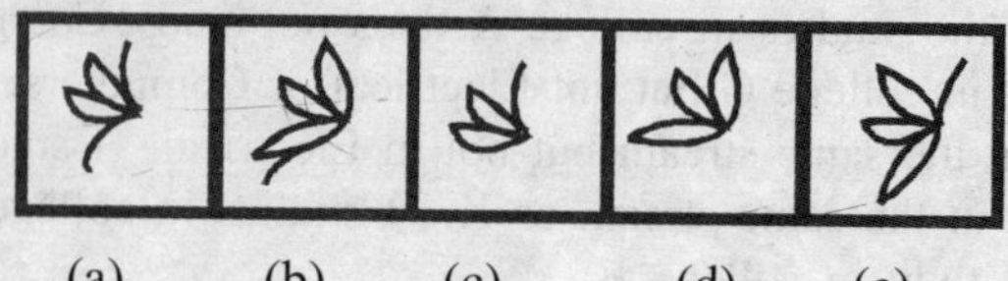

(a) (b) (c) (d) (e)

137. **Problem Figures**

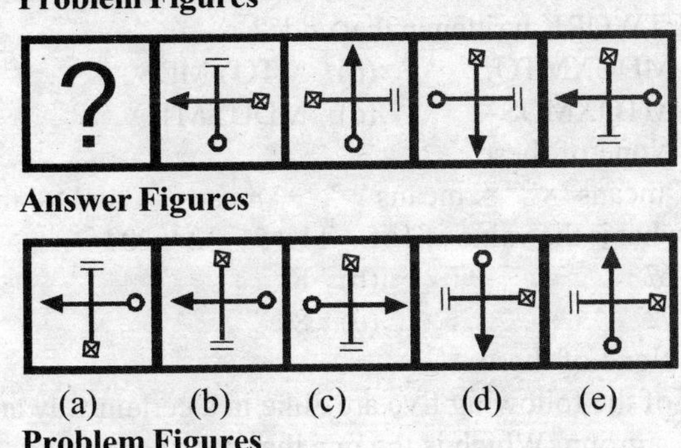

Answer Figures

(a) (b) (c) (d) (e)

138. **Problem Figures**

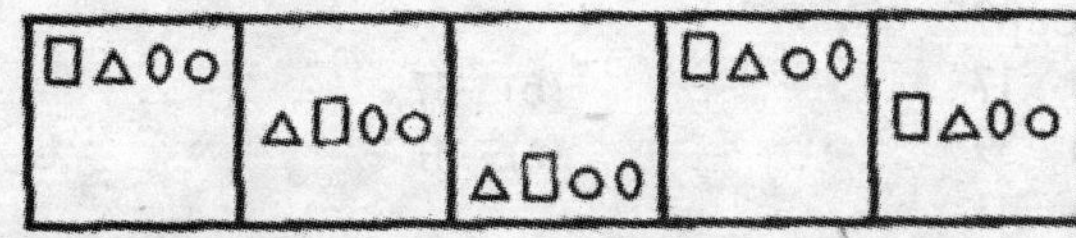

Answer Figures

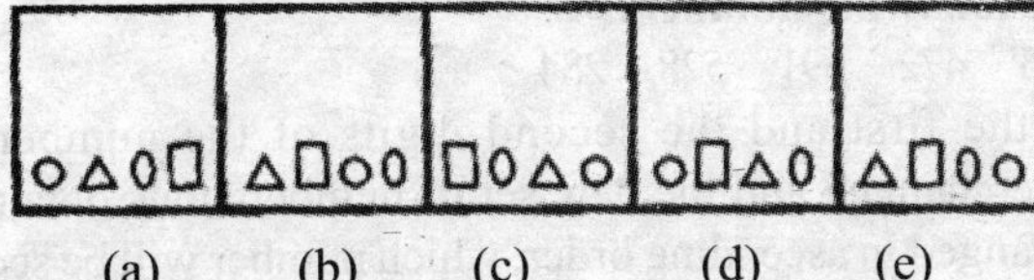

(a) (b) (c) (d) (e)

139. **Problem Figures**

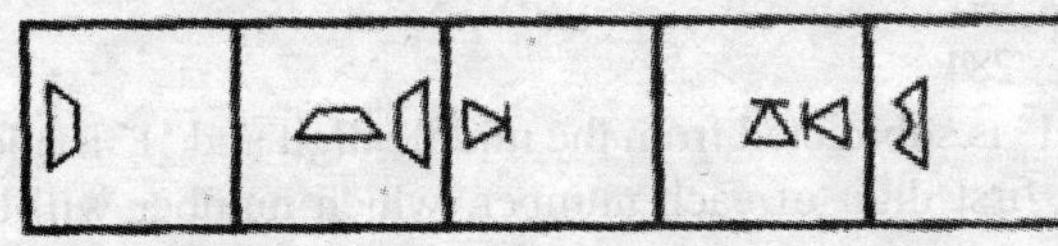

Answer Figures

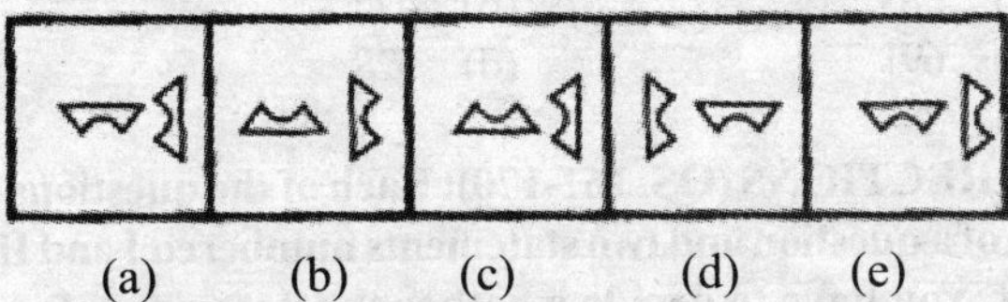

(a) (b) (c) (d) (e)

140. **Problem Figures**

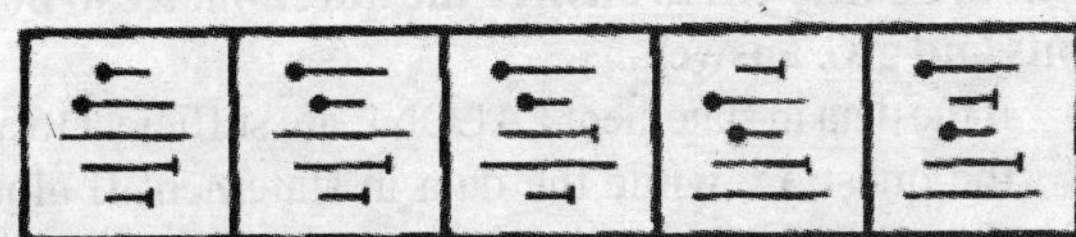

Answer Figures

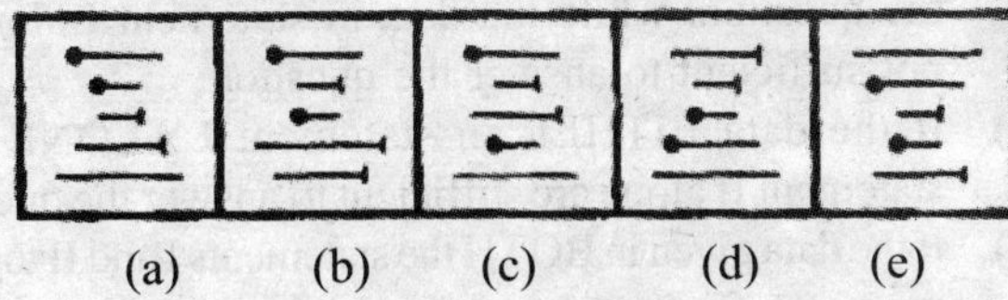

(a) (b) (c) (d) (e)

DIRECTIONS (QS. 141-145): In each question below a sentence with four words printed in bold type is given. These we indicated as (a), (b), (c) and (d). One of these four words may be either wrongly spelt or inappropriate in the context of the sentence. Find out the word which is wrongly spelt or inappropriate, if any. The letter of that word is your answer. If all he four words are correctly spelt and also appropriate in the context of the sentence, mark (e) i.e. 'All Correct' as your answer.

141. His derogatory (a) remark humiliated (b) me, but I kept my cool (c) and didn't allow my work to be affected (d) by it. All Correct. (e)

142. The suspected (a) criminals (b) who were accused (c) of snatching ladies necklesses (d) were finally booked. All Correct. (e)

143. The objective (a) of the programme (b) is to entertain (c) the spectators. (d) All Correct. (e)

144. Enforcement of laws and clean and efficiency (a) administration are fundamental (b) functions of the government machinery (c) known as bureaucracy. (d) All Correct. (e)

145. The quantification (a) of intellectual property is more complicating (b) than most pricing because today it is relatively (c) inexpensive (d) to make copies of most intellectual property. All Correct. (e)

Directions (Qs. 146-150): Below is given passage followed by several possible inferences which can be drawn from the facts stated in the passage. You have to examine each inference separately in the context of the passage and decide upon its degree of truth or falsity. Mark answer

(a) if the inference is "definitely true" i.e. it properly follows from the statement of fact given;

(b) if the inference is "probably true" though not "definitely true" in the light of other fact given;

(c) if the data are inadequate i.e. from the facts given you cannot say whether the inference is likely to be true or false;

(d) if the inference is "probably false" i.e. though not "defiantly false" in the light of the fact given;

(e) if the inference is "definitely false" i.e. it cannot possibly be drawn from the facts given or it contradicts the given facts.

Sub-Saharan Africa whose GDP grew at less than 3% a year through entire 1990s, grew 5.1% in 2004 and at 5.2% in 2005 and is projected to grow at 5.6% in the fiscal year ending 2006. In other words, India is growing about 1.5% a year faster than Sub-Saharan Africa. If India is merely doing somewhat better than the worst performing region in the world, there is no reason to get euphoric. Why is the world economy faring so well that even the worst historical performers are suddenly looking good? Africans are the fragments of the former Soviet Union are patting themselves on the back for reforming and becoming efficient. The world economy has hit a gold patch, and rising global tides has lifted all boats, even most pitiful ones. India has benefited from the rising tide like all others. But it is illusory to think that policies and projects will always keep improving.

146. India's projected economic growth of the current fiscal year is around 7%.

147. India's economy is way above the perennially low performing countries in the world.

148. Indian economy my be above to sustain present rate of growth in the coming years without major changes in its economics policies.

149. In the past, world economy has never grown at the present rate.
150. Average Economics growth of breakaway Soviet Republics is about 6% at present.

DIRECTIONS (QS. 151-155): In each question below is given a statement followed by two assumptions numbered I and II. An assumption is something supposed or taken for granted. You have to consider the statement and following assumptions and decide which the assumption is implicit in the statement. Give answer

(a) if only assumption I is implicit;
(b) if only assumption II is implicit;
(c) if only either I or II implicit;
(d) if only neither I nor II is implicit;
(e) if only both I and II are implicit.

151. **Statement:** "Anybody found in use of unfair means will be debarred from all further examinations conducted by the board" – an ultimatum to the examinees by the examining body.
Assumptions:
I. Henceforth the students may refrain from using unfair means during examination.
II. A good number of students are found involved in use of unfair means.
152. **Statement:** "Visit our showroom for quality products", – an advertisement by a garment factory.
Assumptions:
I. Majority of the people are interested in buying only good quality garments.
II. The word "quality product" may attract the customers.
153. **Statement:** "All children upto the age of 12 years should be brought to the Civic Health Care Centres in the city once in a month for free checkup" – an appeal from Civic Health Care Department in the city.
Assumptions:
I. Public largely prefer the Health Care Centres run by civic authorities to the privately run Health Care Centres.
II. Children upto the age of 12 years are susceptible to suffer from various disease.
154. **Statement:** "There should be a common examination board for the entire country conducting HSC examinations" – the opinion expressed by a group of parents and students.
Assumptions:
I. Various examination boards may be varying evaluation standards across the States.
II. Students passing through the stricture boards may be at a disadvantage at the time of taking admission to professional colleges based on performance in HSC examinations.
155. **Statement:** "Basic knowledge of computer operations is essential" - a condition stipulated by an organisation for recruitment of officers.
Assumptions:
I. Officers having knowledge of computer operations my 'perform to the desired level.
II. There may not be adequate number of applicants having knowledge of computer operations.

156. In a certain code EXHAUST is written as VUWBDWG, how is NETWORK written in that code?
(a) MDUXMTQ (b) MTQYMDS
(c) MTQXMDS (d) MDUYMTQ
(e) None of these
157. If '+' means '×', '×' means '÷', '÷' means '–' and '–' means '+'; what is the value of 165 ÷ 11 +5 – 32 × 20?
(a) 67 (b) 82
(c) 72 (d) 87
(e) None of these
158. Four of the following five are alike in a certain way and so form a group. Which is the one that does not belong to the group?
(a) 17 (b) 37
(c) 39 (e) 41
(e) 43

***Directions (Qs. 159-160)*: These questions are based on the following numbers.**

385 472 691 528 284

159. If the first and the second digits of the numbers are interchanged and the new set of numbers thus obtained is arranged in ascending order, which number will be second?
(a) 385 (b) 472
(c) 691 (d) 528
(e) 284
160. If '1' is subtracted from the middle digit and '1' is added to the first digit of each number, which number will be the largest?
(a) 385 (b) 472
(c) 691 (d) 528
(e) 284

DIRECTIONS (QS. 161-170): Each of the questions below consists of a question and two statements numbered I and II given below it. You have to decide whether the data provided in the statements are sufficient to answer the question. Read both the statements and give answer

(a) if the data in statement I ALONE are sufficient to answer the question, while the data in statement II alone are not sufficient to answer the question;
(b) if the data in statement II ALONE are sufficient to answer the question, while the data in statement I alone are not sufficient to answer the question;
(c) if the data EITHER in statement I ALONE or in statement II alone are sufficient to answer the question;
(d) if the data given in BOTH the statements I and II together are not sufficient to answer the question;
(e) if the data in BOTH the statements I and II TOGETHER are necessary to answer the question.

161. What is the value of a two-digit number?
I. The product of the digits is 0.
II. One of the digits is 6.
162. What is the value of a two-digit number?
I. The product of the digits is 0.
II. The difference between the digits is 9.
163. What is the value of a two-digit number?
I. The difference between the digits is 4.
II. The product of the digits is 0.

164. What is the value of a two-digit number?
   I. The difference between the digits is 9.
   II. The sum of the two digits is 9 and one of the digits is also 9.

165. How much was the per cent profit on selling a product.
   I. The total profit was Rs 175
   II. A rebate of 2.5% on the labelled price was given

166. Is the given number odd?
   I. The number is not divisible by 5.
   II. The number is not divisible by 3, 6, or 7.

167. What is the per cent rate of simple interest per annum?
   I. The amount doubles in 6 years with the interest rate.
   II. The interest amount is Rs 1,600 for the first year.

168. What is the length of a train which crosses a pole in 20 seconds?
   I. The train crosses a 300 metres long platform in 35 seconds.
   II. The speed of train is 72 km/hour.

169. How much is the height of a triangle ABC.
   I. The measure of the three sides is 3, 5 and 6 cm.
   II. One of the angles is 90°.

170. What is the difference between the ages of Madhu and Shweta?
   I. The sum of their ages is 75 years and the ages are in the ratio of 3 : 2 or 2 : 3.
   II. madhu is 45 years old and the respective ratio of ages of Shweta and Madhu is 2 : 3.

DIRECTIONS (QS. 171-174): Study the following graphs and answer accordingly. The following pie-chart shows the percentage of number of students passed in PO examination from different parts of the country in 1999.

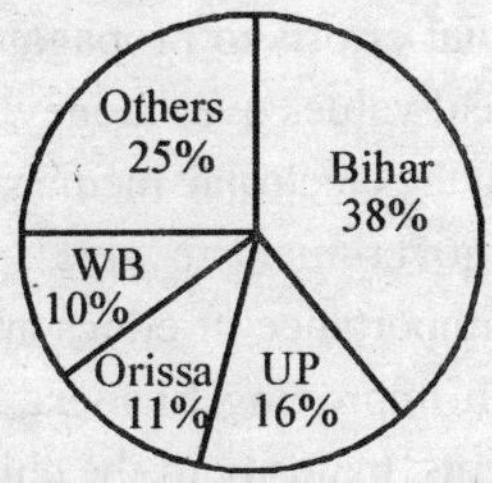

The following graph shows the percentage of students who passed their graduation (freshers) in 1999.

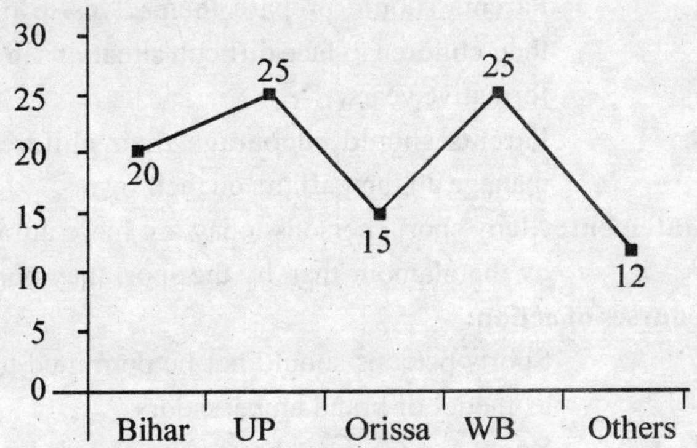

171. If in 1999 the total passed candidates from different parts of the country was 650, then how many non-fresher candidates from Bihar passed the examination in 1999?
   a) 2000 (b) 195
   (c) 198 (d) 204
   (e) 188

172. If in 1999 total number of fresher from WB was 160, then how many non-fresher candidates passed the exam from Others?
   (a) 1398 (b) 1588
   (c) 1608 (d) 1408
   (e) Can't be determined

173. If total passed candidates from UP in 1999 was 112, what is the ratio between the number of freshes from Bihar and that of non-freshers from Orissa?
   (a) 760 : 187 (b) 187 : 760
   (c) 40 : 11 (d) 11 : 40
   (e) None of these

174. If there is an increase of 10% and 20% candidates from Bihar and Others in the year 2000 respectively, and the number of total passed candidates from Orissa in 1999 was 77, what would be the approximate total passed candidates from Bihar and Others in 2000?
   (a) 210 (b) 480
   (c) 450 (d) 550
   (e) 500

DIRECTIONS: (QS. 175-180) : The second figure in the first unit of the problem figurs a certain relationship to the first figure. Similarly one of the figures in the answer figure bears the same relationship to the first figure in the second unit. You are to, therefore, locate the figure which would fit the questionmark.

175. Problem Figures

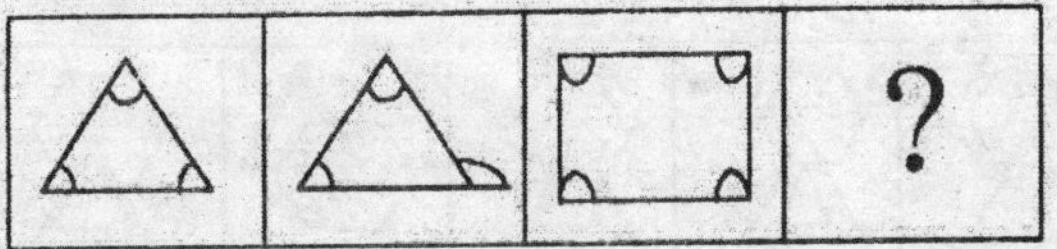

Answer Figures

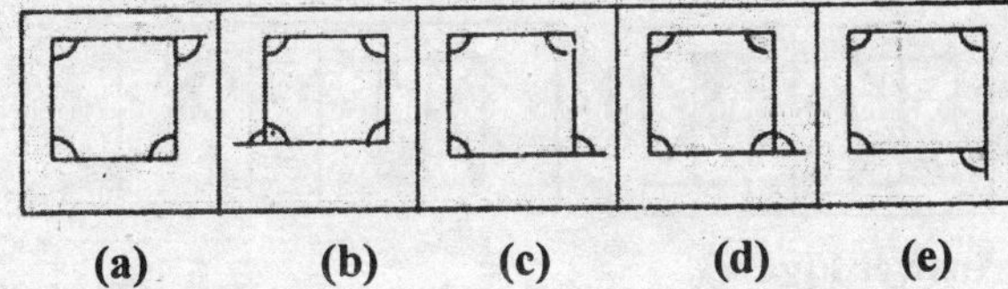

176. Problem Figures

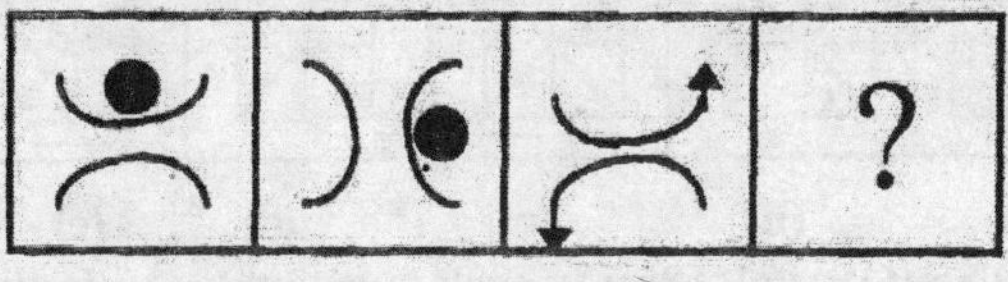

Answer Figures

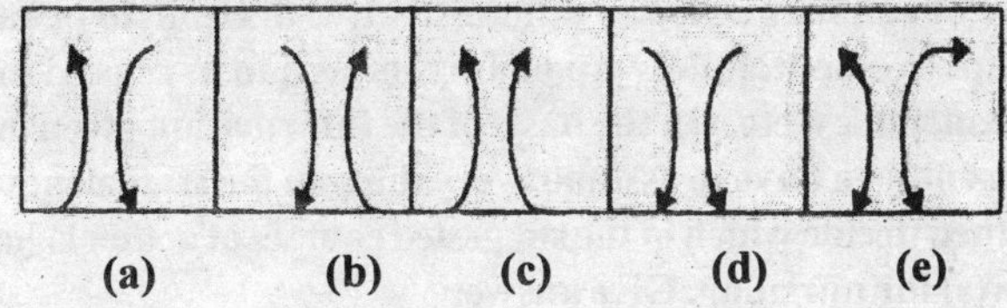

177. Problem Figures

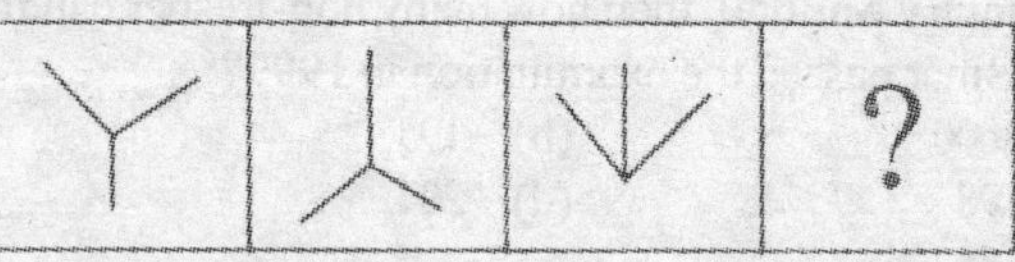

Answer Figures

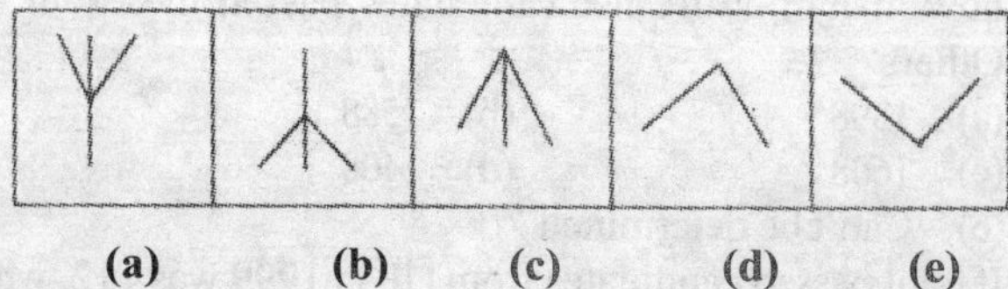

(a) (b) (c) (d) (e)

178. Problem Figures

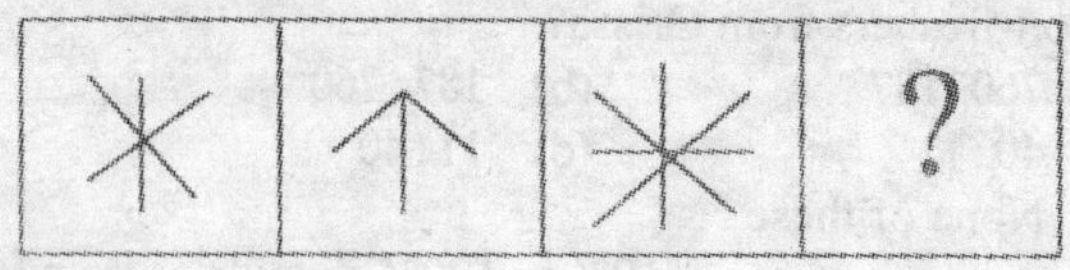

Answer Figures

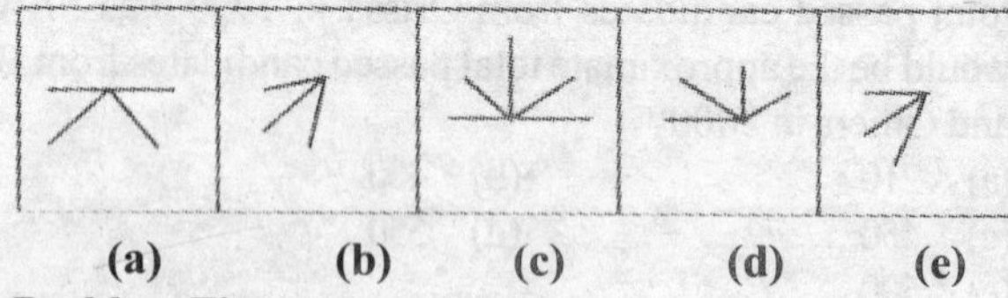

(a) (b) (c) (d) (e)

179. Problem Figures

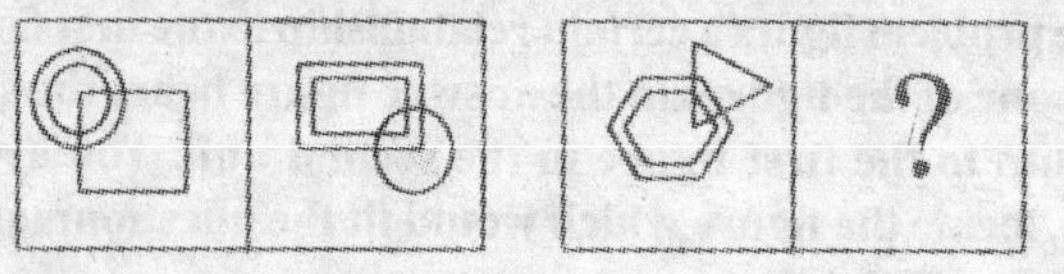

Answer Figures

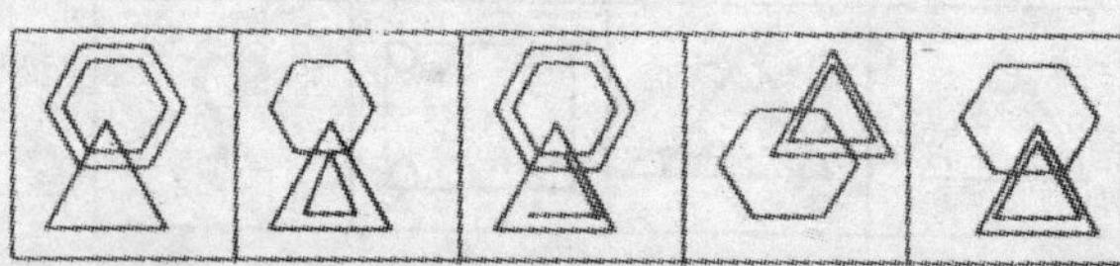

180. Problem Figures

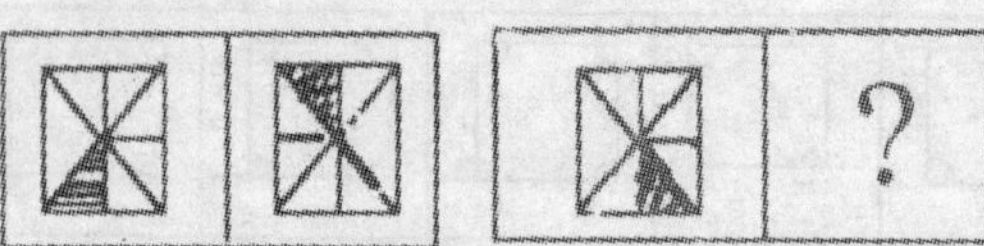

Answer Figures

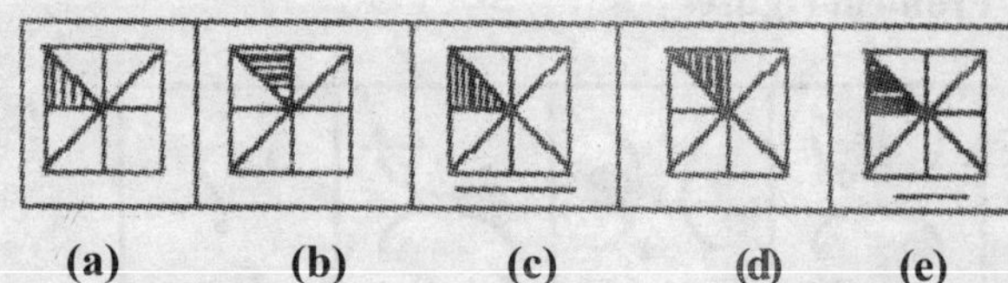

(a) (b) (c) (d) (e)

DIRECTIONS (QS. 181-185): In each question below is given a statement followed by two courses of action numbered I and II. A course of action is a step or administrative decision to be taken for improvement, follow-up or further action in regard to the problem, policy, etc. On the basis of the information given in the statement, you have to assume every thing in the statement to be true, then decide which of the suggested courses of action logically follow(s) for pursuing. Give answer

(a) if only I follows;
(b) if only II follows;
(c) if either I or II follows;
(d) if neither I nor II follows;
(e) if both I and II follow.

181. **Statement:** The number of students suffering from depression during examination days is increasing every year.

Courses of action:

I. The schools and colleges should set up counselling centres within the campus to provide psychological support.

II. Efforts should be made to minimise the pressure from parents and society.

182. **Statement:** Computers have become a part of life and getting a job without computer knowledge has become very difficult.

Courses of action:

I. Computers related subjects should be made compulsory at college level for the disciplines.

II. Students should be advised to join computer-coaching classes, simultaneously while pursuing college education.

183. **Statement:** With the change in value system, money assumed topmost importance nowadays, ultimately leading to criminal activities.

Courses of action:

I. Social service organisations should make special efforts to propagate the importance of ethical values over money.

II. Print the electronic media should be advised by the government to give special emphasis on the importance of ethics and value systems.

184. **Statement:** With improving financial status of the urban parents, majority of the children are pampered and find it difficult to struggle when faced with adverse situations.

Courses of action:

I. Parents should prepare themselves to orient their children to face difficult situations in their formative years.

II. Parents should encourage their children to manage all their affairs on their own.

185. **Statement:** Many sports persons today are more attracted by the glamour than by the sport they pursue.

Courses of action:

I. Sports persons should not be permitted to act as model of brand ambassadors.

II. Sports persons should be paid higher compensation for their achievements in sport.

DIRECTIONS (QS. 186-190): Following are the conditions for selection of IT Officers in an organisation. The candidate must

(I) be an engineer in IT/ Computers/ Electronics or M.C.A. with 1st class with securing minimum 65% marks.

(II) have an experience of working in the related area at least for two yeas after acquiring the desired qualification .

(II) have passed the selection test with at least 0% marks.

(IV) be not less than 21 years and not more than 30 years of age as on 1.2.2006.

However, if a candidate fulfills all the above criteria except

(i) at (II) above, but has an experience of one year and has obtained at least 70% marks at the degree examination the case may be referred to the Chairman and Managing Director of the organisation.

(ii) at (IV) above but less than 32 years of age and has minimum 5 years post-qualification experience of working in the related area, the case may be referred to the Divisional Head of the organisation.

In each question below, detailed information of one candidate is provided. You have to read the information provided carefully and decide which of the following courses of actions you will adopt as regarding status of the candidate based on the conditions stated above. You are not to assume anything other than the information provided in each question. All these cases are given to you as on 1.2.2006.You have to indicate your decision by marking answers to each question as follows.

(a) if the candidate is to be selected.
(b) if the candidate is not to be selected.
(c) if the data is not adequate to take the decision.
(d) if the case is to be referred to the Divisional Head.
(e) if the case to be referred to the Chairman and Managing Director.

186. Sujata Bhatt, is an IT engineer passed out in 1999, with 72% marks. She is working as a Software Engineer since June 2000. Her date of birth is 23rd December 1975. She has cleared the selection test with 65% marks.

187. Nisha Chavan has passed out M.C.A. with 68% marks in the year 2003 and has passed selection test with 62% marks. She has been working as Clerk-cum-Cashier in a Cooperative Bank since 2003. Her date of birth is 16.7.1983.

188. Aditya Jshi is an Electronics Engineer passed with 72% marks in 2002, and is MBA-Finance passed in 2004 with 70% marks. He started working as a software manager in May 2004, immediately after completing MBA. He was born on 23rd October 1979. He has secured 66% marks in selection test.

190. Nilesh Zaveri has passed engineering examination in 2001 with 72% marks and thereafter passed MCA in 2003. He has been working for last two years since September 2003. He has recently completed 25 years of age.

DIRECTIONS (QS. 191-200): In the following passage there are blanks, each of which has been numbered. These numbers are printed below the passage and against each, five words are suggested, one of which fits the blank appropriately. Find out the appropriate words without changing the meaning of the passage.

Regulatory commissions must be **(191)** but also be accountable to some authority. The packing of regulatory commissions with retired or retiring government employees has skewed membership to **(192)** men with administrative experience but **(193)** management skills, or **(194)** there a managerial mindset in state electricity enterprises. Governments have done nothing to correct this.

The electricity system in India is today a heavy **(195)** on society, on state government finances and an **(196)** to growth and social justice **(197)** of perennial debates and reversals, the government must keep reiterating policies and aggressively **(198)** support and implement the Act, **(199)** monitor the policies **(200)** stronger incentives and penalties to make State Electricity Boards (SEBs) more enterprising and professional.

191. (a) formed (b) established (c) independent (d) subsidiary (e) functioning

192. (a) older (b) young (c) mature (d) sober (e) sycophant

193. (a) adequate (b) essential (c) lacked (d) no (e) exceptional

194. (a) has (b) is (c) was (d) merely (e) only

195. (a) loss (b) weight (c) expenditure (d) disadvantage (e) burden

196. (a) obstacle (b) incentive (c) empowerment (d) initiative (e) overture

197. (a) because (b) in spite (c) instead (d) worried (e) tired

198. (a) revising (b) implementing (c) using (d) devising (e) utilising

199. (a) reluctantly (b) intermittently (c) obviously (d) aggressively (e) sparingly

200. (a) eradicate (b) subsidise (c) prevent (d) inculcate (e) introduce

ANSWERS WITH EXPLANATIONS

1. (e) Concrete is the substance used to make buildings.Others are parts of building.
2. (d) Goods are stored in godown.
3. (b) $R \to \%, I \to 7, S \to 5, K \to 2$.
4. (d) I N S T R U C T I O N

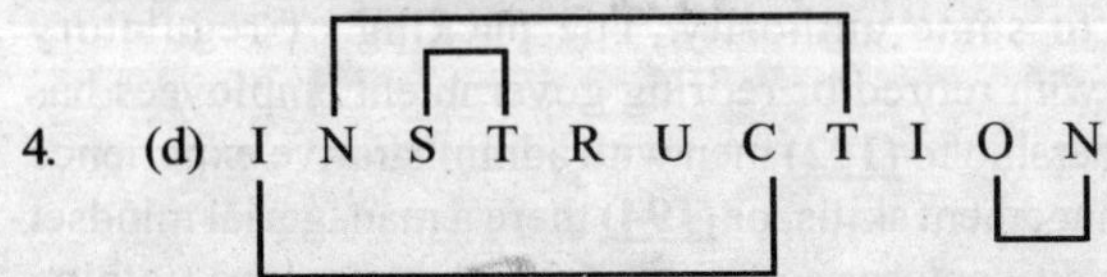

It is clear from the above diagram, NT, ST, NO and CI are four pairs.

5. (e) $P \to 1$ $M \to 2$ $R \to 5$ $E \to 3$
$I \to 7$ $S \to 4$ $V \to 8$ $A \to 9$
$A \to 9$ $G \to 0$ $T \to 6$ $E \to 3$
$E \to 3$
Hence, $S \to 4, I \to 7, E \to 3, G \to 0, E \to 3$.

6. (a) A —1st Place→ 1 B —2nd Place→ 2
E —5th Place→ 5 C —3rd Place→ 3
G —6th Place→ 7 D —4th Place→ 4
B —2nd Place→ 2 F —5th Place→ 6
I —9th Place→ 9
Similarly,
2 —2nd Place→ B
3 —3rd Place→ C
5 —5th Place→ E
4 —4th Place→ D
9 —9th Place→ I

7. (a) Each letter moves – 1 place.
B → A (–1), E → D (–1), G → F (–1), K → J (–1) Similarly P → O (–1), S → R (–1), V → U (–1), Y → X (–1)

8. (d) WFB TGD QHG [NIK]
+2 +3 +4
–3 –3 –3
+1 +1 +1

9. (a) BMX DNW FOU [HPR]
+1 +1 +1
+2 +2 +2
–1 –2 –3

10. (c) As
K O R T P J W O
+5 –5 +5 –5

Similarly, F I N R [K D S M]
+5 –5 +5 –5

11. (b) In each of the other choices, the numbers have only 2 prime factors. Only 90 has 3 prime factors.
12. (e) In each of the other choices, all letters are moving forward by a fixed number, in MSP, S and P are moving backwards.
13. (a) All other publications are in English, Hindustan is in Hindi.
14. (b) Sun is a star, all others are planets.
15. (e) All others are in ascending order of alphabet.

From Qs. 16 – 25

	1999		2000		2001		2002		2003		2004		2005	
	In	Ex	In	Ex	In	Ex	In	Ex	In	Ex	In	Ex	In	ex
Company A	10	5	13	7.5	18.2	9.75	30.94	13.16	52.59	18.4	92.04	25.7	165.67	38.6
Company B	20	10	22	10.5	25.3	11.02	31.6	11.57	47.40	13.89	75.9	16.66	144.21	23.33

16. (e) Income of company B in 1999 = Rs. 20 crores; Percentage increase in 2000 = 10; Hence income in 2000 = 22 crores.
17. (d) Since the figures are not given for growth of 1999, the expenditure for 1998 cannot be calculated.
18. (a) Income of A increases 30%, 40%, 70%, 70%, 75% and 80% successively. Applying these percentages on 10 crores, we get 13 crores, 18.2 crores, 30.94 crores, 52.59 crores, 92.04 crores. Hence in 2004 it is close to 90 crores.
19. (a) Income of A in 2000 = 13 crores
expenditure in 2000 = 7.50 crores.
$$\text{Hence profit \%} = \frac{13 - 7.50}{7.50} \times 100 = 73.33\%.$$
20. (a) Income of B in 2001 = 25.3 crores
expenditure = 11.025 crores
Hence Profit = (25.3 – 11.025) crores = 14.275 crores.
21. (c) Income of Company A increases by 30% (in 2000), 40% (in 2001), and 70% in (in 2002). Hence, income of Company A = 13 crores (in 2000), 18.2 crores (in 2001) and 30.94 crores (in 2002).
22. (b) Income of B increases by 10% (in 2000), 15% (in 2001), 25% (in 2002), 50% (in 2003), and 60% (in 2004). Hence, income of Company B is 22, 25.3, 31.6, 47.40 and 75.9 crores respectively. Hence in 2004 it is close to 76 crore.
23. (c) Income of A is 18.2 crores in 2001. In 1999 it was 10 crores, hence required percentage = $\frac{18.2}{10} \times 100 = 182$
24. (e) Income of B in 2003 is 47.4 crores, and expenditure is 13.9 crores, hence profit = 35.5 crores approx.
$$\text{Hence percentage profit} = \frac{33.5}{13.9} \times 100 = 241 \approx 240\%$$
25. (c) The percent profit was not more in each year for Company B.

For (Qs 26–30)

The correct order of the sentences to form a meaningful paragraph is AEFDBC. Because A and E ask questions and F is attempting to explain them.

26. (a) 27. (e) 28. (e) 29. (b) 30. (c)
31. (b) should be checked ...
32. (d) 'to' should follow succumb.

33. (e)
34. (c) How the burglar got into ...
35. (a) Said to be necessarily
36. (d) In each subsequent step a new design appears at one of the end. Existing design shift half-a-side in anti-clockwise direction.
37. (a) In each subsequent step one line segment is added in upper design horizontally and vertically respectively. The lower desingn rotates 90° in clockwise direction.
38. (c) The whole figure rotates by 90° anticlockwise direction. A new design appears at one of the end in every three figures.
39. (c) The whole figure rotates by 90° anticlockwise direction and the inner designs move two places in anticlockwise direction after rotation.
40. (d) The whole figure rotates by 90° anticlockwise direction and a new design appears at the clockwise end while existing two design shift one place towards anticlockwise end.
41. (d) **Statement I:** Sky is clear → *de ra fa*
Statement II: Make it clear → *de ga jo*
Hence, the code for sky is either *ra* or *fa*
42. (a) **Statement I:** Mohan is the only son of Divya's mother-in-law means Mohan is husband of Divya.
Statement II: Does not show any relation between Mohan and Divya.
Hence, (a) is the correct option.
43. (e) **Statement I:**

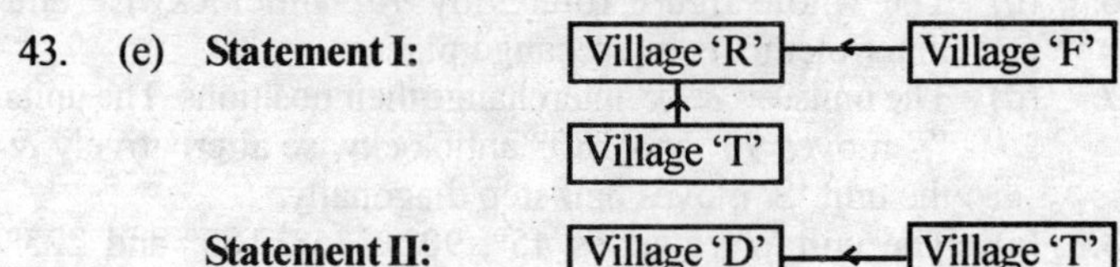

Statement II: Village 'D' ← Village 'T'

Hence, both the statements I and II together are necessary to answer the question.
44. (a) **Statement I:** H is the only daughter of X (mother) and M (father).
Statement II: No information about M's children.
Hence, (a) is the correct option.
45. (c) **Statement I:** Sunil's rank from top is 5th.
Statement II: Sunil's rank from top is 5th.
Hence, either statement is sufficient to answer the question.
46. (a)

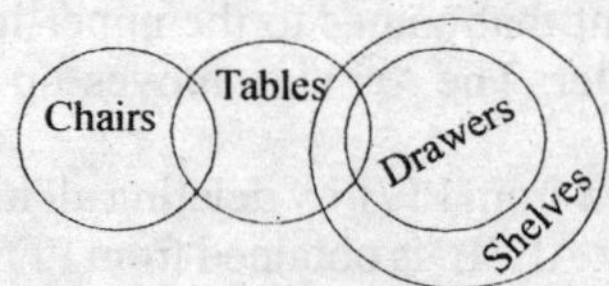

Hence conclusions I. ✓ II. ✗ III. ✓
47. (c)

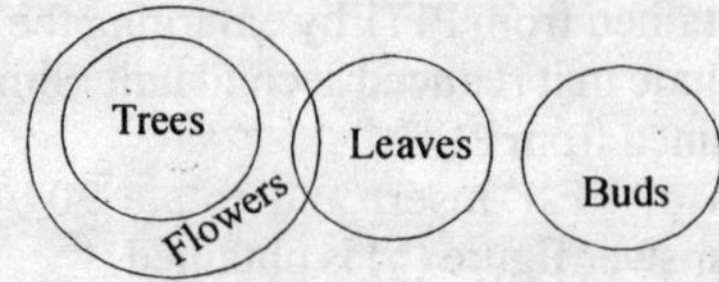

Hence conclusions I. ✗ II. ✗ III. ✗
But I and II are complementary pairs.
48. (e)

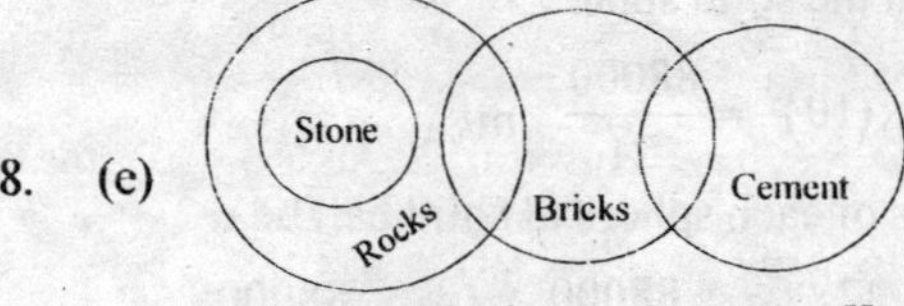

Hence conclusions I. ✗ II. ✗ III. ✗
But II and III are complementary pairs.
49. (e)

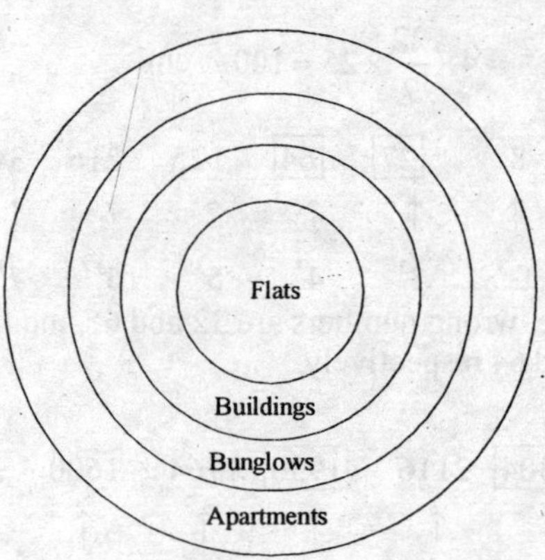

Hence conclusions I. ✓ II. ✓ III. ✓
50. (b)

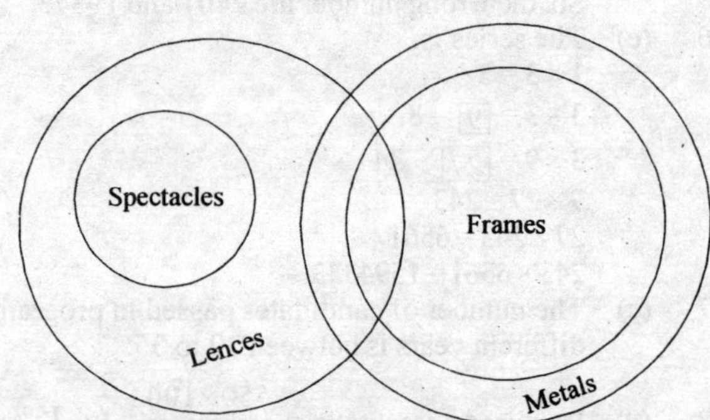

Hence conclusions I. ✓ II. ✗ III. ✗
51. (a) Let number of female and male be x and $3x$ respectively.
At the first stop:

No. of males	No. of females
$\frac{3x-m}{(x-f)+6}=\frac{2}{1}$	$3x-m, (x-f)+6$

$\Rightarrow 3x - m = 2x - 2f + 12$
Also, $m + f = 16$ $\Rightarrow x = 28 - 3f$
$\therefore$ For $f = 4$, $x = 16$
$\therefore$ Total number of passengers in the beginning $= (x + 3x) = 4x = 64$.
52. (c) Let they meet after x minutes
According to the question,

$$\left(\frac{3.75\times5}{18}\right)x+\left(\frac{4.5\times5}{18}\right)x=726$$

or $\frac{5}{18}x\ (3.75+4.5)=726$

or $\left(\frac{5\times8.25}{18}\right)x=726$

$\therefore x=\left(\frac{726\times18}{5\times8.25}\right)$ sec $=\left(\frac{726\times18}{5\times8.25\times60}\right)$ min $= 5.28$ min

53. (d) Volume of the solid sphere

$= \frac{4}{3} \times \frac{22}{7} \times (10)^3 = \frac{88000}{21}$ cm³

Let radius of each spherical solid ball be r.

$\therefore\ 8 \times \frac{4}{3} \times \frac{22}{7} \times r^3 = \frac{88000}{21} \Rightarrow r^3 = \frac{88000}{21} \Rightarrow r = 5$

$\therefore$ Surface area of each ball

$= 4\pi r^2 = 4 \times \frac{22}{7} \times 25 = 100\pi$ cm²

54. (b) 1 8 [27] [64] 125 216 343 512

↑ ↑ ↑ ↑ ↑ ↑ ↑ ↑

1^3 2^3 3^3 4^3 5^3 6^3 7^3 8^3

Hence, wrong numbers are 32 and 65 and it should be 27 and 64 respectively.

55. (d)

2500 [2304] 2116 [1936] 1764 1600 1444

↑ ↑ ↑ ↑ ↑ ↑ ↑

$(50)^2$ $(48)^2$ $(46)^2$ $(44)^2$ $(42)^2$ $(40)^2$ $(38)^2$

So, the wrong number are 2401 and 1937.

56. (c) The series is:

$1 \times 3 = 3$

$3 \times 3 = \boxed{9}$ 8

$3 \times 9 = \boxed{27}$ 24

$9 \times 27 = 243$

$27 \times 243 = 6561$

$243 \times 6561 = 1594323$

57. (c) The number of candidates passed in programme C for different years is between 20 to 35.

58. (d) Required percentage $= \frac{550 \times 100}{800} = 68.75\%$

59. (a) Required percentage for the year

$2001 = \frac{160-110}{110} \times 100 = 45.45$

$2002 = \frac{190-160}{160} \times 100 = 18.75$

$2003 = \frac{300-190}{190} \times 100 = 57.89$

$2004 = \frac{350-300}{300} \times 100 = 16.66$

60. (e) Required difference

$= (450+500+600+800+750+800) - (420+180+370+440+400+510)$

$= 1520$

61. (a) Required percentage for programme:

$A = \frac{600 \times 100}{850} = 70.58$ $B = \frac{200 \times 100}{300} = 66.66$

$C = \frac{30 \times 100}{70} = 42.85$ $D = \frac{460 \times 100}{1800} = 25.55$

$E = \frac{37 \times 100}{100} = 37$ $F = \frac{155 \times 100}{400} = 38.75$

62. (e) Let the no. of boys and girls be $3x$ and $2x$ respectively. Now, according to the question,

$\frac{3x}{2x+6} = \frac{6}{5} \Rightarrow 15x = 12x + 36 \Rightarrow 3x = 36$

$\therefore x = 12$ $\therefore$ No. of boys $= 12 \times 3 = 36$

63. (b) $x^2 - 7x + 12 = 0,$

$\Rightarrow x^2 - 4x - 3x + 12 = 0$

$\Rightarrow (x-4)(x-3) = 0$

Hence the factors are $(x-4)(x-3)$.

The roots are 3 or 4.

64. (c) Let the speed of boat in still water be x km/hr and speed of current be y km/hr.

Then, $\frac{10}{x+y} = 2 \Rightarrow 2x + 2y = 10$ ...(i)

and $\frac{10}{x-y} = 5 \Rightarrow 5x - 5y = 10$ ...(ii)

From (i) and (ii), $x = 3.5$ km/hr.

65. (d) Cost price = Rs 4500 $\left(\frac{100}{100-10}\right)$ = Rs $\frac{4500 \times 100}{90}$

= Rs 5000

Selling price = Rs 5000 $\left(\frac{100+10}{100}\right)$ = Rs $\frac{5000 \times 110}{100}$

= Rs 5500.

66. (b) The whole figure rotates by 90° anticlockwise and inner elements interchange places.

67. (d) The units '=' & 'x' interchange their positions. The units '?' moves 90° and 180° anticlockwise alternatively & the unit 'S' moves half step diagonally.

68. (a) The unit 'α' revolves 45°, 90°, 135°, 180° and 225° anticlockwise in the subsequent figures. The unit 'β' revolves 45° clockwise and the unit 'γ' revolves 90° clockwise.

69. (c) The unit '<' reverses its direction from the top to the bottom in a set order. All the three units move from the left to the right and from the right to the left in their respective positions.

70. (d) The square, triangle and circle move in the order

The element that comes to the centre, gets enlarged and the element that comes to the upper-left corener becomes smaller. The '+' sign moves up and down vertically.

71. (c) PF/2 is obtained from PF/1 by deleting all its outer two units. Similarly, AF/'B' is obtained from PF/3.

72. (c) PF/2 is obtained from PF/1 when inside unit changes its direction and join themselves and outer unit remains the same. Similarly, AF/'C' is obtained from PF/3.

73. (d) PF/2 is obtained from PF/1 by enlarging the innermost unit to include in it reduced second unit. Similarly, AF/'D' is obtained from PF/3.

74. (a) Two units of PF/1 insert and rotate 90° clockwise similarly answer figure (b) is obtained

75. (d) In each subsequent step a new design appears in every row.

76. (a) Benevolent and malevolent are opposites.

77. (d) Ambitious and unmotivated are opposites.
78. (c) Reliance and dependence are same.
79. (b) Crafty and cunning are same.
80. (d) Innocent is opposite of guilty.
81. (e) Envious and jealous are same.
82. (a) Lively is opposite of sluggish.
83. (c) Envisage and foresee are same.
84. (b) Inspire is same as stimulate.
85. (e) Liberal and tolerant are same.
86. (d) M| ≥ |N and H | ≤ | Q and Q | ≥ | M. We cannot get a relationship between H, Q and M.
87. (b) C | > | B, L | < | S and S | ≤ | C. There is no relationship between B and S. But since L | < | S | ≤ |C, then C | > | L is true .
88. (e) 1| ≥ | H, E | > | F and I | = | F. We get E | >| I, hence I is wrong, also E | > | I | ≥ | H hence E | > | H.
89. (c) V | = | O, R | ≥ | V and O | ≥ | B. Hence R | ≥ | V | = | O | ≥ |B. Either I or II is true.
90. (d) L | > | U, T | = | L and U | ≤ | W. We cannot get a relationship between T and W hence I is wrong. II may or may not be true.

For (Qs. 91-95):

On the basis of given information we have the following table.

Leander	Shoes	Reebok
Gopichand	Sportswear / Rackets	Nike
Sachin	Diet Coke	Coca Cola
Anand	Mineral Water / Rackets	Pepsi / Adidas
Bhutia	Mineral Water / Rackets	Pepsi / Adidas

Now, we can answer the given questions.

91. (a) 92. (d) 93. (b) 94. (c) 95. (a)
96. (b) 5 men from 19 and 5 women from 20

$\therefore$ No. of ways $= {}^{19}C_5 \times {}^{20}C_5$

97. (c) We can have 2, 3, 4 or 5 men. Hence we add all the cases to get 350 + 350 + 105 + 7 = 812.
98. (b) Only 4 seats are left which are among P and R, hence ${}^{18}C_4 = 3060$.
99. (d) No. of lecturers = 11 + 10 = 21

No. of ways $= \frac{\lfloor 21}{\lfloor 6 \times \lfloor 15} = 54264$

100. (e) No. of women professors = 7

No. of men professors – 5

No. of ways $= {}^7C_2 \times {}^5C_2 = \frac{\lfloor 7}{\lfloor 2 \times \lfloor 5} \times \frac{\lfloor 5}{\lfloor 2 \times \lfloor 3}$

$= \frac{7 \times 6}{2} \times \frac{5 \times 4}{2} = 210$

101. (c) The author wants us to stop debating and implement policies.
102. (c) Stated in the first paragraph.
103. (d) Uncertainty about payment is mentioned, hence option (d).
104. (b) Refer to the second paragraph. "State governments have not implemented agreed plans to ensure repayment when due..."
105. (a) All the factors are mentioned in the passage.
106. (a) Refer to the third paragraph. "The Delhi model has worked. But it receives no public support."
107. (d) Clearly, populist measures would go against financial wellbeing.
108. (d) It is stated in the passage that the enforcement of the reforms was inadequate.
109. (c) Directly mentioned in the passage.
110. (a) Distance means "the amount of space between two places or things"
111. (c) Delusion means "a false belief of openion about yourself or your situation"
112. (e) The root word of viability is viable. Viable means "capable of developping and surviving independetly"
113. (b) The root word of forcefully is forceful. Forceful means "expressing opinions firmly and clearly in a way that persuades other people to belive them".
114. (d) Impede mans " delay or stop the progress of something.
115. (e) Unboundling is opposite of bundling mans integrating.

For (Qs. 116 -120):

Student	College	Stream
M	G	Electronics
T	D	Computer
K	C	Electronics
Q	B	Electrical
R	A	Electrical
P	E	Computer
H	F	Electronics

116. (c) 117. (b) 118. (b) 119. (c) 120. (a)

For (121-125):

Simply follow the rules of the codes and do these sums.

121. (c) X$DTFX (Because 1st and last digits are odd.)
122. (a) $%HFD# (No any condition.)
123. (c) HK$T%H (Because 1st and the last digits are even.)
124. (b) D%$HK# (Because 1st digit is odd and the last digit is even.)
125. (e) HTMK#H (Because Ist and the last digits are even.)
126. (e) Since $x = + 4.3$, nothing can be said about x and y.
127. (a) Solving the quadratic equations we get $x = -2$ or -3, $y = -5$ or -6. Hence in both cases $x > y$.
128. (b) $x = 8,\ y = -8,\ x > y$.
129. (a) x > y.
130. (e) Nothing can be said about the relationship.
131. (e) Two of the matchsticks change direction every time.
132. (c) 3 and 5 lines are added alternately to the diagram.
133. (d) Direction changes 45 degrees and one line should be added.
134. (d) Every time one additional square is shaded.
135. (a) The side with two arms should be pointing downwards.
136. (a) Notice the direction and add two lines.
137. (d) Dark arrow should point upwards and its end should be crossed.
138. (e) From problem figure 1 to 4 two designs of right change their places with each other and from problem figure 2 to 5, two designs of left change their places with each other. In the same way from problem figure 3 to answer figure two designs of right will change their places with each other. Thus the answer figure (e) is obtained.
139. (E) From problem figure 1 to 2 and 3 to 4 the design turning over horizontally situates toward right side and the design rotating through 90° anticlockwise situates in the middle. As per this rule the answer figure (E) is obtained.

140. (c) In each subsequent figure design change their places as below:

● 1
● 2
● 3
● 4
● 5

From problem 1 to 2 designs 1 and 2
From problem 2 to 3 designs 3 and 4
From problem 3 to 4 designs 5 sets up at top
From problem 4 to 5 designs 1 and 2 and 5 to answer figure design 3 and 4 change their places with each other thus the answer figure (c) is obtained.

141. (e) No correction required.
142. (d) It should be "necklaces".
143. (c) It should be "entertain".
144. (a) It should be "efficient".
145. (b) It should be "complicated".
146. (b) Since India is faster than Africa which is 5.2%, the rate of 7% is probably true for India but not definitely true.
147. (e) India is stated to be "somewhat better" hence the statement that it is "way above" is definitely false.
148. (d) The author says that it is illusory to think that we will keep improving. Hence India can probably not keep improving without a change in policies.
149. (c) The world economy has hit a golden patch but we have no information about growth rates of the past.
150. (b) Since Russia is clubbed with Africa we can say that it is also growing at the same rate, hence probably true.
151. (a) We can only conclude I but we cannot say anything about the number of people doing this.
152. (b) The advertisement is given to attract customers, hence (b) is correct but we cannot say what the majority is interested in.
153. (b) The notice is given to help the children who are susceptible but we cannot say what they prefer.
154. (e) Both statements are implicit.
155. (d) We can neither say anything about managers nor about the number.
156. (e) The first and last letters are interchanged and the letters move +2 steps. Hence last letter is E(F)G and first letter is T(U)V. Similarly last letter should be N(O)P and first letter should be K(L)M.
157. (e) Given expression becomes: $165-11\times5+32\div20=111.6$
158. (c) Each of the other numbers is prime.
159. (b) The numbers become 835, [742], 961, 258 and 824.
160. (c) The numbers become

475 562 [781] 618 374

The largest number = 781

Hence, required number is in option (c).

161. (e) We need both statements. From I, we get one digit is 0. From II we get that the number has to be 60.
162. (e) From statement I, we get one digit is 0. From statement II, we get the number is 90.
163. (e) From statement I, we get one digit is 0. From statement II, we get the number is 40.
164. (b) If we know that the sum is 9 and one digit is 9 then the other digit must be 0.
165. (d) From both the statements we cannot calculate cost price, hence both are not sufficient.
166. (d) Even from both statements we will get both odd number (13) and even number (16).
167. (a) We can find out the rate from the first statement only.
168. (c) We can solve the equation by using either statement I or II.
169. (d) We don't know how the triangle is placed, height cannot be certain.
170. (c) We can find the difference by using either statement I and II.
171. (c) Total passed candidates = 650

Now, no. of passed candidates from Bihar = 38% of 650 = 247.

No. of non-fresher candidates from Bihar

$$=80\% \text{ of } 247=\frac{80\times247}{100}=197.6=198$$

172. (d) Non-fresher candidates passed the exam from Others

$$=\frac{160}{25}\times100\times\frac{25}{10}\times\frac{88}{100}=1408$$

173. (e) No. of freshers from Bihar $=112\times\frac{38}{16}\times\frac{20}{100}$

No. of non-freshers from Orissa $=112\times\frac{11}{16}\times\frac{85}{100}$

$$\therefore \text{Required ratio}=\frac{112\times\frac{38}{16}\times\frac{20}{100}}{112\times\frac{11}{16}\times\frac{85}{100}}=152:1$$

174. (e) Total passed candidates from Bihar and Other in 2000

$$=\frac{38}{11}\times77\times\frac{110}{100}\times\frac{25}{11}\times77\times\frac{120}{100}=500\,(\text{approx}).$$

175. (c) The angle comes outside to the right side of the figure.
176. (a) The figure moves by an angle of 90° in clockwise direction.
177. (c) The figure moves by an angle of 180°.
178. (a) Top portion of the disign is deleted.
179. (d) The two figures interchange their place and number.
180. (a) The shaded portion inside the figure moves two boxes forward in clockwise direction.
181. (a) Only 1 follows. We cannot minimise pressure from society as it is not under our control.
182. (c) Either the student can study at college or they can join coaching classes.
183. (e) Both the statements will help in educating about value systems.
184. (e) Both the statements follow as they can help people to acquire responsibility.
185. (c) Either the activity can be banned or playyers can be encouraged to concentrate on play.
186. (a) She fulfills all the conditions, hence she should be selected.
187. (b) She doesnot fulfill (ii) of havine experience in a related area.
188. (b) He does not fulfill (i) hence should not be selected.
189. (a) He fulfill all the conditions, hence should be selected.
190. (c) Data about marks obtained in selection test is not given.
191. (c) The word must match with the statement given after "but".
192. (a) Since the workers are retired, the word has to be "older".
193. (d) They have experience but no skills.
194. (b)
195. (e) Since the word used is heavy, it has to be a burden.
196. (a) Match the word with burden.
197. (c) Social justice intead of perennial debates
198. (b) Instead of debates the policies should be implemented.
199. (d) Use a positive word in this blank.
200. (e) The only suitable word is "introduce".

MAHARASHTRA

CET

MOCK TEST - 1

☛ *INSTRUCTIONS :*

- **There are 200 questions in this test. You will be given 150 minutes to complete the test.**
- **Each question carries 1 mark. There is no negative marking.**

1. How many such pairs of letters are there in the word MEDICAL each of which has as many letters between them in the word as in the English alphabet?
(a) One (b) Two
(c) Three (d) None
(e) More than three

2. Four of the following five are alike in a certain way and so from a group. Which is the one that DOES NOT belong to that group?
(a) Green (b) Yellow
(c) Grey (d) Red
(e) Blue

3. If it is possible to form a three digit number which is the perfect square of a two-digit odd number with the third, the fifth and the eighth digits of the number 532784691, which of the following will be the second digit of that two-digit odd number? If more than one such number can be formed, give @ as the answer and if no such number can be formed, give © as the answer.
(a) 1 (b) 7
(c) 9 (d) @
(e) ©

4. In a certain code MISTAKEN is written as SRHLOFLB. How is GROUNDED written in that code?
(a) CDCMTNQF (b) TNQFCDCM
(c) EFEOTNQF (d) TNQFEFEO
(e) None of these

5. If 'tree' means 'mountain', 'mountain' means 'water', 'water' means 'jungle', 'jungle' means 'bus', 'bus' means 'truck'; and 'truck' means 'house'; then where do the fish live?
(a) Water (b) Jungle
(c) Mountain (d) Bus
(e) Truck

6. Pointing to a boy Neha said 'He is the son of my grandfather's only child'. How is Neha related to the boy?
(a) Sister (b) Cousin
(c) Aunt (d) Can not be determined
(e) None of these

7. Four of the following five are alike in a certain way and so from a group. Which is the one that DOES NOT belong to that group?
(a) Iron (b) Aluminium
(c) Copper (d) Steel
(e) Procelain

8. What should come next in the following letter sequence?
AABABCABCDABCDEABCDEFABCDEFGA BCDEFG
(a) A (b) I
(c) H (d) B
(e) None of these

DIRECTIONS (Qs. 9-10) : Complete the following series.

9. The next three terms of the series 121143165 are
(a) 789 (b) 246
(c) 187 (d) 209
(e) None of these

10. The next three terms of the series 814265098 are
(a) 386 (b) 194
(c) 943 (d) 650
(e) None of these

Space for Rough Work

DIRECTIONS (Qs. 11-12) : In each of these questions, various terms of a series are given with one term missing as shown by (?). Choose the missing term :

11. QPO, SRQ, UTS, WVU, (?)
    (a) XVZ (b) YXW
    (c) ZYA (d) VWX
    (e) None of these
12. 19, 2, 38, 3, 114, 4, (?)
    (a) 228 (b) 352
    (c) 256 (d) 456
    (e) None of these
13. There are two words to the left of the sign :: which are connected in some way. The same relationship obtains between the third word and one of the four alternatives under it. Find the correct alternative.
    Flying : Bird :: Creeping : ?
    (a) Aeroplane (b) Snail
    (c) Ground (d) Flower
    (e) None of these
14. A pair of words is given, followed by four pairs of words as alternatives. Choose the correct pair in which the words bears the same relationship to each other as the words of the given pair bear.
    Teeth : Chew ::
    (a) Mind : Think (b) Sweater : Heat
    (c) Food : Taste (d) Eyes : Flicker
    (e) None of these

DIRECTIONS (Qs. 15-16): In each of the following questions, four alternatives are given, out of which three are alike in a certain way while one is different. Choose the odd one.

15. (a) Jupiter (b) Saturn
    (c) Venus (d) Sun
    (e) None of these
16. (a) 80 – 9 (b) 64 – 8
    (c) 36 – 6 (d) 7 – 49
    (e) None of these

DIRECTIONS (Qs. 17-26): In each of the questions given below which one of the five answers figures should come after the problem figures, if the sequence were continued?

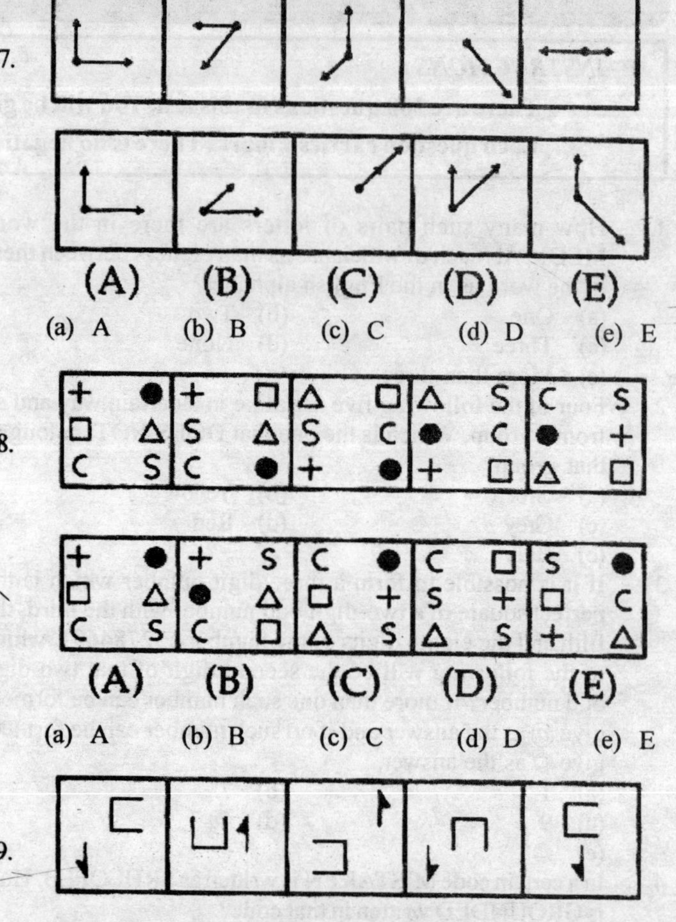

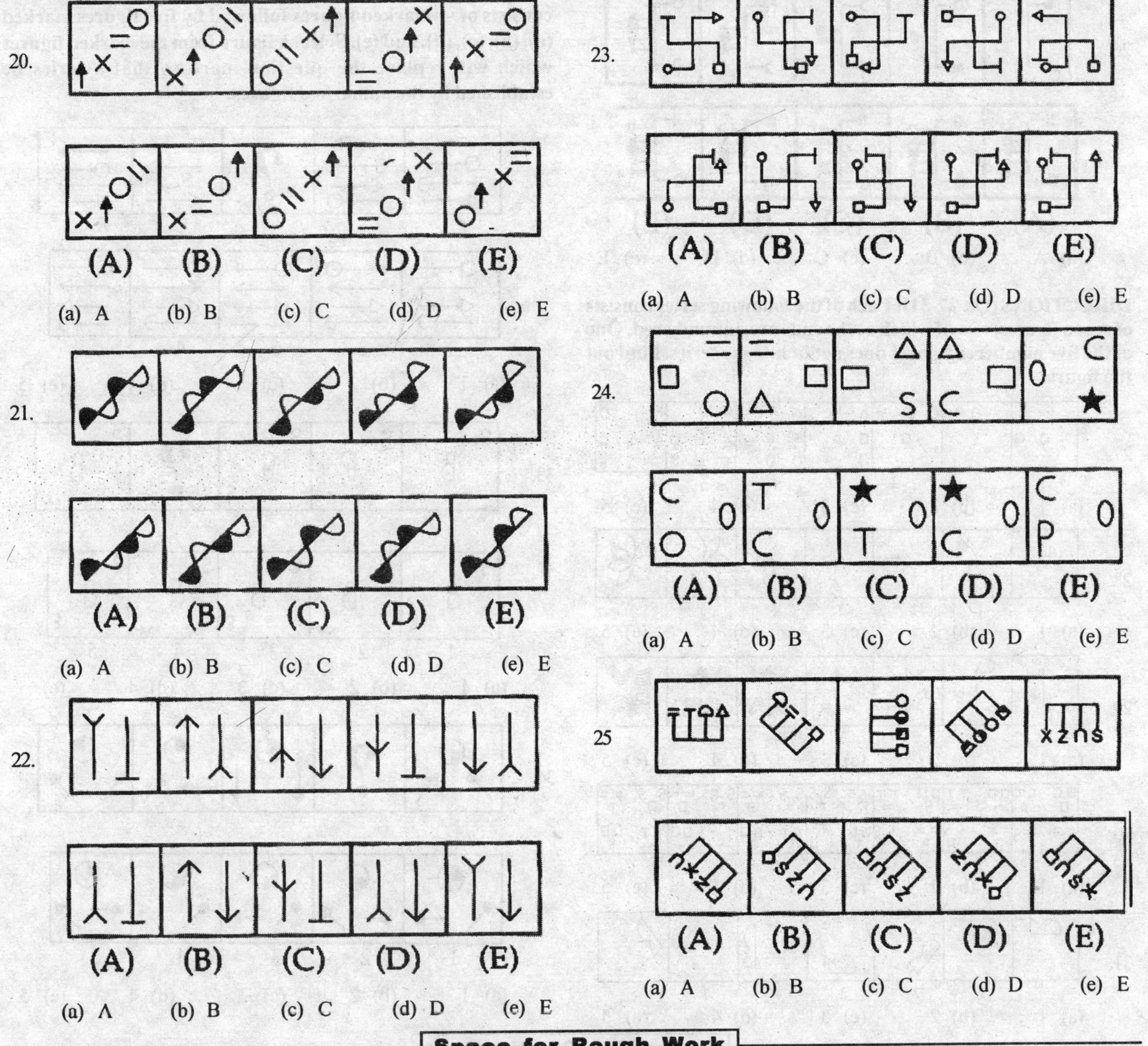

Space for Rough Work

26.

(A) (B) (C) (D) (E)

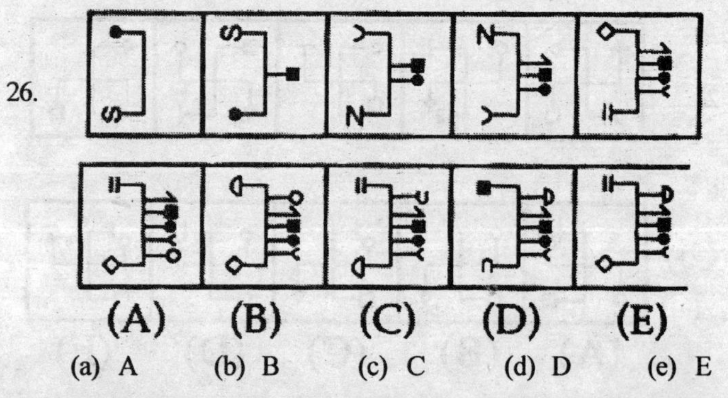

(a) A (b) B (c) C (d) D (e) E

DIRECTIONS (Qs. 27-31): Each of the following series consists of seven figures, two of which at the ends are unnumbered. One of the five numbered figures does not fit into the series. Find out the figure.

27.

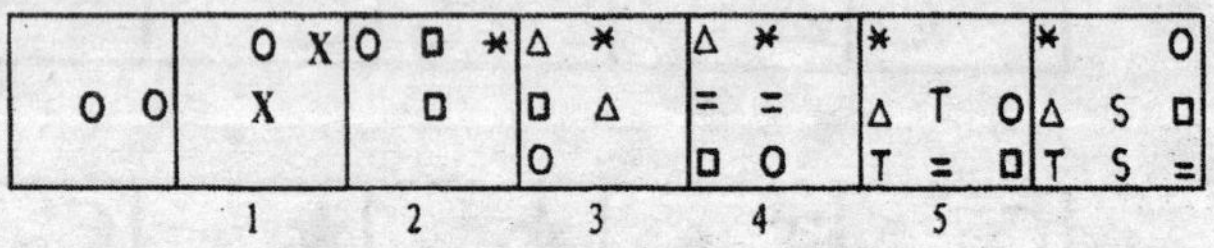

(a) 1 (b) 2 (c) 3 (d) 4 (e) 5

28.

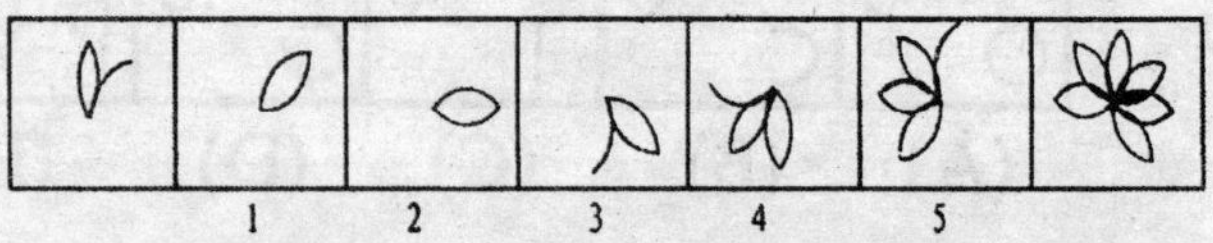

(a) 1 (b) 2 (c) 3 (d) 4 (e) 5

29.

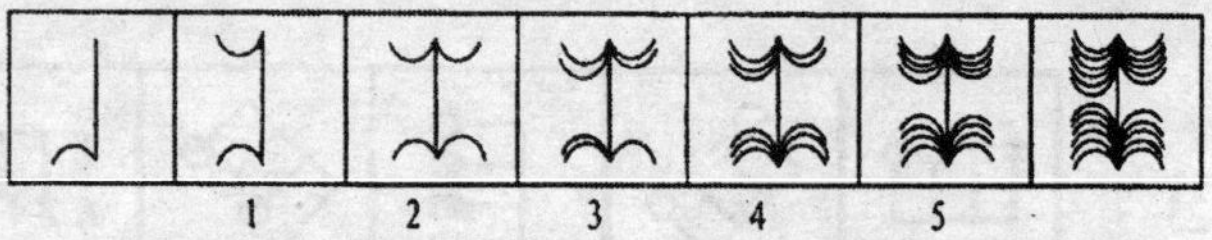

(a) 1 (b) 2 (c) 3 (d) 4 (e) 5

30.

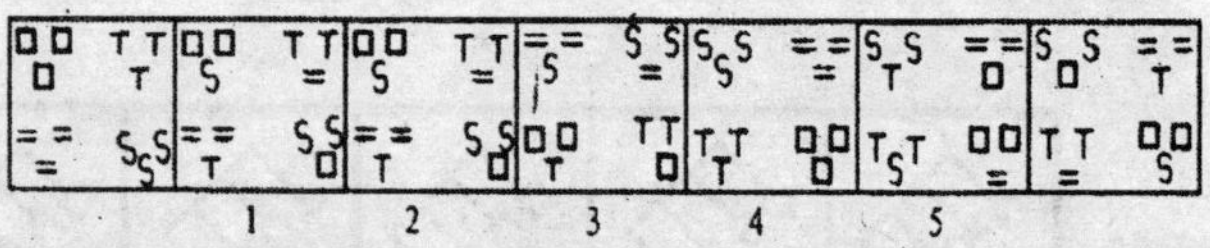

(a) 1 (b) 2 (c) 3 (d) 4 (e) 5

31.

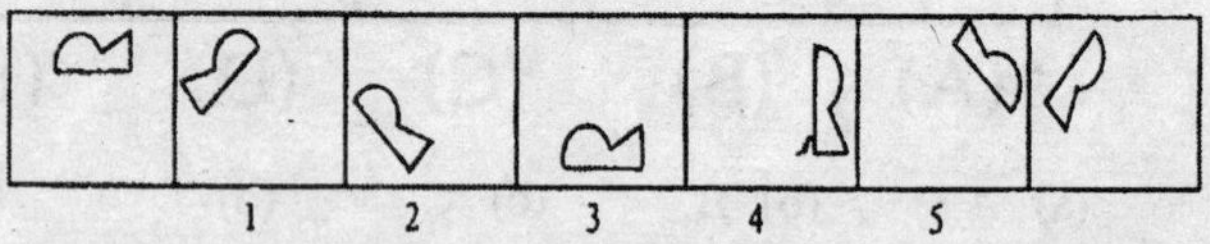

(a) 1 (b) 2 (c) 3 (d) 4 (e) 5

DIRECTIONS (Qs. 32-41): Each of the following questions consists of unmarked figures followed by five figures marked (a), (b), (c), (d), and (e). Select a figure from the marked figures which will replace the question mark so that a series be established by the unmarked figures.

32.

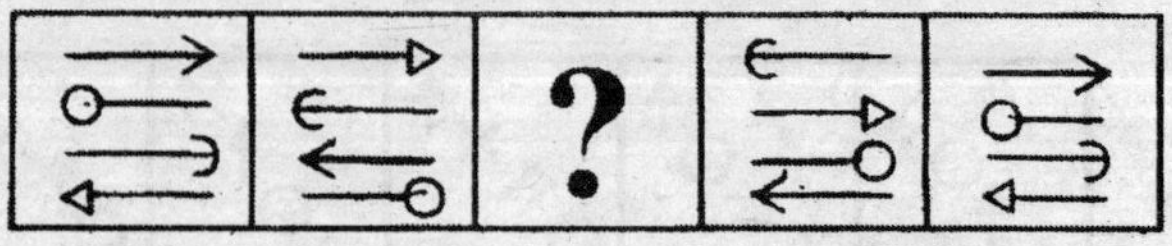

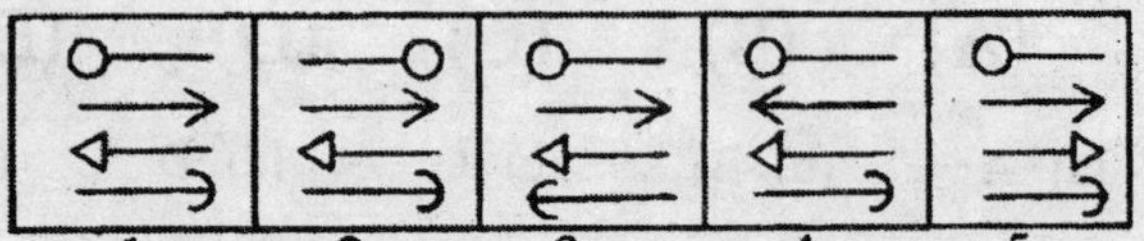

1 2 3 4 5

(a) 1 (b) 2 (c) 3 (d) 4 (e) 5

33.

1 2 3 4 5

(a) 1 (b) 2 (c) 3 (d) 4 (e) 5

34.

1 2 3 4 5

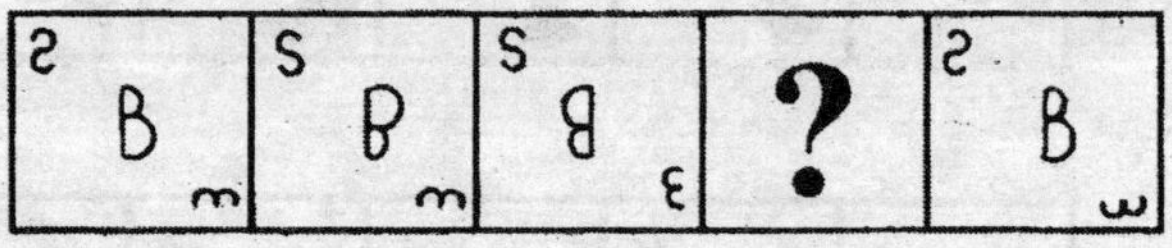

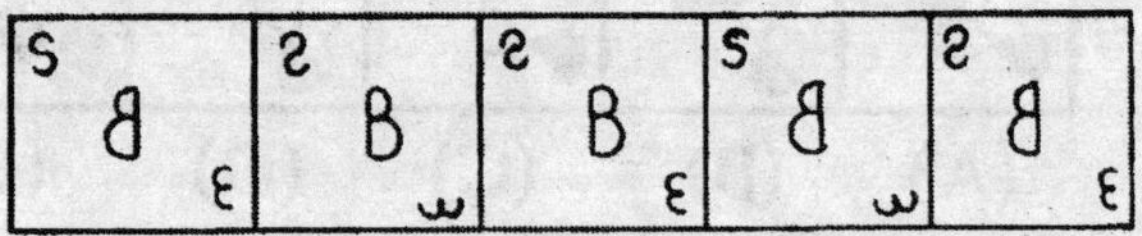

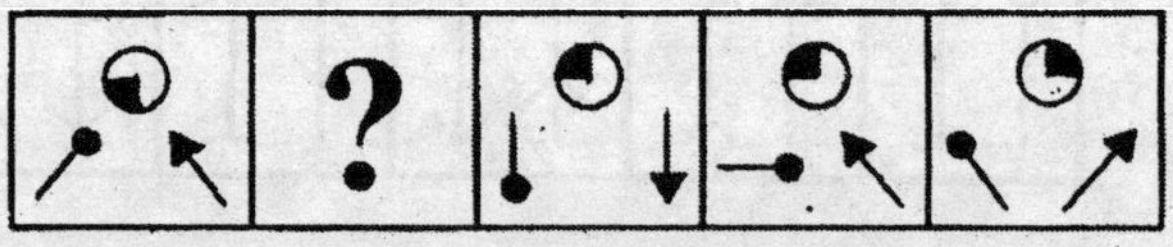

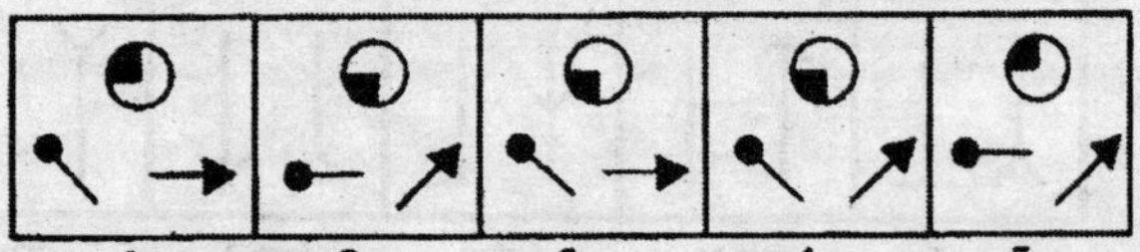

(a) 1 (b) 2 (c) 3 (d) 4 (e) 5

Space for Rough Work

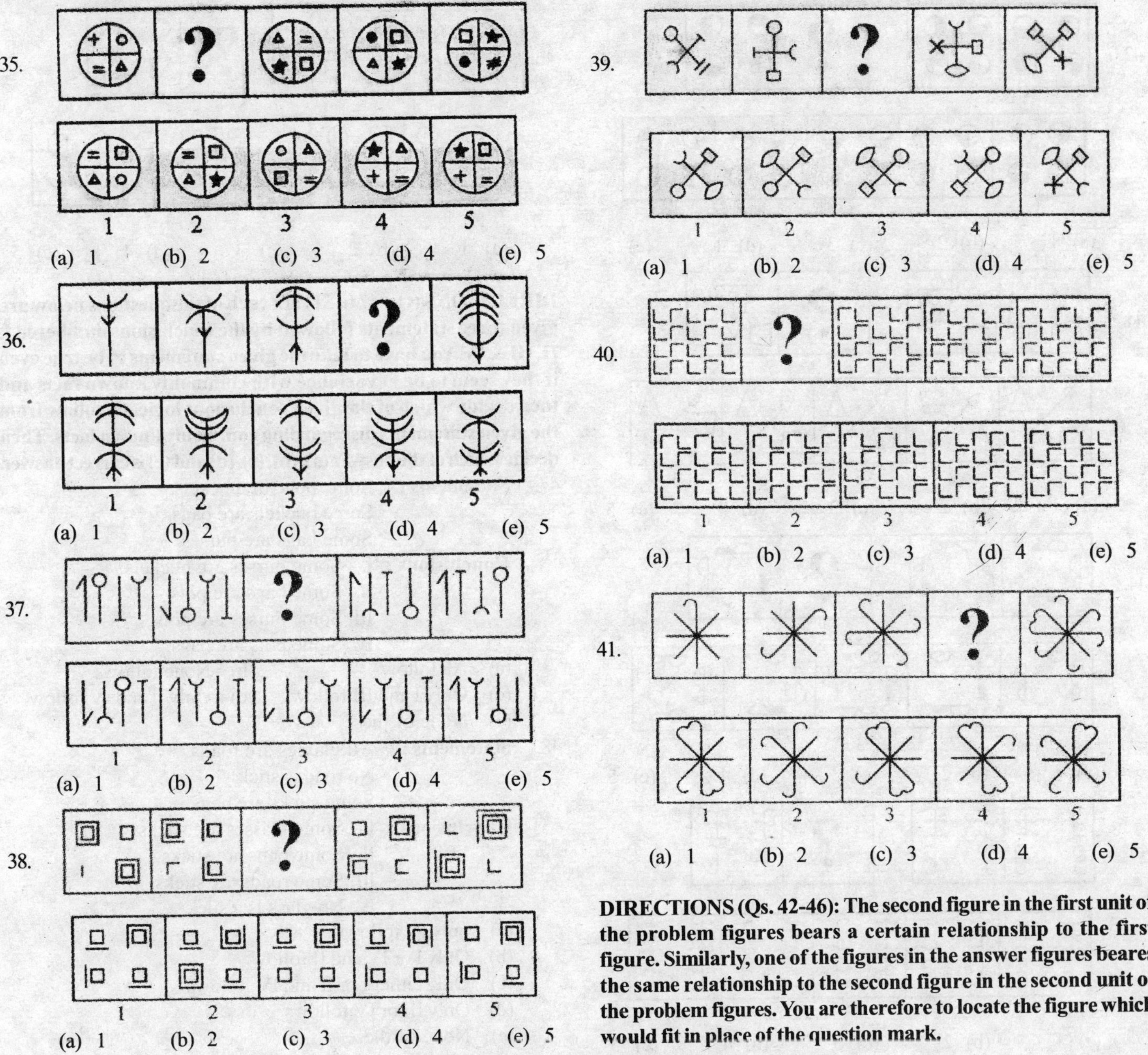

35. (a) 1 (b) 2 (c) 3 (d) 4 (e) 5

36. (a) 1 (b) 2 (c) 3 (d) 4 (e) 5

37. (a) 1 (b) 2 (c) 3 (d) 4 (e) 5

38. (a) 1 (b) 2 (c) 3 (d) 4 (e) 5

39. (a) 1 (b) 2 (c) 3 (d) 4 (e) 5

40. (a) 1 (b) 2 (c) 3 (d) 4 (e) 5

41. (a) 1 (b) 2 (c) 3 (d) 4 (e) 5

DIRECTIONS (Qs. 42-46): The second figure in the first unit of the problem figures bears a certain relationship to the first figure. Similarly, one of the figures in the answer figures beares the same relationship to the second figure in the second unit of the problem figures. You are therefore to locate the figure which would fit in place of the question mark.

Space for Rough Work

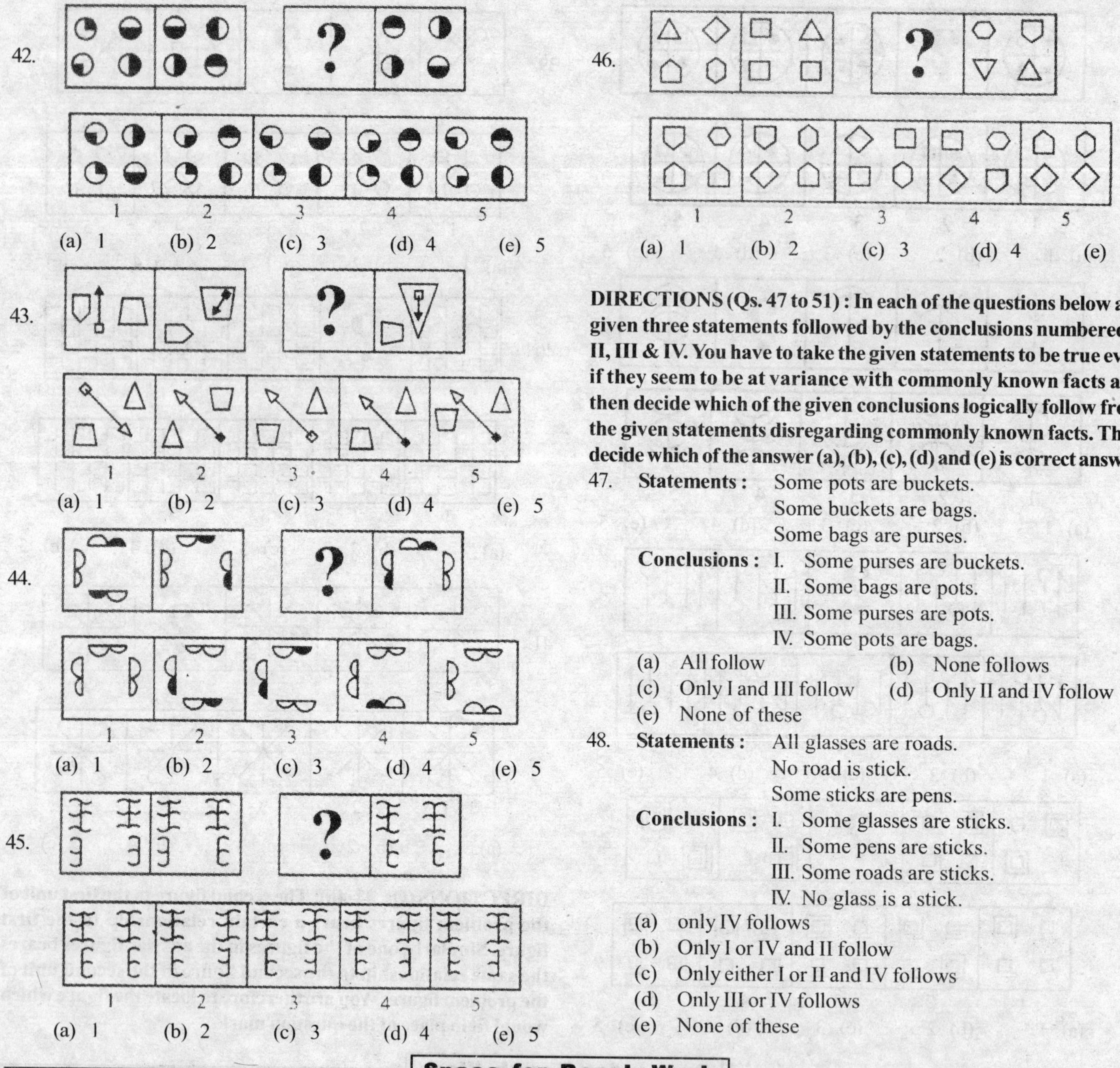

42.

(a) 1 (b) 2 (c) 3 (d) 4 (e) 5

43.

(a) 1 (b) 2 (c) 3 (d) 4 (e) 5

44.

(a) 1 (b) 2 (c) 3 (d) 4 (e) 5

45.

(a) 1 (b) 2 (c) 3 (d) 4 (e) 5

46.

(a) 1 (b) 2 (c) 3 (d) 4 (e) 5

DIRECTIONS (Qs. 47 to 51) : In each of the questions below are given three statements followed by the conclusions numbered I, II, III & IV. You have to take the given statements to be true even if they seem to be at variance with commonly known facts and then decide which of the given conclusions logically follow from the given statements disregarding commonly known facts. Then decide which of the answer (a), (b), (c), (d) and (e) is correct answer.

47. **Statements :** Some pots are buckets.
Some buckets are bags.
Some bags are purses.

Conclusions : I. Some purses are buckets.
II. Some bags are pots.
III. Some purses are pots.
IV. Some pots are bags.

(a) All follow (b) None follows
(c) Only I and III follow (d) Only II and IV follow
(e) None of these

48. **Statements :** All glasses are roads.
No road is stick.
Some sticks are pens.

Conclusions : I. Some glasses are sticks.
II. Some pens are sticks.
III. Some roads are sticks.
IV. No glass is a stick.

(a) only IV follows
(b) Only I or IV and II follow
(c) Only either I or II and IV follows
(d) Only III or IV follows
(e) None of these

Space for Rough Work

49. **Statements :** Some ice are ring.
No ring is paint.
Some rings are gold.
Conclusions : I. No gold is paint.
II. No ice is gold.
III. Some rings are paints.
IV. All golds are ring.
(a) None follows (b) Only I and III follow
(c) Only I and II follow (d) Only III and IV follow
(e) None of these

50. **Statements :** No candle is bell.
Some shoes are bells.
All tables are shoes.
Conclusions : I. Some tables are bells.
II. No table is bell.
III. Some shoes are candles.
IV. No flower is fruit.
(a) Only I and IV follow (b) Only I and II follow
(c) Only III and IV follow (d) None follows
(e) None of these

51. **Statements :** Some cats are rats.
Some rats are ants.
Some ants are flies.
Conclusions : I. Some flies are ants.
II. Some ants are not rats.
III. No rat is fly.
IV. No cat is fly.
(a) Only I and IV follow
(b) Only II follows
(c) Only I and II follow
(d) Only II and III follows
(e) None of these

DIRECTIONS (Qs. 52 - 54) : In the series of terms given in each of the questions below, identify the term which does not fit in the series.

52. 1 C V, 5 F U, 9 I T, 15 L S, 17 O R
(a) 9 JT (b) 13 LS
(c) 5 FU (d) 17 OR
(e) None of these

53. B 0 R, G 3 U, E 3 P, J 7 S, H 9 N
(a) E 3 P (b) H 9 A
(c) J 7 S (d) G 3 U
(e) None of these

54. G 4 T, J 10 R, M 20 P, P 43 N, S 90 L
(a) S 90 L (b) J 10 R
(c) M 20 P (d) P 43 N
(e) None of these

DIRECTIONS (Qs. 55 - 59) : In each of the following questions, a statement is given followed by two conclusions I and II. Give answer

(a) if ONLY conclusion I follows;
(b) if ONLY conclusion II follows;
(c) if EITHER I or II follows;
(d) if NEITHER I nor II follows;
(e) if BOTH I and II follow.

55. **Statement :** This book, 'Z' is the only book which focuses its attention on the problem of poverty in India between 1950 and 1980.
Conclusions : I. There was no question of poverty before 1950.
II. No other books deals with poverty in India during 1950 to 1980.

56. **Statement :** The Electricity Board of state X has given ultimatum to the farmers to either regularise their electric connection by the end of June 2000 or face the legal procedure.
Conclusions : I. The Electricity Board of state X has failed to provide regular connection to the farmers.
II. As the farmers of state X have small farms they don't need electricity for agriculture.

57. **Statement :** 'We follow some of the best and effective teaching learning practices used by leading institutes all over the world'. —A statement of professor of MN Institute.
Conclusions : I. The MN Institute is one of the leading institutes of the world.
II. Whatever is being followed by world's leading institutes will definitely be good and useful.

Space for Rough Work

58. **Statement :** In the absence of national health insurance or social security cover, a person with limited resources has to depend on government hospitals, which are crowded, overburdened and understaffed.

Conclusions : I. National health insurance is meant only for the affluent sections of society.

II. The government hospitals provide treatment on nominal charges or free.

59. **Statement :** We do not need today in India extraordinary specialists but those trained ordinary doctors who are dedicated to their profession.

Conclusions : I. We should promote medical profession with dedicated ordinary doctors rather than promoting high specialised medical education.

II. Extraordinary specialists are not dedicated to their profession.

DIRECTIONS (Qs. 60 - 64) : Study the following information carefully and answer the questions that follow :

Madhu and Shobha are good in Dramatics and Computer Science. Anjali and Madhu are good in Computer Science and Physics. Anjali, Poonam and Nisha are good in Physics and History. Nisha and Anjali are good in Physics and Mathematics. Poonam and Shobha are good in History and Dramatics.

60. Who is good in Computer Science, History and Dramatics?
(a) Anjali (b) Madhu
(c) Shobha (d) Nisha
(e) None of these

61. Who is good in Physics, Dramatics and Computer Science?
(a) Shobha (b) Poonam
(c) Madhu (d) Anjali
(e) None of these

62. Who is good in Physics, History and Dramatics?
(a) Poonam (b) Shobha
(c) Madhu (d) Anjali
(e) None of these

63. Who is good in History, Physics, Computer Science and Mathematics?
(a) Poonam (b) Nisha
(c) Madhu (d) Anjali
(e) None of these

64. Who is good in Physics, History and Mathematics but not in Computer Science?
(a) Madhu (b) Poonam
(c) Nisha (d) Anjali
(e) None of these

DIRECTIONS (Qs. 65-68) : Study the following information carefully and answer the questions that follow.

Six products U, V, W, X, Y and Z are to be placed in display windows of a shop. There are six display windows – numbered 1, 2, 3, 4, 5, 6 and one product is to be put in one window. Moreover, U cannot be immediately to the left or immediately to the right of V. W must be immediately to the left of X. Z cannot be in window number 6 :

65. Which of the following products cannot be placed in window no. 1 ?
(a) U (b) V
(c) W (d) X
(e) None of these

66. If X is placed in window no. 3, then W must be placed in which window ?
(a) 1 (b) 2
(c) 4 (d) 5
(e) None of these

67. If U is placed in window no. 5, then which of the following products must be placed in window no. 6 ?
(a) V (b) W
(c) X (d) Y
(e) None of these

68. Five boys took part in a race. Raj finished before Mohit but behind Gaurav. Ashish finished before Sanchit but behind Mohit. Who won the race ?
(a) Raj (b) Gaurav
(c) Mohit (d) Ashish
(e) None of these

Space for Rough Work

DIRECTIONS (Qs. 69-73) : Read the following information and then answer the questions that follow :

Group Captain Malhotra is choosing the last part of his crew for the spaceship COSMOS, with which he plans to land on the moon. He needs 4 more crew members of whom at least two must be pilots, the others being engineers. The pilots are to be selected from Dalbir, Eric and Farid and the engineers from Lal, Monty, Naveen and Paul. Eric will not crew with Lal and Dalbir and Paul will not crew with Naveen.

69. If Naveen is chosen, which of the following must be other members of the crew?
(a) Farid, Lal and Monty
(b) Dalbir, Eric and Monty
(c) Eric, Farid and Monty
(d) Eric, Farid and Paul
(e) None of these

70. If Paul is chosen, which candidates will not be chosen to be on the crew ?
(a) Dalbir, Eric and Monty
(b) Dalbir, Eric and Farid
(c) Dalbir, Farid and Lal
(d) Eric, Farid and Lal
(e) None of these

71. Given the above statements about the relationships among the potential crew members, which of the following must be true?
(I) If Dalbir is rejected, then Monty must be chosen.
(II) If Dalbir is rejected, then Farid must be chosen.
(III) If Dalbir is chosen, then Paul must also be chosen.
(a) (II) only (b) (III) only
(c) (I) and (II) only (d) (I) and (III) only

72. If Lal is chosen as an engineer, which of the following could be the other members of the crew?
(I) Dalbir, Farid and Monty
(II) Dalbir, Farid and Naveen
(II) Dalbir, Farid and Paul
(a) (I) only (b) (II) only
(c) (III) only (d) (I) and (III) only
(e) None of these

73. Which of the following statements must be true?
(I) If Group Captain Malhotra chooses Lal, then Farid also must be chosen.
(II) If Group Captain Malhotra chooses Monty, then Naveen must also be chosen.
(III) Lal and Naveen never crew together.
(a) (I) only (b) (I) and (II) only
(c) (I) and (III) only (d) (II) and (III) only
(e) None of these

DIRECTIONS (Qs. 74 - 79) : Read the following information and answer the questions that follow :

In a certain code language, 481 means Sky is blue. 246 means Sea is deep and 698 means Sea looks blue.

74. What number is the code for 'sky' ?
(a) 4 (b) 8
(c) 1 (d) None of these
(e) 6

75. What number is the code for 'is' ?
(a) 8 (b) 1
(c) 4 (d) 2
(e) None of these

76. What number is the code for 'looks' ?
(a) 4 (b) 8
(c) 6 (d) 9
(e) None of these

77. What number is the code for 'sea' ?
(a) 2 (b) 8
(c) 6 (d) 4
(e) None of these

78. What number is the code for 'blue' ?
(a) 8 (b) 6
(c) 1 (d) 9
(e) None of these

79. What number is the code for 'deep' ?
(a) 4 (b) 2
(c) 6 (d) 1
(e) None of these

Space for Rough Work

DIRECTIONS (Qs. 80-84): Below is given passage followed by several possible inferences which can be drawn from the facts stated in the passage. You have to examine each inference separately in the context of the passage and decide upon its degree of truth or falsity. Mark answer

(a) if the inference is "definitely true" i.e. it properly follows from the statement of fact given;
(b) if the inference is "probably true" though not "definitely true" in the light of other fact given;
(c) if the data are inadequate i.e. from the facts given you cannot say whether the inference is likely to be true or false;
(d) if the inference is "probably false" i.e. though not "defiantly false" in the light of the fact given;
(e) if the inference is "definitely false" i.e. it cannot possibly be drawn from the facts given or it contradicts the given facts.

Construction industry in India has always enjoyed a special position. We have proved that India is in tune with the times and has not left any stone untouched to compete against the best in international market. Yet, it is the time when other powers are paying attention to developing this sector internationally status. Foundation of an economy lies on its infrastructure. Construction industry has to play a vital role in power, port, road, house construction, railways and industry. Labour-intensive Indian construction industry has to pass through acute changes although it is a bit late. It has to face challenges like advanced designing, odd decision and a growth of demand of work in time, greater mechanisation and intensive construction prevalent in developed countries. The emphasis, is laid on modern techniques adopted in construction and high quality in less time.

80. Indian companies can put their gain to maximum by adopting modern equipment and by reducing the time of project.
81. The policy-makers of India have failed to understand the importance of construction industry.
82. The Indian construction companies have to establish themselves in international market.
83. Construction industry in India has been labour- oriented for years.
84. The construction industry of developed nations of better quality compared to India.

DIRECTIONS (Qs. 85-87) : In each of following questions, a statement is given followed by two assumptions numbered I and II. Consider the statement and the following assumptions and decide which of the assumptions is implicit. Give answer :

(a) if ONLY assumption I is implicit;
(b) if ONLY assumption II is implicit;
(c) if EITHER I or II is implicit;
(d) if NEITHER I nor II is implicit;
(e) if BOTH I and II are implicit.

85. **Statement :** In case of any difficulty about this case, you may contact our company's lawyer.
Assumptions : I. Each company has a lawyer of its own.
II. The company's lawyer is thoroughly briefed about this case.

86. **Statement :** "The programme will start at 6 p.m. but you can come there upto 7 p.m. or so and still there is no problem."
Assumptions : I. The programme will continue even after 7 p.m.
II. The programme may not even start by that time.

87. **Statement :** Health is the foundation of well-being, virtue, prosperity, wealth, happiness and salvation.
Assumptions : I. Happiness results in health and well-being.
II. People desire to be happy, prosperous and virtuous.

88. If CIGARETTE is coded as GICERAETT, then DIRECTION will be coded as :
(a) IRDCTIONE (b) NOIETCRID
(c) RIDTCENOI (d) NORTECDII
(e) None of these

89. If × means +, ÷ means – , – means × and + means ÷, then $8 \times 7 - 8 + 40 \div 2 = ?$
(a) 1 (b) $7\frac{2}{5}$
(c) $8\frac{3}{5}$ (d) 44
(e) None of these

Space for Rough Work

90. Anuj started walking positioning his back towards the sun. After sometime, he turned left, then turned right and then towards the left again. In which direction is he going now?
(a) North or South (b) East or West
(c) North or West (d) South or West
(e) None of these

DIRECTIONS (Qs. 91 & 92) : What number will replace the question mark (?) in the questions below ?

91. 1 2 3 2 10 12
2 5 12 10 16 13
1 2 1 ? 10 24
(a) 5 (b) 11
(c) 13 (d) 8
(e) None of these

92. 3 8 10 2 ? 1
6 56 90 2 20 0
(a) 0 (b) 3
(c) 5 (d) 7
(e) None of these

DIRECTIONS (Qs. 93 - 97) : In each of the following questions, a statement is given followed by two courses of action numbered I and II. Decide which of the cources of action logically follow and give answer

(a) if **ONLY** I follows
(b) if **ONLY** II follows
(c) if **EITHER** I or II follows
(d) if **NEITHER** I nor II follows
(e) if **BOTH** I and II follow

93. **Statement :** The company 'X' has decided to give 10% increase in salary to its employees from next month.
Courses of action : I. The accounts department will have to prepare new salary statement for all employees before due date.
II. Employees' association should ask for more rise in the salary considering the market condition.

94. **Statement :** The meteorological department has predicated good monsoon this year for the tenth consecutive year and this will result in good crop yield.
Courses of action : I. The Government should off-load the stores before harvesting.
II. The Government should provide chemical fertilisers to farmers immediately.

95. **Statement :** Most of the development plans develop in papers only.
Courses of action : I. The incharges should be instructed to supervise the field-work regularly.
II. The supply of paper to such departments should be cut short.

96. **Statement :** The cinema halls are incurring heavy loss these days as people prefer to watch movies in home on TV than to visit cinema halls.
Courses of action : I. The Cinema halls should be demolished and residential multistorey buildings should be constructed there.
II. The cinema halls should be converted into shopping malls.

97. **Statement :** The alert villagers collectively caught a group of dreaded dacoits armed with murderous weapons.
Courses of action : I. The villagers should be provided sophisticated weapons.
II. The villagers should be rewarded for their courage and unity.

DIRECTIONS (Qs. 98-103) : These questions are based on the following information.

During one week, a human resource director conducts five interviews for a new job, one interview per day, Monday through Friday. There are six candidates for the job- Ram, Shyam, Trilochan, Usha, Veena, and Kishore. No more than two candidates are interviewed more than once. Neither Shyam nor Usha nor Veena is interviewed more than once,

Space for Rough Work

and no other candidate is interviewed more than twice. The schedule of interviews is subject to the following conditions:

- If Trilochan is interviewed, then Trilochan must be interviewed on both Monday and Friday.
- If Shyam is interviewed, then Usha is also interviewed, with Shyam's interview taking place earlier than Usha's interview.
- If Ram is interviewed twice, then Ram's second interview takes place exactly two days after Ram's first interview.
- If Veena's is interviewed, then Kishore is interviewed twice, with Veena's interview taking place after Kishore's first interview and before Kishore's second interview.
- If Usha is interviewed then Ram is also interviewed, with Usha's interview taking place on a day either immediately before or immediately after a day on which Ram is interviewed.

98. Which of the following could be a complete and accurate list of candidates the human resources director interviews and the days on which those interviews take place ?
(a) Monday : Shyam; Tuesday : Usha; Wednesday : Ram; Thursday : Kishore; Friday : Ram;
(b) Monday : Shyam; Tuesday : Kishore; Wednesday : Ram; Thursday : Kishore; Friday : Usha
(c) Monday : Trilochan; Tuesday : Ram; Wednesday : Shyam; Thursday : Ram; Friday : Trilochan;
(d) Monday : Trilochan; Tuesday : Ram; Wednesday : Kishore; Thursday : Veena; Friday : Trilochan;
(e) None of these

99. If Veena is interviewed on Tuesday, then which one of the following MUST BE true ?
(a) Trilochan is interviewed on Friday
(b) Usha is not interviewed on Thursday
(c) Ram is not interviewed
(d) Shyam is not interviewed.
(e) None of these

100. If Kishore is not interviewed, then which one of the following MUST BE true ?
(a) Ram is interviewed on Thursday
(b) Shyam is interviewed on Tuesday
(c) Trilochan is interviewed on Monday
(d) Usha is interviewed on Wednesday.
(e) None of these

101. If Shyam is interviewed, then which one of the following could be true ?
(a) Kishore is interviewed on both Tuesday and Wednesday
(b) Usha is interviewed on Monday
(c) Veena is interviewed on Tuesday
(d) Shyam is interviewed on Thursday
(e) None of these

102. If neither Usha nor Trilochan is interviewed, then each of the following MUST BE true EXCEPT :
(a) Ram is interviewed on Monday.
(b) Ram is interviewed on Thursday
(c) Veena is interviewed on Tuesday
(d) Kishore is interviewed on Wednesday
(e) None of these

103. If both Usha and Veena are interviewed, then which one of the following is a complete and accurate list of the days on which Kishore could be interviewed ?
(a) Monday, Friday
(b) Tuesday, Thursday
(c) Monday, Wednesday, Friday
(d) Tuesday, Wednesday, Thursday
(e) None of these

104. An electric wire is sold only in multiples of 1 metre, and a customer required several lengths of wire, each 85cm long. To avoid any wastage and to minimise labour, he should purchase minimum lengths of
(a) 8.5 metres (b) 17 metres
(c) 1.7 metres (d) 1 metre
(e) None of these

105. The captain of a cricket team of 11 players is 25 years old and the wicket-keeper is 3 years older. If the age of these two players are replaced by that of another two players, the average of the cricket team drops by 2 years. Find the average age of these two players.
(a) 15 years (b) 15.5 years
(c) 17 years (d) 16.5 years
(e) None of these

Space for Rough Work

DIRECTIONS (Qs. 106- 110): In the following questions two equations numbered I and II are given. You have to solve both the equations and give answer

(a) if $p > q$ (b) if $p \geq q$
(c) if $p < q$ (d) if $p \leq q$
(e) if $p = q$ or the relationship between p and q can not be established.

106. I. $p^2 = 23409$
II. $q = \sqrt{23409}$

107. I. $4p + 3q = 19$
II. $5p + 5q = 27$

108. I. $14p^2 + 51p + 7 = 0$
II. $18q^2 - 79q = 9$

109. I. $11p^2 + 27p + 10 = 0$
II. $12q^2 - 19q = 10$

110. I. $p = |q|$
II. $q^2 = 256$

DIRECTIONS (Qs.111 - 113) : These questions are based on the figure given below.

Mid-year Prices of Essential Commodities

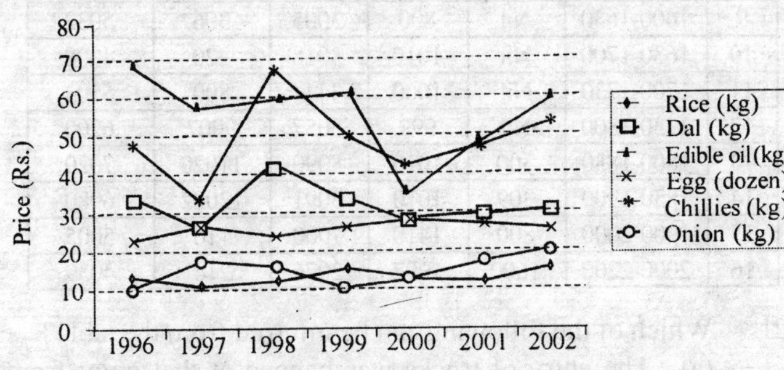

111. During 1996-2002, the number of commodities that exhibited a net overall increase and a net overall decrease, respectively, were
(a) 3 and 3 (b) 2 and 4
(c) 4 and 2 (d) 5 and 1
(e) None of these

112. The number of commodities that experienced a price decline for two or more consecutive years is
(a) 2 (b) 3
(c) 4 (d) 5
(e) None of these

113. For which commodities did a price increase immediately follow a price decline only once in this period?
(a) Rice, Edible oil & Dal (b) Egg and Dal
(c) Onion only (d) Egg and Onion
(e) None of these

DIRECTIONS (Qs.114-118) : Study the following graphs carefully & answer the questions given below.

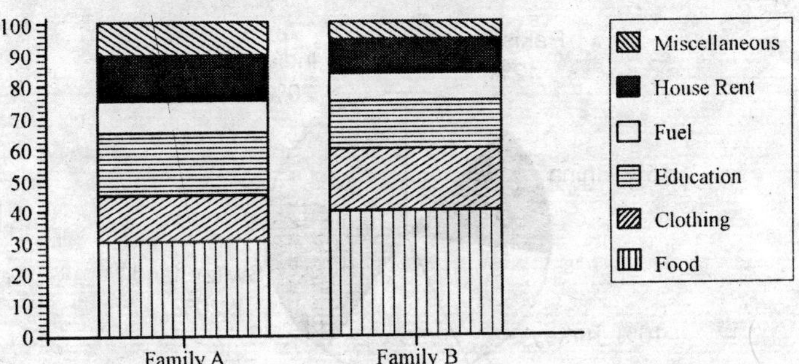

114. What fraction of the total expenditure is spent on education in family A?
(a) $\frac{13}{21}$ (b) $\frac{2}{3}$
(c) $\frac{9}{13}$ (d) $\frac{1}{5}$
(e) None of these

115. If the total expenditure on family B is Rs 10000, then money spent on clothes by this family during the year is
(a) Rs 200 (b) Rs 600
(c) Rs 2000 (d) Rs 6000
(e) None of these

116. If the total annual expenditure of family A is Rs 30000, the money spent on food, clothes and house rent is
(a) Rs 18500 (b) Rs 18000
(c) Rs 21000 (d) Rs 15000
(e) None of these

Space for Rough Work

117. If both the families have the same expenditure, which one spends more on education and miscellaneous together?
(a) A (b) B
(c) Both spends equal amount
(d) Data inadequate (e) None of these

118. What percentage is B's expenditure on food over A's expenditure on food, taking equal total expenditure?
(a) 10% (b) 70%
(c) 133.33% (d) 75%
(e) None of these

DIRECTIONS (Qs. 119-120) : Refer to the pie-charts given below and answer the questions that follow :

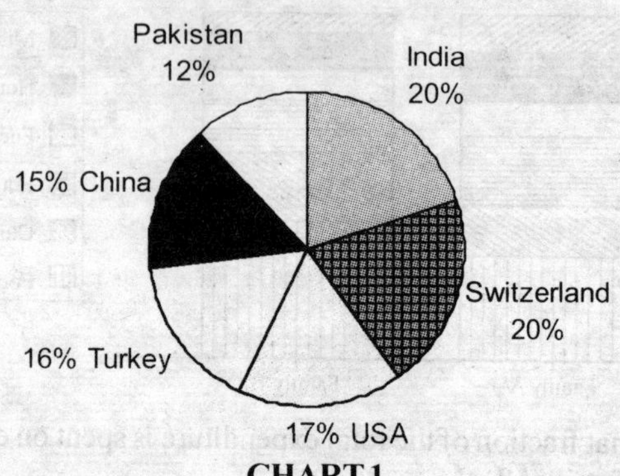

CHART 1

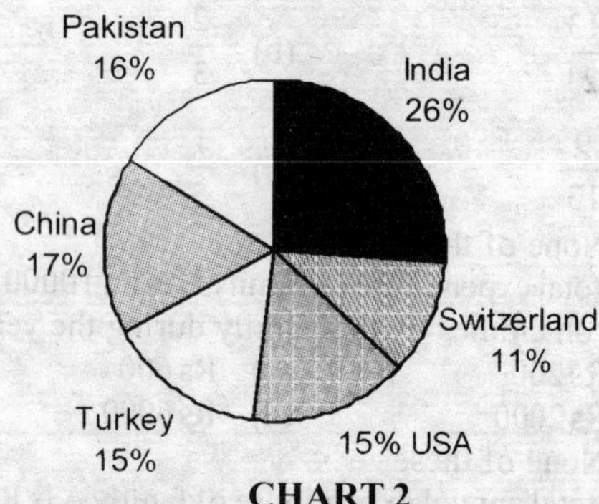

CHART 2

Chart 1 shows the distribution by value of top 6 suppliers of MFA Textiles in 1995. Chart 2 shows the distribution by quantity of top 6 suppliers of MFA Textiles in 1995. The total value is 5760 million Euro (European currency). The total quantity is 1.055 million tonnes.

119. The country, which has the highest average price, is
(a) USA (b) Switzerland
(c) Turkey (d) India
(e) None of these

120. The average price in Euro/kg for Turkey is roughly
(a) 6.20 (b) 5.60
(c) 4.20 (d) 4.80
(e) None of these

DIRECTIONS (Qs. 121-125) : Study the following table to answer the given questions.

Number of vehicles passing through a point of a city at different time slots on a particular day

Slot No.	Time slot	Trucks	Buses	Cars	Two-wheeler	Auto-Rickshaw
1	0600-0800	1008	2001	570	209	5055
2	0800-0900	706	1500	800	605	5000
3	0900-0930	200	1000	5000	15000	6329
4	0930-1000	202	1208	6000	12000	7001
5	1000-1100	Nil	1510	15050	8000	5000
6	1100-1300	Nil	2200	3000	200	4850
7	1300-1500	Nil	2250	3047	175	4900
8	1500-1600	Nil	1200	6899	220	5000
9	1600-1630	Nil	800	3005	306	5032
10	1630-1700	Nil	1010	3018	220	4908
11	1700-1730	Nil	1000	4444	800	5503
12	1730-1800	Nil	999	5057	9007	6200
13	1800-1830	300	1010	8090	11020	7020
14	1830-1900	309	1010	5091	12002	6980
15	1900-2000	800	1410	7000	110	5005
16	2000-2200	1600	1907	2076	214	4039

121. Which of the following can be inferred from the table?
(a) The entry of trucks was banned at that point from 1000-1800.
(b) More people travel by public transport.
(c) The city has more number of two-wheelers than cars.
(d) It is difficult to collect data for equal duration of time slots.
(e) None of these

Space for Rough Work

122. Of the given vehicles, how many passed through the point from 0800-0830?
(a) 8611 (b) 4305
(c) 1722
(d) Can not be determined
(e) None of these

123. During which of the following one-hour time periods did maximum number of buses pass through the point?
(a) 0800-0900 (b) 0900-1000
(c) 0600-0700 (d) 1800-1900
(e) None of these

124. Of the 16 slots given, for which slot number did the maximum number of given vehicles pass through the point?
(a) 13 (b) 14
(c) 3 (d) 5
(e) None of these

125. During 1000-1100, the average number of persons on a bus, car, two-wheeler and auto-rickshaw was 60, 2.5, 1.5 and 2 respectively. How many persons approximately did pass through the point these four vehicles during 1000-1100?
(a) 1,18,240 (b) 1,50,225
(c) 37,564 (d) 1,65,000
(e) None of these

DIRECTIONS (Qs. 126-130) : Study the pie-chart carefully to answer the following questions.

Percentage of students studying different specialisations in a management institute

Total number of students = 4500

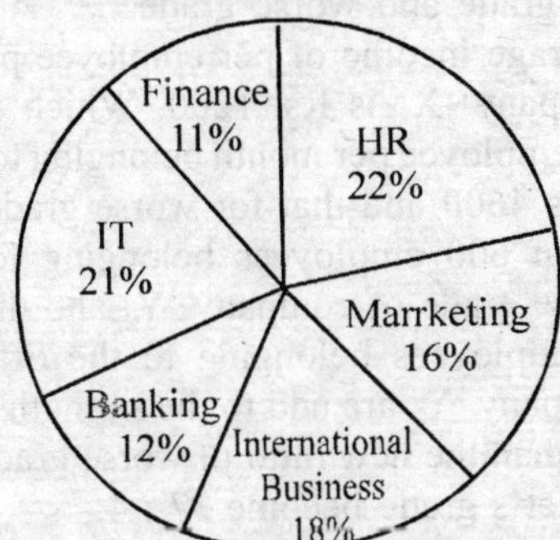

Ratio of men to women in each specialisation

Specialisation	Men	Women
HR	2	3
Marketing	7	5
International Business	5	1
Banking	17	10
IT	1	2
Finance	5	4

126. What is the total number of men studying in the institute?
(a) 1665 (b) 2421
(c) 2025 (d) 1954
(e) None of these

127. The number of women studying Marketing is approximately what per cent of the total number of students in the institute?
(a) 5 (b) 12
(c) 15 (d) 7
(e) None of these

128. What is the total number of men studying Banking and International Business?
(a) 1125 (b) 297
(c) 1015 (d) 594
(e) None of these

129. The number of women studying Finance is what per cent of the number of men studying the same?
(a) 80 (b) 65
(c) 95 (d) 70
(e) None of these

130. In which specialisation do the maximum number of women study?
(a) HR (b) IT
(c) Marketing (d) Finance
(e) None of these

Space for Rough Work

DIRECTIONS (Qs. 131-135) : Each of the questions below consists of a question and two statements numbered (I) and (II) given below it. You have to decide whether the data provided in the statements are sufficient to answer the question. Read both the statements and give answer

(a) if Statement (I) ALONE is sufficient, but statement (II) ALONE is not sufficient;
(b) if Statement (II) ALONE is sufficient, but statement (I) ALONE is not sufficient;
(c) if BOTH statements TOGETHER are sufficient;
(d) if BOTH statements TOGETHER are insufficient;
(e) Statement (I) ALONE or statement (II) ALONE is sufficient.

131. A train crosses another train running in the opposite direction in x seconds. What is the speed of the train?
I. Both the trains have the same length and are running at the same speed.
II. One train crosses a pole in 5 seconds.

132. 50% of the people in a Steeltown have blue eyes and blond hair. What per cent of the people in Steeltown have blue eyes but do not have blond hair?
I. 70% of the people in Steeltown have blond hair.
II. 60% of the people in Steeltown have blue eyes.

133. What is the area of 1 metre wide pathway constructed around all the sides of a rectangular field?
I. Area of the field and the path together is 187 sq. cm.
II. Breadth and the length of the field are in the ratio of 3 : 5 respectively.

134. What was the total compound interest on a sum after three years?
I. The interest after one year was Rs 100 and the sum was Rs 1000.
II. The difference between simple and compound interest on a sum of Rs 1000 at the end of two years was Rs 10.

135. What is the present age of the Mother?
I. Father's age is eight years more than the Mother's age. Father got married at the age of 28 years.
II. Present age of the Father is 30 years. Four years back the ratio of Mother's age to Father's age was 12 : 13.

136. Out of the four teams A, B, C and D which team is not likely to win as per the opinion poll?
I. As per the opinion poll, chances of team C's winning are more than that of team A but not as much as that of team B, whose chances of winning are more than that of team A.
II. As per the opinion poll team C's chances of winning are less than that of team B but not less than that of team D, whose chances of winning are more than that of team A.

137. How many employees of bank 'X' opted for VRS?
I. 18% of the 950 officer cadre employees and 6% of the 1100 of all other cadre employees opted for VRS.
II. 28% of the employees in the age group of 51 to 56 and 17% of the employees in all other age groups opted for VRS.

138. The area of a playground is 1600 square metres. What is its perimeter?
I. It is a perfect square playground
II. It costs Rs 3200 to put a fence around the playground at the rate of Rs 20 per metre.

139. Who among P, Q, R, S, T and U teaches Biology? Each person teaches one subject amongst English, Hindi, Biology, History, Geography and Sanskrit.
I. P and U do not teach Hindi, Biology, History or Geography. Q and S do not teach Biology or Geography. T does not teaches Geography.
II. P and U teach English and Sanskrit but not necessarily respectively. Similarly, Q and S teach either Hindi or History.

140. What is the total number of employees in the company 'X' ? There are only two categories of employees, i.e. officer's grade and worse grade.
I. Average income of per employee per month in the company 'X' is Rs. 1200. Which average income per employee per month belonging to officer's grade is Rs 4600 and that for worse grade is Rs. 1100.
II. When 600 employees belonging for the category worse grade of company 'Y' and the same number of employees belonging to the officer's grade of company 'Y' are add to the strength of the company 'X' than the new ratio of worse grade employees to officer's grade become 37 : 4.

Space for Rough Work

141. What is the value of m – n ÷ 37?
    I. m is the largest possible six-digit number and n is the smallest possible six-digit number.
    II. The diffierence between m and n is known.

142. There are 450 boxes to load on a truck. A and B working independently but at the same time take 30 minutes to load the truck. How long should it take B working by himself to load the truck?
    I. A loads twice as many boxes as B.
    II. A would take 45 minutes by himself.

143. P and Q worked together for 5 days. Then Q left the work and the work was finished by P alone in 8 days. How many days would Q alone take to finish the work if P had left?
    I. P and Q together can do the work in 10 days.
    II. P alone can do the work in 16 days.

144. A, B and C are positive integers. Is their product an even number?
    I. A is an even number.
    II. The product of A and B is an even number and that of A and C is also an even number.

145. By selling a product for Rs. 100 how much profit was earned?
    I. 20% profit would have been earned if it had been sold for Rs. 90.
    II. The profit was one–third of the purchase price.

DIRECTIONS (Qs. 146-150) : These questions are based on the table & information given below.

The amount of money invested (in rupees crore) in the core infrastructure areas of two districts, Chittoor and Khammam, in Andhra Pradesh, is as follows :

Chittoor District			Khammam District		
Core Area	**1995**	**1996**	**Core Area**	**1995**	**1996**
Electricity	815.2	1054.2	Electricity	2065.8	2365.1
Chemical	389.5	476.7	Chemical	745.3	986.4
Thermal	632.4	565.9	Thermal	1232.7	1026.3
Solar	468.1	589.6	Solar	1363.5	1792.1
Nuclear	617.9	803.1	Nuclear	1674.3	2182.1
Total	**2923.1**	**3489.5**	**Total**	**7081.6**	**8352**

146. By what percent was the total investment in the two districts more in 1996 as compared to that in 1995?
    (a) 14% (b) 21%
    (c) 24% (d) 18%
    (e) None of these

147. Approximately how many times the total investment in Chittoor was the total investment in Khammam?
    (a) 2.8 (b) 2.0
    (c) 2.4 (d) 1.7
    (e) None of these

148. The investment in Electricity and Thermal Energy in 1995 in these two districts formed what percent of the total investment made in that year?
    (a) 41% (b) 47%
    (c) 52% (d) 55%
    (e) None of these

149. In Khammam district, the investment in which area in 1996 showed the least percent increase over the investment in that area in 1995?
    (a) Electricity (b) Chemical
    (c) Solar (d) Nuclear
    (e) None of these

150. If the total investment in Khammam shows the same rate of increase in 1997, as it had shown form 1995 to 1996, what approximately would be the total investment in Khammam in 1997 (in Rs. crore?)
    (a) 9,850 (b) 10,020
    (c) 9,170 (d) 8,540
    (e) None of these

DIRECTIONS (Qs.151-155): In each of these questions, in the given sentences, a part of the sentence is underlined. Beneath each sentence, four different ways of phrasing the underlined part are indicated. Choose the best alternative.

151. Expect for you and I, everyone brought a present to the party.
    (a) With the exception of you and I, everyone brought
    (b) Except for you and I, everyone had brought
    (c) Except for you and me, everyone brought
    (d) Except for you and me, everyone had brought
    (e) None of these

152. Although I calculate that he will be here any minute, I cannot wait much longer for him.
    (a) Although I reckon that he will be here
    (b) Although I think that he will be here
    (c) Because I am confidant that he will be here
    (d) Because I calculate that he will be here
    (e) None of these

153. We want the teacher to be him who has the best rapport with the students.
   (a) We want the teacher to be he
   (b) We want him to be the teacher
   (c) We desire the teacher to be him
   (d) We anticipate the teacher to be him
   (e) None of these

154. Today this is a totally different world than we have seen in the last decade.
   (a) than what we seen
   (b) then we have seen
   (c) from what we seen
   (d) from what we have seen
   (e) None of these

155. Although he was the most friendly of all present and different from the others, he hadn't hardly any friends except me.
   (a) different from the others, he hardly had any friends except I
   (b) different than the others, he hardly had any friends except me
   (c) different than the others, he hardly had any friends except I
   (d) different from the others, he hardly had any friends except me
   (e) None of these

DIRECTIONS (Qs. 156-160): Rearrange the following six statements (A), (B), (C), (D), (E) and (F) in the proper sequence to form a meaningful paragraph; then answer the questions given below them.

(A) A computer, to corroborate further, can do simulations for a civilian product, for rapid prototyping or the suitability of market conditions for a future product; it can also simulate performance of a fighter aircraft or weapon performance.

(B) But they are the basis for their market dominance as well.

(C) While India needs to pay more attention to economic areas and employment generation, both crucial to making her a developed country, attention should also be paid to the strategic sectors.

(D) Such 'dual technologies' are closely guarded by the developed countries under the premise of non-proliferation of nuclear weapons or missiles.

(E) The confluence of civilian and defence technologies is leading to a situation where most new tecnologies are basically 'dual use' in nature.

(F) A carbon-composite material, for an example to substantiate this point, can go into making a tennis racquet or a calipar device for polio-affected patients and also for a missile system.

156. Which of the following should be the FOURTH statement after rearrangement?
   (a) A (b) B (c) C (d) D (e) E

157. Which of the following should be the FIFTH statement after rearrangement?
   (a) A (b) B (c) C (d) D (e) E

158. Which of the following should be the SECOND statement after rearrangement?
   (a) A (b) B (c) C (d) D (e) E

159. Which of the following should be the SIXTH (LAST) statement after rearrangement?
   (a) A (b) B (c) C (d) D (e) E

160. Which of the following should be the FIRST statement after rearrangement?
   (a) A (b) B (c) C (d) D (e) E

DIRECTIONS (Qs. 161-170) : In each of these questions four words are given marked A, B, C and D. Two of these words are most nearly the SAME or OPPOSITE in meaning. Identify those two words:

161. A. Umpteen B. Waspish
   C. Countless D. Testimony
   (a) A-C (b) B-C
   (c) C-D (d) A-B
   (e) None of these

162. A. Buffoon B. Scholar
   C. Candid D. Gullible
   (a) A-D (b) B-C
   (c) C-D (d) A-B
   (e) None of these

Space for Rough Work

163. A. Pandemonium B. Realm
C. Sporadic D. Tranquility
(a) A-B (b) B-C
(c) C-D (d) A-D
(e) None of these

164. A Fidgety B. Elation
C. Nervous D. Exuberant
(a) B-C (b) A-B
(c) B-D (d) A-C
(e) None of these

165. A. Oblivious B. Kudos
C. Conscious D. Adulation
(a) A-B (b) B-C
(c) B-D (d) C-D
(e) None of these

166. A. Iconoclast B. Critic
C. Luscious D. Naive
(a) A-C (b) A-B
(c) B-C (d) B-D
(e) None of these

167. A. Lugubrious B. Cheerful
C. Welter D. Gaffe
(a) B-D (b) A-B
(c) C-D (d) B-D
(e) None of these

168. A. Paltry B. Oriental
C. Occidental D. Obnoxious
(a) A-D (b) B-D
(c) B-C (d) C-D
(e) None of these

169. A. Exorbitant B. Moderate
C. Ephemeral D. Mammoth
(a) A-B (b) C-D
(c) B-C (d) A-D
(e) None of these

170. A. Peccable B. Lassitude
C. Jeopardy D. Perfect
(a) B-C (b) A-D
(c) C-D (d) B-D
(e) None of these

DIRECTIONS (Qs. 171–180): Read the following passage carefully and answer the questions given below it.

Management is a set of processes that can keep a complicated system of people and technology running smoothly. The most important aspects of management include planning, budgeting, organizing, staffing, controlling and problem solving. Leadership is a set of processes that creates organizations in the first place or adapts them to significantly changing circumstances. Leadership defines what the future should look like, aligns people with that vision, and inspires them to make it happen despite the obstacles. This distinction is absolutely crucial for our purposes here. Successful transformation is 70 to 90 percent leadership and only 10 to 30 percent management. Yet for historical reasons, many organisations today don't have much leadership. And almost everyone thinks about the problem here as one of managing change.

For most of this century, as we created thousands and thousands of large organisations for the first time in human history, we didn't have enough good managers to keep all those bureaucracies functioning. So many companies and universities developed management programmes and hundreds and thousands of people were encouraged to learn management on the job. And they did. But, people were taught little about leadership. To some degree, management was the main item on the twentieth-century agenda because that's what was needed. For every entrepreneur or business builder who was, a leader, we needed hundreds of managers to run their ever growing enterprises.

Unfortunately for us today, this emphasis on management has often been institutionalized in corporate cultures that discourage employees from learning how to lead. Ironically, past success is usually the key ingredient in producing this outcome. The syndrome, as I have observed it on many occasions, goes like this: success creates some degree of marked dominance, which in turn produces much growth. After a while keeping the ever larger organisation under control becomes the primary challenge. So attention turns inward, and managerial competencies are nurtured. With a strong emphasis on management but not leadership,

Space for Rough Work

bureaucracy and an inward focus take over. But with continued success, the result mostly of market dominance, the problem often goes unaddressed and an unhealthy arrogance begins to evolve. All of these characteristics then make any transformation effort much more difficult.

Arrogant managers can over evaluate their current performance and competitive position, listen poorly, and learn slowly. Inwardly focussed employees can smother those who want to respond to shifting conditions. And the lack of leadership leaves no force inside these organisations to break out of the morass.

171. What is the main topic of the passage?
   (a) Importance of management schools in the present I context I
   (b) Good managers
   (c) Importance of leadership in an organisation
   (d) Management and success of an organisation
   (e) None of these

172. Why did companies and universities develop programmes to prepare managers in large numbers?
   (a) Companies and universities wanted to generate funds through these programmes
   (b) Organisations wanted to create communication network through trained managers
   (c) Large number of organisations were created and they needed managers in good numbers
   (d) Only trained managers could lead an organisation to success
   (e) None of these

173. Which of the following statements is not true according to the passage?
   (a) Bureaucratic culture smothers those who want to change conditions
   (b) Leadership involves carrying out important functions such as budgeting and planning
   (c) Pressure on managers comes mostly from within
   (d) Leadership has the potential to establish direction
   (e) None of these

174. Management education was emphasized in the management programmes because:
   (a) motivating employees was thought to be done by managers
   (b) organisations wanted to create a powerful guiding coalition
   (c) establishing direction was the main force of organisations
   (d) management was the main item of agenda in organisations
   (e) None of these

175. What is the historical reason for many organisations not having leadership?
   (a) Leaders allow too much complacency in organisations
   (b) Leaders are not adept in carrying out managerial functions and organisations need good managers only
   (c) The view that leaders are born and not made
   (d) Socio-political pressure
   (e) None of these

176. Which of the following is similar in meaning to the underlined word 'nurtured' as used in the passage?
   (a) Created   (b) Developed
   (c) Surfaced   (d) Thwarted
   (e) None of these

177. What according to the author is leadership?
   (a) Inspiring people to realise the vision
   (b) Planning and budgeting resources
   (c) Carrying out the crucial function of manager
   (d) Keep the technology running smoothly
   (e) None of these

178. Which of the following characteristics help organisations in their transformations efforts ?
   (a) Bureaucratic and inward looking approach
   (b) A strong and dogmatic culture
   (c) Emphasis on leadership rather than management
   (d) Emphasis on customer satisfaction
   (e) None of these

Space for Rough Work

179. Why were people taught little about leadership in management programmes?
(a) Enough study material was not available
(b) Leadership was considered a political phenomenon
(c) Focus of these programmes was on developing managers
(d) None of the above
(e) None of these

180. Which of the following statements is false according to the passage?
(a) Bureaucracy fosters arrogant culture
(b) Leadership competencies are nurtured only in very large- size organisations
(c) Successful transformation in organisation is largely possible because of leadership
(d) Managers tend to stifle innovation
(e) None of these

DIRECTIONS (Qs.181-183) : Pick out the nearest correct meaning or SYNONYM of the words given below:

181. Which one of the following words very nearly replaces ADVICE?
(a) council (b) counsel
(c) practice (d) proposal.
(e) None of these

182. Which of the following words very nearly means 'ROUGH'?
(a) coarse (b) refine
(c) rude (d) crude
(e) None of these

183. Which of the following words means MISERABLE?
(a) object (b) obstruct
(c) abject (d) abstract
(e) None of these

DIRECTIONS (Qs. 184-185): Pick out the ANTONYM of the words given below:

184. IMPLICATE
(a) appease (b) exonerate
(c) adore (d) advocate
(e) None of these

185. VACILLATING
(a) fascinating (b) fanaticism
(c) indolence (d) resolute
(e) None of these

Directions (Qs. 186-190) : In each of the following sentences four words or phrases have been underlined marked (a), (b), (c) and (d). Only one underlined part in each sentence is not acceptable in Standard English.Choose one word or phrase that must be changed for the sentence to be correct.
If all the four parts are correct, mark (e) i.e. 'All correct' as your answer.

186. I have seen as bad or (a) worse scenes of disorder (b) at the English fair than (c) in any other (d) Australian mining town All correct (e)

187. The officers are now (a) perfectly (b) happy fishing, boating, shooting, playing cricket and other sports (c) All correct (d) (e)

188. While in conversation with a (a) high military officer he told me (b) that at the headquarters (c) nothing was known (d) All correct (e)

Space for Rough Work

189. The fear (a) of an impending invasion (b) has more to do than even the debasing of the coinage (c) with the financial (d) difficulties All correct (e)

190. His assistants have (a) and are still (b) doing excellent (c) work for the (d) organization All correct (e)

DIRECTIONS (Qs. 191-200) : In the following passage there are blanks, each of which has been numbered. These numbers are printed below the passage and against each, five words are suggested, one of which fits the blank appropriately. Find out the appropriate word in each case.

The Government seems to be in right earnest to ensure more **191** in governance. The Prime Minister's announcement that his Government is **192** drafting legislation to **193** the citizen's right to information is indeed welcome . Though the talk on the right to information is not new, we may **194** the bill to be brought early this time. The previous Government had set up a high-level committee to **195** a draft bill. But nothing has been heard about the matter since, **196** the committee did quite some work. The issue, however, has come to such a pass that a solution cannot be **197** further. Sunlight is the best disinfectant, a foreign judge once said, while **198** the unwarranted secrecy in an administrative system. When those in authority know that people have the right to ask questions and the government is under the **199** to provide them with answers, **200** of authority, or of public finances, for personal or party ends is less likely to happen.

191. (a) strictness (b) rudeness (c) leniency (d) economy (e) transparency

192. (a) personally (b) busy (c) not (d) reluctantly (e) absolutely

193. (a) presumption (b) absolve (c) curb (d) question (e) establish

194. (a) expect (b) wait (c) try (d) frustrate (e) appeal

195. (a) level (b) regard (c) prepare (d) enact (e) unearth

196. (a) even (b) as (c) because (d) until (e) though

197. (a) found (b) expected (c) delayed (d) looked (e) longed

198. (a) nurturing (b) criticising (c) demanding (d) appreciating (e) upholding

199. (a) pretention (b) affect (c) substance (d) obligation (e) property

200. (a) misuse (b) governance (c) dishonour (d) curbing (e) breach

Space for Rough Work

MAHARASHTRA CET - MOCK TEST 1

RESPONSE SHEET

NAME : .... DATE : ....

	(A)	(B)	(C)	(D)		(A)	(B)	(C)	(D)		(A)	(B)	(C)	(D)		(A)	(B)	(C)	(D)
1.					51.					101.					151.				
2.					52.					102.					152.				
3.					53.					103.					153.				
4.					54.					104.					154.				
5.					55.					105.					155.				
6.					56.					106.					156.				
7.					57.					107.					157.				
8.					58.					108.					158.				
9.					59.					109.					159.				
10.					60.					110.					160.				
11.					61.					111.					161.				
12.					62.					112.					162.				
13.					63.					113.					163.				
14.					64.					114.					164.				
15.					65.					115.					165.				
16.					66.					116.					166.				
17.					67.					117.					167.				
18.					68.					118.					168.				
19.					69.					119.					169.				
20.					70.					120.					170.				
21.					71.					121.					171.				
22.					72.					122.					172.				
23.					73.					123.					173.				
24.					74.					124.					174.				
25.					75.					125.					175.				
26.					76.					126.					176.				
27.					77.					127.					177.				
28.					78.					128.					178.				
29.					79.					129.					179.				
30.					80.					130.					180.				
31.					81.					131.					181.				
32.					82.					132.					182.				
33.					83.					133.					183.				
34.					84.					134.					184.				
35.					85.					135.					185.				
36.					86.					136.					186.				
37.					87.					137.					187.				
38.					88.					138.					188.				
39.					89.					139.					189.				
40.					90.					140.					190.				
41.					91.					141.					191.				
42.					92.					142.					192.				
43.					93.					143.					193.				
44.					94.					144.					194.				
45.					95.					145.					195.				
46.					96.					146.					196.				
47.					97.					147.					197.				
48.					98.					148.					198.				
49.					99.					149.					199.				
50.					100.					150.					200.				

MAHARASHTRA CET

MOCK TEST - 2

*** INSTRUCTIONS :**

- **There are 200 questions in this test. You will be given 150 minutes to complete the test.**
- **Each question carries 1 mark. There is no negative marking.**

1. In a certain code MAIN is written as IMNA and GOAL is written as AGLO. How is DUSK written in that code?
   (a) SDKU (b) SUKD
   (c) UKDS (d) USKD
   (e) None of these
2. Four of the following five are alike in a certain way and so form a group. Which is the one that DOES NOT belong to that group?
   (a) 12 (b) 24
   (c) 42 (d) 18
   (e) 32
3. How many such letters are there in the word CATEGORY each of which is as far away from the beginning of the word as when they are arranged in alphabetical order?
   (a) One (b) Two
   (c) Three (d) None
   (e) More than three
4. The position of the first and the fifth digits in the number 89123647 are interchanged. Similarly the positions of the second and the sixth digits are interchanged and so on. Which of the following will be the fourth digit from the right end after the arrangement?
   (a) 9 (b) 1
   (c) 8 (d) 2
   (e) None of these
5. In a certain code language '*nik ka pa*' means 'who are you'; '*ka na ta da*' means 'you may come here'; and '*ho ta sa*' means 'come and go'; what does '*nik*' mean in that code language?
   (a) Who (b) are
   (c) who or are (d) data inadequate
   (e) None of these
6. How many meaningful English words can be formed with the letters LESA using each letter only once in each word?
   (a) None (b) One
   (c) Two (d) Three
   (e) More than three
7. In a certain code BEND is written as 5%7@ and DREAM is written as @2%48. How is MADE written in that code?
   (a) 84@% (b) 8@4%
   (c) 85@% (d) 84%5
   (e) None of these

DIRECTIONS (Qs. 8 & 9) : Complete the following series.

8. The next three terms of the series 813213246 are
   (a) 742 (b) 987
   (c) 542 (d) 638
   (e) None of these
9. The next three terms of the series 28204492188 are
   (a) 299 (b) 436
   (c) 380 (d) 456
   (e) None of these

DIRECTIONS (Qs. 10 & 11) : In each of these questions, various terms of a series are given with one term missing as shown by (?). Choose the missing term :

10. YEB, WFD, UHG, SKI, (?)
    (a) QOL (b) TOL (c) QGL (d) QNL
    (e) None of these
11. AZ, CX, FU, (?)
    (a) IR (b) JQ (c) IV (d) KP
    (e) None of these

Space for Rough Work

12. In the following question, there are two words to the left of the sign :: which are connected in some way. The same relationship obtains between the third word and one of the four alternatives under it. Find the correct alternative.
Clock : Time :: Thermometer : ?
(a) Heat (b) Radiation
(c) Energy (d) Temperature
(e) None of these

13. In the following questions, a pair of words is given, followed by four pairs of words as alternatives. Choose the correct pair in which the words bears the same relationship to each other as the words of the given pair bear.
Eyes : Tears ::
(a) Sea : Water (b) Volcano : Lava
(c) Heart : Artery (d) Hunger : Bread
(e) None of these

DIRECTIONS (Qs. 14 & 15) : In each of the following questions, four alternatives are given, out of which three are alike in a certain way while one is different. Choose the odd one.

14. (a) JUDGE (b) SCANT
(c) CROWD (d) FLUSH
(e) None of these

15. (a) Thiamine (b) Niacin
(c) Trypsin (d) Riboflavin
(e) None of these

DIRECTIONS (Qs. 16 - 28) : In each questions given below which one of the five answer figures should come after the problem figures, if the sequence were continued?

16.

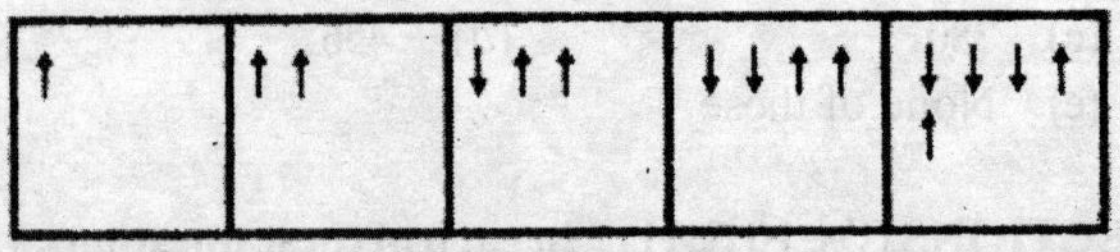

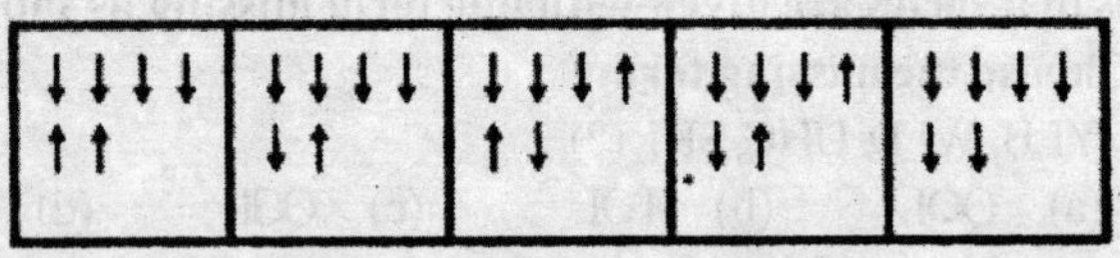

(A) (B) (C) (D) (E)

(a) A (b) B (c) C (d) D (e) E

17.

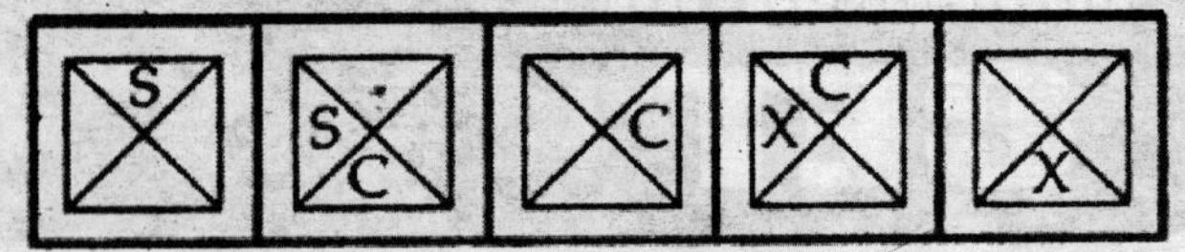

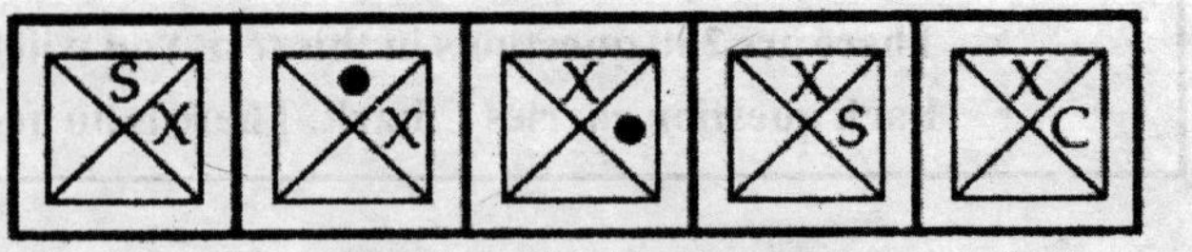

(A) (B) (C) (D) (E)

(a) A (b) B (c) C (d) D (e) E

18.

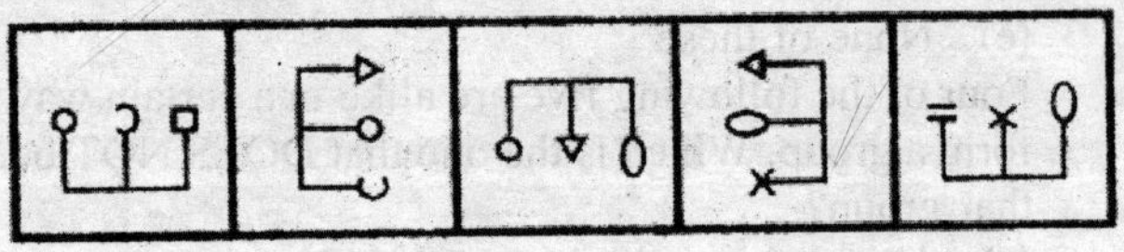

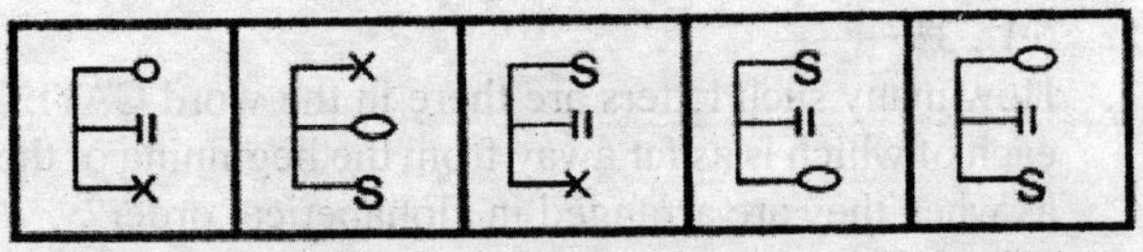

(A) (B) (C) (D) (E)

(a) A (b) B (c) C (d) D (e) E

19.

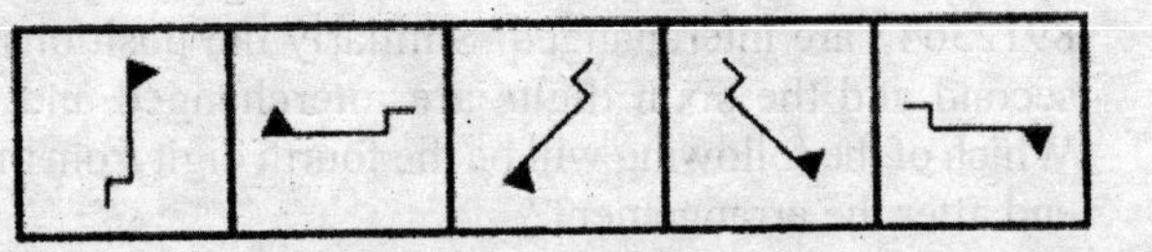

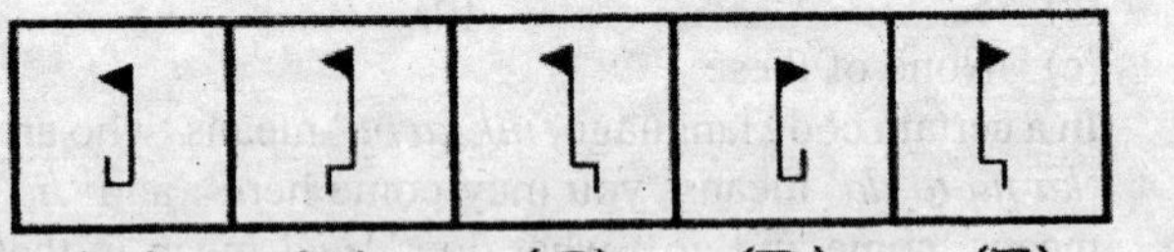

(A) (B) (C) (D) (E)

(a) A (b) B (c) C (d) D (e) E

Space for Rough Work

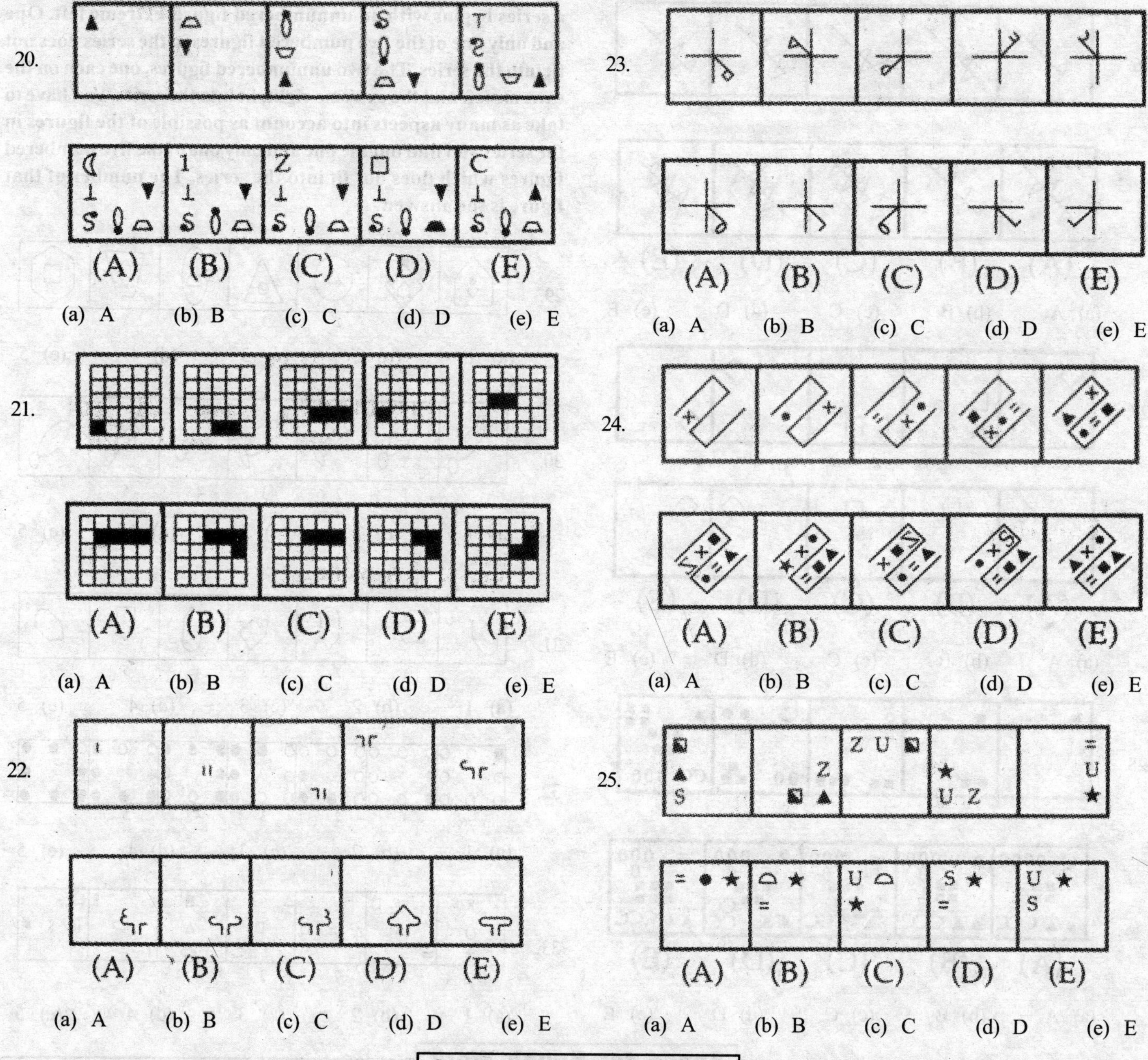

20. (a) A (b) B (c) C (d) D (e) E

21. (a) A (b) B (c) C (d) D (e) E

22. (a) A (b) B (c) C (d) D (e) E

23. (a) A (b) B (c) C (d) D (e) E

24. (a) A (b) B (c) C (d) D (e) E

25. (a) A (b) B (c) C (d) D (e) E

Space for Rough Work

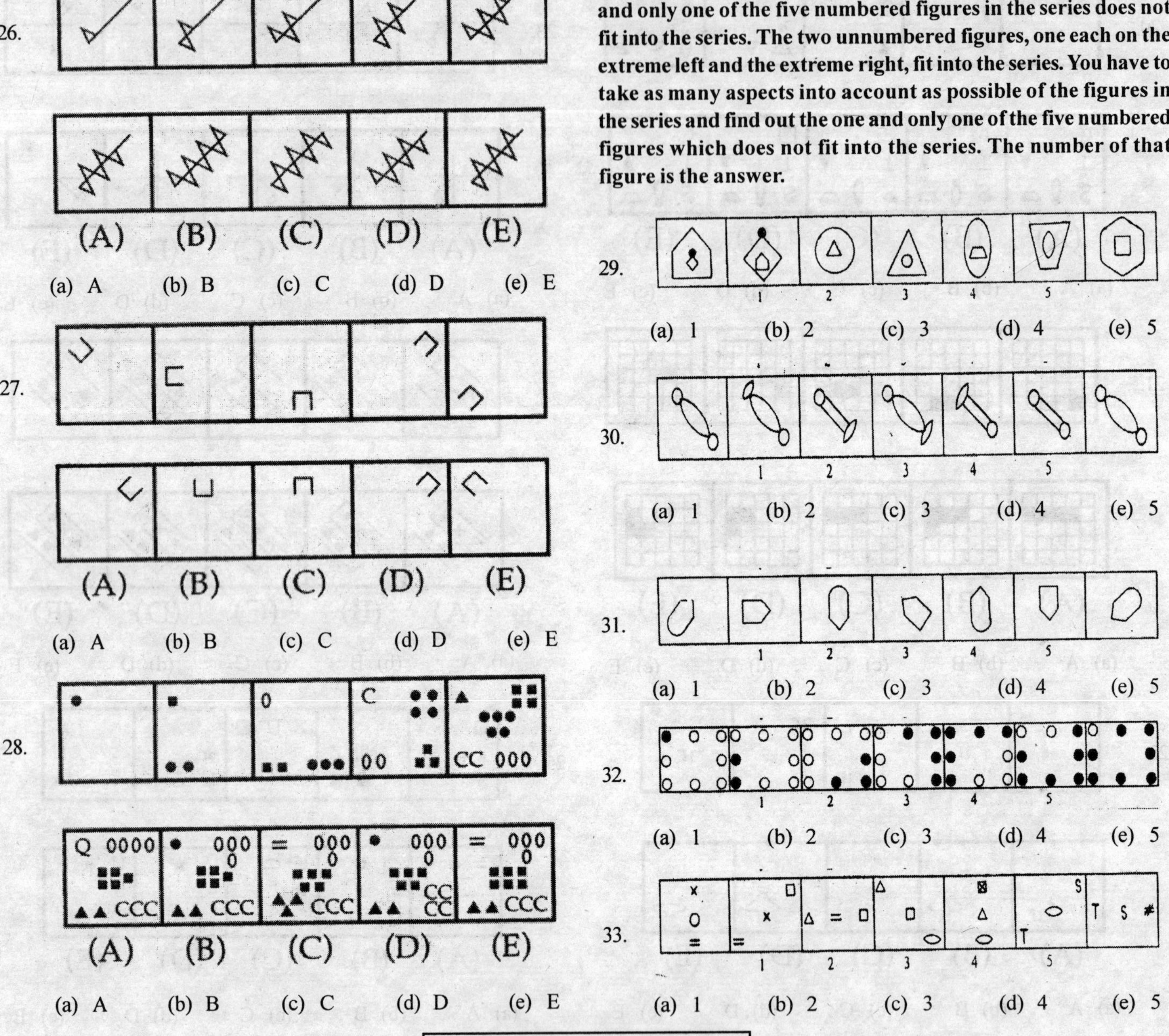

26. (a) A (b) B (c) C (d) D (e) E

27. (a) A (b) B (c) C (d) D (e) E

28. (a) A (b) B (c) C (d) D (e) E

DIRECTIONS (Qs. 29 - 33) : In each of the following questions, a series begins with an unnumbered figure extreme left. One and only one of the five numbered figures in the series does not fit into the series. The two unnumbered figures, one each on the extreme left and the extreme right, fit into the series. You have to take as many aspects into account as possible of the figures in the series and find out the one and only one of the five numbered figures which does not fit into the series. The number of that figure is the answer.

29. (a) 1 (b) 2 (c) 3 (d) 4 (e) 5

30. (a) 1 (b) 2 (c) 3 (d) 4 (e) 5

31. (a) 1 (b) 2 (c) 3 (d) 4 (e) 5

32. (a) 1 (b) 2 (c) 3 (d) 4 (e) 5

33. (a) 1 (b) 2 (c) 3 (d) 4 (e) 5

Space for Rough Work

DIRECTIONS (Qs. 34 - 38) : In each of the following questions the first two figures are related to each other in a certain way. Find out the figure from (a), (b), (c), (d) and (e) so that the second pair will have the similar relationship and can be placed at "question mark".

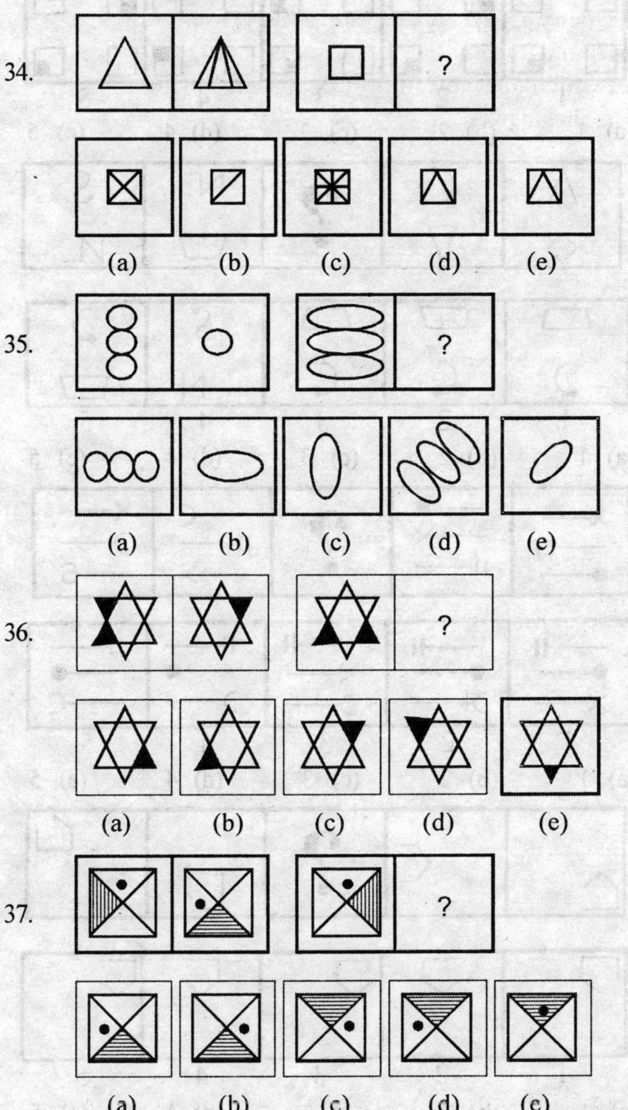

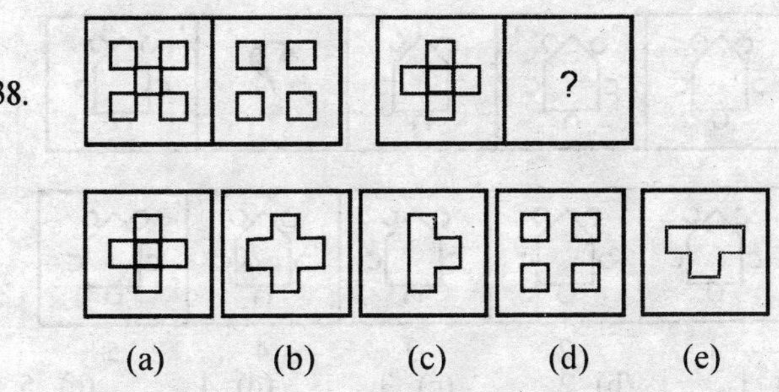

DIRECTIONS (Qs. 39 - 48) : Each of the following questions consists of unmarked figures followed by five figures marked (a), (b), (c), (d) and (e). Select a figure from the marked figures which will replace the question mark so that a series be established by the unmarked figures.

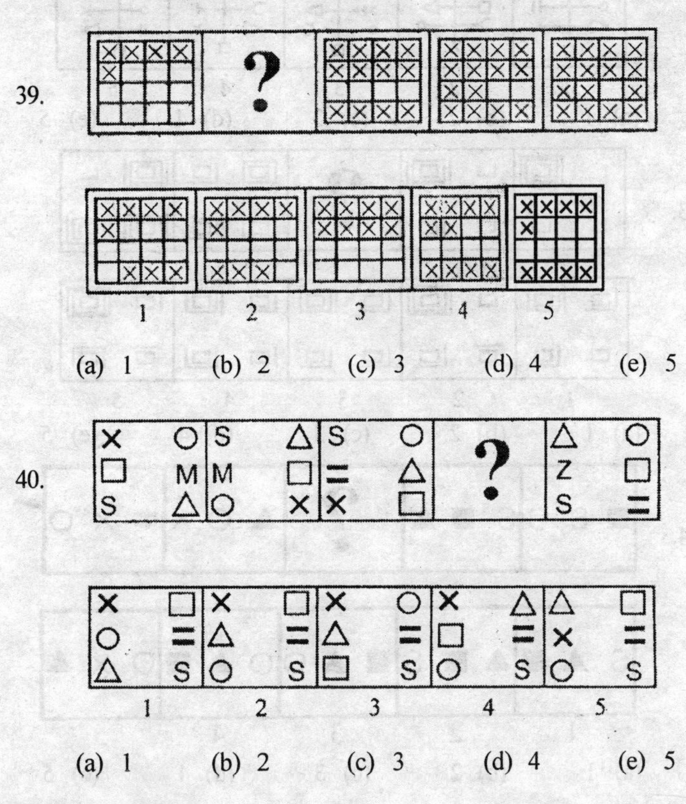

Space for Rough Work

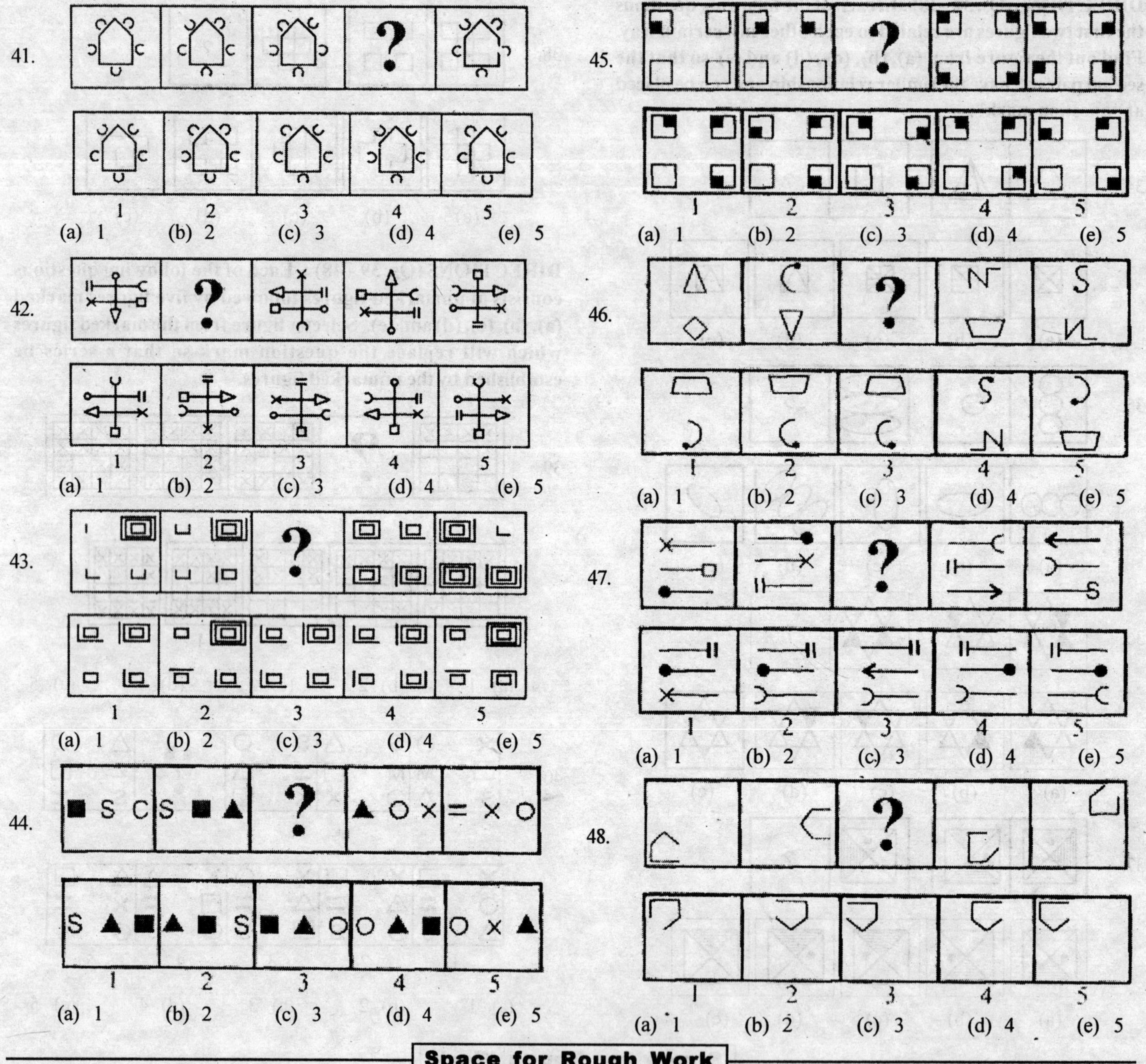

41. (a) 1 (b) 2 (c) 3 (d) 4 (e) 5

42. (a) 1 (b) 2 (c) 3 (d) 4 (e) 5

43. (a) 1 (b) 2 (c) 3 (d) 4 (e) 5

44. (a) 1 (b) 2 (c) 3 (d) 4 (e) 5

45. (a) 1 (b) 2 (c) 3 (d) 4 (e) 5

46. (a) 1 (b) 2 (c) 3 (d) 4 (e) 5

47. (a) 1 (b) 2 (c) 3 (d) 4 (e) 5

48. (a) 1 (b) 2 (c) 3 (d) 4 (e) 5

Space for Rough Work

DIRECTIONS (Qs. 49 - 53) : In each question below are given three statmenets followed by three or four conclusions numbered I, II, III and IV you have to take the given statements to be true if they seem to be at variance with commonly known facts. Read all the conclusions and then decide which of the given conclusions logically follow from the given statements, disregarding commonly known facts.

49. **Statements :** All books are notes.
Some notes are pencils.
No pencil is paper.
Conclusions : I. Some notes are books.
II. Some pencils are books.
III. Some books are papers.
IV. No book is a paper.
(a) Only I and either III or IV follow
(b) Either III or IV follows
(c) Only I and III follow
(d) Only III follows
(e) None of these

50. **Statements :** Some tables are chairs.
No cupboard is table.
Some chairs are cupboards.
Conclusions : I. Some chairs are not tables.
II. All chairs are either tables or cupboards.
III. Some chairs are tables.
IV. All chairs are tables.
(a) Only I and IV follow
(b) Only either II or III follows
(c) Only I and III follows
(d) Either II or III and I follow
(e) None of these

51. **Statements :** No table is fruit.
No fruit is window.
All windows are chairs.
Conclusions : I. No window is table.
II. No chair is fruit.
III. No chair is table.
IV. All chairs are windows.
(a) None follows (b) All follow
(c) Only I and II follow (d) Only III and IV follow
(e) None of these

52. **Statements :** No man is sky.
No sky is roaD.
Some men are roads.
Conclusions : I. No road is man.
II. No road is sky.
III. Some skies are men.
IV. All roads are men.
(a) None follows (b) Only I follows
(c) Only I and III follow (d) Only II follows
(e) None of these

53. **Statements :** All papers are books.
All bags are books.
Some purses are bags.
Conclusions : I. Some papers are bags.
II. Some books are papers.
III. Some books are purses.
(a) Only I follows (b) Only II and III follow
(c) Only I and III follow (d) Only I and II follow
(e) None of these

54. Find the missing letter in the series : C4X, F9U, I16R, ?
(a) L25P (b) L250
(c) L27P (d) L25O
(e) None of these

DIRECTIONS (Qs. 55 -59) : : In each of the following questions, a statement is given followed by two courses of action numbered I and II. Decide which of the cources of action logically follows and give answer :
(a) if only I follows;
(b) if only II follows;
(c) if either I or II follows;
(d) if neither I nor II follows.
(e) if both I and II follow.

55. **Statement :** There was waterlogging in the major part of the city due to heavy rain during past few days and the people residing in those areas were forced to shift to other areas.
Courses of action : I. The Government should arrange food and shelter for the displaced people.
II. The fire brigade should be put on high alert to cope with the situation.

Space for Rough Work

56. **Statement :** The 'M' State Government has decided henceforth to award the road construction contracts through open tenders only.

Courses of action : I. The 'M' state will not be able to get the work done swiftly as it will have to go through tender and other procedures.

II. Henceforth the quality of roads constructed may be far better.

57. **Statement :** ABC LtD. company has decided to launch free education up to class X for the children of its employees from June 2000.

Courses of action : I. The company should reduce its other expenditures to save money for the plan.

II. The company will have to prepare details for the execution of the plan.

58. **Statement :** Many private sector banks have reduced interest rate on housing loans in comparison to public sector banks.

Courses of action : I. The case should be raised before the regulatory authority for investigation by the public sector banks as they cannot follow such reduction.

II. Public sector banks must adopt such policy to remain in competition.

59. **Statement :** The proposed strike by the transporters would paralyse day-to-day life of the people.

Courses of action : I. City administrators should engage the transporters successfully in negotiations on their demands in order to pre-empt their strike.

II. City administrators should arrange for alternative public transportation system during the strike.

DIRECTIONS (Qs. 60 - 62) : Read the following information carefully and answer the questions given below :

Six persons A, B, C, D, E and F took up a job with a firm in a week from Monday to Saturday. Each of them joined for different posts on different days. The posts were of — Clerk, Officer, Technician, Manager, supervisor, and Sales Executive, though not respectively.

F joined as a Manager on the first day. B joined as a Supervisor but neither on Wednesday nor on Friday. D joined as a Technician on Thursday. Officer joined the firm on Wednesday. E joined as a Clerk on Tuesday. A joined as a Sales Executive.

60. Who joined the firm on Wednesday?
(a) B (b) C
(c) B or C (d) Data inadequate
(e) None of these

61. Who was the last person to join the firm?
(a) E (b) F
(c) A (d) B
(e) None of these

62. On which of the following days did the Sales Executive join?
(a) Tuesday (b) Thursday
(c) Saturday (d) Wednesday
(e) None of these

DIRECTIONS (Qs. 63 - 66) : Read the following information carefully and answer the question that follow :

Six boys A, B, C, D, E and F are marching in a line. They are arranged according to their height, the tallest being at the back and the shortest in front,

F is between B and A.

E is shorter than D but taller than C who is taller than A.

E and F have two boys between them.

A is not the shortest among them.

63. Where is E ?
(a) Between A and B
(b) Between C and A
(c) Between D and C
(d) In front of C
(e) None of these

64. Who is the tallest ?
(a) B (b) D (c) F (d) A
(e) None of these

Space for Rough Work

65. If we start counting from the shortest, which boy is fourth one in the line ?
(a) E (b) A (c) D (d) C
(e) None of these

66. Who is the shortest ?
(a) C (b) D (c) B (d) F
(e) None of these

DIRECTIONS (Qs. 67 - 70) : A goldsmith has five gold rings, each having a different weight. They are labelled as D, E, F, G and H. Their peculiarities are given in the following five statements

Statement 1 : Ring D weighs twice as much as ring E.
Statement 2 : Ring E weighs four and a half times as much as ring F.
Statement 3 : Ring F weighs half as much as ring G.
Statement 4 : Ring G weighs half as much as ring H.
Statement 5 : Ring H weighs less than ring D but more than ring F.

67. If these rings are sold according to their weights, which ring will fetch the highest value in rupees?
(a) D (b) G
(c) F (d) H
(e) None of these

68. Ring H is heavier to which of the following two rings ?
(a) G and E (b) G and F
(c) D and F (d) D and E
(e) None of these

69. Which of the following is the lightest in weight?
(a) D (b) E
(c) F (d) G
(e) None of these

70. Which of the following represents the descending order of the weights of the rings ?
(a) D, E, H, G and F (b) F, D, G, E and H
(c) H, F, G, D and E (d) E, G, H, D and F
(e) None of these

71. Six products U, V, W, X, Y and Z are to be placed in display windows of a shop. There are six display windows – numbered 1, 2, 3, 4, 5, 6 and one product is to be put in one window. Moreover, U cannot be immediately to the left or immediately to the right of V. W must be immediately to the left of X. Z cannot be in window number 6 :
If X is placed in window no. 3, then W must be placed in which window ?
(a) 1 (b) 2 (c) 4 (d) 5 (e) None of these

DIRECTIONS (Qs. 72 - 76) : Study the following information and answer the questions given below:

In a certain code, the symbol for 0 (zero) is @ and for 1 is $. There are no other symbols for all other numbers greater than one. The numbers greater than 1 are to be written only by using the two symbols given above. The value of the symbol for 1, doubles itself every time it shifts one place to the left. Study the following example:

'0' is written as @ '1' is written as $
'2' is written as $@ '3' is written as $$
'4' is written as $@@ and so on

72. Which of the following will represent 11?
(1) $@$$ (2) @$$@
(3) $$@@ (4) $@$@@
(5) None of these

73. Which of the following will represent 8?
(1) $$@@ (2) @$$@
(3) $$@@ (4) @@$$
(5) None of these

74. Which of the following numbers will be represented by $$@$?
(1) 8 (2) 11 (3) 13 (4) 12
(5) None of these

75. Which of the following will represent the value of the product $3 \times 3 + 1$?
(1) $$@$ (2) $@$@
(3) $@@$$ (4) $$$
(5) None of these

76. Which of the following numbers will be represented by $@@@$?
(1) 22 (2) 31 (3) 14 (4) 17
(5) None of these

DIRECTIONS (Qs. 77 - 82) : Below is given passage followed by several possible inferences which can be drawn from the facts stated in the passage. You have to examine each inference separately in the context of the passage and decide upon its degree of truth or falsity. *Mark answer*

(a) if the inference is 'definitely true', i.e. it properly follows from the statement of facts given;
(b) if the inference is 'probably true' though not 'definitely true' in the light of the facts given;

Space for Rough Work

(c) if the 'data are inadequate', i.e. from the facts given you cannot say whether the inference is likely to be true or false;

(d) if the inference is 'probably false' though not 'definitely false' in the light of the facts given;

(e) if the inference is 'definitely false', i.e. it cannot possibly be drawn from the facts given or it contradicts the given facts;

Cotton acreage in India during the current year has fallen by 10% as cotton growers have moved on cultivation of other cash crops. This is the result of the cotton glut in world markets post-September 11 and the consequent slowdown in the world economy. But this scenario brought with it benefits to one segment of the industry-yarn manufacturers-as they get higher prices for their produce. Some yarn manufacturers had stocked up low-priced cotton last year. The combined effect of all this is evident in the rise in net profits and net margins of yarn manufacturers.

77. World economy witnessed an upward trend during pre-September 11 perioD.
78. The farmers will again grow cotton next year due to increased price of cotton yarn.
79. Land used for growing cotton in India is conducive to grow other cash crops.
80. The yarn manufacturers have marginally suffered during post-September 11 perioD.
81. There has been a huge drop in the supply of cotton during the current year.
82. There has been shortage of cotton in the world market last year.

DIRECTIONS (Qs. 83 - 87) : In each of the following questions, a statement is given followed by two assumptions numbered I and II. Consider the statement and the following assumptions and decide which of the assumptions is implicit. Give answer

(a) if ONLY assumption I is implicit;
(b) if ONLY assumption II is implicit;
(c) if EITHER I or II is implicit;
(d) if NEITHER I nor II is implicit;
(e) if BOTH assumplious are implicit.

83. **Statement :** Nobody can predict as to how long our country would take to contain the unfortunate and disastrous terrorist activities.
Assumptions : I. It is impossible to put an end to terrorist activities.
II. Efforts to control the terrorist activities are on.

84. **Statement :** You know that your suit is excellent when people ask about your tailor who tailored the suit.
Assumptions : I. People do not ask about your tailor if your suit is not gooD.
II. The people want to know the criterion of an excellent suit.

85. **Statement :** Even with the increase in the number of sugar factories in India, we still continue to import sugar.
Assumptions : I. The consumption of sugar per capita has increased in India.
II. Many of the factories are not in a position to produce sugar to their fullest capacity.

86. **Statement :** Highly brilliant and industrious students do not always excel in the written examination.
Assumptions : I. The written examination is good mainly for mediocre students.
II. The brilliant and industrious students cannot always write good answer in the exam.

87. **Statement :** The coffee powder of company X is quite better in taste than the much advertised coffee of company Y.
Assumptions : I. If your product is not good, you spend more on advertisement.
II. Some people are tempted to buy a product by the advertisement.

88. In a code, CORNER is written as GSVRIV. How can CENTRAL be written in that code?
(a) DFOUSBM (b) GIRXVEP
(c) GJRYVEP (d) GNFJKER
(e) None of these

89. If L denotes ×, M denotes ÷, P denotes + and Q denotes –, then 16 P 24 M 8 Q 6 M 2 L 3 = ?
(a) $\frac{13}{2}$ (b) $-\frac{1}{6}$ (c) $14\frac{1}{2}$ (d) 10
(e) None of these

90. From her home, Prerna wishes to go to school. From home, she goes towards North and then turns left and then turns right, and finally she turns left and reaches school. In which direction her school is situated with respect to her home?
(a) North - east (b) North - west
(c) South - east (d) South - west
(e) None of these

Space for Rough Work

DIRECTIONS (Qs. 91 - 93) : In each of the following number series, two terms have been put within brackets. Mark your answers as

(a) if BOTH the bracketed terms are RIGHT;
(b) if the FIRST bracketed term is right and the SECOND is wrong;
(c) if the FIRST bracketed term is wrong and the SECOND is right;
(d) if BOTH the bracketed terms are WRONG;
(e) if EITHER the bracketed terms are RIGHT.

91. (2), 5, (12), 25, 41, 61
92. 3, 10, 29, (66), (127), 218
93. 4, 6, 10, (12), 16, (14), 22

Direction (Qs. 94-97) : These questions are based on the context given below.

Following are the conditions of promotion from junior Officer's Cadre to Senior Officer's Cadre in an organization. The candidate must

(i) have completed at least 5 years in the organization.
(ii) have secured 65% marks in the written test for promotion.
(iii) have secured 60% marks in the Group Discussion.
(iv) have secured 70% marks in the interview.
(v) have good record of his work performance.
(vi) have good communication skill and get along well with his colleagues.
(vii) not be more than 40 years and less than 30 years as on 1-9-2003.
(viii) have good academic record with an average of at least 65% marks.

However, in the case of a candidate who

(ix) satisfies all other conditions except (4) above but has secured 75% marks in the written test and 65% marks in the Group Discussion, the case is to be referred to the General Manager (Personnel)-GM (P) for the decision.
(x) satisfies all other criteria except (8) above but has secured an average of more than 60% marks, the case is to be referred to the Managing Director (MD) of the organization.

Now read the information provided in the case of each candidate in each of the questions given below and decide on the basis of the information provided and based on the above conditions, which of the courses of action you would suggest. These cases are given to you as on 5.9.2003. You are not to assume anything.

(a) if the case is to be referred to MD;
(b) if the candidate is not to be promoted;
(c) if the candidate is to be promoted.
(d) if the case is to be referred to GM (P);
(e) if the case to be referred to either MB or GM (P).

94. 33 years old Renu has a good academic record with an average of 68% marks and has good communication skill. She has completed six years in the organization. She has secured 63% marks in Group Discussion, 71% marks in interview and 68% marks in written test for promotion. She gets along well with her colleagues and has good record of her work performance.

95. Venkatesh, who is 38 years old, has good academic record with an average of 61% marks. He has secured 65% marks in the written test for promotion, 72% marks in interview and 63% marks in Group discussion. He has good communication skill and gets along well with his colleagues. He has good record of his work performance and has completed 7 years in the organization.

96. 34 years old Madhu has secured 60% marks in written promotion test, 72% marks in interview and 69% marks in Group Discussion. She has good communication skill and gets along well with her colleagues. Her record of work performance is good and she has completed $6\frac{1}{2}$ years in the organization.

97. Tarun has completed 6 years in the organization. He is 34 years old and has a good academic record with an average of 68% marks. He has secured 66% marks in interview and 76% marks in the written test for promotion. He has good communication skill, gets along well with his colleagues and his work performance is gooD.

98. A sum of money is divided among A, B and C in the ratio of $3\frac{3}{4}:4:5.5$. If the lowest share is Rs 30, then the total amount of money is
(a) Rs 212 (b) Rs 106 (c) Rs 53 (d) Rs 159
(e) None of these

99. A man started running at a distance of 225 metre from the train. If the speed of the man is 6 km/h, then how much time should the train wait so that the man will be just able to catch it ?
(a) $2\frac{1}{4}$ min (b) 3 min (c) $4\frac{1}{4}$ min (d) $4\frac{1}{2}$ min
(e) None of these

Space for Rough Work

100. A rectangular paper, when folded into two congruent parts had a perimeter of 34 cm for each part folded along one set of sides and the same is 38 cm when folded along the other set of sides. What is the area of the paper?
(a) 140 cm^2 (b) 240 cm^2
(c) 560 cm^2 (d) 280 cm^2
(e) None of these

101. Which number will come next in the following series 8,15,28,53, ?
(a) 98 (b) 106 (c) 100 (d) 102
(e) None of these

102. Find the missing number in the series :
6, 12, 21, ?, 48
(a) 38 (b) 40 (c) 45 (d) 33
(e) None of these

103. There are 4 numbers. The H.C.F. of each pair is 3 and the L.C.M. of all the 4 numbers is 116. What is the product of 4 numbers?
(a) 9782 (b) 9396 (c) 9224 (d) 9100
(e) None of these

104. A batsman makes a score of 87 runs in the 17th inning and thus increases his average by 3. Find his average after 17th inning.
(a) 36 (b) 39
(c) 42 (d) 45
(e) None of these

105. Rajan got married 8 years ago. His present age is $\frac{6}{5}$ times his age at the time of his marriage. Rajan's sister was 10 years younger to him at the time of his marriage. The age of Rajan's sister is:
(a) 32 years (b) 36 years
(c) 38 years (d) 40 years
(e) None of these

DIRECTIONS (Qs. 106 - 110) : In the following questions two equations numbered I and II are given. You have to solve both the equations and give answer
(a) if $a > b$ (b) if $a \geq b$
(c) if $a < b$ (d) if $a \leq b$
(e) if $a = b$ or the relationship between p and q can not be established.

106. I. $2a + 5b = 7$
II. $-a + 4b = 16$

107. I. $a^2 + 8 = 89$
II. $b - 3 = 6$

108. I. $a^2 - 7a - 18 = 0$
II. $b^2 + 9b + 18 = 0$

109. I. $a^2 = 3249$
II. $b = 57$

110. I. $a^2 - 8a = 48$
II. $b^2 + 9b + 20 = 0$

DIRECTIONS (Qs. 111 - 114) : These questions are based on the graph given below.
The sales & profits of IVP LtD. are given for five years form 93 - 94 to 97 - 98

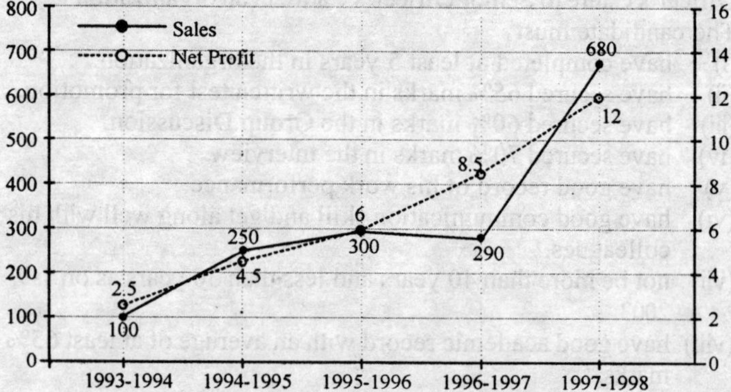

111. For which year had the percentage increase in profit been highest over the previous year
(a) 96-97 (b) 94-95 (c) 95-96 (d) 97-98
(e) None of these

112. For which of the following year has the profit per unit sales been highest over the previous year
(a) 93-94 (b) 94-95 (c) 95-96 (d) 97-98
(e) None of these

113. For which year has the percentage increase in expenses over the previous year been lowest
(a) 96-97 (b) 94-95 (c) 95-96 (d) 97-98
(e) None of these

Space for Rough Work

114. It can be inferred from the given data that profit per unit sales
(a) is non-decreasing over the given period of time
(b) is decreasing over the given period of time
(c) remains constant over the given period of time
(d) cannot determine
(e) None of these

DIRECTIONS (Qs. 115 - 119) : Study the following graphs carefully and answer the questions given below.

Sales and production of Khadi and Village Industries

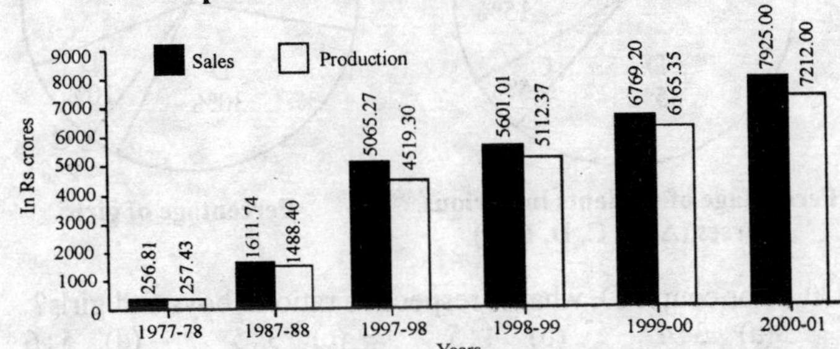

Number of persons employed in khadi and village industries.

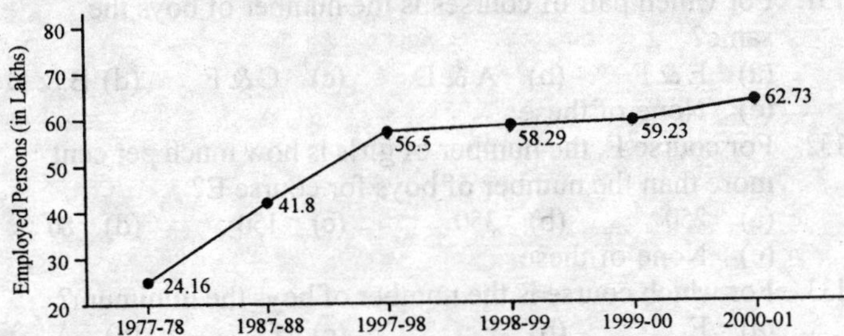

Note : Assume that the periods (years) are in succession.

115. During which period did the sales witness the highest growth as compared to the previous period?
(a) 1997-98 (b) 1987-88 (c) 2000-2001
(d) 1999-2000 (e) None of these

116. During which period the ratio of sales to production was the lowest?
(a) 1977-78 (b) 1997-98 (c) 1999-2000
(d) 2000-2001 (e) None of these

117. In which period was the production per employee the lowest?
(a) 1998-99 (b) 1997-98 (c) 1977-78
(d) 2000-2001 (e) None of these

118. In which period was the production per thousand employees the highest?
(a) 1998-99 (b) 1997-98 (c) 1977-78
(d) 2000-2001 (e) None of these

119. During which period was the ratio to sales of production the highest?
(a) 1977-78 (b) 1987-88 (c) 1997-98
(d) 1998-99 (e) None of these

DIRECTIONS (Qs. 120 - 123) : Study the following graph carefully and answer the question based on it.

Production of rose in various states

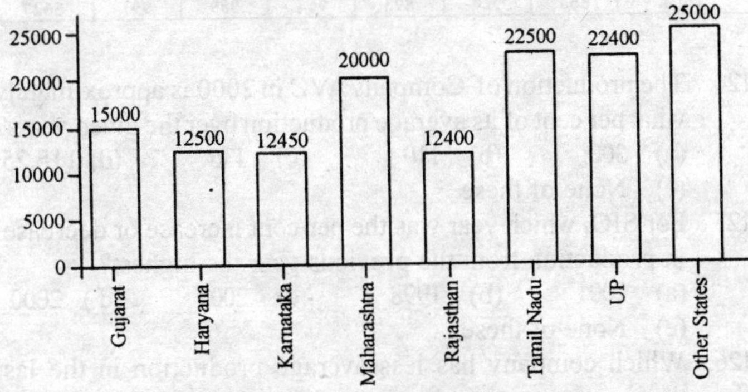

120. Which of the following state(s) contribute(s) less than 10 per cent in the total rose production?
(a) Only Rajasthan
(b) Rajasthan, Karnataka
(c) Rajasthan, Karnataka, Haryana
(d) Rajasthan, karnataka, Haryana and Gujarat
(e) None of these

121. By what percentage rose production of other states is more than that of the Maharashtra?
(a) 25 (b) 30 (c) 20 (d) 15
(e) None of these

Space for Rough Work

122. What is the approximate average production of roses (in thousands) across all the states?
(a) 21 (b) 20 (c) 19 (d) 18
(e) None of these

123. Approximately what percentage of the total rose producation is shared by the other states
(a) 10 (b) 20 (c) 30 (d) 40
(e) None of these

DIRECTIONS (Qs. 124 - 129) : Study the following table to answer the given questions.

Production (in crore units) of six companies over the years

Company	Years						Total
	1997	1998	1999	2000	2001	2002	
TP	103	150	105	107	110	132	707
ZIR	75	80	83	86	90	91	505
AVC	300	300	300	360	370	340	1970
CTU	275	280	281	280	285	287	1688
PEN	25	30	35	40	42	45	217
SIO	85	87	89	91	92	96	540
Total	**863**	**927**	**893**	**964**	**989**	**991**	**5627**

124. The production of Company AVC in 2000 is approximately what per cent of its average production over the given years?
(a) 300 (b) 110 (c) 136 (d) 118.25
(e) None of these

125. For SIO, which year was the per cent increase or decrease in production from the previous year the highest?
(a) 2001 (b) 1998 (c) 2002 (d) 2000
(e) None of these

126. Which company has less average production in the last three years compared to that of first three years?
(a) No company (b) CTU (c) ZIR
(d) TP (e) None of these

127. The total production of the six companies in the first two given years is what per cent of that of last two given years? (round off up to two decimal places)
(a) 87.08 (b) 104.55 (c) 90.40 (d) 10.62
(e) None of these

128. For ZIR, which of the following is the difference between production in 2002 and that in 2001?
(a) 10,00,00,000 (b) 1,00,00,000
(c) 10,00,000 (d) 40,00,000 (e) None of these

129. For how many companies did the production increase every year from that of the previous year?
(a) One (b) Two (c) Three (d) Four
(e) None of these

DIRECTIONS (Qs. 130 - 134) : Study the following pie-graphs to answer the given questions.

Total students: 1200 (800 girls + 400 boys)

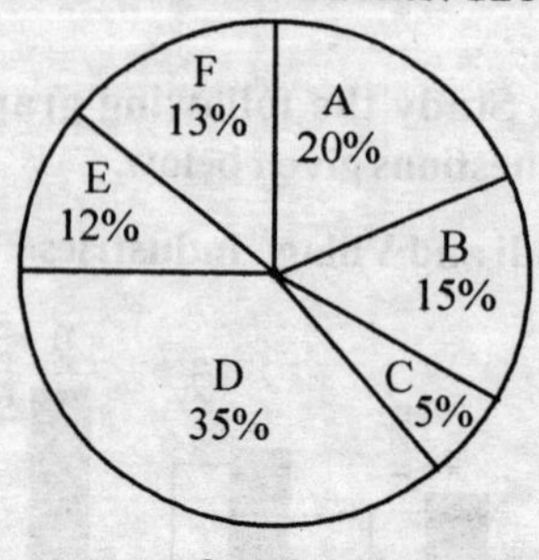

Percentage of students in various courses (A, B, C, D, E, F)

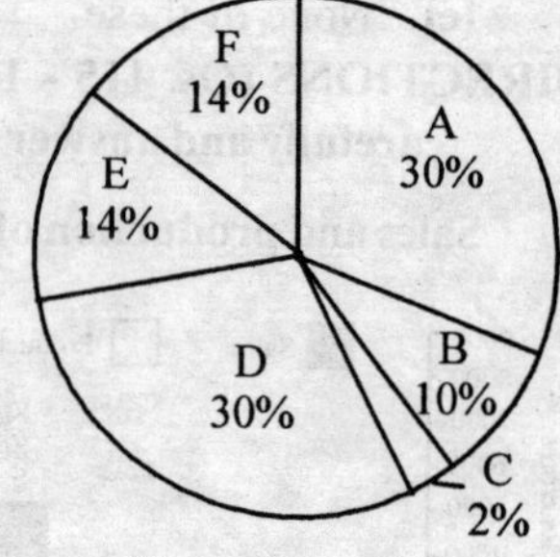

Percentage of girls

130. For course D, what is respective ratio of boys and girls?
(a) 3 : 4 (b) 4 : 5 (c) 3 : 5 (d) 5 : 6
(e) None of these

131. For which pair of courses is the number of boys the same?
(a) E & F (b) A & D (c) C & F (d) B & D
(e) None of these

132. For course E, the number of girls is how much per cent more than the number of boys for course E?
(a) 250 (b) 350 (c) 150 (d) 80
(e) None of these

133. For which course is the number of boys the minimum?
(a) E (b) F (c) C (d) A
(e) None of these

134. How many girls are there in course C?
(a) 44 (b) 16 (c) 40 (d) 160
(e) None of these

DIRECTIONS (Qs. 135 - 139) : The question consists of a question and two statements numbered (I) and (II) given below it. You have to decide whether the data provided in the statements are sufficient to answer the question. Read both the statements and give answer

(a) if the question can be answered with the help of BOTH the statements but not with the help of either statement itself;

(b) if the question can NOT be answered even with the help of BOTH the statements;

(c) if the question can be answered with the help of statement II ALONE;

(d) if the question can be answered with the help of statement I ALONE;

(e) if EITHER the statement I or II is sufficient.

135. The sum of cubes of three consecutive odd numbers is what per cent of the sum of the squares of the same nos.?

I. The average of those nos. is 21.

II. The product of those nos. is 2688.

136. What is the speed of a boat?

I. The boat covers a distance of 48 km in 6 hours while running upstream.

II. It covers the same distance in 4 hours while running downstream.

137. What is the number x if

I. The LCM of x and 18 is 36.

II. The HCF of x and 18 is 2.

138. Is the figure ABCD a rectangle?

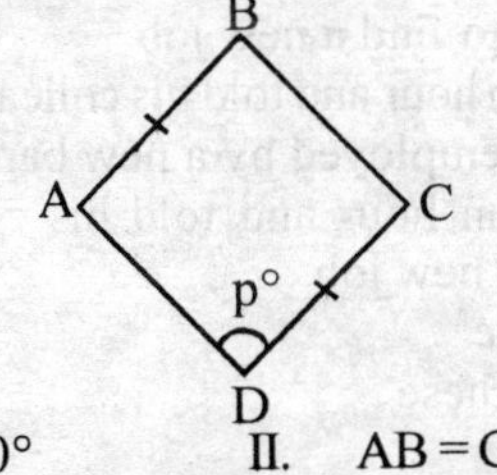

I. p = 90° II. AB = CD

139. What is the width of a stone slab of length 4 metres and thickness $\frac{1}{16}$th of the length?

I. Volume of the slab is 2 cu metres.

II. Surface area of the slab is 19 sq metres.

DIRECTIONS (Qs. 140 - 149) : Each of the questions below consists of a question and two statements numbered (I) and (II) given below it. You have to decide whether the data provided in the statements are sufficient to answer the question. Read both the statements and give answer

(a) if statement (I) ALONE is sufficient, but statement (II) alone is not sufficient;

(b) if statement (II) ALONE is sufficient, but statement (I) alone is not sufficient;

(c) if BOTH statements TOGETHER are sufficient, but NEITHER statement alone is sufficient;

(d) if EACH statement ALONE is sufficient;

(e) if BOTH statement TOGETHER are not sufficient.

140. What was the total compound interest on a sum after three years?

(I) The interest after one year was Rs. 100 and the sum was Rs. 1000.

(II) The difference between simple and compound interest on a sum of Rs. 1000 at the end of two years was Rs. 10.

141. How many hours a day must 4 pumps work to empty a conical tank in 1 day?

(I) 3 pumps working 8 hours a day can empty another tank in 2 days.

(II) The other tank has twice the floor area and one and a half times the depth of the original tank.

142. By selling a product at 20% profit, how much profit was earned?

(I) The difference between cost and selling price is Rs.40.

(II) The selling price is 120 per cent of the cost price.

143. How much is the average salary of the 30 assembly workers? The foreman is paid a salary of Rs 12,000.

(I) The total salary paid to the 30 assembly workers and the foreman is Rs. 312,000

(II) The foreman's salary is 120% of the average salary of the 30 assembly workers.

144. A bag contains coins of one-rupee, 50 -paise and 25–paise denominations. The total amount in the bag is Rs.500 . To find the total number of 50–paise coins, which of the following information is sufficient?

(I) The number of the coin is in the ratio 3 : 4 : 5.

(II) The number of one rupee–coins is one– fourth the total number of coins in the bag.

145. Two trains of length 80 m and 100 m are moving in opposite directions on parallel tracks. If they cross each other in 36 second, how much time will they take to pass each other if they move in the same direction?

(I) First one train passes a pole in one minute.

(II) The other train also passes a 120 m long railway bridge in one minute.

Space for Rough Work

146. Kundu and Puttu can do a work in 12 days. In how many days will Puttu compoete the work working alone?
    (I) Kundu can complete the work in 36 days.
    (II) Kundu is half as efficient as Puttu.

147. In the diagram shown, is ΔABC isosceles ?

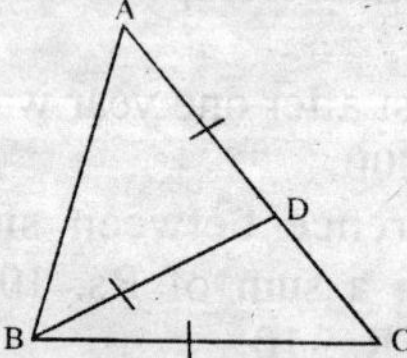

    (I) $BC = BD = DA$ (II) BD bisects $\angle ABC$

148. The speed of a 110 metres long running train 'X' is 45 per cent more than the speed of another 160 meters long train 'Z' running in opposite direction. What is the speed of the train 'Z'?
    (I) The two train crossed each other in 6.5 seconds.
    (II) The difference between the speed of the two trains was 28 km/hr.

149. A man holding 7 cards in his hanD. Four are 'nines' and three are 'fives'. How many cards does he lay on the table?
    (I) He lays a card on the table if the number on the card is divisible by 3.
    (II) He lays a card on the table if and only if the number n is divisible by 3.

DIRECTIONS (Qs. 150 - 154) :In each of these questions, in the given sentences, a part of the sentence is underlineD. Beneath each sentence, four different ways of phrasing the underlined part are indicateD. Choose the best alternative.

150. Since we are living in Bombay for five years, we are reluctant to move to another city.
    (a) Being that we living
    (b) Since we were living
    (c) Since we have been living
    (d) Being that we have been living
    (e) None of these

151. As a child, my parents took me to Jammu to visit my grandmother.
    (a) When I was a child, my parents took me to Jammu to visit my grandmother
    (b) My parents took me, as a child, to Jammu to visit my grandmother
    (c) My parents took me to Jammu to visit my grandmother as a chilD.
    (d) A child, my parents took me to Jammu to visit my grandmother
    (e) None of these

152. Anyone interested in the use of computer can learn much if you have access to a state-of-the-an microcomputer.
    (a) if he has access to (b) if access is available to
    (c) by access to (d) from access to
    (e) None of these

153. Start the motor, and then you should remove the blocks.
    (a) Start the motor, then removing the blocks
    (b) Starting the motor, the blocks should then be removed
    (c) Start the motor and then remove the blocks
    (d) Starting the motor remove the blocks
    (e) None of these

154. The Vice President of the local bank spoke for a half an hour and told his colleague that he, his colleague, must consider finding a new job, or accept a reduction in salary.
    (a) for a half hour and told his colleague that he must consider to find a new job
    (b) for half an hour and told his colleague that the colleague must get employed by a new bank
    (c) for half an hour and told his colleague to consider finding, a new job
    (d) no change
    (e) None of these

DIRECTIONS (Qs. 155 - 159) : In each of these questions a disarranged sentence is given in which words or phrases are lettered A, B, C, D .... You are to arrange these to form a meaningful sentence.

155. A. Still, Sophie might need open-heart surgery later in life and now be more prone to respiratory infections.
    B. But with the news that his infant daughter Sophie has a hole in her heart, he appears quite vulnerable.
    C. While the condition sounds bad, it is not life threatening, and frequently corrects itself.
    D. Sylvester Stallone has made millions and built a thriving career out of looking invincible.
    (a) DCAB (b) DBAC
    (c) DBCA (d) DCBA
    (e) None of these

Space for Rough Work

156. A. That Hollywood is a man's world is certainly true, but it is not the whole truth.
B. Even Renaissance film woman, Jodie Foster, who hosts this compendium of movie history, confesses surprise at this.
C. She says that she had no idea that women were so active in the industry even in those days.
D. During the silent era, for example, female screenwriters outnumbered males 10 to 1.
(a) ADBC (b) ABDC
(c) DCAB (d) ABCD
(e) None of these

157. A. The Saheli Program, run by the US Cross-Cultural Solutions, is offering a three week tour of India that involves more than frenzied sightseeing.
B. Participants interested in women's issues will learn about arranged marriages, dowries and infanticide.
C. Holiday packages include all sorts of topics , but female infanticide must be a first for tourism.
D. Interspersed with these talks and meetings are visits to cities like New Delhi and Agra, home to the Taj Mahal.
(a) ACDB (b) CDBA
(c) ADBC (d) CABD
(e) None of these

158. A. Its business decisions are made on the timely and accurate flow of information.
B. It has 1700 employees in 13 branch and representative offices across the Asia-Pacific region.
C. For employees to maintain a competitive edge in a fast-moving field, they must have quick access to J P Morgan's proprietary trade related data.
D. J P Morgan is one of the largest banking institutions in the U S and a premier international trading firm.
(a) DBAC (b) DCBA
(c) CDAB (d) DCAB
(e) None of these

159. A. Something magical is happening to our planet.
B. Some are calling it a paradigm shift.
C. It's getting smaller.
D. Others call it business transformation.
(a) ABDC (b) ACDB
(c) ABCD (d) ACBD
(e) None of these

DIRECTIONS (Qs. 160 - 170) :In each of these questions four words are given marked A, B, C and D. Two of these words are most nearly the same are opposite in meaning. Identify those two words:

160. A. Affected B. Desolate
C. Anxious D. lonely
(a) B –D (b) A – C (c) B – C (d) A – D
(e) None of these

161. A. Gaucherie B. Dexterity
C. Eulogise D. Dearth
(a) B-C (b) C-D (c) A-B (d) B-D
(e) None of these

162. A. Fallacious B. Pusillanimity
C. Fortitude D. Fallible
(a) B-C (b) A-B (c) C-D (d) A-D
(e) None of these

163. A. Incarcerate B. confine
C. Impeccable D. Felicitate
(a) A-B (b) C-D (c) B-D (d) B-C
(e) None of these

164. A. Disinterested B. comprehensible
C. Emulate D. Impartial
(a) C-D (b) B-C (c) A-D (d) C-A
(e) None of these

165. A. Inamorata B. Beloved
C. Imbecile D. Novice
(a) A-C (b) A-B (c) C-D (d) B-C
(e) None of these

166. A. Adumbrate B. Overshadow
C. Zany D. Vulpine
(a) A-B (b) B-C (c) C-D (d) D-A
(e) None of these

167. A. Cantankerous B. Querulous
C. Amicable D. Occult
(a) B-D (b) D-A (c) A-C (d) B-C
(e) None of these

168. A. Jouisance B. Joyousness
C. Betrothed D. Usurp
(a) A-B (b) B-C (c) C-D (d) B-D
(e) None of these

169. a hunky-dory B. Choleric
C. Shoddy D. Enervate
(a) B-C (b) C-D (c) A-C (d) D-A
(e) None of these

Space for Rough Work

170. A. Certitude B. Hoipolli
C. Certainty D. Hostile
(a) C-B (b) A-B (c) A-C (d) B-D
(e) None of these

DIRECTIONS (Qs. 171 - 179) : Read the following passage carefully and answer the questions given below it.

Icicles- two meters long and, at their tips, as bright and sharp as needless- hang from the eaves: wild ice stalactites, dragon's teeth. I peer through them to see the world transformed to abstract whiteout. Little dervish snow tornadoes twirl across the blank. The car is out there somewhere, represented by a subtle bump in the snow-fielD. The old jeep truck, a larger beast, is up to its door handles, like a sinking remnant: dinosaur yelding to ice age. The town's behemoth snow-plow passes on the road, dome light twirling, and casts aside a frozen doe that now lies, neck broken, upon the roadisde snow-bank, soon to vanish under the snowfall still to come.

There is double-jointed consiciousness at work in the dramatics of big weather. Down in the snowstorm, we are as mortal as the deer. I sink to my waist in a drift, I panic, my arms claw for an instant, like a drowning swimmer's in the powder. Men up and down the storm collapse with cornoaries, snow shovels in their hands, gone a deathly colour, like frost-bitten plums.

Yet when we go upstairs to consult the Weather Channel, we settle down, as cosy gods do, to hover high above the earth and watch the play with a divine perspective. Moist air labelled L for low rides up the continent from the Gulf of Mexico and collides with the high that has slid down from the North Pole. And thus is whipped up the egg-white fluff on the studio map that, down in the frozen, messy world, buries mortals.

An odd new metaphysics of weather: It is not that weather has necessarily grown more apocalyptiC. The famous "Winter of the Blue Snow" of 1886-87 turned rivers of the American West into glaciers that when they thawed, carried along inundation of dead cattle. President Theodore Roosevelt was virtually ruined as a rancher by the weather that destroyed 65% of his herD. In 1811 Mississippi River flowed northward briefly because of the New Madrid earthquake.

What's new in America is the theatre of it. Television does not create weather any more than it creates contemporary politics. However, the ritual ceremonies of televised weather have endowed a subject often previously banal with an amazing life as mass entertainment, nationwide interactive precoccupation and a kind of immense performance art.

What we have is weather as electronic American Shintosim , a casual but almost mystic daily religion wherein nature is not inert but restless, stirring alive with kinetic fronts and meanings and turbulent expectations (forecasts, variables, prophecies). We have installed an elaborate priesthood and technology of interpretation: acolytes and satellites preside over snow and circuses. At least major snowstorms have about them an innocence and moral neutrality that is more refreshing than the last national television spectacle, the O.J. Simpson trial.

One attraction is the fact that these large gestures of nature are apolitical. The weather in its mirabilis mode can, of course, be dragged into the op-ed page to start a macro-argument about global warning or amicro-spat over a mayor's fecklessness in deploying snowplows. Otherwise, traumas of weather do not admit of political interpretation. The snow Shinto reintroduces an element of what is almost charmingly uncontrollable in life. And, as shown last week, surprising , even as the priests predict it. This is welcome- a kind of idological relief-in a rather stupidly politicised society living under the delusion that everything in life (and death) is arguable, politicised society living under the delusion that everything in life (and death) is arguable, political and therefore manipulable - from diet to DNA . None of the old earthbound Marxist who-Whom here in meteorology, but rather sky gods that bang around at higher altitudes and leave the earth in its misery, to submit to the sloppy collateral damage.

The moral indifference of weather, even when destructive, is somehow stimulating. Why ? The sheer levelling force is pleassing. It overrides routine and organises people into a shared moment that will become a punctuating memory in their lives (" Lord, remember the blizzard in '96?").

Or perhaps one's reaction is no more complicated than a child's delight in dramatic disruption. Anyone loves to stand on the beach with a hurricane coing- a darkly lashing Byronism in surf and wind gets the blood up. The god's or child , part of the mind welcomes big weather -floods and blizzards. The coping, grown-up-human part curses it, and sinks.

The paradox of big weather: it makes people feel important even while it dramatised their insignificance. In some ways, extreme weather is a brief moral equivalent of war- as stimulating as war can sometimes be, though without most of the carnage.

The sun rises upon diamond- scattered snow-fields and glistens upon the lucent dragon's teeth. In the distance , three deer, roused from their shelter under pines, venture forth. They struggle and plunge undulously through the opulent white.

Space for Rough Work

Upstairs, I switch on the Shinto Weather Channel and the priests at the map show me the next wave - white swirls and eddies over Indiana, heading ominously east.

171. The author's reaction to the snowstorm may be said to be
(a) fascinated (b) scared
(c) cynical (d) deadpan
(e) None of these

172. How many vehicles does the author mention in the passage?
(a) One (b) Two
(c) Three (d) Four
(e) None of these

173. Which of the following was not the result of the 'Winter of Blue Snow' ?
(a) It almost ruined Theodore Roosevelt
(b) It made the Mississippi flow northward
(c) It turned rivers into glaciers
(d) It killed a lot of cattle
(e) None of these

174. The author compares the weather bulletin channel reportage to
(a) a war (b) the O.J .Simpson trial.
(c) a ritual ceremony (d) a theatre.
(e) None of these

175. According to the author, one of the greatest attractions of the weather is that
(a) it is politicised (b) it is a political
(c) it is reckless (d) it is beautiful
(e) None of these

176. The moral indifference of the weather is stimulating in spite of being destructive because
(a) it shows no mercy
(b) it organises people into a shared moment
(c) Both (a) and (b)
(d) Neither (a) and (b)
(e) None of these

177. Which of the following is not true of the weather ?
(a) it is a moral equivalent of war
(b) it is pleasantly manipulable.
(c) it is a levelling force
(d) it dramatised man's insignificance
(e) None of these

178. What is most probably the physical position of the author of the passage ?
(a) In his house (b) In a snowstorm
(c) In his office (d) In a funk
(e) None of these

179. The word ' undulously' in the context of the passage means
(a) unduly (b) indomitable
(c) powerful (d) curved
(e) None of these

DIRECTIONS (Qs. 180 - 182) : Pick out the nearest correct meaning or SYNONYM of the word(s) given below:

180. Quote is what one of the following words means;
(a) sight (b) sigh
(c) sue (d) cite
(e) None of these

181. Harmony is the nearest equivalent of which of the following words
(a) cemetery (b) ceremony
(c) symmetry (d) hierarchy
(e) None of these

182. Which of the following words means mishap
(a) incident (b) ceremony
(c) advent (d) affectation
(e) None of these

DIRECTIONS (Qs. 183 - 185) : Pick out the ANTONYM of the words given below:

183. RECKLESS
(a) modest (b) awkward
(c) celebrated (d) cautious
(e) None of these

184. INSULT
(a) Humiliation (b) Credulity
(c) Degradation (d) Honour
(e) None of these

185. ABANDON
(a) Roost (b) Forfeit
(c) quit (d) Forsake
(e) None of these

DIRECTIONS (Qs. 186 - 190) : In each of the following sentences four words or phrases have been underlineD. Only one underlined part in each sentence is not acceptable in Standard English, Pick up the part (a), (b), (c) or (d). If all the four words are correctly spelt and also appropriate in the content of the sentence, mark (e) i.e. 'All correct' as your answer.

Space for Rough Work

186. There is something more in the (a) fact that the (b) guns have (c) or are about (d) to be sent abroad. All correct (e).

187. The (a) deceased lord along with (b) his brother started a (c) business in India (d) All correct (e).

188. He relieved (a) the monotony of book peddling (b) by becoming (c) an assistant to a conjuror or to other (d) similar engagements. All correct (e)

189. You have been (a) more able to withstand (b) the treaties (c) than did he (d). All correct (e)

190. It is hoped that with the medical fee being withdrawn (a) and men can be tested (b) and finally accepted (c), a large number of people will come forward (d). All correct (e)

DIRECTIONS (Qs. 191 - 200) : In the following passage there are blanks, each of which has been numbered. These numbers are also printed below the passage and against each five words are suggested, one of which fits the blank appropriately. Find out the appropriate word in each case.

A good percentage of the population of India is tribal. The tribal live in the hills and forests of the country and have been little **191** by the **192** currents of the plains. Practically all the states of India have their tribal population. The tribes are numerous, computed to about 200, some living in **193** regions in the dense forests, and others on the borders of villages. Some tribes are **194** to a few souls, while others like the Santhals, run into millions and are steadily **195** in numbers. During the British Period some of them were known as 'criminal tribes' for they showed **196** respect for the Indian Panel Code. After independence they have been named Scheduled Tribes. Under modern conditions isolation, however, has become **197** and the hill tribes are getting **198**. The cultural traffic is two-way. Social reformers are taking civilisation to the hills, and the tribes, **199** their old occupations of hunting and **200** farming, are setting in villages, towns and cities as labourers and industrial workers.

191. (a) affected (b) domiciled (c) motivated (d) deprived (e) favoured
192. (a) financial (b) proud (c) cultural (d) unruly (e) swift
193. (a) comfortable (b) marshy (c) wild (d) unpopulated (e) inhospitable
194. (a) devoted (b) confined (c) susceptible (d) related (e) attached
195. (a) constant (b) deteriorated (c) developing (d) increasing (e) decreasing
196. (a) abundant (b) genuine (c) superficial (d) exorbitant (e) scant
197. (a) crucial (b) necessary (c) difficult (d) convenient (e) indispensable
198. (a) civilized (b) demoralised (c) wiped-out (d) entertained (e) reduced
199. (a) escaping (b) with (c) enhancing (d) leaving (e) continuing
200. (a) productive (b) primitive (c) profitable (d) cultivatable (e) scientific

Space for Rough Work

MAHARASHTRA CET - MOCK TEST 2

RESPONSE SHEET

NAME : .... DATE : ....

	(A)	(B)	(C)	(D)		(A)	(B)	(C)	(D)		(A)	(B)	(C)	(D)		(A)	(B)	(C)	(D)
1.					51.					101.					151.				
2.					52.					102.					152.				
3.					53.					103.					153.				
4.					54.					104.					154.				
5.					55.					105.					155.				
6.					56.					106.					156.				
7.					57.					107.					157.				
8.					58.					108.					158.				
9.					59.					109.					159.				
10.					60.					110.					160.				
11.					61.					111.					161.				
12.					62.					112.					162.				
13.					63.					113.					163.				
14.					64.					114.					164.				
15.					65.					115.					165.				
16.					66.					116.					166.				
17.					67.					117.					167.				
18.					68.					118.					168.				
19.					69.					119.					169.				
20.					70.					120.					170.				
21.					71.					121.					171.				
22.					72.					122.					172.				
23.					73.					123.					173.				
24.					74.					124.					174.				
25.					75.					125.					175.				
26.					76.					126.					176.				
27.					77.					127.					177.				
28.					78.					128.					178.				
29.					79.					129.					179.				
30.					80.					130.					180.				
31.					81.					131.					181.				
32.					82.					132.					182.				
33.					83.					133.					183.				
34.					84.					134.					184.				
35.					85.					135.					185.				
36.					86.					136.					186.				
37.					87.					137.					187.				
38.					88.					138.					188.				
39.					89.					139.					189.				
40.					90.					140.					190.				
41.					91.					141.					191.				
42.					92.					142.					192.				
43.					93.					143.					193.				
44.					94.					144.					194.				
45.					95.					145.					195.				
46.					96.					146.					196.				
47.					97.					147.					197.				
48.					98.					148.					198.				
49.					99.					149.					199.				
50.					100.					150.					200.				

MAHARASHTRA CET

MOCK TEST - 3

☛ ***INSTRUCTIONS :***

- **There are 200 questions in this test. You will be given 150 minutes to complete the test.**
- **Each question carries 1 mark. There is no negative marking.**

1. Which of the following will be the second digit of the second largest number after reversing the positions of the digits in each of the following five numbers?
513 468 726 397 684
(a) 9 (b) 1
(c) 6 (d) 2
(e) 8

2. How many such pairs of letters are there in the word HEART–BURN each of which has as many letters between them in the word as in the English alphabet?
(a) One (b) Two
(c) Three (d) More than three
(e) None of these

3. In a row of children facing South, Neha is fifth to the right of Robin. Ashok is twelfth to the right of Robin. Ashok is twelfth to the right of Neha and twenty eighth from the left end. What is Robin's position from the left end?
(a) 11th (b) 13th
(c) 14th (d) Data inadequate
(e) None of these

4. In a certain code RAID is written as 5126 and NEAR is written as 7315. How is DINE written in that code?
(a) 6253 (b) 6273
(c) 6723 (d) 1273
(e) None of these

5. In a certain code language 'you could to there' is written as' *la na pa da*' and 'could you come back' is written as '*ha ta da la*'. how is 'back' written in that code language?
(a) *ha* (b) *ta*
(c) *ha* or *ta* (d) Data inadequate
(e) None of these

6. How many such digits are there in the number 3246759, each of which will occupy the same position when rearranged in ascending order as in the number?
(a) None (b) One
(c) Two (d) Three
(e) More than three

7. How many such pairs of letters are there in the word RECRUIT each of which has as many letters between them in the word as they have in the English alphabet?
(a) One (b) Two
(c) Three (d) None
(e) More than three

8. How many such pairs of letters are there in the word DISTURB, each one has as many letters between its two letters in the word as there are between them in the English alphabet?
(a) 4 (b) 5
(c) 3 (d) 2
(e) None of these

9. Ganesh is 7th to the left of Akshay in a row of boys facing North. Vijay, who is 20th from the left end of the row is 7th to the right of Akshay. If Kamlesh who is 3rd to the right of Ganesh is 20th from the right end of the row, how many boys are there in the row?
(a) 30
(b) 28
(c) 26
(d) Cannot be determined
(e) None of these

Space for Rough Work

DIRECTIONS (Qs. 10 & 11) : Complete the following series.

10. The next three terms of the series 137153163 are
    (a) 786 (b) 524
    (c) 127 (d) 611
    (e) None of these
11. The next three terms of the series 13102164129 are
    (a) 778 (b) 612
    (c) 542 (d) 388
    (e) None of these
12. Various terms of a series is given with one term missing as shown by (?). Choose the missing term :
    2Z5, 7Y7, 14X9, 23W11, 34V13, (?)
    (a) 27U24 (b) 45U15
    (c) 47U15 (d) 27V14
    (e) None of these
13. In the series of terms given in the question below, identify the term which does not fit in the series.
    What will be the next term in : BDF, CFI, DHL, ?
    (a) CJM (b) EIM (c) EJO (d) EMI
    (e) None of these

DIRECTIONS (Qs. 14 & 15) : In each of the following questions, there are two words to the left of the sign :: which are connected in some way. The same relationship obtains between the third word and one of the four alternatives under it. Find the correct alternative in each question.

14. Man : Walk :: Fish : ?
    (a) Swim (b) Eat
    (c) Live (d) Sleep
    (e) Fly
15. Import : Export :: Expenditure : ?
    (a) Deficit (b) Revenue
    (c) Debt (d) Tax
    (e) None of these
16. A pair of words is given, followed by four pairs of words as alternatives. Choose the correct pair in which the words bears the same relationship to each other as the words of the given pair bear.
    Lawn : Grass ::
    (a) Wool : Sheep (b) Skin : Goat
    (c) Pelt : Fur (d) Rice : Farm
    (e) None of these

DIRECTIONS (Qs. 17 & 18) : In each of the following questions, four alternatives are given, out of which three are alike in a certain way while one is different. Choose the odd one.

17. (a) Rose (b) Lotus
    (c) Marigold (d) Lily
    (e) None of these
18. (a) 22, 4, 5 (b) 34, 4, 8
    (c) 37, 4, 9 (d) 54, 4, 13
    (e) None of these

DIRECTIONS (Qs. 19-28) : In each of the questions given below which one of the five answer figures on the bottom should come after the problem figure on the top, if the sequence were continued?

19.

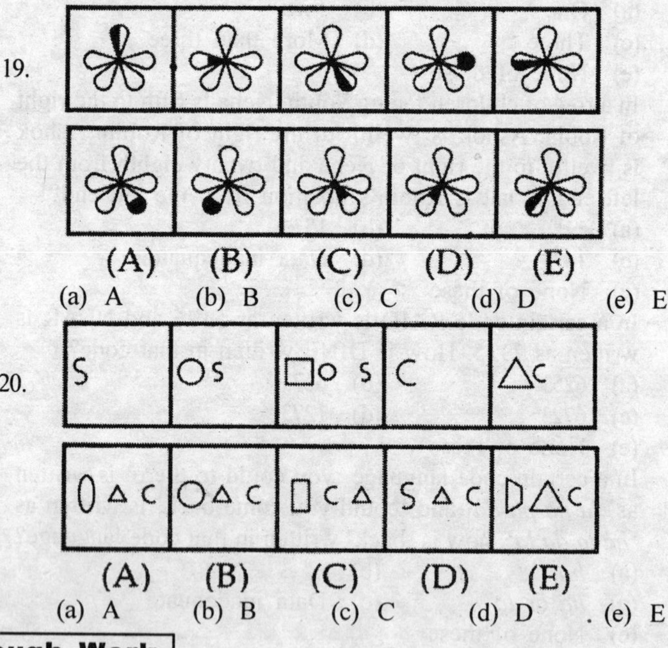

(a) A (b) B (c) C (d) D (e) E

20.

(a) A (b) B (c) C (d) D (e) E

Space for Rough Work

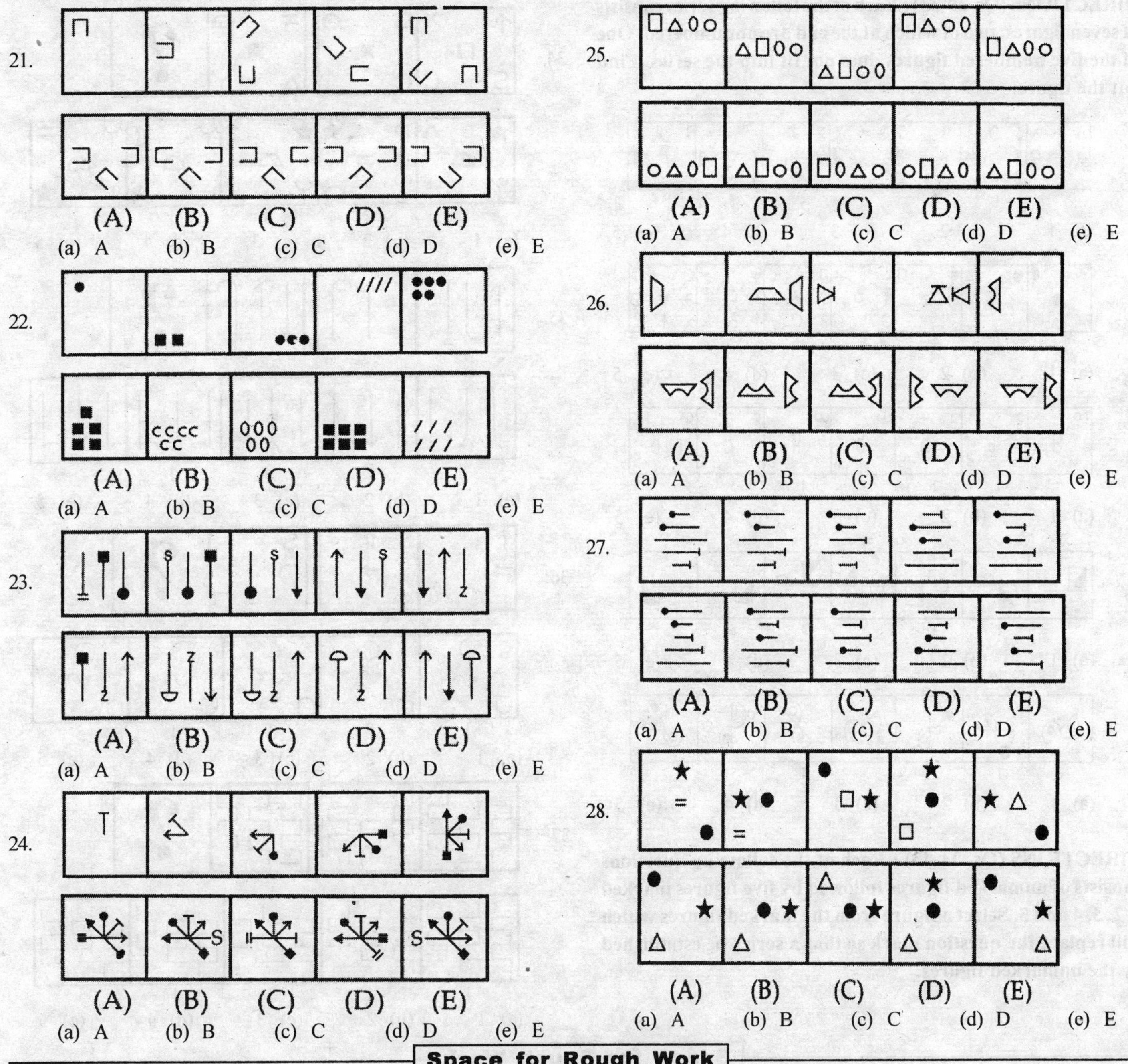
21.
(A) (B) (C) (D) (E)
(a) A (b) B (c) C (d) D (e) E
22.
(A) (B) (C) (D) (E)
(a) A (b) B (c) C (d) D (e) E
23.
(A) (B) (C) (D) (E)
(a) A (b) B (c) C (d) D (e) E
24.
(A) (B) (C) (D) (E)
(a) A (b) B (c) C (d) D (e) E
25.
(A) (B) (C) (D) (E)
(a) A (b) B (c) C (d) D (e) E
26.
(A) (B) (C) (D) (E)
(a) A (b) B (c) C (d) D (e) E
27.
(A) (B) (C) (D) (E)
(a) A (b) B (c) C (d) D (e) E
28.
(A) (B) (C) (D) (E)
(a) A (b) B (c) C (d) D (e) E
Space for Rough Work

DIRECTIONS (Qs. 29-33) : Each of the following series consists of seven figures, two of which at the end are unnumbered. One of the five numbered figures does not fit into the series. Find out the figure.

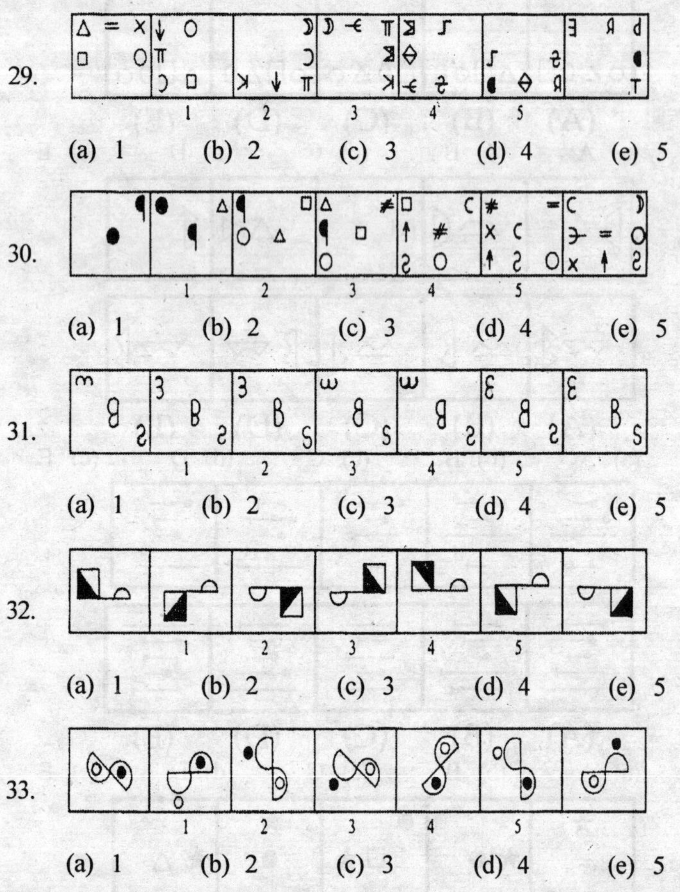

29. (a) 1 (b) 2 (c) 3 (d) 4 (e) 5

30. (a) 1 (b) 2 (c) 3 (d) 4 (e) 5

31. (a) 1 (b) 2 (c) 3 (d) 4 (e) 5

32. (a) 1 (b) 2 (c) 3 (d) 4 (e) 5

33. (a) 1 (b) 2 (c) 3 (d) 4 (e) 5

DIRECTIONS (Qs. 34-43) : Each of the following questions consists of unmarked figures followed by five figures marked 1, 2, 3, 4 and 5. Select a figure from the marked figures which will replace the question mark so that a series be established by the unmarked figures.

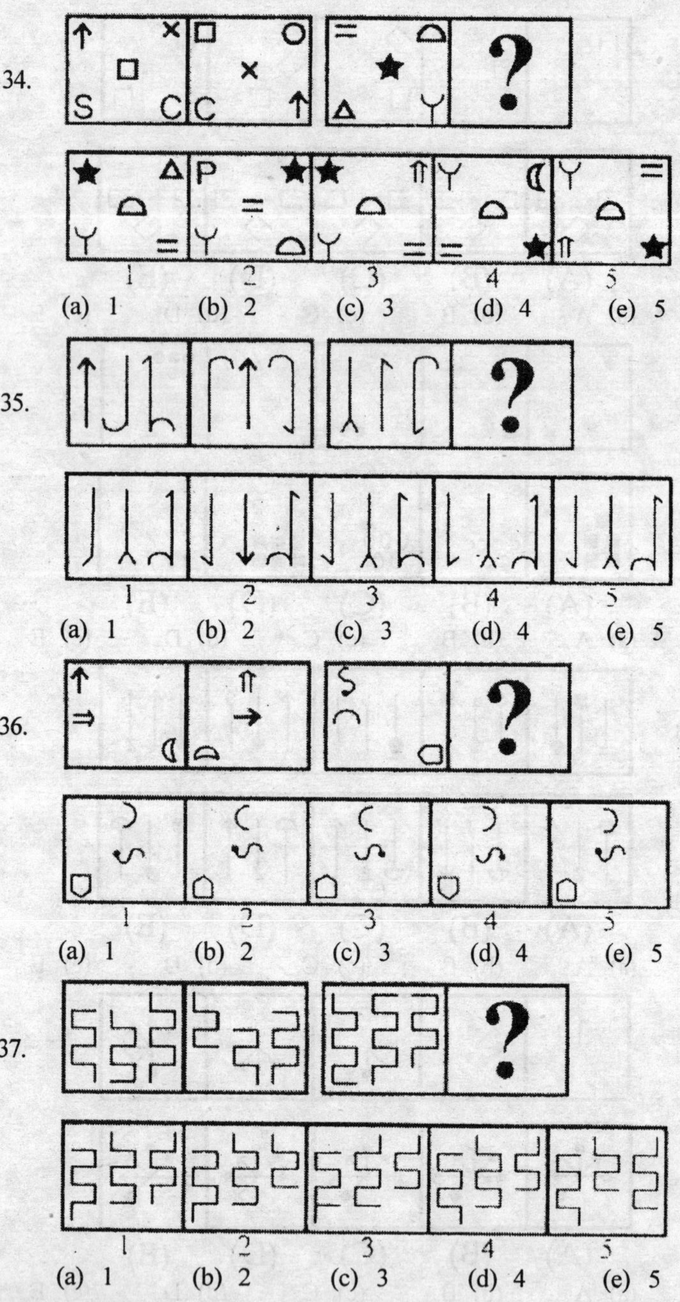

34. (a) 1 (b) 2 (c) 3 (d) 4 (e) 5

35. (a) 1 (b) 2 (c) 3 (d) 4 (e) 5

36. (a) 1 (b) 2 (c) 3 (d) 4 (e) 5

37. (a) 1 (b) 2 (c) 3 (d) 4 (e) 5

Space for Rough Work

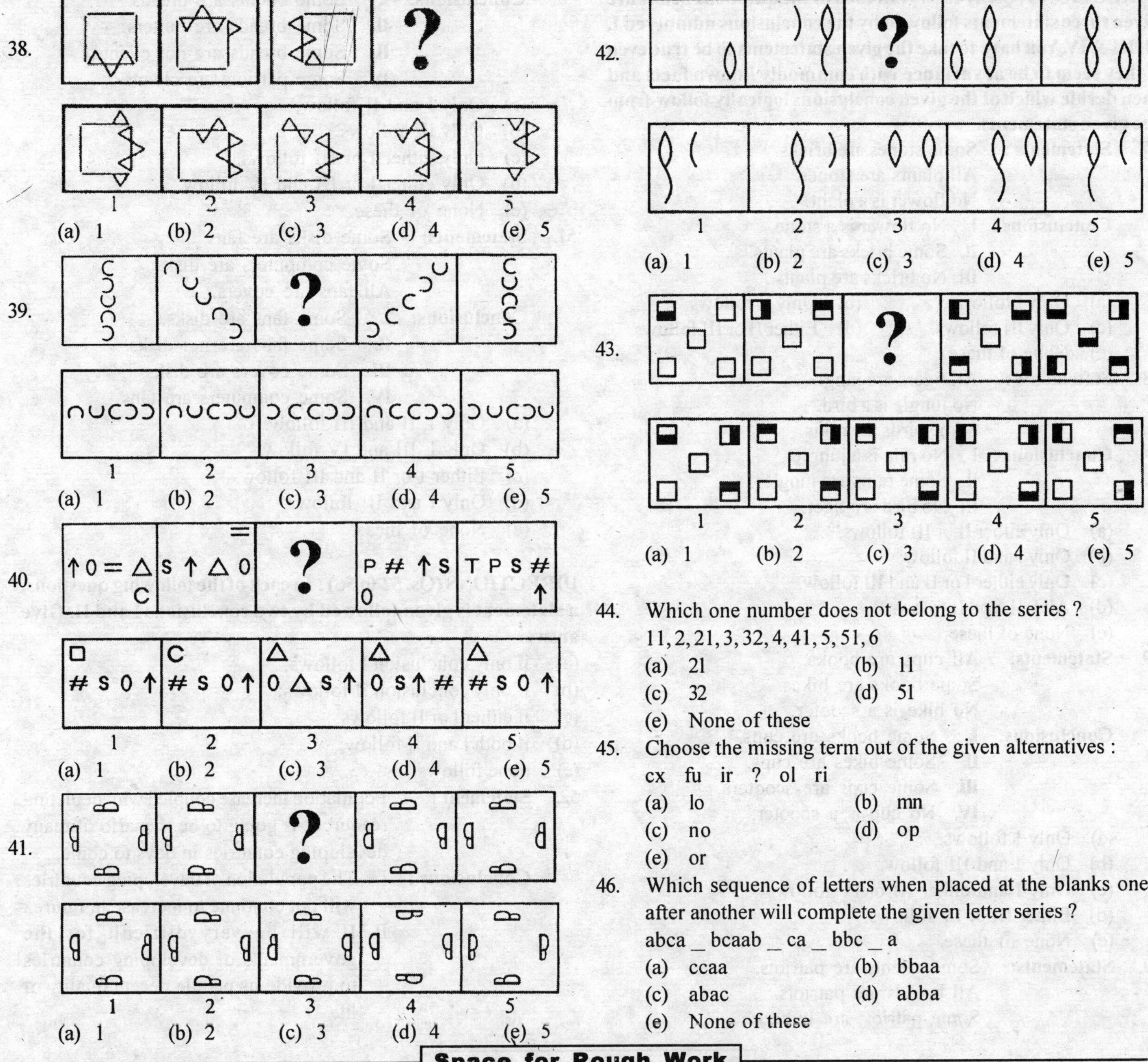

44. Which one number does not belong to the series ?
11, 2, 21, 3, 32, 4, 41, 5, 51, 6
(a) 21 (b) 11
(c) 32 (d) 51
(e) None of these

45. Choose the missing term out of the given alternatives :
cx fu ir ? ol ri
(a) lo (b) mn
(c) no (d) op
(e) or

46. Which sequence of letters when placed at the blanks one after another will complete the given letter series ?
abca _ bcaab _ ca _ bbc _ a
(a) ccaa (b) bbaa
(c) abac (d) abba
(e) None of these

Space for Rough Work

DIRECTIONS (Qs. 47 to 51) : In each of the questions below are given three statements followed by the conclusions numbered I, II, III & IV. You have to take the given statements to be true even if they seem to be at variance with commonly known facts and then decide which of the given conclusions logically follow from the given statements.

47. **Statements :** Some stones are bricks.
All plants are stones.
No flower is a plant.
Conclusions : I. No flower is a stone.
II. Some bricks are plants.
III. No bricks are plants.
(a) Only I follows. (b) Only II follows.
(c) Only III follows. (d) Either II or III follows.
(e) None of these

48. **Statements :** All tigers are jungles.
No jungle is a bird.
Some birds are rains.
Conclusions : I. No rain is a jungle.
II. Some rains are jungles.
III. No bird is a tiger.
(a) Only either II or III follows.
(b) Only I and II follow.
(c) Only either I or II and III follow.
(d) All I, II, and II folow.
(e) None of these

49. **Statements:** All cups are books.
Some books are bikes.
No bike is a scooter.
Conclusions: **I.** Some books are cups.
II. Some bikes are cups.
III. Some cups are scooters.
IV. No cup is a scooter.
(a) Only I follows.
(b) Only I and III follow.
(c) Only I and either III or IV follow.
(d) Either III or IV follows.
(e) None of these.

50. **Statements:** Some clients are patriots.
All breads are patriots.
Some patriots are butters.
Conclusions: **I.** Some clients are breads.
II. Some breads are butters.
III. Some breads are not clients
IV. Some patriots are clients
(a) Only I and II follow.
(b) Only IV follows.
(c) Only either I or III follows.
(d) Only either I or III and IV follow.
(e) None of these.

51. **Statements:** Some disks are fans
Some computers are disks.
All fans are covers.
Conclusions: **I.** Some fans are disks.
II. Some fans are not disks.
III. Some covers are disks.
IV. Some computers are fans.
(a) Only I, II and III follow.
(b) Only I, III and IV follow.
(c) Either I or II and III follow.
(d) Only I and III follow.
(e) None of these.

DIRECTIONS (Qs. 52 to 56) : In each of the following questions, a statement is given followed by two conclusions I and II. Give answer

(a) if only conclusion I follows;
(b) if only conclusion II follows;
(c) if either I or II follows;
(d) if both I and II follow;
(e) none follows.

52. **Statement :** Population increase coupled with depleting resources is going to be scenario of many developing countries in days to come.
Conclusions : I. The population of developing countries will not continue to increase in future.
II. It will be very difficult for the governments of developing countries to provide its people decent quality of life.

Space for Rough Work

53. **Statement :** All the organised persons find time for rest. Sunita, inspite of her very busy schedule, finds time for rest.

Conclusions : I. Sunita is an organised person.

II. Sunita is an industrious person.

54. **Statement :** Quality has a price tag. India is allocating lots of funds to education.

Conclusions : I. Quality of education in India would improve soon.

II. Funding alone can enhance quality of education.

55. **Statement :** Yes, I know honesty is the primary concern for discharging the duties of a police officer and my officers are aware of this. — Statement of police commissioner of city S.

Conclusions : I. The statement of police commissioner of city S is absolutely right.

II. The statement of police commissioner of city S is not absolutely right.

56. **Statement :** Modern man influences his destiny by the choice he makes unlike in the past.

Conclusions : I. Earlier there were less options available to man.

II. There was no desire in the past to influence the destiny.

DIRECTIONS (Qs. 57-59) : Study the following information carefully and answer the questions given below :

Five friends Yash, Neeraj, Mehul, Ram and Prakash are students of five different disciplines – Medical, Engineering, Architecture, Arts, Management. Each plays a different musical instrument Sitar, Tabla, Sarod, Guitar and Violin.

Mehul, a medical student, does not play Sarod or Sitar or Guitar.

Prakash is neither a student of Engineering nor Management.

Ram, who plays Tabla, is an Arts student.

Neither Prakash nor Yash plays Sarod.

57. Who among the following plays Sarod?
(a) Yash (b) Neeraj
(c) Prakash (d) Mehul
(e) Data inadequate

58. The guitarist is a student of which of the following disciplies?
(a) Engineering
(b) Either Engineering or Management
(c) Both Engineering and Management
(d) Data inadequate
(e) None of these

59. Who among the following plays Sitar?
(a) Yash (b) Neeraj
(c) Prakash (d) Data inadequate
(e) None of these

DIRECTIONS (Qs. 60-62) : Answer the questions that follow on the basis of following information :

A team of experts for conducting interviews consists of seven experts – Bhushan, Cyriac, Pramila, Ram, Suresh, Shekhar and Unni. Of these Bhushan, Cyriac and Pramila are experts in social sciences while Suresh and Unni are experts in basic sciences. Ram and Shekhar have exposure in both basic sciences and social sciences. Three panels have to be formed for the interview with a restriction that a panel should have representation from experts with social sciences and basic sciences background. Moreover, at least one member should be an expert of only one area.

60. If Cyriac does not like to be a member of panel with Ram, and Unni was in a panel with Shekhar, then the expert who did not participate in the interview was :
(a) Pramila (b) Cyriac
(c) Bhushan (d) Any of these
(e) None of these

61. If Pramila did not participate in the interview, then who was the person most likely to be with Unni ?
(a) Suresh (b) Bhushan
(c) Pramila (d) Any of these
(e) None of these

62. Unni does not like to be with Shekhar; Ram does not like to be with Pramila and Bhushan had Suresh as the partner. If both Ram and Pramila attended the interview, then who was the partner to Cyriac?
(a) Cyriac did not attend the interview
(b) Shekhar (c) Pramila
(d) Unni (e) None of these

Space for Rough Work

DIRECTIONS (Qs. 63-66) : Study the following information carefully and answer the questions given below it :

(i) Seven subjects Sociology, Psychology, English, History, Geography, Economics and Hindi are taught between Monday and Friday by five persons A, B, C, D and E.

(ii) Each person teaches at least one subject. At least one subject is taught every day. No person teaches two subjects on the same day. B teaches Sociology on Wednesday. History is taught by E but not on Monday or Thursday. English is taught on Monday by A. Geography and Economics are taught on Monday and Tuesday respectively. D teaches only one subject Psychology on Tuesday. Geography is not taught by E or B.

63. Who teaches Geography?
(a) C (b) E
(c) B (d) A
(e) Data inadequate

64. Which subject is taught on Friday?
(a) Hindi (b) Economics
(c) History (d) English
(e) Data inadequate

65. Who teaches Economics?
(a) E (b) A
(c) B (d) C
(e) Data inadequate

66. Which subject is taught on Thursday?
(a) History (b) Economics
(c) English (d) Data inadequate
(e) None of these

DIRECTIONS (Qs. 67-69): Study the information given below to answer these questions:

I. There is a family of 5 persons A, B, C and E.
II. They are working as a doctor, a teacher, a lawyer and a farmer.
II. B, an unmarried teacher, is the daughter of A.
IV. E, a lawyer, is the brother of C.
V. C is the husband of the only married couple in the family.
VI. A, a farmer, is a father of two sons and an unmarried daughter.
VII. Daughter - in- law of a is a doctor.

67. Which of the follows is a group of female members in the faimly ?
(a) D and E (b) B and D
(c) A, C and E (d) B and C
(e) None of these

68. Which of the following is the married couple?
(a) C and D (b) A and B
(c) A and D (d) B and D
(e) None of these

69. Which of the following is a group of male members in the faimly?
(a) B and D (b) A, B and C
(c) A, C and E (d) A, C and D
(e) None of these

DIRECTIOS (Qs. 70 to 72) : Read the information given below to answer these questions.

a, b, c, d, e, f, g, h and i are nine houses. c is 2 km east of b. a is 1 km north of b and h is 2 km south of a. g is 1 km west of h while d is 3 km east of g and f is 2 km north of g. i is situated just in the middle of b and c while e is just in middle of h and d.

70. Distance between e and g is :
(a) 2 km (b) 1 km
(c) 5 km (d) 1.5 km
(e) None of these

71. Distance between a and f is :
(a) 1.41 km (b) 3 km
(c) 2 km (d) 1 km
(e) None of these

72. Distance between e and i is :
(a) 4 km (b) 2 km
(c) 1 km (d) 3 km
(e) None of these

DIRECTIONS (Qs.73 to 76) : In a defence message, GET AWAY, FIRE BACK-WARDS, MOVE SLOW is coded as BEN CDCI, QHOE PCTL DCOXU, ZMWE VFMD.

Based on this coding scheme, spot the codes for the words given in the questions below :

73. OVER
(a) MWOE (c) MWZO
(c) MWEO (d) MWED
(e) None of these

Space for Rough Work

74. DEADLY
(a) XECXEI (b) XENXFI
(c) XECXEL (d) XECXFI
(e) None of these

76. REWARD
(a) OEDNXE (b) OTDCOX
(c) OEDCOX (d) OEDCOU
(e) None of these

76. GREAT
(a) BOENC (b) BOEQN
(c) BOECN (d) BOEHC
(e) None of these

DIRECTIONS (Qs.77 to 83) : Below is given passage followed by several possible inferences which can be drawn from the facts stated in the passage. You have to examine each inference separately in the context of the passage and decide upon its degree of truth or falsity. *Mark answer*

(a) if the inference is 'definitely true', i.e. it properly follows from the statement of facts given;
(b) if the inference is 'probably true' though not 'definitely true' in the light of the facts given;
(c) if the 'data are inadequate', i.e. from the facts given you cannot say whether the inference is likely to be true or false;
(d) if the inference is 'probably false' though not 'definitely false' in the light of the facts given;
(e) if the inference is 'definitely false', i.e. it cannot possibly be drawn from the facts given or it contradicts the given facts;

Procurement of wheat is in full swing in the north-western states of India. By June end, public agencies are likely to end up with food grain stocks of about 40 to 42 million tones, the highest ever witnessed in the history of this country. This stock should be more than sufficient to ensure that country's "food security" is not endangered even if India faces two consecutive droughts. But strangely enough, while the granaries overflow, there is still widespread hunger in the country even without a drought. The estimates of poverty are being debated, but broadly one-third of India seems to remain underfed. And this co-existence of grain surpluses with large-scale hunger should make any serious policy-maker think and examine the existing policy mix with a view to ensure faster economic growth and reduction in poverty.

77. India's foodgrains stock has been satisfactory over the past few years.
78. India, at present, is one of the countries in the world to have sufficient food for its people.
79. The distribution of food grains to the masses has remained a problem area for India.
80. The policy of India needs to be revamped to reduce the extent of poverty in the country.
81. India always maintains food grain stocks to withstand two consecutive droughts.
82. More than 30 per cent of population in India do not even get two times meals per day.
83. The policy-makers in India are unaware of prevalent hunger.

DIRECTIONS (Qs. 84 to 88) : In each of following questions, a statement is given followed by two assumptions numbered I and II. Consider the statement and the following assumptions and decide which of the assumptions is implicit. Give answer

(a) if ONLY assumption I is implicit;
(b) if ONLY assumption II is implicit;
(c) if EITHER I or II is implicit;
(d) if BOTH I and II are implicit;
(e) if NEITHER I nor II as implicit.

84. **Statement :** The state government 'X' is committed to restrict smoke levels on the roads of the metropolis as per the desired parameters.
Assumptions : I. It is possible to determine the smoke levels.
II. A committed government can carry forward welfare measures for its people.

85. **Statement :** Unemployment allowance should be given to all unemployed Indian youth above 18 years of age.
Assumptions : I. There are unemployed youth in India who need monetary support.
II. The government has sufficient funds to provide allowance to all unemployed youth.

Space for Rough Work

86. **Statement :** A Notice Board at a ticket window : 'Please come in queue.'

Assumptions : I. Unless instructed people will not form queue.

II. People any way want to purchase tickets.

87. **Statement :** The Government of India has decided to start a track II dialogue with its neighbour to reduce tension in the area.

Assumptions : I. The neighbouring country may agree to participate in the track II dialogue.

II. The people involved in track II dialogue may be able to persuade their respective Governments.

88. **Statement :** The X-Airlines has temporarily suspended flights to a few destinations for the next four days due to the strike call given by the Pilots' Association.

Assumptions : I. The airlines may be able to restore all the flights after four days.

II. The Pilots' Association may withdraw the strike call within four days.

89. If VICTORY is coded as YLFWRUB, then how can SUCCESS be coded in that code language ?

(a) VXEEIVV (b) VXFFHVV
(c) VYEEHVV (d) VXFFIVV
(e) None of these

90. If L denotes ÷, M denotes ×, P denotes + and Q denotes , then which of the following statements is true?

(a) $32 \text{ P } 8 \text{ L } 16 \text{ Q } 4 = -\frac{3}{2}$

(b) $6 \text{ M } 18 \text{ Q } 26 \text{ L } 13 \text{ P } 7 = \frac{173}{13}$

(c) $11 \text{ M } 34 \text{ L } 17 \text{ Q } 8 \text{ L } 3 = \frac{38}{3}$

(d) $9 \text{ P } 9 \text{ L } 9 \text{ Q } 9 \text{ M } 9 = -17$

(e) None of these

91. One day, Ravi left home and cycled 10 km southwards, turned right and cycled 5 km and turned right and cycled 10 cm and turned left and cycled 10 km. How many kilometres will he have to cycle to reach his home straight?

(a) 10 km (b) 15 km
(c) 20 km (d) 25 km
(e) None of these

DIRECTIONS (Qs. 92 to 94) : In each of these questions, various terms of a series are given with one term missing as shown by (?). Choose the missing term :

92. QPO, SRQ, UTS, WVU, (?)

(a) XVZ (b) YXW (c) ZYA (d) VWX
(e) None of these

93. 19, 2, 38, 3, 114, 2, (?)

(a) 228 (b) 352 (c) 256 (d) 456
(e) None of these

94. YEB, WFD, UHG, SKI, (?)

(a) QOL (b) TOL (c) QGL (d) QNL
(e) None of these

DIRECTIONS (Qs. 95 to 99) : In each of the following questions, a statement is given followed by two courses of action numbered I and II. Decide which of the cources of action logically follows and give answer

(a) if ONLY I follows
(b) if ONLY II follows
(c) if EITHER I or II follows
(d) if BOTH I and II follows
(e) if none follows.

95. **Statement :** The meteorological department has issued a notification forecasting less rainfall during next year's monsoon.

Courses of action : I. The farmers should be advised to be ready for the eventuality.

II. The Government should make arrangement to provide water to the affected areas.

Space for Rough Work

96. **Statement :** The Asian Development Bank has approved a $ 285 million loan to finance a project to construct coal ports by Paradip and Madras Port Trusts.

Courses of action : I. India should use financial assistance from other international financial organisations to develop such ports in other places.

II. India should not seek such financial assistance from the international financial agencies.

97. **Statement :** There are more than 200 villages in the hill area of Uttar Pradesh which are severely damaged due to cyclone and it causes an extra burden of Rs 200 crore on State Government for relief and rehabilitation work.

Courses of action : I. People of hill area should be shifted to other safer places.

II. State Government should ask more financial support from Central Government.

98. **Statement :** Orissa and Andhra Pradesh have agreed in principle to set up a joint control board for better control, management and productivity of several inter-state multipurpose projects.

Courses of action : I. Other neighbouring states should set up such control boards.

II. The proposed control board should not be allowed to function as such joint boards are always ineffective.

99. **Statement :** Footpaths of a busy road are crowded with vendors selling cheap items.

Courses of action : I. The help of police should be sought to drive them away.

II. Some space should be provided to them where they can earn their bread without blocking footpaths.

DIRECTIONS (Qs. 100–106): Read the following information carefully and answer the following questions:

Following are the criteria for organising interview of such candidates as have been selected from the promotion to officer's grade from assistant grade in the PRS Industrial Group Limited.

The candidate to be called for interview must

(i) be a graduate with minimum 50% marks;

(ii) have minimum five years' experience in the clerical cadre job;

(ii) have obtained at least 'C' ratings in performance (speed of work) and the quality of work each during the last three years. For this five ratings A, B, C, D and E-have been created on the basis of "Performance Appraisal Report" with the lowest ratings of A and the highest ratings of E;

(iv) have obtained at least 'D' ratings in the approach of work (dependability) and in the flexibility of work each for his/her works in the last three years. For this, seven ratings A, B, C, D, E, F and G have been formulated on the basis of "Performance Appraisal Report" with lowest ratings of A and the highest ratings of G.

However, in case of a candidate who fulfills all other criteria EXCEPT

(a) (i) above, but has passed Graduation Exam and has got 'E' ratings in the approach of work in the last three years, may be referred to the Assistant Manager (Personnel).

(b) (ii) above, but has experience of three years in clerical cadre job and has got at least 'D' ratings in the quality of work for his/her works in the last three years, may be referred to the Deputy Manager (Personnel).

Based on these criteria and information provided against each candidate, decide the course of action. You are not to assume anything. If the data provided are not adequate to decide the given course of action, your answer will be "Data inadequate". All the candidates fulfil the criterion of age. Give answer

(a) if data inadequate;

(b) if not to be selected;

(c) if selected for the interview;

(d) if case is referred to the Assistant Manager;

(e) if case is referred to the Deputy Manager.

Space for Rough Work

100. Mohammed Sheikh is a brilliant post-graduate in Science and has secured 63% and 55% marks in graduation and post graduation respectively. He has 'E' grade for dependability and flexibility in Performance Appraisal Report for last four years. He has got 'C' rating for quality of work and speed of work. He joined the Bank four years ago.
101. Kiran Bala is a young lady and laborious assistant who joined this organisation six years ago after passing B. Commerce Exam. The ratings being given to her for the last 4 years are 'D' and 'C' respectively for quality of work and speed of work. She is one of the leaders of the clerks. She has got 'D' ratings for flexibility of work for the last 5 years.
102. Mandar Bhave has passed his Graduation in Science and Diploma in Business Management with 58% and 62% respectively. He is good player of chess. His rating on PAR are 'D' for 'dependability' and 'flexibility' whereas he has 'C' rating for 'quality of work' and 'D' rating for 'speed of work' for the last 4 years.
103. Anubhav Rege is with the company for last seven years. For the last 4 years he has 'D' rating for 'quality of work', 'C' rating for 'speed of work', 'E' rating for 'dependability' an 'D' rating for 'flexibility'. His marks in graduation and post-graduation are 46% and 50% respectively. He is very fond of cultural activities.
104. Shivasundaram has got 'D' rating since he joined the bank three years ago on quality of work, speed of work, dependability and flexibility. He has passed his graduation and postgraduation with 52% and 47% marks respectively. Shivasundaram is a popular employee because of his social activities.
105. Seema Mukhi is working in the clerical cadre for last five-and-a-half years. She has got 'D' and 'E' ratings respectively on 'flexibility' and 'dependability' and 'C' rating for 'quality of work' and 'speed of work' for last four years. She has obtained 55% and 48% at SSC and graduation respectively.
106. Anthony Cruz is a sportsman and is Vice-Captain of cricket team of PRS Industries Ltd. He is working with the company for last seven years in the clerical cadre. The rating being given to him for the last 3 years is 'C' and 'D' grade for quality of work and speed of work respectively. Similarly, he has 'D' grade for dependability and flexibility in PAR. He is an Arts Graduate with 54% of marks.
107. A and B are two alloys of gold and copper prepared by mixing metals in the ratio 7 : 2 and 7 : 11 respectively. If equal quantities of the alloys are melted to form a third alloy C, the ratio of gold and copper in C will be:
(a) 5 : 7 (b) 5 : 9 (c) 7 : 5 (d) 9 : 5
(e) None of these
108. The length and breadth of the floor of the room are 20 feet and 10 feet respectively. Square tiles of 2 feet length of different colours are to be laid on the floor. Black tiles are laid in the first row on all sides. If white tiles are laid in the one-third of the remaining and blue tiles in the rest, how many blue tiles will be there?
(a) 16 (b) 24
(c) 32 (d) 48
(e) None of these
109. Three wheels can complete respectively 60,36,24 revolutions per minute. There is a red spot on each wheel that touches the ground at time zero. After how much time, all these spots will simultaneously touch the ground again?
(a) 5/2 seconds (b) 5/3 seconds
(c) 5 seconds (d) 7.5 seconds
(e) None of these
110. Nine men went to a hotel. 8 of them spent Rs 3 each over their meals and the ninth spent Rs 2 more than the average expenditure of all the nine. The total money spent by all of them was
(a) Rs 26 (b) Rs 40
(c) Rs 29.25 (d) Rs 27
(e) None of these
111. If three numbers are added in pairs, the sums equal 10, 19 and 21. The numbers are
(a) 4, 6, 10 (b) 6, 4, 15
(c) 3, 5, 10 (d) 2, 5, 15
(e) None of these
112. Sameer bought 10 kg of tea at Rs 45 per kg and 8 kg at Rs 50 per kg. He mixed both the brands and sold it at a total profit of Rs 32. What was the selling price per kg of the mixture?
(a) Rs 48 (b) Rs 50
(c) Rs 49 (d) Rs 47
(e) None of these

Space for Rough Work

DIRECTIONS (Qs. 113 to 117) : Study the following table carefully and answer the questions given below

Number of students studying in different faculties in seven institutions

Institution	Faculty				
	Arts	Commerce	Science	Engineering	Management
A	125	187	216	98	74
B	96	152	198	157	147
C	144	235	110	164	127
D	165	138	245	66	36
E	215	196	287	86	66
F	184	212	195	112	97
G	225	206	182	138	89

113. What is the percentage of students studying Science with respect to the total number of students studying in the institute G?
(a) 17.20 (b) 12.70
(c) $21\frac{2}{3}$ (d) 20
(e) None of these

114. Out of the total students of the institute 'D', approximately what percentage of students study Management?
(a) 9 (b) 8
(c) 10 (d) 5
(e) None of these

115. The total number of students studying Arts in institutes A, B and C together is approximately what per cent of the total number of students Commerce in institutes D, E, F and G together?
(a) 50 (b) 45
(c) 55 (d) 53
(e) None of these

116. What is the percentage of students studying Engineering in institute C with respect to the total students of all institutions studying Engineering? (rounded to the nearest integer)
(a) 20 (b) 18
(c) 21 (d) 19
(e) None of these

117. In which institution, the percentage of students studying Commerce with respect to the total students of the institution is maximum?
(a) F (b) E
(c) C (d) A
(e) None of these

DIRECTIONS (Qs. 118-122) : Study the following tables carefully and answer the questions given below:
Number of cars (In thousands) of different models and colours sold in two Metro Cities in a year

Model	Metro M					Metro H				
	Colour					Colour				
	Black	Red	Blue	White	Silver	Black	Red	Blue	White	Silver
A	40	25	55	75	15	45	32	40	60	20
B	20	35	60	80	20	30	37	39	81	35
C	35	30	50	90	35	40	42	41	6	37
D	45	40	45	85	40	35	39	37	90	42
E	50	35	35	60	30	50	44	43	77	22
F	55	42	40	65	52	47	34	45	87	17

Space for Rough Work

118. The difference between the white- coloured cars sold in the two metros of which of the following models is the minimum?
(a) A (b) C
(c) D (d) B
(e) None of these

119. The total number of the blue-coloured cars of model 'E' and 'D' sold in Metro H is exactly equal to number of white-coloured cars of which model in Metro M?
(a) B (b) F
(c) C (d) A
(e) None of these

120. What is the difference between the number of blue-coloured cars of model 'C' sold in Metro M and number of red-coloured cars of model 'F' sold in Metro H?
(a) 8,000 (b) 10,000
(c) 12,000 (d) None of these
(e) None of these

121. The total number of silver-coloured cars sold in Metro H is approximately what percentage of that in Metro M?
(a) 130 (b) 140
(c) 90 (d) 100
(e) None of these

122. In Metro M the number of cars sold was maximum for which of the colour-model combination?
(a) White-C (b) Blue-B
(c) Silver-B (d) White-D
(e) None of these

DIRECTIONS (Qs. 123 to 127) : Study the following chart to answer the questions given below.

Village	%population below poverty line
A	45
B	52
C	38
D	58
E	46
F	49
G	51

Proportion of population of seven villages in 1995

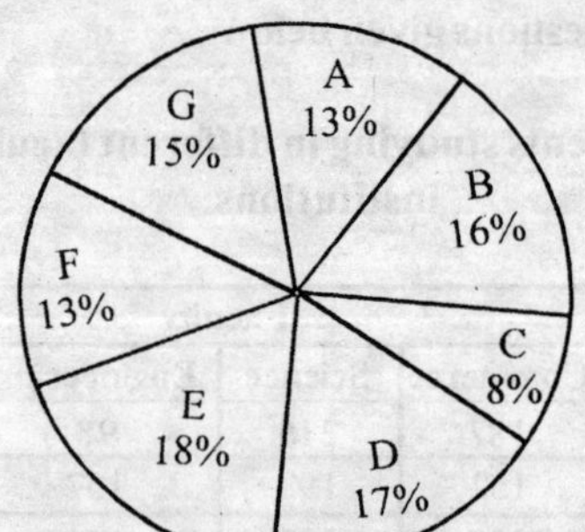

123. In 1996, the population of villages A as well as B is increased by 10% from the year 1995. If the population of village A in 1995 was 5000 and the percentage of population below poverty line in 1996 remains same as in 1995, find approximately the population of village B below poverty line in 1996.
(a) 4000 (b) 4500 (c) 3000 (d) 3500
(e) None of these

124. If in 1997 the population of village D is increased by 10% and the population of village G is reduced by 5% from 1995 and the population of village G in 1995 was 9000, what is the total population of villages D and G in 1997?
(a) 19770 (b) 19200 (c) 18770 (d) 19870
(e) None of these

125. If in 1995 the total population of the seven villages together was 55,000 approximately, what will be population of village F in the year below poverty line?
(a) 3000 (b) 2500 (c) 4000 (d) 3500
(e) None of these

126. If the population of village C below poverty line in 1995 was 1520, what was the population of village F in 1995?
(a) 4000 (b) 6000 (c) 6500 (d) 4800
(e) None of these

127. The population of village C is 2000 in 1995. What will be the ratio of population of village C below poverty line to that of the village E below poverty line in that year?
(a) 207 : 76 (b) 76 : 207
(c) 152 : 207 (d) Data inadequate
(e) None of these

Space for Rough Work

DIRECTIONS (Qs. 128-132) : Refer to the pie-chart given below:

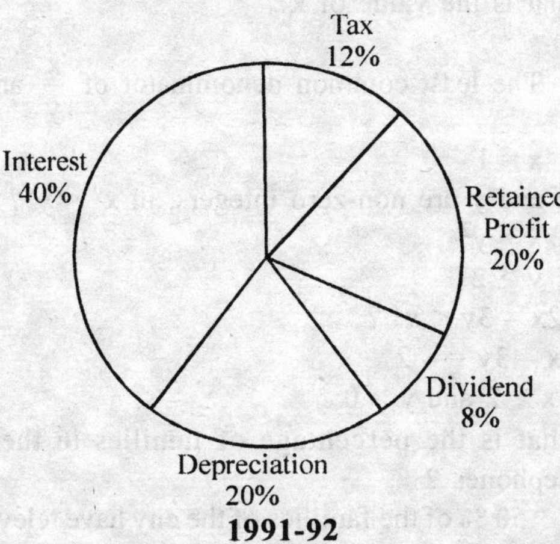

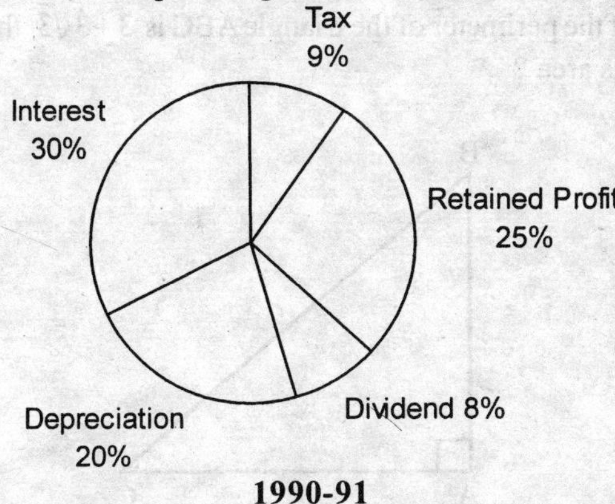

128. The operating profit in 1991-92 increased over that in 1990-91 by
(a) 23% (b) 22%
(c) 25% (d) 24%
(e) None of these

129. The Interest burden in 1991-92 was higher than that in 1990-91 by
(a) 50% (b) 25 lakh
(c) 90% (d) 41 lakh
(e) None of these

130. If, on an average, 20% rate of interest was charged on borrowed funds, then the total borrowed funds used by this company in the given two years amounted to ....
(a) 221 lakh (b) 195 lakh
(c) 368 lakh (d) 515 lakh
(e) None of these

131. The retained profit in 1991-92, as compared to that in 1990-91 was
(a) higher by 2.5% (b) higher by 1.5%
(c) lower by 2.5% (d) lower by 1.5%
(e) None of these

132. The equity base of these companies remained unchanged. Then the total dividend earning (in lakh rupees) by the share holders in 1991-92 is
(a) 10.4 lakh (b) 9 lakh
(c) 12.8 lakh (d) 15.6 lakh
(e) None of these

DIRECTIONS (Qs. 133-137): The question consists of a question and two statements numbered (I) and (II) given below it. You have to decide whether the data provided in the statements are sufficient to answer the question. Read both the statements and give answer

(a) if the question can be answered with the help of both the statements but not with the help of either statement itself;
(b) if the question can not be answered even with the help of BOTH the statements;
(c) if the question can be answered with the help of statement II ALONE;
(d) if the question can be answered with the help of statement I ALONE;
(e) if the question can be answered with the help of EITHER statement I or II.

Space for Rough Work

133. What is the first term of an arithmetic progression of positive integers?
   I. Sum of the squares of the first and second term is 116
   II. The fifth term is divisible by 7.

134. Navni is three times as efficient as Avantika. In how many days can Avantika alone do the whole work?
   I. Both of them together can complete the work in 15 days.
   II. Navni alone can do the whole work in 20 days.

135. There are 450 boxes to load on a truck. A and B working independently but at the same time take 30 minutes to load the truck. How long should it take B working by himself to load the truck?
   I. A loads twice as many boxes as B.
   II. A would take 45 minutes by himself.

136. What is the rate of interest p.c.p.a?
   I. Difference between compound interest and simple interest on an amount of Rs 10,000 for two years is Rs 225.
   II. The amount doubles itself on simple interest in $6\frac{2}{3}$ years.

137. Sanju works for 3 days and leaves the job. In how many days will Sanju alone finish the entire work?
   I. Swamitra finishes the remaining work in 12 days.
   II. Sanju and Swamitra together can finish the work in 6 days.

DIRECTIONS (Qs. 138-150) : Each of the questions below consists of a question and two statements numbered (I) and (II) given below it. You have to decide whether the data provided in the statements are sufficient to answer the question. Read both the statements and give answer.

(a) if statement (I) ALONE is sufficient, but statement (II) alone is not sufficient.
(b) if statement (II) ALONE is sufficient, but statement (I) alone is not sufficient
(c) if BOTH statements TOGETHER are sufficient, but NEITHER statement alone is sufficient.
(d) if EACH statement ALONE is sufficient
(e) if BOTH statements together are NOT sufficient.

138. In the fraction $\frac{x}{y}$, where x and y are positive integers, what is the value of x?
   I. The least common denominator of $\frac{x}{y}$ and $\frac{1}{3}$ is 6.
   II. $x = 1$

139. Is x and y are non-zero integers, in $x^y < y^x$?
   I. $x = y^2$
   II. $y > 2$

140. Is $2x - 3y < x^2$?
   I. $2x - 3y = -2$
   II. $x > 2$ and $y > 0$

141. What is the percentage of families in the city have telephones ?
   (I) 50 % of the families of the city have televisions.
   (II) 30% of the television owners of the city have telephones.

142. If the perimeter of the triangle ABC is $3+3\sqrt{3}$ then what is its area ?

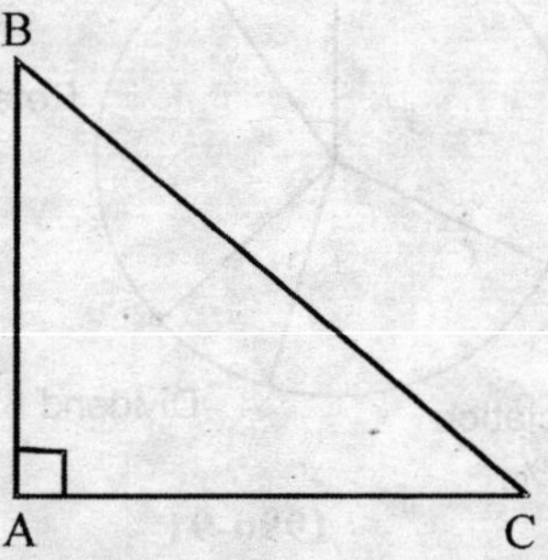

   (I) Side AC ≠ Side AB
   (II) Angle ABC = 30°

143. How many chocolates can Sheena buy if she has to spend 20% of her budget on vegetable and 30% on groceries ?
   (I) Sheena has Rs 50 with her.
   (II) Each chocolate costs 50 paise.

Space for Rough Work

144. How many litres of a chemical can be stored in a cylindrical tank if the radius of the tank is 5 metres?
(I) The height of the tank is 5 m.
(II) The temperature is 70°F.

145. In ΔABC, find r if AB = 5 and q = 40°

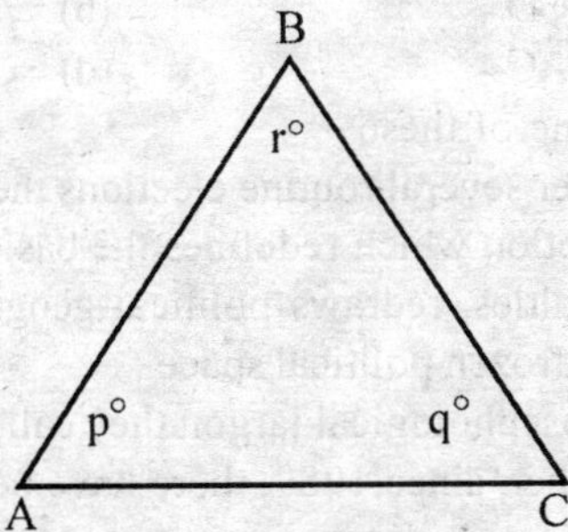

(I) BC = 5
(II) r > p

146. What was Mr. Srinivasulu's combined income for the year 1994-1999? In 1994, he made Rs 10,00, 000.
(I) His average yearly income for the years 1994-1999 was Rs. 12,00,000
(II) In 1999, his income was Rs 20,00,0000

147. A certain book shop sold 92 copies of Bill Gate's book 'Business at the speed of thought' during the first day. What precentage of his stock of this book did he sell on that day ?
(I) The total number of books with this title on stock is 230.
(II) There are a total of 1000 books in his store.

148. What selling price should be marked on the article ?
(I) Discount of 5% is to be given and profit percentage should be double the discount. Purchase cost is in the range of Rs. 300 – Rs 400.
(II) 10% discount is to be allowed and 15% profit is to be obtained on the purchase cost of Rs 200 of the article.

149. At present, how many villagers are voters in village 'X'?
(I) There were 860 voters in village 'X' in the list prepared for the last election.
(II) The present list of village 'X' has 15% more voters than the list for the last election.

150. "You must submit your application within 10 days from the date of release of this advertisement." What is the exact date before which the application must be submitted?
(I) The advertisement was released on 18th February.
(II) It was a leap year.

DIRECTIONS (Qs. 151-155): In each of these questions, in the given sentences, a part of the sentence is underlined. Beneath each sentence, four different ways of phrasing the underlined part are indicated. Choose the best alternative.

151. He does not smoke, nor he drinks.
(a) nor he does drink
(b) neither he does drink
(c) nor does he drink
(d) none of these
(e) no change

152. She wished that her career could be as glamorous as the other women but not willing to work as they had.
(a) as glamorous as the other women's
(b) more glamorous than the career of the other women/
(c) glamorous
(d) none of these
(e) no change

153. Although he is liable to make political enemies with the decision, the Finance Minister will propose severe tax cuts that may both stimulate business and reduce the availability of loans.
(a) liable from (b) able to
(c) of a mind to (d) none of these
(e) no change

154. No matter what experience you have had with forest fires, if you would have witnessed the fire roaring down through the canyon, you would have been terrified.
(a) if you witnessed
(b) if you had witnessed
(c) if you could witness
(d) none of these
(e) no change

Space for Rough Work

155. Eaten in Portugal only, the <u>Indians viewed the potato with suspicion for they</u> assumed it had poisonous properties since only the white skinned people consumed it.
   (a) Indians viewed the potato with suspicion for they
   (b) Indians were suspicious of the potato and they
   (c) potato was viewed with suspicion by Indians who
   (d) potato was suspicious to Indians, and it was
   (e) no change

DIRECTIONS (Qs. 156-160): In each of these questions a disarranged sentence is given in which words or phrases are lettered A, B, C, D .... You are to arrange these to form a meaningful sentence.

156. A. It begins with an ordinary fever and a moderate cough
   B. India could be under attack from a class of germs that cause what is called atypical pneumonias.
   C. Slowly, a sore throat progresses to bronchitis and then pneumonia and respiratory complications.
   D. It appears like the ordinary flu, but baffled doctors find that the usual drugs don't work.
   (a) ABCD (b) BDCA
   (c) ADCB (d) BCDA
   (e) None of these
157. A. Chemists mostly don't stock it: only a few government hospitals do but in limited quantities
   B. Delhi's building boom is creating a bizarre problem : snakes are increasingly biting people as they emerge from their disturbed underground homes.
   C. There isn't enough anti snake serum, largely because there is no centralised agency that distributes the product.
   D. If things don't improve, more people could face paralysis, and even death.
   (a) BCAD (b) DBCA
   (c) ABCD (d) CABD
   (e) None of these
158. A. But the last decade has witnessed greater voting and political participation by various privileged sections
   B. If one goes by the earlier record of mid-term elections, it is likely that the turnout in 1998 will drop by anything between four and six percentage points over the already low polling of 58 per cent in 1996.
   C. If this trend offsets the mid-term poll fatigue, the fall may not be so steep.
   D. Notwithstanding a good deal of speculation on this issue, it is still not clear that who is benefitted from a lower turnout.
   (a) BACD (b) ABCD
   (c) DBAC (d) CBDA
   (e) None of these
159. A. After several routine elections there comes a 'critical' election which redefines the basic pattern of political loyalties, redraws political geography and opens up the frozen political space
   B. In psephological jargon they call it realignment.
   C. Rather, since 1989, there have been a series of semi-critical elections.
   D. On a strict definition, none of the recent Indian elections qualifies as a critical election.
   (a) ABCD (b) ABDC
   (c) DBAC (d) DCBA
   (e) None of these
160. A. Since then, intelligence tests have been mostly used to separate dull children in school from average or bright children, so that special education can be provided to the dull
   B. In other words, intelligence tests give us a norm for each age.
   C. Intelligences expressed as intelligence quotient and tests are developed to indicate what an average child of a certain age can do--what a 5 year old can answer, but a 4-year-old cannot, for instance.
   D. Binet developed the first set of such tests in the early 1900s to find out which children in school needed special attention.
   E. Intelligence can be measured by tests.
   (a) CDABE (b) DECAB
   (c) EDACB (d) CBADE
   (e) None of these

Space for Rough Work

DIRECTIONS (Qs. 161-170): : In each of these questions four words are given marked A, B, C and D. Two of these words are most nearly the same or opposite in meaning. Identify those two words:

161. A. Hood wink B. Sincere
C. Gauche D. Fiasco
(a) A-B (b) B-C
(c) B-D (d) A-C
(e) None of these

162. A. Flummox B. Enlighten
C. Fastidious D. Esoteric
(a) A-B (b) B-C
(c) D-C (d) A-D
(e) None of these

163. A. Exorcise B. Bedevil
C. Diatribe D. Hyperbole
(a) A-C (b) B-D
(c) D-A (d) A-B
(e) None of these

164. A. Draconian B. Cruel
C. Bliss D. Noble
(a) A-C (b) B-D
(c) A-B (d) C-D
(e) None of these

165. A. Deify B. Blasphemy
C. Deluge D. Hubris
(a) B-D (b) B-C
(c) C-D (d) A-B
(e) None of these

166. A. Clandestine B. Cosmopolitan
C. Graceful D. Furtive
(a) A-B (b) B-C
(c) C-D (d) A-D
(e) None of these

167. A. Bellicose B. Affront
C. Peaceful D. Adroit
(a) A-B (b) B-C
(c) B-D (d) A-C
(e) None of these

168. A. Frugal B. Spendthrift
C. Anomaly D. Anathema
(a) A-B (b) B-C
(c) C-D (d) A-D
(e) None of these

169. A. Asinine B. Besolted
C. Tranquil D. Knowledgeable
(a) A-B (b) B-C
(c) C-D (d) A-D
(e) None of these

170. A. Crass B. Nexus
C. Elegant D. Credulous
(a) B-D (b) A-D
(c) A-C (d) C-B
(e) None of these

DIRECTIONS (Qs. 171-180): Read the following passages carefully and answer the questions given below it.

PASSAGE - 1

Economic growth involves both benefits and costs. The desirability of increasing production has frequently been challenged in recent years and some have even mentioned that economic growth is merely a quantitative enlargement that has no human meaning or value:

However, economic growth is an increase in the capacity to produce goods and service that people want. Since the product of economic growth can be measured by its value to someone, it is important to ask whose standard of valuation counts.

In the U.S. the value of a product is what purchasers pay for it. That is determined by the purchaser's preferences combined with condition of supply which in turn reflects various other factors, such as natural and technological circumstances of those who supply capital and labour. The value by which we measure a product, synthesize all these factors. Gross National Product (GNP) is the market value of the nation's total output of goods and service. GNP is not a perfect measure of all the activities involved in economic output. It does not account for the deterioration or improvement in the environment even when they are incidentally results of the production process. On the other hand, it does not count as "Product", many benefits provided as side effect of the economic process. It does not include productive but unpaid work (such as that done by a home maker) and it does not reckon with such other factor as the burdensomeness of work, the length of the work, week and so forth. Nonetheless the GNP concept makes

Space for Rough Work

an important contribution to our understanding of how the economy is working while it is not a complete measure of economic productivity and even less so of "welfare". The level and rate of the increase of GNP are clearly and positively associated with what most people throughout the world see as an improvement in the quality of life. In the long run, the same factor results in a growing GNP and in other social benefits: size and competence of population, state of knowledge, amount of capital and the effectiveness with those are combined and Utilized.

171. The main purpose of the passage is to :
   (a) argue for the value of increased economic output
   (b) explain the disadvantages of measuring the life using a scale of material effluence
   (c) define GNP
   (d) contrast the American and European GNP
   (e) None of these

172. The rhetorical purpose of the fourth para of the passage is to :
   1. Anticipate objection to what the GNP fails to take into account.
   2. Cite example of "Products", the GNP ought to include.
   3. Develop the definition of the GNP with specific details.
   (a) 1 only (b) 2 only
   (c) 1,2 and 3 (d) 3 only
   (e) None of these

173. We can infer from the passage that of the following, the factor that does not influence the growth of GNP is :
   (a) the capital available in the country
   (b) a dependence on spiritual values
   (c) the efficiency of the production process
   (d) the condition of the population
   (e) None of these

174. The critic of the limitations of the measurement of GNP might cite its failure to consider all of the following except :
   (a) steady increase in worker's leisure time
   (b) the widespread existence of chemicals in the rivers
   (c) the valuation of family household management
   (d) the value of time a salaried stock broker spends on research
   (e) None of these

PASSAGE - 2

As heart disease continues to be the number one killer in the United States, researchers have become increasingly interested in identifying the potential risk factors that trigger heart attacks. High-fat diets and "life in the fast lane" have long been known to contribute to the high incidence of heart failure.
But according to new studies, the list of risk factors may be significantly longer and quite surprising.

Heart failure, for example, appears to have seasonal and temporal patterns. A higher percentage of heart attacks occur in cold weather and more people experience heart failure on Monday than on any other day of the week. In addition, people are more susceptible to heart attacks in the first few hours after waking. Cardiologists first observed this morning phenomenon in the mid-1980 and have since discovered a number of possible causes. An early-morning rise in blood pressure, heart rate and concentration of heart stimulating hormones, plus a reduction of blood flow to the heart, may all contribute to the higher incidence of heart attacks between the hours of 8.00 A.M. and 10.00 A.M.
In other studies, both birthday and bachelorhood have been implicated as risk factors. Statistics reveal that heart attack rates increase significantly for both females and males in the few days immediately preceding and following their birthdays. And unmarried men are more at risk for heart attacks than their married counterparts. Though stress is thought to be linked in some way to all of the aforementioned risk factors, intense research continues in the hope of future comprehending why and how heart failure is triggered.

175. What does the passage mainly discuss?
   (a) Cardiology
   (b) Diet and stress as factors in heart attacks
   (c) Seasonal and temporal patterns of heart attacks
   (d) Risk factors in heart attacks
   (e) None of these

176. The underlined word 'potential' could best be replaced by which of the following '?
   (a) Harmful (b) Possible
   (c) Unknown (d) Primary
   (e) None of these

Space for Rough Work

177. According to the passage which of the following is not a possible cause of many heart attacks?
(a) Decreased blood flow to the heart
(b) Increased blood pressure
(c) Lower heart rate
(d) Increase in hormones
(e) None of these

178. Which of the following is cited as a possible risk factor?
(a) Getting married (b) Rainy weather
(c) Eating fatty foods
(d) Driving fast (e) None of these

179. As used in the passage, which of the following could best replace the underlined word 'reveal' ?
(a) Observe (b) Show
(c) Explain (d) Mean
(e) None of these

180. Which of the following does the passage infer?
(a) We now fully understand how the risk factors trigger heart attacks
(b) We do not fully understand how the risk factors trigger heart attacks
(c) We have not identified risk factors associated with heart attacks
(d) We have recently begun to study how risk factors trigger heart attacks
(e) None of these

DIRECTIONS (Qs. 181-183): Pick out the nearest correct meaning or SYNONYM of the word(s) given below:

181. Which of the following words means **unlawful**
(a) elicit (b) draw
(c) illegitimate (d) illicit
(e) None of these

182. One of the following words means **haughty**
(a) imperial (b) imperious
(c) adamant (d) empire
(e) None of these

183. One of the following words means wise
(a) momentous (b) pragmatic
(c) judicious (d) delay
(e) None of these

DIRECTIONS (Qs. 184-187): Pick out the ANTONYM of the words given below:

184. OFFEND
(a) angry (b) hate
(c) force (d) respect
(e) None of these

185. INDICT
(a) condemn (b) reprimand
(c) acquit (d) allege
(e) None of these

186. OBSCENE
(a) decent (b) objectionable
(c) condemnable (d) jealousy
(e) None of these

187. LIBERATE
(a) imprison (b) enclose
(c) liberal (d) conceal
(e) None of these

Directions (Qs. 188-192): In each of the following sentences four words or phrases have been underlined. Only one underlined part in each sentence is not acceptable in Standard English, Pick up the part (a), (b), (c), (d). If all four words are correct, mark (e) i.e., 'All correct' as your answer.

188. Several guests noticed (a) Mr. Peter fall (b) back in his (c) chair and gasping (d) for breath All correct (e)

189. A long (a) life is good if one (b) be (c) happy and has (d) friends All correct (e)

190. The entire (a) party is for the (b) Bill ready to (c) stake their (d) political existence All correct (e)

Space for Rough Work

191. He has suffered (a) from a similar (b) attack but milder as (c) that (d) of last year All correct (e)

192. Our strongest (a) reason for (b) siding with the (c) communists is because (d) our father is a communist All correct (e)

DIRECTIONS (Qs. 193–200): In the following passage, there are blanks, each of which has been numbered. These numbers are printed below the passage and against each, five words are suggested, one of which fits the blank appropriately. Find out the appropriate word in each case.

Actually everyday we are engaged in this business of 'reading' people. We do it **193**. We want to figure others out. So we **194** make guesses about what others think, value, want and feel and we do so based on our **195** beliefs and understandings about human nature. We do so because if we can figure our **196** and intentions of others the possibility of them **197** or hurting us **198** and this will help us to **199** a lot of unnecessary pain and trouble. We also make second-guesses about what they will do in future, how they will **200** if we make this or that response.

193. (a) vehemently (b) practically (c) actually (d) incessantly (e) virtually
194. (a) ably (b) constantly (c) partly (d) largely (e) positively
195. (a) futuristic (b) proactive (c) reactive (d) decorative (e) assumptive
196. (a) manifestations (b) expressions (c) motives (d) hopes (e) prospects
197. (a) tricking (b) blaming (c) furthering (d) alarming (e) criticising
198. (a) lessens (b) happens (c) questions (d) deepens (e) laments
199. (a) approach (b) direct (c) avoid (d) implement (e) prepare
200. (a) solve (b) apply (c) plan (d) approach (e) respond

Space for Rough Work

MAHARASHTRA CET - MOCK TEST 3

RESPONSE SHEET

NAME : ....   DATE : ....

	(A)	(B)	(C)	(D)		(A)	(B)	(C)	(D)		(A)	(B)	(C)	(D)		(A)	(B)	(C)	(D)
1.					51.					101.					151.				
2.					52.					102.					152.				
3.					53.					103.					153.				
4.					54.					104.					154.				
5.					55.					105.					155.				
6.					56.					106.					156.				
7.					57.					107.					157.				
8.					58.					108.					158.				
9.					59.					109.					159.				
10.					60.					110.					160.				
11.					61.					111.					161.				
12.					62.					112.					162.				
13.					63.					113.					163.				
14.					64.					114.					164.				
15.					65.					115.					165.				
16.					66.					116.					166.				
17.					67.					117.					167.				
18.					68.					118.					168.				
19.					69.					119.					169.				
20.					70.					120.					170.				
21.					71.					121.					171.				
22.					72.					122.					172.				
23.					73.					123.					173.				
24.					74.					124.					174.				
25.					75.					125.					175.				
26.					76.					126.					176.				
27.					77.					127.					177.				
28.					78.					128.					178.				
29.					79.					129.					179.				
30.					80.					130.					180.				
31.					81.					131.					181.				
32.					82.					132.					182.				
33.					83.					133.					183.				
34.					84.					134.					184.				
35.					85.					135.					185.				
36.					86.					136.					186.				
37.					87.					137.					187.				
38.					88.					138.					188.				
39.					89.					139.					189.				
40.					90.					140.					190.				
41.					91.					141.					191.				
42.					92.					142.					192.				
43.					93.					143.					193.				
44.					94.					144.					194.				
45.					95.					145.					195.				
46.					96.					146.					196.				
47.					97.					147.					197.				
48.					98.					148.					198.				
49.					99.					149.					199.				
50.					100.					150.					200.				

MAHARASHTRA

CET

MOCK TEST - 4

☛ *INSTRUCTIONS :*

- **There are 200 questions in this test. You will be given 150 minutes to complete the test.**
- **Each question carries 1 mark. There is no negative marking.**

1. M is brother of T, T is sister of R, P is mother of M and wife of H. How many sons does H have?
(a) Two (b) Three
(c) Four (d) Data inadequate
(e) None of these

2. If it is possible to form a number which is the perfect square of a two digit odd number with the second, the fifth and the seventh digits of the number 54321789 using each only once, which of the following will be that two digit odd number? If no such number can be formed, give '99' as the answer and if more than one such number can be formed, give 100 as the answer–
(a) 29 (b) 27
(c) 39 (d) 99
(e) 200

3. Four of the following five are alike in a certain way and so form a group. Which is the one that does not belong to that group?
(a) Brinjal (b) Gourd
(c) Pumpkin (d) Spinach
(e) Tomato

4. What will be next term in the following series?
A, B, B, D, C, F, D, H, E, J, ?
(a) N (b) O
(c) K (d) F
(e) None of these

5. Shyam walked 6 metres facing towards East, then took a right turn and walked a distance of 9 metres. He then took a left turn and walked a distance of 6 metres. How far is he from the starting point?
(a) 15 metres (b) 21 metres
(c) 18 metres (d) Cannot be determined
(e) None of these

6. If the positions of the first and the sixth letters in the word CONTAGIOUS are interchanged, similarly the positions of the second and the seventh letters are interchanged and so on. Which letter will be the second to the right of the fifth letter from the right?
(a) O (b) N
(c) I (d) T
(e) None of these

7 In a certain code DRAUGHT is written as CQBVHIU and CONCISE is written as BNODJTF. How will PROBLEM be written in that code?
(a) OSNCMFN (b) OQPCMFN
(c) QSNAMEN (d) OQPCKDN
(e) None of these

DIRECTIONS (Qs. 8-10) : Complete the following series.

8. The next three terms of the series 151620294 are
(a) 436 (b) 570
(c) 287 (d) 698
(e) None of these

9. The next term of accompanying series is
LXF, MTJ, NPN, OLR, ?
(a) PHV (b) PIU
(c) PJW (d) PKX
(e) None of these

10. In the series of terms given in each of the questions below, identify the term which does not fit in the series.
1 C V, 5 F U, 9 I T, 15 L S, 17 O R
(a) 9 IT (b) 15 LS
(c) 5 FU (d) 17 OR
(e) None of these

Space for Rough Work

11. There are two words to the left of the sign :: which are connected in some way. The same relationship obtains between the third word and one of the four alternatives under it. Find the correct alternative.
Import : Export :: Expenditure : ?
(a) Deficit (b) Revenue
(c) Debt (d) Tax
(e) None of these

12. A pair of words is given, followed by four pairs of words as alternatives. Choose the correct pair in which the words bears the same relationship to each other as the words of the given pair bear.
Telephone : Ring : : .... : ....
(a) Door : knock (b) Gate : open
(c) Door : wood (d) Lock : key
(e) None of these

DIRECTIONS (Qs. 13 & 14) : In each of the following questions, four alternatives are given, out of which three are alike in a certain way while one is different. Choose the odd one.

13. (a) USTO (b) OOT
(c) TTOU (d) SST
(e) None of these

14. (a) Grams (b) Litres
(c) Tonnes (d) Quintals
(e) None of these

DIRECTIONS (Qs. 15-20) : In each questions given below which one of the five answer figures should come after the problem figures, if the sequence were continued?

15.

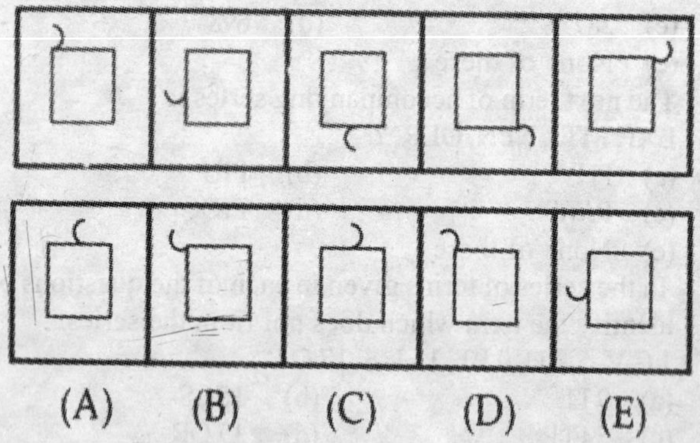

(A) (B) (C) (D) (E)

(a) A (b) B (c) C (d) D (e) E

16.

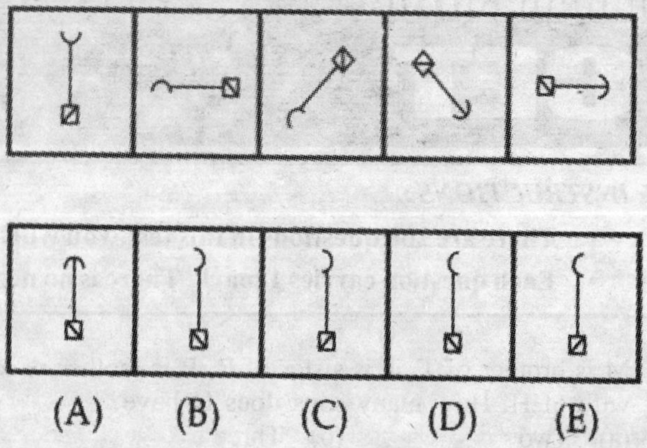

(A) (B) (C) (D) (E)

(a) A (b) B (c) C (d) D (e) E

17.

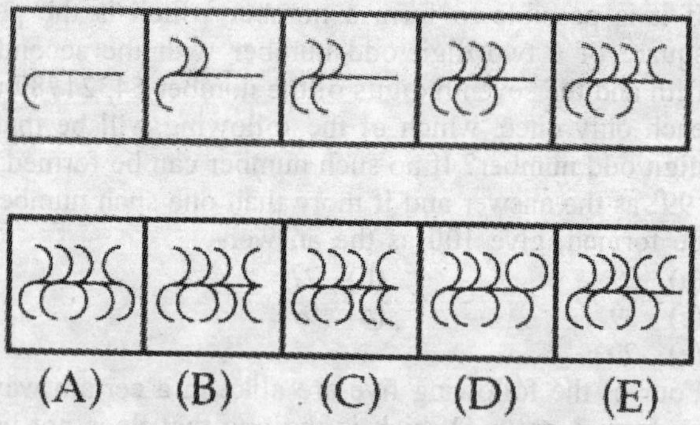

(A) (B) (C) (D) (E)

(a) A (b) B (c) C (d) D (e) E

18.

S ■ ■ Z Z L L = = ▲
⌓ Z L S ■ = ▲ Z L ⊠

▲ ⊠ ▲ L ⊠ = ▲ ⊠ ▲ L
⌓ = = ⌓ ⌓ ▲ O = = ⌓

(A) (B) (C) (D) (E)

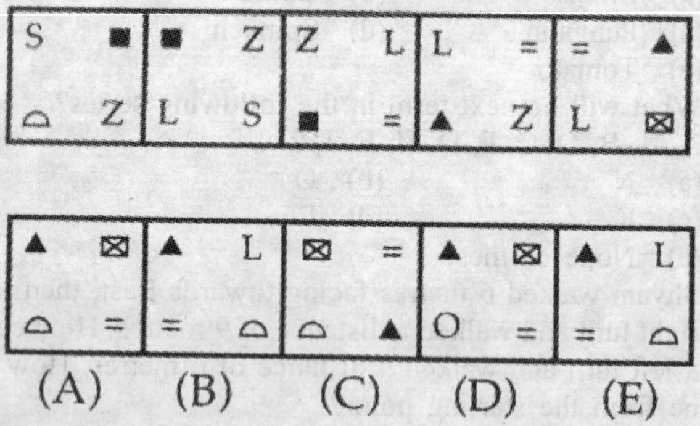

(a) A (b) B (c) C (d) D (e) E

Space for Rough Work

19.

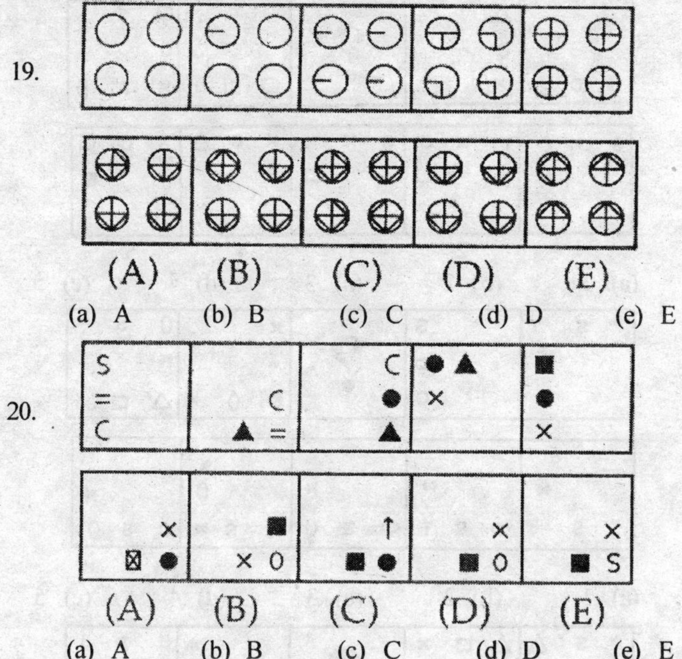

(a) A (b) B (c) C (d) D (e) E

20.

(a) A (b) B (c) C (d) D (e) E

DIRECTIONS (Qs. 21-25): In each of the following questions a series begins with an unnumbered figure on the extreme left. One and only one of the five numbered figures in the series does not fit into the series. The two unnumbered figures one each on the extreme left and the extreme right fit into the series. You have to take as many aspects into account as possible of the figures in the series and find out the one and only one of the five numbered figure which does not fit into the series. The number of that figure is the answer.

21.

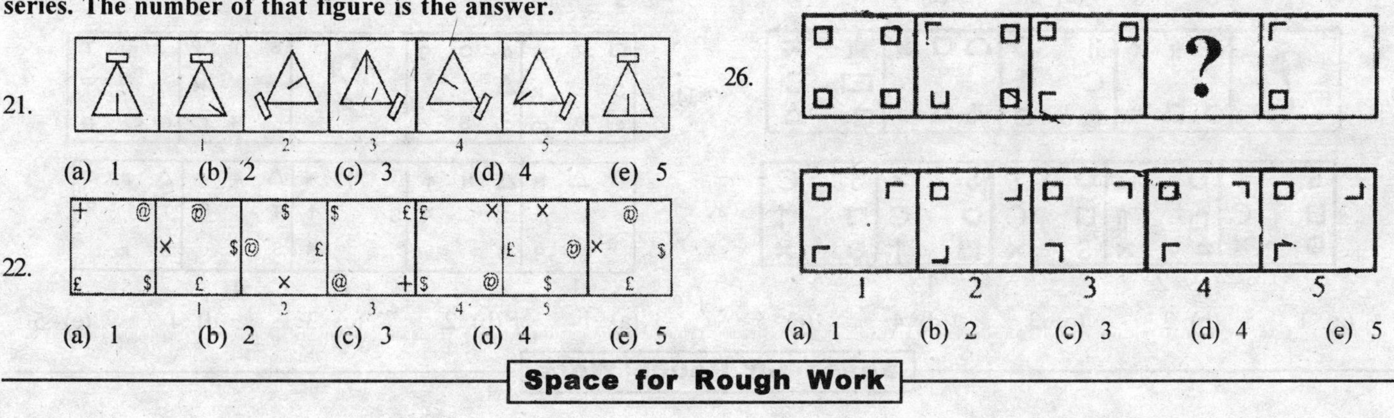

(a) 1 (b) 2 (c) 3 (d) 4 (e) 5

22.

(a) 1 (b) 2 (c) 3 (d) 4 (e) 5

23.

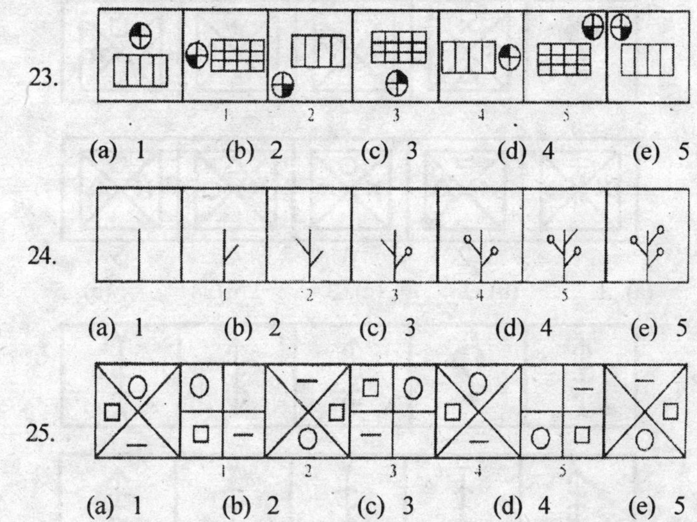

(a) 1 (b) 2 (c) 3 (d) 4 (e) 5

24.

(a) 1 (b) 2 (c) 3 (d) 4 (e) 5

25.

(a) 1 (b) 2 (c) 3 (d) 4 (e) 5

DIRECTIONS (Qs. 26–35): In each of these questions there are two sets of figures. The figures on the left are Problem Figures (four figures and one question–marked space) and those on the right are Answer Figures indicated by number 1, 2, 3, 4 and 5. A series is established if one of the five answer figures is placed at the question marked space. Figures form a series if they change from left to right according to the same rule. The number of the Answer Figure which should be place in the question–marked space is the answer. All the five figures, i.e., four Problem Figures and one Answer Figure placed in the question–marked space, should be considered forming the series.

26.

(a) 1 (b) 2 (c) 3 (d) 4 (e) 5

Space for Rough Work

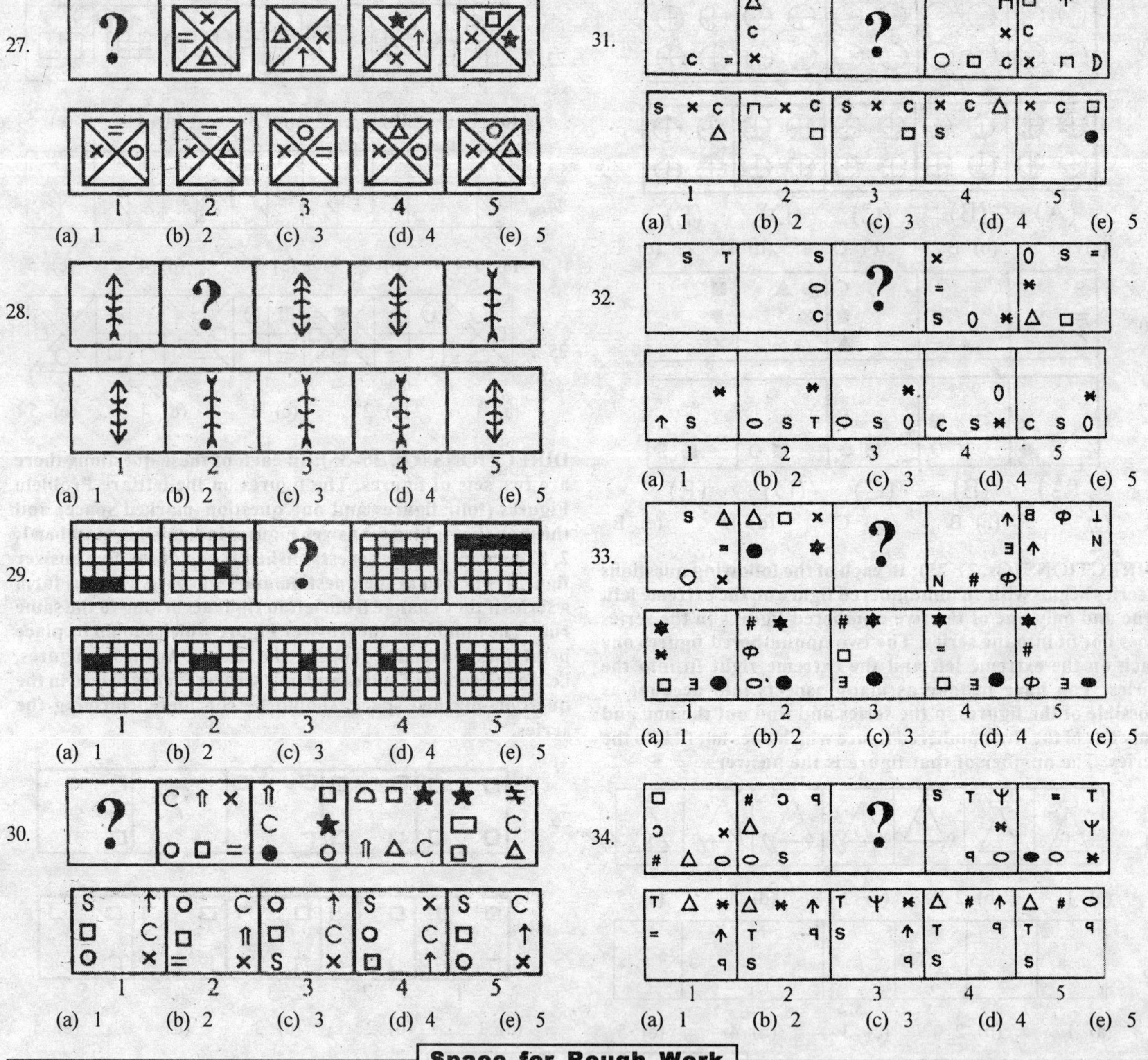

27. (a) 1 (b) 2 (c) 3 (d) 4 (e) 5

28. (a) 1 (b) 2 (c) 3 (d) 4 (e) 5

29. (a) 1 (b) 2 (c) 3 (d) 4 (e) 5

30. (a) 1 (b) 2 (c) 3 (d) 4 (e) 5

31. (a) 1 (b) 2 (c) 3 (d) 4 (e) 5

32. (a) 1 (b) 2 (c) 3 (d) 4 (e) 5

33. (a) 1 (b) 2 (c) 3 (d) 4 (e) 5

34. (a) 1 (b) 2 (c) 3 (d) 4 (e) 5

Space for Rough Work

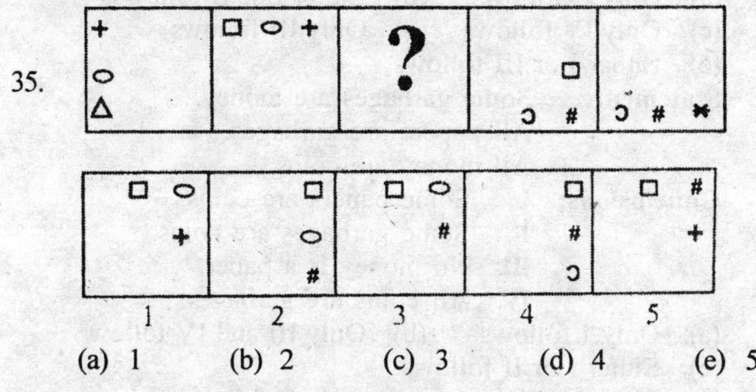

35. (a) 1 (b) 2 (c) 3 (d) 4 (e) 5

DIRECTIONS (Qs. 36–40): The first figure in the first unit of the problem figures bears a certain relationship to the second figure. Similarly, one of the figures in the answer figures bears the same relationship to the second figure in the second unit of the problem figures. You are therefore to locate the figure which would replace the question mark.

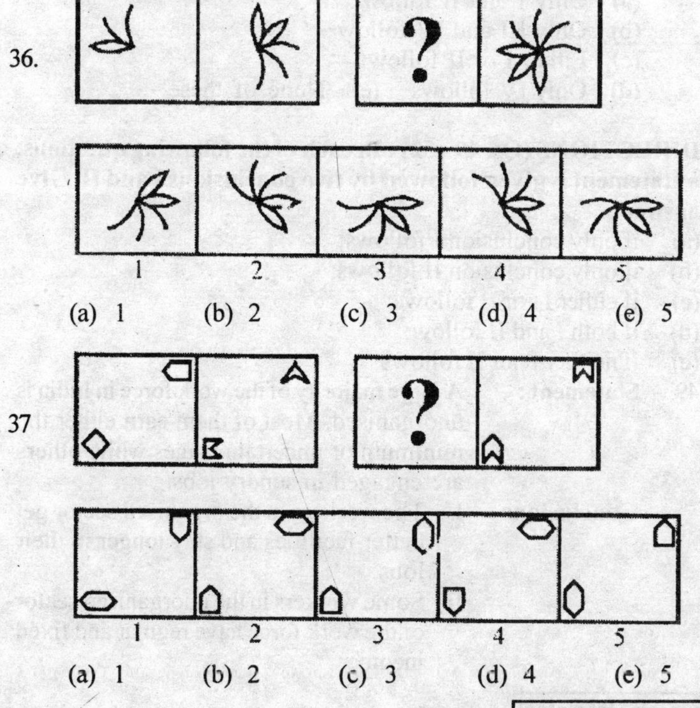

36. (a) 1 (b) 2 (c) 3 (d) 4 (e) 5

37. (a) 1 (b) 2 (c) 3 (d) 4 (e) 5

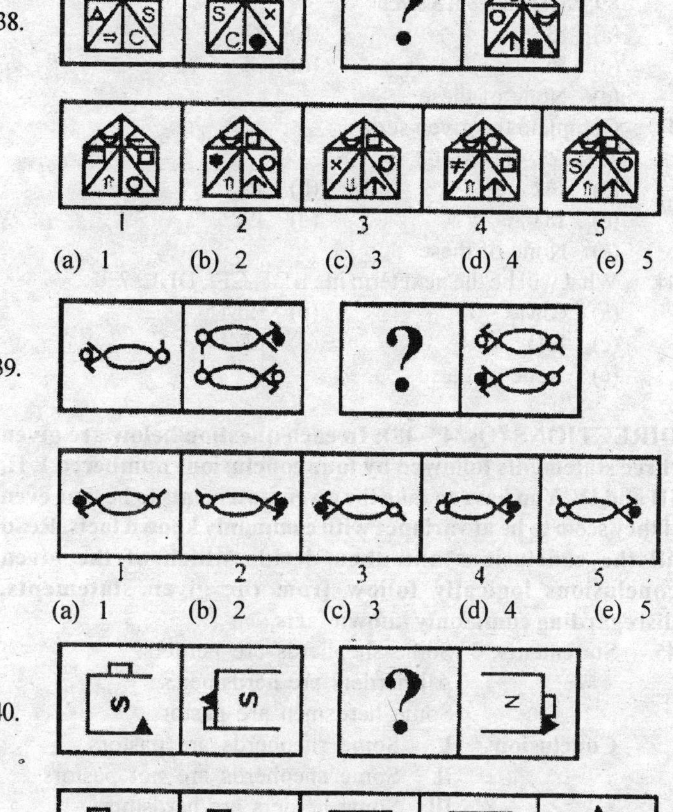

38. (a) 1 (b) 2 (c) 3 (d) 4 (e) 5

39. (a) 1 (b) 2 (c) 3 (d) 4 (e) 5

40. (a) 1 (b) 2 (c) 3 (d) 4 (e) 5

41. Two trains, one from Howrah to Patna and the other from Patna to Howrah, start simultaneously. After they meet, the trains reach their destinations after 9 hours and 16 hours respectively. The ratio of their speeds is:

(a) 2 : 3 (b) 4 : 3
(c) 6 : 7 (d) 9 : 16
(e) None of these

Space for Rough Work

42. Which one of the numbers is wrong in the series given below ?
89, 78, 86, 80, 85, 82, 83
(a) 83 (b) 82
(c) 86 (d) 78
(e) None of these

43. Complete the given series.
3, 12, 27, 48, 75, 108, ?
(a) 147 (b) 162
(c) 183 (d) 192
(e) None of these

44. What will be the next term in : BDF, CFI, DHL, ?
(a) CJM (b) EIM
(c) EJO (d) EMI
(e) None of these

DIRECTIONS (Qs. 45-48): In each question below are given three statements followed by four conclusions numbered I, II, III and IV. You have to take the given statements to be true even if they seem to be at variance with commonly known facts. Read all the conclusions and then decide which of the given conclusions logically follow from the given statements, disregarding commonly known facts.

45. **Statements:** Some shepherds are herders.
All herders are herdsmen.
Some herdsmen are pastors.
Conclusions: **I.** Some shepherds are pastors.
II. Some shepherds are not pastors
III. Some herders are herdsmen.
IV. Some shepherds are herdsmen.
(a) Only I, III and IV follow
(b) Only II, III and IV follow
(c) Only I and IV follow
(d) Either I or II and IV follow
(e) Only III, IV and either I or II follow

46. **Statements:** Some pads are not symbols.
All symbols are letters.
Some letters are boxes.
Conclusions: **I.** Some boxes are pads.
II. Some pads are not boxes.
III. Some pads are not letters.
IV. All symbols are boxes.
(a) Only II follows (b) Either I or II follows
(c) Only IV follows (d) Only III follows
(e) Either I or III follows

47. **Statements:** Some garbages are money.
All papers are garbages.
All money are coins.
Conclusions: **I.** Some papers are coins.
II. Some garbages are coins.
III. No money is a paper.
IV. All coins are garbages.
(a) Only I follows (b) Only III and IV follow
(c) Either I or II follows
(d) Only IV follows (e) Only II follows

48. **Statements:** Some pants are shirts.
No face is a pant.
No pant is a flower.
Conclusions: **I.** No flower is a face.
II. No face is a flower.
III. Some shirts are not faces.
IV. Some shirts are pants.
(a) Only I and II follow
(b) Only III and IV follow
(c) Either I or II follows
(d) Only IV follows (e) None of these

DIRECTIONS (Qs. 49 - 52) : In each of the following questions, a statement is given followed by two conclusions I and II. Give answer :
(a) if only conclusion I follows;
(b) if only conclusion II follows;
(c) if either I nor II follows;
(d) if both I and II follow;
(e) if neither I nor II follows.

49. **Statement :** A large majority of the work force in India is unorganised. Most of them earn either the minimum or uncertain wages while others are engaged in sundry jobs.
Conclusions : I. The workers in the organised sector get better facilities and stay longer in their jobs.
II. Some workers in the unorganised sector of the work force have regular and fixed income.

Space for Rough Work

50. **Statement :** It is almost impossible to survive and prosper in this world without sacrificing ethics and morality.

Conclusions : I. World appreciates some concepts but may not uphold it.

II. Concept of ethics and morality are not practicable in life.

51. **Statement :** Research has proved that people eating high fat diets coupled with decreased level of exercises are prone to heart diseases.

Conclusions : I. People should reduce their high-fat diet as a preventive method.

II. People must have sufficient level of exercise to reduce their chances of having heart disease.

52. **Statement :** From the next academic year, students will have the option of dropping Mathematics and Science for their school leaving certificate examination.

Conclusions : I. Students who are weak in Science and Mathematics will be admitted.

II. Earlier students did not have the choice of continuing their education without taking these subjects.

DIRECTIONS (Qs. 53 & 54) : Read the following information to answer the questions given below :

(i) Five boys are standing in a line facing the wall wearing red, green, yellow, white and blue dress.

(ii) The yellow-dressed boy is not standing at any end of the line

(iii) The red-dressed boy is not standing at any end of the line.

53. The boy in the middle wears which coloured-dress?
(a) Green
(b) Blue
(c) Either Green or Blue
(d) Cannot be determined
(e) None of these

54. Who is to the right of yellow-dressed boy?
(a) Data inadequate (b) White
(c) Green (d) Blue
(e) None of these

DIRECTIONS (Qs. 55-57) : Study the given information carefully and answer the questions that follow :

(i) There are six friends A, B, C, D, E and F.

(ii) Each one is proficient in one of the games, namely Badminton, Volleyball, Cricket, Hockey, Tennis and Polo.

(iii) Each owns a different coloured car, namely, yellow, green, black, white, blue and red.

(iv) D plays Polo and owns a yellow coloured car.

(v) C does not play either Tennis or Hockey and owns neither blue nor yellow coloured car.

(vi) E owns a white car and plays Badminton.

(vii) B does not plays Tennis, he owns a red coloured car.

(viii) A plays Cricket and owns a black car.

55. Who plays Volleyball?
(a) B (b) C
(c) F (d) Data inadequate
(e) None of these

56. Which coloured car F owns?
(a) Green (b) Blue
(c) Either Green or Blue
(d) Data inadequate
(e) None of these

57. Which of the following combinations of colour of car and game played is not correct?
(a) Yellow — Polo (b) Green — Tennis
(c) Black — Cricket (d) Red — Hockey
(e) None of these

DIRECTIONS (Qs. 58 - 62) : Study the given information carefully and answer the questions that follow :

(i) A, B, C, D, E, F and G are sitting on a wall and all of them are facing east.

(ii) C is on the immediate right of D.

(iii) B is at an extreme end and has E as his neighbour.

(iv) G is between E and F.

(v) D is sitting third from the south end.

58. Who is sitting to the right of E?
(a) A (b) C
(c) D (d) G
(e) None of these

Space for Rough Work

59. Which of the following pairs of people are sitting at the extreme ends?
(a) AB (b) AE
(c) CB (d) Cannot be determined
(e) None of these

60. Name the person who should change places with C such that he gets the third place from the north end.
(a) E (b) F
(c) G (d) D
(e) None of these

61. Immediately between which of the following pairs of people is D sitting?
(a) AC (b) AF
(c) CE (d) CF
(e) None of these

62. Which of the conditions (i) to (v) given above is not required to find out the place in which A is sitting?
(a) (i) (b) (ii)
(c) (iii) (d) All are required
(e) None of these

DIRECTIONS (Qs. 63 - 65) : These questions based on the diagram given below showing four persons stationed at the four corners of a square piece of a plot as shown :

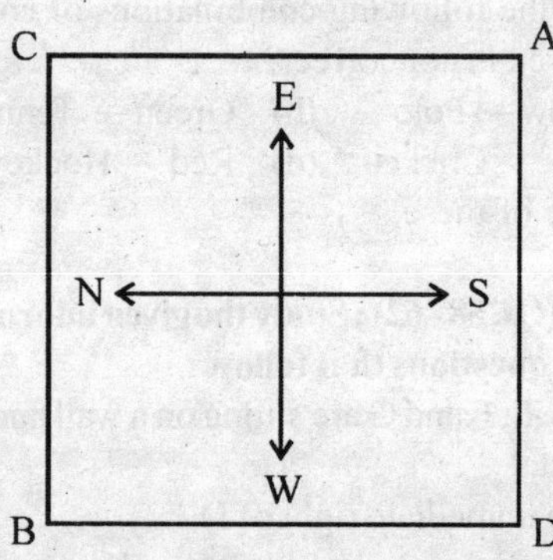

63. A starts crossing the plot diagonally. After walking half the distance, he turns right, walks some distance and turns left. Which direction is A facing now ?
(a) North-east (b) North
(c) North-west (d) South-east
(e) None of these

64. From the original position given in the above figure, A and B move one arm length clockwise and then cross over to the corners diagonally opposite; C and D move one arm length anti-clockwise and cross over to the corners diagonally opposite. The original configuration ABCD has now changed to
(a) CBDA (b) DACB
(c) BDAC (d) ACBD
(e) None of these

65. From the original position, B and D move one and a half length of sides clockwise and anti-clockwise respectively. Which one of the following starements is true ?
(a) B and D are both at the mid point between A and C.
(b) B is at the midpoint between A and C, and D is at the corner originally occupied by A.
(c) D is at the midpoint between A and C, and B is at the corner originally occupied by C.
(d) B and D are both at the midpoint between A and D.
(e) None of these

DIRECTIONS (Qs. 66 - 69) : Read the following information to answer these questions :

(i) In a family of six persons : A, B, C, D, E and F there are two married couples.
(ii) D is grandmother of A and mother of B.
(iii) C is wife of B and mother of F.
(iv) F is the grand-daughter of E.

66. What is C to A ?
(a) Grandmother (b) Mother
(c) Wife (d) Cannot be determined
(e) None of these

67. How many male members are there in the family?
(a) Three (b) Four
(c) One (d) Cannot be determined
(e) None of these

68. Which of the following is true?
(a) A is sister of F (b) D has two grandsons
(c) B has two daughters
(d) has one grandson (e) None of these

69. Who among the following is one of the couples?
(a) DE (b) EB
(c) BC (d) Cannot be determined
(e) None of these

Space for Rough Work

DIRECTIONS (Qs. 70 -73) : In a secret way of writing INDIA HAS WON FIRST GOLD MEDAL is written as JEZJU OUV SEF PJ DVB REQZ ITZUQ. Bearing the method in mind, pick up the code from the answer choices for each given word.

70. FOOT
    (a) PEEB (b) SEEZ
    (c) BEEB (d) CEEA
    (e) None of these
71. DIESEL
    (a) ZJTVTQ (b) ZJEVTQ
    (c) BZTETV (d) LEEB
    (e) None of these
72. WOOD
    (a) SEEZ (b) BEEZ
    (c) ZEES (d) LEEB
    (e) None of these
73. TAILOR
    (a) BUTQEP (b) BUJQED
    (c) ZUTQED (d) SUTQED
    (e) None of these

DIRECTIONS (Qs. 74-78): Below is given passage followed by several possible inferences which can be drawn from the facts stated in the passage. You have to examine each inference separately in the context of the passage and decide upon its degree of truth or falsity. Mark answer

(a) if the inference is "definitely true" i.e. it properly follows from the statement of fact given;
(b) if the inference is "probably true" though not "definitely true" in the light of other fact given;
(c) if the data are inadequate i.e. from the facts given you cannot say whether the inference is likely to be true or false;
(d) if the inference is "probably false" i.e. though not "defiantly false" in the light of the fact given;
(e) if the inference is "definitely false" i.e. it cannot possibly be drawn from the facts given or it contradicts the given facts.

India's export of readymade garments increased by almost 11 per cent in value terms during April 2002 at $ 324 million over the same period last year. As per provisional data compiled by the Apparel Export Promotion Council (AEPC), readymade garment exports were higher by 10.9 per cent in value terms compared to $ 292.2 million in April 2001. In terms of quantity, exports in April 2002 were 16.8 percent higher at 94 million pieces compared to 80.8 million pieces in the same month a year earlier. Exports in rupee terms increased by over 16 per cent at Rs 1587.3 crore compared to Rs 1368.9 crore a year earlier.

74. Apparel Export Promotion Council (AEPC) releases authentic data, and one can believe it.
75. India's export of readymade garments is increasing every year in both value terms as well as rupee terms.
76. In 2001, there was a recession in garment export.
77. Readymade garments' export is a good option for skilful unemployed persons to deal in.
78. Readymade garments' export in 2001 was more than readymade garments' import in 2001.

DIRECTIONS (Qs. 79-83) : In each of following questions, a statement is given followed by two assumptions numbered I and II. Consider the statement and the following assumptions and decide which of the assumptions is implicit. Give answer :

(a) if only assumption I is implicit.
(b) if only assumption II is implicit.
(c) if either I or II is implicit.
(d) if both I and II are implicit.
(e) if none assymption is implicit

79. **Statement :** Try to steal this camera from our store — a display on a departmental store.
    Assumptions : I. People want to own a camera.
    II. The store has a video monitoring system to detect stealing.
80. **Statement :** Never before such a lucid book was available on the topic.
    Assumptions : I. Some other books were available on this topic.
    II. You can write lucid books on very few topics.
81. **Statement :** "Get rid of your past for future, get our new-generation fridge at a discount in exchange of old". — An advertisement.
    Assumptions : I. The sales of the new fridge may increase in the coming months.
    II. People prefer to exchange future with past.

Space for Rough Work

82. **Statement :** The party president has directed that no member of the party will give press briefing or interviews to government and private T.V. channels about the discussion in scheduled meeting of the party.

Assumptions : I. Party members will observe this directive of the president.

II. The general public will not come to know about the happenings in the scheduled meeting of the party.

83. **Statement :** The end of a financial year is the ideal time to take a look at the performance of various companies.

Assumptions : I. All the companies take such a review at the end of a financial year.

II. The performance data of various companies is available.

84. If FRIEND is coded as HUMJTK, how is CANDLE written in that code?

(a) EDRIRL (b) DCQHQK
(c) ESJFME (d) FYOBOC
(e) None of these

85. If '–' means '×' ; '×' means '+' ; '+' means '÷' and '÷' means '–' then $40 \times 12 + 3 - 6 \div 60 = ?$

(a) 44 (b) 7.95
(c) 16 (d) None of these
(e) None of these

86. Rasik walks 20 m North. Then, he turns right and walks 30 m. Then he turns right and walks 35 m. Then he turns left and walks 15 m. Then he again turns left and walks 15 m. In which direction and how many metres away is he from his original position?

(a) 15 metres West (b) 30 metres East
(c) 30 metres West (d) 45 metres East
(e) None of these

DIRECTIONS (Qs. 87 & 88) : In each of these questions, various terms of a series are given with one term missing as shown by (?). Choose the missing term :

87. AZ, CX, FU, (?)

(a) IR (b) JQ
(c) IV (d) KP
(e) None of these

88. 2Z5, 7Y7, 14X9, 23W11, 34V13, (?)

(a) 27U24 (b) 45U15
(c) 47U15 (d) 27V14
(e) None of these

DIRECTIONS (Qs. 89 & 90) : In each of the following questions, a statement is given followed by two courses of action numbered I and II. Decide which of the cources of action logically follows and give answer :

(a) if only I follows;
(b) if only II follows;
(c) if either I or II follows;
(d) if both I and II follows;
(e) if none follows;

89. **Statement :** A recent study shows that children below five years die in the cities of the developing countries mainly from diarrhoea and parasitic intestinal worms.

Courses of action : I. Governments of the developing countries should take adequate measures to improve the hygienic conditions in the cities.

II. Children below five years in the cities of the developing countries need to be kept under constant medication.

90. **Statement :** There has been a significant droop in the water level of all the lakes supplying water to the city.

Courses of action : I. The water supply authority should impose a partial cut in supply to tackle the situation.

II. The Government should appeal to all the residents through mass media for minimum use of water.

Space for Rough Work

DIRECTIONS (Qs. 91 - 93) : In each of the following questions, a statement is followed by three courses of action numbered I, II and III. Decide which of the three given courses of action logically follows for pursuing and then give the answer.

91. **Statement :** Suicides are on the rise among youths, particularly due to unemployment.

Courses of action : I. A committee should be made to find out the main cause of the rise in cases of suicide.

II. People should be discouraged from indulging in love affairs and encouraged to get self-employed.

III. Parents of wards should be instructed to nurse their words if they observe that their wards if they observe that their wards are facing critical circumstances.

(a) All I, II and III (b) Only I and II
(c) Only I and III (d) both I and II
(e) None of these

92. **Statement :** Indian Railways are absolutely dependent on government subsidies and lack concentration on transportation activities.

Courses of action : I. A committee should be constituted to look into the matter.

II. Railways should explore new areas to generate revenues.

III. Railways should concentrate on hiving off non-core activities such as design and manufacture of rolling stock, construction, housing etc. to private sectors.

(a) Only I (b) Only I and II
(c) Only II and III (d) All follow
(e) None of these

93. **Statement :** The chairman of the car company announced in the meeting that all trial of its first product the new car model 'M' are over and company plans to launch its car in the market after six months.

Courses of action : I. The network of dealers is to be finalised and all legal, financial and other matters in this connection will have to be finalised shortly.

II. The company will have to make plan for product other than car.

III. Material, managerial and other resources will have to be in fine tune to maintain production schedule.

(a) Only I and II (b) Only I
(c) All the three (d) Only II
(e) None of these

DIRECTIONS (Qs. 94–102): Study the following information carefully and answer the questions given below:

Following are the criteria for granting admission to the candidates in the Post–Graduate course in Software Technology:

The candidate must

(A) have engineering degree with 65% marks.
(B) not be more than 28 years of age as on 1.12.2000.
(C) have obtained at least 50% marks in the entrance test.
(D) pay a sum of Rs 1,00,000 at the time of admission as course fee.

however if a candidate fulfils all the criteria except:

(I) D above, but can pay the fee in two instatments, the case may be referred to the Director of the Institute.
(II) B above, but he/she has passed post–graduation exam in science with 75% marks, his/her case may be referred to the Admission Co–ordinator.

Based on the above criteria and information provided against each candidate take a decision in each case. you are not to assume anything. If the data given are not adequate to take a decision mark your answer 'Data inadequate'. The following cases are given to you as on 1.12.200. Give answer:

(a) If the candiadate is to be admitted;
(b) If the candiadate is not to be admitted;
(c) If the case is to be referred to the Director;
(d) If the case is to be referred to the Admission Co–ordinator;
(e) If data are inadequate.

Space for Rough Work

94. Sneha was 26 years old as on 3rd march, 2000. She has secured 75% marks inb postgraduation in chemistry and she is ready to pay Rs 1,00,000 at the time of admission. She has secured 72% marks in graduation in engineering and the entrance test.

95. Ashutosh has secured 62% and 68% marks in the entrance test and graduation in engineering respectively. He was 27 years old as on 1 April, 2000. He can pay Rs 1,00,000 at the time of admission.

96. Rishikant was 26 years old as on 22 January, 1997. he has secured 65% marks in graduation in engineering and 83% marks in postgraduation in physics. He has secured 60% marks in the entrance test. He is ready to pay Rs 1,00,000 at the time of admission.

97. Damodar was born on 19 May, 1975. He has secured 60% and 73% marks in the entrance test and postgraduation respectively. He is ready to pay Rs 1,00,000 at the time of admission.

98. Khemchand has secured 69% and 65% marks in graduation in engineering and the entrance test respectively. He was born on 10 November, 1973. He is ready to pay Rs 75,000 at the time of admission and the rest Rs 25,000 after three months.

99. Gopal passed graduation in engineering at the age of 22 years and secured 62% marks in the entrance test. he is ready to pay Rs 1,00,000 at the time of admission.

100. phoolan has secured 82% marks in postgraduation in science. her date of birth is 25 June 1979. She has secured 65% marks in the entrance test and is ready to pay Rs 1,00,000 at the time of admission.

101. Sajid was 24 years old as on 3rd October 1998. he has secured 65% marks in engineering degree and 70% marks in the entrance test. He has also completed his postgraduation in physics with 81% marks. He is ready to pay Rs 1,00,000 in two instalments.

102. Amrita has secured 65% marks in engineering graduation and 75% marks in postgraduation. She was born on 2nd September 1971. She can pay Rs 1,00,000 at the time of admission.

103. Three containers have their volumes in the ratio 3 : 4 : 5. They are full of mixtures of milk and water. The mixtures contain milk and water in the ratio of (4: 1), (3 : 1) and (5 : 2) respectively. The contents of all these three containers are poured into a fourth container. The ratio of milk and water in the fourth container is:
(a) 4 : 1 (b) 151 : 48
(c) 157 : 53 (d) 5 : 2
(e) None of these

104. The ratio between the length and the breadth of a rectangular park is 3 : 2. If a man cycling along the boundary of the park at the speed of 12km / hr completes one round in 8 minutes, then the area of the park (in sq. m) is:
(a) 15360 (b) 153600
(c) 30720 (d) 307200
(e) None of these

105. Number of students who have opted the subjects A, B, C are 60, 84, 108 respectively. The examination is to be conducted for these students such that only the students of the same subject are allowed in one room. Also the number of students in each room must be same. What is the minimum number of rooms that should be arranged to meet all these conditions?
(a) 28 (b) 60
(c) 12 (d) 21
(e) None of these

106. The mean of 30 values was 150. It was detected on rechecking that one value 165 was wrongly copied as 135 for the computation of the mean. Find the correct mean.
(a) 151 (b) 149
(c) 152 (d) 153
(e) None of these

107. A father said to his son, "I was as old as you are at present at the time of your birth." If the father's age is 38 years now, the son's age five years back was:
(a) 14 years (b) 19 years
(c) 33 years (d) 38 years

Space for Rough Work

108. Five litres of water is added to a certain quantity of pure milk costing Rs 3 per litre. If by selling the mixture at the same price as before, a profit of 20% is made, what is the amount of pure milk in the mixture?
(a) 22 litres (b) 25 litres
(c) 27 litres (d) 24 litres
(e) None of these

109. A tyre has two punctures. The first puncture along would have made the tyre flat in 9 minutes and the second alone would have done it in 6 minutes. If air leaks out at a constant rate, how long does it take both the punctures together to make it flat?
(a) $1\frac{1}{2}$ minutes (b) $3\frac{1}{2}$ minutes
(c) $3\frac{3}{5}$ minutes (d) $4\frac{1}{4}$ minutes
(e) None of these

110. Two numbers are such that if the first be added to 5 times the second, their sum becomes 52, and if the second be added to 8 times the first, their sum becomes 65. The two numbers are
(a) 9, 7 (b) 3, 7
(c) 7, 9 (d) 7, 3
(e) None of these

DIRECTIONS (Qs. 111-115) : Study the following table carefully to answer these questions.

Percentage of marks obtained by six students in six subjects

Student	Subjects					
	A (Out of 60)	B (Out of 40)	C (out of 80)	D (out of 50)	E (out of 120)	F (out of 75)
P	80	65	58	68	75	87
Q	55	70	67	74	88	78
R	74	54	72	84	62	76
S	68	76	82	56	72	64
T	75	68	64	72	80	72
U	82	78	75	67	68	82

111. What is the total marks obtained by student R is subjects B, D and E?
(a) 200 (b) 138
(c) 168 (d) 156
(e) None of these

112. What is the average marks obtained by all the students in subject C? (rounded off to the nearest integer)
(a) 56 (b) 58
(c) 54 (d) 54
(e) None of these

113. What is the average percentage of marks obtained by all the students in subject A?
(a) $73\frac{2}{3}$ (b) $43\frac{2}{5}$
(c) $72\frac{1}{3}$ (d) $48\frac{3}{5}$
(e) None of these

114. Approximately what is the overall percentage of marks obtained by student Q in all the Subjects?
(a) 77 (b) 72
(c) 78 (d) 74
(e) None of these

115. What is the total marks obtained by all the students together in subject E?
(a) 522 (b) 488
(c) 445 (d) 534
(e) None of these

DIRECTIONS (Qs. 116-120) : Study the chart and give the answer of follwoing questions.

Selling of the car in UK according to the colours

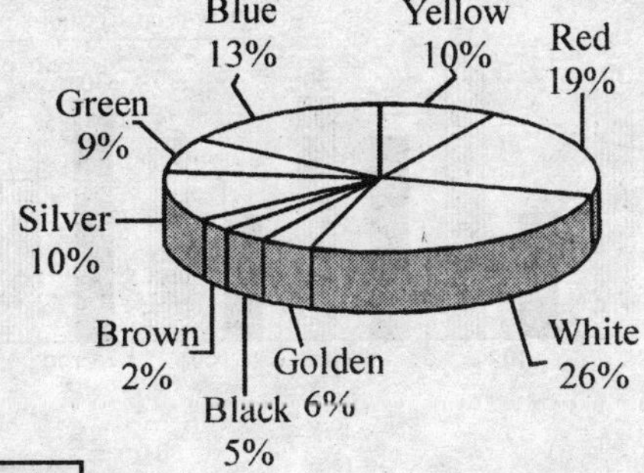

Space for Rough Work

116. 50% of all the cars consisted of which colours of car?
 (a) Black, Gloden, Blue, Red
 (b) Blue, Black, Red, Silver
 (c) White, Golden, Blue, Black
 (d) White, Blue, Green, Black
 (e) None of these

117. Cars of which colour are 20% less popular than white coloured cars?
 (a) Black (b) Golden
 (c) Red (d) Blue
 (e) None of these

118. Cars of which colour are 13% less popular than white cars?
 (a) Blue (b) Green
 (c) Silver (d) Yellow
 (e) None of these

119. Cars of which colour when increased by two per cent and then combined with that of red cars will make 30 per cent of the total?
 (a) Golden (b) Blue
 (c) Black (d) Red
 (e) None of these

120. If in a certain period the total production of all cars was 95400 then how many more blue cars were sold than green?
 (a) 2580 (b) 3618
 (c) 2850 (d) 3816
 (e) None of these

DIRECTIONS (Qs. 121 - 125) : Study the following graph carefully and answer the question given below.

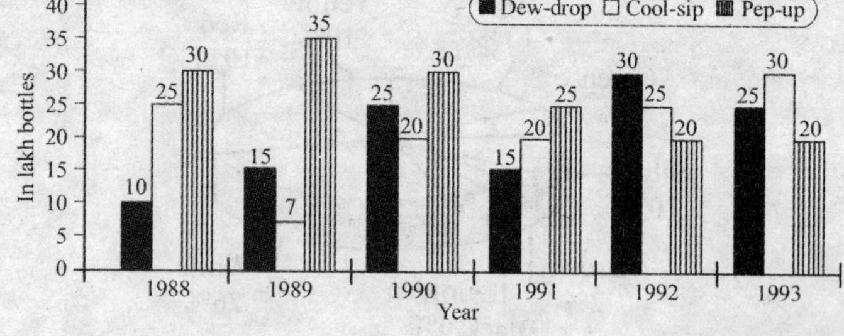

121. In which year was the sale of 'Pep-up' the maximum?
 (a) 1990 (b) 1991
 (c) 1992 (d) 1993
 (e) None of these

122. In the case of which soft drink was the average annual sale maximum in the given period?
 (a) pep-up only (b) Cool-sip only
 (c) Dew-drop only (d) Cool-sip and Dew-drop
 (e) None of these

123. In the case of Cool-sip drink, what was the approximate per cent increase in sale in 1992 over its sale in 1991?
 (a) Less than 20% (b) 20%-25%
 (c) 25% (d) 31%-35%
 (e) None of these

124. In the year 1990, what was the difference between the number of 'Pep-up' and 'Cool-sip' bottles sold?
 (a) 50,00,000 (b) 5,00,000
 (c) 50,000 (d) 10,00,000
 (e) None of these

125. What was the approximate per cent drop in sale of 'Pep-up' in 1990 over its sale in 1989?
 (a) 5 (b) 12
 (c) 14 (d) 28
 (e) None of these

DIRECTIONS (Qs. 126-130) : Study the following data carefully to answer the questions that follow.

Details of Statewise distribution of candidates appeared in an Examination

Statewise distribution of candidates appeared
Total candidates appeared = 1,20,000

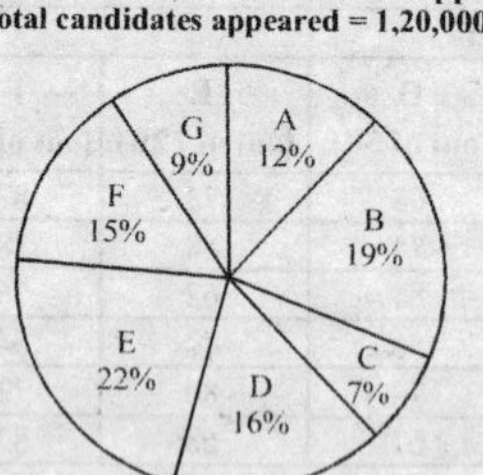

Ratio of male and female candidates appeared

State	Ratio
A	5 : 7
B	11 : 8
C	3 : 4
D	9 : 7
E	5 : 6
F	8 : 7
G	4 : 5

Space for Rough Work

126. The number of female candidates appeared from State 'C' is equal to the number of male candidates apperared in the examination from which state?
(a) A (b) D
(c) E (d) G
(e) None of these

127. What is the ratio of the number of male candidates appeared in the examination from state A to that from state E?
(a) 1 : 2 (b) 1 : 1
(c) 2 : 1 (d) 6 : 7
(e) None of these

128. The total number of female candidates appeared from states E & G together is what per cent of the total number of candidates appeared in the examination from all the states?
(a) 13 (b) 11
(c) 17 (d) 15
(e) None of these

129. What is the total number of male candidates appeared in the examination from states B and F together?
(a) 16,800 (b) 18,4000
(c) 13,200 (d) 22,800
(e) None of these

130. The number of female candidates appeared from state 'D' is what per cent of the total number of candidates appeared in the examination from all the states?
(a) 9 (b) 8
(c) 8.5 (d) 7
(e) None of these

DIRECTIONS (Qs.131 - 145) : The question consists of a question and two statements numbered (I) and (II) given below it. You have to decide whether the data provided in the statements are sufficient to answer the question. Read both the statements and give answer

(a) if the question can be answered by using one of the statements ALONE, but cannot be answered using the other statement alone;
(b) if the question can be answered by using EITHER statement alone;
(c) if the question can be answered by using BOTH statements TOGETHER, but cannot be answered using either statement alone;
(d) if the question CANNOT be answered even by using BOTH statements TOGETHER;
(e) if the question can be answered by using statement I ALONE.

131. What is the area of a circular region X?
I. Area of the square inscribed in the circular region X is 98 sq cm.
II. The perimeter of the circular region X is equal to the perimeter of square Z having area 121 cm^2.

132. Find the number of males and females in a party.
I. The ratio of males and females is 3 : 2
II. The number of males is 50% more than the number of females.

133. What will be the cost of painting the four walls and the roof of a room with length, width and height as 7 metres, 5 metres and 2.5 metres respectively. The room has one door and two windows.
I. Cost of painting per square metre is Rs 72.
II. Area of window is half of the area of the door.

134. A, B and C are integers. Is B an even number?
I. (A + B) is an odd number.
II. (C + B) is an odd number.

135. The towns A, B and C lie on a straight line. C is between A and B. The distance from A to B is 100 miles. How far is it from A to C?
I. The distance from A to B is 25% more than the distance from C to B.
II. The distance from A to C is $\frac{1}{4}$ the distance from C to B.

136. What is Sunil's position in a row of forty students?
I. There are sixteen students towards the left of Sunil.
II. There are twenty-three student towards the right of Sunil ?

137. A person bought 2 kg of rice from a shop. But when he entered the next shop he found that the price was less. He calculated that if he bought 6 kg from that shop his average price would be Rs. 20. Then what is the price in the first shop?
I. The price in the second shop was Rs 18 per kg.
II. The difference in the prices was Rs 8 per kg.

Space for Rough Work

138. A fly crawls around the outside of a circle once. A second fly crawls around the outside of a square once. Which fly travels farther?
(I) The diagonal of the square is equal to the diameter of the circle.
(II) The fly crawling around the circle takes more time to complete his journey than the fly crawling around the square.

139. Is the number $\frac{M}{3}$ an odd integer? (You may assume that $\frac{M}{3}$ is an integer)
(I) M = 3K, where K is an integer.
(II) M = 6J + 3, where J is an interger.

140. A worker is hired for 6 days. He is paid Rs. 5 more for each day of work than he was paid for the preceding day. How much was he paid for the first day of the work ?
(I) His total wages for 6 days were Rs. 900.
(II) He was paid less than Rs 100 on the first day.

141. How much cardboard will it take to make an open cubical box with no top ?
(I) The area of the bottom of the box is 4 square metres.
(II) The volume of the box is 8 cubic metres.

142. How much minimum marks will be require to pass an examination?
(I) Student A secured 32% marks in that examination and he failed by 1 mark. Student B secured 36% marks in the same examination and his marks was 1 more than the minimum pass marks.
(II) Student A secured 30% of full marks in the examination and he failed by 2 marks. If he had secured 5 more marks his percentage of marks would have been 40%.

143. In the given figure P, Q and R are centres of three equal circles. What is the area of the shaded portion in the figure shown below ?

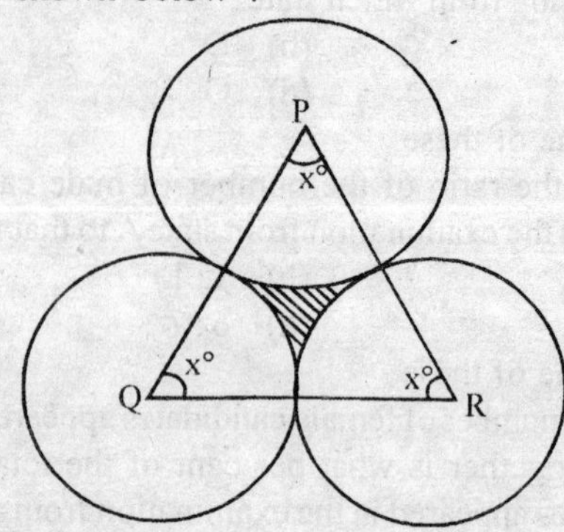

(I) QR is known.
(II) The triangle is an equilateral triangle.

144. What number is opposite the face bearing number 5 of the same dice when it is thrown by different persons? Note that the dice bears the numbers 1 to 6 on different faces of the dice.
(I) When Renu throws the dice on a table, she observes that the visible surfaces bear the numbers 3, 6 and 5, while, when her sister throws the dice, she observes that the visible surfaces are 1, 4 and 5.
(II) When Tulika throws the same dice, she finds herself unable to see the three faces bearing the numbers 1, 3 and 5 while when her brother Shivendra throws the dice he finds himself able to see the three faces bearing the numbers 6, 4 and 5.

145. Find the length of AB?
If $\angle YBC = \angle CAX = \angle YOX = 90°$

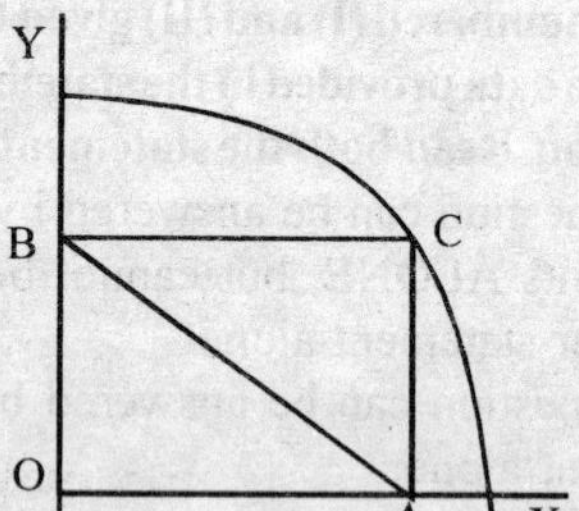

(I) Radius of the Arc is given
(II) OA = 5

Space for Rough Work

DIRECTIONS (Qs.146 - 150) : In each question below is given a statement followed by two assumptions lettered A and B. An assumption is something supposed or taken for granted. You have to consider the statement and following assumptions and decide which the assumption is implicit in the statement. Give answer

(a) if only assumption A is implicit;
(b) if only assumption B is implicit;
(c) if only either A or B implicit;
(d) if only neither A nor B is implicit;
(e) if none assumption is implicit.

146. A certain bakery sells brown bread in 250 gm loaves and 450 gm loaves, and all loaves of the same size sell for the same price per loaf regardless of the number of loaves purchased. What is the price of a 450 gm loaf in this bakery?
A. The total price of a 250 gm loaf and a 450 gm loaf of this bread is Rs 24.00
B. The total price of two 250 gm loaves and one 450 gm loaf of this bread is Rs 34.00

147. What is the ratio of x to y?
A. x is 4 more than twice y
B. The ratio of $0.5x$ to $2y$ is 3 to 5

148. If r and s are integers, is r + s divisible by 3?
A. s is divisible by 3 B. r is divisible by 3

149. Is the integer n odd?
A. n is divisible by 3 B. n is divisible by 5

150. If p and q are positive integers and pq = 24, what is the value of p?
A. $\frac{q}{6}$ is an integer B. $\frac{p}{2}$ is an integer

DIRECTIONS (Qs. 151 -155) : In each of these questions, in the given sentences, a part of the sentence is underlined. Beneath each sentence, four different ways of phrasing the underlined part are indicated. Choose the best alternative.

151. <u>Though he was more faster than his opponent on the field,</u> his chances of winning the race was low as he lacked the killer instinct.
(a) Though he was more faster than his opponent on the field
(b) As he was more faster than his opponent on the field
(c) Though he was more fast from his opponent on the field
(d) Though he was faster than his opponent on the field
(e) None of these

152. The local library has recommended that the books put up for the used book sale <u>should be in good condition and should have no writing in them or be underlined.</u>
(a) and should have no writing in them or be underlined
(b) and should not have writing in them or not be underlined
(c) and contain no writing or underlining
(d) without containing writing or underlining
(e) None of these

153. The news of her employment soon <u>circulated around the small town.</u>
(a) circulated round the small town
(b) circulated in the small town
(c) was circulating across the small town
(d) was circulating within the small town
(e) None of these

154. It is <u>the craziness for speeding that is maddening</u> that is responsible for many motor accidents.
(a) the craziness for speeding that is mad
(b) the mad craze for speed
(c) the mad craze for speeding
(d) the craze for speeding that is maddening
(e) None of these

155. <u>If they cooperate together by dividing up the work</u>, they shall be over with the work faster.
(a) if they cooperate together by dividing the work
(b) if they cooperate by dividing up the work
(c) if they cooperate by dividing the work
(d) if they cooperate together by division of work
(e) None of these

Space for Rough Work

DIRECTIONS (Qs. 156 -159) : In each of these questions a disarranged sentence is given in which words or phrases are lettered P, Q, R, S .... You are to arrange these to form a meaningful sentence.

156. A. If caught in the act, they were punished, not for the crime, but for allowing themselves to be caught another lash of the whip
B. The bellicose Spartans sacrificed all the finer things in life for military expertise.
C. Those fortunate enough to survive babyhood were taken away from their mothers at the age of seven to undergo rigorous military training.
D. This consisted mainly of beatings and deprivations of all kinds like going around barefoot in winter, and worse starvation so that they would be forced to steal food to survive.
E. Male children were examined at birth by the city council and those deemed to weak to become soldiers were left to die or exposure.
(a) BECDA (b) ECADB
(c) BCDAE (d) ECDAB
(e) None of these

157. A. This very insatiability of the photographing eye changes the terms of confinement in the cave, our world.
B. Humankind lingers unregenerately in Plato's cave, still revelling, its age-old habit, in mere images of truth.
C. But being educated by photographs is not like being educated by older images drawn by hand ; for one thing, there are a great many more images around, claiming our attention.
D. The inventory started in 1839 and since then just about everything has been photographed, or so it seems
E. In teaching us a new visual code. Photographs alter and enlarge our notions of what is worth looking at and what we have a right to observe.
(a) EABCD (b) BDEAC
(c) BCDAE (d) ECDAB
(e) None of these

158. A. To be culturally literate is to possess the basic information needed to thrive in the modern world
B. Nor is it confined to one social class; quite the contrary.
C. It is by no means confined to "culture" narrowly understood as an acquaintance with the arts.
D. Cultural literacy constitutes the only sure avenue of opportunity for disadvantaged children, the only reliable way of combating the social determinism that now condemns them.
E. The breadth of that information is great, extending over the major domains of human activity from sports to science.
(a) AECBD (b) DECBA
(c) ACBDE (d) DBCAE
(e) None of these

159. A. Michael Hofman, a poet and translator, accepts this sorry fact without approval or complaint
B. But thanklessness and impossibility do not daunt him
C. He acknowledges too - in fact he returns to the point often - that best translators of poetry always fail at some level.
D. Hofman feels passionately about his work, and this is clear from his writings.
E. In terms of the gap between worth and rewards, translators come somewhere near nurses and street - cleaners.
(a) EACDB (b) ADEBC
(c) EACBD (d) DCEAB
(e) None of these

DIRECTIONS (Qs. 160-163) : In each of these questions, there are three sentences given as (A), (B) and (C). Find out which two or three sentences convey the same meaning.

160. (A) The Manager would like you to help him locate the fault.
(B) If you help him locate the fault, the Manager would like you.
(C) The Manager desires that you should provide him the necessary assistance to locate the fault.
(a) (A) and (B) (b) (A) and (C)
(c) (B) and (C) (d) All of the above
(e) None of these

Space for Rough Work

161. (A) Although the strike of transporters continues, I shall come.
(B) I shall come if the strike of transporters continues.
(C) Even though I come, the strike of transporters is going to continue.
(a) (A) and (B) (b) (A) and (C)
(c) (B) and (C) (d) None of these
(e) None of these

162. (A) Should you need a visa, you must submit an application along with your passport and a copy of income tax returns.
(B) Unless you do not submit an application along with your passport and a copy of income tax returns, you will not get visa.
(C) If you submit your application along with your passport and a copy of income tax returns, you do not need visa.
(a) (A) and (B) (b) (A) and (C)
(c) (B) and (C) (d) All (A), (B) and (C)
(e) None of these

163. (A) The judge remarked that not all the accused were really guilty.
(B) The judge remarked that some of the accused were guilty while others were not.
(C) The judge remarked that all those who were accused included some who were not really guilty.
(a) (A) and (B) (b) (A) and (C)
(c) (B) and (C) (d) All of the above
(e) None of these

DIRECTIONS (Qs. 164-167): Choose the correct option for the given blanks.

164. Pipes are not a safer .... to cigarettes because, though pipe smokers do not inhale, they are still ....
higher rates of lung and mouth cancers than non-smokers.
(a) alternative - subject to
(b) answer - responsible for
(c) preference - tree from
(d) rejoinder- involved in
(e) None of these

165. Because of its tendency to .... most Indian art is............. Japanese art, where symbols have been minimized and meaning has been conveyed by using the method of the merest suggestion.
(a) overdraw - similar to
(b) understate - reminiscent of
(c) imitate - superior to
(d) sentimentalism - supportive of
(e) None of these

166. In the absence of native predators, to stop the spread of their population, the imported goats...........to such an inordinate degree that they over-grazed the countryside and .... the native vegetation.
(a) thrived- threatened
(b) suffered - abandoned
(c) propagated - cultivated
(d) dwindled-eliminated
(e) None of these

167. The analysis of anything but .... the coach's report was but those of us who have learned to discount such dismal .... are optimistic.
(a) malicious - benefits
(b) sanguinary - traps
(c) pessimistic - confusion
(d) pleasant - prognostications
(e) None of these

DIRECTIONS (Qs. 168 - 177) : Read the following passage carefully and answer the questions given below it.

PASSAGE I

We call a man irrational when he acts in a passion, when he cuts off his nose to spite his face. He is irrational because he forgets that, by indulging the desire which he happens to feel most strongly at the moment, he Will thwart other desires which in the long run are more important to him. If men were rational, they would take a more correct view of their own interest than they do at present; and if all men acted from enlightened self-interest, the world would be a paradise in comparison to what it is. I do not maintain that there is nothing better than self-interest as a motive to action, but I do maintain that self-interest, like altruism, is better when it is enlightened than when it is unenlightened. In an ordered community it is very rarely to a man's interest to do anything which is very harmful to others. The less rational a man is, the oftener he will fail to perceive how what injures others also injures him, because hatred or envy Will blind him. Therefore, although I do not pretend that enlightened self-interest is the highest morality, I do maintain that, if it became common; it would make the world an immeasurably better place than it is.

Rationality in practice may be defined as the habit of remembering all our relevant desires, and not only the one which happens at the moment to be strongest. Like rationality in opinion, it is a matter of degree. Complete rationality is no doubt an unattainable ideal, but so long as we continue to classify some men as lunatics it is clear that we think some men more rational than others. I believe that all solid progress in the world consists of an increase in rationality, both practical and theoretical. To preach an altruistic morality appears to me somewhat useless, because it will appeal only to those who already have altruistic desires. But to preach rationality is somewhat different, since rationality helps us to realise our own desire on the "(hole, whatever they may be. A man is rational in proportion as his intelligence informs and controls his desires. I believe that the control of our acts by our intelligence is ultimately what is of most importance, and that alone will make social life remain possible as, science increases the means at our disposal for injuring each other. Education, the press, politics, religion-in a word, all the great forces in the world-are at present on the side of irrationality, they are in the hands of men who flatter King Demos in order to lead him astray. The remedy does not lie in anything heroically cataclysmic, but in the efforts of individuals towards a more sane and balanced view of our relations to our neighbours and to the world. It is to intelligence, increasingly side-spread, that we must look for the solution of the ills from which our world is suffering.

168. What is the central idea of the passage?
   (a) The problems of the world can best be solved by rationality and enlightened self-interest
   (b) Altruism and rationality are the main' indicators of intelligence
   (c) Altruism can make this world a heaven
   (d) Man is absolutely irrational
   (e) None of these

169. What is the author's attitude to modem development in science and communications?
   (a) Cynical about their use
   (b) Sceptical about the uses they are put to
   (c) One of cautious acceptance
   (d) One of concern about their harmful potential
   (e) None of these

170. Rationality, according to the passage, means mainly:
   (a) having regard for others
   (b) intelligent control of one's desires
   (c) the ability to cultivate a balanced view of one's surroundings
   (d) power to resist yielding to strong passions
   (e) None of these

171. The author feels that it is impractical to appeal to altruism because:
   (a) not all people are altruistic by nature
   (b) altruism is weaker than rationality
   (c) altruism is more refined than rationality
   (d) none of the above
   (e) None of these

172. 'The King Demos' refers to :
   (a) populace (b) politician
   (c) scientist (d) despot
   (e) None of these

PASSAGE II

Both plants and animals of many sorts show remarkable changes in form, structure, growth habits and even mode of reproduction in becoming adapted to different climatic environment, types of food supply or mode of living. This divergence in response to evolution is commonly expressed by altering the form and function of some pans of the organism, the original identification of which is clearly discernible. For example, the creeping foot of the snail is seen in related marine pteropods to be modified into flapping organ useful for swimming, and is changed into prehensile arms that bear suctorial disks in the squids and other cephalopods. The limbs of modes of life-for swift running (cursorial) as in the horse and antelope, for swinging in trees (arboreal) as in the

Space for Rough Work

monkeys, for digging (fossorial) as in the moles and gophers, for flying (volant) as in the bats, for swimming (aquatic) as in the seals, whales and dolphines and for other adaptations. The structures or organs that show main change in connection with this adaptive divergence are commonly identified readily as homologous, in spite of great alterations. Thus, the finger and wristbones of a bat and whale, for instance, have virtually nothing in common except that they are definitely equivalent elements of the mammalian limb.

173. Which is the most appropriate title for the passage based on its content?
(a) Evolution (b) Our Changing Bodies
(c) Adaptive Divergence. (d) Changes in Organs
(e) None of these

174. The author provides information that would answer which of the following questions:
1. What factors cause change in organism?
2. What is the theory of evolution?
3. Could structurally different organs be similar in evolution?
(a) 1 only (b) 2 only
(c) 1 and 3 only (d) 1, 2 and 3
(e) None of these

175. The author organises the passage by:
(a) comparison and contrast
(b) general statements followed by examples
(c) hypothesis and proof
(d) definition of key terms
(e) None of these

176. Which of the following words could best be substituted to 'homologous' (underlined) without substantially changing the author's meaning?
(a) Divergent (b) Corresponding
(c) Altered (d) Tactile
(e) None of these

177. The author's style can best be described as :
(a) objective (b) humorous
(c) esoteric (d) patronising
(e) None of these

DIRECTIONS (Qs. 178 - 180) :Pick out the nearest correct meaning or SYNONYMS of the word given below:

178. Find out the word meaning "Attachment":
(a) Affinity (b) Influence
(c) Causation (d) Appendage
(e) None of these

179. Which one of the following words means "weary"?
(a) Tired (b) Fatigued
(c) Sentimental (d) Emotional
(e) None of these

180. The property inherited by a person from his ancestors is:
(a) Parsimony (b) matrimony
(c) heritage (d) patrimony
(e) None of these

DIRECTIONS (Qs. 181 - 183) :Pick out the ANTONYM of the words given below:

181. LIBERATE
(a) imprison (b) enclose
(c) liberal (d) conceal
(e) None of these

182. MELANCHOLY
(a) depressed (b) prejudiced
(c) reckless (d) cheerful
(e) None of these

183. LEGITIMATE
(a) valid (b) extend
(c) unlawful (d) distinguished
(e) None of these

184. TERMINATION
(a) endeavouring (b) beginning
(c) amendment (d) phasing
(e) None of these

DIRECTIONS (Qs. 185 - 190): In each of the following sentences four words or phrases have been underlined. Only one underlined part in each sentence is not acceptable in Standard English, Pick up the part (a), (b), (c) or (d). If all four words are correct, mark (e) i.e., 'All correct' as your answer.

185. Such startling (a) never (b) have neither (c) can and never will be (d) offered again All correct (e)

Space for Rough Work

186. The persecutors laid (a) a heavy fine on an (b) old man who being (c) unable to pay the soldiers were dragging him (d) to the prison All correct (e)

187. He feels (a) his troubles as much (b) or even more (c) than they (d) All correct (e)

188. She told them if they (a) heard (b) any one (c) knocking not to (d) open the door All correct (e)

189. For (a) this delightful (b) excursion it was felt by the members (c) that it was due to (d) the secretary All correct (e)

190. He wishes (a) to tax not only (b) the luxuries (c) of the rich but also the necessities (d) of the poor All correct (e).

DIRECTIONS (Qs. 191 - 200) :In the following passage there are blanks, each of which has been numbered. These numbers are also printed below the passage and against each five words are suggested, one of which fits the blank appropriately. Find out the appropriate word in each case.

A good percentage of the population of India is tribal. The tribal live in the hills and forests of the country and have been little **191** by the **192** currents of the plains. Practically all the states of India have their tribal population. The tribes are numerous, computed to about 200, some living in **193** regions in the dense forests, and others on the borders of villages. Some tribes are **194** to a few souls, while others like the Santhals, run into millions and are steadily **195** in numbers. During the British Period some of them were known as 'criminal tribes' for they showed **196** respect for the Indian Panel Code. After independence they have been named Scheduled Tribes. Under modern conditions isolation, however, has become **197** and the hill tribes are getting **198**. The cultural traffic is two-way. Social reformers are taking civilisation to the hills, and the tribes, **199** their old occupations of hunting and **200** farming, are setting in villages, towns and cities as labourers and industrial workers

191. (a) mere (b) moderate (c) retarding (d) vehement (e) dull
192. (a) obstinate (b) constitute (c) persist (d) repeat (e) normalise
193. (a) go (b) scramble (c) mount (d) yield (e) crop
194. (a) sustained (b) suspicious (c) horrific (d) erratic (e) favourable
195. (a) lists (b) trades (c) services (d) inventories (e) details
196. (a) lists (b) trades (c) services (d) extent (e) deposit
197. (a) support (b) ignore (c) propel (d) prolong (e) insulate
198. (a) position (b) promote (c) process (d) pass (e) form
199. (a) hurrying (b) passing (c) pairing (d) gobbling (e) throwing
200. (a) keep (b) make (c) feed (d) grow (e) fight

Space for Rough Work

MAHARASHTRA CET - MOCK TEST 4

RESPONSE SHEET

NAME : .... DATE : ....

	(A)	(B)	(C)	(D)		(A)	(B)	(C)	(D)		(A)	(B)	(C)	(D)		(A)	(B)	(C)	(D)
1.					51.					101.					151.				
2.					52.					102.					152.				
3.					53.					103.					153.				
4.					54.					104.					154.				
5.					55.					105.					155.				
6.					56.					106.					156.				
7.					57.					107.					157.				
8.					58.					108.					158.				
9.					59.					109.					159.				
10.					60.					110.					160.				
11.					61.					111.					161.				
12.					62.					112.					162.				
13.					63.					113.					163.				
14.					64.					114.					164.				
15.					65.					115.					165.				
16.					66.					116.					166.				
17.					67.					117.					167.				
18.					68.					118.					168.				
19.					69.					119.					169.				
20.					70.					120.					170.				
21.					71.					121.					171.				
22.					72.					122.					172.				
23.					73.					123.					173.				
24.					74.					124.					174.				
25.					75.					125.					175.				
26.					76.					126.					176.				
27.					77.					127.					177.				
28.					78.					128.					178.				
29.					79.					129.					179.				
30.					80.					130.					180.				
31.					81.					131.					181.				
32.					82.					132.					182.				
33.					83.					133.					183.				
34.					84.					134.					184.				
35.					85.					135.					185.				
36.					86.					136.					186.				
37.					87.					137.					187.				
38.					88.					138.					188.				
39.					89.					139.					189.				
40.					90.					140.					190.				
41.					91.					141.					191.				
42.					92.					142.					192.				
43.					93.					143.					193.				
44.					94.					144.					194.				
45.					95.					145.					195.				
46.					96.					146.					196.				
47.					97.					147.					197.				
48.					98.					148.					198.				
49.					99.					149.					199.				
50.					100.					150.					200.				

MAHARASHTRA
CET
MOCK TEST - 5

☛ *INSTRUCTIONS :*

- **There are 200 questions in this test. You will be given 150 minutes to complete the test.**
- **Each question carries 1 mark. There is no negative marking.**

1. A boy has 3 library cards and 8 books of his interest in the library. Of these 8, he does not want to borrow chemistry part II unless Chemistry part I is also borrowed. In how many ways can he choose the three books to be borrowed ?
(a) 56 (b) 27
(c) 26 (d) 41
(e) None of these

2. *A* and *B* play a game where each is asked to select a number from 1 to 5. If the two numbers match, both of them win a prize. The probability that they will not win a prize in a single trial is
(a) $\frac{1}{25}$ (b) $\frac{24}{25}$
(c) $\frac{2}{25}$ (d) $\frac{4}{25}$
(e) None of these

3. A cricket club has 15 members, of whom only 5 can bowlers. If the names of the 15 members are put into a box and 11 drawn at random, then the chance of obtaining an eleven containing at least 3 bowlers is
(a) $\frac{7}{13}$ (b) $\frac{6}{13}$
(c) $\frac{11}{15}$ (d) $\frac{12}{13}$
(e) None of these

4. Between two ends in your study, are displayed your five favourite puzzle books. If you decide to arrange five books in every possible combination and moved just one book every minute, how long would it take you?
(a) 1 hour (b) 2 hours
(c) 3 hours (d) 4 hours
(e) None of these

5. Seven women and seven men are to sit around a circular table such that there is a man on either side of every woman. The number of seating arrangements is
(a) $(7!)^2$ (b) $(6!)^2$
(c) $6! \times 7!$ (d) $7!$
(e) None of these

DIRECTIONS (Qs. 6-10): *What should come in place of the question mark (?) in the following questions?*

6. $1\frac{3}{4}+1\frac{5}{8}-2\frac{4}{5}+\frac{1}{2}=?$
(a) $2\frac{7}{40}$ (b) $1\frac{7}{40}$
(c) $2\frac{3}{40}$ (d) $1\frac{3}{40}$
(e) None of these

Space for Rough Work

7. $14 \times 18.6 \div 12 + 19.3 = ?$
   (a) 41 (b) 33.5
   (c) 291.9 (d) 8.32
   (e) None of these

8. $8^{4.2} \times 64^{2.1} \times 7^{8.4} \times 56^{3.5} = 56^{?}$
   (a) 18.2 (b) 9.8
   (c) 11.9 (d) 12.6
   (e) None of these

9. $69012 - 20167 + (51246 \div 6) = ?$
   (a) 57385 (b) 57286
   (c) 57476 (d) 57368
   (e) None of these

10. $\frac{128 \div 16 \times ? - 7 \times 2}{7^2 - 8 \times 6 + ?^2} = 1$
   (a) 17 (b) 16
   (c) 18 (d) 14
   (e) 3

DIRECTIONS (Qs.11-15) : *The first figures in the first unit of the problem figures bears a certain relationship to the second figure. Similarly one of the figures in the answer figures bears the **same relationship** to the second figure in the second unit of the problem figures. You are, therefore, to locate the figure which would fit in the question mark.*

11. Problem Figures

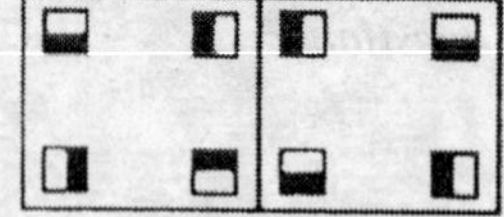

Answer Figures

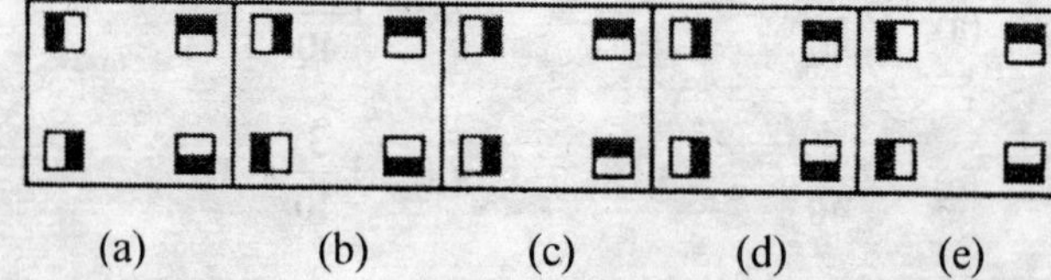

(a) (b) (c) (d) (e)

12. Problem Figures

Answer Figures

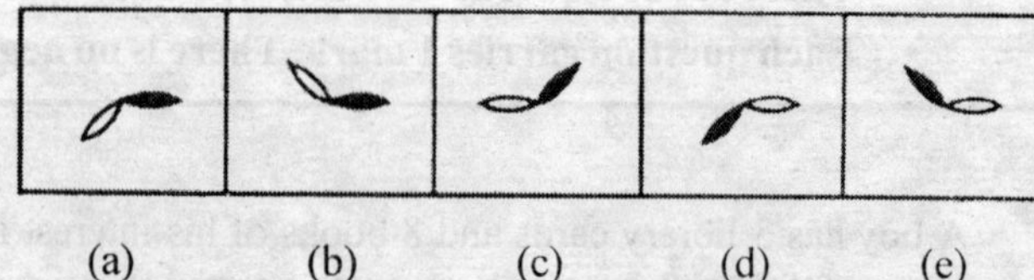

(a) (b) (c) (d) (e)

13. Problem Figures

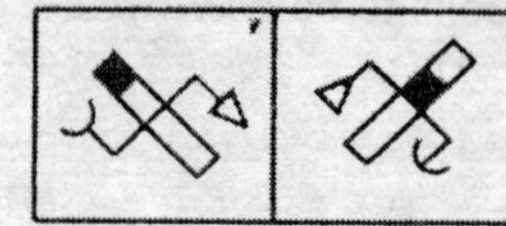

Answer Figures

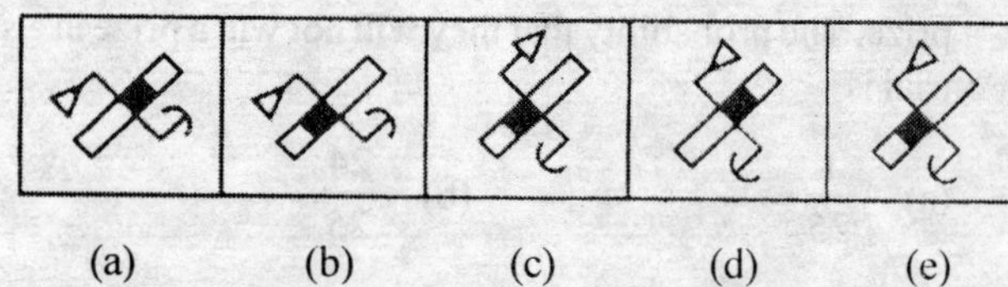

(a) (b) (c) (d) (e)

14. Problem Figures

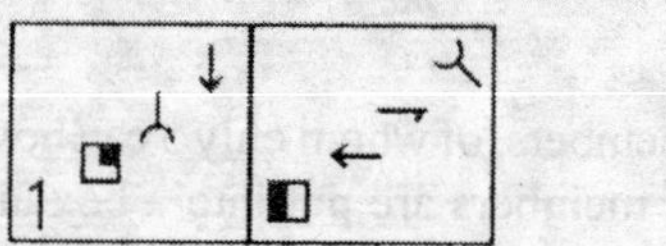

Answer Figures

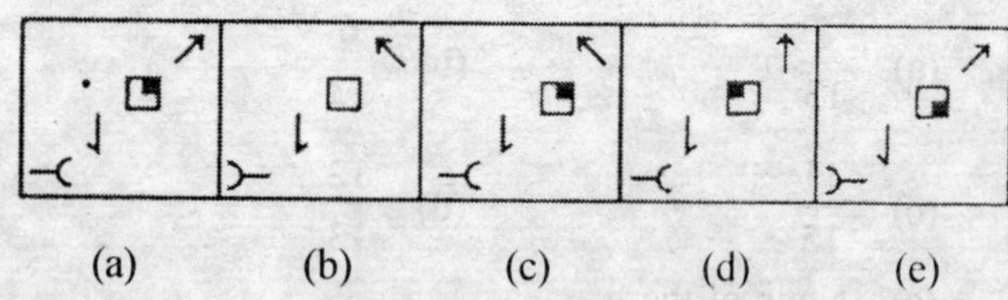

(a) (b) (c) (d) (e)

Space for Rough Work

15. Problem Figures

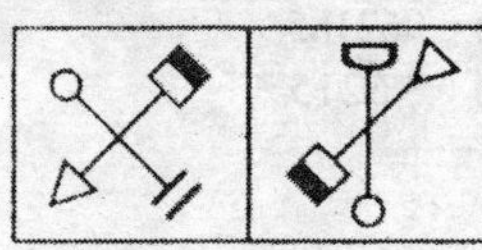

Answer Figures

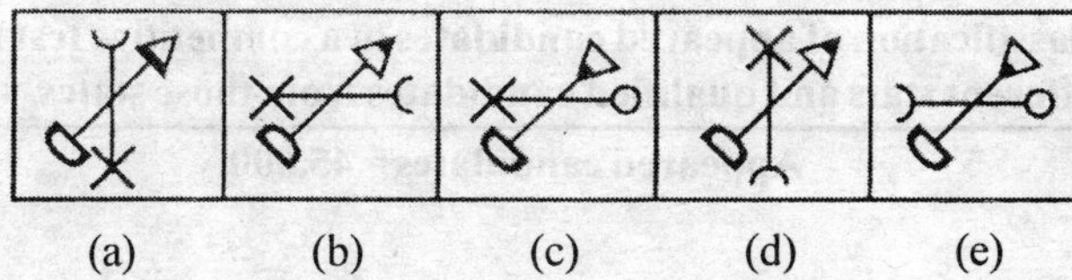

(a) (b) (c) (d) (e)

DIRECTIONS (Qs. 16-20) : *In each of these questions, a statement is followed by two courses of action numbered I and II. Assume everything in the statement to be true, and decide which of the suggested course(s) of action logically follow(s) for pursuing.*

Mark answer as :

(a) if only I follows
(b) if either I or II follows
(c) if only II follows
(d) if neither I nor II follows
(e) if both I and II follow.

16. **Statement :** There has been significant drop in the water level of all the lakes supplying water to the city.

Courses of action :

I. The water supply authority should impose a partial cut in supply to tackle the situation.

II. The government should appeal to all the residents through mass media for minimal use of water.

17. **Statement :** A large number of people visiting India from country 'X' has been tested positive for carrying viruses of a killer disease.

Courses of action :

I. The Government of India should immediately put a complete ban on people coming to India from country 'X' including those Indians who are settled in country 'X'.

II. The Government of India should immediately set-up detection centres at all its airports and seaports to identify and quarantine those who are tested positive.

18. **Statement :** The prices of foodgrains and vegetables have substantially increased due to prolonged strike call given by the truck owners association.

Courses of action :

I. The government should immediately make alternative arrangement to ensure adequate supply of foodgrains and vegetables in the market.

II. The government should take steps to cancel the licences of all vehicles belonging to the association.

19. **Statement :** There have been an unprecedented increase in the number of requests for berths in most of the long distance trains during the current holiday season.

Courses of action :

I. The railway authority should immediately increase the capacity in each of these trains by attaching additional coaches.

II. The people seeking accommodation should be advised to make their travel plan after the holiday

20. **Statement :** While laying pipes for one of the utility companies a huge fire broke out due to damage done to the gas pipeline.

Courses of action :

I. All the licences of the utility company should immediately be suspended pending enquiry into the incidence.

II. People residing in the area should be advised to stay indoors to avoid burn injuries.

DIRECTIONS (Qs.21-25): *What* ***approximate*** *value should come in place of the question mark (?) in the following questions? (You are not expected to calculate the exact value).*

21. $63.9872 \times 9449.8780 \div 243.0034 = (?)^2$

(a) 2489 (b) 2500
(c) 50 (d) 45
(e) 150

22. $5237.897 - 6629.010 + 7153.999 - 2205.102 = ?$

(a) 6340 (b) 4688
(c) 5240 (d) 3558
(e) 6290

23. $4985.0346 \div 215.987 - 3768.112 \div 206.868 = ?$

(a) 8 (b) 5
(c) 18 (d) 11
(e) 15

Space for Rough Work

24. $\sqrt{956240} = ?$
(a) 978 (b) 864
(c) 1009 (d) 647
(e) 783

25. 459% of 849.947 + 266% of 6284.012 – 1486.002 = ?
(a) 20330 (b) 12640
(c) 15000 (d) 22160
(e) 19130

DIRECTIONS (Qs. 26-30) : *Study the following letters and their corresponding digit codes followed by certain conditions of coding and answer the questions given below them by finding out which of the digit combinations given in (a), (b), (c) and (d) is the coded form of the letter groups given in each question and mark your answers accordingly. If none of the coded forms represents the letter group mark answer as (e), i.e. None of these.*

Letter :	P	N	A	J	I	R	E	B	U	K
Digit :	5	3	9	1	4	6	2	7	0	8

Conditions :

(1) If both the first and the last letters in the group are vowels both should be coded as*.

(2) If both the first and the last letters in the group are consonants both should be coded as #.

26. RBUKAE
(a) 670982 (b) 607892
(c) 670892 (d) #70892
(e) None of these

27. PIAEBN
(a) 542973 (b) #4927#
(c) *4927* (d) 549273
(e) None of these

28. NAPKJI
(a) *95814 (b) 395814
(c) *9581* (d) 359814
(d) None of these

29. KUNAJB
(a) #0391# (b) 803917
(c) #0391* (d) *0391*
(e) None of these

30. AREJPK
(a) 962150 (b) 962185
(c) #6215# (d) * 6215 *
(e) None of these

Directions (Qs. 31-35) : *These questions are based on the following pie charts.*

Classification of appeared candidates in a competitive test from different stats and qualified candidates from those states.

Appeared candidates = 45,000.

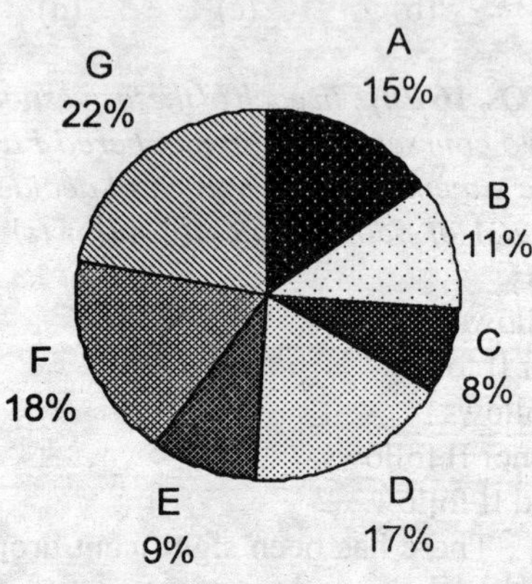

Qualified candidates = 9000.

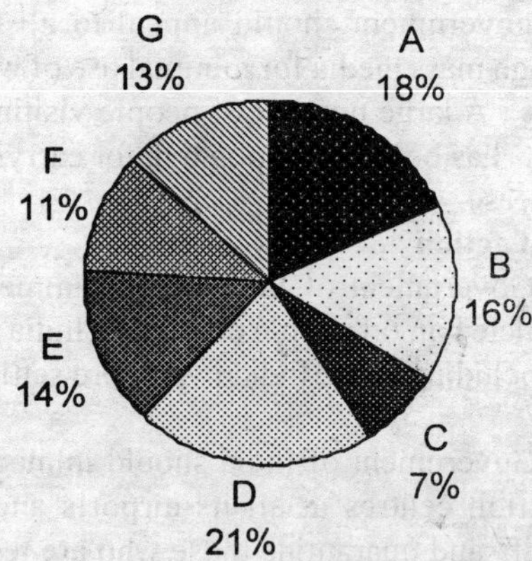

Space for Rough Work

31. What is the ratio of the number of appeared candidates from States C and E together to that of the appeared candidates from States A and F together ?

(a) 17:33 (b) 11:13
(c) 13:27 (d) 17:27
(e) None of these

32. In which state, the percentage of qualified candidates with respect to that of appeared candidates is minimum ?

(a) C (b) F
(c) D (d) G
(e) None of these

33. What is the difference between the number of qualified candidates of States D and those of G ?

(a) 690 (b) 670
(c) 780 (d) 720
(e) None of these

34. What is the percentage of qualified candidates with respect to appeared candidates from States B and C taken together? (rounded to two decimal places)

(a) 23.11 (b) 24.21
(c) 21.24 (d) 23
(e) None of these

35. What is the ratio between the number of candidates qualified from Staes B and D together to the number of candidates appeared from State 'C' respectively ?

(a) 8:37 (b) 11:12
(c) 37:40 (d) 7:37
(e) None of these

DIRECTIONS (Qs. 36-40): *Rearrange the following six sentences (A), (B), (C), (D), (E) and (F) in the proper sequence to form a meaningful paragraph, then answer the questions given below them.*

A. Total forgiveness for a mistake committed generates a sense of complacency towards target achievement among the employees

B. In such a situation the work ethos gets distorted and individuals get a feeling that they can get away with any lapse.

C. The feeling that they develop is 'whether I produce results or not, the management will not punish me or does not have the guts to punish me.'

D. Also excess laxity damages management credibility, because for a long time, the management has maintained that dysfunctional behaviour will result in punishment, and when something goes wrong, it fails to take specific punishment, and when something goes wrong, it fails to take specific punitive action.

E. The severity of the punishment may be reduced , by modifying it, but some action must be taken against the guilty so as to serve as a reminder for all others in the organization

F. Moreover, it helps establish the management's image of being firm, fair and yet human.

36. Which of the following should be the **FIRST** sentence?

(a) A (b) B
(c) C (d) D
(e) E

37. Which of the following should be the **SECOND** sentence?

(a) A (b) B
(c) C (d) D
(e) E

38. Which of the following should be the **THIRD** sentence?

(a) A (b) B
(c) C (d) D
(e) E

39. Which of the following should be the **FOURTH** sentence?

(a) A (b) B
(c) C (d) D
(e) E

40. Which of the following should be the **FIFTH** sentence?

(a) A (b) B
(c) C (d) D
(e) E

DIRECTIONS (Qs. 41-45) : *In each of the following questions a series begins with unlettered figure on the extreme left. One and only one of the five lettered figures in the series does not fit into the series. The two unlettered figures one each on the extreme left and the extreme right fit into the series. You have to take as many aspects into accunt as possible of the figures in the series and find out the one and only one of the five lettered figures which does not fit into the series. The letterand of that figures is the answer.*

41.

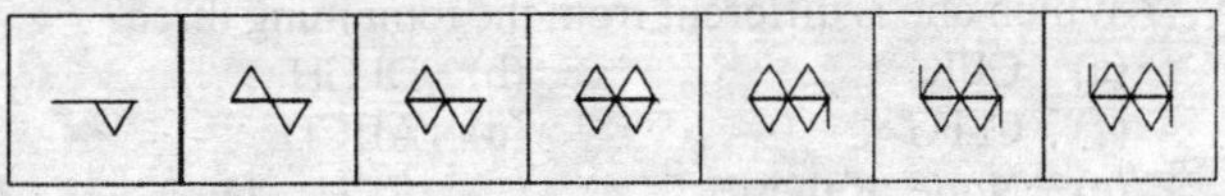

(a) (b) (c) (d) (e)

Space for Rough Work

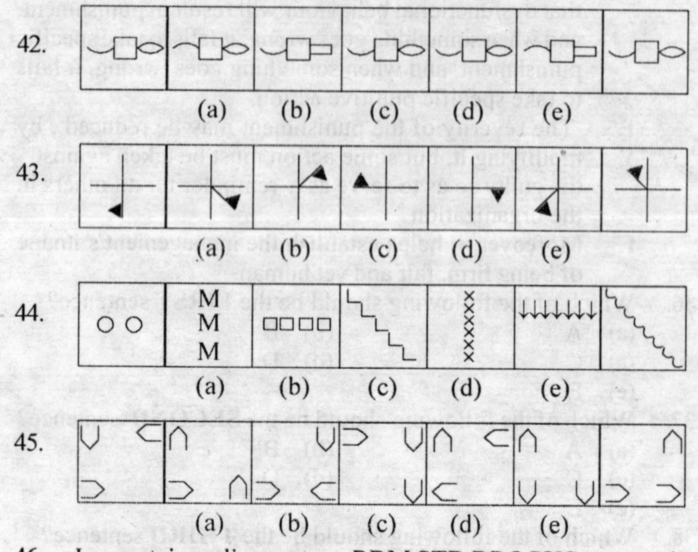

42. (a) (b) (c) (d) (e)

43. (a) (b) (c) (d) (e)

44. (a) (b) (c) (d) (e)

45. (a) (b) (c) (d) (e)

46. In a certain coding system, RBM STD BRO PUS means 'the cat is beautiful'. TNH PUS DIM STD means 'the dog is brown'. PUS DIM BRO PUS CUS means 'the dog has the cat'. What is the code for 'has' ?
(a) CUS (b) BRO
(c) DIM (d) STD
(e) None of these

47. If NAXALITE is written in a certain code as LYVYJGRC' how will INTEGRATE be written in the same code ?
(a) LGRECYPRC (b) GLRCEPYRC
(c) PYWMNOPQR (d) BLACKHOLE
(e) None of these

48. If the second, third, fifth, eighth and ninth letters of the word CONTEMPLATION are combined to form a meaningful word, what will be the middle letter of that word ? If more than one such words can be formed, your answer is X and if no such word can be formed, your answer is Y.
(a) X (b) O
(c) A (d) Y
(e) None of these

49. Which one is different from the remaining three?
(a) GIJK (b) DFGH
(c) CEFG (d) ABCD
(e) None of these

50. One morning after sunrise, Reeta and Kavita were talking to each other face to face at Tilak square. If Kavita's shadow was exactly to the right of Reeta, then which direction was Kavita facing?
(a) North (b) South
(c) East (d) Data inadequate
(e) None of these

DIRECTIONS (Qs. 51-55) : *Study the following graph carefully to answer the questions that follow.*

Number of cars sold by two companies A and B over the years

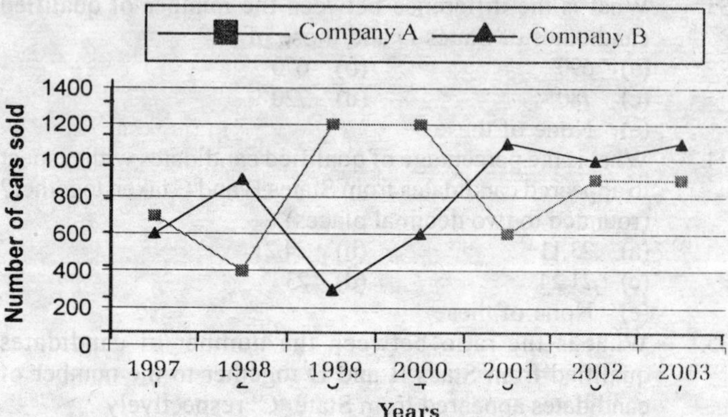

51. Sales in the year 2001 for Company A forms what per cent of total sales of Company A for all the years together ? (rounded off to two decimal points)
(a) 19.64 (b) 18.30
(c) 22.46 (d) 24.19
(e) None of these

52. Which of the following combinations of year and percentage rise in sales from the previous year for Company A is correct ? (Percentage rounded off to two decimal points)
(a) 2000 – 99.85 (b) 2001 – 83.33
(c) 1998 – 43.21 (d) 2003 – 7.68
(e) None of these

53. Total sales of Company B for the years 1997, 1998 and 2001 together is what per cent of the total sales of Company B for all the years together ? (rounded off to two decimal points)
(a) 24.37 (b) 35.64
(c) 28.81 (d) 37.29
(e) None of these

Space for Rough Work

54. What is the ratio of total sales of Company A to the total sales of Company B over the years ?
    (a) 26 : 29 (b) 27 : 31
    (c) 53 : 51 (d) 56 : 59
    (e) None of these
55. During which year was percentage rise/fall in sales from the previous year the highest for Company A ?
    (a) 1999 (b) 2001
    (c) 1998 (d) 2000
    (e) None of these

DIRECTIONS (Qs. 56-60) : *Read the following passage carefully to answer these questions based on the respective passage and the opinion of the author only.*

The tripartite arrangement of the Universal Being into the subjective, objective and the principle of an intermediary consciousness, namely, Adhyatma, Adhibhuta and Adhidaiva, raises also the question of the whole range of theological enunciations, since the Adhidaiva is the divinity that controls the subjective and the objective sides of experience Adhyatma and Adhibhuta - and at the same time rises above them in an instantaneous act of transcendence by not belonging either to the subjective or the objective side, though immanently present in both the sides, without which there cannot be a conscious relation between the subject and the object.

The descent, or may we say ascent, of the hierarchy of subject-object relations in the history of the creation of the universe, may be said to be constituted of an infinite series of degrees of lesser and larger dimensions, the relation becoming grosser and more inscrutable as the degrees come downwards in descent and enlarging in greater and greater perspicuity and transcendence as the degrees ascend towards the Absolute. In as much as these degrees of ascent and descent are spread out everywhere in the universe, differing in quantity and quality in accordance with the corresponding degree of inclusiveness and transparency obtaining between the subjective and objective sides, it appears that these Adhidaiva divinities are countless in number and these are, in fact, the many gods of popular religious worship.

Are there really many gods? The answer is yes, and no. There are many gods, because there are many degrees of the subject-object relation obtaining successively in a sequential order of the manifestation of the universe, and these being transcendentally operative powers beyond the subject and the object, they are verily gods, the shining ones, the conscious relation without which perception or knowledge would be impossible. But, in fact, the gods are not many, since their manifoldness is just a nomenclature designating the levels of consciousness through which the Absolute descends in terms of several subject-object relations in the story of creation.

The Indian religious perspective visualises, adores and worships many a god, the god of the house or the family, the god of the village or the community, the god of the town, the god of the nation, the god of war, and the god of peace, and as on, because these concepts of many divinities follow automatically from the concept of there being many superphysical causes behind the multitudinous variety of events and occurrences in the world of Nature. For anything that happens there is a god behind it, just because nothing can happen unless it is caused by something which itself is not the happening. Millions are, therefore, the gods in number, but there are no million gods, even as the million rays of the sun cannot be regarded as anything but a single projection of the omni-faced solar beam. The Indian religious system adores such gods as Sri Ganesa, or Ganapati; Devi in the form of Durga, Lakshmi and Sarasvati; Siva, known also as Rudra; Vishnu, called also Narayana; Surya or the divinity in the Sun; and Skanda, or Kartikeya or Kumara, the second son of Siva. The sections of people that devote themselves to one or the other of these gods are supposed to form a specific pattern of religious approach, these being six as mentioned, related to the six gods of worship (Shanmata). The philosopher Acharya Sankara is credited by tradition with the work of having established these six ways of divine worship (Shanmata-Sthapanacharya). These six modes of worship form the six systems of spiritual approach, known as Ganapatya, Sakta, Saiva, Vaishnava, Saura, and Kaumara religious traditions.

The worship of these divinities is carried on either privately in one's house, or openly in public temples. In either case the method of worship is the same, namely, the procedure usually adopted in inviting and adoring a king, or a royal personage, with all the paraphernalia of gorgeous and detailed hospitality commencing from the initial salutation, or prostration or greeting, on the coming

Space for Rough Work

of the guest, till he is given a loving farewell after he is treated to every kind of satisfaction, such as being offered a seat, bathed, dressed, garlanded, offered delicious food, given wafer for washing, consecrated with the waving of beautifully decorated flames lamps, offered a suitable gift, and permitted to leave with the dignity and honour of the ruler or the royal patron. The procedure adopted in public temples is more detailed, including periodical festivals, especially the most important one known as the car-festival (Rathotsava), during which special occasion the deity is installed in a chariot looking like a moving temple, pulled with ropes by thousands of devotees gathered to participate in the celebration.

However, the greatest gods of the central religion of India are Brahma, Vishnu and Siva, with their various Avataras, or incarnations, elaborately eulogised in the eighteen Puranas, each god being glorified through a set of six specified texts out of these eighteen cosmic histories. With these Divinities are associated also their Powers, or Saktis, namely, Sarasvati, Lakshmi and Durga or Parvati, respectively.

This is the popular religion of the masses, which overwhelms public life in India even today, irrespective of the basic religion being founded on the hymns of the Veda-Samhitas, the Upanishads, and the Bhagavad-Gita. Humanity, and with it religious history, seems to have found it necessary, through the march of time, to accommodate itself to more and more emotional, aesthetic and epic forms of the envisagement of reality than the pure sublimity of the metaphysical and universal characterisations of the highest spiritual aim.

The propulsion to posit gods and divinities in a realm beyond the earth, a heaven of light and peace, is to be seen in every system of religious thinking and worship, only the designations, visualisations, etc., differing in accordance with the ethnic, geographical and cultural background of the people. 'A higher than oneself' is an imperative need for anyone to survive in a state of assured protection and fulfilment of one's eternal hopes and longings.

56. According to the passage, the Adhidaiva divinity:
(a) helps the subjective experience of many objective divinities
(b) pervades every aspect of the Universal Being
(c) is present in the subconscious of the subject
(d) is the cornerstone of mainstream religious beliefs.
(e) None of these

57. The hierarchy of divinities reflects:
(a) the varying degrees of separation between the Adhyatma and the Adhibhuta.
(b) The consciousness of various existences.
(c) Subject-object relations in varying degrees of dimensions.
(d) All of the above.
(e) None of these

58. Any subject-object relation is defined by:
(a) It's place in the hierarchy of Gods.
(b) It's appreciation of cosmic consciousness vis a-vi s its creator.
(c) Two methods chosen to merge the two aspects of being.
(d) A certain level of consciousness of the Absolute.
(e) None of these

59. According to the passage, the various spiritual approaches of the Indian religious system have been outlined by:
(a) The Vedas
(b) The Shamala
(c) Acharya Sankara
(d) The Upanishads
(e) None of these

60. Which of the following cannot be concluded from the passage?
(a) The Indian religious perspective assigns divine courses to natural events.
(b) The rituals accompanying religious worship are numerous and detailed.
(c) The powers of the greatest Gods are female in nature
(d) The purana's purpose is to eulogese the Gods.
(e) None of these

DIRECTIONS (Qs.61-65): *In each of these questions a few statements are followed by four conclusions numbered I, II, III and IV. Consider the given statements to be true even if they seem to be at variance with commonly known facts. Read all the conclusion(s) and then decide which of the given conclusion(s) logically follow(s) from the given statements.*

Space for Rough Work

61. **Statements:**
A. All mirrors are phones.
B. Some phones are gadgets.
C. All gadgets are mirrors.
Conclusions :
I. Some gadgets are phones.
II. Some gadgets are mirrors.
III. Some gadgets are not mirrors.
IV Some mirrors are phones.
(a) Only I and II follow
(b) None follows
(c) Only II and II follow
(d) Either II or IV follow
(e) All follow

62. **Statements :**
A. All rackets are jackets.
B. No cow is cat.
C. Only cats are dogs.
Conclusions :
I. Some rackets are not cats
II. Some cats are jackets.
III. Some rackets are cats.
IV. No dog is a cow.
(a) Only II and IV follow
(b) Only either I or III and IV follow
(c) Only III and IV follow
(d) Only I and IV follow
(e) All follow

63. **Statements :**
A. All stairs are lifts.
B. No lift is an escalator.
C. Some escalators are helicopters.
D. Some lifts are planes.
Conclusions :
I. No stairs is an escalator.
II. Some helicopters are not escalators.
III. Some stairs are planes.
IV. Some helicopters are escalators.
(a) Only I and IV follow
(b) Only I and either II or IV follow
(c) Either II or IV follows
(d) Only I, III or IV follow
(e) All follow

64. **Statements :**
A. Some grapes are apples.
B. Some apples are papayas.
C. All papayas are mangoes.
D. No mango is banana.
Conclusions :
I. No banana is papaya
II. Some apples ae mangoes.
III. Some bananas are grapes.
IV. No banana is grape
(a) Only I and II follows
(b) Only either III or IV follows
(c) Only I and either III or IV follow
(d) I, II and either III or IV follow
(e) None of these

65. **Statements :**
A. All flowers are trees.
B. Some trees are stars.
C. Some stars are clouds.
D. No cloud is rock.
Conclusions :
I. No rock is star.
II. Some stars are flowers
III. Some rocks are flowers
IV. Some rocks are stars
(a) None follows
(b) Only either I and IV follows
(c) Only I follows
(d) Only III and IV follow
(e) All follow

DIRECTIONS (Qs. 66-70) : *Find the next term in the given series in each of the questions below.*

66. 198, 194, 185, 169, ...
(a) 136 (b) 144
(c) 9 (d) 92
(e) None of these

Space for Rough Work

67. 6, 9, 7, 10, 8, 11, ...
    (a) 12 (b) 13
    (c) 9 (d) 14
    (e) None of these
68. 5, 6, 8, 9, 11, ...
    (a) 15 (b) 12
    (c) 17 (d) 20
    (e) None of these
69. 245, 125, 65, 35, 20, ...
    (a) 15 (b) 10
    (c) 12.5 (d) 2
    (e) None of these
70. 0, 2, 6, 12, 20, ...
    (a) 38 (b) 30
    (c) 45 (d) 60
    (e) None of these

DIRECTIONS (Qs. 71-75) : *Each of the following questions consists of unmarked figures followed by five figures marked a, b, c, d and e. Select a figure from the marked figures which will continue the series established by the unmarked figures.*

71. Problem Figures

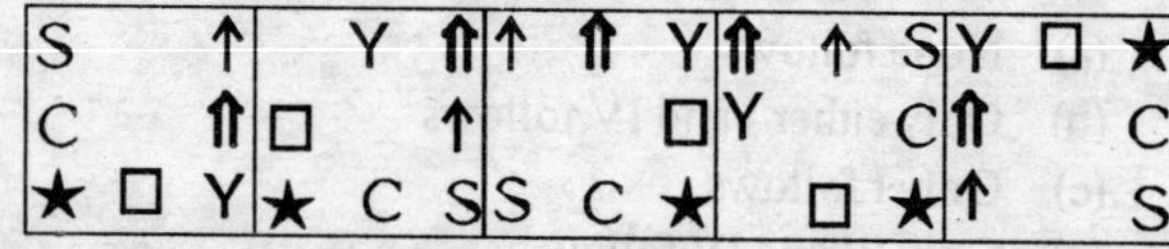

Answer Figures

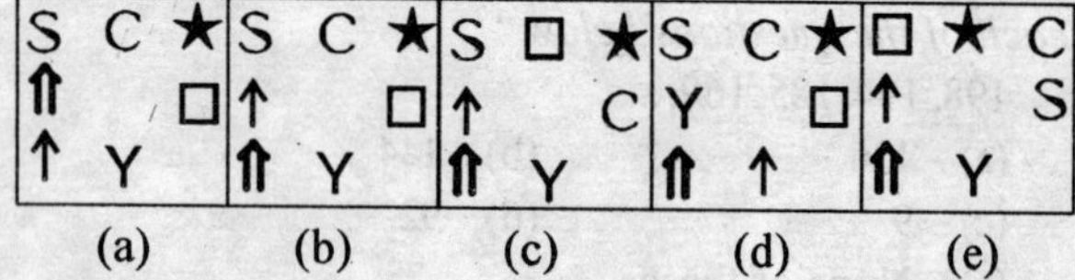

(a) (b) (c) (d) (e)

72. Problem Figures

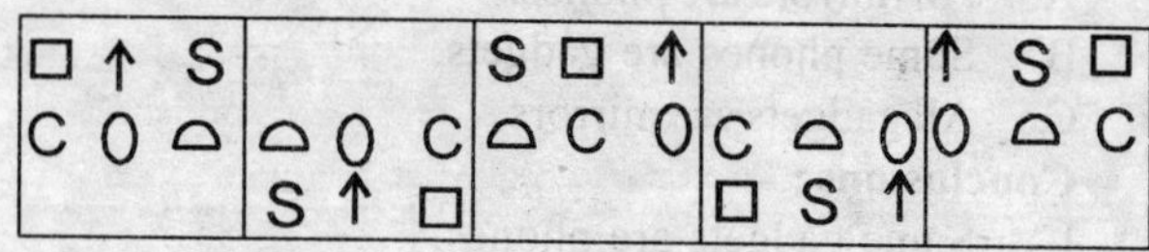

Answer Figures

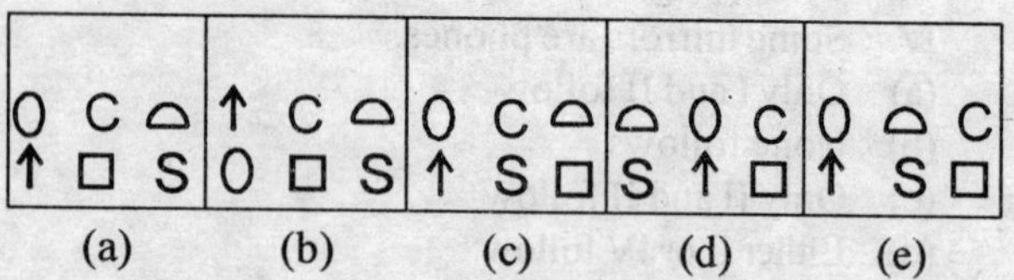

73. Problem Figures

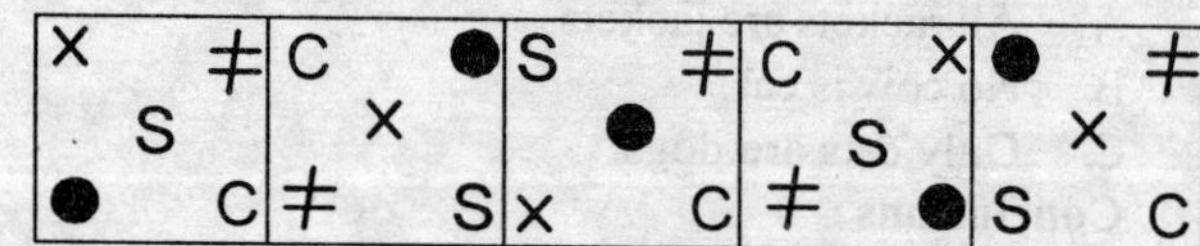

Answer Figures

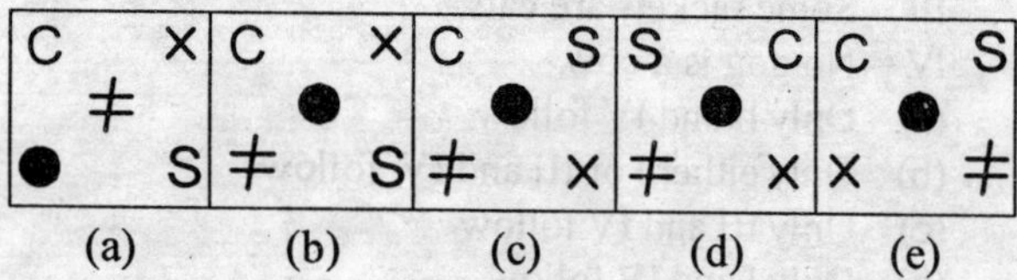

74. Problem Figures

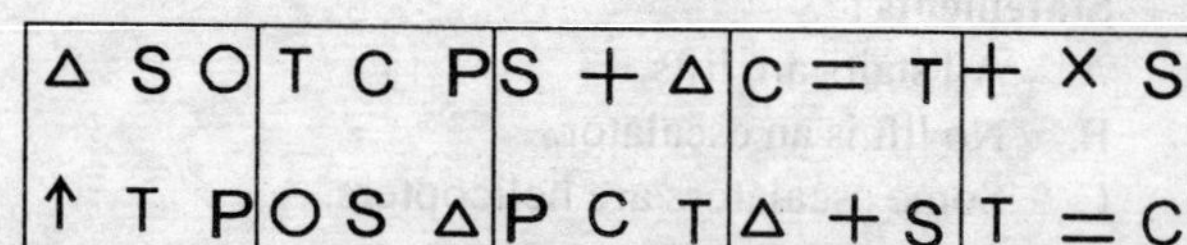

Answer Figures

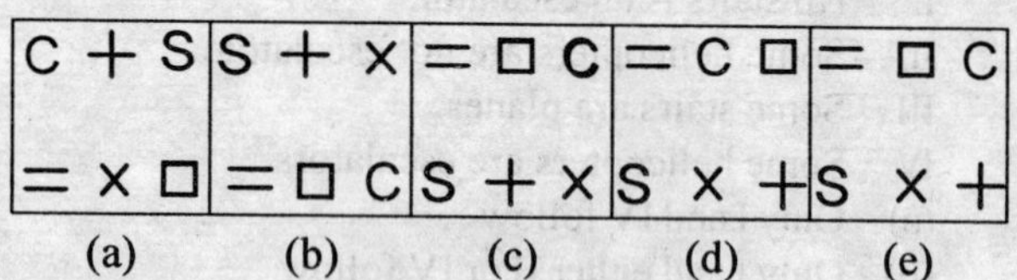

Space for Rough Work

75. Problem Figures

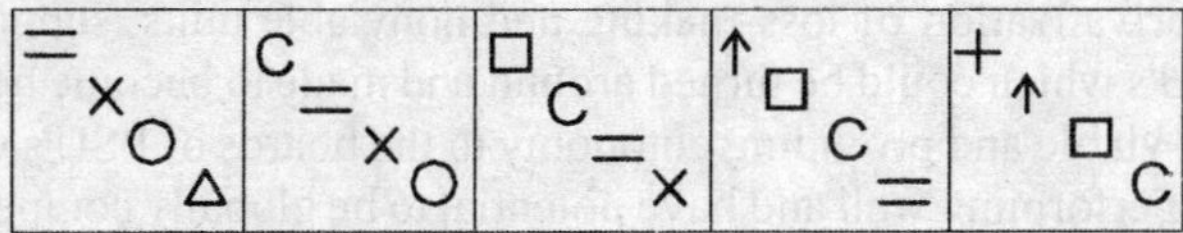

Answer Figures

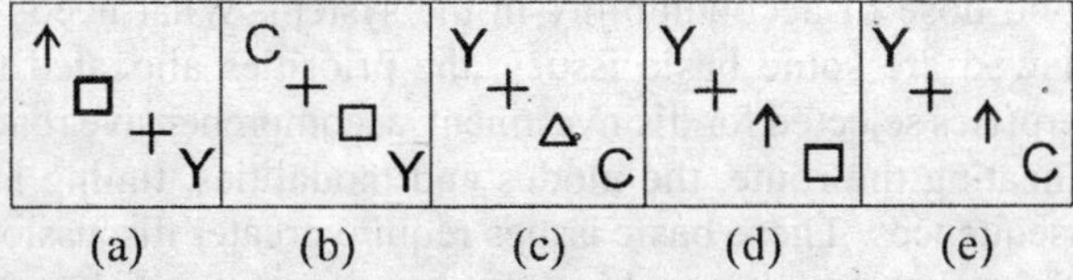

(a) (b) (c) (d) (e)

76. A, B, C, D, E, F and G are sitting in a line facing east. C is immediate right of D. B is at the extreme ends and has E as his neighbour. G is between E and F. D is sitting third from the south end. Who are the persons sitting at the extreme ends?
(a) A and E (b) A and B
(c) F and B (d) C and D
(e) None of these

77. Mohan is the son of Arun's father's sister. Prakash is the son of Reva, who is the mother of Vikas and grandmother of Arun. Pranab is the father of Neela and the grandfather of Mohan. Reva is the wife of Pranab. How is the wife of Vikas related to Neela?
(a) Sister (b) Sister-in-law
(c) Niece (d) Wife
(e) None of these

78. Five students participated in the scholarship examination "Sudha scored higher than Puja. Kavita scored lower than Suma but higher than Sudha. Mamta scored between Puja and Sudha." Who scored lowest in the examination?
(a) Puja (b) Kavita
(c) Mamta (d) Sudha
(e) None of these

79. My friend and I started walking simultaneously towards each other from two places 100 m apart. After walking 30 m, my friend turns left and goes 10 m, then he turns right and goes 20 m and then turns right again and comes back to the road on which he had started walking. If we walk with the same speed, what is the distance between us at this point of time ?
(a) 50 m (b) 20 m
(c) 30 m (d) 40 m
(e) None of these

80. If NARGRUED is the code for GRANDEUR, then Which word is coded as SERPEVRE?
(a) PERSEVER (b) PRESEVER
(c) PERSERVE (d) PRESERVE
(e) None of these

Directions (Q. 81-85): *Study the following information carefully and answer the questions given below it:*

Digits in the numbers are to be coded as follows

Digit	7	3	5	0	2	1	6	4	9	8
Code	N	H	L	T	F	D	R	Q	G	P

Following conditions are to be observed:

(i) If the first digit is even and the last digit is odd they are to be coded as $ and @ respectively.
(ii) If the first digit is odd and the last digit is even they are to be coded as # and £ respectively.
(iii) If 0 is preceded as well as followed by an odd digit then 0 is to be coded as*.
(iv) If 0 is preceded as well as followed by even digit then 0 is to be coded as ↑.
(v) 0 is not considered as either even or odd.

81. What will be the code for 1375490 ?
(a) DHNLQGT (b) # HNLQG£
(c) DHNLQG* (d) £HNLQG#
(e) None of these

82. $ Q R L * H @ is the code for which of the following numbers?
(a) 8456037 (b) 8465032
(c) 6475031 (d) 6460539
(e) Data inadequate.

83. Q L P ↑ R N T is the code for which of the following numbers?
(a) 4570680 (b) 4780650
(c) 6580470 (d) Data inadequate
(e) None of these

84. What will be the code for 7620486 ?
(a) £RE ↑ QP# (b) #RF ↑ QP£
(c) #RF*QP£ (d) £RF*QP#
(e) None of these

Space for Rough Work

85. What will be the code for 36250098?
(a) #RFL**G£ (b) $RFLTTG@
(c) #RFLTTG£ (d) $RFL**G@
(e) None of these

DIRECTIONS (Qs. 86-90) : *Read the following passage carefully to answer these questions based on the respective passage and the opinion of the author only.*

The public sector is at the cross roads ever since the launch of economic reforms programme in India. The pendulum has been swinging between survival and surrender. It is the result of a confluence of several factors: a shift in global economic environment, the emergence of the market economy and myths surrounding the performance of the public sector. So virulent has been the onslaught that it is becoming axiomatic that by the very concept, the public sector is inefficient and resource waster whereas private enterprise is resource efficient.

The reform programme in India commenced with the policy of restricting the public sector supported by greater public participation. With the passage of time, the process of liberalization has shifted to privatization in a disguised form couched as strategic role. In the wake of the recent hot pursuit of the wholesale privatization programme a lively and poignant debate has emerged. It provides a golden opportunity to introspect and revisit the issue.

At the very outset, it must be made clear that in the worldwide liberalized economic environment and very high stake of the state in most public sector undertakings disinvestment policy seeks to differentiate closed or bankrupt enterprises from the private sector, a fact deliberately overlooked by the champions of privatization. These undertakings need immediate attention. They are an unnecessary drain on the public exchequer. A high priority area for the disinvestment programme ought to be these enterprises but under one or the other argument these remain unattended, may be it involves a tough task. If these cannot be sold lock, stock and barrel asset stripping is the only option. Obviously the government cannot realise good price from these assets but their disposal will help to stop the drain. If the assets are depreciated or become obsolete, then there is no point in holding on to them indefinitely and take to softer option of selling the vibrant and highly profit-making organisations to reduce the budgetary deficit. Non performers exist both in public and private sectors. Why condemn the public sector as a whole? Better option will be closure or privatization of loss-making and nonviable units, supporting PSU's which could be turned around and made to become healthy and viable and providing autonomy to the boards of PSU's which are performing well and have potential to be globally competitive be welcomed. With public participation in the PSU's there will be a good dose of accountability in the system. What needs to be reviewed are some basic issues: the priorities allocated to the enterprises selected for disinvestment, a .comprehensive road map delineating the route, the modes and modalities, timing and its consequences. These basic issues require greater discussion and participative decision-making. In any event, the disinvestment programme in respect of the closed and non-revivable units is a must if the drain of further resources is to be prevented.

Let it be understood that PSU's are a big repository of value and it will take quite some time for privatization programme to materialise despite the desire to expedite the process. Until then if a vacuum emerges attended by uncertainty, it will do a great harm to the investments which were made with such great dedication although desired now.

The government has withdrawn a budgetary support over the last decade. If some support is extended, it is largely directed to closed or losing enterprise which have no fortune.

86. The basic issue(s) requiring greater discussion and participative decision making regarding the dis-investment programme is/are :
(a) the priorities allocated to the enterprises selected for disinvestment
(b) a comprehensive road-map delineating the route
(c) the modes and modalities, timings and its consequence
(d) all of these
(e) None of these

87. "The public sector is inefficient and resources waster whereas private enterprise is resource-efficient". This opinion is due to :
(a) a shift in global economic environment
(b) the emergence of market economy
(c) the myths surrounding the performance of the public sector
(d) all of these
(e) None of these

Space for Rough Work

88. The reform programme in India, started with the policy of restructuring of PSUs, has got shifted to :
(a) liberalisation (b) privatization
(c) globalisation (d) Urbanisation
(e) None of these

89. What were made with great dedication earlier, but now derided?
(a) disinvestment
(b) investments in PSUs
(c) wholesale privatisation programme
(d) strategic plans
(e) None of these

90. According to the author, non-performers exist in :
(a) government (b) public sector
(c) private sector (d) public and private sectors
(e) None of these

DIRECTIONS (Qs.91-95) : *In each of the questions given below which one of the five answer figures on the bottom should come after the problem figures on the top, if the sequence were continued ?*

91. Problem Figures

Answer Figures

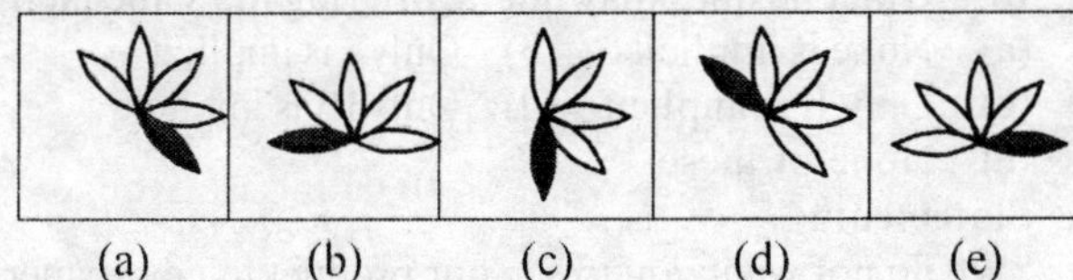

(a) (b) (c) (d) (e)

92. Problem Figures

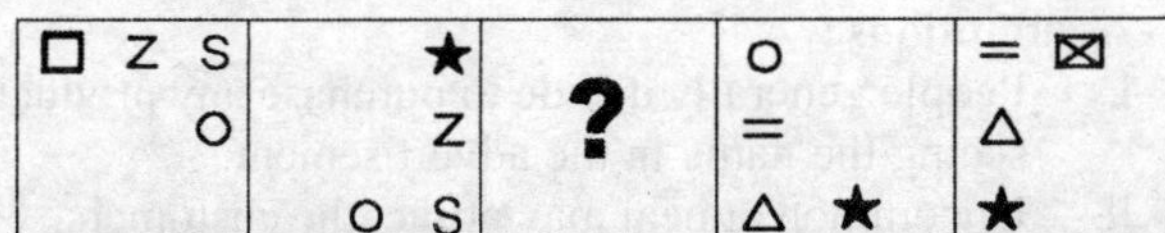

Answer Figures

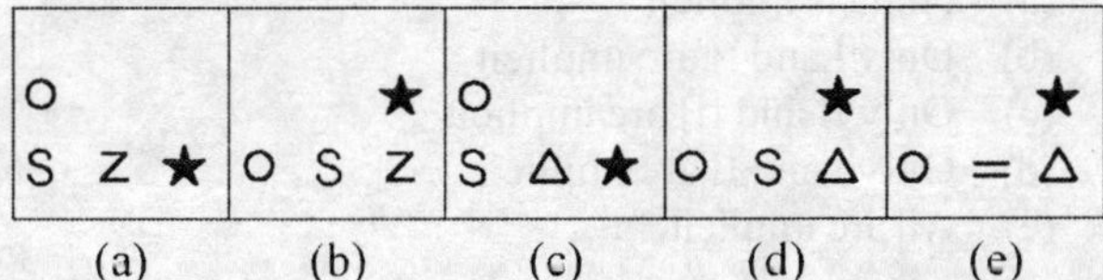

(a) (b) (c) (d) (e)

93. Problem Figures

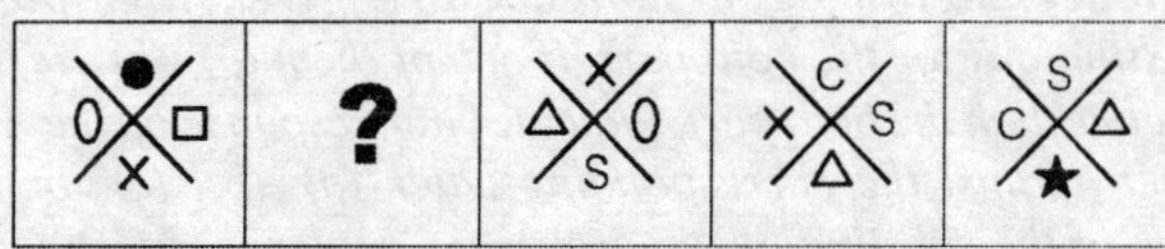

Answer Figures

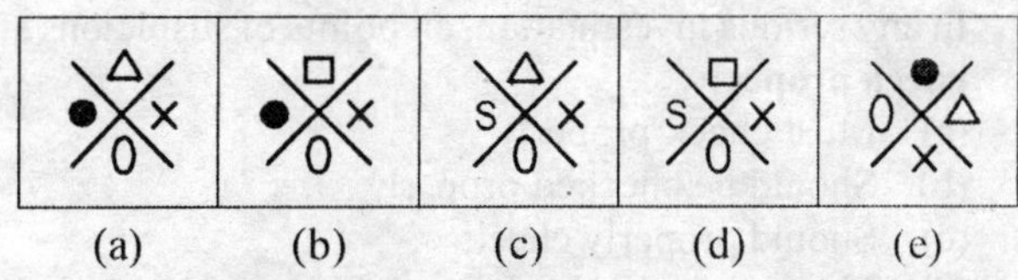

(a) (b) (c) (d) (e)

94. Problem Figures

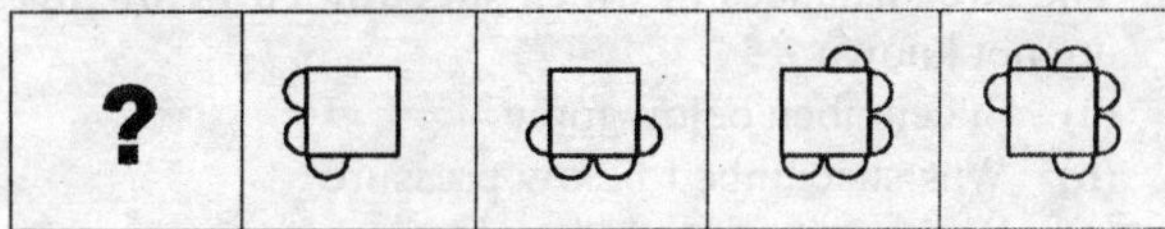

Answer Figures

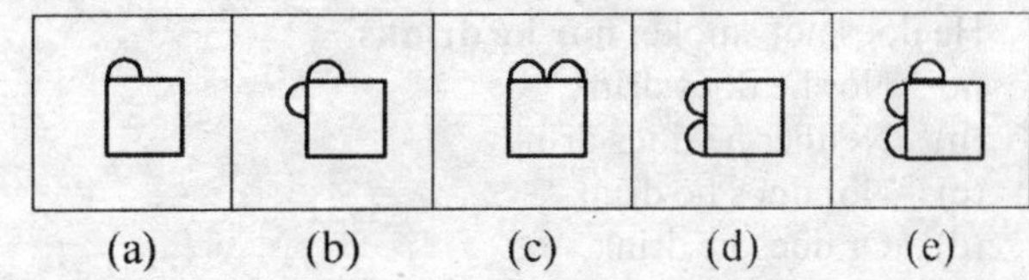

(a) (b) (c) (d) (e)

95. Problem Figures

Answer Figures

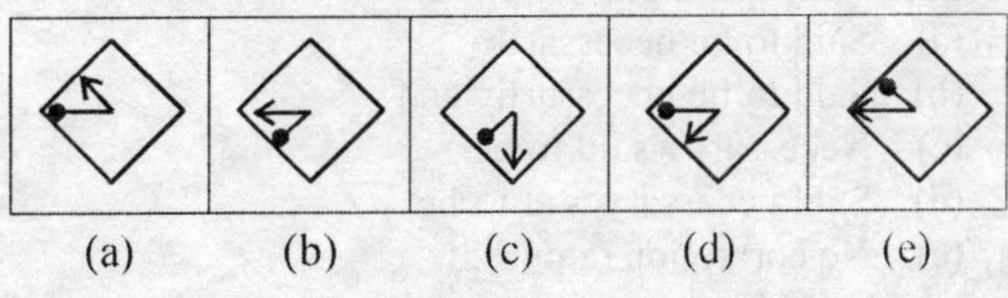

(a) (b) (c) (d) (e)

Space for Rough Work

DIRECTIONS (Qs. 96-100) : *Look at the bold part of each sentence. Below each sentence are given four possible substitutions for the bold part. If one of them (a), (b), (c) or (d) is better than the bold part, indicate your response on the Answer Sheet against the corresponding letter (a), (b), (c) or (d). If none of the substitutions improves the sentence, indicate (e) as your response on the Answer Sheet. Thus a 'No' improvement' response will be signified by the letter (e).*

96. In any serious investigation, all points of suspicions **should check properly.**
   (a) Must check properly
   (b) Should be checked properly
   (c) Should properly check
   (d) Must properly check
   (e) No correction required

97. The circumstances in which **succumbed below pressure,** are not known.
   (a) Succumbed below force
   (b) Was succumbed below pressure
   (c) Was succumbing below force
   (d) Succumbed to pressure
   (e) No correction required

98. He does not smoke, **nor he drinks**
   (a) Nor he does drink
   (b) Neither he does drink
   (c) Nor does he drink
   (d) Or does he drink
   (e) No correction required

99. **How did the burglar got** into the bank is a mystery.
   (a) How did the burglar get
   (b) What did the burglar get
   (c) How the burglar got
   (d) Why did the burglar get
   (e) No correction required

100. What most of the people think right cannot be **said to be necessary and** right?
   (a) Said to be necessarily
   (b) Said to be necessarily and
   (c) Necessarily said to be
   (d) Said necessary and to be
   (e) No correction required

DIRECTIONS (Qs. 101 - 105) : *A statement is followed by three assumptions marked I, II and III. Check whether these assumptions are implicit in the statement or not. Possible combinations of assumptions are given against options (a), (b), (c), (d) and (e). Choose the appropriate one.*

101. **Statement :**
"Buy pure and natural honey of company X"an advertisement in a newspaper.
Assumptions :
I. Artificial honey can be prepared.
II. People do not mind paying more for pure and natural honey.
III. No other company supplies pure honey.
   (a) Only I is implicit
   (b) Only I and II are implicit
   (c) Only I and III are implicit
   (d) All are implicit
   (e) None is implicit

102. **Statement :**
"Fly with us and experience the pleasure of flying"–an advertisement by an airlines.
Assumptions :
I. More passengers may be attracted to travel by the airline after reading the advertisement.
II. People generally may prefer an enjoyable flight.
III. Other airlines may not be offering the same facilities.
   (a) None is implicit (b) Only I is implicit
   (c) Only II is implicit (d) Only III is implicit
   (e) None of these

103. **Statement :**
"We do not want you to see our product in newspaper, visit our shop to get a full view"– an advertisement.
Assumptions :
I. People generally decide to purchase any product after seeing the name in the advertisement.
II. Uncommon appeal may attract the customers.
III. People may come to see the product.
   (a) None is implicit
   (b) Only I and II are implicit
   (c) Only II and III are implicit
   (d) Only I and II are implicit
   (e) All are implicit

Space for Rough Work

104. **Statement :**
"Use Riya cold cream for fair complexion" an advertisement.
Assumptions :
I. People like to use cream for fair complexion.
II. People are easily fooled.
III. People respond to advertisements.
(a) Only I is implicit (b) Only I and II are implicit
(c) Only II is implicit (d) Only I and III are implicit
(e) All are implicit

105. **Statement :**
"Smoking is injurious to health"–a warning printed on the cigarette packets.
Assumptions :
I. People read printed matter on the cigarette packet.
II. People take careful note of warning.
III. Non-smoking promotes health.
(a) Only I is implicit (b) Only I and II are implicit
(c) Only II is implicit (d) All are implicit
(e) None is implicit

DIRECTIONS (Qs. 106-110) : *Answer the questions on the basis of the following information :*
The following is the wholesale price index (WPI) of a select list of items with the base year of 1993-94. In other words, all the item prices are made 100 in that year (1993-94). Prices in all other years for an item are measured with respect to its price in the base year. For instance, the price of cement went up by 1% in 1994-95 as compared to 1993-94. Similarly, the price of power went up by 3% in 1996-97 as compared to 1993-94.

	1993-94	1994-95	1995-96	1996-97	1997-98	1998-99	1999-2000	2000-01	2001-02	2002-03
All items	100	102.0	102.5	104.00	103.00	105.00	106.0	108.00	107.0	106.0
Cement	100	101.0	100.5	103.0	102.50	103.50	103.1	103.80	103.7	104.0
Limestone	100	102.0	102.5	102.75	102.25	103.00	104.0	105.00	104.5	105.0
Power	100	101.5	102.5	103.00	103.50	104.00	106.0	107.00	107.5	108.0
Steel	100	101.5	101.0	103.50	104.00	104.25	105.0	105.50	106.0	105.5
Timber	100	100.5	101.5	102.00	102.50	102.00	103.0	103.50	104.0	104.5
Wages	100	101.5	103.0	103.50	104.00	104.25	104.0	104.75	104.9	105.3

106. Let us suppose that one bag of cement (50 kgs) consumes 100 kgs of limestone and 10 units of power. The only other cost item in producing cement is in the form of wages. During 1993-94, limestone, power and wages contributed, respectively, 20%, 25% and 15% to the cement price per bag. The average operating profit (% of price per cement bag) earned by a cement manufacturer during 2002-03 is closest to
(a) 40% (b) 39.5%
(c) 38.7% (d) 37.5%
(e) None of these

107. Steel manufacturing requires the use of iron ore, power and manpower. The cost of iron ore has followed the All Items index. During 1993-94 power accounted for 30% of the selling price of steel, iron ore for 25%, and wages for 10% of the selling price of steel. Assuming the cost and price data for cement as given in the previous questions, the operating profit (% of selling price) of an average steel manufacturer in 2002-03.
(a) is more than that of a cement manufacturer
(b) is less than that of a cement manufacturer
(c) is the same as that of a cement manufacturer
(d) cannot be determined
(e) None of these

Space for Rough Work

108. Which item experienced continuous price rise during the ten-year period ?
(a) Power (b) Cement
(c) Wages (d) Limestone
(e) None of these

109. Which item(s) experienced only one decline in price during the ten-year period ?
(a) Steel and Limestone
(b) Steel and Timber
(c) Timber
(d) Timber and Wages
(e) None of these

110. Standing on a rock, Ravi said that Madurai was more than 3 km but less than 8 km from there. Prabhu said that it was more than 6 km but less than 10 km from there. If both of them are correct, how far is Madurai from the rock ?
(a) 8 km (b) 6 km
(c) 7 km (d) Cannot be determined
(e) None of these

DIRECTIONS (Qs.111-115) : *Read the following passage carefully to answer these questions based on the respective passage and the opinion of the author only.*

In peacetime, the personal looms to the foreground and history recedes; in wartime, the personal either constitutes history, or is subsumed by it. Thus, the literary romance may be especially to aftermath.

Aptly then, Shirley Hazzard's "The Great Fire" begins in occupied Japan in 1947. Her protagonist, Aldred Leith, a decorated British major, has been sent by the army to report on the condition of Hiroshima. When pressed by his minder to explain the strategy behind dropping the atomic bomb, Leith submits: "By then, neither side was interested in sparing anyone, even themselves".

Early in his posting in the nearby town of Kure, Leith is captivated by the precocious daughter of a widely disliked brigadier. Helen is 17, Leith in his early thirties, and her parents strenuously oppose his courtship. Helen's beloved older brother is dying of a rare disorder, and her unpleasant parents have dumped the boy's daily care entirely on their daughter. At length, her parents wrench Helen from her would-be lover and her brother both, shipping their son to California to die alone, and whisking Helen to New Zealand, a world away from her mature admirer.

As sweetly as Ms. Hazzard evokes the thwarted romance, it is hard for her backdrop not to steal the show. The time is marked by unease. Peace is nominal. The civil war is roiling in China. A confrontation between America and the Soviet Union threatens yet a third world war that these exhausted characters haven't the energy to contemplate. The conquerors in Japan are tainted by guilt over the bomb and by contempt for their charges. In passing, Helen's mother despairs from on high of "their awful gardens". The gardens would not be all that this shrew notices.

Indeed, it is the survivors' struggle to triumph over backdrop - to force the personal to the fore again, that constitutes Ms. Hazzard's subject matter: "Having expected, repeatedly, to die from the great fires into which his times had pitched him, [Leith] had recovered a great desire to live completely; by which he meant, with her". Love's redemption may be an age-old theme, but it is no mean feat to recover one's concern for simple individual happiness after so much collective suffering.

For a novel 20 years in the writing - Ms. Hazzard's last, "The Transit of Venus", won the National Book Critics' Circle Award in 1981 - "The Great Fire" has a surprising quietness. Yet this is the hush you hear after a shoe has dropped, and not the misleading tranquillity that precedes disaster. There is a ring in the air. Moreover, the novel's pervasive sense of composure proceeds from its sentences, which are meticulous and thankfully free of creative writing school overload. Many books are noisy with chatter and frou-frou, as writers take wild scatter-shots at their subjects in the hope that a few lines will hit the target. Ms Hazzard's prose is restful in its exactitude; every sentence strikes its mark.

If her text is never ostentatious, Ms. Hazzard has a knack for deft, unexpected word choice. Leith dreads the arrival in Helen of "a charmless good sense", or in Japan "the chronic anticlimax of nightfall". A military minion is "hysterical with importance".

Her descriptive powers are as muscular when depicting characters as they are with this uniquely shell-shocked era. Of an elderly woman: "Beauty, long since drained of erotic appeal, had remained a habit". Of a couple: "The shared error of their marriage had grown to be a bond".

Space for Rough Work

Owing to a classical tradition, Ms. Hazzard's dialogue is more articulate than strict realism would dictate. Yet to put so much wisdom into the mouths of her characters constitutes a form of authorial generosity. Remarks a woman in London, "You'll find they keep saying, 'Britain is finished' - and with such complacency, as if it were a solution." Or Leith will opine, *"Things,* Helen, the sad silly evidence of things. We're told that possessions are ephemeral, yet my God how they outlast us - the clock on the bedside table, the cough drops, the diary with appointment for that very day."

Though sporting an unusually large cast, "The Great Fire" never feels crowded. While hopscotching between Japan, Hong Kong, Britain and New Zealand, the novel maintains a remarkable sense of geographical unity - as if, after a world war of such dimension, anywhere on the planet begins to feel, depressingly, like the same place. Given the richness of these several settings and the nuanced nature of these many characters, lesser authors might have been tempted to write a doorstop. If nothing else, perhaps Ms. Hazzard deserves America's National Book Award, for which "The Great Fire" has recently been short-listed, for achieving the effect of one of those pretentious, capital-B big books in fewer than 300 exquisitely crafted pages.

111. The aim of the passage is to
   (a) acquaint the reader with Shirley Hazzard's book - "The Great Fire".
   (b) critique the book "The Great Fire" by Shirley Hazzard.
   (c) argue a case for "The Great Fire" winning America's National Book Award.
   (d) both (a) and (b).
   (e) None of these

112. The book is said to "aptly" start in "occupied Japan in 1947" because
   (a) it is a literary romance and therefore needs to have the backdrop of an interesting period.
   (b) it is a literally romance that should ideally take place in peacetime.
   (c) the aftermath of war provides a perfect backdrop for a literary romance
   (d) Japan in 1947 was a turbulent and interesting place.
   (e) None of these

113. One may conclude from the passage that Ms Hazzard's defining characteristic in writing is
   (a) that she makes her characters mouth the philosophy inherent in the story
   (b) that she expresses herself in a clear and straight forward manner.
   (c) that she favours an underlying tone of wisdom in her book.
   (d) that she paints a vivid picture of the historical backdrop to her story.
   (e) None of these

114. The author views the writer's work as a
   (a) process (b) means to an end
   (c) craft (d) collage
   (e) None of these

115. One only infer from the passage that auther considers the dialogues in the book to be
   (a) Archaic (b) Exaggerated
   (c) Unreal (d) Verbose
   (e) None of these

DIRECTIONS (Qs. 116-120) : *In each of the following questions in four out of the five figures, element I is related to element II in the same particular way. Find out the figure in which element I is not so related to element II.*

116.

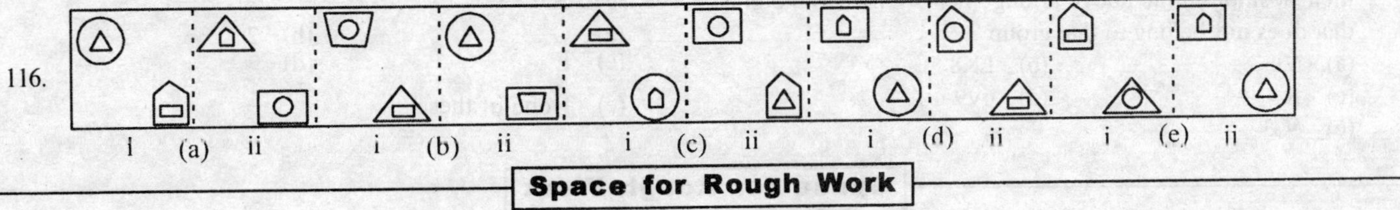

Space for Rough Work

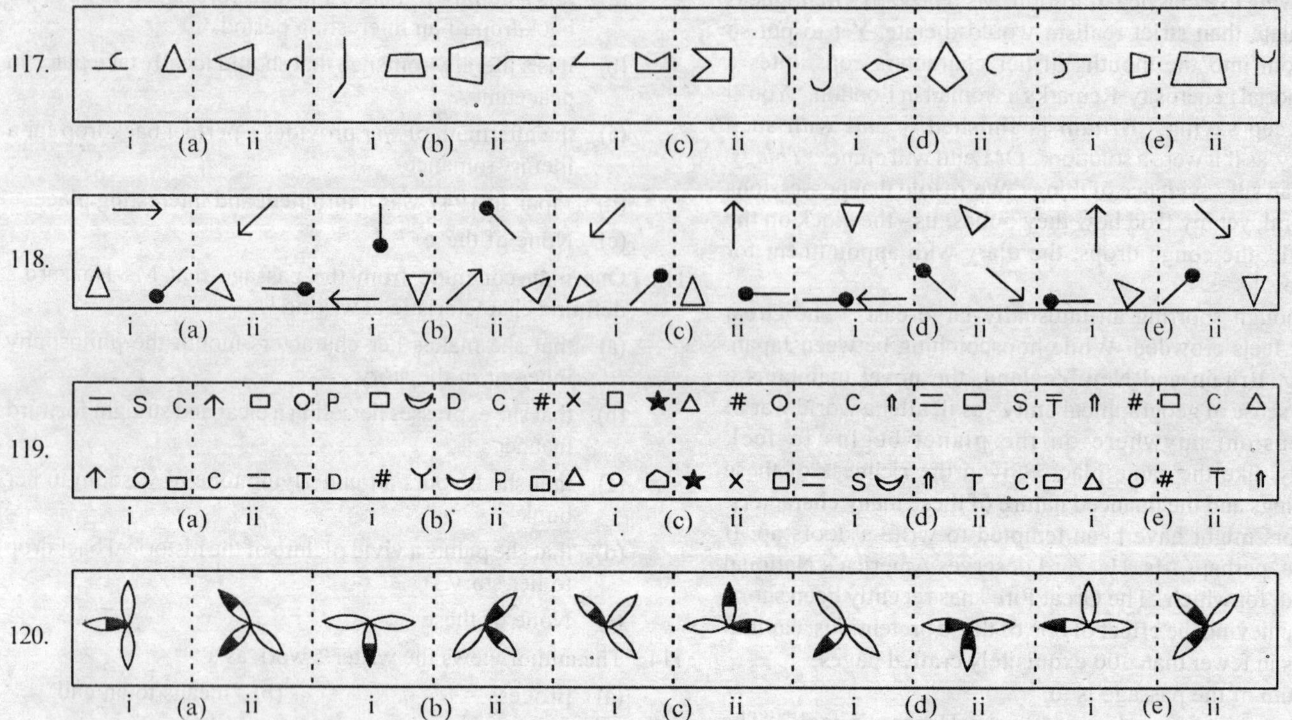

DIRECTIONS (Qs. 121-125) : *Study the following arrangement carefully and answer the questions given below :*

P 1 % T R A 5 # D M 7 K ★ E G 2 8 $ H 3 1 4 V U 6 F ⊕ 9 Z

121. How many such symbols are there in the above arrangment, each of which is immediately preceded by a consonant and also immediately followed by a consonant ?
   (a) None (b) One
   (c) Two (d) Three
   (e) More than three

122. Four of the following five are alike in a certain way based on their position in the above arrangement. Which is the one that **does not** belong to that group ?
   (a) VIF (b) EK8
   (c) R % # (d) 6V9
   (e) $G3

123. How many such vowels are there in the above arrangement, each of which is immediately preceded by a digit and immediately followed by a consonant ?
   (a) None (b) One
   (c) Two (d) Three
   (e) More than three

124. Which of the following is exactly in the middle between the fifth element from the left end and the seventh element from the right end?
   (a) G (b) 2
   (c) E (d) ★
   (e) None of these

Space for Rough Work

125. If the positions of last twelve elements in the above arrangement are reversed, which of the following will be the eigth element to the right of the eleventh element from the left ?
(a) H (b) I
(c) ⌖ (d) 9
(e) None of these

DIRECTIONS (Qs. 126 - 130) : *These questions are based on the information and bar chart given below:*

Essel World is one of the best known and the first amusement park in Mumbai and attracts a large number of visitors every year. The number of visitors visiting the park is very high on Sundays and holidays and during the winter vacations, while it is very less on weekdays and is negligible during the rains. The following graph gives the number of visitors of Essel World in each of the years from 1991-92 to 1997-98.

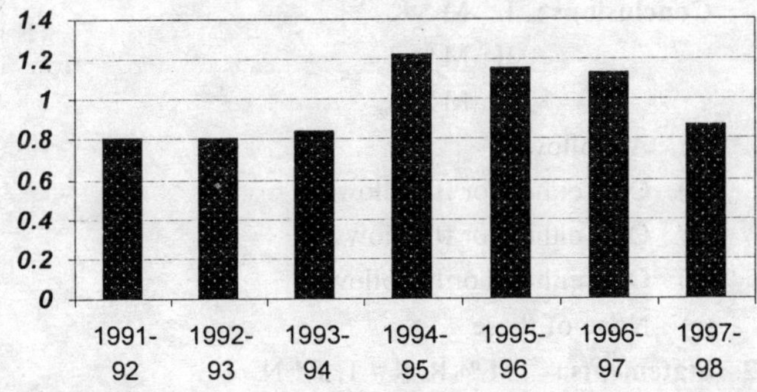

126. The highest percentage growth in the number of visitors was in
(a) 1992 – 93 (b) 1993 – 94
(c) 1994 – 95 (d) 1995 – 96
(e) None of these

127. The average annual growth rate from 1991 – 92 to 1997-98 is
(a) 3.13 % (b) 2.08%
(c) 3.54% (d) 3.75%
(e) None of these

128. What will be the approximate number of visitors in 1998 – 99 assuming the same annual growth rate for the given period ?
(a) 1,00,000 (b) 10,00,000
(c) 1,00,00,000 (d) 10,00,00,000
(e) None of these

129. The lowest percentage change in the number of visitors is in
(a) 1992 – 93 (b) 1993 – 94
(c) 1995 – 96 (d) 1996 – 97
(e) None of these

130. Essel World's revenue was maximum in
(a) 1993 – 94 (b) 1994 – 95
(c) 1996 – 97 (d) Data insufficient
(e) None of these

DIRECTIONS (Qs. 131-134) : *Read the following information and answer the questions given below.*

(i) Rajiv, a medical representative (M. R.), has to meet 7 doctors M, N, O, P, Q, R and S on a particular day between 9 am and 4 pm.

(ii) He takes 30 minutes with each doctor and keeps a gap of 25 minutes between two appointments for travel and preparation except after 5th visit, when he takes 50 minutes' break for lunch, travel and preparation.

(iii) He has to meet doctor M immediately before Q but immediately after R, who is the third doctor to be met.

(iv) 'S' does not give time for M.R. before 9:30 am and after 10.30 Am. 'P' and 'N' meet MR between 2 pm and 3:30 pm only.

131. Who among the following is likely to be the first doctor of that day?
(a) S (b) O
(c) R (d) Q
(e) None of these

132. Who will be the last doctor to be visited by him on that day?
(a) N (b) P
(c) Either N or P (d) Data inadequate
(e) None of these

133. At what time is he likely to meet doctor 'S'?
(a) 9:55 am (b) 9:30 am
(c) 9 am (d) Data inadequate
(e) None of these

Space for Rough Work

134. If doctor 'R' asks him to visit again 25 minutes after his sheduled seventh visit is over, then at what time can he meet doctor 'R'?
(a) 3:55 pm (b) 3:40 pm
(c) 3:25 pm (d) 3:50
(e) None of these

135. The letters L, M, N, O, P, Q, R, S and T in their order are substituted by nine integers 1 to 9 in that order. 4 is assigned to P. The difference between P and T is 5. The difference between N and T is 3. What is the integer assigned to N?
(a) 5 (b) 4
(c) 6 (d) 7
(e) None of these

DIRECTIONS (Qs 136-140): *Fill in the blanks in the following sentences using the most appropriate word or words from the options given :*

136. When listening to the chanting of the scriptures, the listener does not encounter the musician's individual personality .... the chant merely .... both the musical and religious rules of the period.
(a) however-represents
(b) rather-communicates
(c) moreover-reflects
(d) in addition-conveys

137. After listening to the pleas for ...., the judge was .... and gave the convicted man the maximum punishment allowed by law.
(a) activity-abrasive (b) fortitude-formidable
(c) clemency-unmoved (d) multiplicity-noisome
(e) None of these

138. She was a/an .... liar who had mastered the art of making untrue statements in a manner that sounded ....
(a) congenial-creditable
(b) incorrigible-plausible
(c) convincing-illogical
(d) blatant-incongruous
(e) None of these

139. We can coax physical nature into .... many of our wishes but we cannot .... authority over it or make it change its ways one jot
(a) granting- empower
(b) satiating- display
(c) satisfying- exercise
(d) stimulating- exercise
(d) None of these

140. War has been, throughout history, the chief .... of social cohesion; and since science began, it has been the strongest .... to technical progress.
(a) reason-encouragement
(b) origin-boost
(c) cause-provocation
(d) source-incentive
(d) None of these

DIRECTIONS (Qs. 141-145) : *In the following questions, the symbols %, *, @, $ and # are used with the following meaning as illustrated below :*

'P @ Q' means 'P is not smaller than Q'.
'P # Q' means 'P is not greater than Q'.
'P % Q' means 'P is neither greater than nor equal to Q'.
'P * Q' means 'P is neither smaller than nor greater than Q'.
'P $ Q' means 'P is neither smaller than nor equal to Q'.

141. **Statements :** T $ K, K # R, R * M
Conclusions : I. M * K
II. M % T
III. M $ K
(a) All follows
(b) Only either I or III follows
(c) Only either I or II follows
(d) Only either II or III follows
(e) None of these

142. **Statements :** M % R, R # T, T * N
Conclusions : I. N * R
II. N $ R
III. N $ M
(a) All follows
(b) Only either I or II follows
(c) Only either I or II and III follows
(d) Only either I or III and II follows
(e) None of these

Space for Rough Work

143. **Statements :** V @ M, A $ M, R # V
Conclusions : I. R # A
II . V @ A
III. R $ M
(a) Only I follows (b) Only II follows
(c) Only III follows (d) None of follows
(e) All follow

144. **Statements :** B * D, D @ H, H % F
Conclusions : I. B * F
II . B $ F
III. D $ F
(a) None follows
(b) Only either I or II follows
(c) Only either I or II and III follows
(d) Only III follows
(e) All follow

145. **Statements :** J # N, K @ N, T $ K
Conclusions : I . J % T
II. T $ N
III . N @ J
(a) None follows
(b) Only I or II follow
(c) Only I and III follow
(d) Only II and III follow
(e) All follow

DIRECTIONS (Qs. 146 - 150) : *Study the information given below to answer these questions :*

(i) Six plays A, B, C, D, E and F are to be organised from Monday to Saturday, i.e from 5th to 10th-one play each day.
(ii) There are two plays between C and D and one play between A and C.
(iii) There is one play between F and E and E is to be organised before F.
(iv) B is to be organised before A, not necessarily immediately.
(v) The organisation does not start with B

146. The organisation would start from which play ?
(a) A (b) F
(c) D (d) Cannot be determined
(e) None of these

147. On which date the play E is to be organised ?
(a) 5th (b) 7th
(c) 6th (d) Cannot be determined
(e) None of these

148. The organisation would end with which of the following plays?
(a) A (b) D
(c) B (d) Cannot be determined
(e) None of these

149. On which day the play B is organised ?
(a) Tuesday (b) Friday
(c) Thursday (d) Wednesday
(d) None of these

150. Which of the following is the correct sequence of organising plays?
(a) AECFBD (b) DFECBA
(c) BDEFCA (d) DBECFA
(e) None of these

DIRECTIONS (Qs. 151-155) : *In each of the following questions, a related pair of figures is followed by five numbered pairs of figures. Select the pair that has a relationship similar to that in the original pair. The best answer is to be selected from a group of fairly close choices.*

151. 

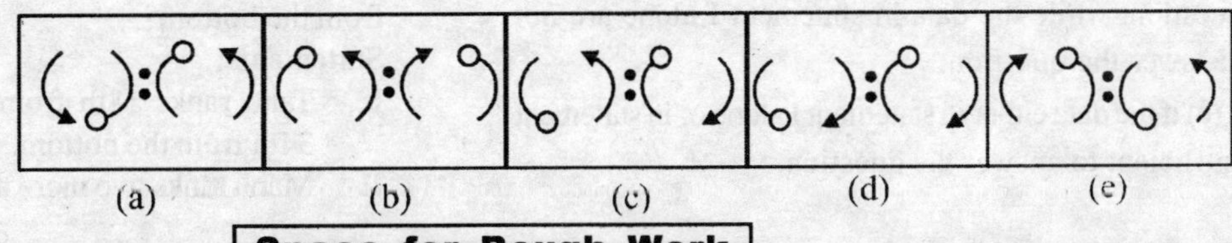
(a) (b) (c) (d) (e)

Space for Rough Work

152.
153.
154.
155.

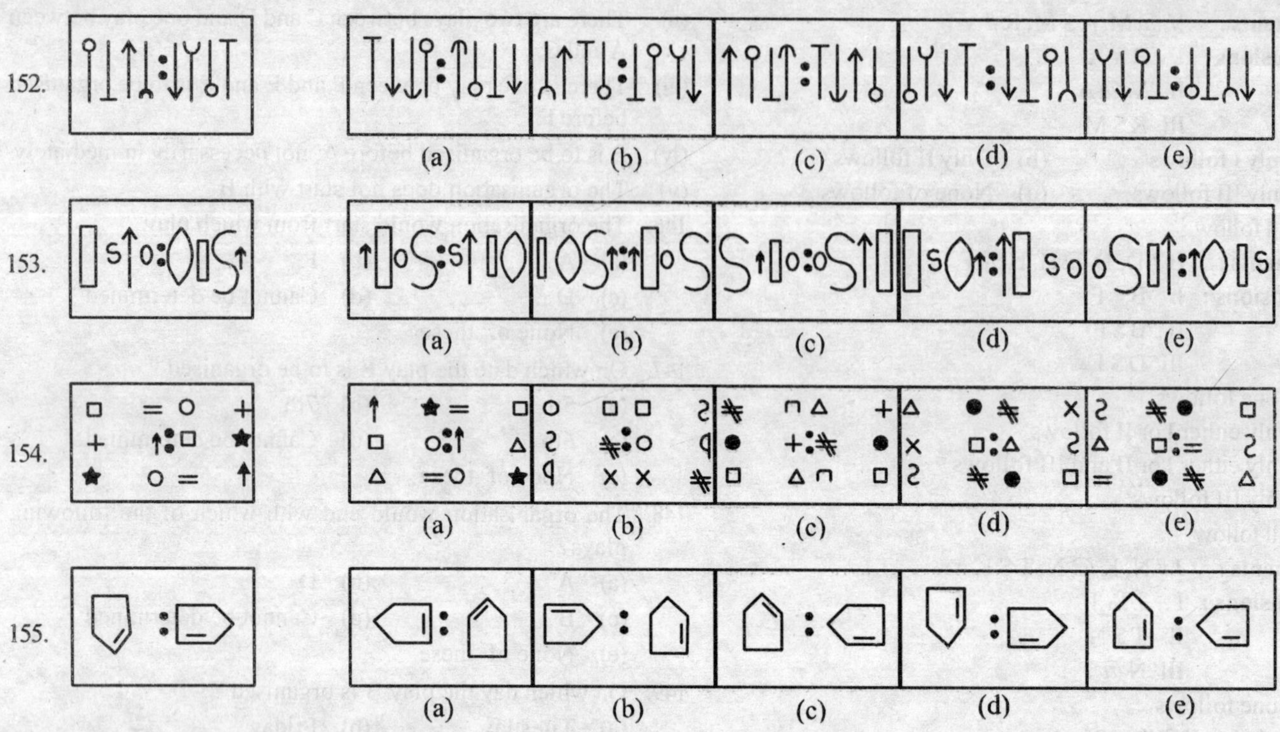

DIRECTIONS (Qs. 156-160): *Each of the questions below consists of a question and two statements numbered I and II given below it. You have to decide whether the data provided in the statements are sufficient to answer the question. Read both the statements and*

Give answer (a) if the data in statement I alone are sufficient to answer the question, while the data in statement II alone are not sufficient to answer the question.

Give answer (b) if the data in statement II alone are sufficient to answer the question, while the data in statement I alone are not sufficient to answer the question.

Give answer (c) if the data either in statement I alone or in statement II alone are sufficient to answer the question.

Give answer (d) if the data even in both the statements I and II together are not sufficient to answer the question.

Give answer (e) if the data in both the statements I and II together are necessary to answer the question.

156. How is Omprakash related to Rajesh?

Statements:

I. Omprakash is the father-in-law of Riya, who is the brother's wife of Rajesh's only uncle.

II. Seema, the only daughter of Omprakash's wife Sanjana's only uncle, is the wife of Rajesh.

157. If Anu ranks 14th from the top in her class.what is her rank from the bottom?

Statements:

I. Tanu ranks 18th from the top in the same class and 34th from the bottom.

II. Manu ranks two more than Anu in a class of 50 students.

Space for Rough Work

158. On which day is Sameer's interview scheduled?

Statements:

I. Tony correctly remembers that it is before Friday but after Tuesday.

II. Tinku correctly remembers that it is before Thursday but after Monday.

159. Which direction is Prem facing?

Statements:

I. If he turns 135° to his left, he will face West.

II. If he turns 180° to his right, he will be opposite Anu, who is facing East.

160. Five friends are sitting around a circular table facing the centre. Who is sitting immediately to the left of Kunal?

Statements:

I. Kunal is sitting third to the left of Anil, who sits between Surender and Gajendra.

II. Surender is sitting to the left of Anil and only one person is sitting between Kunal and Surender.

DIRECTIONS (Qs. 161-164) : *Study the following information carefully to answer these questions:*

Following are the qualifications necessary for the recruitment of librarian in a state University.

The candidate must :

A. have a Master's Degree in Library Science with at least 55% marks or its equivalent grade and a consistently good academic record.

B. have one year specialisation in an area of Information Technology/ Archives and Manuscript-keeping Master's Degree in an area of thrust in the institution.

C. have at least ten years experience as a Deputy Librarian in university.

D. bear an evidence of innovative library service and organisation of published work.

In the case of a candidate who

E. has a 15 years experience as a College Librarian, the case may be referred to the Vice Chancellor.

F. has obtained less than 55% marks in Library Science but has 13 years experience as a Deputy Librarian in a University, the case may be referred to the Registrar of the University for his consideration.

G has M.Phil / Ph. D. Degree in Library Science / Information science / Documentation / Archives and Manuscript-keeping but has only ten years experience as a College Librarian, the condition at (A), may be waived.

Based on the above conditions and the information provided against each of the candidates in the questions given below, decide which of the following courses of action should be taken against each candidate.

Mark your answer as :

(a) if the candidate is to be selected.

(b) if the candidate is not to be selected.

(c) if the data is inadequate.

(d) if the case is to be referred to the Registrar.

(e) if the case is to be referred to the vice chancellor.

161. Rahul Sehgal, an M.Phil. in Library Science, has been a Deputy Librarian in the Rohilkhand University since 27th August, 1980. He also bears Master's Degree in Archives and Manuscript keeping. He holds the evidence of innovative organisation of published works of the college students doing Ph.D.

162. Sanjay Verma has been a Deputy Librarian in the IMS university since 1973. He holds an evidence of contributing library service in the same institution. He has a Master's Degree in Library Science with 53% marks.

Space for Rough Work

163. Ramesh Singhania holding a Ph.D. degree in Library Science has one year specialisation in Archives and Manuscript-keeping. He has been a Deputy Librarian in the Assam university since 11th April, 1982. He also bears a certificate of innovative library service in a public library for three years.

164. Sunil Garewal has been a College Librarian since 15th December, 1975. He holds an M.Phil. Degree in Library Science.

165. A boy has 3 library cards and 8 books of his interest in the library. Of these 8, he does not want to borrow chemistry part II unless Chemistry part I is also borrowed. In how many ways can he choose the three books to be borrowed ?
(a) 56 (b) 27
(c) 26 (d) 41
(e) None of these

DIRECTIONS (Qs. 166-170) : *Study the following information carefully and answer the questions given below:*

(i) A, B, C, D, E, F and G are seven persons wearing a shirts of different colours – white, red, black, green, yellow, blue and violet – and trousers of different colours – blue, red, white, black, cream, yellow and indigo. The persons, colour of the shirt and colour of the trousers above and not necessarily in the same order. No person is wearing shirt and trousers of same colour.

(ii) B is wearing red shirt and is not wearing cream or yellow trousers. D is wearing green shirt and indigo trousers. Colour of A's shirt and F's trousers is same. Colour of E's shirt and C's trousers is same. G is wearing blue shirt and E is wearing blue trousers. F is not wearing any yellow dress. Red and blue is not the combination of shirt and trousers of any of the persons.

166. What is the colour of A's trousers?
(a) White (b) Red
(c) Blue (d) Data inadequate
(e) None of these

167. What is the colour of G's trousers?
(a) Red (b) Cream
(c) White (d) Indigo
(e) None of these

168. Who wears violet shirt?
(a) C (b) F
(c) C or F (d) Data inadequate
(e) None of these

169. What is the colour of F's shirt?
(a) Blue (b) Violet
(c) Green (d) Data inadequate
(e) None of these

170. What is the colour of B's trousers?
(a) Red (b) White
(c) Indigo (d) Data inadequate
(e) None of these

DIRECTIONS (Qs. 171-175) : *Given below are pairs of events 'A' and 'B'. You have to read both the events 'A' and 'B' and decide their nature of relationship. You have to assume that the information given in 'A' and 'B' is true and you will not assume anything beyond the given information in deciding the answer.*

Mark answer as :

(a) If 'A' is the effect and 'B' is its immediate and principal cause.
(b) If 'A' is the immediate and principal cause and 'B' is its effect.
(c) If 'A' is an effect but 'B' is not its immediate and principal cause.
(d) If 'B' is an effect but 'A' is not its immediate and principal cause.
(e) None of these

171. **Event : (A)** The 1,000-rupee note is being printed once again.
Event : (B) The 1,000-rupee note went out of circulation in 1978.

172. **Event : (A)** The country's fiscal deficit has widened over the years.
Event : (B) The govt has desided to abolish posts meant for carrying out obsolete functions.

173. **Event : (A)** Two pistols disappeared from a police training institute.
Event : (B) An old woman was shot dead with a pistol in the vicinity of the institute.

174. **Event : (A)** University 'X' and its affiliated colleges have hiked the fees.
Event : (B) The govt has reduced the subsidy on higher education.

Space for Rough Work

175. **Event : (A)** Pradeep, father of a Class XII student, logged on to the website *www.cbse.nic.in* at 11 am on May 31.

Event : (B) The CBSE results for class XII were announced on May 31.

DIRECTIONS (Qs. 176-180) : *Each of these questions is followed by three statements. You have to study the question and all the three statements given to decide whether any information provided in the statement(s) is not required while answering the question.*

176. On a shopping trip, Mr. X purchased a camera worth 30% of the money he had. How much money did he have originally?
1. Apart from purchasing a camera, he also purchased a radio worth Rs 900.
2. After purchasing the radio, he still had one-fourth of the original amount.
3. Mr. X sold the camera for Rs 720 at a profit of 20%

(a) Either 1 and 2 together or 3 alone.
(b) Only 3
(c) Only 1 and 2 together
(d) Any two of them
(e) None of these

177. Is the average of the largest and the smallest of four given numbers greater than the average of the four numbers ?
1. The difference between the largest and the second largest numbers is less than the difference between the second largest and the second smallest numbers.
2. The difference between the largest and the second largest numbers is greater than the difference between the second smallest and the smallest numbers.
3. The difference between the largest and the second smallest numbers is greater than the difference between the second largest and the smallest numbers

(a) Only 1 (b) Either 2 or 3
(c) 1 and either 2 or 3 (d) Any two of them
(e) None of these

178. A water tank has been filled with two filler taps P and Q and a drain pipe R. Taps P and Q fill at the rate of 14 and 12 litres per minute respectively. What is the capacity of the tank ?
1. Tap R drains out at the rate of 6 litres per minute
2. If all the three taps are opened simultaneously, then the tank is filled in 4½ hrs.
3. Tap R drains the filled tank in 15 hrs.

(a) 2 and either 1 or 3 (b) Either 2 or 3
(c) 2 and 3 together (d) Any one of them
(e) None of these

179. What is the cost of carpeting a rectangular hall?
1. Angle between the width and hypotenuse is 30°.
2. The perimeter of the hall is 60 m.
3. The cost of carpeting the hall is Rs 125 per square metre.

(a) Any two of them (b) Any one of them
(c) None (d) 2 and either 1 or 3
(e) Only 2

180. A, B and C secured 45%, 50% and 60% marks respectively in Biology. D's marks in Biology are 10 more than A's marks and 20 less than C's marks. Find out the total marks of the four students.
1. For the students, total marks allotted for Biology are 800.
2. Total of D's and A's marks is 190.
3. C has obtained 120 marks.

(a) 1 and 2 are sufficient
(b) Only 3 is sufficient
(c) Either 1 and 2 together or 3 alone is sufficient
(d) None
(e) Only one

DIRECTIONS (Qs. 181-185) : Five incomplete sentences are given. You have to obtain correct option from among 10 common options to complete the question statements.

A. damaging
B. you are greeting
C. so humid that
D. of being killed
E. to enter the nation
F. who are greeting
G as humid as
H. for being killed
I. the nation will enter
J. damage

181. It is good form to use the name of the person ....

(a) Only 'A' (b) Only 'B'
(c) Both 'A' and 'B' (d) Only 'C'
(e) None of these

Space for Rough Work

182. He was frightened ....
(a) Only 'C' (b) Only 'B'
(c) Both 'C' and 'D' (d) Only 'D'
(e) None of these

183. The impact of two vehicles can cause a lot of .... to both.
(a) Only 'J' (b) Only 'F'
(c) Both 'E' and 'F' (d) Only 'H'
(e) None of these

184. The weather in the far north is not .... it is down south.
(a) Only 'F' (b) Only 'G'
(c) Both 'G' and 'H' (d) Only 'H'
(e) None of these

185. After the election .... a new stage.
(a) Only 'I' (b) Only 'E'
(c) Both 'I' and 'J' (d) Only 'H'
(e) None of these

DIRECTIONS (Qs. 186-190) : In the following questions, each word in capital letters is followed by three words lettered by A, B and C. Choose the word(s) which is/are similar in meaning from the options given below :

186. BONHOMIE
A. Friendliness B. Wrath
C. Very
(a) Only 'A' (b) Both 'A' and 'B'
(c) Only 'C' (d) All 'A', 'B' and 'C'
(e) None of these

187. COLLAPSE
A. Rise B. Failure
C. Debt
(a) Only 'A' (b) Both 'A' and 'B'
(c) Only 'C' (d) All 'A', 'B' and 'C'
(e) None of these

188. BASHFUL
A. Upset B. Discreet
C. Shy
(a) Only 'A' (b) Both 'A' and 'B'
(c) Only 'C' (d) All 'A', 'B' and 'C'
(e) None of these

189. APOLITICAL
A. Not interested in politics
B. Terrorist
C. Antipolitical
(a) Only 'A' (b) Both 'A' and 'B'
(c) Only 'C' (d) All 'A', 'B' and 'C'
(e) None of these

190. APPEASE
A. Agitate B. Pacify
C. Qualify
(a) Only 'A' (b) Both 'A' and 'B'
(c) Only 'C' (d) All 'A', 'B' and 'C'
(e) None of these

191. Four boys and three girls stand in queue for an interview. The probability that they will stand in alternate positions is:
(a) 1/34 (b) 1/35
(c) 1/17 (d) 1/68
(e) None of these

192. Excluding stoppages, the speed of a train is 45 km/h and including stoppages, it is 36 km/h. For how many minutes does the train stop per hour ?
(a) 10 min. (b) 12 min.
(c) 15 min. (d) 18 min.
(e) None of these

DIRECTIONS (Qs. 193-200): *In the following passage there are blanks, each of which has been numbered. These numbers are printed below the passage and against each, five words are suggested, one of which fits the blank appropriately. Find out the appropriate word in each case.*

Trust is the basis of human relationship. As trust between people grows, **193** change and interpersonal dynamics are transformed. Diverse skills and abilities become **194** and appreciated as strengths. People begin to **195**one another's attitudes and feelings. They learn to be **196** instead of playing roles. As trust grows the barriers that prevent **197** and openness lessen. People become more expressive, impulsive, frank and spontaneous. Their communication is efficient and clear. They risk **198** and confrontation, opening the doors to deeper communication, involvement and commitment. Congestion and **199** lessen. The flow of data is open and **200**.

Space for Rough Work

193. (a) motivations (b) behaviours
(c) patterns (d) aspirations
(e) commitments

194. (a) obvious (b) necessary
(c) essential (d) recognised
(e) prominent

195. (a) accept (b) participate
(c) pronounce (d) inculcate
(e) relate

196. (a) advocates (b) possessed
(c) exponents (d) indifferent
(e) themselves

197. (a) snobbery (b) egoism
(c) brashness (d) boasting
(e) candour

198. (a) conflict (b) persuasiveness
(c) dedication (d) propensity
(e) jealousy

199. (a) pervasiveness (b) boundaries
(c) sluggishness (d) blocking
(e) enthusiasm

200. (a) unanimous (b) uncritical
(c) uninhabited (d) uncanny
(e) unusual

Space for Rough Work

MAHARASHTRA CET - MOCK TEST 5

RESPONSE SHEET

NAME : ....

DATE : ....

	(a)	(b)	(c)	(d)	(e)		(a)	(b)	(c)	(d)	(e)		(a)	(b)	(c)	(d)	(e)		(a)	(b)	(c)	(d)	(e)
1.						51.						101.						151.					
2.						52.						102.						152.					
3.						53.						103.						153.					
4.						54.						104.						154.					
5.						55.						105.						155.					
6.						56.						106.						156.					
7.						57.						107.						157.					
8.						58.						108.						158.					
9.						59.						109.						159.					
10.						60.						110.						160.					
11.						61.						111.						161.					
12.						62.						112.						162.					
13.						63.						113.						163.					
14.						64.						114.						164.					
15.						65.						115.						165.					
16.						66.						116.						166.					
17.						67.						117.						167.					
18.						68.						118.						168.					
19.						69.						119.						169.					
20.						70.						120.						170.					
21.						71.						121.						171.					
22.						72.						122.						172.					
23.						73.						123.						173.					
24.						74.						124.						174.					
25.						75.						125.						175.					
26.						76.						126.						176.					
27.						77.						127.						177.					
28.						78.						128.						178.					
29.						79.						129.						179.					
30.						80.						130.						180.					
31.						81.						131.						181.					
32.						82.						132.						182.					
33.						83.						133.						183.					
34.						84.						134.						184.					
35.						85.						135.						185.					
36.						86.						136.						186.					
37.						87.						137.						187.					
38.						88.						138.						188.					
39.						89.						139.						189.					
40.						90.						140.						190.					
41.						91.						141.						191.					
42.						92.						142.						192.					
43.						93.						143.						193.					
44.						94.						144.						194.					
45.						95.						145.						195.					
46.						96.						146.						196.					
47.						97.						147.						197.					
48.						98.						148.						198.					
49.						99.						149.						199.					
50.						100.						150.						200.					

MAHARASHTRA CET

MOCK TEST - 6

☛ ***INSTRUCTIONS :***

- **There are 200 questions in this test. You will be given 150 minutes to complete the test.**
- **Each question carries 1 mark. There is no negative marking.**

1. A bag has 4 red and 5 black balls. A second bag has 3 red and 7 black balls. One ball is drawn from the first bag and two from the second. The probability that there are two black balls and a red ball is

   (a) $\frac{14}{45}$ (b) $\frac{11}{45}$

   (c) $\frac{7}{15}$ (d) $\frac{9}{54}$

   (e) None of these

2. An article manufactured by a company consists of two parts *X* and *Y*. In the process of manufacture of part *X*, 9 out of 104 parts may be defective. Similarly, 5 out of 100 are likely to be defective in the manufacture of the part *Y*. The probability that the assembled product will not be defective, is

   (a) $\frac{253}{416}$ (b) $\frac{361}{416}$

   (c) $\frac{322}{416}$ (d) $\frac{422}{416}$

   (e) None of these

3. The number of ways in which a committee of 3 ladies and 4 gentlemen can be appointed from a meeting consisting of 8 ladies and 7 gentlemen, if Mrs. X refuses to serve in a committee if Mr. Y is its member, is

   (a) 1960 (b) 3240

   (c) 1540 (d) 700

   (e) None of these

4. There are three events A, B and C, out of which one and only one can happen. The odds are 8 to 3 against A, 5 to 2 against B. Find the odds against C .

   (a) 43 : 34 (b) 43 : 77

   (c) 34 : 43 (d) 77 : 43

   (e) None of these

5. In a certain city, all telephone numbers have six digits, the first two digits always being 41 or 42 or 46 or 62 or 64. The number of telephone numbers having all six digits distinct is

   (a) 8400 (b) 7200

   (c) 9200 (d) 8000

   (e) None of these

DIRECTIONS (Qs. 6-10) : *The first figure in the first unit of the problem figures bears a certain relationship to the second figure. Similarly, one of the figures in the answer figures bears the same relationship to the second figure in the second unit of the problem figures. You are therefore to locate the figure which would replace the question mark.*

6. 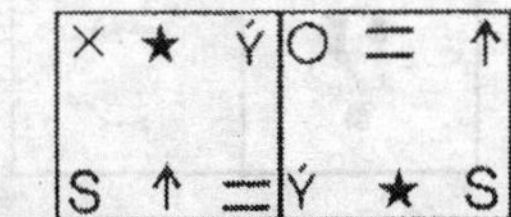

   ?

   (a) (b) (c) (d) (e)

Space for Rough Work

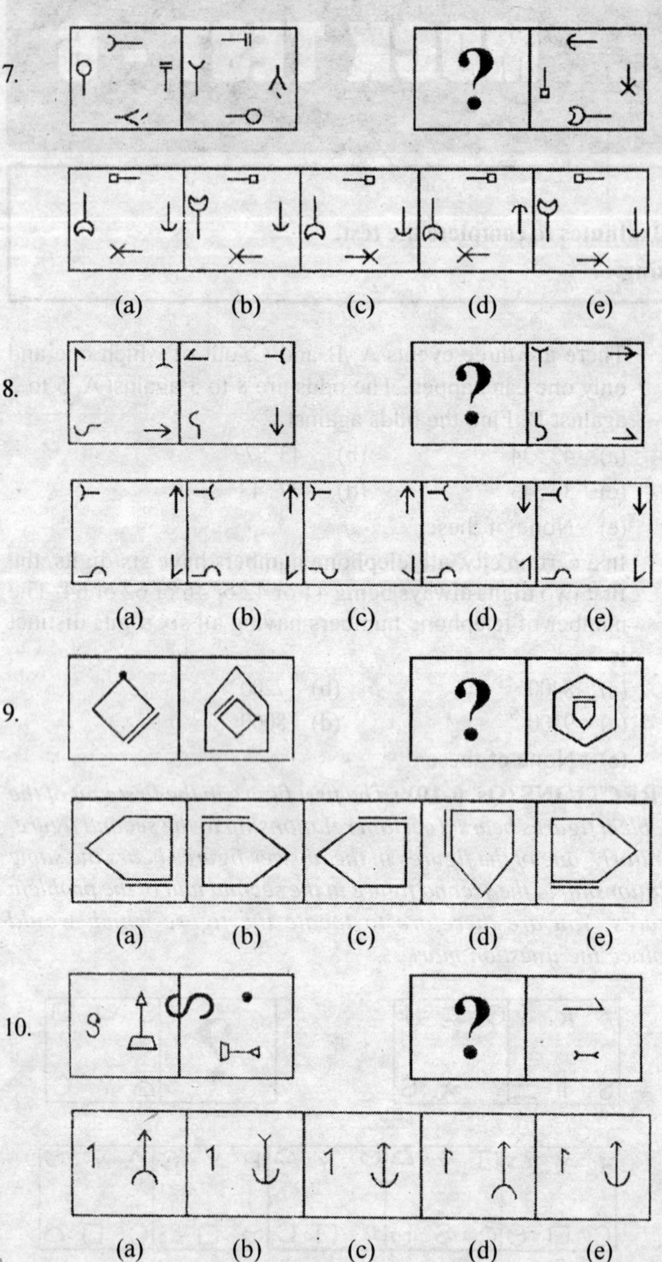

DIRECTIONS (Qs. 11-15) : *In each of the questions below, there are two or three statements followed by four conclusions numbered I, II, III and IV. You have to take the given statements to be true even if they seem to be at variance with commonly known facts and then decide which of the given conclusions logically follow (s) from the given statements.*

11. **Statement :**

Some singers are rockers.
All rockers are westerners.

Conclusions :

I. Some rockers are singers.
II. Some westerners are rockers.
III. Some singers are westerners.
IV. Some singers are not westerners.

(a) I, II, and III follow (b) I, II and IV follow
(c) II, III and IV follow (d) I, III and IV follow
(e) None of these

12. **Statements :**

No Indian is an Asian.
Some Americans are Indians.

Conclusions :

I. Some Indians are not Asians.
II. Some Asians are not Americans.
III. Some Americans are not Asians.
IV. All Americans are Asians.

(a) Either III or IV follows (b) Either I or II follows
(c) I and III follow (d) Either II or III follows
(e) None of these

13. **Statements :**

Some charts are darts.
All darts are carts.
Some carts are smarts.

Conclusions :

I. Some charts are carts.
II. Some carts are darts.
III. Some darts are smarts.
IV. Some smarts are charts.

(a) Only I and II follow (b) Only II and III follows
(c) I and III follow (d) I, III and IV follow
(e) None of these

Space for Rough Work

14. **Statements :**

Some big are small.

No small is large.

Some large are tiny.

Conclusions :

I. Some large are not big

II. No big is large

III. Some small are not tiny

IV. Some big are not tiny.

(a) Only I follows (b) Only II follows

(c) Only III follows (d) None of follows

(e) None of these

15. **Statements :**

No killer is a sweater.

No jacket is a sweater.

Some jackets are roses.

Conclusions :

I. Some roses are sweaters.

II. Some roses are not sweaters.

III. No killer is a jacket.

IV. Some jackets are killers.

(a) Either I or II and III follow

(b) Either III or IV and II follow

(c) Either II or III follows

(d) Either I or II and either III or IV follow

(e) None of these

DIRECTIONS (QS. 16 - 20) : *Study the following line graphs which show the production (in, 0000 units) and percentage exported of scooters,. Motorbikes and cars respectively over the years.*

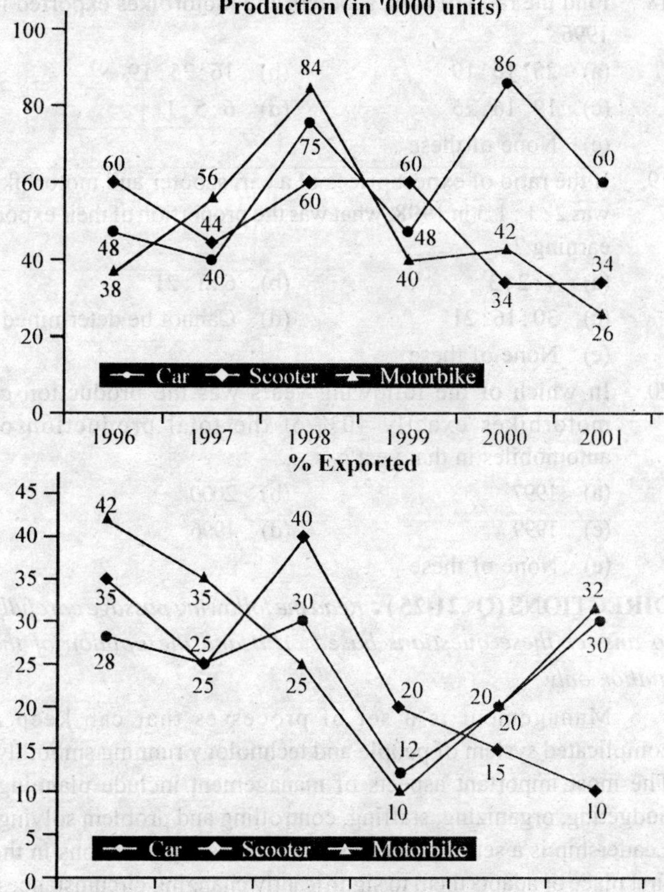

16. In which of the following years was the production of cars more than 50% of the total production?

(a) 2000 (b) 2001

(c) 1998 (d) 1996

(e) None of these

17. Find the total number of automobiles exported in the year 1999 :

(a) 2,27,600 (b) 2,07,600

(c) 2,17,600 (d) 2,20,000

(e) None of these

Space for Rough Work

18. Find the ratio of cars, scooters and motorbikes exported in 1996:
    (a) 25 : 16 : 19 (b) 16 : 25 : 19
    (c) 19 : 16 : 25 (d) 6 : 5 : 1
    (e) None of these
19. If the ratio of export prices of a car, scooter and motorbike was 2 : 1 : 1.5 in 1998, what was the proportion of their export earning ?
    (a) 4 : 2 : 3 (b) 6 : 1 : 21
    (c) 30 : 16 : 21 (d) Cannot be determined
    (e) None of these
20. In which of the following years was the production of motorbikes exactly 40% of the total production of automobiles in that year?
    (a) 1997 (b) 2000
    (c) 1999 (d) 1996
    (e) None of these

DIRECTIONS (Qs.21-25) : *Read the following passage carefully to answer these questions based on it and the opinion of the author only.*

Management is a set of processes that can keep a complicated system of people and technology running smoothly. The most important aspects of management include planning, budgeting, organizing, staffing, controlling and problem solving. Leadership is a set of processes that creates organizations in the first place or adapts them to significantly changing circumstances. Leadership defines what the future should look like, aligns people with that vision, and inspires them to make it happen despite the obstacles. This distinction is absolutely crucial for our purposes here. Successful transformation is 70 to 90 percent leadership and only 10 to 30 percent management. Yet for historical reasons, many organisations today don't have much leadership. And almost everyone thinks about the problem here as one of managing change.

For most of this century, as we created thousands and thousands of large organisations for the first time in human history, we didn't have enough good managers to keep all those bureaucracies functioning. So many companies and universities developed management programmes and hundreds and thousands of people were encouraged to learn management on the job. And they did. But, people were taught little about leadership. To some degree, management was the main item on the twentieth-century agenda because that's what was needed. For every entrepreneur or business builder who was, a leader, we needed hundreds of managers to run their ever growing enterprises.

Unfortunately for us today, this emphasis on management has often been institutionalized in corporate cultures that discourage employees from learning how to lead. Ironically, past success is usually the key ingredient in producing this outcome. The syndrome, as I have observed it on many occasions, goes like this: success creates some degree of marked dominance, which in turn produces much growth. After a while keeping the ever larger organisation under control becomes the primary challenge. So attention turns inward, and managerial competencies are nurtured. With a strong emphasis on management but not leadership, bureaucracy and an inward focus take over. But with continued success, the result mostly of market dominance, the problem often goes unaddressed and an unhealthy arrogance begins to evolve. All of these characteristics then make any transformation effort much more difficult.

Arrogant managers can over evaluate their current performance and competitive position, listen poorly, and learn slowly. Inwardly focussed employees can smother those who want to respond to shifting conditions. And the lack of leadership leaves no force inside these organisations to break out of the morass.

21. Why did companies and universities develop programmes to prepare managers in large numbers?
    (a) Companies and universities wanted to generate funds through these programmes
    (b) Organisations wanted to create communication network through trained managers
    (c) Large number of organisations were created and they needed managers in good numbers
    (d) Only trained managers could lead an organisation to success
    (e) None of these

Space for Rough Work

22. Management education was emphasized in the management programmes because:
    (a) motivating employees was thought to be done by managers
    (b) organisations wanted to create a powerful guiding coalition
    (c) establishing direction was the main force of organisations
    (d) management was the main item of agenda in organisations
    (e) None of these
23. What according to the author is leadership?
    (a) Inspiring people to realise the vision
    (b) Planning and budgeting resources
    (c) Carrying out the crucial function of manager
    (d) Keep the technology running smoothly
    (e) None of these
24. Which of the following characteristics help organisations in their transformations efforts ?
    (a) Bureaucratic and inward looking approach
    (b) A strong and dogmatic culture
    (c) Emphasis on leadership rather than management
    (d) Emphasis on customer satisfaction
    (e) None of these
25. Why were people taught little about leadership in management programmes?
    (a) Enough study material was not available
    (b) Leadership was considered a political phenomenon
    (c) Focus of these programmes was on developing managers
    (d) Managers are market-oriented persons
    (e) None of the above

DIRECTIONS (Qs. 26-30) : *Rearrange the following six sentences (A), (B), (C), (D), (E) and (F) in the proper sequence to form a meaningful paragraph, then answer the questions given below them.*

A. Picture a termite colony, occupying a tall mud hump on an African plain

B. Hungry predators often invade the colony and unsettle the balance.

C. The colony flourishes only if the portion of soldiers to workers remain roughly the same, so that the queen and the workers can be protected by the soldiers, and the queen and the soldiers can be serviced by workers.

D. But its fortunes are presently restored, because the immobile queen walled in well below ground level, lays eggs not only large enough numbers, but also in the varying proportions required.

E. The hump is alive with worker termites and solider termites going about their distinct kind of business.

F. How can we account for her mysterious ability to respond like this to events on the distant surface

26. Which of the following should be the **FIRST** sentence?
    (a) A (b) B
    (c) C (d) D
    (e) E
27. Which of the following should be the **SECOND** sentence?
    (a) A (b) B
    (c) C (d) D
    (e) E
28. Which of the following should be the **THIRD** sentence?
    (a) A (b) B
    (c) C (d) D
    (e) E
29. Which of the following should be the **FOURTH** sentence?
    (a) A (b) B
    (c) C (d) D
    (e) E
30. Which of the following should be the **FIFTH** sentence?
    (a) A (b) B
    (c) C (d) D
    (e) E

DIRECTIONS (Qs. 31-35) : *In each of these questions a group of letters is given followed by four combinations of numbers codes lettered (a), (b), (c) and (d). The group of letters is to be coded with the numbers codes and the condition given below. The 'serial number of the number combination', which correctly represents the letter group, is your answer.*

Letters	D	J	K	Q	H	V	N	E	B	A
Numbers Codes	3	9	7	6	4	8	2	1	5	0

Conditions : If the first or the last letter or both in the letter group is /are a vowel then the same is/are to be coded by symbol #.

Space for Rough Work

31. EHNDJV
(a) #42389 (b) 142398
(c) #42398 (d) 14239#
(e) None of these

32. KQDJNH
(a) 763942 (b) 736924
(c) #36924 (d) #63924
(e) None of these

33. AJNVQE
(a) #9286# (b) 09286#
(c) #92861 (d) 092861
(e) None of these

34. QHJVND
(a) 648923 (b) 649823
(c) #49823 (d) 64892#
(e) None of these

35. JKEDHA
(a) 97#34# (b) 971340
(c) 971430 (d) 97134#
(e) None of these

DIRECTIONS (Qs.36-40) : *What will come in place of the question mark (?) in the following equations ?*

36. $2567 \div 17 \times 3 = ? + 180$
(a) 51 (b) 271
(c) 273 (d) 73
(e) None of these

37. $\frac{3}{8}$ of $\frac{4}{7}$ of $\frac{7}{12}$ of 1375= ?
(a) 185 (b) 175
(c) 285 (d) 275
(e) None of these

38. $10^{7.5} \times 5^{2.5} \times 2^{2.5} = 10^{?}$
(a) 10 (b) 12.5
(c) 9.5 (d) 11.5
(e) None of these

39. 56% of 958 + 67% of 1008 = ?% of 2000
(a) 60.592 (b) 47.622
(c) 42.86 (d) 91.455
(e) None of these

40. $(?)^2 + (164)^2 = (307)^2 - 272$
(a) 151 (b) 189
(c) 211 (d) 259
(e) None of these

DIRECTIONS (Qs. 41-45) : *Each of the following series consists of seven figures, two of which at the ends are unnumbered. One of the five numbered figures does not fit into the series. Find out the figure.*

41.
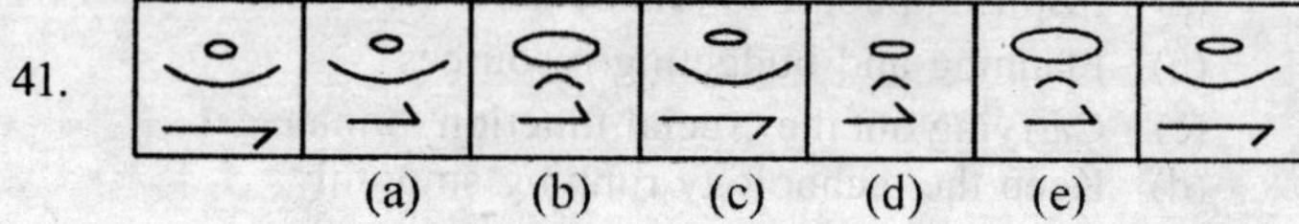

42.
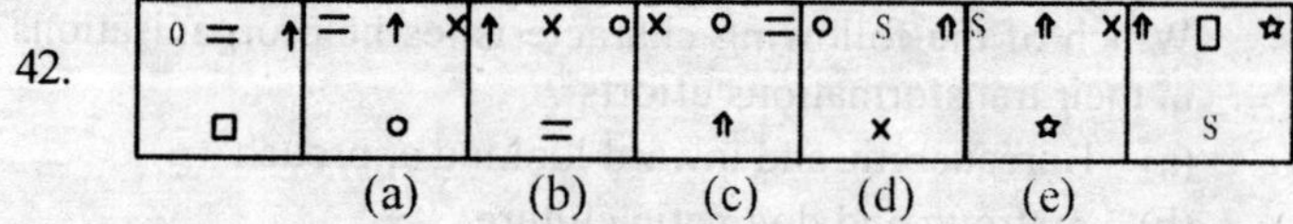

43.
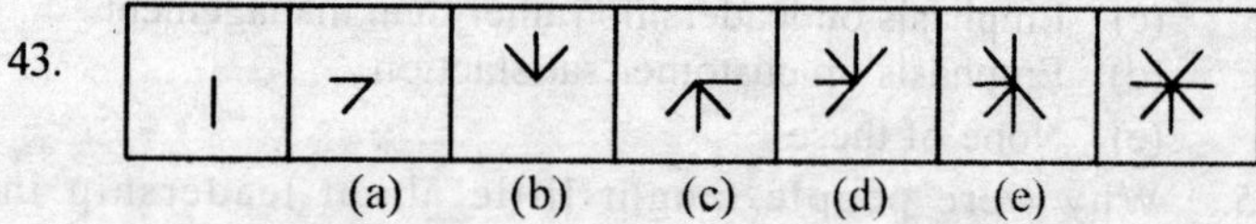

44.
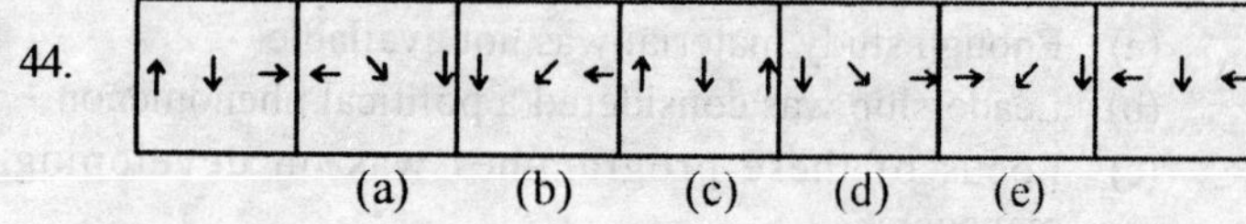

45.
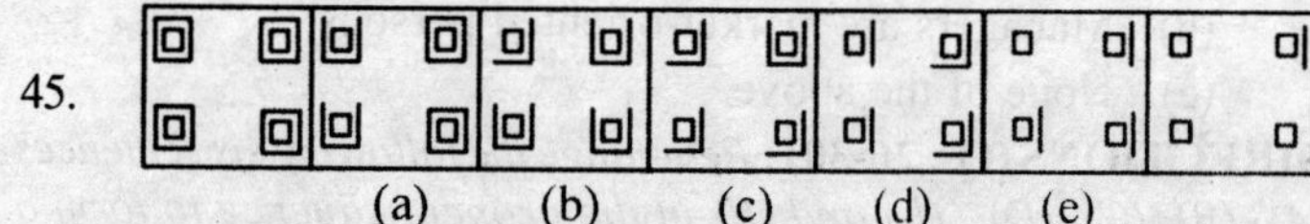

DIRECTION (Qs. 46 - 50) : *In each of these questions, a sentence has one or two blanks, each blank indicating the something has been omitted. Beneath the sentence are given four words or a set of word. Choose the word or the set of words for each blank that best fits the meaning of the sentence as a whole.*

Space for Rough Work

46. He was .... very clever, but he .... performed excellently.
(a) certainly- obviously
(b) never- also
(c) not- always
(d) rarely- seldom
(e) None of these

47. A .... analysis of these substances will show that they differ ....
(a) random- minutely
(b) detailed- essentially
(c) careful- completely
(d) final- Structurally
(e) None of these

48. When the .... polished the stones, they gleamed with a breath-taking brilliance.
(a) graphologist (b) cosmetologist
(c) lapidary (d) beagle
(e) None of these

49. As .... head of the organisation, he attended social functions and civil meetings, but had no .... in the formulation of company policy.
(a) hypothetical-vote
(b) titular-voice
(c) nominal-competition
(d) former-pride
(e) None of these

50. The perpetual spinning of particles is much like that of a top, with one significant difference, unlike the top, the particles have no need to be wound up, for .... is one of their .... properties.
(a) revolution- radical
(b) rotation- intrinsic
(c) motion- intangible
(d) acceleration- hypothetical
(e) None of these

DIRECTIONS (51-55) : *These questions are based on the table and the pie charts given below :*

Global Top Brands

Brand	Rank in 2002	Rank in 2003	Value in 2003 in $ billion
Coca-cola	2	1	70.3
Microsoft	1	2	65.2
IBM	3	3	51.8
GE	5	4	42.3
Intel	4	5	31.1
Nokia	10	6	29.4
Disney	7	7	28.0
McDonald's	6	8	24.7
Marlboro	9	9	22.2
Mercedes	8	10	21.4

Split-up by value of top 5 brands of luxury goods in 2003 (Value $18.9 billion)

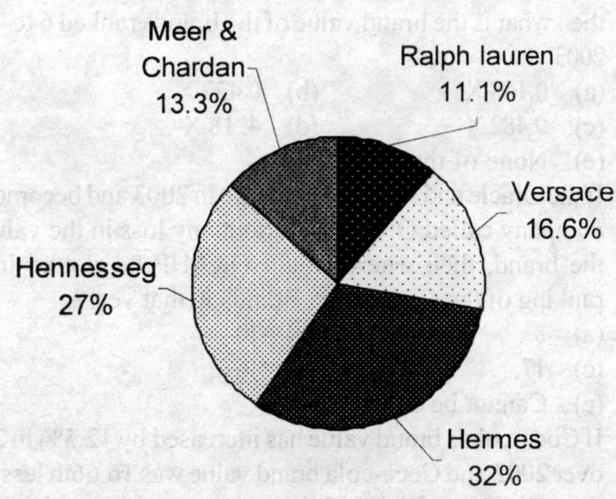

Space for Rough Work

Split-up by value of top 5 brands of Technology in 2003
(Value $160 billion)

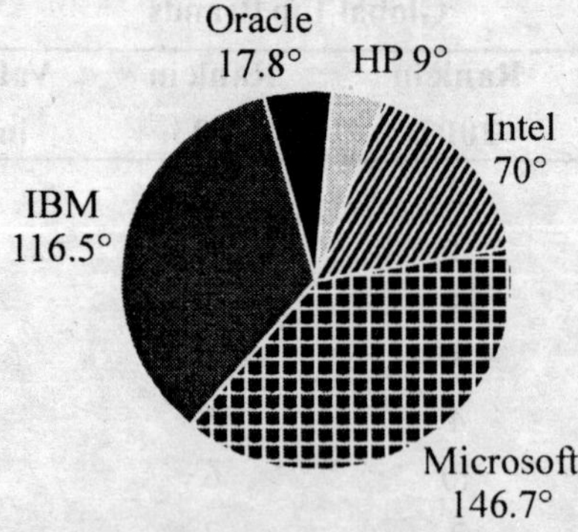

51. What is the difference in the value of Global Top Brands which have an improved ranking in 2003 over that of 2002 and those whose ranking has deteriorated from 2002 to 2003?
(a) $ 4 million (b) $ 4 billion
(c) $ 400 million (d) $ 40 million
(e) None of these

52. If the brand value of the Global Top 5 brands in 2003 is X, then what is the brand value of the brands ranked 6 to 10 in 2003?
(a) 0.148 X (b) 0.422 X
(c) 0.482 X (d) 4. 18 X
(e) None of these

53. If the Oracle and HP were to merge in 2003 and become one company called ORAHP, without any loss in the value of the brand, then where would ORAHP be slotted in the ranking of the Global Top Brands in that year?
(a) 8 (b) 10
(c) 17 (d) 16
(e) Cannot be determined

54. If Coca-cola's brand value has increased by 12.5% in 2003 over 2002 and Coca-cola brand value was 16.66th less than that of Microsoft in 2002 then what was the brand value of Microsoft in 2002?
(a) $ 62. 48 billion (b) $ 79.11 billion
(c) $ 68 billion (d) $ 74.97 billion
(e) None of these

55. If Ralph Lauren and Hermes were to join hands and form a superbrand called 'Ralher' then what would be the rating if 'Ralher' be in the Global Top Brands in 2003 given that Oracle is ranked 87th and HP is ranked 71st in the list in 2003?
(a) Greater than 10 and less than 70
(b) Greater than 10 and less than 71
(c) Between 71 and 87
(d) Greater than 88 and less than 100
(e) None of these

DIRECTIONS (Qs. 56-60): *Use the following series of elements (alpha-number-symbol) to answer these questions. Every two-digit number (given in brackets) is to be treated as single number.*

2 ★ 8 5 6 B 9 $ Q 3 E 1 7 R D 4 £ (13) U ● K (18) A (14) P

56. Four of the following five groups of elements are alike in a certain way and so form a group. Which one **does not** belong to that group ?
(a) 2 ★ 8 (b) 5 6 B
(c) Q $ 9 (d) 1 3 E
(e) D R 7

57. If each alphabet has a value of zero, each symbol (i.e., ★, $ and ●) has a value equivalent to the square of the numeral that immediately precedes the symbol or the value of 1 if it is not immediately preceded by a numeral, what will be the sum of the values of the first 10 elements of the series starting from the left end ?
(a) 118 (b) 46
(c) 79 (d) 107
(e) None of these

58. If each of the letters in the above series of elements is given a value equivalent to its serial number in the English alphabet, what will be the difference between the sum of the consonants and the sum of the vowels used in the series ?
(a) 109 (b) 41
(c) 82 (d) 27
(e) None of these

Space for Rough Work

59. Which of the following groups of elements will come in the place of the question-mark in the series of elements given below?
6 8 2 $ B 5 E Q 9 ? £ D 7
(a) ● (13) 4 (b) 4 (13) ●
(c) U £ D (d) ● (13) £
(e) None of these

60. BQ in the above series is related in ER in a similar way as AP is related to
(a) RD (b) U ●
(c) KA (d) Q 3
(e) 6 B

DIRECTIONS (Qs. 61-65) : *Find out the* ***approximate*** *value which should come in place of the question mark in the following questions. (You are not expected to find the exact value.)*

61. $\sqrt{45689} = ?$
(a) 180 (b) 415
(c) 150 (d) 210
(e) 300

62. $\frac{(10008.99)^2}{10009.001} \times \sqrt{3589} \times 0.4987 = ?$
(a) 3000 (b) 300000
(c) 3000000 (d) 5000
(e) 9000000

63. 399.9+ 206 × 11.009= ?
(a) 2800 (b) 6666
(c) 4666 (d) 2400
(e) 2670

64. $\frac{2}{5} + \frac{7}{8} \times \frac{17}{19} \div \frac{6}{5} = ?$
(a) 1 (b) $\frac{1}{2}$
(c) $2\frac{1}{2}$ (d) $\frac{3}{4}$
(e) $\frac{9}{11}$

65. $(299.99999)^3 = ?$
(a) 27000000 (b) 9000000000
(c) 180000 (d) 2.7×10^9
(e) 2700000

DIRECTIONS (Qs. 66-70) : *Each of the questions below consists of a question and two statements numbered (I) and (II) given below it. You have to decide whether the data provided in the statements are sufficient to answer the question. Read both the statements and give answer*

(a) if statement (I) alone is sufficient, but statement (II) alone is not sufficient.
(b) if statement (II) alone is sufficient, but statement (I) alone is not sufficient
(c) if both statements together are sufficient, but neither statement alone is sufficient.
(d) if each statement alone is sufficient
(e) if both statements together are sufficient

66. What is the volume of a given cylinder? It is given that the cylinder is within the cube touching all the vertical faces and a cone is inside the cylinder. It is also given that heights are same with the same base.
(I) Volume of the cone is known.
(II) Total surface area of the cube is known.

67. Is $n^x - n$ divisible by x? It is given that x and n are natural numbers.
(I) Value of n is known.
(II) Value of x is known.

68. Is $\frac{5^{2(abc)}+1}{abcabc}$ the simplest form of a fraction? It is given that a, b and c are natural numbers.
(I) c is an odd number.
(II) a, b and c are odd numbers.

Space for Rough Work

69. What is the sum of the perimeter of the circle denoted by centre O and the triangle AFG shown in the given figure?

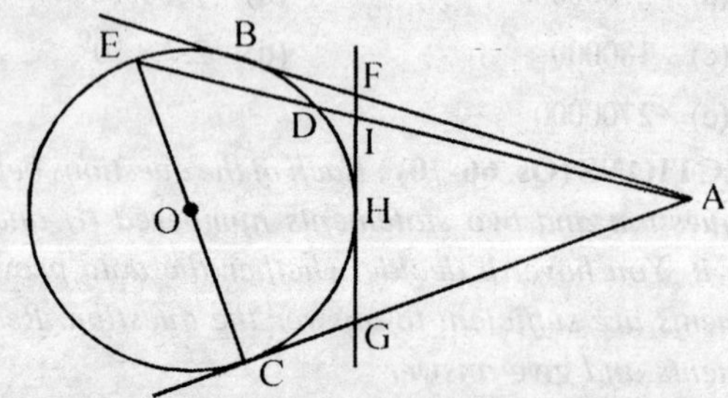

(I) Lengths of AD and DE are known.

(II) Lengths of AC and ED are known.

70. On a stretch of water there is no current from P to Q but there is current from Q to R. In such a circumstance, Vicky takes 3 hours to row downstream from P to R and 3½ hours upstream from R to P. Suppose the circumstances change and now the earlier current is there all the way from P to R. How long will Vicky take to row from R to P in the changed circumstances?

(I) Ratio of the speed of Vicky in still water and that of the stream is 6 : 1.

(II) In the changed circumstances, his downward journey would have taken $2\frac{3}{4}$ hrs.

DIRECTIONS (Qs. 71-75) : *In each of the questions given below which one of the five answer figures on the right should come after the problem figures on the left, if the sequence were continued ?*

71. **Problem Figures**

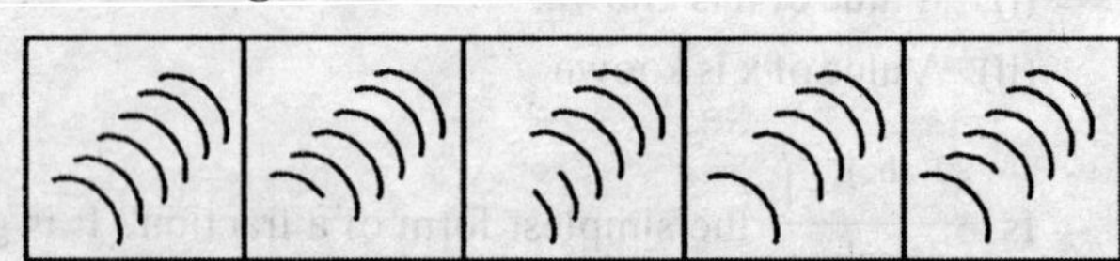

Answer Figures

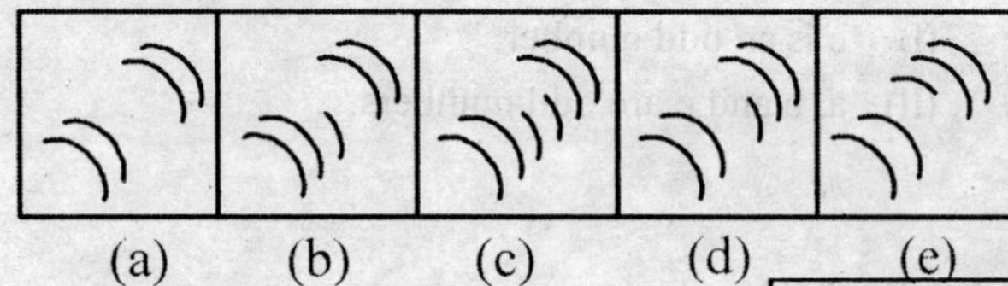

(a) (b) (c) (d) (e)

72. **Problem Figures :**

Answer Figures :

(a) (b) (c) (d) (e)

73. **Problem Figures :**

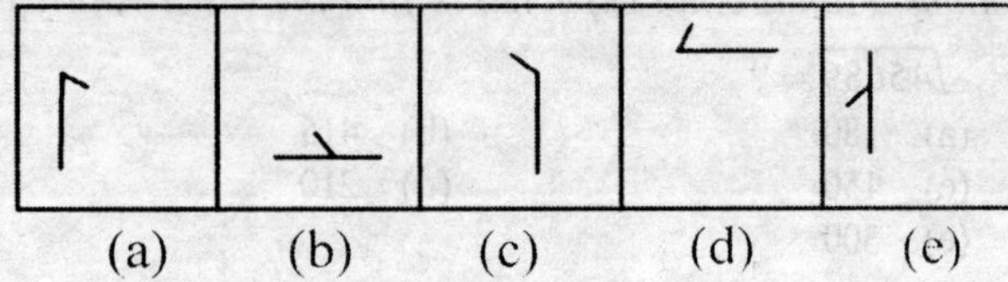

(a) (b) (c) (d) (e)

Answer Figures :

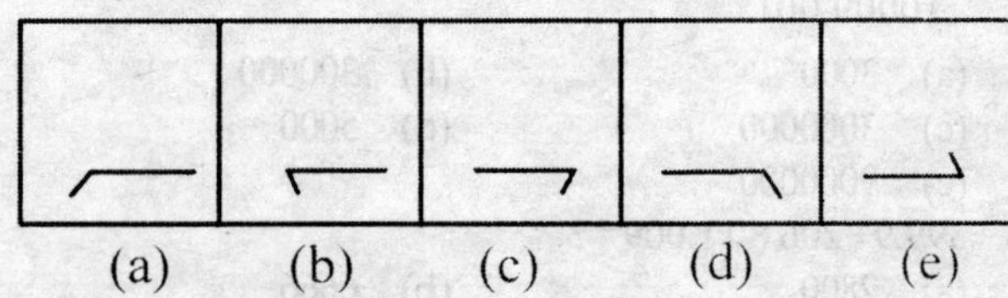

(a) (b) (c) (d) (e)

74. **Problem Figures :**

Answer Figures :

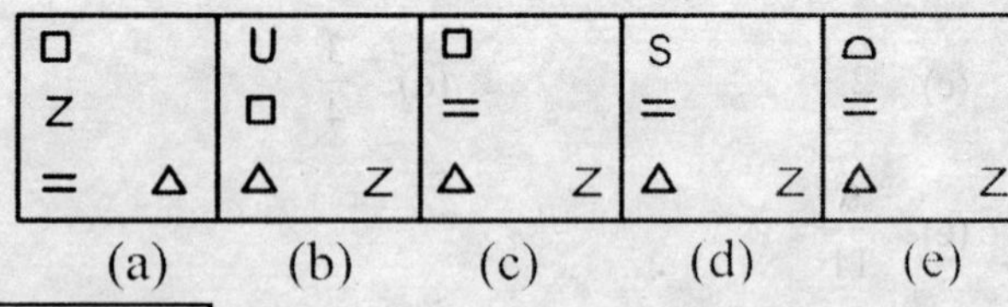

(a) (b) (c) (d) (e)

Space for Rough Work

75. **Problem Figures :**

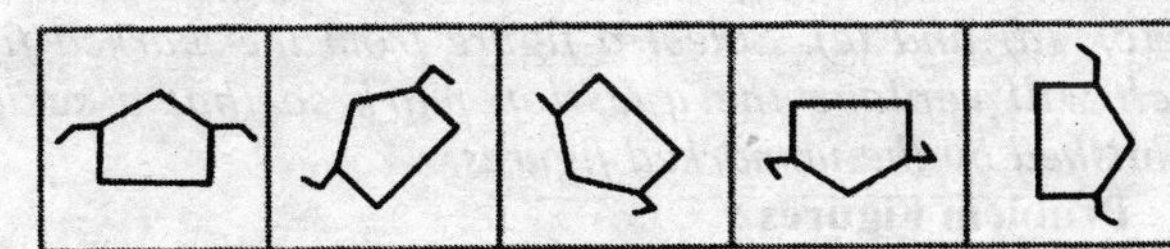

Answer Figures :

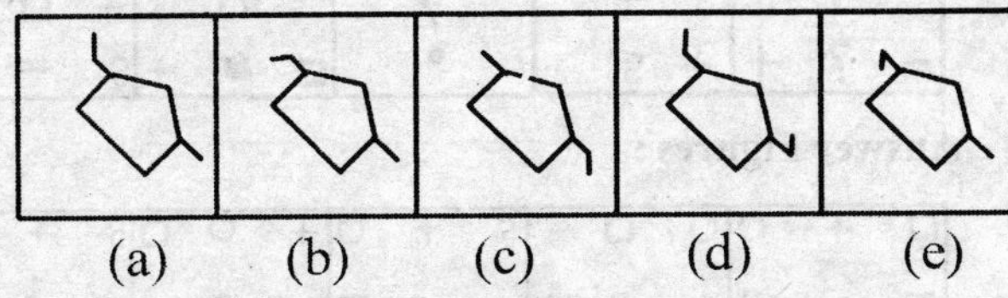

(a) (b) (c) (d) (e)

DIRECTIONS(Qs. 76-80): *What will come in place of the question mark (?) in the following number series?*

76. 2 9 30 105 ? 2195

(a) 432 (b) 426
(c) 440 (d) 436
(e) None of these

77. 3 4 12 45 ? 1005

(a) 152 (b) 198
(c) 144 (d) 192
(e) None of these

78. 1 3 9 31 ? 651

(a) 97 (b) 127
(c) 129 (d) 109
(e) None of these

79. 5 ? 4 7.5 17 45

(a) 3.5 (b) 3
(c) 2.5 (d) 2
(e) None of these

80. 15 30 ? 40 8 48

(a) 10 (b) 20
(c) 18 (d) 12
(e) None of these

81. In a certain code language, 134 means good and tasty 478 means see good pictures and 729 means pictures are faint. Which of the following numerical symbols stands for **see** ?

(a) 1 (b) 2
(c) 7 (d) 8
(e) None of these

82. In a certain code, EASE is written as GUCG. How is CUT written in that code ?

(a) UWE (b) VWE
(c) EWU (d) CWF
(e) None of these

83. If only the consonants in the word MEAT are changed in such a way that each of them becomes the next letter in the English alphabet and the remaning letters are kept unchanged, then how many meaningful words can be formed with the new set of letters using each letter only once in a word ?

(a) Four (b) Two
(c) Three (d) One
(e) None of these

84. Unscramble the letters in the given words and find the odd one out.

(a) UMRSME (b) EIWNTR
(c) PIGRSN (d) LCUOD
(e) None of these

85. At an enquiry office at a railway station, a passenger was told that a train for New Delhi has left 15 minutes ago, but after every 45 minutes a train leaves for New Delhi. The next train will leave at 8.30 p.m. At what time was this information given to the passanger ?

(a) 7.45 pm (b) 8.00 pm
(c) 8.15 pm (d) 8.05 pm
(e) None of these

Space for Rough Work

DIRECTIONS (Qs. 86-90) : *Study the following letters and their corresponding digit codes followed by certain conditions of coding and answer the questions given below them by finding out which of the digit combinations given in (1), (2), (3) and (4) is the coded form of the letter groups given in each question and mark your answers accordingly. If none of the coded forms represents the letter group mark answer as (5), i.e. None of these.*

Number	1	2	3	4	5	6	7	8	9
Symbol	x	*	?	÷	$	•	+	!	Δ

Conditions :

(i) If any number begins by odd number then the odd number is symbolised by @.

(ii) If any number ends by even number then the even number is symbolised as ©.

86. Which of the following will be the symbol of 673258 ?
(a) • + ? * $!
(b) @ + ? * !
(c) @ ? + $ * !
(d) • + ? * $ ©
(e) None of these

87. Which of the following will be the symbol of 236475 ?
(a) ? * • ÷ *x*
(b) © ? • ÷ + @
(c) *x* ? • ÷ + @
(d) © ? 1 ÷ + $
(e) None of these

88. Which of the following will be the symbol of 846721?
(a) © ÷ • + * *x*
(b) ! ÷ © ? • + @
(c) ! ÷ • + * *x*
(d) © ÷ • + * *x*
(e) None of these

89. Which of the folowing will be the symbol of 178524?
(a) @ + ! $ *©
(b) *x* + ! $ ©
(c) @ + !$ * ÷
(d) * + ! $ ÷
(e) None of these

90. Which of the following will be the symbol of 25486 ?
(a) *$ ÷ Δ
(b) *$ ÷ !©
(c) ©$ ÷ !•
(d) *$! ÷ •
(e) None of these

DIRECTIONS (Qs. 91-95) : *Each of the following questions consists of unmarked figures followed by five figures marked (a), (b), (c), (d) and (e). Select a figure from the marked figures which will replace the question mark so that a series be established by the unmarked figures.*

91. **Problem Figures :**

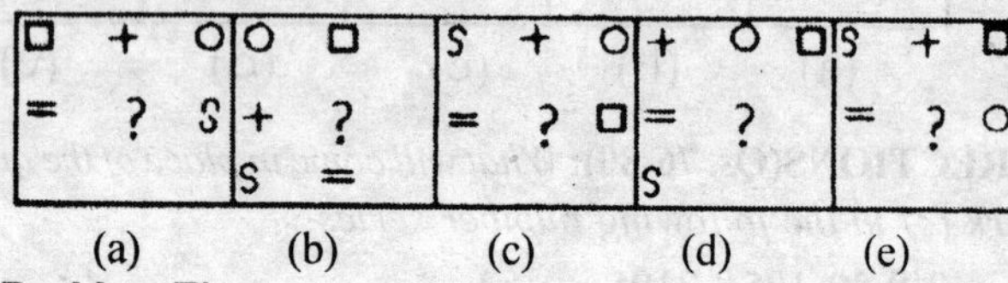

Answer Figures :

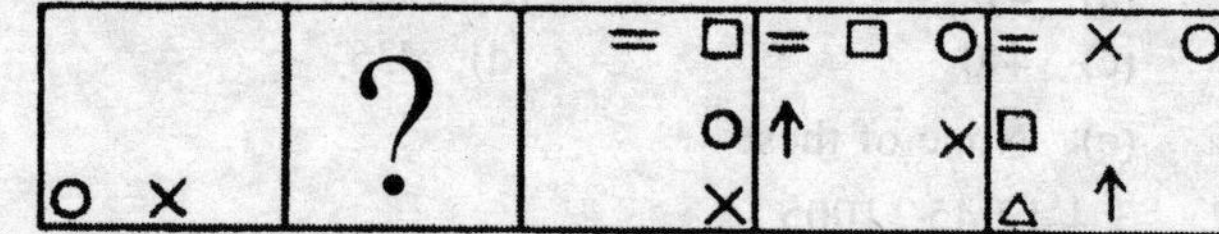

(a) (b) (c) (d) (e)

92. **Problem Figures :**

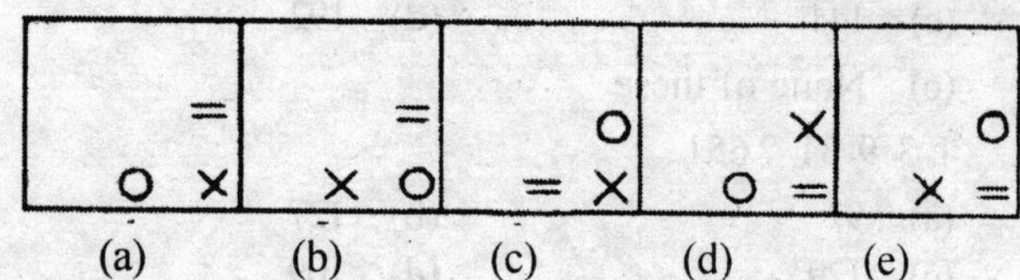

Answer Figures :

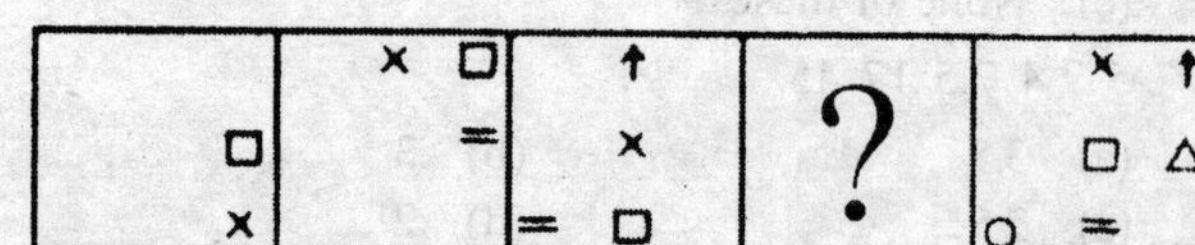

(a) (b) (c) (d) (e)

93. **Problem Figures :**

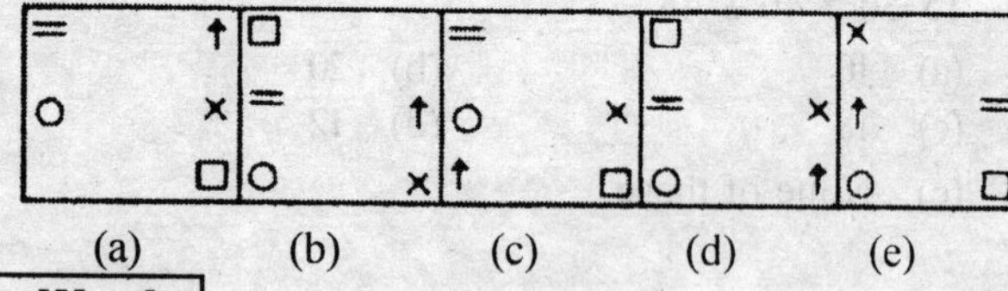

Answer Figures :

(a) (b) (c) (d) (e)

Space for Rough Work

94. **Problem Figures :**

Answer Figures :

(a) (b) (c) (d) (e)

95. **Problem Figures :**

Answer Figures :

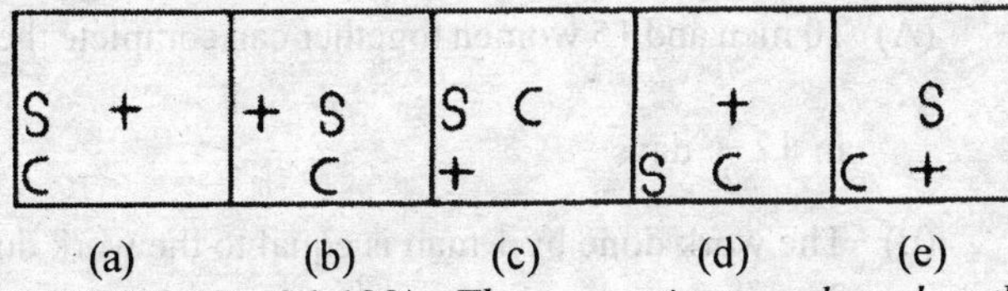

(a) (b) (c) (d) (e)

DIRECTIONS (Qs. 96-100) *: These questions are based on the following information :*

There are five high schools A, B, C, D and E in a certain town. Total number of high school students of the town is 1800. The strength of school A is 20% and that of B is 37.5% of the total number of students of the town. D and E have equal strengths. 40% students of A know only one language–Hindi. 60% students of D know only one language–English. There are 111 more students in B who know Hindi exclusively than the number of students of D who know English only. 55 students of C know Hindi but not English. 15 students of D know both the languages. The strength of C is 37.5% of the strength of A. Two-fifths of students of B know both the languages. The number of students of C who know English but not Hindi is 40 less than the number of the same category of B. 97 students of E know only English and 20% students of A know both the languages. 28 students of E know both the languages.

96. What is the percentage of the number of students who know both the languages?
(a) 22.33 (b) 22.66
(c) 22.22 (d) 22.5
(e) None of these

97. What is the difference between the number of students who know English and those who know Hindi exclusively?
(a) 250 (b) 200
(c) 400 (d) 360
(e) None of these

98. The number of students who know only Hindi of C is how many times those who know both the languages of the same school?
(a) $4\frac{2}{3}$ (b) $3\frac{1}{3}$
(c) $4\frac{1}{3}$ (d) $3\frac{2}{3}$
(e) None of these

99. Find the percentage of the number of students who know Hindi exclusively.
(a) 44.44 (b) 55.55
(c) 33.33 (b) 22.22
(e) None of these

100. Mohan is thirteenth from the left end in a row of children. Prabir is twelfth from the right end and eighteenth from the left end. How many children are towards the right of Mohan in that row?
(a) 12 (b) 17
(c) 18 (d) 15
(e) None of these

DIRECTIONS (Qs. 101 - 105) : *A word in capital letters is followed by four words. Choose the word that is most nearly opposite in meaning to the word given in capital letters.*

101. PREDILECTION
(a) Antipathy (b) Ignorance
(c) Dissonance (d) Disharmony
(e) None of these

102. DOCILE
(a) Unmanageable (b) Dutiful
(c) Submissive (d) Painful
(e) None of these

Space for Rough Work

103. EQUIVOCAL
(a) Mistaken (b) Quaint
(c) Clear (d) Universal
(e) None of these

104. PROSAIC
(a) Pensive (b) Imaginative
(c) Rhetorical (d) Pacified
(e) None of these

105. LEVITY
(a) Praise (b) Blame
(c) Solemnity (d) Frivolity
(e) None of these

DIRECTIONS (Qs. 106-110) : *The following questions are accompanied by three statements (A), (B) and (C). You have to determine which statements(s) is/ are sufficient/ necessary to answer the questions.*

106. How much minimum marks are required to pass an examination ?
(A) Student A secured 38% marks in the examination and failed by 8 marks. Student B secured 42% marks in the same examination and got 12 more than the minimum pass marks.
(B) Student A secured 35% of the total marks in the examination and failed by 23 marks. If he had secured 25 more marks, his percentage of marks would have been 40%.
(C) A student will be declared passed if he secures 39.60% of the total marks.
(a) Any two of them (b) Only A
(c) C and either A or B (d) Either A or B only
(e) None of these

107. What will be the share of R in the profit earned by V, R and A together ?
(A) They together invested an amount of Rs 54000 for a period of one year.
(B) R's investment was 25% less than V's and 50% more than A's.
(C) The profit of V is Rs 4000 more than that of A.
(a) Only A and B together
(b) B and either A or C only
(c) Only B
(d) Only B and C together
(e) None of these

108. What was the profit earned on the cost price by Mahesh by selling an article ?
(A) He got 15% concession on the labelled price in buying that article.
(B) He sold it for Rs 3060
(C) He earned a profit of 2% on the labelled price.
(a) Only A and B together are required
(b) Only B and C together are required
(c) Only either A or C and B together are required
(d) All A, B and C together are required
(e) None of these

109. 15 men and 20 women work together for 5 days and then 5 men and 8 women leave the group. In how many days will the remaining work be finished by the remaining people ?
(A) 10 men and 15 women together can complete the work in $17\frac{1}{2}$ days
(B) The work done by 1 man is equal to the work done by 2 women.
(C) 20 men alone can do the entire work in 15 days.
(a) Any one of them (b) Either A or C
(c) Only B (d) Any two of them
(e) None of these

110. What is the cost of flooring a rectangular hall ?
(A) The length and the breadth of the hall are in the ratio of 3 : 2.
(B) The length of the hall is 48 m and the cost of flooring is Rs 850 per square metre.
(C) The perimeter of the hall is 160 m and the cost of flooring is Rs 850 per square metre.
(a) Only A and B (b) Only A and C
(c) Only C (d) Any two of the three
(e) None of these

Space for Rough Work

DIRECTIONS (Qs. 111-114) : *Read the following information to answer the questions that follow.*

For getting selected as a Marketing Manager in a company, a candidate must :

I. be a graduate with at least 50% marks.

II. have secured at least 40% marks in the Written Test.

III. not be less than 24 years and more than 29 years as on October 10, 1997.

IV. should have work experience of atleast two years as an officer. However, if a candidate.

V. fulfils all other criteria except (IV) above but has a Diploma in Marketing Management, his/her case is to be referred to the Director, Marketing.

VI. fulfils all other criteria except (III) above but has worked as Marketing Officer atleast for three years, his/her case is to be referred to the Director, Markeing.

Based on the above criteria and the information given in each of the questions below you have to take the decision in respect of each case. You are not to assume anything. These cases are given to you as on October 10, 1997. Give answer

(a) if the canddate is to be appointed.

(b) if the candidate is not to be appointed.

(c) if the data given are not sufficient to take the decision.

(d) if to be referred to the General Manager, Marketing.

(e) none of these

111. Amit Khanna, born on 5 June, 1973, has done his Post-Graduation in Marketing Management with first class. He has secured 50% marks in the Written Test. He has been working in an organisation as a Marketing Officer for the last four years.

112. Rohit Verma has been working in an organisation as on officer for the last ten years. His date of birth is 17 February, 1964. He has secured 60% marks in the Degree Examination and 40% marks in the Written Test.

113. Manju Sharma is a first class Graduate and has a Diploma in Marketing Management. She has secured 50% marks in the Written Test. She was 23 years old as on 5th September 1996.

114. Suman Malhotra is a Graduate with first class and has secured 60% marks in the Written Test. She has been working as an officer for the last three years. She was born on 20th May 1972.

115. A man pointing to a photograph says, "The lady in the photograph is my nephew's maternal grandmother and her son is my sister's brother-in-law. How is the lady in the photograph related to his sister who has no other sister?

(a) Mother (b) Cousin

(c) Mother-in-law (d) Sister-in-law

(e) None of these

DIRECTIONS (Qs. 116-120) : *Study the following graphs and answer the questions that follow :*

CIRCULATION OF MAGAGZINES

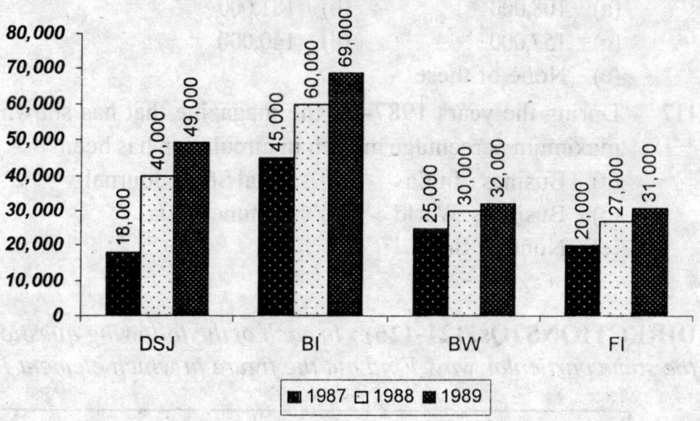

Abbreviations

BI : Business India,

DSJ : Dalal Street Journal

BW : Business World

FI : Fortune India

(Note : Figures are hypothetical and do not reflect actual circulation of the magazines.)

Space for Rough Work

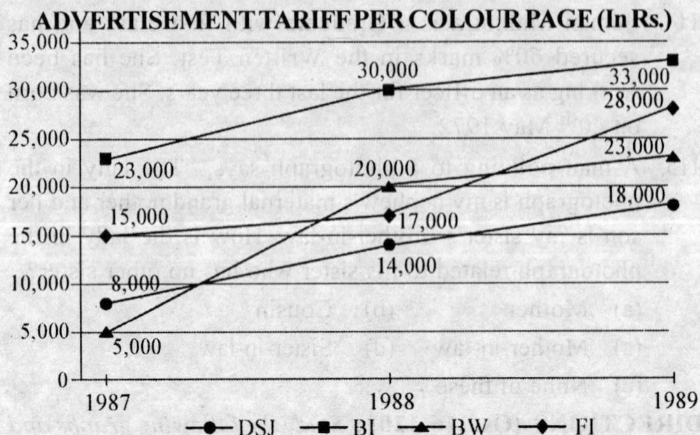

116. The total circulation figure for the four magazines together in 1988 was approximately
(a) 108,000 (b) 181,000
(c) 157,000 (d) 140,000
(e) None of these

117. During the years 1987-89, the magazine that has shown maximum percentage growth in circulation has been
(a) Business India (b) Dalal Street Journal
(c) Business World (d) Fortune India
(e) None of these

118. In 1989, if Fortune India was to charge the same rate to its advertisers as Dalal Street Journal was charging a year ago, their cost of advertisement per thousand copies in Fortune India would
(a) decrease by 50%
(b) increase by Rs. 140
(c) decrease by Rs. 400
(d) increase by 25%
(e) None of these

119. In 1988, the advertisement cost for colour page per thousand copies was the lowest for
(a) Business India (b) Dalal Steel Journal
(c) Business world (d) Fortune India
(e) None of these

120. The advertisement cost of colour page per thousand copies for business world has, from 1987 to 1988
(a) remained the same
(b) decreased by Rs. 200
(c) increased by Rs. 466
(d) increased by Rs. 200
(e) None of these

DIRECTIONS (Qs. 121-125) : *In each of the following questions, in four out of the five figures element I is related to element II in the same particular way. Find out the figure in which element I is not so related to element II.*

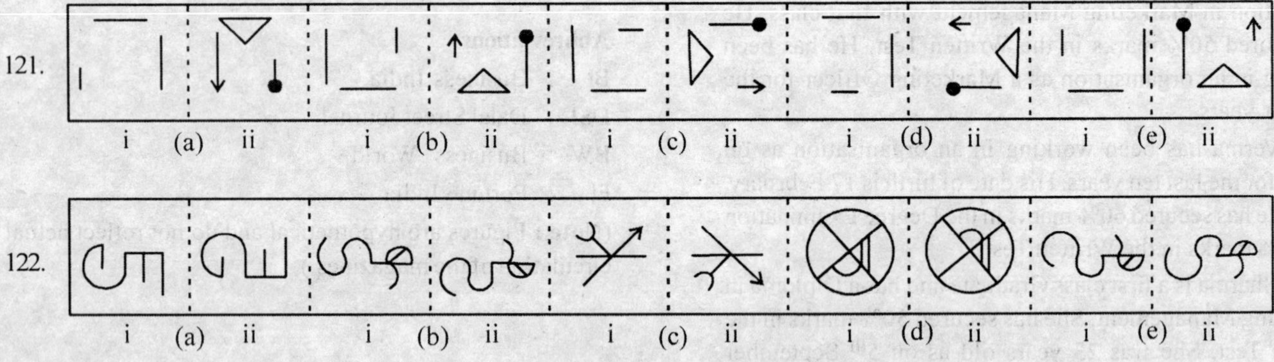

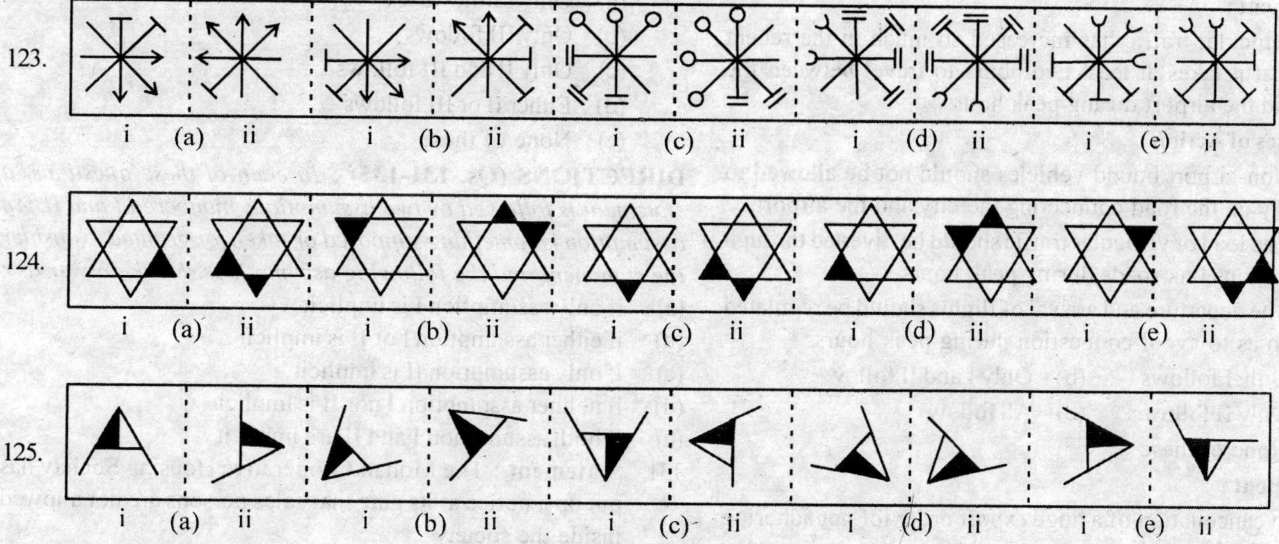

DIRECTIONS (Qs. 126-130) : *Each of these questions has a statement followed by three suggested Courses of Action numbered I, II and III. Assume everything in the statement to be true, and decide which of the given Courses of Action logically follows for pursuing:*

126. **Statement :**

Drinking water supply to New Bombay has been suspended till further orders from Maharashtra Pollution Control Board following pollution of Patalganga river, caused by discharge of effluents from some chemical industries.

Courses of Action :

I. The industries responsible for discharging effluents into the river should be asked to close down immediately.

II. The river water should immediately be treated chemically before resuming supply.

III. The Pollution Control Board should check the nature of effluents being discharged into the river by industries at regular intervals.

(a) All follow (b) Only II and III follow
(c) Only I follows (d) Only III follows
(e) None of these

127. **Statement :**

The Department of Education has recommended that the primary level admission to Government and Government-aided schools should be done purely by random selection and not by admission tests. This is necessitated as the number of admission seekers are much more than the available seats.

Courses of Action :

I. The Government should instruct the private schools also to follow the same practice.

II. The Government should set up an independent body to regulate the primary level admissions.

III. The schools should be asked to select students only from those who stay in the neighbouring areas of the school.

(a) None follows (b) Only II and III follow
(c) Only I follows (d) Only III follows
(e) None of these

Space for Rough Work

128. **Statement :**

The vehicular traffic has increased so much in the recent past that it takes at least two hours to travel between the city and the airport during peak hours.

Courses of Action :

I. Non-airport bound vehicles should not be allowed to ply on the road connecting the city and the airport.

II. The load of vehicular traffic should be diverted through various link roads during peak hours.

III. The departure and arrival of flights should be regulated so as to avoid congestion during peak hours.

(a) Only I follows (b) Only I and II follow
(c) Only II follows (d) All follow
(e) None of these

129. **Statement :**

Due to cancellation of a huge export order for not adhering to the time frame, the company is likely to get into incurring losses in the current financial year.

Courses of Action :

I. The officer-in-charge of the production should be immediately suspended.

II. The goods manufactured for the export order should be sold to other party.

III. The company should change its machinery to maintain the time frame.

(a) None follows (b) Only I and II follow
(c) Only II follows (d) All follow
(e) None of these

130. **Statement :**

A devastating earthquake has ravaged the city killing hundreds of people and rendering many more homeless.

Courses of Action :

I. The entry of outsiders into the city should be stopped.

II. The civic administration should immediately make alternate temporary housing arrangement for the victims.

III. The affected people should immediately be shifted to a safer place.

(a) Only I follows
(b) Only III follows
(c) Only II and III follows
(d) Either II or III follows
(e) None of these

DIRECTIONS (Qs. 131-135) : *In each of these questions, a statement is followed by two assumptions numbered I and II. An assumption is something supposed or taken for granted. Consider the statement and the following assumptions. Mark answer as :*

(a) if only assumption I is implicit
(b) if either assumption I or II is implicit
(c) if only assumption II is implicit
(d) if neither assumption I nor II is implicit
(e) if both assumption I and II are implicit

131. **Statement :** The Mohan Cooperative Housing Society has put up a notice at its gate that sales persons are not allowed inside the society .

Assumptions :

I. All the sales persons will stay away from the Mohan Cooperative Housing Society.

II. The security guard posted at the gate may be able to stop the sales persons entering the society.

132. **Statement :** Bank 'A' has announced reduction of half percentage on the interest rate on retail lending with immediate effect.

Assumptions :

I. Other banks may also reduce their retail lending rates to be in competition.

II. The bank 'A' may be able to attract more customers for availing retail loans.

133. **Statement :** The government has decided to hold the employers responsible for deducting tax at source for all its employees.

Assumptions :

I. The employers may still not arrange to deduct tax at source for its employees.

II. The employees may not allow the employers to deduct tax at source.

Space for Rough Work

134. **Statement :** The Union Government has decided to withdraw existing tax relief on various small savings schemes in a phased manner to augment its tax collection.

Assumptions :

I. People may still continue to keep money in small savings schemes and also pay taxes.

II. The total tax collection may increase substantially.

135. **Statement :** Because of incidental arrival of cyclone, at least this year the government should take help of army to rehabilitate cyclone-affected people.

Assumptions :

I. For every incidental incidence the government should take help of army.

II. To prevent the havoc caused by cyclone, some precautionary scheme is being made.

DIRECTIONS (Qs.136-140) : *Read the following passage carefully to answer these questions based on it and the opinion of the author only.*

Have you ever come across a painting by Picasso, Mondrian, Miro, or any other modem abstract painter of this century, and found yourself engulfed in a brightly coloured canvas which your senses cannot interpret? Many people would tend to denounce abstractionism as senseless trash. These people are disoriented by Miro's bright, fanciful creatures and two-dimensional canvases. They click their tongues and shake their heads at Mondrian's grid works, declaring that the poor guy played too many scrabble games. They silently shake their heads in sympathy for Picasso, whose gruesome, distorted figures must be a reflection of his mental health. Then, standing in front of a work by Charlie Russell, the famous western artist, they'll declare it a work of God. People feel more comfortable with something they can relate to and understand immediately without too much thought. This is the case with the work of Charlie Russell. Being able to recognise the elements in his paintings-trees, horses and cowboys-gives people a safety line to their world of 'reality'. There are some who would disagree when I say abstract art requires more creativity and artistic talent to produce a good piece than does representational art, but there are many weaknesses in their arguments.

People who look down on abstract art have several major arguments to support their beliefs. They feel that artists turn abstract because they are not capable of the technical drafting skills that appear in a Russell; therefore, such artists create an art form that anyone is capable of understanding and that is less time consuming, and then parade it as artistic progress. Secondly, they feel that the purpose of art is to create something of beauty in an orderly, logical composition. Russell's compositions are balanced and rational; everything sits calmly on the canvas, leaving the viewer satisfied that he has seen all there is to see. The modem abstractionists, on the other hand, seem to compose their pieces irrationally. For example, upon seeing Picasso's Guernica, a friend of mine asked me, 'What's the point? Finally, many people feel that art should portray the ideal and real. The exactness of detail in Charlie Russell's work is an example of this. He has been called a great historian because his pieces depict the lifestyle, dress, and events of the times. His subject matter is derived from his own experiences on the trial, and reproduced to the smallest detail.

I agree in part with many of these arguments, and at one time even endorsed them: But now, I believe differently. Firstly, I object to the argument that abstract artists are not capable of drafting. Many abstract artists, such as Picasso, are excellent draftsmen. As his work matured, Picasso become more abstract in order to increase the expressive quality of his work. Guernica was meant as a protest against the bombing of that city by the Germans. To express the terror and suffering of the victims more vividly, he distorted the figures and presented them in a black and white journalistic manner. If he had used representational images and colour, much of the emotional content would have been lost and the piece would not have caused the demand for justice that it did. Secondly, I do not think that a piece must be logical and aesthetically pleasing to be art. The message it conveys to its viewers is more important. It should reflect the ideals and issues of its time and be true to itself, not just a flowery, glossy surface. For example, through his work, Mondrian was trying to present a system of simplicity, logic and rational order. As a result, his pieces did end up looking like a scrabble board. He sees with his eyes. This is the reality he reproduces on' canvas. To the abstract artist, reality is what 'he feels about what his eyes see. This is the reality he interprets on canvas. This can be illustrated by Mondrian's Trees series. You can actually see the progression from the early recognisable, though abstracted trees, to his final solution, the grid system.

Space for Rough Work

A cycle of abstract and representational art began with the first scratching of prehistoric man. From the abstractions of ancient Egypt' to representational, classical Rome, returning to abstractionism in early Christian art and, so on up to the present day, the cycle has been going on. But this day and age may witness its death through the camera. With film, there is no need to produce finely detailed, historical records manually. The camera does this for us more efficiently. May be, representational art would cease to exist. With abstractionism as the victor of the first battle, may be that a different kind of cycle will be touched off. Possibly, some time in the distant future, thousands of years from now, art itself will be physically non-existent. Some artists today believe that once they have planned and constructed a piece in their mind, there is no sense in finishing it with their hands. It has already been done and can never be duplicated.

136. The author argues that many people look down upon abstract art because they feel that:
(a) modern abstract art does not portray
(b) abstract artists are unskilled in matters of technical drafting
(c) abstractionists compose irrationally
(d) all of the above
(e) none of these

137. According to the author, people feel comfortable with representational art because:
(a) they are not engulfed in brightly coloured canvases
(b) they understand the art without putting too much strain on their minds
(c) paintings like Guernica do not .have a point
(d) they do not have to click their tongues and shake their heads in sympathy
(e) none of these

138. In the author's opinion, Picasso's Guernica created a strong demand for justice since:
(a) it was a protest against the German bombing of Guernica
(b) it was a mature work of Picasso, painted when the artist's drafting skills were excellent
(c) Picasso managed to express the emotional content well with his abstract depiction
(d) it depict, the terror and sufferings of the victims in a distorted manner
(e) none of these

139. The author acknowledges that Mondrian's pieces may have ended up looking like scrabble board because:
(a) Mondrian was trying to convey the message of simplicity and rational order
(b) Mondrian learned from his Trees series to evolve a grid system
(c) Mondrian believed in 'grid works' approach to abstractionist painting
(d) many people declared that he played too many scrabble games
(e) none of these

140. The main difference between the abstract artist and the representational artist ill matter of the 'ideal' and the 'real', according to the author, is :
(a) how each chooses to deal with 'reality' on his or her canvas
(b) the superiority *of* interpretation of reality over production of reality
(c) the different values attached by each to being a historian
(d) the varying levels of drafting skills and logical thinking abilities
(e) none of these

DIRECTIONS (Qs. 141-145) : *In each of the following questions, a related pair of figures is followed by five numbered pairs of figures. Select the pair that has a relationship similar to that in the original pair. The best answer is to be selected from a group of fairly close choices.*

141. **Problem Figures** **Answer Figures**

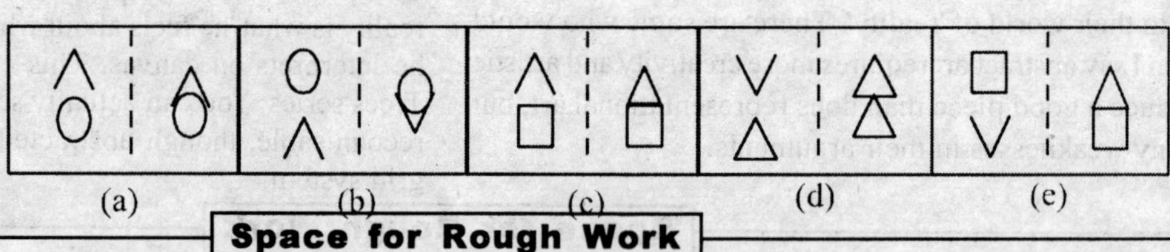

(a) (b) (c) (d) (e)

Space for Rough Work

142. **Problem Figures** **Answer Figures**

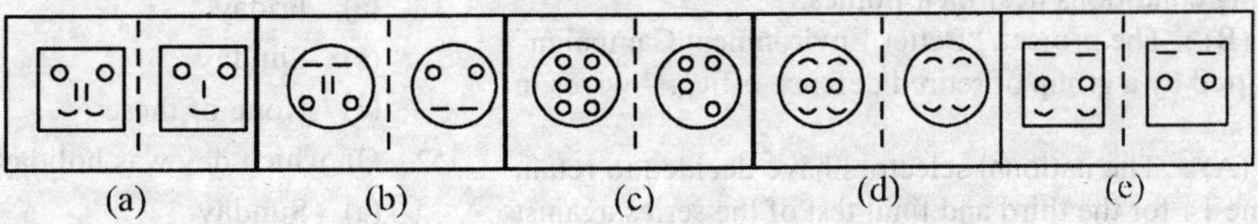

143. **Problem Figures** **Answer Figures**

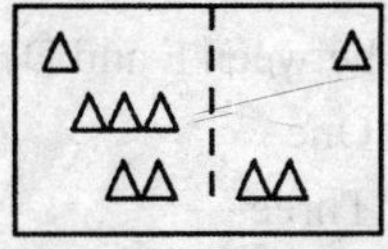

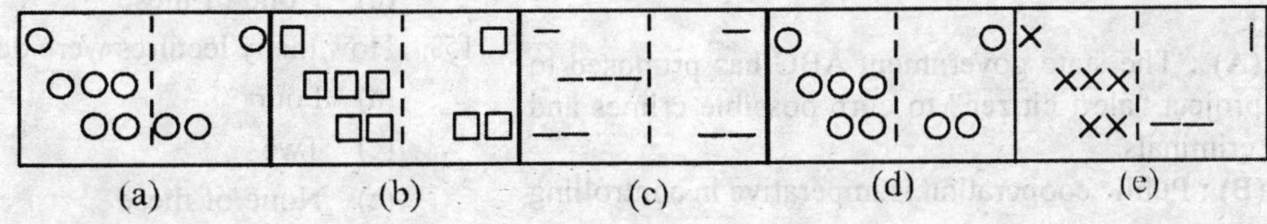

144. **Problem Figures** **Answer Figures**

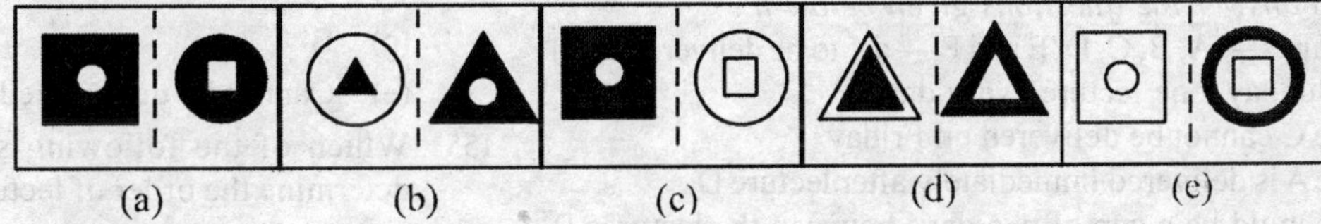

145. **Problem Figures** **Answer Figures**

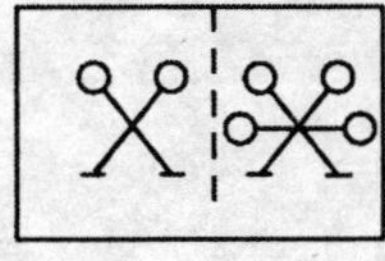

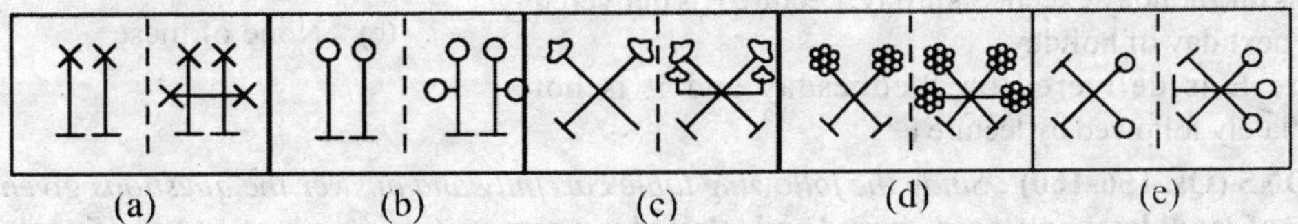

DIRECTIONS (Qs. 146-150) : *Given below are pairs of events 'A' and 'B'. You have to read both the events and decide their nature of relationship. You have to assume that the information given in 'A' and 'B' is true and you are not to assume anything beyond the given information in deciding the answer.* ***Mark answer***

(a) if 'A' is the effect and 'B' is its immediate and principal cause;
(b) if 'A' is the immediate and principal cause and 'B' is its effect;
(c) if 'A'; is an effect but 'B' is not its immediate and principal cause;
(d) if 'B' is an effect but 'A' is not its immediate and principal cause; and
(e) None of these

146. **Event (A) :** A gay 14-year-old youth is expelled from a prestigious private school.
Event (B) : The youth has announced he is in love with a schoolmate.

147. **Event (A) :** The Duchess hinted in a newspaper that she would like to marry Andrew again.
Event (B) : Britain's prince Andrew has ruled out remarrying his ex-wife, the Duchess of York.

Space for Rough Work

148. **Event (A) :** A handful of women have managed to transform the living conditions near their homes.

Event (B) : The project, "Better Environment Campaign" was started by a group of retired defence officers' wives in 1995.

149. **Event (A) :** The national selectors have decided to retain the same 14 for the third and final test of the series against New Zealand.

Event (B): India has won the second test against New Zealand.

150. **Event (A) :** The state government ABC has proposed to start a project "alert citizen" to curb possible crimes and nab the criminals.

Event (B) : Public cooperation is imperative in controlling crime.

DIRECTIONS (QS. 151-155) : *Study the following information carefully and answer the questions given below it:*

Six lectures — A, B, C, D, E and F — are to be delivered from Monday to Sunday, one lecture every day.

(i) Lecture C cannot be delivered on Friday.
(ii) Lecture A is delivered immediately after lecture D.
(iii) There should be a gap of two days between the lectures B and F.
(iv) There is one holiday except Saturday. Lecture F is delivered on the next day of holiday.
(v) Lecture E is delivered on Wednesday and it is not immediately followed by lecture F.

151. On which day was lecture D delivered?
(a) Friday (b) Saturday
(c) Sunday (d) Thursday
(e) None of these

152. On which day was holiday?
(a) Sunday (b) Friday
(c) Thursday (d) Cannot be determined
(e) None of these

153. How many lectures were delivered between F and D?
(a) Four (b) One
(c) Two (d) Three
(e) None of these

154. Which of the following was the last lecture?
(a) A (b) C
(c) B (d) D
(e) Cannot be determined

155. Which of the following statements is not necessary to determine the order of lectures?
(a) (i) (b) (ii)
(c) (v) (d) (i) and (ii)
(e) None of these

DIRECTIONS (Qs. 156-160) : *Study the following table carefully and answer the questions given below it.*

The number of candidates appeared, passed and selected in a competitive examination from five states over the years.

State	A			B			C			D			E		
Year	A	P	S	A	P	S	A	P	S	A	P	S	A	P	S
1995	850	215	25	1050	245	35	990	195	28	1080	300	36	1120	240	40
1996	880	240	20	980	230	30	650	150	28	1150	320	38	960	180	26
1997	750	180	22	1120	210	28	840	180	25	995	280	42	885	177	32
1998	920	290	36	890	190	32	780	160	32	975	260	39	1040	220	30
1999	960	300	32	950	225	40	1020	220	36	888	240	32	980	280	34
2000	820	250	28	1180	200	38	930	215	35	864	216	30	900	228	24

A = Appeared, P = Passed, S = Selected

Space for Rough Work

156. In the year 1995 which state had the lowest percentage of candidates selected over the candidates appeared ?
(a) A (b) B
(c) C (d) D
(e) None of these

157. During which of the following years the passing percentage over appeared is the highest from state D ?
(a) 2000 (b) 1999
(c) 1998 (d) 1997
(e) None of these

158. Total number of of candidates selected from state A is approximately what percentage of the total number of candidates selected from state B ?
(a) 72 (b) 88
(c) 85 (d) 80
(e) None of these

159. During which of the following years the percentage of candidates selected over passed is the lowest for state B?
(a) 1995 (b) 1996
(c) 1998 (d) 1999
(e) None of these

160. What is the ratio between number of candidates passed from state A in 1996 to that from state E in 1999 ?
(a) 6 : 7 (b) 14 : 15
(c) 13 : 16 (d) 12 : 16
(e) None of these

DIRECTIONS (Qs. 161 - 165): *Each of these questions has a bold part. Choose the option that best replaces the bold part.*

161. The number of children seeking admission to this college has risen sharply this year, **even though it may be only temporarily.**
(a) even though the rise may be only temporary.
(b) but it may be a temporary rise only.
(c) but the rise may be only temporary.
(d) but such a rise may only be a short lived one.
(e) no correction required

162. The political masters of the health care system have not listened to professional health planners because it **has not been profitable for them to do that thing.**
(a) has not been profitable for them to do so.
(b) has not been profitable for them to do that thing.
(c) has been unprofitable for them to do that thing.
(d) has been unprofitable for them to do so.
(e) no correction required

163. Most bacterial population grown in controlled conditions will quickly expand to limit the food supply, **produce toxic waste products that inhibit further growth, and reached the equilibrium state within a relatively short time.**
(a) Will have produced toxic waste products that inhibit further growth and also will reach an equilibrium state within a relatively short time.
(b) Producing toxic waste products that inhibit further growth, and reached the equilibrium state within a relatively short time.
(c) Will then produce a toxic waste product that inhibits further growth and thus reached an equilibrium state in a very short time.
(d) Produce toxic waste products that inhibit further growth and reach equilibrium .
(e) no correction required

164. It could be argued that the most significant virtue of a popular democracy is not the right to participate in the selection of leaders, **but rather that it affirms** our importance in the scheme of things.
(a) but rather is affirmation of
(b) but rather than it affirm
(c) but rather it's affirmation in terms of
(d) but instead of that, its affirming that
(e) no correction required

Space for Rough Work

165. Long popular among the connoisseurs of Indian music, Ravi Shankar first impressed western listeners with his phenomenal technical virtuosity, **but they soon came to appreciate his music as an artful** expression of an older culture's musical insight.
   (a) but it soon occurred that they appreciated his artful music as an
   (b) but they soon came to appreciate his music as an artful
   (c) but soon this was surpassed by an appreciation of it as an artful
   (d) which was soon surpassed by an even deeper appreciation of it as an artful
   (e) no correction required.

Directions (Q. 166-170): *In the questions given below, certain symbols are used with the following meanings:*

A @ B means A is greater than B.

A * B means A is either greater than or equal to B.

A # B means A is equal to B.

A $ B means A is either smaller than or equal to B.

A + B means A is smaller then B.

Now in each of the following questions, assuming the given statements to be true, find which of the two conclusions I and II given below them is/are definitely true?

Give answer

(a) : if only conclusion I is true

(b) : if only conclusion II is true

(c) : if either conclusion I or II is true

(d) : if neither conclusion I nor II is true

(d) : if both conclusions I and II are true

166. **Statements :** B + D; E $ T; T * P; P @ B
   Conclusions : I. P$D
   II. P @ D

167. **Statements :** E * F; G $ H; H # E; G @ K
   Conclusions: I. H @ K
   II. H * F

168. **Statements :** P $ Q; N # M; M @ R; R * P
   Conclusions : I. P + N
   II. Q $ M

169. **Statements :** D + T; E $ V; F * T; E @ D
   Conclusions : I. D $ V
   II. D + F

170. **Statements : T * U; U $ W; V @ L; W + V**
   Conclusions : I. V @ T
   II. L # W

DIRECTIONS (Qs.171-175) : *Read the following passage carefully to answer these questions based on it and the opinion of the author only.*

We are the failed generation-we who are now in our 40s and 50s. We do not have to look far to realise that our generation has failed. The India we inherited was wonderful, but the one that we have bequeathed our children is degraded in every way. We are the citizens of transition, with personal memories of our childhood when we lived in a good, simple world where laws and morals had their place. And now we have first-hand experience of an India stifled by corruption and injustice, with breakdowns on every front.

There is no point getting defensive about our failure. There is no point denying it either. Perhaps time has come for us to face up to reality and try and understand why we failed. We were good and talented and grew up in a relatively safe and protected environment. Then why and where did we go wrong? Perhaps we must first rewind a bit.

Our grandparents were the generation of freedom fighters. They were brave and committed men and women fired with a vision of a free India. They made sacrifices, donated money and property, their youth and even lived to achieve their goal. They were incredibly disciplined. And then came our parent's generation. They wanted to build a new India, a modern India where all citizens were equal. They were incredibly thrifty. They worked hard and saved money and believed the best they could give their children was a good education. And then came my generation, born in safety and security. We benefitted from a good education. Our nationalistic goals had whittled down. We only wanted to make a difference. But we did not really manage to because we were incredibly ambitious. We wanted to create a separate identity, push the frontiers of our personal capabilities and professional parameters to a new high. We took pride in being unlike the rest. Highly individualistic, we became the generation that abrogated civic responsibility, that hurt the social fabric-we wanted the best for our family, but community arid country could look after itself.

Sure, we inherited problems from our parents' generation. But we did not do anything to set it right. So they got worse and around us India started to crumble. We saw it, were conscious enough to protest, but not concerned enough to step in and stem the root. We were unconcerned because we were caught up in our own personal pursuits. We love to make a virtue of tolerance and indifference, as also permissiveness. It is indifference, when we do not care deeply enough to do something about our problems. It is not tolerance but permissiveness when we are too lazy to intervene. As we strove to prove our worth in professional pursuits, we happily .left nation building to politicians and bureaucrats. We abdicated our responsibility, our personal role in shaping India's destiny. Politics and civic action soon became too dirty for us to soil our hands, our name, our reputations. Some of us who belatedly want to do something about it, now discover that the system is too atrophied, set in its ways, to let us enter. So we stand outside wringing our hands. Perhaps secretly glad that we cannot enter this murky world. After all, we have accumulated too much to lose and in any case why bother. The system is too far gone and we would be fools to sacrifice the comforts of our cocooned world.

And our children, they worship money. And when it is there parent's money, they love it even more. Nowhere in the world do teenagers spend their parents' money as freely and without compunction as they do here. We are to be blamed for that too because we are being permissive, not liberal. Parents are so involved in their work that they do not have time for third children. They buy children's affection with guilt-money. So kids now have cars, electronic gadgets, designer clothes. India is a fading figment of their parents' nostalgia. All they want is a job that will give them good money so that they can pursue their materialistic pursuits-preferably in America.

But can you blame them? Look at the India they are living in-pollution is high, crime is endemic, brute power is law, civic amenities deplorable, justice non-existent, merit has no place. It is caste or connections that work. There are cases of affluence amidst unbelievable deserts of deprivation. How long is India really sustainable? Can it really remain stable and peaceful amidst such grotesque ills and inequities.

Often we are optimistic because we are afraid to be pessimistic. Impending scenarios scare the living daylights out of LIS. So, we collectively believe that things will improve and gladly cite a variety of instances to prove that there are areas of growth and excellence. We want to be optimistic because we do not want to give in to despair. After all, what is life without hope?

171. The author believes that he belongs to a failed generation because:
(a) India is today stifled with poverty and corruption
(b) he believes he is morally responsible for not being able to handover an unblemished India to the next generation
(c) he believes that his generation has not accepted failure gracefully
(d) he is pessimistic
(e) None of these

172. The author believes that the earlier generation was mainly concerned with:
(a) saving money for their children
(b) changing the face of India
(c) self sacrifice
(d) giving their children a good education
(e) None of these

173. The author thinks that his generation did not succeed in making a difference because:
(a) it overlooked nationalistic goals
(b) its objectives were unrealistic to be met
(c) in its quest for personal excellence, it forgot its duties to the society
(d) it did not manage to create a personal identity for itself
(e) None of these

174. While questioning India's sustainability, the author points out that :
(a) terrorism spread by brutes is rempant
(b) caste divide still exists which over-powers merit
(c) there are pockets of prosperity in the midst of widespread poverty
(d) the pollution rate is alarmingly high causing denudation'
(e) none of these

Space for Rough Work

175. In the opinion of the author the teenagers of today are spoilt by their parents because:
(a) parents want their children to have as nice a childhood as theirs
(b) parents do not have time for their children so that they compensate with luxuries
(c) parents become nostalgic and indulge their children with expensive items
(d) parents want to fulfill their children's dreams of materialistic pursuits in America.
(e) none of these

176. Seven men – A, B, C, D, E, F and G are standing in a queue in that order. Each one is wearing a cap of different colour – violet, indigo, blue, green, yellow, orange and red. D is able to see in front of him green and blue, but not violet. F can see violet and yellow, but not red. G can see caps of all the colours other than orange. If E is wearing an indigo coloured cap, then the colour of the cap worn by F is
(a) Blue (b) Violet
(c) Red (d) Orange
(e) None of these

177. A party consists of grandmother, father, mother, four sons and their wives and one son and two daughters to each of the sons. How many females are there in all?
(a) 14 (b) 16
(c) 18 (d) 24
(e) None of these

178. At my house I am facing east, then I turn left and go 10 m, then turn right and go 5 m, and then I go 5 m towards the south and from there 5 m towards the west. In which direction am I from my house ?
(a) East (b) West
(c) North (d) South
(e) None of these

179. In a certain code, 15789 is written as XTCAL and 2346 is written as NPSU. How is 23549 written in that code ?
(a) NPTUL (b) PNTSL
(c) NPTSL (d) NBTSL
(e) None of these

180. Keshav knows that Sudha's marks are more than 3 but less than 8 in a unit test. Sonia knows that these are more than 6 but less than 10. If both of them are correct, which of the following statements about Sudha's marks is definitely true?
(a) It has only one value
(b) It has any of three values
(c) It has either of two values
(d) It has any of four values
(e) None of these

DIRECTIONS (Qs. 181-185) : *Five incomplete sentences are given. You have to obtain correct option from among 10 common options to complete the question statements.*

A. in addition to earn
B. besides money
C. Towards basic needs
D. for the completion of
E. in
F. over
G many more
H. quite a few more
I. to
J. of

181. Research in the work place reveals that people work for many reasons ....
(a) Only 'A' (b) Only 'B'
(c) Both 'A' and 'B' (d) Only 'C'
(e) None of these

182. The conditions necessary .... this project have not been met.
(a) Only 'C' (b) Only 'E'
(c) Both 'C' and 'D' (d) Only 'D'
(e) None of these

183. The country is ushering .... a new era.
(a) Only 'E' (b) Only 'D'
(c) Both 'E' and 'F' (d) Only 'F'
(e) None of these

184. The present Constitution will see .... amendments but its basic structure will survive.
(a) Only 'F' (b) Only 'H'
(c) Both 'F' and 'G' (d) Only 'G'
(e) None of these

185. In his painting "The three Musicians", Picasso reached a climax in his use .... geometric forms.
(a) Only 'H' (b) Only 'I'
(c) Only 'J' (d) Both 'H' and 'I'
(e) None of these

Space for Rough Work

DIRECTIONS (Qs. 186-190) : *In the following questions, each word in capital letters is followed by three words lettered by A, B and C. Choose the word(s) which is/are similar in meaning from the options given below :*

186. BLAZE
A. Blank B. Beautiful
C. Indifferent
(a) Only 'A' (b) Both 'A' and 'B'
(c) Only 'C' (d) All 'A', 'B' and 'C'
(e) None of these

187. PADDY
A. Race track B. Rice
C. Caress
(a) Only 'A' (b) Both 'A' and 'B'
(c) Only 'C' (d) All 'A', 'B' and 'C'
(e) None of these

188. REPERCUSSION
A. Reaction B. Acceptance
C. Resistance
(a) Only 'A' (b) Both 'A' and 'B'
(c) Only 'C' (d) All 'A', 'B' and 'C'
(e) None of these

189. GOAD
A. Pursue B. Supercede
C. Spur
(a) Only 'A' (b) Both 'A' and 'B'
(c) Only 'C' (d) All 'A', 'B' and 'C'
(e) None of these

190. HOMELY
A. Refined B. Plain
C. Amiable
(a) Only 'A' (b) Both 'A' and 'B'
(c) Only 'C' (d) All 'A', 'B' and 'C'
(e) None of these

DIRECTIONS (Qs. 191-200) : *In the following passage there are blanks, each of which has been numbered. These numbers are printed below the passage and against each, five words are suggested, one of which fits the blank appropriately. Find out the appropriate word in each case.*

India's **191** over the past half century since independence has been unique and **192** in many ways. Yet the record is **193** in relation to what the country set out to achieve and could certainly have been **194**. It is **195** to look at both sides; the alternative is to be **196** down by unrelieved gloom or unwarranted **197**. The fact is that after eight 5-year plans, about 40 per cent of population is **198** below the poverty line. The human development indices are **199** low, placing India at the 126th position in the world table, far below many countries that came into **200** much later than it did.

191. (a) development (b) domination
(c) predicament (d) history
(e) excellence

192. (a) dubious (b) insignificant
(c) desperate (d) special
(e) commendable

193. (a) outshining (b) broken
(c) disappointing (d) brighter
(e) played

194. (a) underplayed (b) accomplished
(c) tampered (d) noteworthy
(e) exaggerated

195. (a) proposed (b) futile
(c) impracticable (d) necessary
(e) suggested

196. (a) laid (b) struck
(c) cooled (d) weighed
(e) brought

197. (a) progress (b) debating
(c) meticulousness (d) haste
(e) complacency

198. (a) much (b) still
(c) obviously (d) found
(e) far

199. (a) deplorably (b) admirably
(c) surprisingly (d) not
(e) amusingly

200. (a) world (b) being
(c) independence (d) compete
(e) India

Space for Rough Work

MAHARASHTRA CET - MOCK TEST 6

RESPONSE SHEET

NAME : .... DATE : ....

	(a)	(b)	(c)	(d)	(e)
1.					
2.					
3.					
4.					
5.					
6.					
7.					
8.					
9.					
10.					
11.					
12.					
13.					
14.					
15.					
16.					
17.					
18.					
19.					
20.					
21.					
22.					
23.					
24.					
25.					
26.					
27.					
28.					
29.					
30.					
31.					
32.					
33.					
34.					
35.					
36.					
37.					
38.					
39.					
40.					
41.					
42.					
43.					
44.					
45.					
46.					
47.					
48.					
49.					
50.					

	(a)	(b)	(c)	(d)	(e)
51.					
52.					
53.					
54.					
55.					
56.					
57.					
58.					
59.					
60.					
61.					
62.					
63.					
64.					
65.					
66.					
67.					
68.					
69.					
70.					
71.					
72.					
73.					
74.					
75.					
76.					
77.					
78.					
79.					
80.					
81.					
82.					
83.					
84.					
85.					
86.					
87.					
88.					
89.					
90.					
91.					
92.					
93.					
94.					
95.					
96.					
97.					
98.					
99.					
100.					

	(a)	(b)	(c)	(d)	(e)
101.					
102.					
103.					
104.					
105.					
106.					
107.					
108.					
109.					
110.					
111.					
112.					
113.					
114.					
115.					
116.					
117.					
118.					
119.					
120.					
121.					
122.					
123.					
124.					
125.					
126.					
127.					
128.					
129.					
130.					
131.					
132.					
133.					
134.					
135.					
136.					
137.					
138.					
139.					
140.					
141.					
142.					
143.					
144.					
145.					
146.					
147.					
148.					
149.					
150.					

	(a)	(b)	(c)	(d)	(e)
151.					
152.					
153.					
154.					
155.					
156.					
157.					
158.					
159.					
160.					
161.					
162.					
163.					
164.					
165.					
166.					
167.					
168.					
169.					
170.					
171.					
172.					
173.					
174.					
175.					
176.					
177.					
178.					
179.					
180.					
181.					
182.					
183.					
184.					
185.					
186.					
187.					
188.					
189.					
190.					
191.					
192.					
193.					
194.					
195.					
196.					
197.					
198.					
199.					
200.					

SOLUTIONS

MOCK TEST - 1

1. (e)

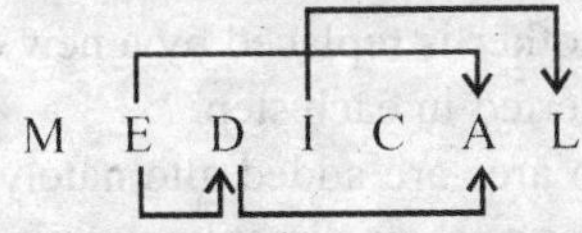

Hence such pairs are ED, EA, DA and IL.

2. (c) All the rest are the colours of spectrum.
3. (b) The third, the fifth and the eighth digits of the number 5 3 2 7 8 4 6 9 1 are 2, 8 and 9 respectively. The number formed with these digits is 2 8 9 which is a perfect square of 17. The second digit of 17 is 7.
4. (d) As, Similarly,

M –1 S, I –1 R, S –1 H, T –1 L | G –1 T, R –1 N, O –1 Q, U –1 F

A +1 O, K +1 F, E +1 L, N +1 B | N +1 E, D +1 F, D +1 E, D +1 O

5. (b) The fish live in water and water means jungle. Therefore fish live in jungle.
6. (d) Gender of Neha is not clear. So relation between them can not be determined.
7. (e) All the rest are metals.
8. (c) A A B A B C A B C D A B C D E A B C D E F A

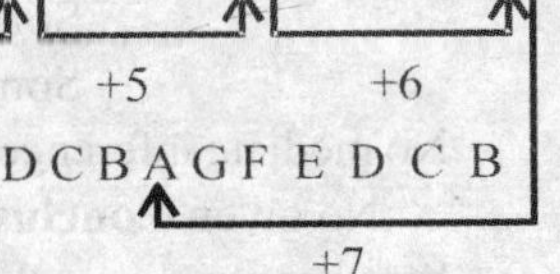

9. (c) In the series $\underset{1+1=2}{\underline{121}}$ $\underset{1+3=4}{\underline{143}}$ $\underset{1+5=6}{\underline{165}}$

∴ the next three terms would be $\underset{1+7=8}{\underline{187}}$.

10. (b) The series 814265098 can be broken as 8, 14, 26, 50, 98 ......
Which is 14 = 2(8) –2, 26 = 2(14) – 2 and so on.
∴ Next no. is = 2(98) –2 = 194
11. (b) Each letter moves +2 steps.
12. (d) 19 × 2 = 38, 38 × 3 = 114, 114 × 4 = 456.
13. (b) As 'Bird' flies, in the same way, 'snails' creeps.
14. (a) Second is the function of the first.
15. (d) All the others are planets.
16. (a) In all other pairs, one number is the square of the other.
17. (d) The smaller arrow moves through 90° and 45° anticlockwise respectively while the bigger one moves through 135° in each subsequent figure clockwise.
18. (c) The movement of design is as follows:

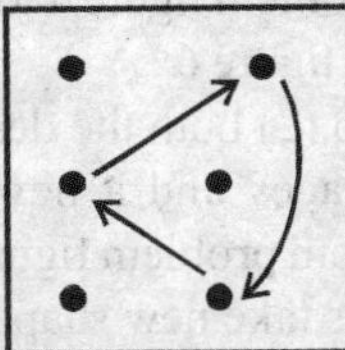

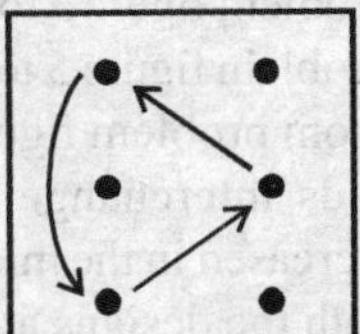

Problem fig. 1 to 2 Problem fig. 2 to 3
Problem fig. 3 to 4 Problem fig. 4 to 5
Problem fig. 5 to answer fig. 6

19. (b) In each subsequent figure the design ⊏ moves through 90° anticlockwise and shifts diagonally halfway while the arrow shifts halfway diagonally and is each time inverted.
20. (a) From problem figure (1) to (2) both the lower designs and both the upper designs inrterchanged their positions. From problem figures (2) and (3) both the upper designs shift lower and vice-vrsa. The same order of change is repeated.
21. (c) From problem figure (1) to (2) both the lower designs reverse. From problem figure. (2) to (3) third design from the bottom reverses. From problem figure (3) to (4) first and fourth designs from the bottom reverse. From problem figure (4) to (5) second design from the bottom reverses. Hence from problem figure (5) to (6) third and fourth designs from the bottom will reverse.
22. (d) The design at right is repeated from problem figure (4). Besides this, from problem figure (1) to (2) the upper of the design at left is reversed. From (2) to (3) this part shifts to centre. From problem figure (3) to (4) this part reverse at its own place. From problem figure (4) to (5) this part shifts to bottom. Hence in problem figure (6) it will reverse at its own place.
23. (d) In each subsequent figure the design moves through 90° clockwise. If 1 to □, 2 to ○, 3 to –, and 4 to Δ are supposed then the order in which they reverse is 1, 2 and 3, 4, 1 and 2 respectively.
24. (e) The movement of the design is as follows :

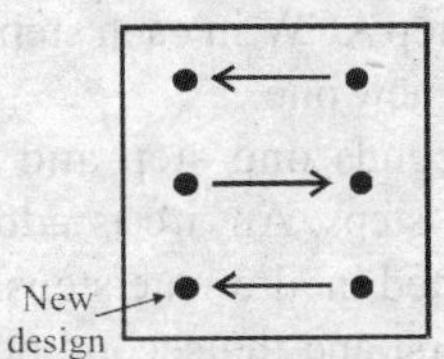

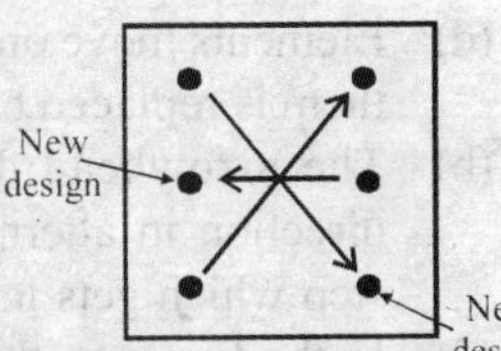

Problem figure 1 to 2 Problem figure 2 to 3
Problem figure 3 to 4 Problem figure 4 to 5
Problem figure 5 to 6

25. (c) In each subsequent figure whole design moves through 90° clockwise. Besides, the small designs change their position as shown below:

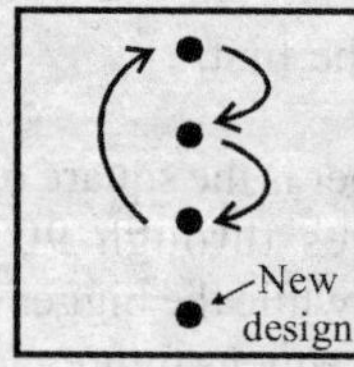

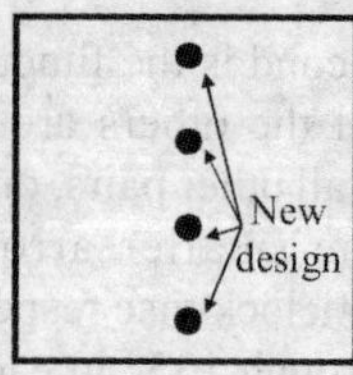

Problem figure 1 to 2 Problem figure 2 to 3
Problem figure 3 to 4 Problem figure 4 to 5
Problem figure 5 to answer figure 6.

26. (e) From problem figure (1) to (2) both the designs at the ends interchange their places and a new design is increased in the middle. From problem figure (2) to (3) both the designs at the ends take new shape while one design in the middle is incresed downward. From problem figure (3) to (4) both the designs at the ends interchange their places a new design in the middle is increased upward. The same order change continues.

27. (a) In each step two similar designs are added replacing one of the pre-existing pair of designs. So there should be two asterisks in place of crosses.

28. (e) In each step the figure rotates by 45° clockwise. The curves forming petals increase/decrease in the order – 1, 0, 1, 2, 3, 4, ...

29. (d) In each subsequent step, 1, 2, 3, 4, 5 ......, curves are added in a set order.

30. (e) The lower designs get interchanged diagonally, when all the three designs at each corner is same. There is no change in next step. Now, the upper two elements interchange columnwise and rowwise in the next two steps. These steps are repeating.

31. (c) In alternate steps the figure rotates by 45° anti-clockwise and gets inverted on its base and rotates by 90° anti-clockwise and changes its direction.

32. (a) In each step the design from the top shifts to third position, second to fourth, third to second and fourth to first after getting inverted.

33. (e) In alternate steps the upper design gets laterally inverted, the middle design gets inverted laterally and vertically, and lower design rotates by 90° anti-clockwise.

34. (c) In alternate steps shading of the upper circle rotates by 90° clockwise, the lower-left design rotates by 90° and 135° anti-clockwise while lower-left rotates by 90° and 135° clockwise.

35. (d) Elements move one step ACW in each step and one of them is replaced by a new one.

36. (b) The arrowhead descends one step and change its direction in alternate steps. An arc is added in each step which gets inverted in alternate steps.

37. (d) In the first step the first and the second designs from the left get inverted vertically while other two interchange places. In the next step the first from left gets inverted laterally, the fourth gets inverted vertically while other two interchange places.

38. (a) In alternate steps one and two line segments from the upper left and two and one from the lower right are lost. While one and two line segments are added to the upper right and one and three line segments to the lower left.

39. (b) In each step the whole figure rotates by 45° clockwise and one of the designs reverses its direction while one end design in another is replaced by a new one.

40. (a) Five L's get inverted in each step.

41. (a) One arc and two arcs are added alternately. The pre-exisiting arcs change their directions while the figure rotates by 45° clockwise. We can't get the last step from option 3 or 4.

42. (e) **From figure II to I:** The shaded part of the upper designs rotates 90° anti-clockwise while that of lower designs rotates 90° clockwise. Halves of shading from the left-column designs is lost.

43. (e) **From figure II to I:** The lower designs shifts half a side clockwise while it rotates by 90° clockwise. The upper closed-ended designs gets reduced in size and inverted. The inside designs (arrow) gets enlarged, rotates by 135° clockwise and is placed in the middle. The designs attached to the tail of the arrow gets unshaded if shaded and vice versa.

44. (c) **From figure II to I:** The designs on RHS shifts one side clockwise, rotates by 90° clockwise and gets inverted vetically. The upper design gets inverted vertically while the design on LHS remains the same.

45. (d) **From figure II to I:** In the upper-left design beginning from upper-left arc, the first, the third and the fourth arcs get inverted. While in the upper-right design, the second, the fifth and the sixth arcs get inverted. The lower-right design gets laterally inverted while there is no change in lower-left design.

46. (b) **From figure II to I:** The upper two designs interchange their positions and the design reaching the right rotates. One and two line segments are added to the lower left and lower-right designs respectively.

47. (b) **Conclusions** : Some buckets are pots. (conversion)
Some bags are buckets. (conversion)
Some purses are bags. (conversion)

No mediate inference follows.
∴ No given **Conclusions** follows.

48. (a) **Statements** : All glasses are roads.
No road is stick.
Conclusions : No glass is stick. (A + E = E-type)
Statements : Some sticks are pens.
Conclusions : Pens are not glass. (E + I = O* type)
Statements : No road is stick.
Some sticks are pens.
Conclusions : Some pens are not road.
(E + I = O* type)

Hence only IV follows.

49. (a) **Statements** : Some ice are rings.
Conclusions : Some rings are ice. (conversion)
Statements : Some rings are gold.
Conclusions : Some gold are ring. (conversion)
↙↗
Statements : No ring is paint.
Conclusions : Some gold are not paint.
(I + E = O-type)
Statements : Some ice are ring.
↙↗
No ring is paint.
Conclusions : Some ice are not paint.
(I + E = O-type)
Statements : No ring is paint.
Conclusions : No paint is ring. (Implication)
Hence none follows.

50. (d) **Statements** : Some shoes are bells.
Conclusions : Some bells are shoes. (conversion)
Statements : No candle is bell.
↙↗
Some bells are shoes.
Conclusions : Some shoes are not candle.
(E + I = O*)
Statements : All tables are shoes.
Conclusions : Some tables are shoes. (Implication)
Some shoes are tables. (conversion)
Statements : No candle is bell.
Conclusions : No bell is candle. (conversion)
Hence none follow.

51. (c) **Statements** : Some cats are rats.
Conclusions : Some rats are cats. (conversion)
Statements : Some rats are ants.
Conclusions : Some ants are rats (conversion)
Statements : Some ants are flies.
Conclusions : Some flies are ants. (conversion)
No mediate inference follows.
Hence, only I and II follow.

52. (b) The numerical parts moves with a difference of + 4. Thus, the correct sequence of the numerical components would be 1, 5, 9, 13, 17 Therefore, 15 LS does not fit in the series.

53. (c) There are two series :
I. B0R E3P H9N
First letter moves + 3 steps forward. The middle numerical component moves + 3, + 6, + 9 .... and the letter in the third position moves 2 steps backwards (– 2).
II. G3U, J7S
The same pattern follows in this series.
Hence, J7S does not fit.

54. (b) The letters of the alphabet on the first positions move + 3 steps forward while the numerical components in the middle move with the following pattern.
× 2 + 1, × 2 + 2, × 2 + 3, × 2 + 4 ....
Therefore, J10R does not fit in the series.

55. (d) The statement doesn't mean that there was no poverty before 1950. So I do not follow. Z focusses its attention on the said problem, that doesn't mean that no other book deals with the issue.

56. (d) If I were true, the Board would not warn farmers to regularise their electric connection. Hence I does not follow. Nothing can be concluded about the size of the farms and their need to electricity for agriculture. Hence II does not follow.

57. (d) II may be an assumption which the professor is assuming before passing his statement. Hence II does not follow. I may or may not be possible. Hence I does not follow.

58. (b) It is clear that either there is no facility for health insurance available or it is available for only affluent sections. Hence I can not definitely be concluded. II follows from the given statement.

59. (c) Only I or II can follow.

For (Qs. 60-64).

	Dramatics	Computer Sec.	Physics	History	Mathematics
Madhu	✓	✓	✓		
Shobha	✓	✓		✓	
Anjali		✓	✓	✓	✓
Poonam	✓		✓	✓	
Nisha			✓	✓	✓

60. (e) none of these
61. (c) Madhu
62. (a) Poonam
63. (d) Anjali
64. (c) Nisha
65. (d) As W is to be placed immediately to the left of X, we cannot place X in window 1.
66. (b) Clearly, W must be placed in window no. 2 as dictated by the restrictions.
67. (d) If U is placed in window no. 5, then Y will placed in window 6.
68. (b) Gaurav – Raj – Mohit – Ashish – Sanchit.
Hence Gaurav won the race.
69. (c) As option (a) means just one pilot, so it is ruled out. Dalbir will not crew with Naveen so (b) is ruled out. Both (c) and (d) are possible, but (c) being earlier option will be the answer.
70. (d) As Eric will not crew with Lal, so (d) is not possible
71. (c) If Dalbir is rejected, either of Naveen or Paul and Monty must be chosen. It is not necessary if Dalbir is chosen, then Farid, Lal and Monty can be chosen.
72. (d) Dalbir and Farid can't be together
73. (c) II is not necessary that Naveen must also be chosen.

For (Qs. 74-79).

'481' means 'sky is blue' .... (i)
'246' means 'sea is deep' .... (ii)
'698' means 'sea looks blue' .... (iii)
From (i) and (ii) ⇒ '4' means 'is'
From (ii) and (iii) ⇒ '6' means 'sea'.

∴ From (ii), '2' means 'deep'
From (i) and (iii) ⇒ '8' means 'blue'
∴ From (iii), '9' means 'looks'
and from (i) '1' means 'sky'

74. (c) 75. (c) 76. (d)
77. (c) 78. (a) 79. (b)
80. (a) From the last sentence it can be inferred.
81. (e) It contradicts the first two sentences of the passage. Hence it is definitely false.
82. (e) The Indian construction companies have already established themselves in international market.
83. (a) The passage talks of "labour-intensive Indian construction industry".
84. (c) It can't be compared from the information given in the passage.
85. (b) No deduction can be made regarding other companies. So, I is not implicit. Since one is advised to contact the company's lawyer in case of any problem, it means that the lawyer is fully acquainted with the case. So, II is implicit.
86. (a) The statement mentions that there is no problem if one comes upto 7 p.m. also. This is clearly mentioned that the programme will continue even after 7 p.m. So, I is implicit. Also, it is clearly mentioned that the programme will start at 6 p.m. So, II is not implicit.
87. (b) I is not implicit. The statement puts it the other way round. That is, health results in happiness. II is implicit, hence the statement.
88. (c) CIG → GIC, ARE → ERA, TTE → ETT
⇒ <u>DIR</u> <u>ECT</u> <u>ION</u> → RIDTCENOI
89. (b) Using the given symbols, we have:

$$\text{Given expression} = 8 + 7 \times 8 \div 40 \quad 2 = 8 + 7 \times \frac{1}{5} \quad 2$$

$$= \frac{37}{5} = 7\frac{2}{5}$$

90. (a) Clearly, there are two possible movements of Anuj as shown below:

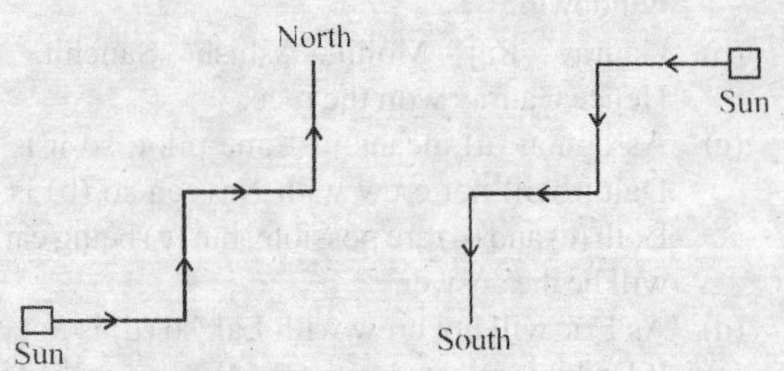

91. (c)

1	2	3	2	10	12
2	5	12	10	16	13
$\frac{1}{4}$	$\frac{2}{9}$	$\frac{1}{16}$	$\frac{?}{25}$	$\frac{10}{36}$	$\frac{24}{49}$

+5 +7 +9 +11 +13

Hence, the missing term is 25 − (2 + 10) = 13.

92. (c) The upper number in each column divides the lower number completely. Hence the correct option is (c) as only 5 divides 20 completely.
93. (a) I is a reasonable course of action. Hence follows. Nothing about the market condition is known from the statement. Hence II does not follow.
94. (a) I is advisable to be prepared for the storage of the new crop. II is not relevant.
95. (a) Clearly, proper supervision alone can see the development in practice. So, only course I follows.
96. (d) I is not a proper way to tackle the problem. Because this action will not help reduce the problem. Hence, I is not advisable. On a similar basis II is also not advisable.
97. (b) I is not advisable because sophisticated weapons must not be provided in lay hands. II is advisable because this will encourage the villagers.
98. (a) (b) is wrong as Shyam can not be interviewed twice.
(c) is wrong as Usha is not there but Shyam is there.
(d) is wrong as Kishore has to be interviewed twice if Veena is interviewed.
99. (d) If Veena is interviewed on Tuesday then Kishore is interviewed on Monday and a day after Tuesday. So we have only 2 days left. If Shyam is interviewed than Usha and then Ram have to be interviewed, which is not possible.
100. (c) If Kishore is not interviewed, then Veena is not interviewed also. Hence Trilochan has to be interviewed on Monday and Friday because one interview is conducted per day.
101. (a) Shyam's interview takes place earlier than Usha's interview. Hence option (b) is ruled out. Option (d) is also ruled out because Ram's inerview is either followed or preceded by Usha's interview.
If Veena is interviewed on Tuesday then Kishore has to be interviewed on Monday and a day later than Tuesday. As Shyam is interviewed so, Usha and Ram have to be there, which can not be adjusted.
102. (d) So Ram, Veena and Kishore have to be interviewed. Both Ram and Kishore have to be interviewed twice.
If Usha is not interviewed, Shyam is also not interviewed. In this case Kishore is not interviewed on Wednesday because if Ram is interviewed twice, then Ram's second interview takes place exactly two days after Ram's first interview.
103. (c) If Usha is there then Ram is there. If Veena is interviewed than Kishore has to be interviewed twice. The possible combinations can be
K V K U R or U R K V K
So, Kishore can be interviewed on Monday, Wednesday or Friday.
104. (b) Required length = LCM of 100 cm and 85 cm
= 1700 cm = 17 m
105. (b) Let average of team = x years
Then, $25 + 28 + S_9 = 11x$ ... (i)
where S_9 is the sum of ages of remaining players
Also, $Np + S_9 = 11(x - 2)$, ... (ii)
where Np is the sum of ages of new players
(i) − (ii) ⇒ 53 − Np = 22
⇒ Np = 31

$$\therefore \text{Average age of new two players} = \frac{31}{2} = 15.5 \text{ years}$$

106. (d) If $p^2 = k$ and $q = \sqrt{k}$ then $p \le q$, whatever be the value of k, where $k > 0$.
107. (a) $p = 2.8, q = 2.6$
108. (c) $p = \frac{-7}{2}, \frac{-1}{7}, q = \frac{9}{2}, \frac{-1}{9}$
109. (c) $p = -2, \frac{-5}{11}; q = 2, \frac{-5}{12}$ $\quad \therefore p < q$
110. (b) $p = 16, q = \pm 16$ $\quad \therefore p \ge q$
111. (c) The graph shows that Rice, Onion, Egg and Chillies increase and Dal & Edible Oil decreases.
112. (d) Commodities showing price decline for 2 or more years consecutively – Rice, Dal, Edible Oil, Egg, Onion.
113. (d) The graph shows that only for Egg & onion, the price decline followed by an increase, only once in the entire period.
114. (d) Money spend on education in family A= (65 –45) = 20% of total expenditure = $\frac{1}{5}$ of total expenditure.
115. (c) Money spend on clothes by family B = (60 – 40)% of total expenditure = Rs $\left(\frac{20}{100} \times 10000\right)$ = Rs 2000
116. (b) Money spend by A on food, clothes & house rent = [30 + (45 – 30) + (90 – 75)]% of total expenditure

$= (60\% \text{ of Rs } 30000) = \text{Rs}\left(\frac{60}{100} \times 30000\right) = \text{Rs } 18000$

117. (a) Money spend by A on education and miscellaneous = [(65–45) + (100 –90)]% = 30%
Money spend by B on education and miscellaneous = [(75 – 60) + (100 – 95)]% = 20%
$\therefore$ Family A spends more on these heads.
118. (c) B's expenditure on food = 40%
A's expenditure on food = 30%

B's percentage over A's $= \left(\frac{40}{30} \times 100\right)\% = 133.33\%$

119. (b) Distribution (value) for USA $= 5760 \times \frac{17}{100} = 979.2$;

Distribution (qty.) for USA $= 1.055 \times \frac{15}{100}$ kg $= .1583$

Distribution (value) Switzerland

$= 5760 \times \frac{20}{100} = 1152$;

Distribution (qty.) for Switzerland

$= 1.055 \times \frac{11}{100} = .11605$

Distribution (value) for Turkey $= 5760 \times \frac{16}{100} = 921.6$;

Distribution (qty.) for Turkey $= 1.055 \times \frac{15}{100} = .1583$

Distribution (value) for India = 1152;

Distribution (qty.) for India $= 1.055 \times \frac{26}{100} = .2743$

Per kg price

USA $= \frac{979.2}{.1583} = 6186$;

Switzerland $= \frac{1152}{.11605} = 9927$;

Turkey $= \frac{921.6}{.1583} = 5822$;

India $= \frac{1152}{.2743} = 4199.7$

$\therefore$ Highest price in Switzerland.

120. (b) Average price in Euro/ kg for turkey

$= \frac{\text{distribution by value}}{\text{distribution by quantity in kg}}$

$= \frac{5760 \times 16/100}{1055 \times 15/100} = 5.82 \approx 5.60$

121. (a) The table depicts the number of vehicles passing through a point of a city at different time slots in a day. On the basis of this we can not obtain the number of two-wheelers and cars in the city. Hence, option (c) is relued out. Option (d) is absured. Option (b) is uncertain.
122. (d) The table shows information about the time slot 0800-0900. We can not determine the number of vehicles passing through the point during 0800-0830.
123. (b)

Time slot	No. of buses passed
0800-0900	1500
0900-1000	1000+1208 = 2208
0600-0700	Cannot be said
1800-1900	1010 + 1010 = 2020

124. (d)

Slot No.	No. of vehicles passed
13	27,440
14	25,392
3	27,529
5	29,560

125. (b) Required number of persons
$= 1510 \times 60 + 15050 \times 2.5 + 8000 \times 1.5 + 5000 \times 2$
$= 90.600 + 37,623 + 12,000 + 10,000 = 1,50,225$

For (Qs: 126-130).

	Specialisation	Total number of students	Male	Female
1	HR	990	396	594
2	Marketing	720	420	300
3	International Business	810	675	135
4	Banking	540	340	200
5	IT	945	315	630
6	Finance	495	275	220
		4500	**2421**	**2079**

126. (b) It is obvious from above.

127. (d) The required per cent $= \dfrac{300 \times 100}{4500} = 6.6\% \approx 7\%$

128. (c) The required number of men $= 675 + 340 = 1015$

129. (a) The required per cent $= \dfrac{220 \times 100}{275} = 80\%$

130. (b) IT is obvious from above table.

131. (d) When the trains are running in opposite direction,

time taken to cross each other $= \dfrac{L_1 + L_2}{S_1 + S_2}$,

Where,
L_1 = Length of I train.
S_1 = Speed of I train.
L_2 = Length of II train.
S_2 = Speed of II train.
(I) $\Rightarrow L_1 = L_2 = L$ (let)
$S_1 = S_2 = S$ (let)

$\Rightarrow 2S = \dfrac{2L}{x} \Rightarrow S = \dfrac{L}{x}$

(II) $\Rightarrow S = \dfrac{L}{5}$

We can't find the value of S even with the help of both statements.

132. (b)

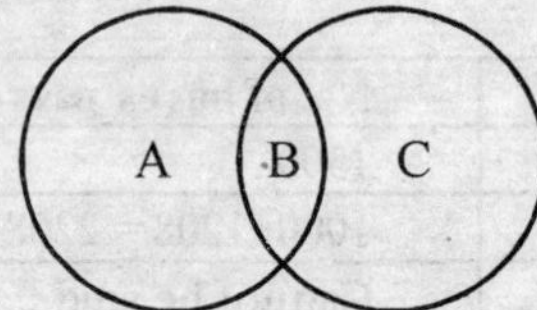

A = People have only blue eyes.
C = People have only blond hair.
B = People have blue eyes and blond hair.
and B = 50%
(I) $\Rightarrow B + C = 70\%$
(II) $\Rightarrow A + B = 60\%$
We have to find 'A'
$\therefore$ Statement (II) alone is sufficient.

133. (c)

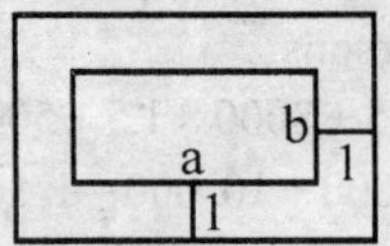

(I) $\Rightarrow (a+2)(b+2) = 187$

(II) $\Rightarrow \dfrac{b}{a} = \dfrac{3}{5}$

With the help of both statements, we can calculate 'b'.

134. (e) (I) $\Rightarrow$ Interest and sum are given and

$$I = P\left(1 + \frac{r}{100}\right)^3 - P$$

$\Rightarrow$ r can be calculated.
$\Rightarrow$ C.I. after three years can be found.
Hence, statement (I) alone is sufficient to answer the question.
(II) $\Rightarrow$ Since, difference between S.I. and C.I. $= P \times \left(\dfrac{r}{100}\right)^n$

$\Rightarrow$ r can be calculated.
Hence, C.I. after three years can be found.
Therefore, statement (II) alone is sufficient to answer the question.

135. (b) Let present age of Mother = x years.
Let present age of Father = y years.
(I) $\Rightarrow y = x + 8$
Hence, from (I) we can't be determined the present age of mother.

(II) $\Rightarrow y = 30$ years and $\dfrac{x-4}{30-4} = \dfrac{12}{13} \Rightarrow \dfrac{x-4}{26} = \dfrac{12}{13}$

Hence, present age of mother (x) can be determined by using statement (II) alone.

136. (b) (I) $\Rightarrow A < C < B$, we have no idea about D.
(II) $\Rightarrow A < D < C < B$

137. (a) Statement (I) gives required information but statement (II) gives information in terms of percentage. Hence (II) is not sufficient.

138. (e) **From (I) :** Area $\rightarrow$ Side $\rightarrow$ Perimeter
From (II) : Since Perimeter $\times$ rate of fencing per metre = Total cost (in rupees)
Hence, each, statement alone is sufficient.

139. (a) **From (I) :** We get the following table

Person	Hindi	Bio	Hist	Geo	Eng	Sanskrit
P	×	×	×	×		
U	×	×	×	×		
Q		×		×		
S		×		×		
T				×		
R						

From the above table R is the person who teaches Geography. Obviously, T teaches Biology.

From (II) : We get the following chart :

Person	Subject
P	English / Sanskrit
U	Sanskrit / English
Q	Hindi / History
S	History / Hindi

From the chart given above, we can conclude that

Person	Subject
R	Biology / Geography
T	Geography / Biology

But, we can't find who among R and T teaches Biology.

140. (c) **From (I) :** We get the ratio of the employees belonging to worse grade and officer's grade by Alligation method.

Worse (W) grade	**Officer's (O) grade**
1100	4600
1200	1200
4600 – 1200 = 3400	1200 – 1100 = 100

Hence the ratio of employees of worse grade to officer's grade = 34

From (II) : Suppose there were 'a' and 'b' employees of worse and officer's grades respectively, in the beginning.

Therefore, according to second statement

$$\frac{a+600}{b+600} = \frac{37}{4} \quad \text{..........(i)}$$

From (I) : $\frac{a}{b} = \frac{34}{1}$ or $a = 34b$

Hence, with the help of value 'a' from statement I we can find out the total strength by using equation (i).

141. (a) (I) ⇒ $m = 999999, n = 100000$

∴ We can find the value of $m - 7 \div 37$

(II) ⇒ $m - n$ = known, but neither the value of 'm' is known nor the value of 'n' is known. So, we cannot find the values of $m - n \div 37$.

142. (e) (I) ⇒ A loaded 300 boxes in 30 minutes and B loaded 150 boxes in 30 minutes. So B should take 90 minutes to load the 450 boxes by himself.

(II) ⇒ A loads 10 boxes per minute, hence A loads 300 boxes in 30 minutes. Therefore, B loaded 150 boxes in 30 minutes and hence, B will take 90 minutes to load all the 450 boxes.

∴ Each statement alone is sufficient to answer the question.

143. (e) (I) ⇒ (P + Q)'s one day work = $\frac{1}{10}$ th part of whole work

∴ (P + Q)'s five days work = $\frac{1}{2}$

∴ Remaining work $= 1 - \frac{1}{2} = \frac{1}{2}$

Now, since in 8 days, P's work = $\frac{1}{2}$ th work

∴ P's one day work = $\frac{1}{16}$ th work

∴ Q's one day work $= \frac{1}{10} - \frac{1}{16} = \frac{3}{80}$ th work

Hence, we can calculate the time taken by Q to finish $\frac{1}{2}$ work.

(II) ⇒ P's one day work = $\frac{1}{16}$ th work

∴ P's eight days work $= \frac{1}{16} \times 8 = \frac{1}{2}$ th work

⇒ P & Q together can do $\frac{1}{2}$ th work in 5 days.

∴ P's five days work $= \frac{1}{16} \times 5 = \frac{5}{16}$ th work

∴ Q's five days work $= \frac{1}{2} - \frac{5}{16} = \frac{3}{16}$ th work

⇒ Q's one day work $= \frac{3}{16 \times 5} = \frac{3}{80}$ th work

⇒ Required time can be calculated.

Hence, each statement alone is sufficient to answer the question.

144. (e) Since the product of any numbers is an even number if and only if at least one of them is an even number.

Now,

(I) ⇒ A is an even number ⇒ Product of A, B, C is even.

(II) ⇒ A × B is an even number and A × C is also an even number.

⇒ at least one of them (A, B, C) is even

⇒ their product is an even number.

∴ Each statement alone is sufficient to answer the question.

145. (e) (I) ⇒ C.P. can be calculated since

$$\text{C.P.} = \frac{\text{S.P.} \times 100}{(100 + \%\text{profit})}$$

Also, since Profit = S.P. – C.P.

$\therefore$ Profit can be calculated using statement (I) alone.

(II) $\Rightarrow$ C.P. $= \frac{1}{3} \times$ Profit and Profit = S.P. – C.P.

Therefore, each statement alone is sufficient to answer the question.

146. (d) Total investment in 1995 = 2923.1 + 7081.6 = 10004.7
Total investment in 1996 = 3489.5 + 8352.0 = 11,841.5

$\therefore$ % increase $= \frac{11841.5 - 10,004.7}{10,004.7} \times 100 = 18.36\%$

147. (c) Total investment in Chittor = 6412.6
Total investment in Khammam = 15433.6

$\therefore \frac{\text{Total investment in Khammam}}{\text{Total investment in Chittor}} = \frac{15433.6}{6412.6} = 2.40$

148. (b) Investment in electricity & thermal energy in 1995 in two districts
= 815.2 + 632.4 + 2065.8 + 1232.7 = 4746.1

% in terms of total investment $= \frac{4746.1}{10,004.7} \times 100 = 47.43$ %

149. (a) % increase in Khammam district in the area of

Electricity $= \frac{2365.1 - 2065.8}{2065.8} \times 100 = 14.5\%$

Chemical $= \frac{986.4 - 745.3}{745.3} \times 100 = 32.34\%$

Solar $= \frac{1792.1 - 1363.5}{1363.5} \times 100 = 31.43\%$

Nuclear $= \frac{2182.1 - 1674.3}{1674.3} \times 100 = 30.32$

Hence highest increase is in the area of chemical.

150. (a) % increase in investment from 1995 to 1996

$= \frac{8352 - 7081.6}{7081.6} = 17.93\%$

Let the investment be x in 1997

$\frac{x - 8352}{8352} = \frac{17.93}{100}$

$\Rightarrow x = 8352 + \frac{17.93 \times 8352}{100}$

$= 9850.3 \approx$ Rs.9850 crores

151. (c) When the word 'except' is used 'me' is used with it instead of I, so the most appropriate form of this phrase will be except for you and me.

152. (a) 'Calculate' is not an appropriate word for this sentence, calculation is done on the basis of available facts with certain fixed rules, whereas according to the sense of the sentence the person is only making a guess or a supposition, thus reckon is the most appropriate word that can be used to replace calculate

153. (a) 'him' is not the right usage because it is a possessive pronoun, and in the sentence it is followed by who, which is used to refer. So the pronoun he should be used. He, who has the best rapport with the students.

154. (d) Different is used with 'from' e.g- 'you are different from Ritu'. Than is used for comparisons, e.g., The world is more populated than it was in our time.

155. (d) When we use the word 'hardly', it implies a negative meaning, there is then no need to use not, so the most suitable use is 'he hardly had any friends'.

156. (a) 157. (b)

158. (d) 159. (c)

160. (e)

161. (a) A. Umpteen means in large number, countless.
B. Waspish means bad tempere
D. Testimony means evidence, proof
Umpteen is synonym to option (c).

162. (d) A. Buffoon means a fool.
B. Scholar means a person with good knowledge.
C. Candid means frank, unbiased
D. Gullible means a person who is easily duped or cheateD.
A-B are antonym in nature.

163. (d) A. Pandemonium means chaos
B. Realm-domain, sphere
C. Sporadic is scattered, occurring casually.
D. Tranquility is peace
Thus, A and D are antonym to each other.

164. (d) A. Fidgety means nervous, restless, uneasy.
B. Elation means to feel proud, cheer
C. Nervous is feeling uneasy.
D. Exuberant means luxuriant, lavish.
A and C are synonym to each other.

165. (d) A. Oblivious is forgetful.
B. Kudos means fame renown.
C. Conscious means being aware of
D. Adulation- to praise excessively
Thus c is antonym to A.

166. (b) A. Iconoclast means critic, dissident rebel.
B. Critic means who says and gives opinion about others.
C. Juscious means succulent, juicy
D. Naive means artless frank.
Thus A and B are synonymous.

167. (b) A Lugubrious means dismal
B. Cheerful means happy, gay
C. Welter is a confused mixture of things or people.
D. Gaffe means a blunder.
Thus A and B are synonymous.

168. (c) A. Paltry means worthless, trifling.
B. Oriental is related to east
C. Occidental is to west.
D. Obnoxious means unpleasant, offensive
Thus B and C are antonym.

169. (a) A. Exorbitant means excessively high price.
B. Moderate means not in extreme, not excessive
C. Ephemeral means short-live.
D. Mammoth large extinct species of elephant.
Thus option (a) shows the antonym variant.

170. (b) A. Peccable means imperfect
B. Lassitude mens weariness.
C. Jeopardy means great danger or risk.
D. Perfect is completely good.
Thus A and D are antonyms.

171. (c) The main concern of the passage is importance of leadership in an organisation. Management and success are only subordinate ideas depending on the leadership in an organisation. Management schools are only referred to, they are not a significant idea in text.

172. (c) This is a factual question. Refer to the first sentence of the second paragraph. It could be inferred from this line that there were many large organisations but not enough managers and this need for good managers led to development of various management programs by companies and universities.

173. (b) This is an incorrect statement as it can be inferred from the passage budgeting and planning are managerial tasks relating to Management and not leadership.

174. (d) Refer to the second last sentence of the second paragraph.

175. (b) (a), (c) and (d) can be eliminated because they are not suggested as such by the passage. (b) can be inferred from the third paragraph of the passage which describes difference between managers and leaders and talks about the importance given to the former in today's world.

176. (b) Developed is nearest in meaning to nurtur.

177. (a) (b), (c) and (d) are the functions of a manager according to the passage and in author's opinion leader's task so different from that of a manager's. A leader is a visionary. Refer to this sentence in the first paragraph "Leadership defines what the future should look like.... despite the obstacles.

178. (c) According to the passage successful transformations is 70 to 90% leadership and only 10-30% management. So, the emphasis should be on leadership rather than management for transformation efforts.

179. (c) Because management was the main item on 20th century agenda and it was manager that were required in large numbers. The focus was on management which is why they were taught little about leadership.

180. (b) The passage does not support this statement. Rather the passage states that leadership is a set of processes that creates organizations at the first place. Size of organizations does not affect leadership.

181. (b) counsel also means 'legal adviser.

182. (d) crude

183. (c) abject means helpless, miserable, despicable situation, obstruct means to hinder, abstract is the literal opposite of.

184. (b) Exonerate means declared free from blame, to implicate means to show that someone is involved in something especially a crime, to appease means to pacify, to adore means to love deeply and respect highly.

185. (d) Fascinating means charming, fanaticism means madness, especially in religious or political matters, indolence means laziness.

186. (a) The underlined portion should be deleted.

187. (d) and indulging in other sports.

188. (b) I was told
The subject should come before the verb.

189. (c) with the debasing of the coinage than

190. (a) have done
The present perfect tense is used to denote an action beginning at some time in the past and continuing upto the moment as the words "ate still doing" in the sentence reveal.

191. (e)	192. (b)	193. (e)
194. (a)	195. (c)	196. (e)
197. (c)	198. (b)	199. (d)
200. (a)		

MOCK TEST - 2

1. (a) As, M A I N → I M N A
   1 2 3 4   3 1 4 2
   and G O A L → A G L O
   1 2 3 4   3 1 4 2
   Similarly, D U S K → S D K U
   1 2 3 4   3 1 4 2
2. (e) All the rest are the multiples of 6.
3. (a) Original word → C A T E G O R Y
   According to alphabet → A C E G O R T Y
   Hence the required letter is only one is Y.
4. (c) 8 9 1 2 3 6 4 7 → 3 6 4 7 8 9 1 2
   ∴ 4th digit from the right end after the rearrangement is '8'.
5. (c) 'nik ka pa' → 'who are you' ..... (1)
   'ka na ta da' → 'you may come here'..... (2)
   and 'ho ta sa' → 'come and go'..... (3)
   From (1) and (2), *ka* → you
   From (2) and (3), *ta* → come
   ∴ '*nik*' → 'who' or 'are'
6. (c) The words formed with the letters L, E, S and A are 'SEAL' and 'SALE'.
7. (a) BEND → 5 % 7 @
   and DREAM → @ 2 % 4 8
   ∴ MADE → 8 4 @ %
8. (d) The series 813213246 can be broken as 8, 13, 21, 32, 46 which is $13 - 8 = 5, 21 - 13 = 8, 32 - 21 = 11, 46 - 32 = 14$ and so on.
   ∴ The next no. would be $= 46 + 17 = 63$.
   And the next no. would be $= 63 + 20 = 83$.
   ∴ The following 3 digits would be 638.
9. (c) The series 282 04492188 can be broken as 2, 8, 20, 44, 92, 188.
   $8 = 2(2) + 4, 20 = 2(8) + 4, 44 = 2(20)+4$ and so on.
   ∴ Next term $= 2(188) + 4 = 380$
10. (a) 1st letter moves –2 steps each time.
   2nd letter moves +1, +2, +3, +4 steps respectively.
   3rd letter moves +2, +3, +4 steps respectively.
11. (b) 1st letter moves +2, +3 and +4 steps respectively.
   2nd letter moves –2, –3 and –4 steps respectively.
12. (d) First is an instrument to measure the second.
13. (b) Second comes out of the first.
14. (a) In other pairs only one vowel is used
15. (c) All except Trypsin are chemical names of vitamins, while trypsin is an enzyme.
16. (a) From problem figure (1) to (2) one line is increased. problem figure (2) to (3) one line is increased at right while the line at left is reversed. The same order of change is repeated from problem figure (3) to (4) and (4) to (5). Hence the order of change will be repeat from problem figure (5) to answer figure (a).
17. (b) From problem figure (1) to (2) the inner design shifts one line anticlockwise and a new design takes place at its next time. From problem figure (2) to (3) one design shifts to next line while previous design disappears. The order of changes is repeated later on.
18. (c) In each subsequent problem figure the design moves through 90° clockwise. Besides, designs at the lines shifts as shown below:

19. (e) The designs move through 90° and 45° respectively anticlockwise in subsequent figure. Besides, from problem figure (1) to (2) the design at the end on line N reverses and from problem figure (2) to (3) the design at the end on the other line ▲ reverses. The same order of changes is repeated.
20. (c) In each subsequent problem figure the previous designs after shifting half line anticlockwise reverse and a new design takes place at the place of previous design.
21. (d) From problem figure (1) to (2) the black square shifts two lines and next to one black square is increased. From problem figure (2) to (3) black squares shift two lines and next to them one black square is increased. From problem figure (3) to (4) one black square shifts two line and two previous designs disappear. The same order is repeated.
22. (b) Upto problem figure (4) one line is increased in each subsequent figure. From problem figure (4) to (5) one semicircle is increased. Hence from problem figure (5) to (6) one semicircle will increase at the second line.
23. (d) From problem figure (1) to (2) the design moves through 180 anticlockwise while the design at the end of line takes a new shape after reversing. From problem figure (2) to (3) the design moves through 90° in the same direction and the design at the end of line takes a new shape after reversing. The same order is repeated.
24. (b) In each subsequent problem figure the upper design shifts down while a new design is formed in place of previous design.
25. (b) The designs are shifting as shown below:

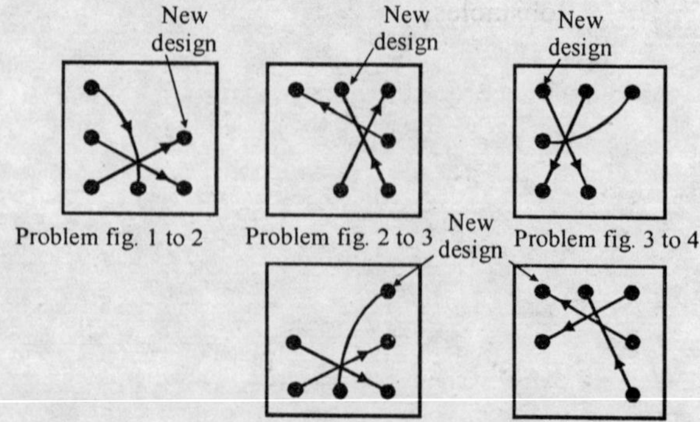

26. (e) In each subsequent problem figure the previous designs are reversed and one Δ is increased next to them.
27. (b) In each subsequent problem figure design shifts $\frac{1}{2}, 1, 1\frac{1}{2}, 2$ and $2\frac{1}{2}$ sides respectively anticlockwise and then moves through 135°, 90°, 45°, 0 and then 135° anticlockwise respectively.

28. (a) In each subsequent problem figure one design is increase in previous designs and these shift one place anticlockwise. Besides a new design takes place at the left upper corner.
29. (e) The outer figure gets reduced and moves inside while the inner figure gets enlarged and moves outside.
30. (b) In each step shape of one of the adjacent design changes. The middle design changes after three steps.
31. (e) In each subsequent steps the figure rotates by 45°, 90°, 135°, 45°, ... clockwise. Similar figure appears alternately.
32. (e) The shaded design move one and two steps anticlockwise and an additional circle on anticlockwise side gets shaded in each step.
33. (e) Elements on the ends alternately interchange their position with the central design. The central design changes its shape. The line on which the design are arranged rotates by 45° clockwise in each step.
34. (d) '∆' gets divided into 3 parts, so will the square.
35. (b) Clearly (b) is the correct option as 3 circles reduce to 1; so will the ellipse.
36. (d) Two black '∆'s reduce to one shifting clockwise.
37. (d) Second figure rotate 90° anticlockwise direction
38. (b) All intersecting lines are removed.
39. (e) In subsequent steps 5, 4, 3, 2, 1 ... crosses are added alternately on upper and lower side.
40. (b) In the first step the upper row designs shift diagonally, the lower row designs shift to upper row, while the middle row designs interchange places. In the next step the lower left designs shifts to the upper right, right column designs move one step down–wards, while the lower right shifts to lower left. The left middle is replaced by a new one.
41. (e) In alternate steps three and four consecutive arcs get inverted.
42. (c) In the first step the lower left shifts to upper left, upper left to top, top to lower left. The upper right shifts to lower right, lower right to bottom and bottom to upper right. In the next step the upper left shifts to top, top to upper right, and upper right to upper left while the lower left shifts to lower right, lower right to bottom and bottom to lower left.
43. (d) In the upper left designs two and three line segments are added alternately while two line segments are added to the lower right design in each step. In subsequent steps 1, 2, 3... line segments are lost from the upper right while 1, 2, 3 line segments are added to the lower left design.
44. (d) In alternate steps the middle design interchanges place with left and right designs respectively.
45. (a) The shading in upper–left and lower–right square moves one side anticlockwise while one step clockwise in upper–right and lower – left.
46. (c) The upper design gets vertically inverted and shifts to lower position in each step.
47. (b) In each step the designs shift from lower to upper and upper to middle and get inverted while a new design appears at lower position.
48. (e) In each step the pentagon shifts one–and–a–half side anticlockwise and one line segment shifts from anticlockwise to clockwise end.
49. (a) **Statements** : All books are notes.
Conclusions : Some books are notes. (Implication)
Some notes are books. (conversion)
Hence I follows.
Statements : Some notes are pencils.
No pencil is paper.
Conclusions : Some note are not paper.
(I + E = O type)
Statements : Some notes are pencils.
Conclusions : Some pencils are notes. (conversion)
Statements : No pencil is paper.
Conclusions : Some pencils are not papers.
(Implication)
No paper is pencil. (Conversion)
Since III and IV form a complementary I-E pair, either of the two must follow.
50. (c) **Statements** : Some tables are chairs.
Conclusions : Some chairs are tables. (conversion)
Hence, III follows.
Statements : No cupboard is table.
Conclusions : Some cupboards are not table.
(Implication)
No table is cupboarD. (conversion)
Statements : Some chairs are cupboards.
Conclusions : Some cupboards are chairs.
(conversion)
Since, no table is cupboarD.
Some cupboards are chairs.
Conclusions : Some chairs are not table.
(E + I = O* type)
Hence, I follows.
51. (a) **Statements** : No table is fruit.
Conclusions :
Some tables are not fruit. (Implication)
No fruit is table. (conversion)
Statements : No fruit is window.
Conclusions : Some fruits are not window.
(Implication)
No window is fruit. (Conversion)
Statements : No fruit is window
All windows are chairs.
Conclusions : Some chairs are not fruit.
(E + A = O* type)
Statements : All windows are chairs.
Conclusions : Some windows are chairs.
(Implication)
Some chairs are windows.
(Conversion)
Hence none follows.

52. (d) **Statements** : No man is sky.
Conclusions : Some men are not sky. (Implication)
No sky is man. (conversion)
Statements : No sky is roaD.
Conclusions : Some skies are not roaD. (Implication)
No road is sky. (conversion)
Hence II follows.
Statements : Some men are roads.
Conclusions : Some roads are men. (conversion)
No sky is man.

Some men are roads.
Some roads are not sky.
(E + I = O* type)
No sky is roaD.

Some roads are men.
Some men are not sky.
(E + I = O* type)
Statements : Some men are roads.

No road is sky.
Conclusions : Some men are not sky. (I + E = O type)
Statements : Some roads are man.

No man is sky.
Conclusions : Some roads are not sky.
(I + E = O type)
Hence, only II follows

53. (b) **Statements** : All papers are books.
Conclusions : Some papers are books. (Implication)
Some books are papers. (conversion)
Hence II follows.
Statements : All bags are books.
Conclusions : Some bags are books. (Implication)
Some books are bags. (conversion)
Statements : Some purses are bags.
Conclusions : Some bags are purses. (conversion)
Statements : Some purses are bags.

All bags are books.
Conclusions : Some purses are books. (I + A = I-type)
Some books are purses. (conversion)
Hence, III follows.

54. (d) C is the 3rd letter, F sixth, I ninth so next letter will be 12th, i.e. L.
The middle numerics are the squares of 2, 3, 4 and so on. So next numeric would be 25.
The last letter follow the order : U is 3rd letter after R, X is 3rd after U. So, R would be 3rd letter after 'O'.
∴ Missing term = L25O.

55. (a) I follows because it will lessen the miseries of affected people. II does not follow. What role can the fire brigade play in a problem caused by heavy rain?

56. (d) Neither talks about what should be done. Both only suggest the probable consequence.

57. (e) Money is very important for the execution of any plan. Reduction in other expenditures will definitely help to raise money. Hence I follows. Any programme can not succeed without a good planning. Hence II follows.

58. (b) Only II follows as I does't provide solution to the problem. Rather it talks about the contrary.

59. (d) The first course should be try their best that transporters don't go on strike. But it necessary that one is prepared with an alternative as well, in case the first course fails.

For (Q. 60-62)

Clearly, C joined as a officer. Since, B joined on neither wednesday nor Friday. Therefore, B joined on Saturday and A joined on Friday. These information can be summerized as follows :

Person	Post	Day
F	Manager	Monday
B	Supervisor	Saturday
D	Technician	Thursday
C	Officer	Wednesday
E	clerk	Tuesday
A	Sales executive	Friday

60. (b) 61. (d)
62. (e)

For (Q. 63-66)

According to the information provided, the order in which the boys stand according to their heights is as follows :

63. (c) Clearly, form the above diagram, E is between D and C.

64. (b) D is the tallest.

65. (d) Counting from the shortest, C is the fourth are in the line.

66. (c) Clearly, from the above diagram, B is the shortest.

For (Q. 67-70)

On the basis in of information provided, we get the following relationship amongst the weights of the various rings.

$D = 2E, \ E = 4.5F$

$F = \frac{G}{2}, \ G = \frac{H}{2}$

Let H = 10, then G = 5, F = 2.5,
$E = 4.5 \times 2.5 = 11.25$ and $D = 11.25 \times 2 = 22.50$

Thus the weights in the decreasing order are as follows
$D > E > H > G > F$.

67. (a) As ling D is the heaviest, it will fetch the highest value.

68. (b) Clearly, H is heavier than G and F.

69. (c) Ring F is the lightest.

70. (a) As marked out above.

71. (b) Clearly, W must be placed in window no. 2 as dictated by the restrictions.

For (Qs. 72-76):

The following are the questions on the conversion of decimal number system into binary number system and vice versa.

72. (a)

2	11	remainder
2	5	1
2	2	1
	1	0

$\therefore (11)_{10} = (1011)_2 = \$@\$\$$

73. (e) $(8)_{10} = (1000)_2 = \$@@@$

74. (c) $\$\$@\$ = (1101)_2$

To convert binary number into decimal number start coming from the right, starting with zero (0).

Now
1 1 0 1
3 2 1 0

$\therefore 1\times 2^3 + 1\times 2^2 + 0\times 2^1 + 1\times 2^0 = 8+4+0+1 = (10)_{10}$

75. (b) 76. (d)

77. (c) According to the passage, world economy witnessed a slowdown during post-September 11 perioD. But-what was the trend of growth of the economy during pre-September 11 period is not known.

78. (d) This will benefit the yarn manufacturers, not the farmers, unless the latter act as the former also.

79. (b) That is why the cotton growers seem to have switched over to other cash crops.

80. (e) Note that yarn manufacturers get benefited in post-September 11 scenario.

81. (b) The passage says nothing about the supply of cotton during the current year. But lack of enthusiasm in cotton growers, fall of cotton acreage and rise in the price of yarn makes the inference probably true.

82. (e) The price of the cotton was very low last year which attracted the yarn manufactures to store cotton. Therefore, the case of shortage is ruled out.

83. (b) I is not implicit. In fact, the statement suggests it is possible to contain terrorist activities. What is disputed is "how long". But II is implicit. The action has begun, though its end is not in sight

84. (a) The statement mentions that if the people ask about the tailor, your suit is gooD. This means that people ask only in the situation when the thing is gooD. So, I is implicit. The criteria of an excellent suit is not mentioneD. So, II is not implicit.

85. (c) Clearly, the need to import sugar could be either due to increase in consumption or the inefficiency of the factories to produce sugar to their fullest capacity. So, either I or II is implicit.

86. (b) What we are being told about brilliant students does not have anything to do with mediocre students. Hence I is not implicit. But II is implicit. This must be the reason why the brilliant students do not always excel.

87. (b) I is not implicit as the company with a bad product might be advertising more because people are not aware of it. According to the statement, the product of company Y is more known because of more advertisement. So, II is implicit.

88. (b) Each letter of the word is moved four steps forward to obtain the code.

89. (d) Using the proper symbols, we have:

Given expression $= 16 + 24 \div 8 - 6 \div 2 \times 3$

$= 16 + 3 - 3 \times 3 = 16 + 3 - 9 = 10.$

90. (b)

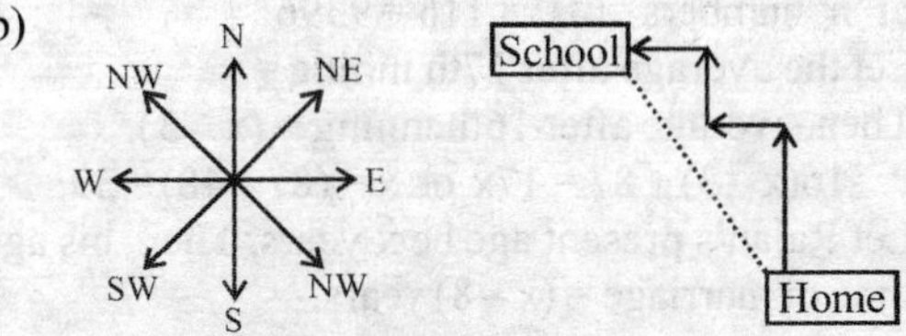

It is clear from the diagram that school is in North-west direction with respect to home.

91. (d) The correct series will be

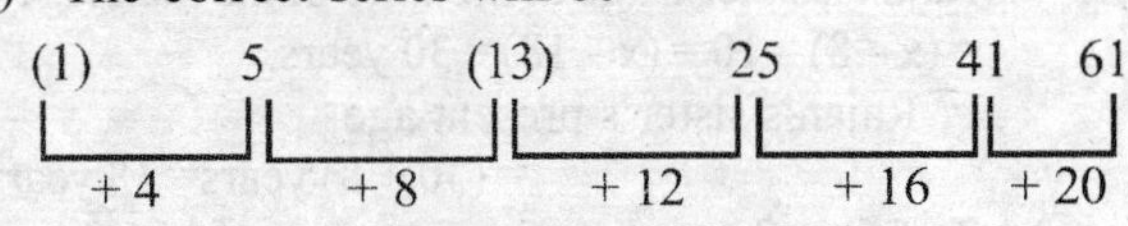

92. (a) 3, 10, 29, (66), (127), 218

1^3+2, 2^3+2, 3^3+2, 4^3+2, 5^3+2, 6^3+2

93. (b) 4 6 10 (12) 16 (18) 22

+6 +6 (above); +6 +6 +6 (below)

94. (c) The candidates satisfies all the conditions and hence is to be promoteD.

95. (a) The candidate satisfy all other conditions except condition (8) and hence the case is to be referred to MD.

96. (b) The candidates does not satisfy condition (2) and no information is given about condition (8). Hence the candidate is not to be promoteD.

97. (d) The candidate satisfies all other conditions except condition (4). Hence the case is to be referred to GM (P).

98. (b) Let A's share $= \text{Rs}\frac{15}{4}x$, B's share = Rs 4x and C's share = Rs 5.5x

Given $\frac{15}{x}x = 30 \Rightarrow x = 8$

$\therefore$ Total amount $= 30 + 32 + 44 = $ Rs 106

99. (a) Time $= \dfrac{225}{6\times\frac{5}{18}} = 135\,\text{sec} = 2\frac{1}{4}$ min.

100. (a) When folded along breadth, we have :

$2\left(\frac{l}{2}+b\right) = 34$ or $l + 2b = 34$ ....(i)

When folded along length, we have :

$2\left(l+\frac{b}{2}\right) = 38$ or $2l + b = 38$ ....(ii)

Solving (i) and (ii), we get :

$l = 14$ and $b = 10$.

$\therefore$ Area of the paper $= (14 \times 10)\ \text{cm}^2 = 140\ \text{cm}^2$.

101. (d) $8 \times 2 - 1 = 15$, $15 \times 2 - 2 = 28$, $28 \times 2 - 3 = 53$, $53 \times 2 - 4 = 102$

102. (d) The common differences between the consecutive terms of the series are 6, 9, 12, 15, etC.

103. (b) ∵ Product of 'n' numbers = (HCF for each pair)^n × LCM of 'n' numbers $= (3)^4 \times 116 = 9396$

104. (b) Let the average after 17th inning = x.
Then, average after 16th inning = (x – 3).
$\therefore\ 16(x-3) + 87 = 17x$ or $x = (87-48) = 39$.

105. (c) Let Rajan's present age be x years. Then, his age at the time of marriage = (x – 8) years.

$$\therefore\ x = \frac{6}{5}(x-8) \Rightarrow 5x = 6x - 48 \Rightarrow x = 48.$$

Rajan's sister's age at the time of his marriage $= (x-8) - 10 = (x-18) = 30$ years.
∴ Rajan's sister's present age $= (30 + 8)$ years $= 38$ years.

106. (c) $2a + 5b = 7$
$-2a + 8b = 32$
$\Rightarrow 13b = 39 \Rightarrow b = 3, a = -4$
$a < b$. Hence option (c) is the correct answer.

107. (d) $a^2 + 8 = 89 \Rightarrow a^2 = 81$
$\Rightarrow a = \pm 9,\ b = 9$
If $a = -9$, then $a < b$
$\therefore\ a \le b$ i.e. option (d)

108. (a) $a^2 - 7a - 18 = 0 \Rightarrow a = 9$ or -2
$b^2 + 9b + 18 = 0 \Rightarrow b = -6, -3$
$\Rightarrow a > b$ i.e., option (a) is the correct answer.

109. (e) $a^2 = 3249$
$a = \sqrt{3249} \Rightarrow a = b$

110. (b) $a^2 - 8a - 48 = 0 \Rightarrow a = 12, -4$
$b^2 + 9b + 20 = 0 \Rightarrow b = -5, -4$
$a \ge b$ i.e. (b)

111. (b) $$\%\text{ increase in profit} = \frac{\text{Change in profit}}{\text{Profit in previous year}}$$

$$\%\text{ increase in the year 1994-95} = \frac{4.5 - 2.5}{2.5} \times 100 = 80\%$$

% increase in the year 1995-96

$$= \frac{6 - 4.5}{4.5} \times 100 = 33.33\%$$

% increase in the year 1996-97

$$= \frac{8.5 - 6}{6} \times 100 = 41.67\%$$

% increase in the year 1997-98

$$= \frac{12 - 8.5}{8.5} \times 100 = 41.2\%$$

Comparing the fractions we can say that % increase in profit is highest over the previous year in the year 1994-95.

112. (a) $$\text{Profit per unit sales} = \frac{\text{profit}}{\text{sales}}$$

$$\text{Profit per unit sale for year 1993-94} = \frac{2.5}{100} = 0.025$$

$$\text{Profit per unit sale for year 1994-95} = \frac{4.5}{100} = 0.016$$

$$\text{Profit per unit sale for year 1995-96} = \frac{6}{300} = 0.02$$

$$\text{Profit per unit sale for year 1997-98} = \frac{12}{680} = 0.0176$$

Hence, profit per unit sales was highest in 1993-94 over previous year.

113. (b)

	Expense	% increase
1996-1997	$290 - 8.5 = 281.5$	shows decrease
1994-1995	$250 - 4.5 = 245.5$	$\frac{245.5 - 97.5}{97.5} = 1.52$
1995-1996	$300 - 6 = 294$	$\frac{294 - 245.5}{245.5} = 0.19$
1997-1998	$680 - 12 = 668$	$\frac{668 - 281.5}{281.5} = 1.37$
1993-1994	$100 - 2.5 = 97.5$	—

114. (d) $$\text{Profit/Unit sale for 1996-1997} = \frac{8.5}{290} = 0.029.$$

So, it is clear from the above data and solution of question 32, that the data is very fluctuating.

115. (b) In 1987-1988, growth in sales = 529%
In 1997-1998, growth in sales = 214%
In 2000-2001, growth in sales = 170%
In 1999-2000, growth in sales = 208%

116. (a) This is the only period when total sales was less than total production.

117. (c) Production per employee (in Rs)

1977-78	1065.52
1987-88	3560.76
1997-98	7998.76
1998-99	8770.57
1999-00	10409.16
2000-01	11496.19

118. (d) From table given in solution (3)

119. (c)

Year	Ratio
1977-78	0.997
1987-88	1.082
1997-98	1.12
1998-99	1.095
1999-00	1.097
2000-01	1.098

120. (c) Total rose producation $= (15 + 12.5 + 12.45 + 20 + 12.4 + 22.5 + 22.4 + 25) \times 1000 = 142250$

$$\text{Now 10\% of total production} = \frac{142250 \times 10}{100} = 14,225.$$

Obviously, Haryana, Karnataka and Rajasthan contribute less than 10% in the total production.

121. (a) Required percentage $= \frac{25-20}{20} \times 100 = 25\%$ (more)

122. (d) Total producation of rose by all the states = 142250

$\therefore$ Average $= \frac{142250}{8} \approx 18$ thousand

123. (b) Required percentage $= \frac{25}{142.25} \times 100 = 17.6\% \approx 20\%$

124. (b) Production of company AVC in 2000 = 360 crore units
Average production of AVC over the given years

$= \frac{1970}{6}$

Hence, required per cent $= \frac{360 \times 6}{1970} \times 100 = 109.64\%$
$\approx 110\%$

125. (c) Apprroximate per cent increase or decrease in production from the previous year for SIO are as follows :

$1998 = \frac{2}{85} \times 100 = 2.35\%$

$1999 = \frac{2 \times 100}{87} = 2.29\%$

$2000 = \frac{2 \times 100}{89} = 2.24\%$

$2001 = \frac{1 \times 100}{91} = 1.09\%$

$2002 = \frac{4 \times 100}{92} = 4.35\%$

Quicker method : See the difference of produced units between two consecutive years. The difference is maximum for 2001 to 2002, and production during all these years is almost same. Hence, in the year 2002, SIO registered maximum increase in production over the previous year.

126. (d) Sum of the productions of companies in the first three years and the last three years is as follows :

Company	First three years	Last three years
TP	358	349
ZIR	238	267
AVC	900	1070
CTU	836	852
PEN	90	127
SIO	261	279

127. (c) Total production of the six companies in first two given years = 863 + 927 = 1790
Again, total production of the six companies in last two given years = 989 + 991 = 1980

Therefore, required per cent $= \frac{1790 \times 100}{1980} = 90.40\%$

128. (b) The required difference = (91 – 92) crore units = 1 × 10000000 = 10000000 units

129 (c) Those companies are: ZIR, PEN and SIO

For (Q. 130-134)

Courses	Total students T = x% of 1200	Number of girls G = y% of 800	Number of boys B = T – G
A	240	240	0
B	180	80	100
C	60	16	44
D	420	240	180
E	144	112	32
F	156	112	44

130. (a) Required ratio = 180 : 240 = 3 : 4

131. (c) Courses are C and F

132. (a) Required % $= \frac{112-32}{32} \times 100 = 250\%$

133. (d) The number of boys for course A = 0

134. (b) Number of girls in course C = 16.

135. (e) Let numbers are $(x-2)$, x and $(x+2)$.
$(I) \Rightarrow (x-2) + x + (x+2) = 3 \times 21$
Hence, we can find value of x.
Then, question can be solved using statement (I) alone.
$(II) \Rightarrow x(x-2)(x+2) = 2688$
Obviously, question can be solved using statement (II) alone.

136. (a) Let the speed of boat = V_b km/h
and the speed of stream = V_s km/h
$(I) \Rightarrow V_b - V_s = 48/6$
$\Rightarrow V_b - V_s = 8$ .... (i)
$(II) \Rightarrow V_b + V_s = 48/4$
$\Rightarrow V_b + V_s = 12$ .... (ii)
On solving (i) and (ii), we can be determined the value of V_B.
Hence, both the statements together are necessary to answer the question.

137. (a) $\because$ Product of two numbers = their HCF × LCM
$\therefore$ Both the statements together are necessary to answer the question.

138. (b) $(I) \Rightarrow p = 90°$
$(II) \Rightarrow AB = CD$
Since, we have no idea about other angles and length of sides AD and BC. Therefore, nothing can be said about ABCD. Hence both the statements together are not sufficient to answer the question.

139. (e) Given : $l = 4$ metres.

$h = \frac{1}{16} \times 4 = \frac{1}{4}$ metre

Let width of slab = b metres
$(I) \Rightarrow l \times b \times h = 2$
Hence, width of slab can be determined by using (I) alone.
$(II) \Rightarrow$ Surface Area = 19 m^2
$\Rightarrow 2(bh + hl + lb) = 19$.
Obviously, question can be answered by using (II) alone.
Hence, each statement alone is sufficient.

140. (d) $\because$ Amount $= P\left(1+\frac{R}{100}\right)^n$

(I) $\Rightarrow$ For P = 1000 and n = 1, A = Rs 1100

$\therefore$ R = 10%

Hence, C.I. after 3 years can be calculateD.

$\therefore$ Statement (I) alone is sufficient to answer the question.

Now, since difference between S.I. and C.I. for 2 years $= P \times \left(\frac{R}{100}\right)^2$

$\therefore$ From (II), R can be calculateD.

Hence, C.I. after 3 years can be determineD.

Therefore, each statement alone is sufficient to answer the question.

141. (c) (I) $\Rightarrow$ Other tank empty in 2(8 + 8 + 8) hours = 48 hours

(II) $\Rightarrow$ Volume of original tank $= \frac{1}{3}$(volume of other tank)

$\Rightarrow$ Original tank empty in 16 hours

$\Rightarrow$ Required number of hours can be calculateD.

142. (a) (I) $\Rightarrow$ Profit = S.P. – C.P. = 40. Hence statement (I) alone is sufficient.

(II) $\Rightarrow$ It's nothing new. Since, if profit = 20% S.P. = 120% of C.P.

143. (d) (I) $\Rightarrow$ Total salary of 30 assembly workers

T_s = Total salary – salary of foreman

and required average $= \frac{T_s}{30}$

(II) $\Rightarrow$ Foreman's salary = 12,000 = 120% of average salary of assembly workers

$\Rightarrow$ Average salary $= \frac{12{,}000 \times 100}{120}$

Hence, each statement alone is sufficient to answer the question.

144. (a) (I) $\Rightarrow$ $3x + 4x(0.50) + 5x(0.25) = 500$

$\Rightarrow 6.25x = 500 \Rightarrow x = 80$

$\therefore$ The total number of 50-paise coins = 4x = 320

But we can't be solved the question using statement (II).

Hence statement (I) alone is sufficient to answer the question.

145. (d) Given : $V_1 + V_2 = \frac{80+100}{36} = 5\,\text{m/s}$

(I) $\Rightarrow$ $V_1 = \frac{80}{60} = \frac{4}{3}\,\text{m/s}$

$\therefore V_2 = 5 - \frac{4}{3} = \frac{11}{3}\,\text{m/s}$

$\therefore$ Required time $= \frac{80+100}{\frac{11}{3}-\frac{4}{3}}$ m/s

(II) $\Rightarrow$ $V_2 = \frac{120+100}{60} = \frac{11}{3}\,\text{m/s}$

Now, $V_1 = 5 - \frac{11}{3} = \frac{4}{3}\,\text{m/s}$

Hence, required time can be calculateD.

$\therefore$ each statement alone is sufficient to answer the question.

146. (d) (I) $\Rightarrow$ Puttu can do the job in $\frac{36 \times 12}{36-18} = 18$ days

(II) $\Rightarrow$ Ratio of efficiency for Kundu : Puttu = 1 : 2

$\therefore$ ratio of days for Kundu : Puttu = 2 : 1

$\therefore$ Puttu will do the job in $12\left(\frac{2+1}{2}\right) = 18$ days and

Kundu will do it in $12\left(\frac{2+1}{1}\right) = 36$ days.

147. (c) (I) $\Rightarrow$ $\angle ABD = \angle BAD = \theta$ (let)

(II) $\Rightarrow$ $\angle ABD = \angle CBD = \theta$

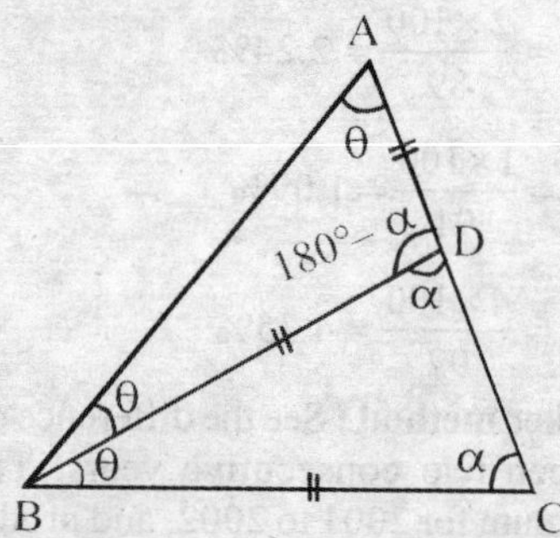

Since BC = BD $\Rightarrow \angle BDC = \angle BCD = \alpha$ (let)

$\therefore$ In ΔABD, $\theta + \theta + (180 - \alpha) = 180^\circ$

$\Rightarrow \alpha = 2\theta$

$\Rightarrow \angle ACB = \angle ABC$

$\Rightarrow \angle AB = \angle AC$

$\Rightarrow \Delta ABC$ is isosceles.

Hence, both statements together are necessary to answer the question.

148. (d) Suppose speed of train Z = x m/s

$\therefore$ Speed of train X = x + 45% of

$x = x + \frac{9}{20}x = \frac{29x}{20}$ m/s

Now , (I) $\Rightarrow$ $\frac{110+160}{6.5} = x + \frac{29x}{20}$

Hence, x can be calculated by statement (I) alone.

(II) $\Rightarrow$ $\frac{29x}{20} - x = 28 \times \frac{5}{18}$

$\therefore$ x can also be calculated using statement (II) alone.

149. (d) (I) ⇒ He lays 4 cards on the table.
(II) ⇒ He lays 4 cards on the table.

150. (c) The tense in this sentence should be the present perfect continous because it refers to an action that started at some time in past and continues till the present time so right use is 'have been living in Mumbai.'

151. (a) As a child, should be followed by a phrase that has 'child' as its subject, i.e., as a child I was taken by my parents to visit Jammu & Kashmir or other ways, we can change the first part of the sentence, the second part describes an action so the first should be an adverb clause. Thus when I was child is the most suitable alternative.

152. (a) 'Anyone' implies a person involveD. So a personal pronoun will be needed to give conditions later in the sentence, there must be a 'he' or 'one' in the sentence. The noun cannot be in the second person but has to be in the third person because 'Anyone' refers to an unknown third person.

153. (c) The use of the modal 'should' is unnecessary in this statement. It is a statement giving directions.

154. (c) The part he, his colleague could easily be eliminated and a simpler form of to + verb can be used to make the sentence more appropriate (a) is grammatically incorrect since it has omitted the article 'an' (b) changes the meaning or intent of the underlined phrase. Thus (c) is the most suitable choice.

155. (c) D is the introductory sentence, B tells us that he may look invincible but he appears quite vulnerable as his daughter Sophie has a hole in her heart, C re-assures that it is not life threatening, and A ends by stating that Sophie might need open-heart surgery later in life.

156. (a) A begins the paragraph with the statement that 'Hollywood is a man's world' is not the whole truth. D shows that during the silent era female screen writers are more than men, B follows by showing Jodie Fosters surprise at this. It is concluded by C which says that Jodie had no idea about the activeness of women even in those days.

157. (d) C introduces the topic for the paragraph, A tells us about the Saheli Program, which offers a three week tour of India. B continues telling us about what the participants will learn about in those three weeks. And D concludes with other activities apart from women's issues.

158. (a) D begins the paragraph telling us about J. P. Morgan, B continues with more details about J. P. Morgan. A tells us about its timely and accurate information which brings about business decisions and it concludes with C which talks about J. P. Morgan's proprietary trade related data.

159. (d) Sentence A beings the paragraph by introducing the topic the magical thing happening to our planet. C states that our planet is getting smaller. B follows in which it says that some are calling it a paradigm shift and in D others call it a business transformation.

160. (a)

161. (c) A. Gaucherie means clumsiness
B. Dexterity means skillful; adroitness
C. Eulogise means praise, extol.
D. Dearth means scarcity.
Thus a and b are antonym to each other.

162. (a) A. Fallacious means mistaken belief, faulty.
B. Pusillanimity is cowardly.
C. Fortitude-courage in pain or adversity.
D. Fallible-one who commits fault.
Thus b is antonym to C.

163. (a) A. Incarcerate means to imprison, confine.
C. Impeccable means flawless.
D. Felicitate is to congratulate
Thus a is synonym of B.

164. (c) A. Disinterested means impartial, not influenced
B. Comprehensible means including all.
C. Emulate is to copy.
D. Impartial means supporting one person or group than another.
Thus both are synonym to each other.

165. (b) A. Inamorata means beloved
B. Beloved means much loved
C. Imbecile is stupid or person of weak intellect.
D. Novice means beginner.
Thus a and b are synonyms.

166. (a) A. Adumbrate means indicate faintly,
B. Overshadow means to throw a shadow over.
C. Zany means a clown, buffoon
D. Vulpine means crafty; cunning
Thus a and b are synonym.

167. (c) A. Cantankerous is bad tempered, quarrelsome
B. Querulous means complaining
C. Amicable means friendly
D. Occult means mysterious.
Thus a is antonym to c

168. (a) A. Jouisance means pleasure, joy.
B. Joyousness means merry, happiness.
C. Betrothed means promise to marry, bind with
D. Usurp means seize or assume right.
Thus a and b are synonymous.

169. (c) A. Hunky-dory means excellent.
B. Choleric means easily angereD.
C. Shoddy means inferior, pretentious.
D. Enervate means to deprive of strength or vigour.
Thus a and c are antonym.

170. (c) A. Certitude means certainty.
B. Hoipolli means common people.
C. Certainty means sure.
D. Hostile means unfriendly, enemy
Thus a is synonymous to C.

171. (a) is the correct option, it can be inferred from the language used by the author.

172. (c) is the correct option, as the vehicles mentioned are A car, A jeep and Snow Plough.

173. (b) is the correct choice, as the Mississippi flowed northwards due to an earthquake.
174. (c) is the correct option, as it can be seen in paragraph five.
175. (b) is the correct choice, as it can be given in paragraph seven.
176. (b) is the best option, as it can be found in the eighth paragraph.
177. (b) Option (b) is the correct choice, as weather is not manipulable as can be inferred from paragraph seven.
178. (a) is the correct option, as he is watching the weather channel in his house.
179. (d) is the correct choice, as it can be inferred from the passage.
180. (c) sight means scene, sue means to file a Suit.
181. (c) cemetery means graveyards, hierarchy means a system of society in which people are graded into different classes according to certain norms.
182. (c) affectation means to pretend
183. (d) Modest means humble, awkward means clumsy, celebrated means distinguisheD.
184. (b) Credulity
185. (a) Roost
186. (c) have been
The present perfect tense is used to express past actions whose time is not given and not definite.
187. (c) had started
The past perfect tense helps in telling us which action happened earlier than the other when both the actions referred to happen in the past. The simple past is used in one clause and the past perfect in the other.
188. (d) or by taking up other
Or is a Co-ordinating Conjunction that joins together two statements or clauses of equal rank or importance.
189. (d) he did
190. (b) men being tested
The present (passive) participle, being tested' ought to be used here to maintain the uniformity in the Sentence.

191. (a) 192. (c)
193. (b) 194. (b)
195. (d) 196. (e)
197. (c) 198. (e)
199. (d) 200. (b)

MOCK TEST - 3

1. (a) According to question, reversing the position of digits of the numbers, we have 315, 864, 627, 793, 486
   ∴ Second largest number is 793, whose second digit is 9.
2. (a) As per question. the required pairs are shown below:

   H E A R T B U R N

   Therefore, only one required pair is 'RU'
3. (a) According to question,

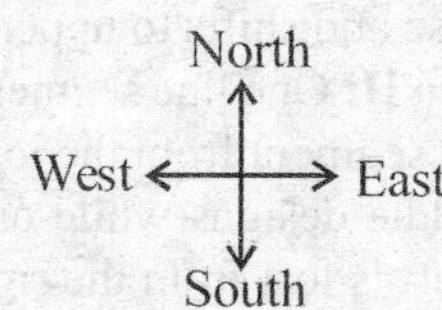

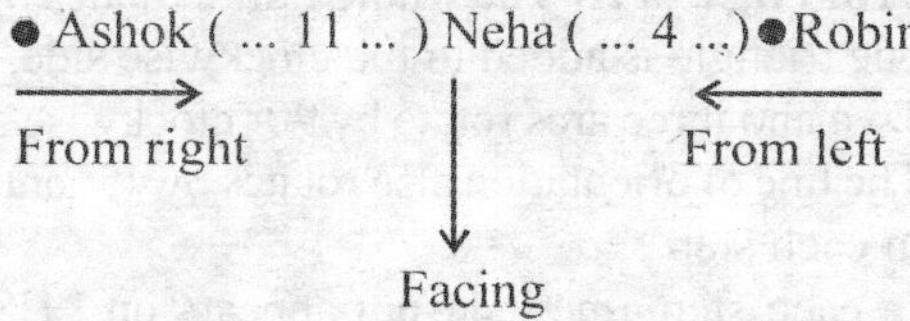

   The number of children is 28 from left in the row upto Ashok. Therefore, the number of children seated before Robin
   $= 28 - (1 + 11 + 1 + 4 + 1)$
   $= 28 - 18 = 10$
   ∴ Position of Robin from left $= 10 + 1 = 11$
4. (b) On comparing,
   R → 5
   A → 1
   I → 2
   D → 6
   N → 7
   E → 3
   ∴ DINE → 6273
5. (c) According to question,
   You could go there → *la na pa da*.........(i)
   and
   could you come back→ *ha ta da la*.......(ii)
   From both equations (i) and (ii)
   go there → *na pa*
   and come back → *ha ta*
   ∴ To find the code for 'back' the data are inadequate, but the code for 'back' will be either *ha* or *ta* surely.
6. (c) 3 2 (4) 6 7 5 (9)
   2 3 (4) 5 6 7 (9)
   After arranging original number digits in ascending order.
7. (a) R E C R U I T
   Only one pair i.e., E – I
8. (a) D I S T U R B
   Hence these pairs are ST, TU, SU and RT
9. (b) N, W, E, S
   o o o o o o o o o o o o o o o o o o o o o o o o o o o o
   G K A V
   Hence, total number of boys = 28
10. (c) The series 137153163 can be broken as 1, 3, 7, 15, 31, 63 where $3 = 2(1) + 1$, $7 = 2(3) + 1$
    $15 = 2(7) + 1$ and so on.
    ∴ The next term is $2(63) + 1 = 127$
11. (d) The series 13102164129 can be broken as 1, 3, 10, 21, 64, 129. Where $3 = 2(1) + 1$, $10 = 3(3) + 1$
    ∴ The next term is $= 3(129) + 1 = 388$
12. (c) 1st number moves +5, +7, +9, +11, +13 steps respectively.
    3rd number moves +2 steps each time.
    2nd letter moves –1 step each time.
13. (c) Clearly, the first, second and third letters of each term are respectively moved one, two and three steps forward to obtain the corresponding letters of the next term. So, the next term is EJO.
14. (a) As a man covers some distance after walking, in the same way, a fish covers some distance after swimming. Hence the correct answer is (a).
15. (b) The words in each pair are antonyms.
16. (c) Second grows on the first. "Pelt" is the skin of an animal with the fur or hair still on it.
17. (b) Here, all except Lotus are flowers, which grow on land while lotus is a water flower. Hence, the answer is (b).
18. (c) In all other groups, the first number is obtained by adding 2 to the product of the second and the third numbers.
19. (d) From problem figure 1 to 2 the black part comes toward centre reaching in the next leaf in anticlockwise direction. And from problem figure 3 to 4 the black part reaching in the next leaf in anticlockwise direction comes toward outer side. In the same way from problem figure 5 to 6 black part will come toward centre reaching in the next leaf in anticlockwise direction. Thus, the answer figure (d) is obtained.
20. (a) From problem 1 to 3 there is increasing of design by one which comes on the left side in the larger shape. Thus the answer figure (a) is obtained.
21. (a) From problem figure 1 to 2 and 3 to 4 the design moves half side ahead anticlockwise rotating through 90°. In the same way from problem figure 5 to 6 the design will change, thus the answer figure (a) is obtained.
22. (b) In each successive problem figure there is increasing of design by one and the design moves anticlockwise one arm ahead, while a new design comes at the designs of even places. Thus the answer figure (b) is obtained.
23. (d) From problem figure 1 to 2 two design from right change their places mutually and the design of left change to a new form at the same place and turns over vertically. From problem figure 2 to 3 two designs of left change

their places mutually and the design of right changes to a new form and turns over vertically the same rule continues further, thus the answer figure (d) is obtained.

24. (b) In each successive problem figure design '⊤' rotates anticlockwise through 45°, 90°, 45°, 90° respectively and a new design of its left and then right is added respectively. Thus the answer figure (e) is obtained.

25. (e) From problem figures 1 to 4 two designs of right change their places with each other and from problem figure 2 to 5, two designs of left change their places with each other. In the same way from problem figure 3 to 6 two designs of right will change their places with each other. Thus the answer figure (e) is obtained.

26. (e) From problem figure 1 to 2 and 3 to 4 the design turning over horizontally situates toward right side and the design rotating through 90° anticlockwise situates in the middle. As per this rule the answer figure (e) is obtained.

27. (c) In each subsequent figure design change their places as below:

• 1
• 2
• 3
• 4
• 5

From problem 1 to 2 designs 1 and 2
From problem 2 to 3 designs 3 and 4
From problem 3 to 4 designs 5 sets up at top
From problem 4 to 5 designs 1 and 2
and 5 to 6 design 3 and 4 change their places with each other thus the answer figure (c) is obtained.

28. (b) In the consecutive figure, the design '•' comes at middle from lower right, at upper left from middle and than at middle. The design '★' comes at left middle from upper middle, at right from left middle and at upper middle from right middle. A new design comes lower left from middle.

29. (a) Designs shift one and one-and-a-half sides anticlockwise alternately. Designs placed at the second and fourth from clockwise end are replaced in one step while the first, third and the fifth designs are replaced in the next step.

30. (c) The designs shift from upper-right position to centre, centre to upper-left and then one step anticlockwise in each consecutive step. Designs are replaced by a new one after three steps. A new design is added in each step at upper-right position.

31. (c) The designs shifts from upper-right position to centre, centre to upper-left and then one step anticlockwise in each consecutive step. Designs are replaced by a new one after three steps. A new design is added in each step at upper-right position.

32. (e) The shading moves alternately to adjacent and opposite corners. The outer design moves one side anticlockwise in each step and gets inverted alternately.

33. (c) The main figure rotates by 45° and 90° anticlockwise alternately. The unshaded circle moves outside and inside in each step while shaded circle moves inside and outside alternately.

34. (c) **From fig I to II:** The upper-right design shifts to centre → upper-left → lower-right → lower-left. The lower-left disappears while a new design appears at upper-right position.

35. (e) **From fig I to II:** The middle design rotates by 180° and interchanges place with left design. The right design gets vertically inverted and the arc attached to it further rotates by 180° anticlockwise.

36. (b) **From fig I to II:** The upper-left and lower-right designs rotate by 90° clockwise and shift to centre and lower-left respectively while the middle-left rotates by 90° anticlockwise and shifts to upper-middle.

37. (a) **From fig I to II:** One line segment from the upper part and one line segment from the lower part are lost from left and middle designs while one line segment from the upper part is lost from the right design.

38. (e) **From fig I to II:** The whole figure rotates by 180° and one triangle is added to the clockwise side.

39. (b) Two and three arcs rotate by 90° clockwise alternately. The line of orientation also rotates by 45° anticlockwise in each step.

40. (e) In each step a new design appears on LHS end. The first from LHS shifts one step towards right. The second from LHS becomes RHS-end and RHS end design becomes second from RHS. The second from RHS moves to anticlockwise corner while the existing corner element is lost.

41. (c) The upper and the lower designs get laternally inverted in one step while the middle row designs get vertically inverted in the next step.

42 (a) The designs move one step anticlockwise in each step while two arcs are added in one step and the designs get laterally inverted in the next.

43. (c) One square on the clockwise side gets shaded in each step while the shaded squares rotate by 90° anticlockwise in each step. The shading of the next square is 180° rotated form of its anticlockwise counterpart.

44. (c) The given sequence is a combination of two series :
I. 11, 21, 32, 41, 51 and II. 2, 3, 4, 5, 6
Clearly, the pattern in I is +10
So, 32 is wrong and should be replaced by (21 + 10) i.e. 31.

45. (a) The first letter of each term is moved three steps forward and the second letter is moved three steps backward to obtain the corresponding letters of the next term.

46. (c) The series is abc/a$\underline{a}$bc/aab$\underline{b}$c/a$\underline{a}$bbc$\underline{c}$/a.

47. (d) **Statements** : Some stones are bricks.
Conclusions : Some bricks are stone. (conversion)
Statements : All plants are stones.
Conclusions : Some plants are stones. (Implication)
Some stones are plants. (conversion)
Statements : No flower is plant.
Conclusions : Some flowers are not plant. (Implication)
No plant is flower. (Conversion)
Statements : No flower is plant.
All plants are stones.

Conclusions : Some stones are not flower. (E + A = O* type)

Since, II and III form a complementary I-E pair, either of two must follow.

48. (c) **Statements :** All tigers are jungles.
Conclusions : Some tigers are jungles. (Implication)
Some jungles are tigers. (conversion)
Statements : No jungle is bird.
Conclusions : Some jungle are not bird. (Implication)
No bird is jungle. (conversion)
Statements : Some birds are rains.
Conclusions : Some rains are birds. (conversion)
Statements : All tigers are jungles.
No jungle is bird.
Conclusions : No tiger is bird. (A + E = E-type)
No bird is tiger. (conversion)
Hence III follows.
Statements : No jungle is bird.
Some birds are rains.
Conclusions : Some rains are not jungle.
(E + I = O* type)
Since I and II form a complementary E-I pair, either of two must follow.

49. (c) Converted 1st statement gives conclusion I. 1st statement + 2 nd statement gives no conclusion. Hence II does not follow. Again, all the given statements don't give *conclusion*. Hence III and IV do not follow. But III and IV make a complementary pair. Hence either III or IV follows.

50. (d) All breads are patriots (A) → conversion → Some patriots are bread (I). Now, ome clients are patriots + ome patriots are breads = I + I = No conclusion. But either I or III follows because they form a complementry I-O pair. All breads are patriots + Some patriots are butters = A + I = No conclusion. Hence II does not follow. IV follows by converting the first statemets.

51. (d) Conclusion I follows from 1st statement Now, 1st statement and 2nd statement gives ome disks are covers (I + A = I). On conversion, this gives conclusion III. No conversion, this gives conclusion III. No other conclusion is possible.

52. (b) With the limited resources and overpopulation it is very hard to provide decent quality of life. Hence II follows.

53. (d) Sunita has a very busy schedule. This means that she is industrious. But still she finds time for rest. This means that she is an organised person. So, both I and II follow.

54. (a) According to the statement, funding is necessary to improve quality and India is allocating funds to education. This means that quality of education will improve in India. So, I follows. But funding alone is sufficient to enhance quality, is not true. So, II does not follow.

55. (c) Either the commissioner is absolutely right or he is not.

56. (a) Clearly, I directly follows from the statement while II cannot be deduced from it.

For (Qs.57-59).

	Discipline					Musical Instrument				
Name	Med	Eng	Ar	Art	Mg	Sit	Tab	Sar	Gui	Viol
Neeraj	×	—	×	×	—	×	×	✓	×	×
Yash	×	—	×	×	—	—	×	×	—	×
Mehul	✓	×	×	×	×	×	×	×	×	✓
Ram	×	×	×	✓	×	×	✓	×	×	×
Prakash	×	×	✓	×	×	—	×	×	—	×

57. (b)

58. (c) Guitarist is either Yash or Prakash. Therefore discipline may be Engineering or Architecture or Management.

59. (c)

60. (d) Three panels can be found as follows:
(i) Unni – Shekhar
Cyriac – Suresh
Bhushan – Ram
Pramila does not participate
OR
(ii) Unni – Shekhar
Cyriac – Suresh
Pramila – Ram
Bhushan does not participate.
OR
(iii) Unni – Shekhar
Pramila – Ram
Bhushan – Suresh
Cyriae does not participate.

61. (b) The possible panel is:
Cyrea – Shekhar
Suresh – Ram
Unni – Bhushan

62. (a) Panel can be follows.
Bhushan – Shuresh
Unni – Ram
Pramila – Shekhar

For (Qs.63-66)

As History is not taught on Monday or Thursday, it must be taught on Friday. Since it is given that at least one subject is taught every day, this helps to match Hindi — Thursday.

As D teaches only one subject (Psychology) and Geography is not taught by E or B and from the information: No person teaches two subjects on the same day, it is clear that C teaches Geography (since A teaches English on Monday).

Hence, the above information can be summerized in table as follows –

Subject	Person	Day
Sociology	B	Wednesday
History	E	**Friday**
English	A	Monday
Geography	C	
Economics	B/E/A/C	Tuesday
Psychology	D	
Hindi	B/E/A/C	**Thursday**

From above table.

63. (a) C teaches Geography.
64. (c) History taught on Friday.
65. (d) From given dates it is not clear.
66. (d) Hindi is taught on Thursday.

For (Qs.67-69)

67. (b)

Persons	Profession	Sex	M/S
A	Farmer	M	
B	Teacher	F	UM
C	Trader	M	M
D	Doctor	F	M
E	Lawyer	M	

68. (a)
69. (c)

For (Qs.70-720).

From the information given, positions of houses are as follows :

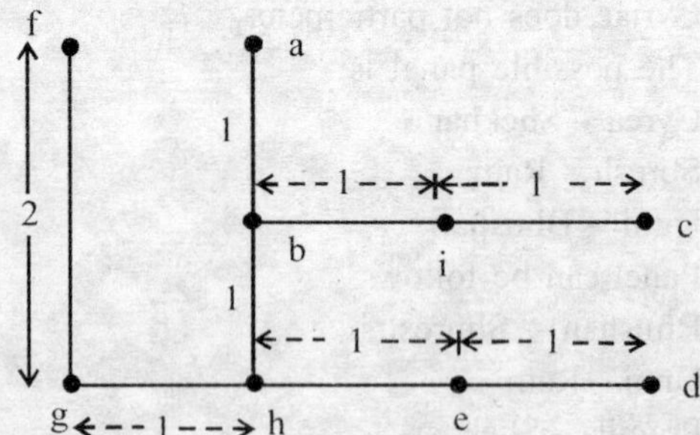

70. (a) Clearly, the distance between e and g is 2 km.
71. (d) From the above diagram, the distance between a and f is 1 km.
72. (c) Clearly, the distance between e and i is 1 km.

For (Qs.73-76)

GET AWAY ≡ BEN CDCI
FIRE BACK-WARDS ≡ QHOE PCTC DCOXU
MOVE SLOW ≡ ZMWE VFMD

Here, G is denoted by B
E is denoted by E
T is denoted by N
A is denoted by C
W is denoted by D
Y is denoted by I
F is denoted by Q
I is denoted by H
R is denoted by O
B is denoted by P
C is denoted by T
K is denoted by L
D is denoted by X
S is denoted by U
M is denoted by Z
O is denoted by M
V is denoted by W
L is denoted by F

73. (c)
74. (d)
75. (c)
76. (c)
77. (c) The given paragraph provides no hint about previous foodgrains stocks.
78. (a) From the third sentence, it can be inferred.
79. (a) From the fifth sentence 'one-third of India seems to remain underfed' we can infer so.
80. (a) From the last line it may be inferred.
81. (d) There is no categorical information. But since the stock this year is making news, it is apparently not a usual case.
82. (b) It is not clear from the passage what are the parameters to determine 'underfed' level. But two times meals may be a criterion.
83. (e) It is cleared from the last sencence of passage.
84. (d) The govt. has promised to bring down the smoke level because it is possible to determine the level. Hence I is implicit. II is implicit because containing pollution is also a welfare measure.
85. (a) I directly follows from the statement and so is implicit. Also, the statement is a suggestion and does not tell about a government policy or its position of funds. So, II is not implicit.
86. (d) The instructions have been given so that people willing to buy tickets may not form a crowd. So, I is implicit. Also, it is clear that people would purchase the tickets even after following the given instructions. So, II is also implicit.
87. (d) A decision to start any short of dialogue with one's neighbour assumes that the neighbour will also participate in it. Hence I is implicit. II is implicit because track II dialogue can be meaningful only when the respective Govts agree to abide by it.
88. (a) Why has the suspension of flights been made for a limited period of four days? It must have been assumed by the authorities of X-Airlines that the crisis may be over after this limited period. Hence, assumption I is implicit. II may or may not be an assumption. Hence, II is not implicit.
89. (b) Each letter of the word is moved three steps forward to obtain the code.
90. (d) Using the proper notations in (d), we get $9 + 9 \div 9 - 9 \times 9 = 9 + 1 - 9 \times 9 = 9 + 1 - 81 = -71$.
$\therefore$ option (d) is true.

91. (b) Here, Ravi starts from home at A, moves 10 km southwards up to B, turns right and moves 10 km up to C, turns right again and moves 10 km up to D and finally turns left and moves 10 km up to E.
Thus, his distance from initial position A = AE
= AD + DE
= BC + DE = (5 + 10) km = 15 km.

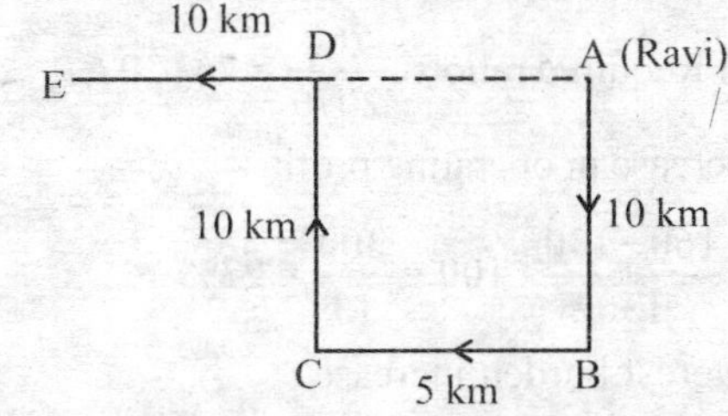

92. (b) Each letter moves +2 steps.
93. (d) 19 × 2 = 38, 38 × 3 = 114, 114 × 4 = 456.
94. (a) 1st letter moves –2 steps each time.
2nd letter moves +1, +2, +3, +4 steps respectively.
3rd letter moves +2, +3, +4 steps respectively.
95. (d) I is advisable because it will prepare the farmer to face the situation well in advance. II is also advisable because it will be helpful to cope with the problem related to water.
96. (a) Clearly, such projects shall be an asset and a source of income to the country later on. So, course I shall follow.
97. (d) Since severe damage has been caused by cyclone, people in affected villages ought to be shifted to safer places. Also, since relief work entails huge amounts, financial help from Central Government is a must. So, both the courses follow.
98. (a) The effectiveness of such Control Boards is established by the fact that Orissa and A.P. have agreed to it for better control of its multipurpose projects. So, only course I follows.
99. (d) The footpaths are meant for an entirely different purpose. So, they need to be kept empty. For this, police has to be sought. Also, the vendors cannot be deprived of a living. So, both the courses follow.

For (Qs.100-106)

	(i)/(a)	(ii)/(b)	(iii)	(iv)
100.	✓	×	✓	✓
101.	–	✓	✓	–
102.	✓	–	✓	✓
103.	(✓)	✓	✓	✓
104.	✓	(✓)	✓	✓
105.	(✓)	✓	✓	✓
106.	✓	✓	✓	✓

For (iii), the candidate should obtain C, D or E ratings. 'B' alone is also sufficient.
For (iv), the candidate should obtain D, E, F or G ratings.
(i) + (ii) + (iii) + (iv) = option (c)
(a) + (ii) + (iii) + (iv) = option (d)
(i) + (b) + (iii) + (iv) = option (e)
(a) + (b) + (iii) + (iv) = option (b)
Anything not fulfilling = option (b)
Anything missing = option (a)

100. (b) He is neither fulfilling criteria (ii) nor (b). For fulfilling (b), he should obtain either D or E ratings for quality of work.
101. (a) Nothing given about her ratings in approach of work and B. Com. marks.
102. (a) We don't know when he joined.
103. (d) 104. (e)
105. (d) 106. (c)
107. (c) Gold in C = $\left(\frac{7}{9}+\frac{7}{18}\right)$ units = $\frac{7}{6}$ units.

Copper in C = $\left(\frac{2}{9}+\frac{11}{18}\right)$ units = $\frac{5}{6}$ units.

$\therefore$ Gold : Copper = $\frac{7}{6}:\frac{5}{6} = 7:5$.
108. (a) Area left after laying black tiles
= [(20 – 4) × (10 – 4)] sq. ft. = 96 sq. ft.
Area under white tiles = $\left(\frac{1}{3}\times 96\right)$ sq. ft = 32 sq. ft.
Area under blue tiles = (96 – 32) sq. ft = 64 sq. ft.
Number of blue tiles = $\frac{64}{(2\times 2)} = 16$.
109. (c) A makes 1 rev. per sec
B makes $\frac{6}{10}$ rev per sec
C makes $\frac{4}{10}$ rev. per sec
In other words A, B and C take 1 , $\frac{5}{3}$ & $\frac{5}{2}$ seconds to complete one revolution.
L.C.M of $1, \frac{5}{3} \& \frac{5}{2} = \frac{\text{L.C.M. of } 1,5,5}{\text{H.C.F. of } 1,3,2} = 5$
Hence, after every 5 seconds the red spots on all the three wheels touch the ground
110. (c) Let the average expenditure of all the ninte be Rs x
Then, 3 × 8 + x + 2 = 9x ⇒ x = 3.25
$\therefore$ Total money spent = 9x = 9 × 3.25 = Rs. 29.25
111. (b) Let the numbers be x, y and z. Then,
x + y = 10 ..... (i) y + z = 19 ..... (ii) x + z = 21 ..... (iii)
Adding (i), (ii) and (iii), we get : 2 (x + y + z) = 50 or (x + y + z) = 25.
Thus, x = (25 – 19) = 6; y = (25 – 21) = 4;
z = (25 – 10) = 15.
Hence, the required numbers are 6, 4 and 15.
112. (c) C. P. of mixture of 18 kg = 10 × 45 + 8 × 50 = Rs 850
$\therefore$ S. P. = C. P. + Profit = 850 + 32 = Rs 882
$\therefore$ S. P. = Rs 882 for 18 kg
$\therefore$ S. P. = Rs $\frac{882}{18}$ per kg = Rs 49 per kg
113. (c) Total number of students studying in institute
G = 225 + 206 + 182 + 138 + 89 = 840
Required % = $\frac{182}{840}\times 100 = 21\frac{2}{3}\%$

114. (d) Total students in institute
$D = 165 + 138 + 245 + 66 + 36 = 650$

Required % $= \frac{36}{650} \times 100 = 5.5\% \approx 5\%$

115. (a) Required % $= \frac{125 + 96 + 144}{138 + 196 + 212 + 206} \times 100$

$= \frac{365}{752} \times 100 = 48.50\%$

116. (a) Required % $= \frac{164}{98 + 157 + 164 + 66 + 86 + 112 + 138}$

$= \frac{164}{821} \times 100 = 19.97\% \approx 20\%$

117. (c) Obviously, the required % is maximum for C.

118. (d) The difference between the white-coloured cars sold is the minimum in B type model.

119. (a) Blue (E + D) = 37 + 43 = 80 = White (B)

120. (d) Required difference = (50 – 34) × 1000 = 16,000

121. (c) Total number of silver coloured cars sold in Metro H
= 20 + 35 + 37 + 42 + 22 + 17 = 173
Total number of silver coloured cars sold in Metro M
= 15 + 20 + 35 + 40 + 30 + 52 = 192

$\therefore$ Required percentage $= \frac{173}{192} \times 100 \approx 90\%$

122. (a) Colour-model combinations of car in Metro M

White – C	Blue – B	Silver – B	White – D
90	60	20	85

123. (d) Population of village B in 1995 $= 5000 \times \frac{16}{13} \approx 6150$

Population of village B in 1996 $= 6150 \times \frac{110}{100} = 6765$

Population below poverty line = 52% of 6765 ≈ 3500

124. (a) Population of village D in 1995 $= 9,000 \times \frac{17}{15} = 10,200$

Population of village D in 1997

$= 10,200 \times \frac{110}{100} = 11,220$

Population of village G in 1997

$= 9,000 \times \frac{95}{100} = 8,550$

Total population of village D and G in 1997
= 11,220 + 8,550 = 19,770

125. (d) Population of village F below poverty line

$= 55000 \times \frac{13}{100} \times \frac{49}{100} \approx 3500$

126. (c) Population of village F in 1995

$= 1520 \times \frac{100}{38} \times \frac{13}{8} = 6500$

127. (b) Population of village C below poverty line

$= 2000 \times \frac{38}{100} = 760$

Population of village E below poverty line

$= \frac{2000}{8} \times 18 \times \left(\frac{46}{100}\right) = 2070$

$\therefore$ Required ratio $= \frac{760}{2070} = 76 : 207$

128. (a) Increase in operating profit

$= \frac{160 - 130}{130} \times 100 = \frac{300}{13} = 23\%$

129. (b) Interest burden increase

$= 0.4 \times 160 - 0.3 \times 130 = 64 - 39 = 25$ lakh

130. (d) Borrowed funds in 1990-91 $= \frac{0.3 \times 130}{0.2} = 195$ lakhs

Borrowed funds in 1991-92 $= \frac{0.4 \times 160}{0.2} = 320$ lakhs

Total = 320 + 195 = 515.

131. (d) Retained Profit in 1990 - 91 = 0.25 × 130 = 32.5
Retained Profit in 1991 - 92 = .2 × 160 = 32

Reduction $= \frac{0.5}{32.5} \times 100 = \frac{100}{65} = 1.5\%$

132. (c) Dividend earning in 1991-92 = 0.08 × 160 = 12.8

133. (d) (II) is useless
(I) shows that the two integers on squaring add up to $116 < 11^2$ which means the integers are less than 10. We further find that the nos. are 10 and 4.

134. (e) Let Navni takes to finish the work = x days
Then Avantika takes to finish the work = 3x days.

(I) $\Rightarrow \frac{1}{x} + \frac{1}{3x} = \frac{1}{15}$

Obviously, x can be determined.

$\therefore$ statement (I) alone is sufficient to answer the question.

(II) ⇒ x = 20 days and since, Avantika takes time = 3x days

Hence, statement (II) alone is sufficient to answer the question.

135. (e) Let B alone whole work in x minutes

$\therefore$ in one minute, work done by B $= \frac{1}{x}$th part of whole work.

$\therefore$ in 30 minutes, work done by B $= \frac{30}{x}$th part of whole work.

(I) $\Rightarrow \frac{30}{x} + \frac{60}{x} = 1$

$\therefore$ Statement (I) alone is sufficient.

(II) ⇒ In 45 min., work done by A = 1

∴ in 30 minutes, work done by A = $\frac{30}{45}$th part of whole work = $\frac{2}{3}$th part of whole work.

Now, $\frac{2}{3}+\frac{30}{x}=1$

Hence, statement (II) alone is sufficient to answer the question.

136. (e) Let rate of interest = r % per year

(I) ⇒ Difference between S.I. and C.I. = $P \times \left(\frac{r}{100}\right)^2$

Hence, r can be determined by using statement (I) alone.

(II) ⇒ S.I. = Amount = P

and S.I. = $\frac{p \times r \times t}{100}$

∴ r can be determined by using statement (II) alone.

137. (a) Let whole work done by Sanju in x days.

∴ work done by Sanju in 3 days = $\frac{3}{x}$th part of whole work.

Remaining work = $1-\frac{3}{x}=\frac{x-3}{x}$

(I) ⇒ Swamitra's work in 12 days = $\frac{x-3}{x}$

⇒ Swamitra's one day work = $\frac{x-3}{12x}$

(II) ⇒ $\frac{1}{x}+\frac{x-3}{12x}=\frac{1}{6}$

Hence, both statements together are sufficient to answer the question.

138. (b) Statement II gives us the answer directly. From statement I, we cannot find the value of x.

139. (b) Statement II alone is enough to answer the question. Hence answer is option (a).

140. (d) **Statement-I**

For the given linear equation 2x – 3y = –2; whatever be the value of 'x' we can get the corresponding value of y. But 2x – 2y = – 2

i.e., L.H.S. = –2

∴ L.H.S. < R.H.S.

ie $2x - 3y < x^2$

Therefore statement 'I' alone is sufficient.

Statement - II

If x > 2 and y > 0 the 2x – 3y may be + ive or – ive but value of 2x – 3y is always less than x^2.

Note: Students are advised to substitute the random value of x and y.

Therefore, statement

Option (c) is the correct answer.

141. (c) Let total families in city = x

(I) ⇒ Families having television = $\frac{x}{2}$

(II) ⇒ Families having telephoes = 30% of $\frac{x}{2}=\frac{3x}{20}$

∴ Required % = $\frac{3x/20}{x}\times 100$

Hence, both statements together are necessary to answer the question.

142. (b) (I) ⇒ It is not sufficient

(II) ⇒ Angles of ΔABC are 30º, 60º and 90º.

⇒ The lengths of the sides are in the ratio $1:2:\sqrt{3}$

(∵ The ratio between the lengths of the sides in a 30º, 60º, 90º triangles is always constant and it is $1:2:\sqrt{3}$)

Since perimeter $= 3+3\sqrt{3}$

⇒ $x+2x+\sqrt{3}x = 3+3\sqrt{3}$

⇒ $x=\sqrt{3}$

∴ Sides of Δ are $\sqrt{3}, 2\sqrt{3}$ and 3

Also since ∠B = 30º

⇒ base = $\sqrt{3}$ and height = 3

Hence, area of triangle can be determined using statement (II) alone.

143. (c) (I) ⇒ For chocolates, Sheena has = 50 – 20% of 50 – 30% of 50 = Rs. 25

(II) ⇒ Number of chocolates = $\frac{\text{Total remaining rupees}}{\text{cost per chocolate}}$

∴ Both statements together are necessary to answer the question.

144 (a) ∵ Storing capacity of tank = volume of tank = $\pi r^2 h$

Here r is given

and (I) ⇒ height(h)

∴ Statement (I) alone is sufficient to answer the question.

(II) ⇒ There is no need of value of temperature to answer the question.

145. (a) (I) ⇒ BC = 5 = AB

⇒ p = q = 40º

⇒ r = 180º – (40 + 40)

Hence, r can be determined by using (I) alone.

(II) ⇒ it is not sufficient to answer the question.

146. (a) (I) ⇒ combined income for the years 1994 to 1999 = average yearly income × total years.

∴ Statement (I) alone is sufficient to answer the question.

(II) ⇒ It is insufficient to answer the question.

147. (a) (I) ⇒ required % = $\frac{92}{230}\times 100$
∴ Statement (I) alone is sufficient to answer the question.
(II) ⇒ We have no need of total number of books.

148. (b) (I) ⇒ The fixed value of CP is not given, so SP of the article cannot be determined
(II) ⇒ Let x be SP of an article
$$x\times\frac{9}{100}=\frac{200\times 115}{100}=255.55$$

149. (c) (I) ⇒ No. of voters in the last election
(II) ⇒ No. of voters at present = 115% of no. of voters in the last election.
∴ Both statements together are necessary to answer the question.

150. (a) (I) ⇒ 18 Feb. + 10 days = 28 Feb.
∴ Statement (I) alone is sufficient to answer the question.
But we can't be determined the exact date using (II).

151. (c) The first part of the sentence uses the auxillary verb'does', since the second part of the sentence is an alternative to the first it must be in the same syntax so there must be the auxillary verb 'does' in the second part as well.

152. (a) The comparison is between the careers of the two women and not a woman and the career of another women. The subject is absent from the sentence but if you complete the sentence you will find it should be- she wished that her career was as glamorous as the other woman's career. In sentences such as these where the noun is hidden, it is helpful to complete the noun to find the correct answer.

153. (d) Liable to means, it is an event that will happen. This is the only phrase which would fit in with the sense of the rest of the sentence. So there will be no change

154. (b) would is a modal and its use here is unnecessary. There is a 'would have' in the second part of the sentence but it should not be repeated in the first one, because the use of 'would have' is done as a possibility of an affect of something done in past. So generally would have will be followed by a past perfect verb.

155. (c) The first part of the sentence is directed at a subject, which is 'eaten in portugal only', i.e., the potato, therefore the comma should be followed by a phrase with potato as its subject and not Indians. Of (c) & (d), (c) is the right option because 'suspicious to Indian' is not an appropriate usage.

156. (c) Sentence A talks about the beginning with ordinary fever and a moderate cough. D states that it appears like flu, but doctors are confused as usual drugs don't work. C tells us that a sore throat progress to respiratory complications. B concludes by saying that India could be under attack from a typical Pneumonias.

157. (a) D introduces the topic which is about a bizarre problem i.e about snakes. C talks about anti snake serum, which is not enough, A follows which states that only government hospitals stock it. B concludes by saying that more and more bitten people could face paralysis.

158. (a) B begins the paragraph stating the earlier record of mid-term elections. A follows as it talks about greater political participation. C logically follows talking about this trend and D ends the paragraph speculating about who is to benefit with lower turnout.

159. (b) A is the beginning to the paragraph talking about the critical election. B states that in psephological language it is called realignment. D states that none of the recent elections in India have been a critical election and C concludes by saying that since 1989, there have been a series of semi-critical elections.

160. (c) E is the statement which begins the passage, D talks about the first set of test for intelligence, this is followed by A on the use of such intelligent tests, C tells us about the intelligence quotient and tests which are developed to indicate what an average child of a certain age can do and B ends the passage.

161. (a) A. Hood wink is to deceive, cheat
B. Sincere means really believing what you say, not pretending
C. Gauche means tactless.
D. Fiasco means failure
Thus A is antonym of B.

162. (a) A. Flummox means bewilder, confuse
B. Enlighten means to give knowledge, clarify
C. Fastidious means not easy to please
D. Esoteric means intelligible to those with special knowledge.
Thus A is antonym to B.

163. (d) A. Exercise means to drive out the evil,
B. Bedevil is confuse, trouble
C. Diatribe is bitter criticism in speech.
D. Hyperbole means exaggeration
Exorcise is to purge the man from evil and bedevil is to trouble thus A is antonym of B.

164. (c) A. Draconian means severe.
B. Cruel mens harsh
C. Bliss means happiness
D. Noble is excellent character, magnanimous.
Thus A is synonym to B.

165. (d) A. Deify to worship as god, make a god of
B. Blasphemy is to show disrespect.
C. Deluge means heavy flood
D. Hubris means pride.
Thus A is antonym to B.

166. (d) A. Clandestine means secretive
B. Cosmopolitan means including masses
C. Graceful means charm
D. Furtive means secretive
Thus A is synonym to D.

167. (d) A. Bellicose means quarrelsome, warlike
B. Affront means insult openly.
C. Peaceful means calm, quiet
D. Adroit means skilful.
Thus A is antonym to C.

168. (a) A. Frugal means economical
B. Spendthrift means extravagant person
C. Anomaly means abnormality
D. Anathema means a curse
Thus A is antonym to B.

169. (d) A. Asinine means stupid, foolish.
B. Besotted means made silly by love
C. Tranquil means calm, peace.
D. Knowledgable means having lot of knowledge.
Thus A is antonym to D.

170. (c) A. Crass means unrefined
B. Nexus means a connection
C. Elegant means refined, graceful
D. Credulous means gullible.
Thus A is antonym to C.

171. (a) While discussing Economic growth, the author is making a case for real value of increased economic input. This value is the human meaning which is not generally included in what is considered as product. GNP in author's opinion is an incomplete measure of economic output.

172. (c) The fourth paragraph cities the lackings in the definition of GNP and mentions factors it does not includes. It also cities examples of "Products" GNP should include like unpaid but productive work of housewives and finally it also develops the definition of GNP by adding certain towards the end of the paragraph.

173. (b) Spiritual values have nothing whatsoever to do with GNP and have not even been mentioned in the passage.

174. (a) We can answer this question by opposite elimination i.e. we will find out which of the given options are not considered by GNP and eliminate them to reach the right answer. The fourth paragraph says GNP does not account for deterioration in environment which means it fails to consider the chemicals in river so, (b) is eliminated. GNP also does not count the productive but unpaid work of a home maker, so, family household management is also not considered by GNP, thus, (c) gets eliminated, the research work done by a stock broker is also productive but unpaid work and, thus, (d) also gets eliminated. So, (a) is our answer.

175. (a) The passage talks chiefly about heart attack and not broadly on cardiology, so, (a) is eliminated. The main theme is not risk factors in heat attack although the paragraph mentions the factor very early in the passage because almost 80% of the passage is devoted to discoursing seasonal and temporal patterns of heart attack, therefore, (c) is the answer and not (d).

176. (b) In the context of the passage 'Potential' can only be replaced by 'possible' of the given options. It does not mean 'unknown', so, (c) is eliminated. Potential may seem similar to primary but in the sentence potential does not mean most important but only factors that can possibly cause the risk of a heart attack.

177. (c) The last sentence of the second paragraph gives several factors which may cause an heart attack and its high rate that can cause an attack and not a low heart rate.

178. (c) Refer to second sentence of the first paragraph.

179. (b) 'Show' is a synonym of 'reveal'.

180. (b) The passage concludes on the hope that we will be able to comprehend in future why and how heart attacks are triggered which means we do not now fully understand the risk factors.

181. (d) Illicit means not sanctioned by law, elicit means to draw a response with difficulty, illegitimate means illegal/un lawful

182. (b) Imperial means of an empire or its rulers, adamant means firmly or stubbornly, determinedly.

183. (c) Judicious means having good sense, momentous means most important, pragmatic means practical, treating in a sensible and realistic way.

184. (d) **Offend** means not to show proper respect or make someone angry, so the opposite will be **respect**.

185. (c) **Indict** means to charge someone with a crime or something wrong. **Accuse** also means the same, **acquit** means to free of charge.

186. (a) **Obscene** means indecent, **objectionable** and **condemnable** mean similar to obscene.

187. (a) **Liberate** is to make someone free and **imprison** is to put in prison, conceal is to hide and **vacillation** is to move from one place or idea to another.

188. (d) gasp
The sentence demands the use of the simple present tense.

189. (c) is
The simple present is used to express general truths.

190. (d) it's
A collective noun takes a singular verb when the collection is thought of as one whole; a plural verb when the individuals of which it is composed are thought *of,* as, The Committee has issued its report. The Committee are divided on one minor point.

191. (c) but milder than
'Than' (her used as a preposition) shows the relation between this year and last year's attack. It is more appropriate than 'as' which generally shows the relation between two similar things.

192. (d) that
The use of the conjunction 'that', to introduce the adverb clause of reason or cause, is more apt here as because means 'for the reason that'.

193. (d) 194. (b)
195. (e) 196. (c)
197. (a) 198. (a)
199. (c) 200. (e)

MOCK TEST - 4

1\. (d) According to question,

$H \xrightarrow{\text{wife}} P \xleftarrow{\text{mother}} M \xleftarrow{\text{brother}} T \xleftarrow{\text{sister}} R$

Since the sex of 'R' is not clear therefore, the data are inadequate.

2\. (a) The second, fifth and seventh digit of the given number are 4, 1 and 8 respectively.
Therefore, required number will be 841, which is a perfect square of 29.

3\. (d) Spinach is leaf vegetable, but all other are the vegetable grow on vein or tree.

4\. (d)

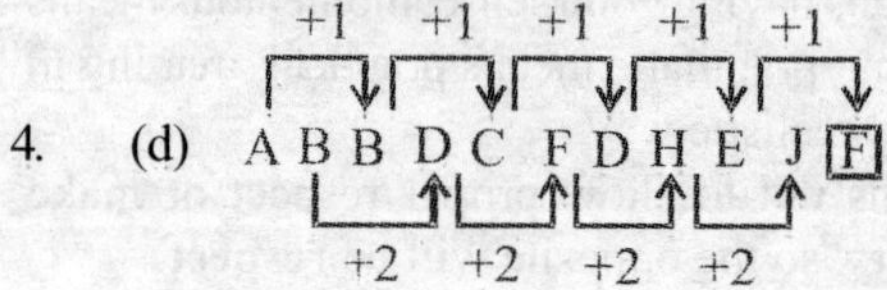

5\. (a)

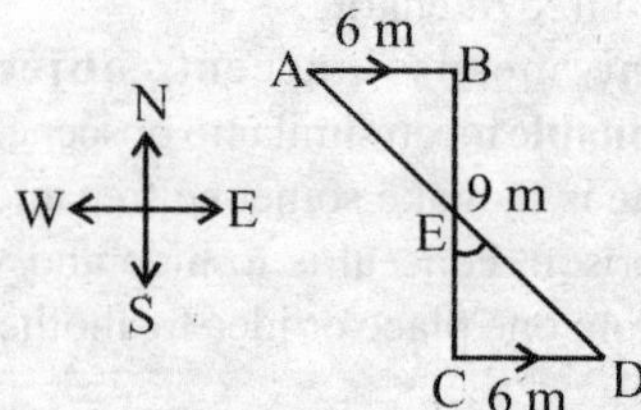

E will be the mid-point of BC and AD.

$AE = \sqrt{6^2 + (4.5)^2}$

and $DE = \sqrt{6^2 + (4.5)^2}$

$AE = 7.5$ m

and $DE = 7.5$ m

$\therefore$ $AD = 7.5 + 7.5 = 15$ m

6\. (b) After changing the letters as directed, we get
G I O U S C O N T A
5th letter from the right is C and second letter to the right of C is N.

7\. (b) As, $D \xrightarrow{-1} C$ and $C \xrightarrow{-1} B$

Similarly, $P \xrightarrow{-1} O$

$R \xrightarrow{-1} Q$ $O \xrightarrow{-1} N$ $R \xrightarrow{-1} Q$

$A \xrightarrow{+1} B$ $N \xrightarrow{+1} O$ $O \xrightarrow{+1} P$

$U \xrightarrow{+1} V$ $C \xrightarrow{+1} D$ $B \xrightarrow{+1} C$

$G \xrightarrow{+1} H$ $I \xrightarrow{+1} J$ $L \xrightarrow{+1} M$

$H \xrightarrow{+1} I$ $S \xrightarrow{+1} T$ $E \xrightarrow{+1} F$

$T \xrightarrow{+1} U$ $E \xrightarrow{+1} F$ $M \xrightarrow{+1} N$

8\. (b) The series 151620294 can be broken as
15, 16, 20, 29, 45 ......
$16 = 15 + 1^2$; $20 = 16 + 2^2$; $29 = 20 + 3^2$; $45 = 29 + 4^2$
$\therefore$ The next term is $45 + 5^2 = 70$.
$\therefore$ The next three terms are 570.

9\. (a) The first letter of each term is moved one step forward, the second letter is moved four steps backward and the third letter is moved four steps forward to obtain the corresponding letters of the next term.

10\. (b) The numerical parts moves with a difference of + 4. Thus, the correct sequence of the numerical components would be 1, 5, 9, 13, 17 Therefore, 15 LS does not fit in the series.

11\. (b) The words in each pair are antonyms.

12\. (a) Ring is related to telephone in the same way as knock is related to door.

13\. (a) Except USTO, all others have at least one letter repeated.

14\. (b) All except litre are units or measurement of the mass of a body.

15\. (a) In each successive problem design ')' moves 1/2, 1, 1/2, 1 arm ahead anticlockwise direction respectively and the design along with this reverses. Thus the answer figure (a) is obtained.

16\. (e) In each successive problem figure the whole design rotates through 90°, 45°, 90° anticlockwise respectively. Alongwith this design '∪' from problem figure 1 to 2 rotates through 90° and the design ⧅ from 2 to 3 rotates 90° anticlockwise. The same rule continues further. Thus, the answer figure (e) is obtained.

17\. (d) In each subsequent problem figure the designs are increasing by two and one respectively and when two designs increase their directions are same.

18\. (d) The designs are changing their places as shown below:

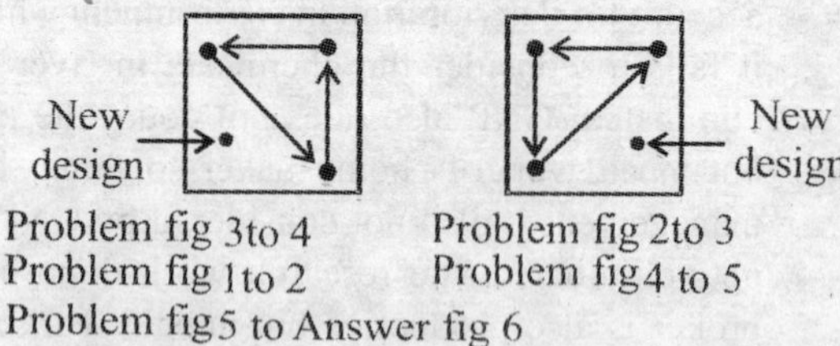

Problem fig 3 to 4 Problem fig 2 to 3
Problem fig 1 to 2 Problem fig 4 to 5
Problem fig 5 to Answer fig 6

19\. (a) In each subsequent figure the number of lines increased in 1, 3, 5, 7 and 9 respectively.

20\. (d) From problem figure (a) to (b) each of all the designs shifts $1\frac{1}{2}$ sides anticlockwise and first design from the left takes a new shape. From problem figure (2) to (3) each design is shifting 1/2 side anticlockwise and the middle design takes a new shape. From P. F. (c) and (d) each design shifts $1\frac{1}{2}$ sides anticlockwise and the last design takes a new shape. The same order of change is reapeated.

21\. (c) The dash rotates by 45° anticlockwiseand shifts half-a-side anticlockwise in each step while the rectangle shifts one side in alternate steps.

22. (d) In alternate steps the designs shift half-a-side and one side anticlockwise while the 'X' changes to plus and vice versa.
23. (a) The circular design rotates by 90° anticlockwisein each step while it shifts half-a-side and one side anticlockwise in alternate steps.
24. (b) A dash and a circle is added in alternate steps.
25. (a) The cross-bars rotate by 45° in each step while the smaller designs shift $1\frac{1}{2}$ and $\frac{1}{2}$ side anticlockwise in alternate steps.
26. (a)
27. (a) 'X' shifts one step clockwise in each step. One of the remaining two designs shifts one step clockwise while the other shifts one step anticlockwise. The designs are replaced by new ones in altermate steps.
28. (d) The end designs and middle designs get inverted in alternate steps.
29. (a) The shaded part moves 3 steps, 3 steps, 0 step, 0 step. The movement is from left to right in one row and right to left in the next upper row.
30. (c) In alternate steps, two designs of one set of designs shift half–a– side anticlockwise. while the third is replaced by a new one and shifts two sides. The middle design of the second set of designs shifts $1\frac{1}{2}$ side, the clockwise design shifts one side, while the third is replaced by a new one and shifts half–a–side anticlockwise.
31. (e) One of the end design is replaced by a new one while a new design is added twice on clockwise and twice on anticlockwise end. The designs move one, one, one–and–a–half, one–and a half side clockwise in subsequent steps.
32. (c) In the first step designs move half–a–side clockwise, the clockwise design is lost and two new designs appear on clockwise side. In the next step the designs move one–and–a half side clockwise . The clockwise design is lost and two new designs are added on anticlockwise side. These two steps go on alternately.
33. (b)
34. (e) Designs move one side and half–a– side clockwise alternately. Beginning from clockwise end, 1st and last, second and fifth, and third and fourth designs respectively are replaced by new ones in subsequent steps.
35. (e)
36. (c) **From fig II to I:** The whole figure rotates by 90° anticlockwise and one petal and a half–petal are lost.
37. (c) **From fig II to I:** The designs interchange places, one of them gets inverted and one part of each moves inward.
38. (b) **From fig II to I:** The middle–right shifts to the upper–left. The lower right shifts to the upper–right and gets unshaded. The upper–right shifts to the lower–left and rotates by 90° clockwise . The lower–left shifts to lower–right. The middle–left shift to middle–right. The upper-left shift to middle-left and is replaced by a new one.
39. (b) **From fig II to I:** The lower design gets inverted laterally while the upper one is lost.
40. (d) **From fig II to I:** The rectangle shifts one–and–a–half sides clockwise while the shaded triangle shifts one–and–a–half sides anticlockwise and gets inverted.
41. (b) Let us name the trains as A and B. Then, (A's speed) : (B's speed) = $\sqrt{b}:\sqrt{a} = \sqrt{16}:\sqrt{9} = 4:3$.
42. (c) The sequence is –11, +9, –7, +5, –3, +1
So, 86 is wrong and should be replaced by (78 + 9) i.e. 87.
43. (a) The numbers are 3×1^2, 3×2^2, 3×3^2, 3×4^2, 3×5^2, 3×6^2, ...
$\therefore$ Missing number = $3 \times 7^2 = 3 \times 49 = 147$
44. (c) Clearly, the first, second and third letters of each term are respectively moved one, two and three steps forward to obtain the corresponding letters of the next term. So, the next term is EJO.
45. (e) Conclusion III follows as an immediate implication of 1st statement. 1st and 2nd statements give conclusion IV [$\because$ I + A = I]. I and II do not follow from the rules of syllogism but they make a complementary pair [I-O pair], so either of them follows.
46. (b) By the rule of syllogism, no conclusion follows. But I and II make a complementary pair [I-O type].
47. (e) 1st and 2nd statements give: Some garbages are coins. Hence II follows but IV does not. 2nd and 1st statement don't give any conclusion. Hence III does not follow. All the given statements don't give conclusion I.
48. (b) E + E = No conclusion. Therefore, I and II can't be obtained from the 2nd and 3rd statements. Converted form of 1st statement give conclusion IV. 2nd statement and 1st statement (a) give conclusion III [$\because$ E+I=O].
49. (b) The workers in the organised sector are not being talked about in the statement. So, I does not follow. It is mentioned that some workers in the unorganised sector are engaged in sundry jobs. This means that they have fixed income. So, II follows.
50. (b) Clearly I is vague and so does not follow. However, II directly follows from the given statement.
51. (d) Both follow because they together take care of the two problems leading to heart diseases.
52. (d) Since the new system gives the students the option of dropping Science and Mathematics, so students weak in these subjects can also be admitted. So, I follows. Also, it is mentioned that the new system will come into effect from the next academic year. This means that it did not exist previously. So, II also follows.
53. (d) Cannot be determined
54. (a) Data inadequate

For (Qs. 55-57).

	Game	Colour of Car
A	Cricket	Black
B	Hockey	Red
C	Volleyball	Green
D	Polo	Yellow
E	Badminton	White
F	Tennis	Blue

55. (b) C plays Volleyball.
56. (b) F owns a blue car.
57. (b) Clearly, the incorrect combination is Green — Tennis.

For (Qs. 58- 62).

C is to the right of D and D is third from south. So, B will be at the extreme end from north because it should have E as its neighhour. G is between E and F. So the sequence is:

B
E
G
F East
D
C
A

58. (d) G is sitting to the right of E.
59. (a) A and B are sitting at the extreme ends.
60. (c) G should change place with C to make it third from north.
61. (d) D is sitting between C and F.
62. (d) All the statements are required to determine the place of A.
63. (c) 64. (a)
65. (a)

For (Qs. 66-69).

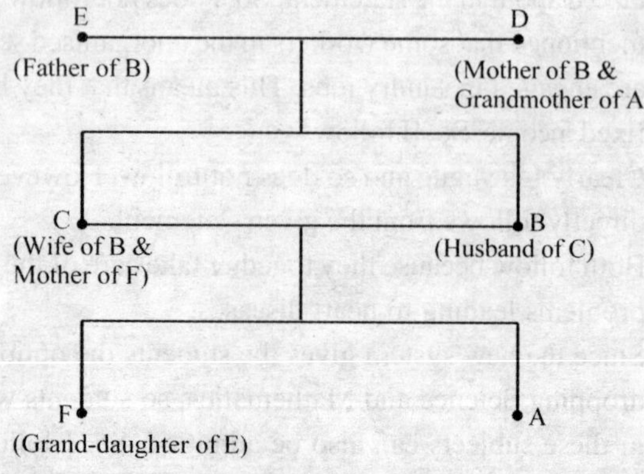

66. (b)
67. (d) : Sex of A is not known
68. (e)
69. (a)
70. (a) We have, F ≡ P, O ≡ E, T ≡ B. hence, code for FOOT is PEEB.
71. (a) We have D ≡ Z, I ≡ J, E ≡ T, S ≡ V, L ≡ Q.
72. (a) W ≡ S, O ≡ E, D ≡ Z
 ⇒ Code for WOOD is SEEZ
73. (b) T → B, A → U, I → J, L → Q, O → E, R → D
 ⇒ Code for TAILOR = BUJQED.
74. (b) Quoting AEPC's provisional data implies that it is likely that the council releases authentic data. Hence, probably true.
75. (c) We have no information about the trend of performance of India's export of readymade garments
76. (c) We have no data of year 2000.
77. (b) The given inference seems to be probably true.
78. (c) We have no data of import. So comparison is not possible.
79. (b) Clearly, the owner of the store warn that one dare not try to steal the camera. So, only II is implicit while I is not.
80. (a) It follows from the statement that books on this topic were available before also but they were not 'lucid'. So, I is implicit. But a general comment as II cannot be made from the given statement. So. II is not implicit.
81. (d) Assumption I is implicit. Why has such advertisement been published by the advertisers? Definitely, the advertiser is assuming the sales to pick up. II is also implicit; that is why advertiser advocates doing so.
82. (d) Clearly, the party president lays down the policies for its members. So, I is implicit. Also, when no party member would publicly reveal the happenings in the meeting, nobody will come to know. So, II is also implicit.
83. (d) Since both I and II follow from the given statement, so both are implicit.
84. (a) The first, second, third, fourth, fifth and sixth letters of the word are respectively moved two, three, four , five, six and seven steps forward to obtain the corresponding letters of the code.
85. (d) $40 + 12 \div 3 \times 6 - 60 = 4$
86. (d) The movements of Rasik from A to F are as shown in figure.
 Since CD = AB + EF, so F lies in line with A.
 Rasik's distance from original position A = AF
 $= (AG + GF) = (BC + DE) = (30 + 15)\text{ m} = 45\text{m}$.
 Also, F lies to the east of A.

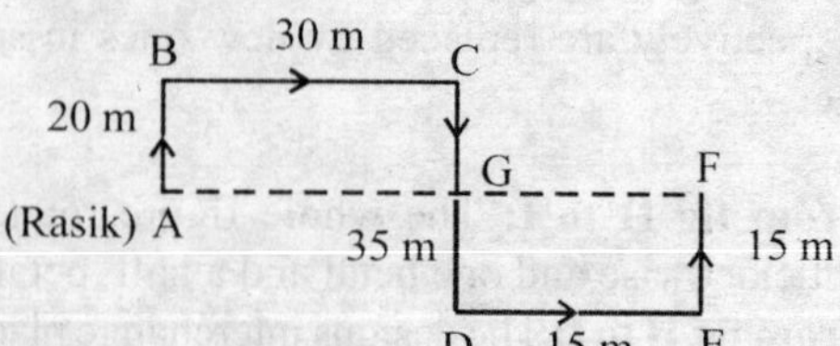

87. (b) 1st letter moves +2, +3 and +4 steps respectively.
 2nd letter moves –2, –3 and –4 steps respectively.
88. (c) 1st number moves +5, +7, +9, +11, +13 steps respectively.
 3rd number moves +2 steps each time.
 2nd letter moves –1 step each time.

89. (d) Clearly, the two diseases mentioned are caused by unhygienic conditions. So, improving the hygienic conditions is a step towards their eradication. Also, constant medication will help timely detection of the disease and hence a proper treatment. So, both I and II follow.

90. (d) I is advisable because partial cut in supply will be useful when water crisis occurs. II is also advisable because minimal use of water by people will help conserve water and ensure smooth supply in future.

91. (d) I is not advisable because it is explicitly mentioned in the statement that unemployment is the main cause of raise in suicide cases. Does love affair lead to suicidal death? Answer is: not necessarily. Hence, II is not advisable. III is advisable because it will help minimise the problem.

92. (d) Clearly all three follows

93. (a) Once the trials are over, the best availability of material, managerial and other resources is necessary to maintain production schedule. Hence III follows.
As mentioned in the statement, 'model M is its first product', so it is necessary to finalise the network of dealers and all matters regarding the sale of the product. Hence I follows. II has no connection with the statement.

94. (a) 95. (a)
96. (d) 97. (e)
98. (c) 99. (e)
100. (e) 101. (c)
102. (e)

103. (c) Let the three containers contain 3x, 4x and 5x litres of mixtures, respectively.

Milk in 1st mix. $= \left(3x \times \frac{4}{5}\right)$ litres $= \frac{12x}{5}$ litres.

Water in 1st mix. $= \left(3x - \frac{12x}{5}\right)$ litres $= \frac{3x}{5}$ litres.

Milk in 2nd mix. $= \left(4x \times \frac{3}{4}\right)$ litres $= 3x$ litres.

Water in 2nd mix. $= (4x - 3x)$ litres $= x$ litres.

Milk in 3rd mix. $= \left(5x \times \frac{5}{7}\right)$ litres $= \frac{25x}{7}$ litres.

Water in 3rd mix. $= \left(5x - \frac{25x}{7}\right)$ litres $= \frac{10x}{7}$ litres.

Total milk in final mix.

$= \left(\frac{12x}{5} + 3x + \frac{25x}{7}\right)$ litres $= \frac{314x}{35}$ litres.

Total water in final mix.

$= \left(\frac{3x}{5} + x + \frac{10x}{7}\right)$ litres $= \frac{106x}{35}$ litres.

Required ratio of milk and water

$= \frac{314x}{35} : \frac{106x}{35} = 157 : 53.$

104. (b) Perimeter = Distance covered in 8 min.

$= \left(\frac{12000}{60} \times 8\right) \text{m} = 1600$ m.

Let length = 3x metres and breadth = 2x metres.
Then, $2(3x + 2x) = 1600$ or $x = 160$.
∴ Length = 480 m and Breadth = 320 m.
∴ Area $= (480 \times 320)\ \text{m}^2 = 153600\ \text{m}^2$.

105. (d) HCF of 60, 84 and 108 is 12 so each room contain 12 students at minimum
So that each room contains students of only 1 subject

∴ Number of rooms $= \frac{60}{12} + \frac{108}{12} + \frac{84}{12} = 21$ rooms

106. (a) Corrected mean $= \frac{150 \times 30 - 135 + 165}{30}$

$= \frac{4500 - 135 + 165}{30} = \frac{4530}{30} = 151$

107. (a) Let the son's present age be x years. Then, $(38 - x) = x$
$\Rightarrow 2x = 38 \Rightarrow x = 19$.
∴ son's age 5 years back = (19 – 5)years = 14 years.

108. (b) Here, S. P. of mixture = C. P. of pure milk = Rs 3 per litre

Now, S. P. of mixture $= \frac{100 + 20}{100} \times$ C.P. of mixture

$\Rightarrow$ C.P. of mixture $= \frac{3 \times 100}{120}$ = Rs 2.5 per litre

Also, C. P of water = Rs 0
By the rule of alligation :

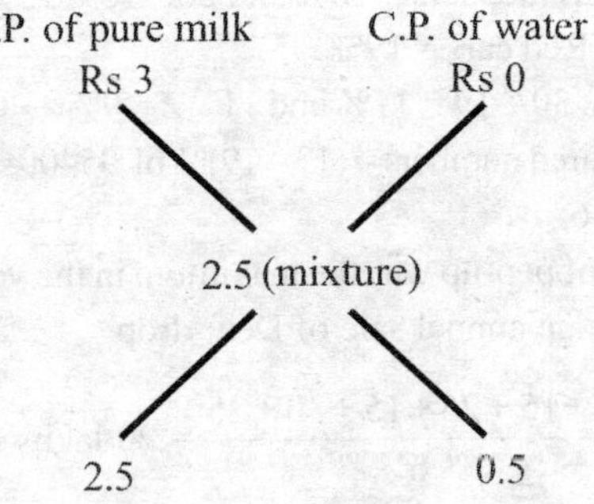

∴ Ratio of pure milk and water in mixture $= \frac{2.5}{0.5} = 5:1$

For five litres of water, quantity of pure milk
= 5 × 5 = 25 litres

109. (c) 1 minute's work of both the punctures $= \left(\frac{1}{9} + \frac{1}{6}\right) = \frac{5}{18}$.

So, both the punctures will make the tyre flat in

$\frac{18}{5} = 3\frac{3}{5}$ min.

110. (c) Let the numebrs be x & y
then $x + 5y = 52$ and $8x + y = 65$
$\Rightarrow x = 7, y = 9$

111. (b) Marks obtained by R in B, D and E = 54 % of 40 + 84% of 50 + 62% of 120 = 21.60 + 42+ 74.40 = 138.

112. (a) Average marks obtained by all the students in C

$$= \left(\frac{58+67+72+82+64+75}{6}\right)\% \text{ of } 80$$

$$= \frac{418}{6} \times \frac{80}{100} = 55.7 \approx 56.$$

113. (c) Average % of marks obtained by all the students in 'A'

$$\% = \frac{(80+55+74+68+75+82)}{6} = \frac{434}{6} = 72\frac{1}{3}\%$$

114. (d) Total marks obtained by Q in all subjects = 55% of 60 + 70% of 40 + 67% of 80 + 74% of 50 + 88% of 120 + 78% of 75
= 33 + 28 + 53.60 + 37 + 105.6 + 58. 5 = 315.7

$$\text{Required \%} = \frac{315.7}{425} \times 100 \approx 74\%$$

115. (d) Total marks obtained by all the students together in subject E = (75 + 88 + 62 + 72 + 80+ 68) % of 120 = 534

116. (c) Option (a) : Black + Golden + Blue + Red = 5 + 6 + 13 + 19 = 43%
Option (b) : Blue + Black + Red + Silver = 13 + 5 + 19 + 10 = 47%
Option (c) : White + Golden + Blue + Black = 26 + 6 + 13 + 5 = 50%

117. (b) % of White cars = 26% and 26 – 20 = 6% ® Golden cars

118. (a) % of White cars = 26% and 26 – 13 = 13% ® Blue cars

119. (e) % of Red cars = 19%
Then, 30 – 19 = 11% and 11 – 2 = 9% → Green

120. (d) Required numbers = (13 – 19)% of 95400 = 4% of 95400 = 3816

121. (e) Sale of pep-up was the maximum in the year 1989.

122. (a) Average annual sale of Dew-drop

$$= \frac{10+15+25+15+30+25}{6} = 20 \text{ lakhs}$$

Average annual sale of Cool-sip

$$= \frac{25+7+20+20+25+30}{6} = 21.16 \text{ lakhs}$$

Average annual sale of Pep-up

$$= \frac{30+35+30+25+20+20}{6} = 26.66 \text{ lakhs}$$

123. (c) $\text{Required \%} = \frac{25-20}{20} \times 100 = 25\%$

124. (d) Required no. = (30 – 20) lakhs = 10,00,000

125. (c) $\text{Required \% drop} = = \frac{35-30}{35} \times 100 \approx 14\%$

For Qs. (126-130).

State	Total	Male	Female
A	14400	6000	8400
B	22800	13200	9600
C	8400	3600	4800
D	19200	10800	8400
E	26400	12000	14400
F	18000	9600	8400
G	10800	4800	6000

126. (d) No. of female candidates appeared from C

$$= 1,20,000 \times \frac{7}{100} \times \frac{4}{7} = 4800$$

Following in the table for male candidates appeared in the examination from different states :

A	B	C	D	E	F	G
6,000	13,200	3,600	10,800	12,000	9,600	4,800

Clearly that state is 'G'.

127. (a) $\text{Required ratio} = \frac{6,000}{12,000} = 1:2$

128. (c) Total no. of female candidates appeared from states E and G together = 14,400 + 6000 = 20,400

$$\text{Required percentage} = \frac{20,400 \times 100}{1,20,000} = 17\%$$

129. (d) The total no. of male candiates appeared in the examination from states B and F together = 13,200 + 9600 = 22,800

130. (d) $\text{Required \%} = \frac{8400}{1,20,000} \times 100 = 7\%$

131. (b) We know that Area of the square inscribed in the circle = $3r^2$, where r is the radius of circle.
(I) ⇒ $3r^2 = 98$
⇒ r can be determined.
⇒ Area of circle can be determined.
(II) ⇒ Area of circle = $\frac{4 \times 121}{\pi}$ [since, the area of a square is x cm^2, then area of circle formed by the same perimeter is $\frac{4x}{\pi}$]
Hence, question can be answered by using each statement alone.

132. (d) Let number of males = M
and number of females = F

(I) ⇒ $\frac{M}{F} = \frac{3}{2}$ ..... (i)

(II) ⇒ $M = F\left(1+\frac{50}{100}\right) = \frac{3}{2}F \Rightarrow \frac{M}{F} = \frac{3}{2}$ ..... (ii)

Since, equations (i) and (ii) are same.
Therefore we can't solve the question even with the help of both statements together.

133. (d) Since the dimension of the window and door is not given, therefore, question can't be solved by using both statements together.

134. (d) (I) $\Rightarrow A+B$ is odd $\Rightarrow$ either A is odd and B is even or A is even and B is odd.
(II) $\Rightarrow C+B$ is odd $\Rightarrow$ either C is odd and B is even or C is even and B is odd.
Hence, question can't be answered even with the help of two statements. Therefore, both statements together are not sufficient to answer the question.

135. (d) AB = 100 miles and AC + CB = 100 miles.

$$\text{(I)} \Rightarrow AB = CB\left(1+\frac{25}{100}\right)$$

$$\Rightarrow 100 = \frac{5}{4}CB \Rightarrow CB = 80 \text{ miles}$$

$$\text{(II)} \Rightarrow AC = \frac{1}{4}(CB)$$

Hence, question can be answered using both statements together.

136. (b) (I) $\Rightarrow$ Sunil is at 17th position from the left end and 40 – 16 = 24th position from the right end.
(II) $\Rightarrow$ Sunil is at 24th position from the right end and 40 – 23 = 17th position from the left end.
$\therefore$ Each statement alone is sufficient to answer the question.

137. (b) Let the price in first shop = Rs x per kg

$$\text{(I)} \Rightarrow \frac{18\times6+x\times2}{8} = 20 \Rightarrow x \text{ can be determined.}$$

$$\text{(II)} \Rightarrow \frac{6x+2(x+8)}{8} = 20 \Rightarrow x \text{ can be determined.}$$

$\therefore$ **Each statement alone is sufficient for answering the question.**

138. (e) Let the diameter of circle = d and side of square = a
Then First fly covers the distance = πd
and Second fly covers the distance = 4a
(I) $\Rightarrow a\sqrt{2} = d$
Hence, conclusion can be drawn.
(II) $\Rightarrow$ We have no idea about their speeds. So statement (II) alone is not sufficient.

139. (a) (I) $\Rightarrow \frac{M}{3} = K$

$\therefore \frac{M}{3}$ may be odd or even. Therefore it is not sufficient to answer the question.

(II) $\Rightarrow \frac{M}{3} = 2J + 1$, which is always odd because J is an integer.
$\therefore$ Statement (II) alone is sufficient to answer the question.

140. (e) Suppose he was paid Rs x for the first day.

$$\text{(I)} \Rightarrow x+(x+5)+(x+10)+(x+15)+(x+20)+(x+25) = 900$$

Hence x can be calculated. Therefore statement (I) alone is sufficient to answer the question.
(II) $\Rightarrow x < 100$.
$\therefore$ Statement (II) is not sufficient to answer the question.

141. (b) (I) $\Rightarrow$ Area of the open cubical box with no top = 4 × 5 = 20 sq m
(II) $\Rightarrow$ Edge of box = 2m.
Therefore required area = $5 \times 2^2 = 20$ sq. m.
Hence we can get answer with statement (I) alone and statement (II) alone.

142. (b) Let the total marks = x
(I) $\Rightarrow$ Minimum pass marks = 32% of x + 1 = 36% of x – 1.
Hence minimum marks can be calculated.
(II) $\Rightarrow$ Minimum pass marks = 30% of x + 2 and 30% of x + 5 = 40% of x
Hence minimum marks can be calculated.
Therefore each statement alone is sufficient for answer the question.

143. (e) Since, all three circles are equal.
$\therefore PQ = QR = PR$
$\Rightarrow \Delta PQR$ is an equilateral triangle.
And area of shaded portion
= Area of Δ – 3 (area of each sector),

where area of sector = $\frac{60°}{360°} \times \pi \times (\text{radius})^2$

and area of $\Delta = \frac{\sqrt{3}}{4}(\text{side})^2$.

(I) $\Rightarrow$ QR is known.
$\Rightarrow$ side of triangle and radius is known.
Hence, statement (I) alone is sufficient to answer the question.
Now, since all three circles are equal, therefore, statement (II) is restatement of the information given in question.

144. (b) (I) $\Rightarrow$ The faces bearing the numbers 1, 3, 4 and 6 are adjacent surfaces of the surface bearing the number 5. Hence 2 is opposite to 5.
(II) $\Rightarrow$ Tulika finds herself able to see the surface bearing the number 2, 4 and 6. While Shivendra can see 6, 4 and 5. From this we can conclude 2 is opposite to 5.

145. (e) Since $\angle YBC = \angle CAX = \angle YOX = 90°$
Hence $AB^2 = OA^2 + OB^2$
therefore we need both the length or any other relation since OACB is a rectangle
Hence OC = AB
Therefore radius = AB
Hence, only statement (I) can give us the answer.

146. (c) Let the price of 250 gm loaf be x and price of 450 gm loaf be y. Using statement A, x + y = 24 ...(1). Also from B, we get 2x + y = 34. So value of y can be easily calculated.

147. (b) From A, we get $x = 2y - 4$. So ratio of x to y cannot be calculated.

From B, we get $\frac{0.5x}{2y} = \frac{3}{5}$. So x : y can be calculated from this equation.

148. (c) Both statements together are required to answer this question. Either statement alone is not sufficient.

149. (d) We cannot determine the answer using either statements or even by combining them.

150. (d) $pq = 24$. $\therefore$ possible pairs are (1, 24), (2, 12), (3, 8), (4, 6), (6, 4), (8, 3), (12, 2) and (24, 1). Using A, if we get q/6 is an integer then q can be 24 or 12 or 6. Using B, if we get p/2 is an integer then p = 4 or 2 (depending on q). Even after the combination of two statements, we get 2 values of p as 2 or 4. So both statements are not sufficient.

151. (d) The comparative degree for verb 'fast' is 'faster' and there is no need to add more to it.

152. (c) The modal 'should' need not be repeated since the conjunction 'and' is being used. The should in the sentence will be used for both the parts.

153. (b) 'in' is the correct preposition to be used with the verb circulated.

154. (c) 'craziness' is no word, the right noun is craze. If that is maddening is chosen it will be follwed by 'that is responsible' which will not be appropriate 'mad craze' is the correct use, and this craze is not for the noun 'speed' but the verb 'speeding', i.e., driving vehicles at high speed.

155. (c) Co-operate has an implicit meaning of together. It means 'work together', so together must be eliminated. Similarly 'dividing' means 'breaking up' so 'up' from 'dividing' must also be eliminated.

156. (a) Sentence B is the beginning to the passage telling us about the Spartans, E tells us more about the way they treated their male children who were too weak to become soldiers. C talks about those babies who survived babyhood, D continues with the rigorous military training refer to C, A ends the passage by stating that the children were punished if they were caught stealing.

157. (c) B is the introduction to the passage, C follows refering to education by older images drawn by hand to be better than being educated by photographs, D talks about the inventory started in 1839 and everything else being photographed after that A refers to the insatiability of the photographing eye and E talks about the new visual code i.e. of photographs altering and enlarging our notions.

158. (a) A talks about being culturally, literate which is needed to thrive in the modern world, E states about the great breadth of that information, C tells us that this information is by no means confined to "culture", B follows stating that nor is it confined to one social class, D ends the passage by stating that cultural literacy is the only reliable way of combating social determinism.

159. (c) E begins the paragraph telling us about the gap between the worth and rewards of translators. A refers to the feelings of Michael Hofman about this sorry fact. C tells us more about this acknowledgement, B continues by saying that he is not daunted by thanklessness and impossibility, D concludes by saying that Hofman is passionated about his work which is clear from his writings.

160. (b) A and C means that the manager wants you to do something. B means after you will do something he will start liking you.

161. (d) Each sentence has different meanings.

162. (d) Same as above.

163. (d) Every sentence has same meaning.

164. (a) (c) is obviously wrong, the second part of (b) does not fit as the pipe smokers are not 'responsible'. (d) is incorrect because rejoinded means reply or retort.

165. (b) (a) is wrong since overdrawing is definitely not an aspect of art. (c) cannot be held true since Indian art cannot be accused of imitation and one form of art can never be judged superior or inferior to other. Among (b) and (d), (b) fits better as it supports the later part of sentence as well.

166. (a) The answer is obvious since the other options are week as one or other word doesnot fit at all.

167. (d) Prognostications means prediction. One may be declared optimistic only when one doesnot take heed of upleasant situations. (a) is wrong because if a report is malicious there is no chance of benefit. (b) is wrong since sanguinary means violent and a report cannot be violent by any means. (c) is wrong because if the analysis is not pessimistic then what is the point of boisting of being optimist.

168. (a) Option (a) is the right answer because the main concern of the passage is with rationality and enlightened self interest. The passage does talk about altruism but it cannot be considered the main theme because neither it is the focus of the passage nor it is the important prospective given through the passage. In fact, rationality and self interest are the running idea of the text and the rest is discussed through them.

169. (d) To say that the author is cynical or even sceptical about their use would not be true. The relevant line in the passage is "prince increases the means at our disposal for injuring each other". This statement best shows the author's concern about their harmful potential. It is not a cautions acceptance. The passage talks only of what science can do i.e. its potential and not what it does i.e. its use. So, (d) will be the right answer.

170. (d) Option (d) is the right answer (a) and (d) can be eliminated straightway. There is a confusion between (b) and (d). Author's opinion of rationality is clear from the line "Rationality in practice may be defined as...... the strongest". The author does not say anything about control of desire. It only urges us to not only remember the strongest desire at particular moment but remember all desire. He asks us to check momentary passing and not all desires. So, (d) is the answer not (b).

171. (a) This is an inference question. The author says that "to preach an altruistic morality..... already have altruistic desire". He means that altruism will appeal only to those who are by Nature altruists and since that is not true, altruistist morality is useless. It is not any comparison between altruism and rationality that affects the appeal of altruism, according to the passage.

172. (b) In the context of the passage, king Demos seems to refer to a man in position of power, he may be a king or a politician.

173. (c) Option (c) is the appropriate choice of a title for the given passage. (b), (d) could be eliminated because they are too simplistic to be the title for a scientific passage. (a) cannot be the title because this passage does not emphasise 'Evolution' as such but adaptation as a response to evolution. Because Adaptation is the central idea in the passage, so, (c) will be the right title.
Tip: Whenever a question asks you to choose a title for the given passage, always choose the one nearest to the central theme of the passage.

174. (c) Question 1 is answered in the first statement of the passage. But the passage does not answer the second question. The third question on the other hand is answered by inference in the second last line of the passage. In fact all the examples of different limbs given in the passage are the organs structurally different but similar or homologous when seen in the chain of evolution. Thus, the passage answers question (a) and (c), so (c) is the right answer.

175. (b) (a) is incorrect there are no comparison or contracts between different ideas. There are only statements and examples, thus, (b) is the right answer. (c) and (d) are also incorrect because there is no hypothesis or definitions in the passage either.

176. (b) 'Homo' means similar or of the same kind. (a), (c) can be eliminated because they are opposite to similar. (d) has no relation with the meaning, 'similarly' (b) is the correct answer, homologous means corresponding'.

177. (a) Because the passage has only factual statements and examples the style can best be called objective. It is not humorous or patronizing. It cannot even be called esoteric because the passage gives general information without using much jargon.

178. (a) Affinity

199. (d) Fatigued

180. (c) heritage

181. (a) **Liberate** is to make someone free and **imprison** is to put in prison, conceal is to hide and **vacillation** is to move from one place or idea to another.

182. (d) **Melancholy** means depressed and is therefore opposite to **cheerful**.

183. (c) **Legitimate** means legal or lawful, **distinguished** means eminent, and **courteous** means polite.

184. (b) The controversy led to a termination of the contract. That is the contract came to an end. The opposite of end is beginning.

185. (c) The-adverb of time, 'never' and not the conjunction 'neither' is to be used. This is also done to never have the construction in the same series.

186. (d) was being dragged by the soldiers
All qualifying words, phrases and clauses should be placed as near as possible to the words to which they refer.

187. (d) them
The Accusative Case of the third person plural 'them' and not the Nominative 'they' is to be used as the other people are the object of the sentence.

188. (d) they were not to open
The infinitive 'to open': like a noun needs a subject which the verb 'were' fulfils.

189. (c) the members felt
The subject usually comes before the verb in a sentence. In English, owing to the fewness of the inflections, the order of the words in a sentence is of the first importance.

190. (d) necesssities
The word above is the plural of the noun 'necessity'.

191. (b)
192. (c)
193. (e)
194. (d)
195. (b)
196. (a)
197. (e)
198. (b)
199. (d)
200. (c)

MOCK TEST - 5

1. (d) Two possibilities are there :
   (i) Chemistry part I is available in 8 books with Chemistry part II.

   or

   (ii) Chemistry part II is not available in 8 books but Chemistry part I is available.

   Total No. of ways $= 1\times {}^6C_1 + {}^7C_3$

   $= 6+\dfrac{7\times6\times5}{3\times2} = 6+35 = 41$

2. (e)

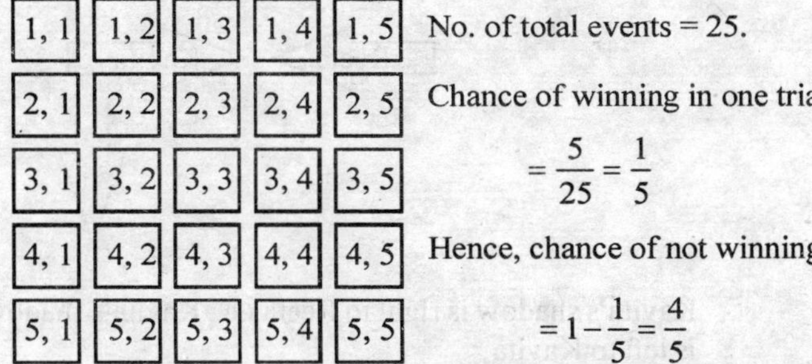

No. of total events = 25.

Chance of winning in one trial

$= \dfrac{5}{25} = \dfrac{1}{5}$

Hence, chance of not winning

$= 1-\dfrac{1}{5} = \dfrac{4}{5}$

3. (d) Chance of selecting an eleven out of 15 members (including 5 bowlers) such that atleast 3 bowlers are included

$$= \frac{{}^{10}C_8\times{}^5C_3 + {}^{10}C_7\times{}^5C_4 + {}^{10}C_6\times{}^5C_5}{{}^{15}C_{11}}$$

$$= \frac{{}^{10}C_2\times{}^5C_2 + {}^{10}C_3\times{}^5C_1 + {}^{10}C_4\times1}{{}^{15}C_4}$$

$$= \frac{45\times10+120\times5+210}{1365} = \frac{1260}{1365} = \frac{12}{13}$$

4. (b) 5 books can be arranged in 5! ways i.e. in 120 ways
   As one book is moved every minute
   $\therefore$ Total time taken in moving all books in all possible ways $= \dfrac{120\times1}{60}$ hrs. = 2 hrs.

5. (c) No. of seating arrangements
   = No. of ways in which men sit
   × No. of ways in which women sit
   $= 6!\times7!$

6. (d) $1\frac{3}{4}+1\frac{5}{8}-2\frac{4}{5}+\frac{1}{2}$

$$= (1+1-2)+\left(\frac{3}{4}+\frac{5}{8}+\frac{1}{2}-\frac{4}{5}\right)$$

$$= \frac{30+25+20-32}{40} = \frac{43}{40} = 1\frac{3}{40}$$

7. (a) $14\times1.55+19.3 = ?$
   $21.7+19.3 = ?$
   $41 = ?$
   $\therefore ? = 41$

8. (c) $8^{4.2}\times64^{2.1}\times7^{8.4}\times56^{3.5}$

$$= 8^{4.2}\times\left(8^2\right)^{2.1}\times7^{8.4}\times56^{3.5}$$

$$= 8^{4.2}\times8^{4.2}\times7^{8.4}\times56^{3.5} = \left(8^{8.4}\times7^{8.4}\right)\times56^{3.5}$$

$$= 56^{8.4}\times56^{3.5} = 56^{(8.4+3.5)} = 56^{11.9}$$

9. (e) $? = 48845+\dfrac{51246}{6} = 48845+8541 = 57386$

10. (e) Work with options we find that the value of ? is 3.

11. (b) From fig. II to I : The right column elements rotate by 90° clockwise while the left column elements rotate by 90° anticlockwise.

12. (a) From fig. II to I : The whole figure rotates by 180°.

13. (e) From fig. II to I : The rectangular element rotates by 90° anticlockwise while its shading moves to end. The bar rotates by 90° clockwise. The end elements get inverted and one of them changes its side.

14. (d)

15. (c) From fig. II to I : One of the bars rotates by 135°clockwise and one of its end element is replaced by a new one. The end elements on the other bar interchange places.

16. (b) Either I or II can be advised. Water supply authority must partial cut in supply to tackle the situation or appeal to all residents for minimal use of water.

17. (c) I is not advisable because from this decision virus negative person would be also affected. II will be the right action to tackle the situation.

18. (a) It is duty of government to make alternative arrangement. So, I is advisable. II is not advisable because it will be extreme action and against of fundamental right.

19. (a) Increased capacity of train will be helpful to tackle the situation, so it is advisable. II is not advisable, what is meaning of this advise for those people who want to utilise holiday. Hence only I follows.

20. (c) I cannot be advised because it can be created problem to continue supply of gas. II is advisable because it will be helpful to save life.

21. (c) $63.9872\times9449.8780\div243.0034$
    $= 64\times9450\div243 = 64\times39 \approx 2496$
    Now, $(?)^2 \approx 2496$
    $\therefore ? \approx 50$

22. (d) $? = 5237.897-6629.010+7153.999-2205.102$
    $= 3557.784 \approx 3558$

23. (b) $4985.0346\div215.987-3768.112\div206.868$
    $\approx 4985\div216-3768\div207 \approx 23-18 \approx 5$

24. (a) $? = \sqrt{956240} \approx 978$
25. (e) $? = 459\% \text{ of } 849.947 + 266\% \text{ of } 6284.012 - 1486.002$
$? = 460\% \text{ of } 850 + 265\% \text{ of } 6285 - 1486$
$= 3910 + 16655 - 1486 = 19079 \approx 19130$
26. (c) RBUKAE $\rightarrow$ 670892
27. (b) PIAEBN $\rightarrow$ #4927#
28. (b) NAPKJI $\rightarrow$ 395814
29. (a) KUNAJB $\rightarrow$ #0391#
30. (e) AREJPK $\rightarrow$ 962158
31. (a) Required ratio $= \frac{8+9}{15+18} = 17:33$
32. (d) Here, do not find the ratio of the no. of qualified candidates to that of the appeared. Simply check the ratio of % qualified candidates with respect to the appeared is the least for which state.
33. (d) Required difference $= (21-13)\% \text{ of } 9000 = 720$
34. (b) Reqd % $= \frac{(16+7)\% \text{ of } 9000}{(11+8)\% \text{ of } 45000} \times 100 = 24.21\%$
35. (c) Reqd ratio $= \frac{(16+21)\% \text{ of } 9000}{8\% \text{ of } 45000} = 37:40$

For (Qs. 36- 40). Excess Laxity in sentence D is to be taken after total forgiveness, therefore D follows A, which is itself is followed by E which speaks of action mentioned in D and it is followed inturn by B and C.

36. (a) 37. (d) 38. (e) 39. (b) 40. (c)
41. (b) Beginning from the right, in each step two line segments forming triangles are added. After four steps one line segment is added.
42. (c) The arc on the left side changes its direction in each step.
43. (c) The flag-like element rotates by 45°, 90°, 135°, 180° .... anticlockwise in subsequent steps and reverses its direction in each step.
44. (b) The no. of elements increases by one in each step. The line of orientation totates by 90° and 45° alternately.
45. (e) The clockwise -end element rotates by 90° clockwise in each step while the other two rotate by 90° anticlockwise and 180° alternately.
46. (a) RBM STD BRO PUS $\equiv$ the cat is beautiful ....(i)
TNH PUS DIM STD $\equiv$ the dog is brown ....(ii)
PUS DIM BRO PUS CUS $\equiv$ the dog has the cat ....(iii)
(i) and (ii) $\Rightarrow$ STD PUS $\equiv$ is
(ii) and (iii) $\Rightarrow$ PUS DIM $\equiv$ the dog
(i) and (iii) $\Rightarrow$ PUS BRO $\equiv$ the cat
$\therefore$ From (iii), CUS $\equiv$ has
47. (b) As,
$N \xleftarrow{-2} L$
$A \xleftarrow{-2} Y$
$X \xleftarrow{-2} V$
$A \xleftarrow{-2} Y$
$L \xleftarrow{-2} J$
$I \xleftarrow{-2} G$
$T \xleftarrow{-2} R$
$E \xleftarrow{-2} C$
$\Rightarrow$ Similarly,
$G \xrightarrow{+2} I$
$L \xrightarrow{+2} N$
$R \xrightarrow{+2} T$
$C \xrightarrow{+2} E$
$E \xrightarrow{+2} G$
$P \xrightarrow{+2} R$
$Y \xrightarrow{+2} A$
$R \xrightarrow{+2} T$
$C \xrightarrow{+2} E$
48. (b) Only one meaningful word 'ALONE' can be made. O is the middle letter.
49 (d) ABCD is different from the remaining three.

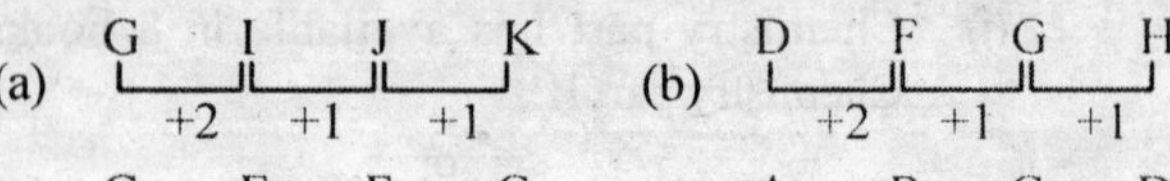

(c) C E F G (+2 +1 +1) (d) A B C D (+1 +1 +1)

50. (a)

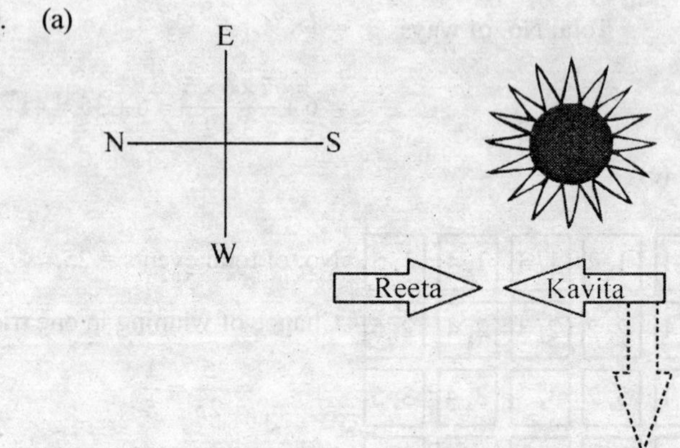

Kavita's shadow is right to Reeta i.e., Kavita's shadow is left to Kavita.
$\therefore$ Kavita is facing North.

51. (a) Required percentage $= \frac{1100 \times 100}{5600} = 19.64\,\%$
52. (b) The correct combinations should be as follows
(i) 2000 — 100%
(ii) 1998 — 50%
(iii) 2003 — 10%
53. (c) The required percentage
$= \frac{(700+400+600)}{5900} \times 100 = \frac{1700}{59} \approx 28.81\,\%$
54. (d) The required ratio $= 5600:5900 = 56:59$
55. (d) It is obvious from the graph.
56. (b) Refer to paragraph 1 - It is said to be 'imminently' present in both the Adhyatma and the Adhibhuta.
57. (c) Refer to paragraph 2.
58. (d) Refer to paragraph 3- last sentence, the Absolute is said to descend through varying levels of consciousness in subject - object relations.
59. (c) Refer to paragraph 4 - last sentence.
60. (c) Refer to paragraph 6 - That the powers are female, is not mentioned.
61. (b)

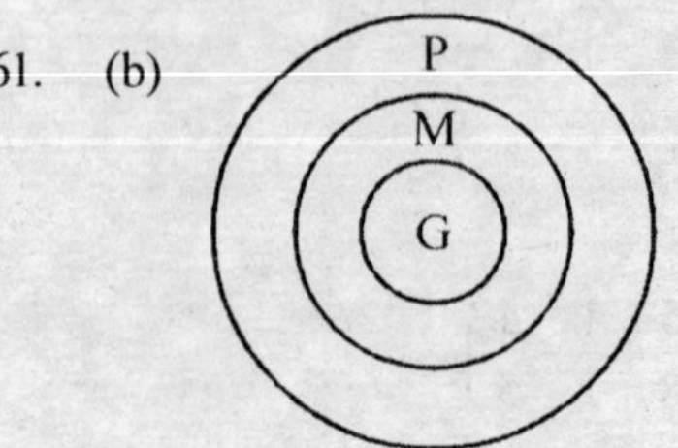

None of the conclusions follows.

62. (b)

63. (b)

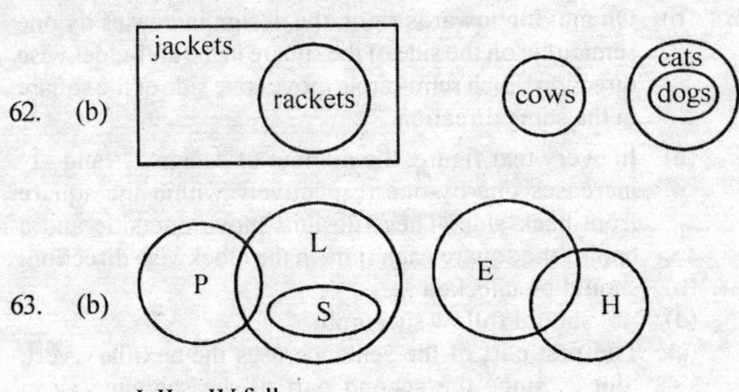

I, II or IV follow.

64. (d)

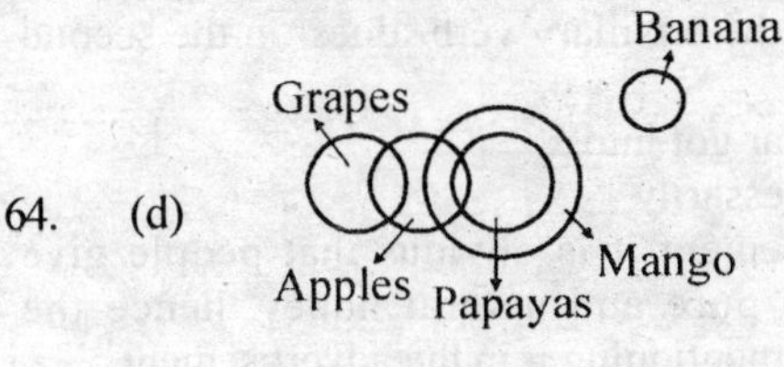

Or

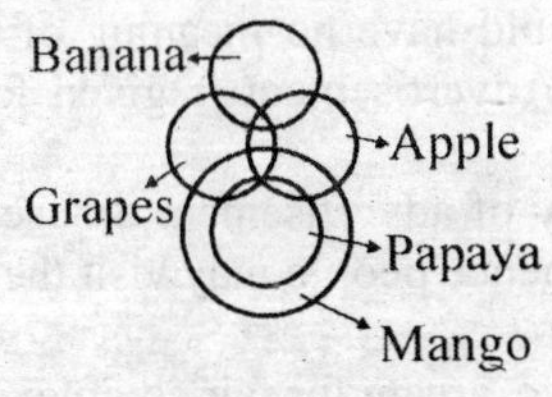

65. (b)

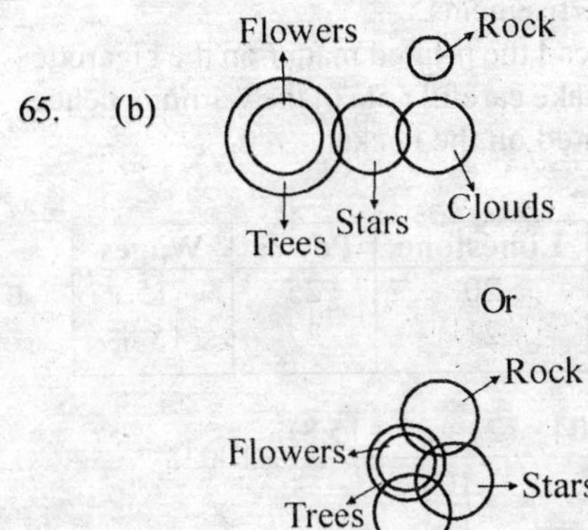

66. (b)

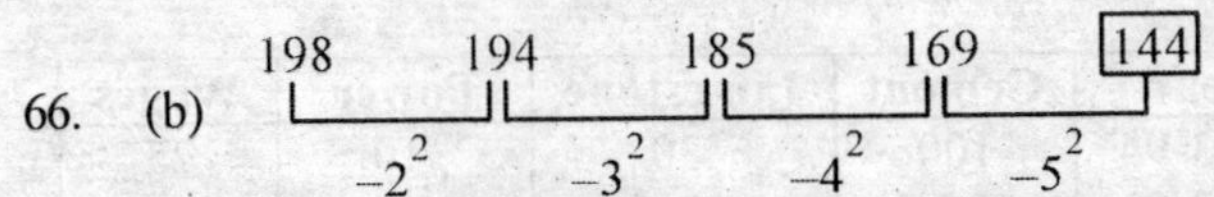

67. (c) The first, third, fifth .... and second, fourth .... terms are groups of consecutive natural numbers.

68. (b) 5, 6, 8, 9, 11, 12 (+1, +2, +1, +2, +1)

69. (c) 245, 125, 65, 35, 20, 12.5 (120, 60, 30, 15, 7.5)

70. (b) 0, 2, 6, 12, 20, 30 (+2, +4, +6, +8, +10)

71. (b) In each step anticlockwise -end element shifts half-a-side clockwise. The second and third elements from anticlockwise end shift to the other side of this element while the order of the remaining four elements get reversed.

72. (a) In each step two elements in each row interchange their positions in a set order while one row shifts from upper to lower and vice versa.

73. (c) In each step three elements shift diagonally downwards alternately on left and right diagonals while the other two interchange positions.

74. (e) In each step a new element appears at upper-middle positions. The upper-middle shifts to lower-middle → upper-left → lower-right → upper-right → lower-left element. The lower-left is lost.

75. (d) In each step a new element appears at upper-left while the elements shift one step downward diagonally. The lower element is lost.

76. (b) The sitting order of the persons are as follows :

B E G F D C A

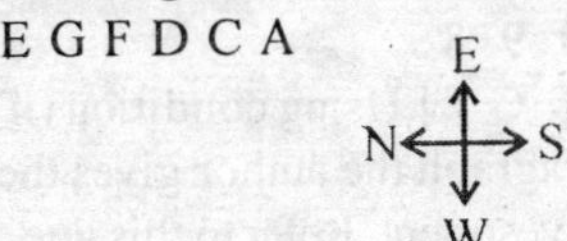

Thus, A and B are sitting at the extreme ends.

77. (b) The relations described in the question can be represented as follows:

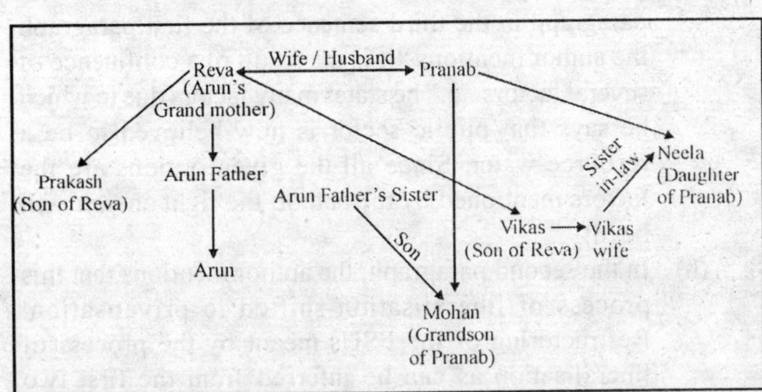

Thus wife of Vikas is sister- in-law of Neela.

78. (a) (i) Sudha > Puja

(ii) Suma > Kavita > Sudha

(iii) Sudha > Mamta > Puja

Now order of score is

Suma > Kavita > Sudha > Mamta > Puja

79. (b) 70 m; 100 m; A (My self); 50 m; B'; 10; A'; 10; 30; B (My friend); 20

When my friend reaches on the previous track (i.e. on B') again, he had travelled a distance of (30 + 10 + 20 + 10) = 70 m. As I walk with the same speed as that of my friend I have walked 70m, but on the straight track. Now, he is just [100 – (30 + 20)] = 50m

from my starting point.
Hence, the distance between us = (70 – 50) = 20m

80. (d) As,

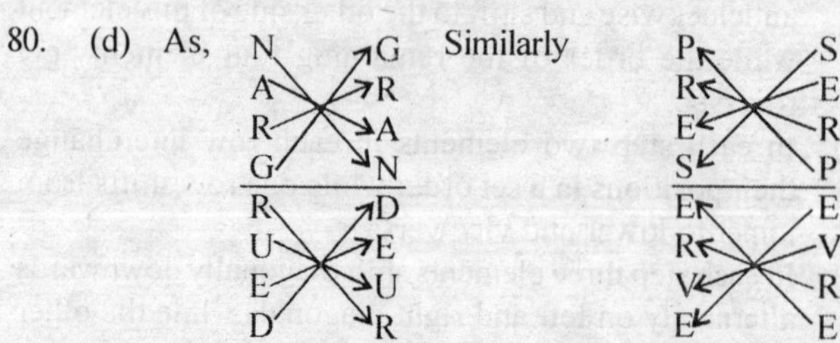

81. (b) 1 3 7 5 4 9 0
\# H N L Q G £ (Using condition (ii))
82. (e) From (i), $ and @ can be replaced by the combination of 2, 4 , 6, 8 and 1, 3, 5, 7, 9 respectively.
83. (e) Using (iv), Q L P ↑ R N T
4 5 8 0 6 7 0
84. (b) 7 6 2 0 4 8 6
\# R F ↑Q P £ [Using condition (ii) and (iv)]
85. (c) 3 6 2 5 0 0 9 8
\# R F L T T G £ [Using condition (ii)]
86. (d) In the third paragraph the author gives the basic issues regarding disinvestment. Refer to this line "whole needs to be reviewed are some basic issues,...." All the given options are mentioned as the basic issues regarding disinvestment.
87. (d) For this question the relevant portion is the first paragraph in the third sentence of the first paragraph the author mentions "It is the result of a confluence of several factors......" he states many factors due to which he says that public sector is new believed to be a resource water. Since all the given options are the factors mentioned by the author, the right answer will be (d).
88. (b) In the second paragraph, the author mentions that this process of liberalisation shifted to privatisation. Restructuring of the PSUs meant by the process of liberalisation as can be inferred from the first two sentences of the second paragraph.
89. (b) In the last line of the fourth paragraph, the author refers to "Great harm to the investments which were made with such great dedication as though derided now". These investments are made in the PSUs as clear from the previous line.
90. (d) The author says in the passage, "Non-performers exist both in public and private sector"
91. (b) On moving towards right, the design increases by one leaf, added beside the last leaf in the clockwise direction. The first dark leaf remains at the same place.
92. (d) On moving towards right all the four designs move one complete and a half side of the figure. In every next figure, the last design is replaced by one new design.
93. (a) On moving towards right, each design formed between the straight lines moves one segment of the figure in the anti-clockwise direction. Starting from the square, each design is replaced by a new design in the same direction.
94. (b) On moving towards right, the design increases by one semicircle on the side of the square in the anti-clockwise direction. Each semi-circle moves one side of the square in the same direction.
95. (d) In every text figure, the number of design '↑' and '↑' increases one-by-one respectively within the square from back side. These designs move one side and a half of the square each time in the clockwise direction.
96. (b) should be checked ...
97. (d) 'to' should follow succumb.
98. (c) The first part of the sentence uses the auxillary verb 'does', since the second part of the sentence is an alternative to the first it must be in the same syntax so there must be the auxillary verb 'does' in the second part as well.
99. (c) How the burglar got into ...
100. (a) Said to be necessarily
101. (a) From the statement it is obvious that people give preference to pure and natural honey, hence the company X is mentioning it in the advertisement.
102. (e) Both I and II are implicit. If people did not want enjoyable flight, there would have no meaning of this kind of advertisement. Advertisement is given for attraction of people.
103. (c) Uncommon way of advertisement arouses interest in the customers, hence people may visit the shop out of curiosity.
104. (d) People like to use, cream for fair complexion and they respond to advertisements.
105. (b) People usually read the printed matter on the cigarette packet and they take careful note of the warning, hence the warning printed on the packet.
106. (c)

Year	Cement	Limestone	Power	Wages
1993-94	100	20	25	15
2002-03	104	21	27	15.8

$$\text{Hence, \% profit} = \frac{104-(21+27+15.8)}{104}\times 100$$

$$= \frac{40.2}{104}\times 100 = 38.7\%$$

107. (b)

Year	Cement	Limestone	Power	Wages
1993-94	100	30	10	25
2002-03	105.5	32.4	10.53	26.5

Hence,

$$\text{profit \%} = \frac{105.5-(32.4+10.53+26.5)}{105.5}\times 100$$

$$= 33.71\ \%$$

108. (a) To answer this question, we have to see only the particular row in the table for the given options and for power it experienced continuous rise.
109. (d) Again for Timber and Wages experienced decline only once for the given period.

110. (d) 7 is a figure which is fulfilling both people's statements.

111. (d) The passage is clearly a book review - as such, it fulfils both the purposes mentioned in (a) and (b).

112. (c) Refer 1st para-the altermath of war if said to be ideal for literary romances and therefore "occupied Japan in 1947" is an "apt" background. Thus (c) is the correct answer.

113. (b) Refer para 6, last sentance and 1st sentance of para 7 - thus (b) is correct.

114. (c) The author says the book is a finely crafted work (last sentance).

115. (c) Refer para 9, "......more articulate than realism would dicale......."

116. (e) The inner elements get enlarged and become outer while the outer elements get reduced in size and become inner. The smaller elements then interchange places.

117. (c) The LHS element rotates by 90° clockwise and gets inverted on the bar. The RHS element gets rotated by 90° anticlockwise. Both the elements interchange places.

118. (d) The upper and the lower left elements rotate by 135° clockwise while lower right element rotates by 135° anticlockwise.

119. (a) The elements move from position 1 to 8 → 3 → 7 → 1. The element at position 2 moves to 9 while a new element appears at 2.

120. (c) The whole figure rotates by 45° anticlockwise. The shading of the half-shaded leaf changes and one more leaf gets shaded in the same fashion.

121. (a) P 1 % T R A 5 # D M 7 K ★ E G 2 8 $ H 3 1 4 V U 6 F ⊕ 9 Z
In the above series there is no consonant symbol-consonant sequence.

122. (e) Except it in each choice second and third elements are second to the left of first elements and third to the right of first element respectively.

123. (a) We have to look for digit- vowel-consonant sequence in the following series.
P 1 % T R A 5 # D M 7 K ★ E G 2 8 $ H 3 1 4 V U 6 F ⊕ 9 Z
There is no such sequence.

124. (c) Elements, between the fifth from the left and the seventh from the right end are :
A 5 # D M 7 K ★ [E] G 2 8 $ H 3 1 4
↑ Middle element

125. (d) After changing the series becomes as follows:
P 1 % T R A 5 # D M 7 K ★ E G 2 8 Z 9 ⊕ F 6 U V 4 1 3 H $
Now, eight element to the right of eleventh from the left, i.e., 9.

126. (c) From visual observation, it is more in the year 1994–95.

127. (b) Required rate $= \frac{0.90-0.80}{0.80} \times \frac{100}{6} = \frac{100}{48}\% = 2.08\%$

128. (b) Number of visitors in 1998 – 99
$= 0.90 \times 1.02 \times 10^6 \approx 10^6$

129. (a) It is minimum for 1992 – 93.

130. (d) No data about the price of ticket is given, hence, question cannot be answered.

For (Qs. 131-134):

Following table represents the time duration in which Rajiv met the doctors:

Orders	Doctors	Duration of meeting	Gap (in minutes)
1	O	9:00 am - 9:30 am	25
2	S	9:55 am - 10:25 am	25
3	R	10:50 am - 11:20 pm	25
4	M	11:45 am - 12:15 pm	25
5	Q	12:40 pm - 1:10 pm	50
6	P/N	2:00 pm - 2:30 pm	25
7	N/P	2:55 pm - 3:25 pm	25
8	R	3:50 pm (visit again)	

131. (b) 132. (c) 133. (a) 134. (d)

135. (c)

L	M	N	O	P	Q	R	S	T
		6		4			9	

136. (b) The part of the sentence is in negative what follows is instead of what is assumed in the first part, so, first blank should have a word that means similar to instead, which is rather.

137. (c) **Clemency** means pardon, a plea to a judge can only be for pardon since the sentence talks about a punishment being given **formidable** means difficult to overcome, and **abrasive** means rough but the most appropriate feeling is that of indifference, so, **unmoved** is the right answer.

138. (b) **Canonical** means pleasant or agreeable, **creditable** means reliable. There is no conversation between being a pleasant liar and appearing reliable, so, this can be eliminated, **incorrigible** is something that cannot be redeemed or reformed, incorrigible is something that can be true. **Alive** that seems **plausible** will be the quality of a liar who has mastered the art of lying so, this is the appropriate selection of words. Illogical and Incongruous (not suitable) will oppose the meaning of the sentence a conveying liar will not tell illogical lies.

139. (c) Authority is 'exercised', so we have two options (c) and (d). The wishes are satisfied according to the meaning of the sentence stimulate means to make more active.

140. (d) Source fits well in the first blank and incentive is the most appropriate choice for the second origin and cause are verbs used for a specific point in time and not throughout history. So, (b) and (c) are eliminated. Of (a) and (d) war is not an encouragement to screens but an incentive.

141. (b) Here, $T > K$ ...(i)
$K \leq R$ ...(ii)
$R = M$ ...(iii)
From (ii) and (iii), we get
$R = M \geq K$ ...(iv)
Now, from (iv) we get $M > K$ (conclusion III) for $M = K$

(conclusion I). Hence, either conclusion I or conclusion III follows. Again, from (i) and (iv) we can't get any specific relationship between 'M' and 'T'. Hence, conclusion II does not follow.

142. (c) Here, $M < R$ ...(i)

$R \leq T$ ...(ii)

$T = N$ ...(iii)

From (i), (ii) and (iii), we get

$T = N \geq R > M$ ...(iv)

Hence, from (iv) we get $N = R$ (conclusion I) or $N > R$ (conclusion II). Hence, either conclusion I or conclusion II follows. Also, from (iv) we get $N > M$ (conclusion III). Hence, conclusion III follows.

143. (d) Here, $V \geq M$ ...(i)

$A > M$ ...(ii)

$R \leq V$ ...(iii)

From (i) and (ii), we can't get any specific relationship between 'V' and 'A'. Hence, conclusion II does not follow. Again from (i) and (iii), we can't get any specific relationship between 'M' and 'R'. Hence, conclusion III does not follow. On the similar basis we can't get any specific relationship between 'A' and 'R' using all (i), (ii) and (iii). Hence, conclusion I does not follow.

144. (b) Here, $B = D$ ...(i)

$D \geq H$ ...(ii)

$H < F$ ...(iii)

From (i) and (ii), we get

$B = D \geq H$ ...(iv)

Now, from (iii) and (iv), we can't get any specific relationship between B and F (or D and F). Hence, no conclusion follows. But, conclusion I and II make a complementary pair. Hence, either conclusion I or conclusion II follows.

145. (d) Here, $J \leq N$ ...(i)

$K \geq N$ ...(ii)

$T > K$ ...(iii)

From (i), (ii) and (iii), we get

$T > K \geq N \geq J$ ...(iv)

From (iv), we get $J < T$ (conclusion I) and $T > N$ (conclusion II). Hence, conclusion I and conclusion II follow. Conclusion III can be obtained from conversion of (i). Hence, conclusion III follows.

For (Qs. 146-150) :

The Organization of the plays will be as follows

5th	6th	7th	8th	9th	10th
Mon	Tue	Wed	Thu	Fri	Sat
D	B	E	C	F	A

146. (c) The organisation would start from play D which is clear from above.
147. (b) E is to be organised on 7th.
148. (a) The organisation would end with the play A on 10th.
149. (a) The play B is organised on 6th which is a Tuesday.
150. (d) The correct sequence of the plays is DBECFA.
151. (c) Elements of the first get vertically inverted in the second.
152. (b) Elements get inverted vertically and first and third, and second and fourth interchange their positions.
153. (a) Elements move one step towards right and right most becomes left most. The smaller elements get enlarged and vice versa.
154. (d) The elements move from $1 \text{ to } 4 \rightarrow 3 \rightarrow 7 \rightarrow 6 \rightarrow 9 \rightarrow 1$.
155. (e) The figure rotates 90° anticlockwise. The line segment moves two steps clockwise.
156. (c) From I Riya is the mother of Rajesh. So, Omprakash is the grandfather of Rejesh.

From II Seema is the cousin of Sanjana. So, their husbands, Omprakash and Rajesh, are brothers-in-law.

157. (c) From I Total number of students in the class $= (18 + 34 - 1) = 51$

So, Anu's rank from the bottom $= 52 - 14 = 38$th

Hence, I alone is sufficient.

From II Here also, the strength of the class is given. So, Anu's rank from the botton* $= (51 - 14) = 37$th.

158. (e) From I Possible days are Wednesday and Thursday.

From II Possible days are Tuesday and Wednesday.

Combining I and II:

The day of interview is Wednesday.

159. (c) From I. Prem is facing North-east.

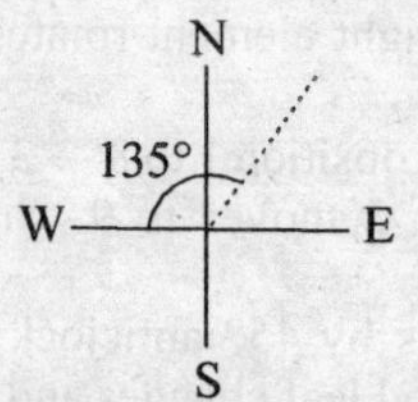

From II. Prem is facing East.

160. (e) From I

Sur/Gaj

Anil Kunal

Gaj/Sur

Hence I alone is not sufficient.

From II

Surendra

Anil Kunal

Hence II alone is also not sufficient.

Combining I and II

Surendra

Anil Kunal

Gajendra

Hence Gajendra sits on the immediate left of Kunal.

161. (a) Condition (G) is fulfilled. So (A) is waived. Hence the candidate is selected.
162. (c) Question does not mention if Sanjay Verma has any specialization in the area of Information Technology/ Archives and Manuscript keeping.
163. (a) Since Mr Ramesh Singhania has fulfilled the conditions of (G) hence (A) is waived. He can therefore be selected.
164. (c) The data about Sunil Garewal's candidature is inadequate.

165. (d) Two possibilities are there :
(i) Chemistry part I is available in 8 books with Chemistry part II.
or
(ii) Chemistry part II is not available in 8 books but Chemistry part I is available.

Total No. of ways $= 1\times 1\times {}^6C_1 + {}^7C_3$

$= 6+\frac{7\times6\times5}{3\times2} = 6+35 = 41$

For (Qs. 166-170) :
The information can be tabulated as below :

Person	Shirt	Trouser
B	red	black/white
D	green	indigo
A	white/black	red
F	black/white/violet	white/black
E	yellow	blue
C	black/white/violet	yellow
G	blue	cream

166. (b) 167. (b) 168. (c) 169. (d) 170. (d)
171. (c) It is true that if the notes had not gone out of circulation, there might have been no need of their re-print. But much time has elasped and a direct causal relationship can't be established.
172. (b) B is an exercise in cutting expenditure, which has become imperative given the widening fiscal deficit.
173. (d) Even a remote connection can't be established with any bit of certainty.
174. (a) Since the subsidy has been reduced, the institutions will have to compensate for it by recovering a large portion from the students.
175. (a) When the results were declared, it was the father's curiosity that led him to the website.
176. (c) Cost of camera = 30% of money Mr. X had (say x)
1 and 2 together are sufficient, as we obtain the following equation, which can be solved to give x.

$\frac{30}{100}\times x + 900 + \frac{1}{4}x = x$

Again, (c), alone is sufficient as from the selling price and profit we can get the cost price, which is equal to 30% of the initial money.
177. (c) If a, b, c and d be the required numbers in ascending order
1 gives $d - c < c - b$ or $b + d < 2c$;
2 gives $d - c > b - a$ or $a + d > b + c$, so 2 is sufficient
3 gives $d - b > c - a$ or $a + d > b + c$, so 3 is sufficient
So, A and either B or C is redundant.
178. (b) 3 alone gives that capacity of tank = $150 \times 60 \times x = 900x$
Equating it to data, from 2,
capacity of tank = $(26 - x) \times 270$
or $900x = (26 - x) \times 270$
or $x = 5400$ litres. So, either of 2 or 3 is redundant.
179. (c) We require the area of the rectangle and the cost of carpeting. For which we require the two sides a and b. 3 is required as it gives the carpeting cost. 1 and 2 separately gives a relation between a and b. So both 1 and 2 are required to give a and b. So all three are required. None is redundant.
180. (d) Given: $A + 10 = C - 20 \Rightarrow C - A = 30$
$\therefore$ C secured 60% marks and A secured 45% marks, therfore 15% of the marks = 30
$\therefore$ A secured 45% marks, i.e. 90
B secured 50% marks, i.e. 100
C secured 60% marks, i.e. 120
D's marks are
$A + 10 = C - 20 = 100$
$\therefore$ None of the statements 1,2 and 3 is required to answer the given question.
181. (b) There is no need for 'who' or 'which' as 'whom' follows the subject 'person' directly and need not be connected through a pronoun.
182. (d) 'of' is the preposition used with frightened.
183. (a) The word here is used as a 'noun' not as a verb thus damage will be the right answer.
184. (b) The right use is 'as + adjective + as'.
185. (b) In the given sentence there is no subject or verb, so the added phrase should be of the form 'subject + infinitive verb.'
186. (a) **Bonhomie** means cheerful, friendly, while **wrath** means extreme anger.
187. (e) **Collapse** means to fell down or lose strength, of the given options the nearest to its meaning is failure.
188. (c) **Bashful** means a shy person, discreet is someone who is cautious and prudent, not showy.
189. (a) Prefix 'a' means 'not' that is most nearest in meaning to 'Not interested in politics.'
190. (e) **Appease** is to calm down. **Pacify** also means to calm down, **agitate** is to be trouble.
191. (b) Total number of possible arrangements for 4 boys and 3 girls in a queue = 7!
When they occupy alternate positions the arrangement would be like
B G B G B G B
Thus, total number of possible arrangements

$= \underset{\text{For boys}}{4\times3\times2} \times \underset{\text{For girls}}{3\times2}$

Required probability $= \frac{4\times3\times2\times3\times2}{7!}$

$= \frac{4\times3\times2\times3\times2}{7\times6\times5\times4\times3\times2} = \frac{1}{35}$

192. (b) Due to stoppges the train travels (45 – 36) = 9 km less in an hour than it could have travelled without stoppages.

Thus train stops per hour for $\frac{9}{45}\times 60 = 12$ min.

193. (b) 194. (e) 195. (a) 196. (e)
197. (e) 198. (a) 199. (d) 200. (b)

MOCK TEST - 6

1. (c) Required probability
= Probability that a ball from bag *A* is red and both the balls from bag *B* are black + Probability that ball from bag *A* is black and one black and one red balls are drawn from bag B

$$= \frac{^4C_1}{^9C_1} \times \frac{^7C_2}{^{10}C_2} + \frac{^5C_1}{^9C_1} \times \frac{^3C_1 \times ^7C_1}{^{10}C_2}$$

$$= \frac{4}{9} \times \frac{7}{15} + \frac{5}{9} \times \frac{7}{15} = \frac{7}{15}$$

2. (b) Probability that the assembled part will not be defective

$$= \frac{95}{104} \times \frac{95}{100} = \frac{361}{416}$$

3. (d) 3 ladies can be appointed out of 7 ladies as 1 is not including in $^7C_3$ ways.
Also, 3 gentlemen can be appointed out of 6 gentlemen as 1 is already member in $^6C_3$ ways.
Hence the required number of ways
$= {^7C_3} \times {^6C_3} = 700$

4. (a) Let A, B, C be three events.
Given: Odd are 8: 3 against A

$$\therefore\ P(A) = \frac{3}{8+3} = \frac{3}{11}$$

Similarly, $P(B) = \frac{2}{5+2} = \frac{2}{7}$

Also we know, $P(A) + P(B) + P(C) = 1$
$\Rightarrow 1 - [P(A) + P(B)] = P(C)$

$$\Rightarrow P(C) = 1 - \left[\frac{3}{11} + \frac{2}{7}\right] = 1 - \left[\frac{21+22}{77}\right] = \frac{77-43}{77} = \frac{34}{77}$$

$\therefore$ Odds against C = 43: 34

5. (a) In each of the case the rest of the 4 digits can be choosen in $8 \times 7 \times 6 \times 5$ ways.
Hence no. of telephone numbers having all 6 distinct digits $= 5 \times (8 \times 7 \times 6 \times 5)$ ways = 8400 ways.

6. (a) **From fig II to I :** The elements move 2 to 9 → 7 → 3 → 8 → 2. The upper left is replaced by a new one.

7. (c) **From fig II to I :** Elements move one side clockwise while they rotate by 90° anti-clockwise.

8. (e) **From fig II to I :** The upper elements rotate by 90° clockwise while the lower ones rotate by 90° anti-clockwise.

9. (e) **From fig II to II :** The outer element is lost. The inner closed-ended element gets enlarged and rotates by 90° anti-clockwise while the adjacent line segment moves one side anti-clockwise further.

10. (d) **From fig II to I :** The upper element rotates by 90° anti-clockwise and gets laterally inverted. The lower element rotates by 90° anti-clockwise and its head reverses its direction. The bigger element gets reduced and vice versa.

11. (a) As positive premises give only positive conclusions.

So, 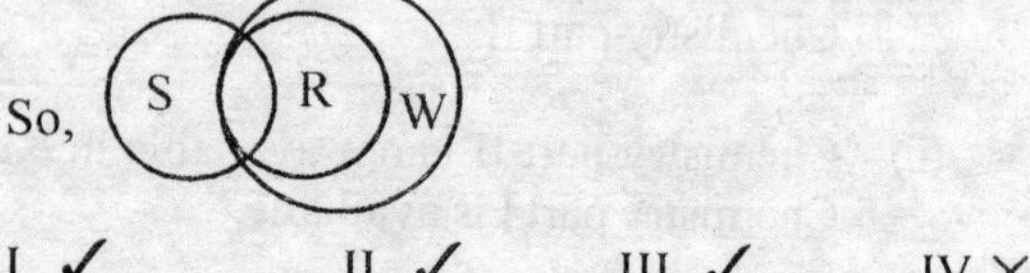

I ✓ II ✓ III ✓ IV ✗

12. (c) As no Indian is an Asian and some being part of all, so statement 1 Follows. Those some Americans who are Indian are not Asians.

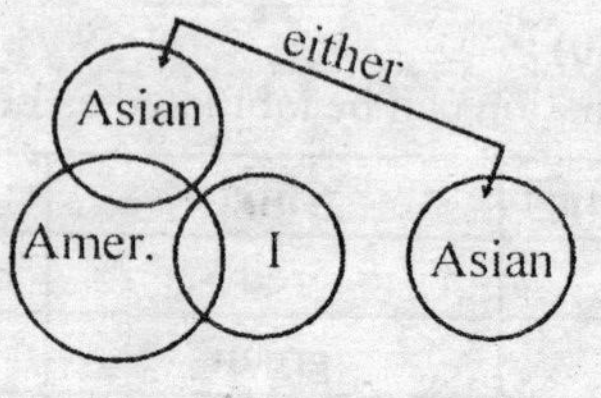

I ✓ II ✗ III ✓ IV ✗

13. (a) There is no correlation among darts and smarts or smarts and charts.

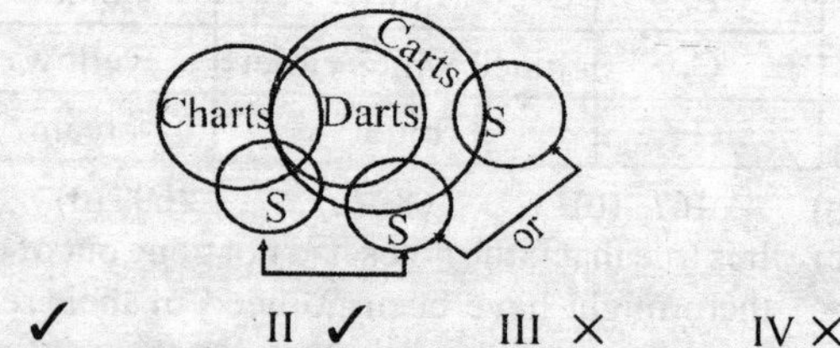

I ✓ II ✓ III ✗ IV ✗

14. (d) Both groups are totally different.

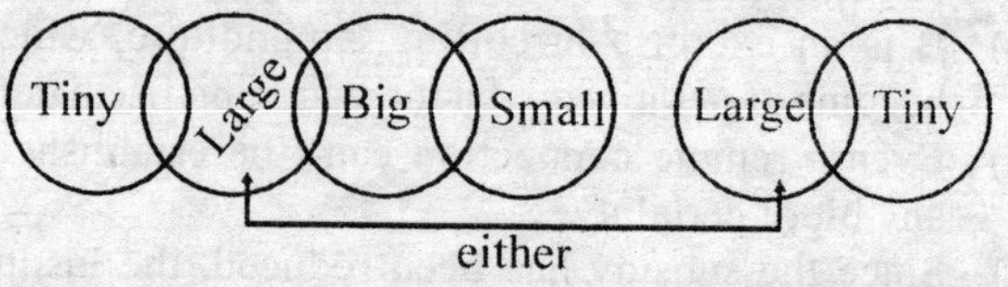

I ✗ II ✗ III ✗ IV ✗

15. (d) I & II and III & IV are mutually exclusive.

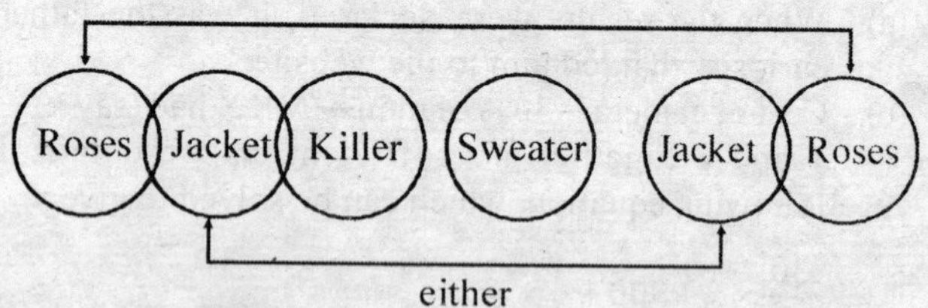

Either I or II
Either III or IV

16. (a) In year 2000 no. of cars = 86 is more than scooter and motorbikes (42+34 = 76) put together. Hence this is the answer.

17. (c) Easier method is as follows :
Motorbike = $40 \times 0.1 = 4$
Scooter = $48 \times 0.12 = 5.76$
Cars = $60 \times 0.2 = 12$
Total = 21.76.
Multiply 21.76 by 10000 = 2,17,600 units.

18. (b) Same as above
Cars = 48×0.28
Scooters = 60×0.35
Motorbikes = 38×0.42
$48 \times 28 : 60 \times 35 : 38 \times 42 \Rightarrow 16 : 25 : 19.$

19. (c) Cars = $75 \times 0.3 \times 2$
Scooter = $60 \times 0.4 \times 1$
Motorbike = $84 \times 0.25 \times 1.5$

$$\frac{75\times3\times2}{10}:\frac{60\times4\times1}{10}:\frac{84\times25\times15}{10\times100}\Rightarrow 30:16:21$$

20. (a) Solving with the help of options. In 1997 motorbike production is 56 ('0000 units).
Total Production = Car + Scooter + Motorbike
= 40 + 44 + 56 = 180 ('0000 units)

$\therefore$ Required % = $\frac{56}{180}\times100 = 40\%$.

21. (c) is the answer. This is a factual question. Refer to the first sentence of the second paragraph. It could be inferred from this line that there were many large organisations but not enough managers and this need for good managers led to development of various management programs by companies and universities.
22. (d) is the answer. Refer to the second last sentence of the second paragraph.
23. (a) is the answer. (b), (c) and (d) are the functions of a manager according to the passage and in author's opinion leader's task so different from that of a manager's. A leader is a visionary. Refer to this sentence in the first paragraph "Leadership defines what the future should look like.... despite the obstacles.
24. (c) According to the passage successful transformations is 70 to 90% leadership and only 10-30% management. So, the emphasis should be on leadership rather than management for transformation efforts.
25. (c) Because management was the main item on 20th century agenda and it was manager that were required in large numbers. The focus was on management that is why they were taught little about leadership.

For Qs. 26-30 Sentence E picturises the termite colony mentioned in sentence A and thus naturally follows it. This is followed by C which also explains a little bit about the colony and then is followed by B and lastly by D, which is linked to B through the restoration of balance that had been unsettled in sentence B.

26. (a) 27. (e) 28. (c) 29. (b) 30. (d)

31. (c)

Letter	E	H	N	D	J	V
Code	#	4	2	3	9	8

Condition is applied.

32. (e)

Letter	K	Q	D	J	N	H
Code	7	6	3	9	2	4

33. (a)

Letter	A	J	N	V	Q	E
Code	#	9	2	8	6	#

Condition is applied.

34. (b)

Letter	Q	H	J	V	N	D
Code	6	4	9	8	2	3

35. (d)

Letter	J	K	E	D	H	A
Code	9	7	1	3	4	#

Condition is applied.

36. (c) $2567 \div 17 \times 3 = ? + 180$
or $151 \times 3 = ? + 180$ or $453 = ? + 180$
$\therefore ? = 453 - 180 = 273$

37. (e) $\frac{3}{8}\times\frac{4}{7}\times\frac{7}{12}\times1375 = \frac{1375}{8} = 171.875 \approx 172$

38. (a) $10^{7.5}\times5^{2.5}\times2^{2.5} = 10^{7.5}\times10^{2.5} = 10^{10}$
Hence, the question mark (?) should be replaced by 10.

39. (a) 56% of $958 + 67\%$ of $1008 = 536.48 + 675.36 = 1211.84$
Now, $1211.84 = ?\%$ of 2000
$\therefore ? = 60.592$

40. (d) $(?)^2 + (164)^2 = (307)^2 - 272$
$\therefore \quad (?)^2 = (307)^2 - 272 - (164)^2$
$= 94249 - 272 - 26896 = 67081$

Hence, ? = $\sqrt{67081} = 259$

41. (a) The size of each element changes after two steps and it resume its originsal size in the next step. The lower two elements also get inverted with the change of size.
42. (a) The elements move one step anticlockwise in each step while the upper middle and lower middle element is replaced alternately by a new one.
43. (d) The main figure rotates by 45°, 90°, 135°, 180° ..... clockwise in subsequent steps while a dash is added on clockwise side in each step.
44. (b) The RHS arrow rotates by 90° clockwise in each step. The LHS arrow rotates by 90° anticlockwise and 180° alternately while the middle arrow follows if 0 = 3 = 6, 1 = 4 then 2 = 5 rule.
45. (e) Beginning from the upper left in anticlockwise direction, 2 and 3 line segments are lost in alternate steps.
46. (c) Since, there is a but between the two parts of the sentence, the passive words should be antonyms. (a) and (d), thus, get eliminated never - also do not fit the sense of the sentence properly thus, not - always are the most suitable fillers for the given sentence.
47. (c) An **analysis** must be careful, it may or may not be detailed and final. It certainly should bot be random, thus, (a) is eliminated of the remaining careful is the most appropriate choice for this sentence.
48. (c) **Graphologist** is one who studies handwriting, while a **cosmetologist** is a person skilled is the art of cosmetics, **Beagle** is a species of dog and lapidary is a person skilled in polishing of atoms.
49. (b) The second blank could either be voice so (c) and (d) are eliminated. **Hypothetic** means something that is assumed and **titular** means a ruler without real authority. So, titular - vote is the appropriate choice of words.

50. (b) If the particles need no wounding then spanning is their natural property, so the filler for second plant should be synonymous to natural or internal. **Radical** means drastic, intrinsic is inbuilt or internal, **intangible** is something that is not available in the physical form, **hypothetical** is assumed. Thus, intrinsic will be the filler for the second gap.

51. (c) The total value of brands Coca coal, GE, Nokia = \$ 142 Bn. (These brands have improved their ranking)
Mircosoft, Intel, MC Donal's and Mercedes have deteriorated ranking total value = \$142.4 Bn = 400 Mn
Difference = 142.4 – 142 = \$0.4 Bn

52. (c) Brand value of top 5 brands in 2003
= \$ 260.7 Bn = X
Brand value of brands ranked 6 – 10 in 2003
= \$125.7 Bn

$$\therefore \frac{125.7}{260.7} = 0.482$$

53. (d) Brand value of HP and Oracle

$$= \frac{160 \times (17.8 + 9)}{360} = \$11.9 \text{ Bn}$$

The 10th ranked brand is valued at 21.4 Bn \$. Hence, we cannot determine the exact ranking of ORAHP in 2003.

54. (d) Brand value of Coca-cola in 2002

$$= \frac{70.3}{112.5} \times 100 = 62.48 \text{ Bn } \$$$

Coca cola's brand value was 16.66%, (i.e., 1/6) less than that of Microsoft in 2002, (i.e., Mircosoft was 6/5 times the value of coca-cola)
∴ Microsoft's brand value in 2002

$$= \frac{62.48 \times 6}{5} = 74.97 \text{ Bn } \$$$

55. (c) Brand value of Ralher in 2003

$$= \frac{32 \times 11.1}{100} \times 18.9 = \$8.15 \text{ Bn}$$

Brand value of Oracle in 2003
= \$4 Bn = 87th rank
Brand value of HP in 2003
= \$8.88 Bn = 71st rank
∴ Since, Ralher's brand value is greater than Oracle's but less than that of HP it must be ranked somewhere between 71 and 87.

56. (d) Other groups consist of consecutive elements.

57. (a) $2 + 2^2 + 8 + 5 + 6 + 0 + 9 + 9^2 + 0 + 3 = 118$
Where value of alphabet = 0; symbol = square of the previous number; number = the value itself.

58. (b) The letters used in the series are *B Q E R D U K A P*. Sum of the positions of consonants according to alphabet = 2 + 17 + 18 + 4 + 11 + 16 = 68. Similarly, sum of the vowels' positions = 5 + 21 + 1 = 27. Hence required difference = 68 – 27 = 41.

59. (e) First element of each group follows the order + 3, + 3, +3... and so on.
Middle element and last element also follow the same trend. Hence (?) should be replaced by R 13.

60. (c) Number of elements between *B* and *Q* is the same as that between *E* and *R*. Similarly, number of elements between *A* and *P* is the same as that between *K* and *A*.

61. (d) $? = \sqrt{45689} = 213.75 \approx 210$

62. (b) $? = \frac{(10008.99)^2}{10009.001} \times \sqrt{3589} \times 0.4987$

$$= \frac{(10009)^2}{10009} \times \sqrt{3600} \times 0.50$$

$$= 10009 \times 60 \times 0.50 \approx 300000$$

63. (e) $? = 399.9 + 206 \times 11.009$

$$= 400 + (200 + 6) \times 11 = 400 + 2200 + 66 \approx 2670$$

64. (a) $? = \frac{2}{5} + \frac{7}{8} \times \frac{17}{19} \div \frac{6}{5} = \frac{2}{5} + \frac{7}{8} \times \frac{17}{19} \times \frac{5}{6}$

$$= \frac{2}{5} + \frac{595}{912} = 0.40 + 0.65 = 1.05 \approx 1$$

65. (a) $? = (299.99999)^3 \approx (300)^3 = 27000000$

66. (d) Since cone is inside cylinder which is within cube
⇒ Diameter of base of cone = height of cone
= diameter of base of cylinder
= height of cylinder = side of cube
(I) ⇒ Volume of cone ⇒ radius and height of cone
⇒ radius and height of cylinder
Hence, volume of cylinder can be determined.
(II) ⇒ Total surface area of cube ⇒ side of cube
⇒ radius and height of cylinder
Hence, volume fo cylinder can be determined.
∴ Each statement alone is sufficient to answer the question.

67. (b) Remember that $n^x - n$ is divisible by x if x is a prime number and the divisibility does not depend on the value of n.
∴ Only statement (II) alone is sufficient to answer the question.

68. (d) (I) ⇒ c is an odd number
⇒ abc is odd [because if last digit of a three-digit number is odd then this three digit number will certainly be odd]
⇒ $5^{2(abc)} + 1$ will be divisible by 13. (∵ $5^{2n} + 1$ is divisible by 13 if n is odd).
And abcabc = 1000 (abc) + abc = abc (1000 + 1) = abc (1001) = abc (7 × 11 × 13)
⇒ abcabc will be divisible by 13.
Hence, statement (I) alone is sufficient to answer question.
(II) ⇒ a, b, c are odd numbers.
⇒ c is odd which is statement (I) and hence same conclusion is drawn.

69. (d) Here AB and AC are tangent segments and ADE is a secant to the circle intersecting it at D and E. FB, FH, HG and GC are also tangent segments.
Since, the lengths of two tangents drawn from an external point to a circle are equal.
$\therefore$ AB = AC, BF = FH and HG = CG ....(i)
Also, we know that
$\Rightarrow AD \times AE = AC^2$ ....(ii)
$\Rightarrow (AE - ED) \times AE = AC^2 \Rightarrow AE^2 - (AE \times ED) = AC^2$
$\Rightarrow AE^2 - AC^2 = AE \times ED$ [$\because \angle ECA = 90°$]
$\Rightarrow EC^2 = AE \times ED$
$\Rightarrow$ Radius of the circle $= \frac{\sqrt{AE \times ED}}{2}$
[$\because$ EC = diameter]
$\Rightarrow$ Perimeter of the circle can be determined if AE and ED are known.
Perimeter of the triangle AFG = AF + FH + HG + GA
= AF + BF + CG + GA [from (i)]
= AB + AC = 2AC [from (i)]
$= 2\sqrt{AD \times AE}$ [from (ii)]
$\Rightarrow$ Perimeter of ΔAFG can be determined if either AC or AD and DE is known.
Hence, to answer the question, any two of AD, DE and AC are required.
$\therefore$ Each statement alone is sufficient to answer the question.

70. (d) Suppose the distance between P and Q is D_1, the distance between Q to R is D_2, the speed of Vicky in still water is x km per hour and the stream flows at the rate of y km per hour.
Hence we have the following information in the question.

$$\frac{D_1}{x} + \frac{D_2}{x+y} = 3 \quad ....(i)$$

$$\frac{D_1}{x} + \frac{D_2}{x-y} = 3\frac{1}{2} \quad ....(ii)$$

$$\frac{D_2}{x-y} - \frac{D_2}{x+y} = \frac{1}{2}$$

$$\Rightarrow 4D_2y = x^2 - y^2 \quad ....(iii)$$

and we have to find out $\frac{D_1 + D_2}{x - y} = ?$

$$(I) \Rightarrow \frac{x}{y} = \frac{6}{1} \Rightarrow x = 6y \quad ....(iv)$$

Putting this value of x in equation (iii) we get the value of D_2 in terms of y. Putting the value of D_2 in equation (i) we get the value of D_1 in terms of y.
Hence we can get $\frac{D_1 + D_2}{x - y}$

$\therefore$ Statement (I) alone is sufficient to answer the question.

$$(II) \Rightarrow \frac{D_1 + D_2}{x+y} = \frac{11}{4} \quad ....(v)$$

Subtracting (v) from (i) we have
$$4D_1y = x(x+y) \quad ...(vi)$$
Now adding (iii) and (vi) we get
$$4D_2y + 4D_1y = x^2 - y^2 + x(x+y)$$
$$\Rightarrow 4y(D_1 + D_2) = (x+y)(x-y+x)$$
$$\Rightarrow 4y(D_1 + D_2) = (x+y)(2x-y)$$
$$\Rightarrow \frac{D_1 + D_2}{x+y} = \frac{2x-y}{4y}$$

From equation (v), $\frac{2x-y}{4y} = \frac{11}{4} \Rightarrow x : y = 6 : 1$

Hence, $\frac{D_1 + D_2}{x-y} = \frac{D_1 + D_2}{(x+y)} \times \frac{(x+y)}{(x-y)}$

Hence statement (II) alone is sufficient to answer the question.

71. (d) From question figure I to II, half portion of one design disappears while from question figure II to III, half portions two designs disappear and half portion of the first design reappears. The same order of changes is repeated.

72. (b) In each subsequent figure the whole design move 90° anticlockwise and two designs shift one place in the same direction but one of the designs shifts along the diagonal while the rest one design takes a new shape.

73. (b) In each subsequent figure the st. line shifts one side anticlockwise and the desh on it shifts half side anticlclwise after reversing.

74. (e) In each subsequent figure the designs are changing their places as shown below and a new design comes at the place of N :

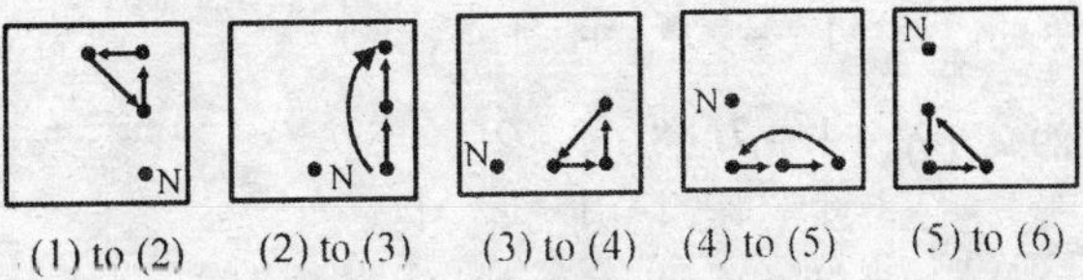

(1) to (2) (2) to (3) (3) to (4) (4) to (5) (5) to (6)

75. (c) In each subsequent figure the main design moves through 45° and 90° anticlockwise respectively while the dashes on it, move through 45° and 90° respectively.

76. (d) The series is × 1 + 1 × 7, × 2 + 2 × 6, × 3 + 3 × 5...

77. (e) 3 4 12 45 [196] 1005
$\times 1 + 1^2$ $\times 2 + 2^2$ $\times 3 + 3^2$ $\times 4 + 4^2$ $\times 5 + 5^2$

78. (c) The series is × 1 + 2, × 2 + 3, × 3 + 4, × 4 + 5 ...

79. (b) The series is × 0.5 + 0.5, × 1 + 1, + 1.5 + 1.5, ...

80. (a) The series is × 2, ÷ 3 , × 4, ÷ 5, ...

81. (d) 134 ≡ Good and tasty ..... (i)
478 ≡ See good pictures .... (ii)
729 ≡ Pictures are faint ... (iii)
From (i) and (ii) 4 ≡ good
and from (ii) and (iii) 7 ≡ pictures

Hence the code for see is 8

82. (b) EASE→GUCG

As,

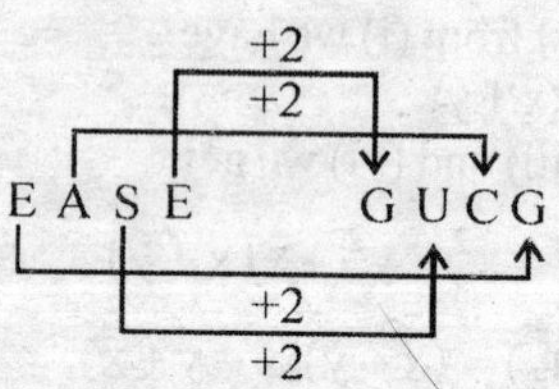

Similarly,

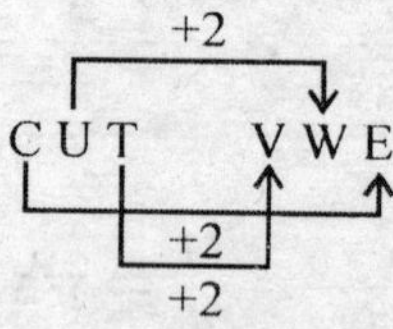

83. (a) M and T are two consonants in the word MEAT. N comes after M and U comes after T. Hence, the letters are N, E, A and U.

84. (d) (a) Summer; (b) Winter ; (c) Spring ; (d) Cloud
All other are name of seasons.

85. (b) Next train for N. Delhi leaves at 8:30 p.m. Since time interval between two trains for N. Delhi is 45 minutes. A train for New Delhi has left 15 minutes ago.
∴ Time of information = 8:30 – 45 + 15 = 8 P.M.

86. (d) 6 7 3 2 5 8
↓ ↓ ↓ ↓ ↓ ↓
● + ? * $ ©
As '8' is the end-number, its symbol will change according to rule (ii).

87. (e) 2 3 6 4 7 5
↓ ↓ ↓ ↓ ↓ ↓
* ? ● ÷ + $

88. (c) 8 4 6 7 2 1
↓ ↓ ↓ ↓ ↓ ↓
! ÷ ● + * x

89. (a) 1 7 8 5 2 4
↓ ↓ ↓ ↓ ↓ ↓
@ + ! $ * ©
As '1' is 1st number, its symbol will change according to rule (i).
similarly '4' is the end-number, its symbol will change according to rule (ii).

90. (b) 2 5 4 8 6
↓ ↓ ↓ ↓ ↓
* $ ÷ ! ©

91. (e) The clockwise element moves to the centre. The second from clockwise end becomes clockwise end element. The central element moves to the anticlockwise end and a new element appears at second place from clockwise end.

92. (b) Elements move half-a-side anticlockwise and a new element appears at anticlockwise end. In each step two of the elements interchange places once at clockwise end and next at anticlockwise end.

93. (c) In each step a new element is added. The cross and the square move together one side clockwise and interchange their places. The movement is restricted to middle and right column.

94. (d) The anticlockwise end element moves half a side clockwise while others are arranged in the reverse order on its anticlockwise side. A new element is added at the anticlockwise end.

95. (a) The element at anticlockwise end moves to centre while the central element moves to the clockwise end. A new elements appears at the anticlockwise end. The other elements reverse their order and move one, one-and-a-half, two.....sides anticlockwise.

For (Qs. 96-100)

We can summarise the information given in the question by the following table:

Schools	Strength	English	Hindi	Both
A	360	144	144	72
B	675	105	300	270
C	135	65	55	15
D	315	189	111	15
E	315	97	190	28
Total	1800	600	800	400

96. (c) % of students who know both the languages
$$= \frac{400}{1800} \times 100 = 22.22\%$$

97. (b) Difference between no. of students knowing English and Hindi = 800 – 600 = 200

98. (d) $\frac{\text{No. of students of C who know Hindi}}{\text{No. of students of C who know both languages}}$
$$= \frac{55}{15} = 3\frac{2}{3}$$

99. (a) % of students who know Hindi only
$$= \frac{800}{1800} \times 100 = 44.4\%$$

100. (e) 18th ⟶ Parbir ⟵ 12th
13th ⟶ Mohan
Total children = (18 – 1) + 12 = 29

101. (a) **Predilection** means a special liking for someone. **Antipathy** means hate for someone or a strong dislike. **Dissonance** is difference of opinion.

102. (a) **Docile** means submissive and therefore can be controlled very easily, **unmanageable** is someone or something that cannot be controlled or managed easily.

103. (c) **Equivocal** means doubtful or ambiguous, **clear** will be opposite to that, **Quaint** means strangely delightful.

104. (c) **Prosaic** means ordinary, whereas **Rhetorical** is impressive, ornate and is meant to influence. **Pensive** means sad and thoughtful.

105. (c) **Levity** means lack of seriousness whereas **solemnity**

means seriousness. **Frivolity** is something that lack a serious intention and can be taken synonymous with levity.

106. (d) (C) doesn't give hint about full marks. From (A) and (B) we can obtain the minimum marks required to pass the examination.

107. (b) B gives relative values of their profit in percentage and A gives total investment. So A & B put together have enough Information to give profit share in percentage terms. B alongwith C can also help in getting actual profit.

108. (d) Data in all statements will enable to calculate the cost price, which is necessary to calculate the profit.

109. (d) As B gives relative working capacity and A gives time taken by the group, so it is enough to get the answer. Difference in days taken to finish the work in A and B will give the required information. B gives relative working capacity and C gives working capacity of men, so these information will be helpful.

110. (d) B gives length and cost/sq mt. Using ratio in A we can calculate the width.
From length in B and perimeter in C we can calculate the width.
From ratio in A and perimeter in B length and width can be calculated.

Number of children towards the right of Mohan $= 29 - 13 = 16$

111. (a) Amit Khanna fulfills all the requirements. Thus, he is to be appointed.

112. (c) We have insufficient information in the case of Rohit Verma.

113. (a) Manju Sharma conforms to all the requirements. Therefore, she is to be appointed.

114. (a) Suman Malhotra fulfills all the requirements. Hence, she is to be appointed.

115. (c)

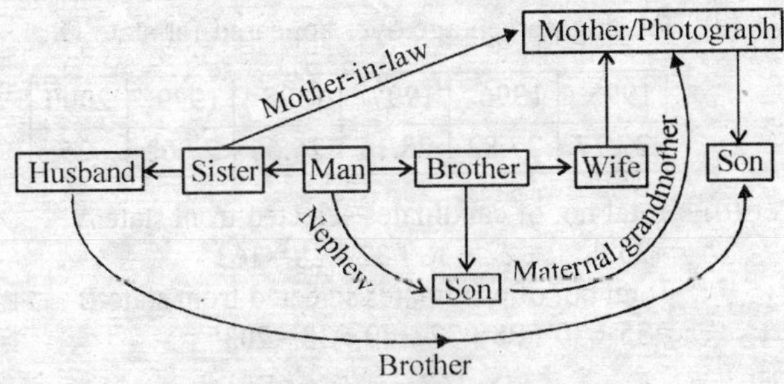

116. (c) Total circulation in 1988
$= 60{,}000 + 40{,}000 + 30{,}000 + 27{,}000 = 157{,}000$
Hence, option (c) is the correct answer.

117. (b) Growth % for Business India $= \frac{69-45}{45} = 53.3\%$

Growth % for Dalal street journal $= \frac{49-18}{18} = 172\%$

Growth % for Business world $= \frac{32-25}{25} = 28\%$

Growth % for Fortune India $= \frac{31-20}{20} = 55\%$

Hence, it is maximum for Dalal Street Journal.

118. (a) Advertising tariff for FI in 1989 is 14,000 per page vis-a-vis 28,000 per page.

$\therefore$ Cost in 1988 $= \frac{28000}{31}$

Cost in 1989 $= \frac{14000}{31}$

$\therefore$ Decrease % $= \frac{28000-14000}{28000} \times 100 = 50\%$

119. (b) Advertissing cost per 1000 copies is given below :
Dalal Street Journal
$= (14{,}000/40{,}000) \times 1000 = \text{Rs. } 350$
Business World
$= (20{,}000/30{,}000) \times 1000 = \text{Rs. } 666$
Fortune India
$= (17{,}000/27000) \times 1000 = \text{Rs. } 629$
Business India
$= (30{,}000/60{,}000) \times 1000 = \text{Rs. } 500$
It is lowest for Dalal Street Journal. Hence, option (b) is the lowest.

120. (c) Advertising cost per 1000 copies of Business World in 1987

$= \left(\frac{5{,}000}{25{,}000}\right) \times 1000 = \text{Rs.}200$

Advertising cost per 1000 copies of Business world in 1988

$= \left(\frac{20{,}000}{30{,}000}\right) \times 1000 = \text{Rs.}666$

Hence, the cost has increased by Rs. 466.

121. (a) The two parallel line segments interchange their positions. An arrowhead is added to the smaller and dot to the bigger line segment. The base line is converted to a triangle in the second figure.

122. (e) The second is the vertically inverted form of the first.

123. (d) The whole figure rotates anticlockwise. The elements on the anticlockwise side reduce by one while elements on clockwise side increase by one.

124. (c) The triangle moves one step clockwise and another triangle on clockwise side of it also gets shaded. The open triangle appears after one step in clockwise direction of the shaded triangle.

125. (a) The figure rotates by 90° clockwise. The shaded pare becomes unshaded and unshaded part becomes shaded. The outer line changes its direction.

126. (a) All the three courses of actions follow in this case. The chemical industries are discharging effluents into the river which may be hazardous hence the chemical factories should be closed down. Now that the water is polluted, it has to be treated chemically before resuming supply, otherwise it may affect those using it. This also gives an example to Pollution Control Board to keep a check to prevent any mishappening at regular intervals.

127. (d) To avoid testing at the primary level admissions the government should take the course of action III .

128. (c) The best option in this case is to divert the load of vehicular traffic through various link roads during peak hours.

129. (b) The officer-in-charge of production should be suspended so as to ensure that this kind of a problem does not happen in future. Also the export order should be sold to the other party.

130. (d) If the entry of outsiders were stopped how would the victims get the help. Hence surely course of action (I) does not follow. Now if the civic administration is making alternate housing arrangements for the victim there is no requirement to shift them and viceversa. Hence II or III follow.

131. (b) After notice all sales persons will stay away from the society. So I is implicit. II is also an assumption because it may be possible that sales persons do not obey notice and security guard posted at the gate. But both assumptions cannot be at the same time. Hence either I or II follows.

132. (b) For compete with bank A other bank may be reduced their retail lending rates. So I is implicit. If other banks do not reduce their retail lending rate then bank A may be able to attract more customers for availing retail loans. But both assumptions cannot be taken at the same time. Hence either I or II follows.

133. (c) I is not implicit because it is against of government decision. II is implicit because employees did not want to deduct tax at source. Hence only II is implicit.

134. (d) Assumption II is supplementary of assumption I and cannot be assumed with statement.

135. (c) Assumption I is not implicit because of the word 'every'. II is implicit because prevention is better than cure.

136. (d) The second paragraph of the passage tests the different arguments that people who do not like abstract are given. All given options are mentioned in the reasons stated by the author, thus (d) is the answer.

137. (b) The other three options are illogical and have nothing to do with the question. (b) is the answer because representational act is direct and not abstract and this is simple to understand so the people don't have strain their head trying to figure out the meaning.

138. (c) The passage states that if piccolos had used representational images much of emotional content would have been last and price would not have caused demand for justice. Thus means Picasso did not use representational images rather he use abstract images. He express the emotional context through abstract depiction.

139. (a) In the third paragraph the passage states "Mondrian was trying to present a system of logic, simplicity and rational order. As a result his pieces did end up looking like a scrabble board".

140. (b) In the third paragraph the author says of the representation act "This is the reality he reproduction on the canvas' and of the abstract at he says "This is the reality he interprets on canvas.

141. (e) The elements get vertically inverted and interchange their position and are attached to each other.

142. (d) The middle elements get lost.

143. (a) The element of the upper and lower row shift one side and half-a-side clockwise respectively while the middle row is lost.

144. (b) The outer element becomes more one and vice versa and the two elements are not similar.

145. (d) Two similar heads are added from the centre.

146. (a) Because of his announcement he has been expelled.

147. (b) Andrew talked so after reading the newspaper.

148. (a) Because of the project they have managed to transform the living conditions near their homes.

149. (a) Because of the term second and third, we can establish the relation between the two sentences.

150. (a) Because of (B), government has started the project "alert citizen" to curb crimes. Hence 'A' is the effect and (B) is the cause.

For(Qs. 151-155) :

The whole information can be tabulated as below:

Day	Lecture
Monday	C
Tuesday	B
Wednesday	E
Thursday	Holiday
Friday	F
Saturday	D
Sunday	A

151. (b) 152. (c) 153. (e) 154. (a) 155. (a)

156. (c) Percentage of candidate selected over appeared

A	B	C	D	E
$\frac{25}{850}\times 100 = 2.94$	$\frac{35}{1050}\times 100 = 3.33$	$\frac{28}{990}\times 100 = 2.82$	$\frac{36}{1080}\times 100 = 3.33$	$\frac{40}{1120}\times 100 = 3.57$

157. (d) Passing percentage over appeared for state D

1995	1996	1997	1998	1999	2000
27.77	27.82	28.14	26.66	27.02	25

158. (d) Total no. of candidates selected from state A

$= 25 + 20 + 22 + 36 + 32 + 28 = 163$

Total no. of candidates selected from state B

$= 35 + 30 + 28 + 32 + 40 + 38 = 203$

$\therefore$ Reqed. % $= \frac{163}{203} \times 100 \approx 80\%$

159. (b) Percentage of candidates selected over passed for state B

1995	1996	1997	1998	1999	2000
14.28	13.04	13.33	16.84	17.77	19

160. (a) Required ratio $= \frac{240}{280} = 6:7$

161. (c) "Even though" warrants this phrase at the beginning of the sentence. "only" can't come at the end. "May only be" is incorrect.

162. (a) The use of 'that thing' is non standard. Replace it with so.

163. (d) The underlined sentence is unnecessarily made bulky and redundant.

164. (c) affirms is the verb form, affirmation is the noun form. This sentence requires the use of the noun form,

165. (b) The original sentence is correct.

166. (c) $B<D$ ...(i), $E \le T$ ...(ii), $T \ge P$ ....(iii), $P>B$...(iv) From (i) and (iv), we get, $P>B<D \Rightarrow$ no conclusion. But the exhaustive possibilities are $P>D, P=D$ and $P<D$. Hence either I or II is true.

167. (e) $E \ge F$ ...(i), $G \le H$ ...(ii), $H=E$ ...(iii), $G>K$ ...(iv) From (ii) and (iv), we get, $H \ge G > K \Rightarrow H > K$. Hence I is true.
From (i) and (iii), we get, $H = E \ge F \Rightarrow H \ge F$. Hence II is true.

168. (a) $P \ge Q$ ...(i), $N=M$ ....(ii), $M>R$...(iii), $R \ge P$ ...(iv)
From (ii), (iii) and (iv), we get, $N=M>R \ge P$
$\Rightarrow N>P$ or $P<N$. Hence I is true.
From (ii), (iv) and (i), we get, $M>R \ge P \le Q \Rightarrow$ No conclusion about the relationship between M and Q can be established.

169. (b) 170. (d)

171. (b) The author believes that they have inherited a wonderful India but what they have given their children it a corrupted country. It is not pessimism or not accepting failure that makes author think his generation as a failed generation

172. (d) Author says that their parents believed that "the best they could give their children is education" (third paragraph).

173. (a) The author talks about his generation in the third paragraph and says that "we wanted to make a deference but we did not really mange to because we were too ambitious". Author believes the his generation was too occupied with personal goals and ambitions to be able to bring about any difference to the national reality.

174. (b) The author says along with other issues that "merit has no place, it is caste or connection that words". (Second last paragraph).

175. (b) The author talks about the 'guilt-money'. Parents do not have sufficient time to spend with their kids to compensate for which they buy them cars, gadgets etc. and this spoils the children in opinion of the author.

176. (c) The colours of the caps of all the seven persons are as follows:
A – Green or Blue (not explicit)
B – Green or Blue (not explicit)
C – Yellow
D – Violet
E – Indigo
F – Red
G – Orange

177. (a)

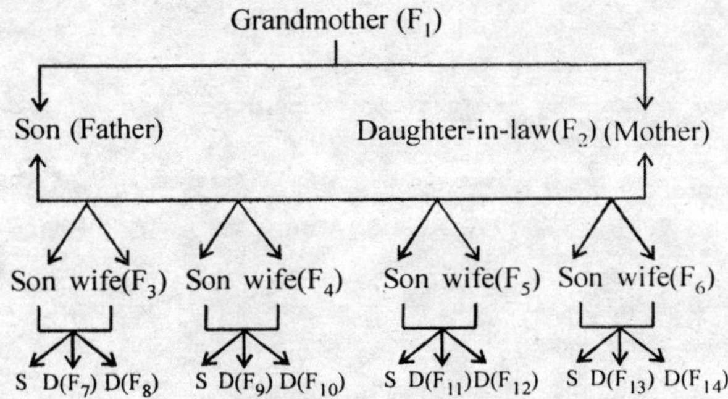

178. (c) Clearly, I am to the north of my house.

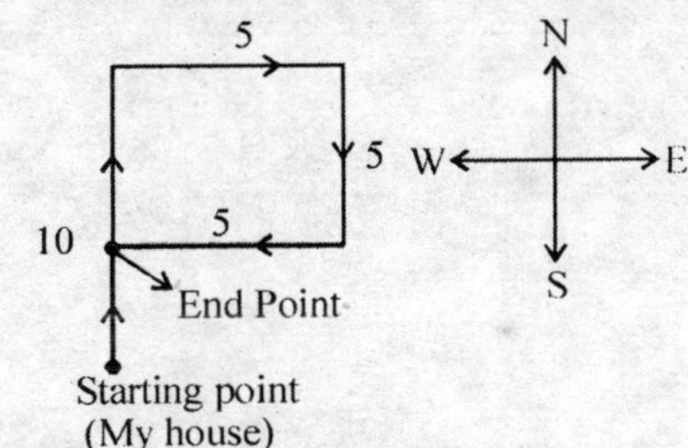

179. (c)

1	5	7	8	9	2	3	4	6
X	T	C	A	L	N	P	S	U

Hence, 23549 will be coded as NPTSL.

180. (a) If the marks are x
3 < x < 8
6 < x < 10
x = 7 satisfies the above conditions.

181. (b) 'Beside' is a preposition meaning 'by the side of' while 'besides' mean in addition to.

182. (d) The right expression is 'conditions necessary for', since the gap is followed by, this. 'complete' should be used in the noun form and not adjective so it will be 'completion of this'.

183. (a) 'in' is the correct preposition to be used with ushering

184. (d) Amendments are countable noun, thus the determiner 'many' will be used. 'Too' need not be used with 'many', and 'quite a few' and 'many' cannot be used together since they give opposite sense.

185. (c) 'Of' is the right preposition to be used with 'use'

186. (c) **Blaze** means excited, **indifference** means not caring about anything or showing a cold attitude, the two meanings are very similar.

187. (e) **Paddy** is another name for rice, **race track** is the track on which a race takes place, **caress** is to touch someone with love and fondness.

188. (a) **Repercussion** means the consequent action or reaction.

189. (c) **Goad** is to stimulate by annoying, **spur** means to stimulate, to **supercede** is to take the place of.

190. (e) **Homely** is simple and informal, **Plain** means simple. **Amiable** is friendly, and **refined** is sophisticated opposite to homely.

191. (d) 192. (e) 193. (c) 194. (b) 195. (d)
196. (d) 197. (e) 198. (b) 199. (a) 200. (b)